PHP4 DEVELOPER'S GUIDE

PHP 4
Developer's
Guide

Blake Schwendiman

McGraw-Hill
New York   Chicago   San Francisco   Lisbon
London   Madrid   Mexico City   Milan   New Delhi
San Juan   Seoul   Singapore   Sydney   Toronto

McGraw-Hill

A Division of The McGraw-Hill Companies

1 2 3 4 5 6 7 8 9 0   AGM/AGM   0 5 4 3 2 1 0

ISBN 0-07-212731-7

The sponsoring editor for this book was Rebekah Young and the production manager was Clare Stanley. It was set in Century Schoolbook by MacAllister Publishing Services, LLC.

Printed and bound by Quebecor Martinsburg.

This book is printed on recycled, acid-free paper containing a minimum of 50 percent recycled, de-inked fiber.

CONTENTS

V

Contents

Contents

Contents

INTRODUCTION

This book was written to provide enough information and examples for programmers to create real-world Web applications using PHP. I say Web applications, rather than Web pages or Web sites, in order to distinguish the role of PHP in Web development. In the past, simple HTML pages with limited interactivity ruled the Web. Today, the Web landscape is significantly more complex. Individuals and businesses expect much more from their Web presence, which drives the requirement for more dynamic, interactive Web applications. PHP is ideal for creating these dynamic Web applications because it was developed expressly for this purpose.

Who Should Use this Book?

This book will be useful to a broad range of Web developers, but the intended audience is intermediate to experienced software developers. PHP is a programming language, not a design or layout language, so previous programming experience is recommended for reading this book. Programmers with a background in C or Perl will find PHP to be very familiar, and Microsoft's *Active Server Pages* (ASP) developers will find PHP similar structurally.

Because this book is not targeted toward beginning programmers, the discussion will focus only briefly on basic programming concepts. It is assumed that the reader already understands programming concepts like functions, variables, and constants.

Conventions

The following conventions are used in this book:

- Code and program output appears in `monospace`.
- Filenames also appears in `monospace`.
- Commands and keywords appears in **boldface**.

Overview

The first section of the book, "Introduction and Overview," provides a brief introduction to PHP and an overview of the language. How to install and configure the tool is covered in this section also.

The second section, "Special Considerations in Web Development," is for programmers moving from traditional application development to Web applications. This section covers concepts like form processing, user interaction, state management, and browser independence.

The next section, "Project Management in Web Development," discusses code and reuse modularity.

The section, "Real-World Examples," is provided to illustrate the use of PHP in realistic development scenarios. This section brings together the concepts of the other sections to show the full interaction between the end-user's browser and the application residing on your Web server.

Finally, a reference section includes a full PHP4 function reference.

Author's Notes

I have been developing Web applications primarily using PHP and ASP for about three years as an independent contractor. PHP has been fundamental to the success of my business because it enables for rapid prototyping and provides the strength and reliability for large Web application delivery.

My goal with this book is to provide a useful tool for programmers. I won't be discussing the differences between PHP and similar tools, and I won't spend much time discussing the history of PHP or providing a general overview. This is available at the PHP Web site, www.php.net. I will, however, illustrate the use of PHP in deploying real-world Web applications. I will also discuss software engineering in Web-based projects, how to leverage existing code in new Web projects, and provide examples of some of the popular third-party tools for PHP.

Some example sites as well as information about my company and me can be found at www.intechra.net. The site also includes my current contact information if you have any feedback on this book.

About the Example Code

Just as an informational note, I developed and tested the example code using PHP 4.0.1 (patch level 2) with Apache 1.3.11 on RedHat Linux 6.1. I also edited the HTML and PHP code in Allaire Corporation's Homesite 4.5.1 on Windows NT.

For testing the smaller code samples, I developed a basic HTML template and simply inserted the relevant PHP code as needed for testing:

```
<html>
        <head>
                    <title>Example Name</title>
        </head>

        <body>
        <!--PHP Code Goes Below -->
        </body>
</html>
```

For larger code samples, the code was typically developed inline with the HTML.

What Is PHP?

PHP is a programming language created to enable Web developers to quickly create dynamic Web applications. PHP officially stands for "PHP: Hypertext Preprocessor." It is an HTML-embedded programming language syntactically similar to C, Perl, and Java. Listing 1 is an example of PHP.

Listing 1: A Basic PHP Example

```
<html>
        <head>
                    <title>A basic PHP example</title>
        </head>
        <body>
                    <?php
                            echo "Hello from PHP!" ;
                    ?>
        </body>
</html>
```

The previous example (if run from a properly configured Web server) can generate the HTML shown in Listing 2.

Listing 2: The Results of Listing 1

```
<html>
        <head>
                            <title?A basic PHP example</title>
```

```
<head>
<body>
            Hello from PHP!
<body>
</html>
```

The PHP preprocessor executes all the code between the <?php and ?> tags embedded in the HTML and returns the results of the included statements as text. This is not a particularly interesting example, but it shows how simply dynamic content can be developed inline with regular HTML. It is also important to note that the code is executed on the Web server, not in the client browser. This means that the browser has no knowledge of the fact that the PHP is used. It simply receives an HTML stream as if it were any other static HTML page. This also presents some challenges to developers who are accustomed to developing traditional applications where the display or user interface code runs on the same machine as the logic code. This is discussed at length in the section titled, "Special Considerations in Web Development."

Why Should I Use PHP?

PHP is a full-fledged programming language that will enable you to create Web applications with all the functionality you need. Beyond providing the programming framework for software development, PHP also provides support for accessing a wide range of databases. This makes creating database-enabled Web applications incredibly simple. PHP also supports services such as IMAP, POP3, NNTP, and HTTP. It can also open raw sockets to provide access to other TCP/IP protocols.

As for server environments, PHP can be used in many configurations. Because the PHP source is distributed, it can be compiled on many different platforms including Linux, FreeBSD, and even Windows. Binary distributions also are available for Win32.

PHP can be configured to run in CGI binary mode or installed as an Apache module or ISAPI extension. Thus, PHP works with almost any Web server from Apache on Linux to IIS on Windows NT. For the most configurable environment, choose a platform and Web server combination that enables you to compile and install PHP yourself. If you prefer to get up and running quickly, you may opt for a binary distribution of PHP.

 **Where Can I Get Support?**

PHP support is available at the PHP Web site and through several news-groups and mailing lists. As of February 2000, approximately 1,400,000 Web domains were using PHP. Because of its popularity, a large number of developers and consultants are available to help answer questions about PHP. For more information about the resources available on the Internet, see the "Resources" section at the end of the book.

ACKNOWLEDGMENTS

I would first like to thank everyone at McGraw-Hill for making this whole thing possible. Special thanks to Rebekah Young for her encouragement and for helping me with the technicalities of writing this book. Thanks to John Steele, the technical editor who provided me with meaningful comments and real-world information to help create this book.

Sincere thanks must go to the development team involved in creating PHP itself. Many of the team were available to help me with this book and I thank them. I take no credit for the reference sections of this book. All credit goes to the hundreds and thousands of hours spent by the PHP team for providing such a cool programming language and such rich documentation.

Thanks to Matt Wilson for allowing me to use the MWeather code as an example in this book. To Nick Bradbury for permission to use TopStyle screenshots and information. To Nate Weiss for help and permission with the WDDX deserializer for JavaScript. To John Kos for all the help with unixODBC and the EasySoft ODBC-ODBC Bridge. To Martin Evans, the lead developer of the ODBC-ODBC Bridge, for developing such a cool product. To Michael Justin for the help with the Scrooge RTF to HTML converter. To Michael C. Battilana for help with the Cloanto Currency Server and the follow-up to ensure that it works on all the discussed platforms. To Sam Ockman for providing permission to use a picture of the Penguin Computing 1U server used throughout the book. To Richard Litofsky for the help with BrowserHawk. To Ali Ersheid for his permission to use the CyberCash documentation in this book. To Joseph Harris (aka CDI) for the FastTemplate class and the other fantastic tools available from The Webmasters.net.

To my parents and brothers for their constant support, even when I was up all night cranking out Apple Basic programs at home in the eighties. To Mrs. Barton, Mr. Wakefield and Mrs. Smith, my high school English teachers who had the most impact on my writing. To Gary Rogers and Jason Wallin for pointing me in the direction of PHP and Linux when I was going down the ASP/Windows path. To Tracy Ard, for providing meaningful comments on this work and for his constant friendship.

Finally and most importantly, thanks to my wife and daughter for allowing me the time to finish this. Now I can get back to jumping on the trampoline with you in the evenings.

ABOUT THE AUTHOR

Blake Schwendiman has been programming since 1980, starting with an Apple IIe and the Basic language. He completed a Bachelor of Science degree at Arizona State University in 1994. Currently Blake is the managing partner of Intechra LLC, `http://www.intechra.net/`, a software consulting and contracting firm in Rexburg, Idaho. Intechra LLC specializes in custom Web software development and in Web development consulting. Blake is married to Holly and has a three-year-old daughter. He can be reached at `blake@intechra.net`.

Building and Installing PHP 4

Introduction

Before delving into the language, it is important to first get PHP installed and running in your environment. Because PHP supports so many Web servers and operating systems, this chapter focuses on providing detailed examples of installing on only a few platforms, while providing enough information so that you can tweak the examples to your specific platform.

The platforms that are discussed in depth in this chapter are Apache on Linux and IIS/PWS on Windows NT. These are common Web server configurations and are different enough to illustrate the required concepts for installing PHP on most platforms. Platform-specific details can also be found at the PHP site, www.php.net.

Downloading PHP

Obviously, the first step in beginning with PHP is to download it. The download section at www.php.net provides several download options. The most current version of PHP is listed at the top of the downloads page. For a *nix server, it is recommended that you download the complete source code and build PHP yourself. The term *nix refers to any Unix-like platform, including Linux, BSD, Solaris, and others. For Windows, it is recommended that you download the binary version of PHP.

From the download page, you can also download a previous version of PHP, the documentation, and related PHP tools. You may want to download a previous version of PHP if you already have PHP code running elsewhere and don't want to risk incompatibilities.

Installing the Binary Version

Once you have obtained a binary distribution of PHP, installation is straightforward. The most common binary installation of PHP is the Windows version. Because some *nix distributions may include a binary distribution of PHP, a brief installation discussion is included here as well.

Windows Binary Installation

With PHP, more than one option is always available for just about everything. The binary PHP download for Windows includes both the *Common Gateway Interface* (CGI) version of PHP and the ISAPI version. If you are running the *Internet Information Server* (IIS) or the *Personal Web Server* (PWS), it is recommended that you use the ISAPI version of PHP. The CGI version requires that the PHP executable be invoked for each page, so it is less efficient than using a dynamically linked library such as an ISAPI extension. The ISAPI version is also inherently more secure than the CGI version, so it is preferred.

Installing the PHP ISAPI Module   If you are using IIS/PWS or another Windows-based Web server that supports ISAPI, then the best choice for security and scalability is to use the PHP ISAPI module. To install the ISAPI module, copy the php4ts.dll and msvcrt.dll files into the Windows system directory (usually \windows\system on Windows 95 and \winnt\system32 on Windows NT). These files must be copied to the system directory for any version of PHP4 to work on Windows. They are shared libraries that must be available for PHP to work correctly. Additionally, you may copy the other DLL files to the system directory if you want, but they do not need to be moved to be used.

Next, IIS or PWS needs to be configured to use the ISAPI module when serving PHP files. This is done by starting the Microsoft Management Console for IIS configuration, which is typically available from the Windows NT Option Pack menu. Figure 1.1 shows the menu hierarchy for locating the application on Windows NT.

Figure 1.1
Starting the IIS
configuration
application

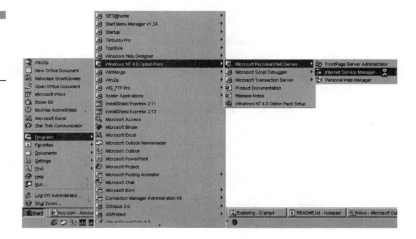

Once the Microsoft Management Console is running, right-click on your Web server node (probably labeled Default Web Site) and select **Properties**, as shown in Figure 1.2. Then on the Properties dialog, select the **Home Directory** tab and click the **Configuration** button. This enables you to add and edit extension mappings.

Click the **Add** button and then enter the information requested. Figure 1.3 shows the process of adding the PHP ISAPI module as a mapping for files with the phtml extension.

Once you have added a mapping, the information appears in the **Application Configuration** dialog. Something that might be useful for testing is to have some extensions map to the PHP ISAPI module and some to the CGI executable. The configuration on my personal Web server is shown in Figure 1.4. The figure illustrates the mappings for PHP version 3, the ver-

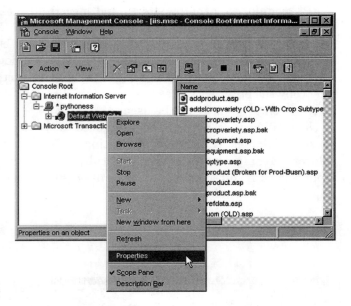

Figure 1.2
Editing the IIS configuration properties

Figure 1.3
Adding an IIS extension mapping

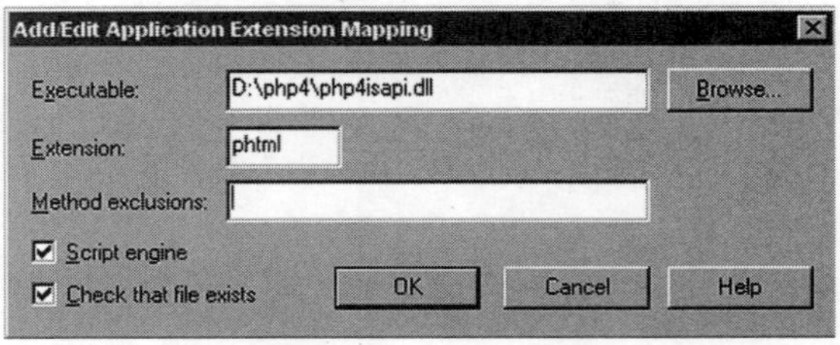

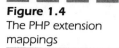

Figure 1.4
The PHP extension
mappings

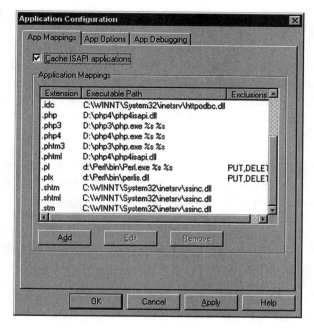

sion 4 CGI executable, and the version 4 ISAPI module. This is useful for testing the differences between version 3 and version 4 PHP code.

After finishing the configuration, you must restart your Web server. This can be done using the **Services** applet in the Windows Control Panel or by issuing the following commands from a command prompt:

```
net stop iisadmin
net start w3svc
```

After restarting, you should create a simple PHP test file such as the following one in Listing 1 and try to browse to the file on your server. If everything is properly configured, you will see the PHP information output.

Listing 1: The Test PHP Script

```
<html>
<head>
      <title>phpinfo()</title>
</head>

<body>
<?php
      phpinfo();
```

```
?>
</body>
</html>
```

It should be noted that PHP ships with a note about the state of the ISAPI module that basically indicates that it is not considered to be of production quality. The statement further suggests that for absolute stability the CGI executable should be used. The next section explains using PHP as a CGI.

Using PHP as a CGI Executable If you are not using an ISAPI-compliant Web server or have other reasons for choosing the CGI executable, the installation is similar to the previous steps. In fact, all the steps are the same except the extension mapping. Rather than selecting the ISAPI DLL, select the php.exe file. The IIS/PWS Web server sends parameters to CGI executables, so the %s %s command-line options should be provided along with the executable name. This can be seen in Figure 1.4 for the .php4 extension.

Other Web servers have methods for specifying the mappings previously discussed. For Apache on Windows, an excellent guide is www.php.net/manual/config-apache-nt.html. Other online resources for using the Windows version of PHP with various Web servers can be located using the search facility at www.php.net.

Other Binary Installations

Some *nix installations provide binary distributions of PHP as part of a Web server installation. Other vendors, such as Red Hat, also distribute binary versions of PHP on their Web site. These come in the form of *Red Hat Package Manager* (RPM) files. The advantage of using an RPM is its ease of installation. Rather than worrying about the build process, the RPM contains a platform-specific build of the tool, ready for use. The downside is that so many variants of the *nix platform exist that determining the right RPM can be challenging for newcomers. Also, the RPM doesn't always set all of the configuration options required for complete installation and use.

If you have an RPM of PHP, you can install it using the command line, rpm -i <rpmfile.rpm>. This installs all the binary files in directories set by the person or company who built the RPM file. These locations are typically correct for most uses. After installation, you must manually configure your

Web server to use the PHP binary files. The method for configuring Apache is explained here. Other Web servers have similar configuration steps.

No matter whether you are using PHP as a CGI binary or as a module, the first configuration step is the same. You must create an association between the file extension and its media type. This is done by adding lines similar to the following:

```
AddType application/x-httpd-php .php
AddType application/x-httpd-php .phtml
AddType application/x-httpd-php .inc
```

The previous directives configure Apache to consider all files with extensions php, phtml, and inc as the media type **application/x-httpd-php**. PHP is then used to process these file types.

Assuming that you have installed the Apache module version of PHP, the next step is to modify the Apache httpd.conf file to load the PHP module:

```
LoadModule php4_module        libexec/libphp4.so
```

If you have installed the CGI executable and want to use it with Apache, you need to edit the httpd.conf file slightly differently. The following configuration directive is similar to the previous directive, but it provides information about the actual PHP binary executable:

```
Action application/x-httpd-php /cgi-bin/php
```

The **Action** directive defines a media type that executes a script when a matching file is requested from the Web server. The correct path to the PHP executable should obviously be given in the directive.

Again, you must restart your Web server to have the new configuration settings take effect. An Apache Web server can be restarted using the following command:

```
/path/to/apachectl restart
```

You should test the configurations by requesting a test PHP script from a Web browser. A sample test script is shown in Listing 1.

The binary distribution of PHP can simplify the process of getting started with PHP on *nix, but it can be problematic. Because of the many variants of *nix, locating a pre-built version of PHP that works on your system can be difficult. In many cases, it will be more time-efficient to download the source version, build PHP, and then install it. This process is discussed next.

Building PHP

If you need the flexibility of a custom PHP creation or if you are considering adding your own extension to the PHP language (discussed in Chapter 11, "Code Reuse"), you must understand how to build PHP. Depending on your platform, you may have no choice but to build PHP yourself because no binary distribution is available.

Building PHP on a *nix Platform

This section provides information for building PHP on a *nix platform. Recall that *nix refers to any Unix-like platform including Linux, BSD, Solaris, and others. Obviously, these platforms have differences, but many of the steps for building will be exactly the same. For more information specific to your platform, use the search facility at www.php.net.

Several ways are available for building PHP for any platform. When building *nix to run Apache, you can build PHP as a binary executable, as a dynamically loaded module, or as a static link library. If you are not using the Apache Web server, you must consult the PHP and Web server documentation for details. By way of recommendation, the dynamically loaded Apache module build is probably best for most applications. When linked statically with Apache, more work is required any time you need to change your PHP configuration. As a CGI executable, security concerns exist.

The next sections assume that you have obtained the latest PHP source and have extracted the files into a directory on your build machine. The build process is essentially the same for each type of build. First, the **configure** script should be run to set the configuration options. Next, the **make** utility is used to perform the actual build. Finally, PHP must be installed and the Web server restarted. The details of the configure script are given in the section for building the CGI executable, so it is recommended that you read this section as an overview.

Building the CGI Executable　Building PHP as a CGI executable is the simplest build method and is a good practice if you have never built a program on *nix before. The complete set of steps is listed in the following code, but it should be noted that some of the steps are not actually required. The optional steps are shown in italic print. The php_dir reference is to be substituted with your specific PHP base directory.

```
cd <php_dir>
rm config.cache
make clean
./configure
make
make install
```

Executing the previous commands will clear any cached configuration settings, delete any existing binary objects, and then build PHP as a CGI executable. Again, this is the simplest form of a build and is intended as an example. In a real build, options originate from the configure script that specifies the attributes of PHP.

The second two lines are optional because they are used to clean up a previous configuration and build process. If you have not previously configured or built PHP, these are not needed. You may also choose to omit these in general when building PHP, but occasionally you need to use them. If you are making significant configuration changes or if you are switching from building the CGI executable to another build type, you may need to execute these commands to have a successful build. Depending on the speed of your build machine, the full configure and build process can take time. Leaving the configuration cache file and binary objects between builds can significantly reduce the build time.

For those new to the process, the configure script checks the system for various tools, files, and other system information. It then creates a build script specific to the platform. If a failure occurs during the configure process, this often indicates that a required tool or file is missing or improperly configured. After the configure script is finished, a cache file named *config.cache* is created that contains information about your system so that the checks don't have to be made again the next time you run configure. If you make significant changes to your system configuration, you may need to delete the cache file before running configure again to ensure that the new changes are recognized.

After the previous commands have completed, a new executable program, php, is available for use. You can test the executable with the following command:

```
php < /dev/null
```

If you see something similar to the following, then you have successfully built and installed PHP as a CGI executable:

```
X-Powered-By: PHP/4.0.2
Content-type: text/html
```

Note that this version of PHP probably doesn't have the features that you need for your application because it was built entirely with default settings. You must run the configure script again to set the options you need for your application, then make PHP, and install it again.

One of the nice things about the current defaults for PHP is that the simple configuration listed previously includes many of the commonly used configuration settings including MySQL database support, sessions, and more. This means that the previous commands will build PHP in such a way that you can begin writing PHP scripts for most uses.

If you need support for a different database or other extension, you will need to set the configure options accordingly. For a list of all current configuration options, run the following command:

```
./configure --help
```

Most configuration options that affect the features of PHP are of the form **--enable-FEATURE** or **--with-PACKAGE**. To add a feature to PHP, use one of the following forms:

```
--enable-FEATURE
--enable-FEATURE=yes
```

To remove a feature from PHP, use the following:

```
--disable-FEATURE
--enable-FEATURE=no
```

A complete listing of the configuration options is given in the reference section at the end of the book. Features using the --enable syntax are typically PHP built-in features, such as the capability to use short tags or ftp support. Packages are typically external modules that can be linked with PHP, such as Oracle database support or Java support. These types of features require external source code and use the following syntax for inclusion:

```
--with-PACKAGE=/path/to/package
```

To exclude a package, use the following:

```
--with-PACKAGE=no
--without-PACKAGE
```

As an example, consider the following configure command:

```
./configure --with-apxs=/www/bin/apxs --with-java --with-
cybercash=/home/blake/m
ck-3.2.0.6-i586-pc-linux-gnulibc2.1 --with-
```

```
unixODBC=/usr/local/unixODBC --disabl
e-debug --enable-track-vars --enable-fin_funcs --with-
snmp=/home/blake/ucd-snmp-
4.1.2 --enable-ucd-snmp-hack
```

The previous configuration command sets up PHP to use the Java, Cybercash®, *Simple Network Management Protocol* (SNMP), and unixODBC packages. The location of the Java files is not given, so the configure script uses the default location for that package. Additionally, the **-with-apxs** feature is selected that causes PHP to be built as a dynamically loaded Apache module, rather than a CGI executable. This is discussed in greater detail later. The other features of the previous configuration are that **debug information** is disabled, and the **track-vars**, **fin-funcs**, and **ucd-snmp-hack** features are enabled. The fin-funcs feature is an extension written for this book (see Chapter 11), but the others are standard PHP configuration elements described in the reference section at the end of the book.

Although the previous configuration does not build the CGI executable, it illustrates the power of configure. Many of the packages that can be included must be downloaded separately. Details about where to obtain the packages can be found in the PHP online documentation at www.php.net.

After building the PHP CGI executable, configure your Web server to use it. To configure the Apache Web server, edit the httpd.conf file and add the following directives:

```
AddType application/x-httpd-php .php
AddType application/x-httpd-php .phtml
AddType application/x-httpd-php .inc
Action application/x-httpd-php /cgi-bin/php
```

The first three directives tell Apache that all files with the extensions php, phtml, and inc are of media type application/x-httpd-php. Then the last directive causes Apache to send any files of the aforementioned media type to the PHP executable. This assumes that you have copied PHP to the **cgi-bin** directory on your Web server.

These directives are the minimum requirement when using PHP with Apache, but the same thing can be accomplished in other ways. Consult an Apache configuration manual for further details.

Building PHP for Static Linking with Apache   Apache enables the option for statically linking additional modules directly into the Apache binary itself. Using this option with PHP increases the security of your server system over the CGI executable version and can improve the performance of your application. The downside of this method is that you have to rebuild Apache each time you build PHP. This can be time-consuming and frustrating because a configuration problem in PHP can cause Apache to fail. However, because application-specific reasons exist for using the statically linked module, it is described in the following paragraphs.

Before configuring and building PHP, it is necessary to configure Apache. Assuming that you have downloaded and extracted the Apache source, use the following commands to configure Apache:

```
cd <apache_dir>
./configure
```

Once this is done, you can configure and build PHP using the following:

```
cd <php_dir>
./configure --with-apache=<apache_dir>
make
make install
```

This<$PHP;static libraries> configures PHP as a static library in Apache. Note that the **--with-apache** configuration is used to cause PHP to be built as a static library and to provide the path to the Apache source. Next, you must build Apache itself using the following:

```
cd <apache_dir>
$ ./configure --prefix=/www --activate-
module=src/modules/php4/libphp4.a
 make
make install
```

The **--prefix** directive may be different in your environment because it specifies where the architecture-independent files are installed. After building and installing Apache with these options, you have a version of Apache with PHP built in. You can then start the Apache server and use a test file, such as that in Listing 1 to test the configuration.

Again, Apache configuration directives in the httpd.conf file may need to be set in order for Apache to properly process PHP files. Based on the extensions you have chosen to represent PHP files, you need to make the appropriate adjustments. Again, the standard configuration is something like the following:

```
AddType application/x-httpd-php .php
AddType application/x-httpd-php .phtml
AddType application/x-httpd-php .inc
```

The build instructions included here show how to build a plain vanilla version of PHP with all the standard defaults. For more information about changing the configuration of the PHP build, see the section on building the CGI executable.

Building PHP as a Dynamically Loaded Apache Module   Building
PHP as a module that can be loaded dynamically by Apache is not significantly different from the other methods already discussed. One advantage
of using this method is that you can rebuild PHP without needing to rebuild
Apache. Also, some of the extensions to PHP (such as Java support) require
that PHP be built as a dynamic object in order to run properly. In order for
Apache to support dynamic modules, it may need to be rebuilt once using
the following configuration options:

```
cd <apache_dir>
make clean
./configure --enable-module=so --enable-rule=SHARED_CORE --
prefix=/www
make
make install
```

In addition to building Apache, the previous commands also prepare the
apxs script that is required for building a dynamic module to be used by
Apache. If you have troubles with the apxs script when trying to build PHP
as a dynamic module, you may need to perform the previous steps to get a
properly configured apxs script. After building Apache with support for
dynamic modules, use the following commands to build PHP:

```
cd <php_dir>
make clean
rm config.cache
./configure --with-apxs=/www/bin/apxs (other options)
make
make install
```

Again, the cleanup commands are optional but are recommended if you
have previously built PHP with a completely different configuration. The
path for the **--with-apxs** configuration directive should be the full path to
the apxs script on your server.

As with the other configuration and build procedures, you must configure Apache to use your preferred PHP file extensions. Once you have done
this, you can start Apache and request a test PHP script.

Summary of Building PHP on a *nix Platform   The intent of this section is not to provide an exhaustive list of all the possible configuration
options, but to illustrate the basic methods for building PHP in its various
forms. If you have not built PHP, you should first attempt to build it with
the most basic configuration and then add options later. Once you become
familiar with the build process, it is easy to test different build configurations and include some of the non-standard extensions.

After building PHP and testing that it is working with your installation of Apache, you should look into the run-time configuration options discussed later in this chapter.

Building PHP for Windows

Building PHP for Windows is a much more complicated process initially than building for *nix. The online documentation recommends using Visual C++ version 6 to build PHP, although version 5 may work. As a note, I tried to use Borland C++ Builder to see if it would also work but had no success. The main problem is the pre-built lib files, because Microsoft and Borland use different object formats. It is conceivable that the Borland compiler could be used, but all the PHP libraries would have to be rebuilt first. The rest of this discussion assumes you are using Visual C++.

Before starting, several additional support files and programs must be downloaded. The following table shows what should be downloaded and gives the current download location at the time of this writing.

The Cygwin tools listed are a set of popular GNU utilities such as *gcc*, *make,* and *bison*. Some of these tools are used by the build process, so you must download and install these files to continue. The other files are required also but are essentially a part of the PHP distribution, not third-party tools. The PHP source code is the same source as that used for building the *nix version.

You also need an unzip utility. I use WinZip® because it inherently handles .tar.gz files without any trouble. Other zip utilities may also provide this capability. To begin, install the Cygwin utilities. You may need to manually add an environment variable to specify the location of the Cygwin installation. If you are running Windows 95, you can add this variable to

Table 1.1

Additional Support File and Program Locations

Download	Location
PHP Source Code	www.php.net/downloads.php
Cygwin tools	http://sources.redhat.com/cygwin/
PHP Win32 Build Tools	www.php.net/extra/win32build.zip
BCMath (Number) Support	www.php.net/version4/downloads/number.tar.gz
Replacement resolv.lib Build Files	www.php.net/version4/downloads/bindlib_w32.zip

your autoexec.bat. On Windows NT, right-click the My Computer icon and select **Properties** from the menu. Then select the **Environment** tab and add a new variable, as shown in Figure 1.5. The variable name to use is CYGWIN and the value is the path where you installed the Cygwin tools.

Next, create a directory and unzip the win32build.zip file into it. Next, launch Visual C++ and from the **Tools** menu, select **Options**. Then select the **Directories** tab, as shown in Figure 1.6. Using the drop-down list labeled "Show directories for," select the option Executable files, and add the

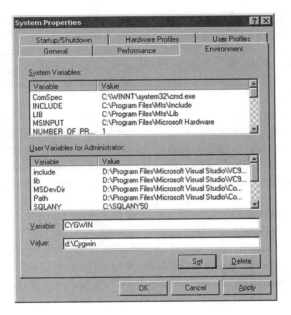

Figure 1.5
Setting the CYGWIN environment variable

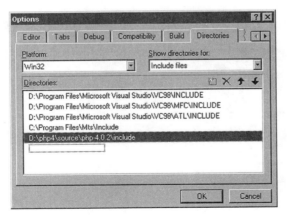

Figure 1.6
Setting the Visual C++ directory options

location of the Cygwin bin directory. Next, select Include files from the drop-down list and add the location of the win32build\include directory (shown in Figure 1.6). Finally, select Library files and add the location of the win32build\lib directory. This sets up the Visual C++ compiler to use the additional tools and files just installed.

The next step is to build the new version of resolv.lib. First, create a new directory and unzip the files from bindlib_w32.zip into it. In Visual C++, open the bindlib.dsp project. From the **Build** menu, select **Set Active Configuration** and choose either the debug or release version of the library based on whether you will be building the debug or release version of PHP. Press the **F7** key to build the library project. When finished, copy the resolv.lib file to the win32build\lib directory.

Next, unpack the PHP source code and the number.tar.gz file using either your unzip utility or the tar utility available with Cygwin. Copy the unpacked files, number.c and number.h, to the ext/bcmath directory in the PHP source tree.

Assuming that you have followed the steps to this point, you are now ready to build PHP. Start Visual C++ and open the php4ts.dsp project file found under the PHP source tree in the win32 directory. This project contains several configurations. The easiest place to start is to build the CGI executable by selecting the release or debug configuration, as shown in Figure 1.7.

Build the project and if all goes well, you have a new custom-built PHP executable available for use. If you need the ISAPI or NSAPI version of PHP, you can simply select the proper build configuration and rebuild. As mentioned before, the hard part of building PHP on Windows is the initial setup. After that has been accomplished, the rest of the process is as simple as on *nix.

Figure 1.7
Selecting the CGI
executable release
configuration

Summary of Building PHP

Building the Windows version of PHP is much harder the first time than the *nix version, but once you have everything configured, it is straightforward. As you become familiar with the build process on either platform, you can begin to develop highly specialized versions of PHP that meet your organization's precise needs. Additionally, if you are inclined to develop extensions for PHP, you must have an understanding of the build process. A discussion of building extensions is given in Chapter 11.

Configuring PHP Run-Time Options

No matter which platform or build of PHP you elect to use, the configuration of run-time options is the same. PHP uses a file, php.ini, to define its run-time behavior. This file is shipped with the PHP source distribution as php.ini-dist and php.ini-optimized. Unless you are familiar with the optimized settings, you should probably begin with the settings in the basic, php.ini-dist file. The first step is to copy and rename the file. The file should be renamed to php.ini and copied to a directory based on your platform, as shown in Table 1.2.

After copying and renaming the configuration file, you can edit it to make changes appropriate to your needs. The php.ini file is subdivided into sections delimited by *[section_name]* similar to Windows standard *ini* files. The file contains ample comments that describe the sections and configuration options. Throughout the remainder of this book, times will occur when specific options need to be set to use the example. Typically, the example

Table 1.2

PHP Platforms and Locations

Platform	php.ini **Location**
Windows	\<windows\> directory, usually \windows on Windows 95 and \winnt on Windows NT
*nix	This can be determined using the phpinfo() function but is typically /usr/local/lib

provides a section name, option name, and value to use. Preferably, you should make the change in the php.ini file and then restart Apache to make the change, but other mechanisms exist for changing the options and those will be discussed here also.

Using the php.ini File

If you find that you need to make a run-time configuration change, the recommended method is to edit the php.ini file and restart the Web server. If you happen to be using the CGI executable version of PHP, you won't need to restart the Web server because the php.ini file is read each time the CGI executable is invoked. By way of example, you can change the way that errors are reported in PHP using the error-reporting configuration items. By default, these items are set to the following values:

```
error_reporting = E_ALL & ~E_NOTICE ; Show all errors except for
notices
display_errors = On ; Print out errors (as a part of the HTML
script)
log_errors = Off ; Log errors into a log file
error_log = syslog ; log errors to syslog
```

The first item sets error reporting to include all the errors except type **E_NOTICE** errors. The next line causes errors to be displayed inline with the HTML script. The next two control the logging of errors to a file. Suppose that for production, you do not want to ever display errors, but prefer all errors to be logged to a particular file. The following configuration changes accomplish this:

```
error_reporting = E_ALL; Show all errors
display_errors = Off ;
log_errors = On ; Log errors into system log
error_log = /tmp/php_log ; log errors to /tmp/php_log
```

This configuration causes all errors including notices to be logged to the file /tmp/php_log. Obviously, the file has to be set with the appropriate permissions for logging to occur.

Because of the number of configuration settings, a full listing is not presented here, but a detailed list is included in the reference section at the end of this book. This section is intended to provide an overview of how the settings are used in general. If you need to set a specific value, you should open the php.ini file in your favorite editor and search for the setting. Typically, you will find enough comments to determine the applicable values.

Other Methods for Changing PHP Run-Time Configurations

Two methods for changing PHP run-time settings don't involve using the php.ini file. The first is to make the changes in your Apache httpd.conf file or in an Apache .htaccess file. You can use the first method if you want to have specific PHP settings for a particular virtual host or directory. The second method is typically used if you do not have direct access to either the php.ini or httpd.conf files. This tends to be the case when using third-party hosting providers. However, it is the least recommended method because the .htaccess file is read and parsed each time a Web page is requested from the same server directory as the file. This results in slower Web server performance overall.

In either case, the method for changing the PHP settings is the same. Use the configuration directives **php_value** and **php_flag** to set the values you need. For example, using the error reporting configuration values previously mentioned, the Apache directives are as follows:

```
<VirtualHost 192.1.1.1>
        ServerAdmin blake@intechra.net
        DocumentRoot /www/hosts/wwwprojects/
        ServerName www.testserver.com
        php_value error_reporting 2047
        php_flag display_errors off
        php_flag log_errors on
        php_value error_log /tmp/php_log
</VirtualHost>
```

Using the previous settings in an httpd.conf file sets specific error-reporting information for the name-based virtual server, www.testserver.com. If other virtual servers use the same physical hardware, they use the values in the php.ini file as usual. This enables you to have different PHP configurations based on which virtual server or directory is being accessed.

If you need to set PHP configuration variables but don't have direct access to either the php.ini or httpd.conf file, you can use the Apache .htaccess file. This is also useful if you have unique settings for a single directory in a large site. For example, you may need special error-reporting settings for one directory because you are debugging it. The following is a sample .htaccess file:

```
php_value error_reporting 2039
php_flag  log_errors off
php_flag  display_errors on
```

Note that in both of the examples of the Apache configuration files that the value of **error_reporting** is set using a number rather than a named

Figure 1.8
The configuration
flexibility of php.ini
and Apache
configuration files

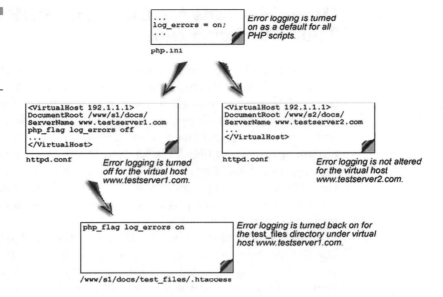

constant. This appears to be the only way to set the values correctly. Therefore, you must remember that when configuring PHP using Apache directives, you don't use any PHP-named constants in the value. Otherwise, you won't get the expected results.

To illustrate the power of the available configuration mechanisms and to clarify the previous examples, see Figure 1.8. It shows how much flexibility is available when configuring PHP for your environment.

Summary

This chapter presented several mechanisms for getting started with PHP. Because of its flexibility and the number of supported platforms, a full description of all the configuration possibilities is impossible. However, using the information provided here and at the PHP site, www.php.net, you should be able to install and configure PHP for your platform.

It should be noted that PHP also provides a large number of native functions for changing configuration settings. Some examples of these functions are the **error_reporting()** and **set_time_limit()** functions. More details about these functions can be found in the reference section at the end of this book.

CHAPTER 2

The Language

Introduction

This chapter provides a brief overview of the PHP programming language. As I mentioned in the introduction to this book, I don't intend to spend much time discussing general programming concepts. Here you will find the PHP syntax for common programming elements such as variables, constants and functions. The examples in this chapter are not intended to demonstrate best programming practices, but simply to illustrate syntax and usage. For a full language reference, check the documentation section at the PHP web site, http://www.php.net.

General Syntax Information

Because PHP is typically embedded within HTML code, there are special tags to delimit PHP code blocks. Using these tags is also known as *escaping from HTML*.

Listing 1: Ways to delimit PHP code blocks within HTML

```
<? echo "short PHP tags method of escaping from HTML<br>"; ?>
<?php echo "escape using full PHP tags<br>"; ?>
<script language="php">
    echo "some HTML editors don't like processing
instructions<br>";
</script>
<% echo "you may prefer ASP-style tags<br>"; %>
```

The first method of delimiting a PHP block is available only if short tags have been enabled. To enable short tags, use the **short_tags()** function, enable the **short_tag_open** configuration setting in the PHP configuration file, or compile PHP with the **-enable-short-tags** option. ASP-style tags are available only if the **asp_tags** configuration setting is enabled. For more information about building and configuring PHP, see the chapters "Building and Installing PHP4" and "Configuration Options."

PHP is syntactically very similar to C. For example, instructions are separated by a semicolon. The ?> tag is an implicit end of statement, so the following examples are syntactically equivalent:

Listing 2: End of statement examples

```
<?php
    echo "Testing, testing...<br>";
```

```
?>
<?php
    echo "Testing, testing...<br>"
?>
```

PHP comments are noted using comment delimiters in the C, C++, or Unix shell style. Single-line comments end at the end of the line or at the end of the current PHP code block, whichever comes first. Do not nest the multi-line C-style comments.

Listing 3: Comments

```
<?php
    echo "Hello, World!<br>";        // This is a 1-line C++ style
comment
    /*      This is a multi-
            line comment block.  */
    echo "Hello, again.<br>";# This is a shell-style comment
?>
<?php
/* The following line will print, "This will
        print nothing."
    */
?>
This will print <?php # echo "something"; ?> nothing.<br>
<?php
    /*
        echo "This is a problem."; /* This comment will cause
                                      a problem */
    */
```

Types

PHP supports the following types: floating-point numbers, integers, strings, arrays, and objects. The variable type is typically determined by the context of the variable instead of being set explicitly by the programmer. This fact is important to remember when developing PHP applications because implicit type conversion can cause some unusual (and difficult-to-find) bugs. For example, the following statement is valid and will result in the number 9 being displayed:

```
print( 3 * "3 little pigs" );
```

To help manage variable types, PHP provides the **gettype()** and **settype()** functions along with some specific type-checking functions such as **is_integer()** and **is_array()**. The function reference at the end of this book provides a full discussion of these functions. Each of the variable types (except objects) is discussed briefly in the following sections. PHP objects are discussed later in this chapter.

Numbers: Integers and Floating-Point

You can specify integers using decimal, octal, or hexadecimal notation. You may specify floating-point numbers in standard and scientific notation. The PHP syntax for each is shown in the following listing.

Listing 4: Number representations

```php
<?php
    $int1 = 523;      // decimal
    $int2 = -523;      // negative decimal
    $int3 = 01013;     // octal representation of 523
    $int4 = 0x20B;     // hex representation of 523
    $float1 = 523.197;     // standard float notation
    $float2 = 5.23197e2;     // scientific float notation
    /* Print all the numbers.
        Displays "523, -523, 523, 523, 523.197, 523.197". */
    print( "$int1, $int2, $int3, $int4, $float1, $float2<br>" );
?>
```

Strings

Strings in PHP are delimited by either double quotes (") or single quotes ('). The difference is how the string is interpreted. If a string is delimited by double quotes, variables within the string will be expanded. You can use the backslash character (\) in double-quoted strings to specify special characters (escape sequences), as shown in Table 2.1.

Table 2.1

Escape sequences in double-quoted strings

Character sequence	Meaning
\n	new line
\r	carriage return
\t	horizontal tab
\\	backslash
\"	double quote
\$	dollar sign

Single-quoted strings do not expand internal variables. Also, the only escape sequences valid within single quoted strings are the backslash (\ \) and single-quote (\') escape sequences. These escape sequences allow for single quotes and backslashes to be present within single-quoted strings. You can concatenate strings by using the dot (.) operator. The section on operators in this chapter has more information about this procedure. Similar to the C programming language, individual characters within a string may be accessed by treating the string as an array of characters.

Listing 5: String examples

```php
<?php
    $aStr1 = "This is a simple string.";
    print( "$aStr1<br>" );
    $aStr2 = "Thatcher";
    print( "$aStr2<br>" );
    $aStr3 = "My name is $aStr2";
        // $aStr3 = "My name is Thatcher"
    print( "$aStr3<br>" );
    $aStr4 = "My name is \$aStr2";
        // $aStr4 = "My name is $aStr2"
    print( "$aStr4<br>" );
    $aStr5 = 'Don\'t evaluate $aStr2';
        // $aStr5 = "Don't evaluate $aStr2"
    print( "$aStr5<br>" );
        // prints "My name is Thatcher and My name is $aStr2"
    print( "$aStr3" . " and " . "$aStr4" );
?>
```

Because of the loosely typed nature of PHP, variables can transition from one type to another based on their context. A number can be converted implicitly to a string when used with a string operator, or a string may be converted to a number to evaluate a numeric statement. When PHP evaluates a string to convert it to a number, it uses the following rules:

- If the string begins with valid numeric data, this data will be the value used.
- If the string does not begin with valid numeric data, the value will be zero (0).
- If the valid numeric data contains any of the characters ., e, or E, the value will be a floating-point type; otherwise, it will be an integer type.

Valid numeric data is an optional sign followed by one or more digits, an optional decimal point, and an optional exponent. The exponent is e or E followed by one or more digits.

Listing 6: Implicit string/number conversion examples

```php
<?php
    $aVar = 123;
    print( "\$aVar = $aVar, type = " . gettype( $aVar ) . "<br>" );

    $aVar2 = $aVar . " implictly converted to string";
    print( "\$aVar2 = $aVar2, type = " . gettype( $aVar2 ) . "<br>"
);

    $aVar3 = $aVar2 + 1;    // implicit cast to integer
    print( "\$aVar3 = $aVar3, type = " . gettype( $aVar3 ) . "<br>"
);

    $aVar3 = $aVar2 * 1.1;    // implicit cast to floating-point
    print( "\$aVar3 = $aVar3, type = " . gettype( $aVar3 ) . "<br>"
);

    $aNotNumber = "abc";
    $aVar4 = $aNotNumber * 1; // attempt to cast to number, returns
0
    print( "\$aVar4 = $aVar4, type = " . gettype( $aVar4 ) . "<br>"
);

    $aIsNumber = "3 little pigs";
    $aVar5 = $aIsNumber + 1; // casts $aIsNumber to integer 3
    print( "\$aVar5 = $aVar5, type = " . gettype( $aVar5 ) . "<br>"
);
?>
```

Arrays

Arrays in PHP behave both like indexed arrays (vectors) and as hash tables (associative arrays). PHP also supports multidimensional arrays. Because of the unique implementation of arrays in PHP, you can index multidimensional arrays numerically on one dimension and associatively on another.

You can create arrays either by using the **list()** or **array()** functions or explicitly specifying each value. The reference section at the end of this book documents the full set of available array-manipulation functions.

Single-dimensional array variables can be expanded within strings just like any other variable. For multidimensional arrays, curly braces must enclose the full variable reference. The following listing shows examples of the different types of arrays.

Listing 7: Initializing and using arrays

```php
<?php
    // Create a simple array explicitly
    $a[0] = "Ryan";
    $a[1] = "Scott";
```

```
    $a[] = "Randall"; // implicitly assigned to index (key) 2
    $a[] = "Sherie";  // implicitly assigned to index (key) 3
    print( "$a[3], $a[2], $a[1], $a[0]<br>" );

    // Create an associative array
    $color["blue"] = "#0000FF";
    $color["green"] = "#00FF00";
    $color["red"] = "#FF0000";
    print( "The hex value for red is {$color['red']}<br>" );

    // Create the same associative array as above, just
    // do it more simply.
    $color = array( "blue" =>  "#0000FF",
                    "green" =>  "#00FF00",
                    "red"   =>  "#FF0000" );
    print( "The hex value for green is {$color['green']}<br>" );

    // Manually create a multi-dimensional array
    $m[0][0] = "Zero Zero";
    $m[0][1] = "Zero One";
    print( "The value of \$m[0][1] is {$m[0][1]}<br>" );

    // Manually create a multi-dimensional associative array
    $counties["Idaho"][0] = "Ada";
    $counties["Idaho"][1] = "Adams";
    $counties["Idaho"][2] = "Bannock";
    $counties["Arizona"][0] = "Apache";
    $counties["Arizona"][1] = "Cochise";
    $counties["Arizona"][2] = "Coconino";
    print( "\$counties['Idaho'][0] = {$counties['Idaho'][0]}<br>"
);
?>
```

Variables and Constants

PHP variables are designated by a dollar sign ($), followed by the name of
the variable. All variable names are case-sensitive. Valid variable names
must start with a letter or underscore followed by a number of letters, numbers, or underscores. For variable names, a letter is considered to be **a-z, A-
Z**, or any ASCII character in the range **127-255 (0x7f - 0xff)**.

Listing 8: Variable name examples

```
<?php
    $variable1 = "Ryan";
    $variable2 = "Scott";
    print( "$variable1, $variable2<br>" ); // prints "Ryan, Scott"
    $1variable = 123;    // invalid variable name
    $_test = "test";        // valid, starts with underscore
    $_testÇ = "test2";     // valid, Ç is ASCII 128
?>
```

Variables can be assigned either by value or by reference. When a variable is assigned by value, the entire value of the original expression is assigned to the destination variable. After the assignment, the original variable is independent, so a change to one variable will not affect the other.

When a variable is assigned by reference, the new variable simply references the original variable. Changes made to either variable will be reflected in the other one. To make an assignment by reference, simply prepend an ampersand (&) to the variable name.

Listing 9: Variable assignments

```php
<?php
    $variable1 = "Ryan";
    $variable2 = $variable1;                // assign by value
    print( "$variable1, $variable2<br>" ); // prints "Ryan, Ryan"
    $variable2 = "Scott";
    print( "$variable1, $variable2<br>" ); // prints "Ryan, Scott"
    $variable3 = &$variable1;                // assign by reference
    print( "$variable1, $variable3<br>" ); // prints "Ryan, Ryan"
    $variable3 = "Katie";
    print( "$variable1, $variable3<br>" ); // prints "Katie, Katie"
?>
```

Predefined Variables

In addition to user-defined variables, PHP provides a number of predefined variables to any script in which it runs. The list of variables available is dependent on the context of the script (for example, whether it is running stand-alone or through a Web server), the version of PHP, and the type of Web server (if present). Because the predefined variable list is dependent on these factors, some variables may not be available in all cases.

PHP also generates variables for cookies and forms submitted via either POST or GET. For a detailed discussion of these variables, see Chapter 3, "Forms and Cookies."

The following sections display a subset of the available variables available when running PHP4 on Apache 1.3.11. Use the **phpinfo()** function to list the variables available in your development environment. You can find a more complete set of predefined variables in the reference section at the end of this book. Table 2.2 shows a subset of the Apache environment variables, Table 2.3 shows a subset of the system environment variables, and Table 2.4 displays a subset of the PHP-generated variables. The arithmetic operators are shown in Table 2.5, Table 2.6 shows the bitwise operators, and Table 2.7 displays the comparison operators. Table 2.8 shows the increment/

decrement operators, and Table 2.9 displays the logical operators. Finally, Table 2.10 shows the assignment operators.

Table 2.2

A Subset of the Apache Environment Variables

Variable	Definition
HTTP_HOST	The contents of the Host: header sent from the browser, if any.
HTTP_USER_AGENT	The contents of User Agent: header sent from the browser. This header denotes the browser that requested the current page, for example, "Mozilla/4.0 (compatible; MSIE 5.01; Windows NT)." For more information about using this variable, see Chapter 9, "Browser Independence."
REMOTE_ADDR	The IP address of the user viewing the current page.
SERVER_PROTOCOL	Name and revision of the protocol by which the page was requested, for example, HTTP/1.1.
GATEWAY_INTERFACE	The revision of the CGI specification used by the server; for example, CGI/1.1.

Table 2.3

A Subset of the System Environment Variables

Variable	Definition
HOSTNAME	The name of the server host
HOSTTYPE	The type of the server computer, for example, i386
PATH	The server's path variable
OSTYPE	The operating system running on the server, for example, Linux

Table 2.4

A Subset of the PHP-Generated Variables

Variable	Definition
PHP_SELF	The filename of the currently executing script
HTTP_COOKIE_VARS	An associative array of variables passed to the current script via HTTP cookies
HTTP_GET_VARS	An associative array of variables passed to the current script via the HTTP GET method
HTTP_POST_VARS	An associative array of variables passed to the current script via the HTTP POST method

Table 2.5

The Arithmetic
Operators

Operator	Name	Example	Result
+	Addition	$a + $b	Sum of $a and $b
-	Subtraction	$a - $b	Difference of $a and $b
*	Multiplication	$a * $b	Product of $a and $b
/	Division	$a / $b	Quotient of $a and $b
%	Modulus	$a % $b	Remainder of $a divided by $b

Table 2.6

The Bitwise
Operators

Operator	Name	Example	Result
&	And	$a & $b	Bits set in both $a and $b are set
|	Or	$a | $b	Bits set in either $a or $b or both are set
^	Xor	$a ^ $b	Bits set in either $a or $b but not both are set
~	Not	~$a	Bits previously set in $a are not set and vice versa
<<	Shift Left	$a << $b	Shift the bits of $a to the left by $b steps
>>	Shift Right	$a >> $b	Shift the bits of $a to the right by $b steps

Table 2.7

The Comparison
Operators

Operator	Name	Example	Result
==	Equal	$a == $b	True if $a is equal to $b
===	Identical	$a === $b	True if $a is equal to $b and they are the same type
!=	Not equal	$a != $b	True if $a is not equal to $b
<	Less than	$a < $b	True if $a is less than $b
>	Greater than	$a > $b	True if $a is greater than $b
<=	Less than or equal to	$a <= $b	True if $a is less than or equal to $b
>=	Greater than or equal to	$a >= $b	True if $a is greater than or equal to $b

Table 2.8

The Increment/
Decrement
Operators

Operator/Example	Name	Result
$a++	Post-increment	Returns $a, and then increments $a by one
++$a	Pre-increment	Increments $a by one, and then returns $a
$a—	Post-decrement	Returns $a, and then decrements $a by one
—$a	Pre-decrement	Decrements $a by one, and then returns $a

Table 2.9

The Logical
Operators

Operator	Name	Example	Result
and	And	$a and $b	True if both $a and $b are true
or	Or	$a or $b	True if either $a or $b is true
xor	Xor	$a xor $b	True if either $a or $b is true, but not both
!	Not	!$a	True if $a is not true
&&	And	$a and $b	True if both $a and $b are true
||	Or	$a or $b	True if either $a or $b is true

Table 2.10

The Assignment
Operators

Operator	Example	Result
=	$a = $b	Assigns the value of $b to $a.
+=	$a += $b	Assigns the value of ($a + $b) to $a. This is identical to $a = $a + $b.
-=	$a -= $b	Assigns the value of ($a - $b) to $a. This is identical to $a = $a - $b.
*=	$a *= $b	Assigns the value of ($a * $b) to $a. This is identical to $a = $a * $b.
/=	$a /= $b	Assigns the value of ($a / $b) to $a. This is identical to $a = $a / $b.
.=	$a .= $b	Assigns the value of ($a . $b) to $a. This is identical to $a = $a . $b.
%=	$a %= $b	Assigns the value of ($a % $b) to $a. This is identical to $a = $a % $b.
|=	$a |= $b	Assigns the value of ($a | $b) to $a. This is identical to $a = $a | $b.
&=	$a &= $b	Assigns the value of ($a & $b) to $a. This is identical to $a = $a & $b.
^=	$a ^= $b	Assigns the value of ($a ^ $b) to $a. This is identical to $a = $a ^ $b.
<<=	$a <<= $b	Assigns the value of ($a << $b) to $a. This is identical to $a = $a << $b.
>>=	$a >>= $b	Assigns the value of ($a >> $b) to $a. This is identical to $a = $a >> $b.

Variable Scope

In general, all PHP variables have single scope. This scope spans both included and required files. Within user-defined functions, local function scope is introduced. Global variables must be declared global inside a function if they are going to be used within the function. Lastly, PHP supports static variables within functions to allow function-local variables to maintain their values between invocations.

Listing 10: Variable scope

```php
<?php
    $aGlobal1 = "This is a test";
    /*
        Include another PHP source file.  The above
        variable, $aGlobal1, will
        be available in the included file.
    */
    include( "example10_inc.php" );
    function DoPrint( )
    {
        /*
            The following will print only the <br>
            since the variable
            $aGlobal1 doesn't have scope
            inside this function.
            This could also cause a undefined since warning.
        */
        print( "$aGlobal1<br>" );
    }
    DoPrint();
    function DoPrint2( )
    {
        global $aGlobal1;
        /*
            The following will print the variable since it has
            been declared global.
        */
        print( "$aGlobal1<br>" );
    }
    DoPrint2();
    function StaticFunc( )
    {
        static $aVal = 0;
        print( "$aVal<br>" );
        $aVal++;
    }
    // The following will print 0, then 1
    StaticFunc();
    StaticFunc();
?>
---     Contents of file, example10_inc.php3:   ---
<?php
    print( "$aGlobal1<br>" );
?>
```

Constants

PHP provides several predefined constants and allows for the definition of additional constants. You can find the full list of predefined constants in the reference section at the end of this book. To define new constants, use the **define()** function. Note that PHP constants are not C-style macros and therefore must be scalar values.

Listing 11: Constants

```php
<?php
    define( "aString", "This is a string constant" );
    define( "aNumber", 1 );
    print( "There is " . aNumber . " constant defined.<br>" );
    print( "Its value is '" . aString . "'<br>" );
?>
```

Operators and Operator Precedence

PHP provides a set of operators that will be very familiar to C/C++ programmers. Tables 2.5 through 2.10 provide a brief description of the available operators.

There are more operators in addition to the operators listed in the preceding tables, but they are harder to categorize. The ternary operator, which is designated with ?:, is available in PHP as in C. The expression $aValue = (expression1) ? (expression2) : (expression3); assigns the value of expression2 to the $aValue variable if expression1 evaluates to true. Otherwise, the $aValue variable receives the value of expression3.

The execution operator is designated by backticks (`) similar to many shell programming languages. The statements within the backticks are executed on the server, and the result may be passed to a variable.

PHP also supports an error-control operator, @. When this operator is prepended to an expression in PHP, any error messages that may be generated are suppressed. Use of this operator allows for more structured error handling if the **track_errors** feature is enabled. When the **track_errors** feature is enabled, any error messages suppressed by the @ operator are stored in the global variable **$php_errormsg**. This variable is overwritten on each error, so the variable should be checked as soon as possible to ensure the error is handled properly.

Listing 12: Some operator examples

```php
<?php
    $aNum1 = 1;
    $aNum2 = 2;

    $aVal   = ( $aNum1 == $aNum2 ) ? "The values are equal" :
                    "The values are different";
    print( "$aVal<br>" ); // prints "The values are different"

    $aVal   = ( 1 == "1" ) ? "The values are equal" :
                    "The values are different";
    print( "$aVal<br>" ); // prints "The values are equal"

    $aVal   = ( 1 === "1" ) ? "The values are identical" :
                    "The values are not identical";
    print( "$aVal<br>" ); // prints "The values are not identical"
    /*
        The following code first sets $aListing
        to the contents of the current server
        directory, then it converts the newlines
        to <br>'s for formatting, then prints the
        results
    */
    $aListing = 'ls -l';  // 'ls' is on *nix systems mostly
    $aFmtList = nl2br( $aListing );
    print( "<br>Directory Listing:<br><b>$aFmtList</b><br>" );
?>
```

Program Flow Control

PHP supports standard flow-control statements such as the **if**, **while**, and **for** loop statements. C programmers will recognize the syntax of each of these statements. Additionally, PHP supports two functions for including source files: **include()** and **require()**.

if, else, elseif

An obviously critical language element, the if statement controls program flow by branching on conditional expressions.

Listing 13: Examples using if, else, and elseif

```php
<?php
    if ( 1 < 2 )
        print( "This will be printed.<br>" );
    else
```

```
            print( "This will not be printed.<br>" );

    $aValue = 2;
    if ( $aValue == 1 )
    {
        // Use curly braces to delimit a statement block
        // Only NEEDED for multiple statement blocks
        print( "\$aValue == 1<br>" );
    }
    elseif ( $aValue == 2 )
    {
        print( "\$aValue == 2<br>" );
    }
    elseif ( $aValue == 3 )
    {
        print( "\$aValue == 3<br>" );
    }
    else
    {
        print( "\$aValue is neither 1, 2 nor 3<br>" );
    }
?>
```

while

The simplest type of loop in PHP, the while loop behaves just as it does in C and other high-level languages.

do..while

Although similar to the while loop, the do..while loop checks the loop condition *after* the first execution of the loop statements. This guarantees that the loop statements will execute at least once.

Listing 14: Examples using while and do..while

```
<?php
    print( "Counting up using <b>while</b>.<br>" );
    $nIndex = 0;
    // prints the numbers 0 through 9
    while ( $nIndex < 10 )
    {
        print( "$nIndex<br>" );
        $nIndex++;
    }

    print( "Counting down using <b>do..while</b>.<br>" );
    // prints the numbers 10 down through 1
    do
    {
```

```
        print( "$nIndex<br>" );
        $nIndex--;
    } while ( $nIndex > 0 );
?>
```

for

The for loop is the most complex looping statement in PHP, but it is syntactically equivalent to the C language **for** statement. The syntax is as follows:

```
for (expr1; expr2; expr3 ) statement
```

The first expression (expr1) is evaluated once at the beginning of the loop. The second expression (expr2) is evaluated at the beginning of each iteration through the loop. If it evaluates to true, the loop continues, and the statement(s) are executed. If the second expression is empty, it is implicitly evaluated as true. At the end of each iteration, expression three (expr3) is evaluated. Any of the three expressions may be empty.

Listing 15: Examples using for

```php
<?php
    // print the numbers 0 through 9
    for ( $nIndex = 0; $nIndex < 10; $nIndex++ )
    {
        print( "$nIndex<br>" );
    }

    /*
        $nIndex is now 10. this example shows that
        any of the three expressions may be empty
        when using the for loop. this is not a
        great idea for code readability, though.
        this prints the numbers 10 down to 1
    */
    for ( ; $nIndex > 0; $nIndex-- )
    {
        print( "$nIndex<br>" );
    }
?>
```

foreach

The foreach statement is a convenient mechanism for iterating arrays. Perl, VBScript, and other languages support a similar construct. PHP supports two syntaxes:

```
foreach( array_expr as value_varname) statement
foreach( array_expr as key_varname => value_varname) statement
```

The first form loops over the given array (array_expr). For each iteration of the loop, the value of the current array element is assigned to the variable (value_varname) and the array pointer is advanced. The second form does the same thing, but additionally assigns the key of the current array element to the variable key_varname.

Listing 16: Examples using foreach

```php
<?php
    $aArray = array( "Red", "Green", "Blue" );
    foreach( $aArray as $aValue )
    {
        print( "The current value is $aValue<br>" );
    }

    $aColorArray = array(    "Red"    =>    "#FF0000",
                             "Green"  =>    "#00FF00",
                             "Blue"   =>    "#0000FF" );
    foreach( $aColorArray as $aKey => $aValue )
    {
        print( "The hex value of $aKey is $aValue<br>" );
    }
?>
```

switch

The switch statement simplifies the evaluation of multiple conditions. It is often used to replace a complex if..elseif..else statement when the code contains multiple occurrences of elseif. The syntax and implementation of the switch statement in PHP is the same as in C. One nice advantage of the PHP implementation is that you can use a string as the switch expression.

For Delphi/Pascal programmers, one of the harder things to remember in a C-style switch statement is the break statement. Occasionally, omitting the break statement in a switch is convenient. The following examples illustrate many of the common uses of the switch statement.

Listing 17: Examples using switch

```php
<?php
    $nIndex = 2;
    // The simplest switch statement
    switch ( $nIndex )
    {
        case 0:
```

```
            print( "zero<br>" );
            break;
        case 1:
            print( "one<br>" );
            break;
        case 2:
            print( "two<br>" );
            break;
}

// Use the 'default' case
$nIndex = 17;
switch ( $nIndex )
{
    case 0:
        print( "zero<br>" );
        break;
    case 1:
        print( "one<br>" );
        break;
    case 2:
        print( "two<br>" );
        break;
    default:
        print( "neither zero, one nor two<br>" );
        break;
}

// Switch on a string
$aColor = "blue";
switch( $aColor )
{
    case "red":
        print( "#FF0000<br>" );
        break;
    case "green":
        print( "#00FF00<br>" );
        break;
    case "blue":
        print( "#0000FF<br>" );
        break;
    default:
        print( "other<br>" );
        break;
}

/*
    failing to remember the break statements will
    cause all the statements after the matching
    condition to be executed.
    if $nIndex is 0, all three print statements
    will execute. if $nIndex is 1, the last two
    print statements will execute.
*/
$nIndex = 0;
switch ( $nIndex )
{
    case 0:
        print( "zero<br>" );
```

```
        case 1:
            print( "one<br>" );
        case 2:
            print( "two<br>" );
    }

    /*
        omitting the break statement can be useful
        in some cases.
    */
    $aColor = "Red";
    switch( $aColor )
    {
        case "red":
        case "Red":
            // The following prints if $aColor is
            // either "red" or "Red"
            print( "#FF0000<br>" );
            break;
        case "green":
        case "Green":
            print( "#00FF00<br>" );
            break;
        case "blue":
        case "Blue":
            print( "#0000FF<br>" );
            break;
        default:
            print( "other<br>" );
            break;
    }
?>
```

break and continue

PHP provides C-style break and continue statements to provide additional
control over the various loop statements. Both statements accept an
optional numeric argument that specifies the number of nested control
structures to break from or continue to.

The break statement ends the execution of the current control structure
(either a loop or a switch statement). The continue statement is used only
with loops. It causes PHP to skip the remainder of the current loop and go
to the beginning of the next iteration.

Most often, break and continue statements are used in deeply nested
loops. For simple loops, the basic conditional statements usually suffice.

Listing 18: Examples using break and continue

```
<?php
    $aArray   = array( 4, 5, 15, 12, 7, 3, 20, 11, 31 );
    $aCurMax = 17;
```

```php
    /*
        check to see if there is a value in the array
        that is greater than the current maximum value.
        this only checks to see if there is a value
        greater than the current it doesn't necessarily
        find the largest value in the array.
    */
    foreach( $aArray as $aValue )
    {
        /*
            this will evaluate to TRUE when the value
            20 is reached. because of the break,
            it won't check the other
            values in the array after 20.
        */
        if ( $aValue > $aCurMax )
        {
            $aCurMax = $aValue;
            break; // could write 'break 1;'
        }
    }
    // prints "The current maximum is 20"
    print( "The current maximum is $aCurMax<br>" );

    // print the odd numbers from 0 to 20
    $nIndex = 0;
    for ( $nIndex = 0; $nIndex < 20; $nIndex++ )
    {
        if ( ( $nIndex % 2 ) == 0 )
            continue; // optionally, 'continue 1;'
        print( "$nIndex<br>" );
    }
?>
```

PHP provides an alternative syntax for the if, while, for, and switch control structures. For each of these structures, the basic form of this syntax is to change the opening brace to a colon (:) and the closing brace to endif, endwhile, endfor, or endswitch, respectively. When you are developing large scripts embedded in HTML, the alternative syntax is useful because it provides a clear indication of the end of the control structure.

Listing 19: Examples using the alternative syntax in an HTML page

```html
<html>
 <head>
  <title>Example 19</title>
 </head>

<body>
<!-- Use PHP to create an option list -->
<form action="someotherpage.phtml" method="post">
 <table>
  <tr>
   <td>
    Select the year you were born:
   </td>
```

```
<td>
  <select name="BirthYear" size="1">
  <?php
   /*
      Generate the option tags for the years 1920-2000
      in reverse order
   */
   $aCurYear = 2000;
   while( $aCurYear >= 1920 ):
    ?>
     <option value="<?php print( $aCurYear ); ?>">
      <?php print( $aCurYear ); ?>
     </option>
    <?php
    $aCurYear--;
   endwhile;
   /*
    assuming there were a lot more text between the
    while and endwhile statements, it might be difficult to
    find the closing semicolon for the while statement
    using the regular syntax.
   */
  ?>
  </select>
  </td>
 </tr>
</table>
</form>
</body>
</html>
```

include and require

PHP provides two mechanisms for including external files: include() and require(). The include() statement is a regular PHP function; require() is a special language construct and has some restrictions on its usage. In both cases, whenever a file is included using either statement, parsing drops out of PHP mode and into HTML mode at the beginning of the target file. The parser resumes PHP mode at the end of the file. This means that any code in the target file that should be executed as PHP script must be included within valid PHP start and end tags.

The include() function is evaluated each time it is encountered and may be contained within loops or conditional statements. This means that files can be conditionally included or groups of files can be included using a loop. The include() function also allows the target file to specify a return value and can assign that value to a variable. The processing of a file in an include() statement terminates if a return statement is encountered.

The require() statement is different from the include() statement in that it is not subject to any control structures. This means that files cannot be conditionally included using require(). The statement will execute one time if it appears within a loop or even if it appears within a conditional statement that evaluates to false. Another difference is that a file in a require() statement will not return a value. Attempting to return a value in a require() statement causes a parse error.

Functions

PHP supports the creation of user-defined functions. Functions do not have to be declared before they are referenced in PHP4. PHP supports the following features with respect to functions: variable function names, variable number of arguments, default arguments, arguments passed by value, and arguments passed by reference. Within a function block, PHP allows for any PHP code to be executed, including code that calls other functions. This capability enables PHP to provide recursive functions. PHP does not support function overloading or the ability to undefine or redefine previously defined functions.

By default, arguments are passed to functions by value. To pass a value by reference, prepend the variable name with an ampersand (&). When using default arguments, any default argument must be to the right of all nondefault arguments. For variable-length argument lists, the **func_num_args()**, **func_get_arg()**, and **func_get_args()** functions are available to retrieve information about the passed arguments. The following examples show general usage of functions in PHP.

Listing 20: Examples of user-defined functions

```php
<?php
    // a basic function
    function ReturnSum( $a, $b )
    {
        return $a + $b;
    }

    // passed by reference
    function StringAppend( &$BaseString, $AddString )
    {
        // because it's passed by reference, the value
        // of $BaseString will be changed outside the
        // scope of this function
        $BaseString .= $AddString;
    }

    // default values
    /*
        This function can be called using either:
```

```
                    PrintAnchorTag( "href", "text" );
                    PrintAnchorTag( "href", "text", "target" );
        */
        function PrintAnchorTag( $aHREF, $aText, $aTarg = "" )
        {
            if ( $aTarg == "" )
            {
              print( "<a href=\"$aHREF\">$aText</a>" );
            }
            else
            {
              print( "<a href=\"$aHREF\" target=\"$aTarg\">$aText</a>"
);
            }
        }

        // variable-length argument list
        function PrintEverything( )
        {
            $aNumArgs = func_num_args();
            for ( $nIndex = 0; $nIndex < $aNumArgs; $nIndex++ )
            {
                $aArgVal = func_get_arg( $nIndex );
                print( "Argument $nIndex: $aArgVal<br>" );
            }
        }

        print( "ReturnSum( 3, 5 ): " . ReturnSum( 3, 5 ) . "<br>" );

        $aString = "Mary had ";
        StringAppend( $aString, "a little lamb" );
        print( "$aString<br>" ); // prints "Mary had a little lamb"

        PrintAnchorTag( "example10.phtml",
                        "See example 10 again" );
        print( "<br>" );
        PrintAnchorTag( "example10.phtml",
                        "See example 10 again, in a new window",
                        "_blank" );
        print( "<br>" );

        print( "Calling PrintEverything( 1, 2, 3, 4, 5 ):<br>" );
        PrintEverything( 1, 2, 3, 4, 5 );
    ?>
```

OO/Classes

PHP supports class creation with a syntax similar to C++. PHP also supports a very basic object implementation that is sufficient for the scope of many Web applications. Single inheritance is available, but multiple inheritance is not. Class constructors exist, but destructors do not. PHP supports (and requires) the **$this** pointer within classes to refer to member variables and methods. The following examples show basic class creation within PHP. You can find more examples later in this book.

Listing 21: Examples of using classes in PHP

```php
<?php
// create a simple class
class ShoppingBasket
{
    var $fItems;
    var $fCurValue;
    /*
        this is the class constructor because it has
        the same name as the class itself. as in
        C++, PHP class constructors may specify
        arguments. in this case, the argument is the initial
        value of the basket, perhaps a mandatory
        shipping charge.
    */
    function ShoppingBasket( $aInitialValue = 0.0 )
    {
        $this->fCurValue = $aInitialValue;
    }
    // add a quantity of named items
    function AddItem( $aName, $aValue, $aQuantity = 1 )
    {
        $this->fItems[$aName]["Quantity"] +=  $aQuantity;
        $this->fItems[$aName]["Value"] = $aValue;
        $this->fCurValue += $aValue * $aQuantity;
        return True;
    }
    function RemoveItem( $aName, $aQuantity = 1 )
    {
        // only remove the quantity of items if there are
        // currently enough available
        if ( $this->fItems[$aName]["Quantity"] > $aQuantity )
        {
            $this->fItems[$aName]["Quantity"] -= $aQuantity;
            $this->fCurValue -= $this->fItems[$aName]["Value"] *
                                $aQuantity;
        }
        else
        {
            return False;
        }
    }
    function PrintBasket( )
    {
        if ( count( $this->fItems ) > 0 )
        {
            print( "Contents of basket:<blockquote>" );
            foreach( $this->fItems as $aKey => $aValue )
            {
                print( "{$aValue['Quantity']} $aKey<br>" );
            }
            print( "Total value: $" .
                    number_format( $this->fCurValue, 2 ) );
            print( "</blockquote>" );
```

```
                        print( "<br>" );
                }
                else
                {
                        print( "<i>Shopping basket is empty</i><br><br>" );
                }
        }
}
/*
        create a new instance of a ShoppingBasket. add some items,
        remove some items, and print the basket each time.
*/
$aBasket = new ShoppingBasket( 3.50 );
$aBasket->PrintBasket();
$aBasket->AddItem( "gizmo", 1.50 ); // add 1 gizmo
$aBasket->PrintBasket();
$aBasket->AddItem( "foobar", 2.10, 6 ); // add 6 foobars
$aBasket->PrintBasket();
$aBasket->RemoveItem( "foobar", 15 );
$aBasket->PrintBasket();
$aBasket->RemoveItem( "foobar", 3 );
$aBasket->PrintBasket();
?>
```

Pattern Matching

PHP supports two types of pattern-matching (or regular expression) functions. The first type is the POSIX-style functions: **ereg()**, **eregi()**, **ereg_replace()**, **eregi_replace()**, and **split()**. Each of these functions accepts a regular expression string as its first argument. PHP uses the POSIX-extended regular expressions as defined by POSIX 1003.2. PHP includes man pages in the regex directory of the PHP distribution that fully describe the POSIX regular expressions.

The second type of pattern matching functions is the Perl-compatible regular expression functions. These functions are all prepended with the **preg_** string. You can find a complete listing and description of these functions in the reference section at the end of this book. The regular expression syntax is the same as is available in Perl 5, with just a few differences. The current implementation of the functions corresponds to Perl 5.005. The differences between the Perl 5.005 implementation and the PHP implementation are documented thoroughly in the PHP documentation available from http://www.php.net.

Summary

This chapter was intended to provide you with a quick overview of the PHP language, not to provide an exhaustive programming primer. Therefore, any discussion of when or why to use a particular language feature was skipped in favor of simply providing sample code to illustrate syntax and functionality. PHP provides all of the features needed to create complex but manageable Web applications. As a language, it is robust enough for almost any task, but it is particularly suited toward Web application development, as the next chapters will illustrate.

## CHAPTER 3

Forms and Cookies

Introduction

When developers build any type of software application, user interaction is the driving factor. HTML provides form elements for gathering user information, and PHP provides a straightforward mechanism for processing those forms. Because PHP was developed as a Web application language, it transparently handles many of the details of forms processing for you. This chapter provides information not only about how to use HTML forms with PHP, but also how to validate and process the form data. For developers moving from desktop application development into Web development, the section, "Special Considerations in Web Development," outlines some important issues that arise when using a Web browser as the display medium. A discussion of cookies is also included in this chapter because of the syntactic similarity of using form elements. Cookies can also provide state management, which is typically needed in conjunction with other user feedback.

File Naming Conventions

In my examples, as in my actual development work, I use the extension *phtml* for PHP scripts that generate HTML pages and either the extension *php* or *php3* for all included code files. I don't use the conventional extension *php* or *php3* for my display pages because I personally think that the *phtml* extension looks better. That's the only reason. For included files, I like to use an extension other than *phtml*, but I like to denote the fact that the included file is a PHP script; therefore, I don't use a generic extension such as *inc*.

You can use any extension for PHP scripts. Whatever extensions you choose to use to denote PHP scripts and PHP include files should all be configured in your Web server. You can configure extensions by using your Web server's configuration options. These options are discussed in Chapter 1, "Building and Installing PHP4." For example, if you use *php* and *inc* to denote PHP scripts and PHP include files, respectively, you should ensure that your Web server is configured to treat both extensions as PHP scripts and to parse the files before sending them to the user's browser. If you fail to do this, a user could download your scripts. Consider the following example:

```
<!-- File: securityhole.phtml -->
<html>
     head>
          <title>Example: Bogus Include File Opens a Security
Hole</title>
     </head>

     <body>
<?php
    /*
         The include file, bogus.inc, has a deliberate error in
it,
         but it also has a database username and password in it.
    */
    include( "bogus.inc" );
    print( "Welcome to my security flaw.<br>" );
?>
     </body>
</html>
<!-- File: bogus.inc -->
<?php
    // This is a PHP include file demonstrating a
    // potential security flaw if you don't
    // configure your web server correctly.
    $aDatabaseIP   = "12.34.56.123";
    $aDatabaseUser = "secretuser";"
    $aDatabasePass = "secretpassword";
    /*
         This nested comment causes an error.
         /* right here */
    */
?>
```

In the preceding example, the main file, *securityhole.phtml*, includes the file *bogus.inc*. The included file contains database connection information, including the user name and password, but it also contains a coding error. When the page *securityhole.phtml* is accessed, the following error is displayed in the user's browser: "**Parse error:** parse error in **bogus.inc** on line **12**."

The interested user may try to look at the *bogus.inc* file by entering its URL on the address bar. If the Web server is configured to treat *inc* files as text (as mine is), the entire text of the included file is conveniently displayed to the user. If the Web server is configured to treat inc files as any other PHP script file, the preceding error message is the only text sent to the Web browser.

In summary, you may use any extensions you want when developing PHP applications, but to avoid potential security risks, always configure your Web server to parse all files that have the extensions you have chosen.

Handling Forms in PHP

HTML provides forms for gathering information from the end-user. In the default PHP configuration, PHP automatically converts all of the form elements to PHP variables when a form is submitted to a PHP script. The following HTML page displays a simple form asking for a user name and password. When the form is submitted to the *post1.phtml* script, the $Username and $Password variables will contain the values submitted as the username and password, respectively.

Listing 1: HTML page and PHP script illustrating a user login

```html
<!-- This is the HTML page, listing1.html -->
<html>
    <head>
        <title>Listing 1 - listing1.html</title>
    </head>

    <body>
        <form action="post1.phtml" method="post">
            UserName: <input type="text" name="Username"><br>
            Password: <input type="password" name="Password"><br>
            <input type="submit" name="Submit" value="Submit">
        </form>
    </body>
</html>
<!-- This is the PHP script, post1.html -->
<html>
    <head>
        <title>Listing 1: post1.phtml</title>
    </head>
    <body>
<?php
    print( "The user name is: $Username<br>" );
    print( "The password is: $Password<br>" );
?>
    </body>
</html>
```

Scalar and Multivalue Form Elements

HTML form elements typically specify a scalar value. The example in Listing 1 is a form that provides two scalar values: user name and password. You also can create a form element that has multiple values, such as a multiselect list. In order to use nonscalar form elements with PHP, you must include the square brackets to denote an array variable in the name of the element. The form in Listing 2 illustrates multivalue form elements.

Listing 2: HTML form with multivalue elements

```html
<form action="displayall.phtml" method="post">
    <table>
        <tr>
            <td valign="top">
                Please select all the colors you like:
            </td>
            <td valign="top">
                <!-- The name includes the array specifier -->
                <select name="Colors[]" size="5" multiple>
                    <option value="Red">Red</option>
                    <option value="Green">Green</option>
                    <option value="Blue">Blue</option>
                    <option value="Purple">Purple</option>
                    <option value="Yellow">Yellow</option>
                </select>
            </td>
        </tr>
        <tr>
            <td valign="top">
                Please enter your address:
            </td>
            <td valign="top">
                <!-- provide three spaces for address
                    information. use the array notation
                    to denote multiple array lines -->
                <input type="text" name="address[]"><br>
                <input type="text" name="address[]"><br>
                <input type="text" name="address[]"><br>
            </td>
        </tr>
        <tr>
            <td colspan="2">
                <input type="submit" name="Submit" value="Submit">
            </td>
        </tr>
    </table>
</form>
```

When the form in Listing 2 is posted to a PHP script, the $Colors[ ] and $address[ ] arrays will contain zero or more values each.

Alternate Method of Retrieving Form Values

PHP provides an alternate method for accessing information submitted to a script. The predefined array variables HTTP_GET_VARS and HTTP_POST_VARS each contain an associative array of elements passed to the script through the HTTP GET or POST method, respectively. The display script in Listing 1 could be rewritten as follows:

```
<!-- This is the PHP script, post2.html -->
<html>
    <head>
        <title>Listing: post2.phtml</title>
    </head>

    <body>
<?php
    print( "The user name is: {$HTTP_POST_VARS['Username']}<br>" );
    print( "The password is: {$HTTP_POST_VARS['Password']}<br>" );
?>
    </body>
</html>
```

In some instances, using the HTTP_GET_VARS or HTTP_POST_VARS variables is preferred over using the global variable names. For instance, you may want to simply display the contents of the entire form for debugging. If you are extremely concerned about Web server performance, there is a performance gain if PHP doesn't have to create global variables for each form element. Therefore, you may choose to configure PHP not to provide the global variable names and simply write your scripts to use the HTTP_GET_VARS and HTTP_POST_VARS variables. To learn more about this configuration directive, see the register_globals configuration option in the reference section at the end of this book.

The following functions demonstrate using the HTTP_GET_VARS and HTTP_POST_VARS variables to display all of the form information passed to a script:

```
function DisplayGetVars()
{
    global $HTTP_GET_VARS;
    DisplayArray( $HTTP_GET_VARS );
}
function DisplayPostVars()
{
    global $HTTP_POST_VARS;
    DisplayArray( $HTTP_POST_VARS );
}
```

Both of the preceding functions depend on the DisplayArray function in Listing 3. This simple function displays all the elements of an array in an HTML table and is recursive to handle array values that are arrays themselves.

Listing 3: The DisplayArray function

```
function DisplayArray( $aArray )
    {
        // Make sure that $aArray is really an array
        // and that it has some values
```

```php
if ( is_array( $aArray ) && ( count( $aArray ) > 0 ) )
{
    // Open the table
    print( "<table border=\"1\">" );
    // Display the table header row
    print( "<tr><th>Key</th><th>Value</th></tr>" );
    // display each key/value pair of the array
    foreach( $aArray as $aKey => $aValue )
    {
        print( "<tr>" );
        // if the current value is an array itself,
        // recurse this function, otherwise just
        // display the value
        if ( !is_array( $aValue ) )
        {
            // if the current value is empty, display
            // that fact
            if ( empty( $aValue ) )
            {
                print( "<td>$aKey</td><td><i>empty</i></td>" );
            }
            else
            {
                print( "<td>$aKey</td><td>$aValue</td>" );
            }
        }
        else
        {
            print( "<td>$aKey (array)</td><td>" );
            DisplayArray( $aValue );
            print( "</td>" );
        }
        print( "</tr>" );
    }
    print( "</table>" );
}
else
{
    print( "<i>empty or invalid</i>" );
}
}
```

Using the previous functions, you can write a generic PHP script to display all submitted form variables. The following script, displayall.phtml, displays all information submitted through HTTP GET, HTTP POST, and all cookies sent by the browser. (Cookies are discussed later in this chapter.)

Listing 4: The displayall.phtml script

```php
<html>
<head>
    <title>Display All Form Elements</title>
</head>
<body>
<?php
    error_reporting( 255 );
```

```
        include( "../include/gen_form_funcs.php" );
?>
<h2>All HTTP_GET_VARS</h2>
<?php
    DisplayGetVars();
?>
<br><br>
<h2>All HTTP_POST_VARS</h2>
<?php
    DisplayPostVars();
?>
<br><br>
<h2>All HTTP_COOKIE_VARS</h2>
<?php
    DisplayCookieVars();
?>
<br><br>
</body>
</html>
```

Using the form in Listing 2, Figures 3.1 and 3.2 show the input form and results of posting the form to the displayall.phtml script, respectively. Note that in Figure 3.2 the HTTP_POST_VARS array contains three elements: Colors, Address, and Submit. The values of the former two elements are arrays, as expected. The value of the Submit element is the same as the caption on the button. Remember that the Submit element is always included in the HTTP_POST_VARS array if you are writing a script to manage these values.

Using Forms to Upload Files

Most modern Web browsers provide a facility for uploading files directly from the user's hard drive to the Web server. PHP supports file uploading directly within the language. This facility is discussed at length in Chapter 5, "Forms and File Uploading."

Using an Image for the Submit Button

Depending on the design requirements of your Web application, you may use images instead of HTML buttons to submit forms to the server. PHP doesn't care whether you use buttons or images, but if you choose to use an image, the x and y coordinates representing where the user clicked (relative

Figure 3.1
The multivalue form
example

to the upper-left corner of the image) will be sent to the server along with the other form data. The coordinate variable names are constructed from the name of the name of the image element with _x and _y appended. For example, in Listing 5, the image element name is SubmitImg. The two coordinate variables that will be included when the form is posted are SubmitImg_x and SubmitImg_y. This mechanism can be handy for implementing server-side image maps.

Listing 5: Example using an image element in a form

```
<!-- This is the HTML page, imgsubmit.html -->
<html>
    <head>
        <title>Using an image instead of a submit button</title>
    </head>
    <body>
        <form action="displayall.phtml" method="post">
            UserName: <input type="text" name="Username"><br>
            Password: <input type="password" name="Password"><br>
            <input type="image" name="SubmitImg" src="submit.gif">
        </form>
    </body>
</html>
```

Figure 3.2
Results of posting the
multivalue form to
displayall.phtml

One note about using the mechanism in Listing 5 is that some browsers provide a default behavior for forms that allows the **Enter** key to be used in lieu of clicking the submit button. When you use an image instead of a standard submit button, this default behavior can still occur. When it does occur, no coordinate information (x or y position) is sent with the form at all.

 # Validating Form Data

This section discusses server-side form validation, not client-side validation. Client-side scripting languages such as JavaScript can be used to validate form elements before they are submitted to the Web server. This validation is recommended when you are developing highly interactive Web applications, but it is not completely reliable given the vast number of browsers and operating environments that may be used. Therefore, all data should be validated at the server even if some validation occurs at the client. PHP provides several methods for validating data including using regular expressions, checking data types, and accessing databases for data lookups.

Data Validation Using Regular Expressions

Probably the most powerful mechanism for validating data is to use regular expressions and the regular expression functions in PHP. Although regular expressions are powerful, they are complex to use if you don't already have some experience with them.

PHP supports two types of regular expressions: POSIX style and Perl style. This discussion will focus on POSIX-style regular expression functions, but similar functionality is available for the Perl-style functions. The Perl-style function names are all prepended with preg_ and are documented in the reference section at the end of this book. Because my experience is with the POSIX-style regular expressions, I will use them in the examples, but keep in mind that the Perl-style functions are faster and more powerful.

The POSIX-style regular expression functions are **ereg()**, **ereg_replace()**, **eregi()**, **eregi_replace()**, and **split()**. For validation, the **ereg()** and **eregi()** functions are used. The general syntax for each function is as follows:

```
int ereg( string pattern, string string [, array regs] )
int eregi( string pattern, string string [, array regs] )
```

Both functions accept a regular expression pattern, a string to be searched, and an optional array variable that stores the matches found of any subexpressions in parentheses in the pattern. Each function returns true if a match for the pattern is found in the string. The **eregi()** function is identical to the **ereg()** function except that it ignores case when matching alphabetic characters.

Avoiding Validation

Although validating input data is important, don't validate anything that you don't have to. Rather, provide input mechanisms that reduce the chance of user error. For example, providing a combo box listing all of the months of the year is less work than validating a month typed by a user. Instead of always using a generic text box, look for places where you can provide a list, check box, or option group instead to minimize user errors.

The following examples illustrate using regular expressions to validate a U.S. postal code format and a date in ISO format (YYYY-MM-DD). Note that these examples validate only the format, not the value.

Listing 6: Validating a U.S. postal code and an ISO date

```php
<?php
    $aCode1 = "83440";
    $aCode2 = "83440-1607";
    $aCode3 = "834";
    $aCode4 = "M6K 3E3";
    $aCodeFormat = "[0-9]{5}(-[0-9]{4})?";
    if ( ereg( $aCodeFormat, $aCode1 ) == True )
        print( "'$aCode1' is valid US postal code format<br>" );
    else
        print( "'$aCode1' is not valid US postal code format<br>" );
    if ( ereg( $aCodeFormat, $aCode2 ) == True )
        print( "'$aCode2' is valid US postal code format<br>" );
    else
        print( "'$aCode2' is not valid US postal code format<br>" );
    if ( ereg( $aCodeFormat, $aCode3 ) == True )
        print( "'$aCode3' is valid US postal code format<br>" );
    else
        print( "'$aCode3' is not valid US postal code format<br>" );
    if ( ereg( $aCodeFormat, $aCode4 ) == True )
        print( "'$aCode4' is valid US postal code format<br>" );
    else
        print( "'$aCode4' is not valid US postal code format<br>" );
    $aDate1 = "2000-06-29";
    $aDate2 = "2000-7-4";
    $aDate3 = "June 29, 2000";
    $aDate4 = "0000-99-99";
    $aDateFormat = "[0-9]{4}-[0-9]{1,2}-[0-9]{1,2}";
    if ( ereg( $aDateFormat, $aDate1 ) == True )
        print( "'$aDate1' is valid ISO date format<br>" );
    else
        print( "'$aDate1' is not valid ISO date format<br>" );
```

```
        if ( ereg( $aDateFormat, $aDate2 ) == True )
            print( "'$aDate2' is valid ISO date format<br>" );
        else
            print( "'$aDate2' is not valid ISO date format<br>" );
        if ( ereg( $aDateFormat, $aDate3 ) == True )
            print( "'$aDate3' is valid ISO date format<br>" );
        else
            print( "'$aDate3' is not valid ISO date format<br>" );
        if ( ereg( $aDateFormat, $aDate4 ) == True )
            print( "'$aDate4' is valid ISO date format<br>" );
        else
            print( "'$aDate4' is not valid ISO date format<br>" );
?>
```

The results of the Listing 6 are as follows:

```
'83440' is valid US postal code format
'83440-1607' is valid US postal code format
'834' is not valid US postal code format
'M6K 3E3' is not valid US postal code format
'2000-06-29' is valid ISO date format
'2000-7-4' is valid ISO date format
'June 29, 2000' is not valid ISO date format
'0000-99-99' is valid ISO date format
```

Developers coming from Perl or those with background in regular expressions will find that validation using regular expressions is straight-forward and powerful. Those developers with limited regular expression background may choose other mechanisms for data validation such as those described in the next two sections.

Data Validation Using Type Checking

In some cases, simply checking the type of data at the server, while ignoring the actual values, may be sufficient. This method works for validating simple types such as strings and numbers, but offers little more. When it is used in conjunction with other custom validation code, it can be powerful enough for many applications. The following example simply checks the type of the variable to ensure that only numbers are accepted.

Listing 7: Validating numbers using type checking

```
<?php
    $aValue1 = "123";
    $aValue2 = "123.446";
    $aValue3 = "1.56e18";
    $aValue4 = "3 little pigs";
    if ( is_numeric( $aValue1 ) == True )
        print( "'$aValue1' is a number<br>" );
```

```
    else
        print( "'$aValue1' is not a number<br>" );
    if ( is_numeric( $aValue2 ) == True )
        print( "'$aValue2' is a number<br>" );
    else
        print( "'$aValue2' is not a number<br>" );
    if ( is_numeric( $aValue3 ) == True )
        print( "'$aValue3' is a number<br>" );
    else
        print( "'$aValue3' is not a number<br>" );
    if ( is_numeric( $aValue4 ) == True )
        print( "'$aValue4' is a number<br>" );
    else
        print( "'$aValue4' is not a number<br>" );
?>
```

In Listing 7, the first three values are validated as numbers; the last is not. For more type-checking functions, see the **is_xxx()** functions and the *Variable Functions* list in the reference section at the end of the book.

The Validator Class

One of the beautiful things about open-source software is the availability of great open-source tools to complement the original product. You can find third-party tools for PHP in many places. The Webmasters Net (http://www.thewebmasters.net) provides some great open-source classes and source modules. For data validation, the Validator class provides an array of functions that can simplify your efforts and save time. Among the validation functions are the **is_email()**, **is_url()**, and **is_phone()** functions for validating e-mail addresses, URLs, and phone numbers, respectively. For more information about this class and others provided by The Webmasters Net, see the section, "PHP Tools and Extras," on the Webmasters Net Web site.

Listing 8: Validating data using the Validator class

```
<?php
    error_reporting( 0 );
    include( "../include/class.Validator.php3" );
    $aValidator = new Validator;
    $aPhoneNum1 = "(208) 359-1540";
    $aPhoneNum2 = "+1 208-359-1540";
    $aPhoneNum3 = "support@intechra.net";
    if ( $aValidator->is_phone( $aPhoneNum1 ) == True )
        print( "'$aPhoneNum1' is a valid phone number<br>" );
    else
        print( "'$aPhoneNum1' is not a valid phone number<br>" );
    if ( $aValidator->is_phone( $aPhoneNum2 ) == True )
        print( "'$aPhoneNum2' is a valid phone number<br>" );
    else
```

```
                    print( "'$aPhoneNum2' is not a valid phone number<br>" );
          if ( $aValidator->is_phone( $aPhoneNum3 ) == True )
                    print( "'$aPhoneNum3' is a valid phone number<br>" );
          else
                    print( "'$aPhoneNum3' is not a valid phone number<br>" );
          /*
                    The is_email function checks not only for a valid email
                    address format, but also checks to see if the host
                    is a real Internet host. This obviously requires an
                    Internet connection to succeed. At the time this was
                    written, the host 'invalidhost.com' was not registered.
          */
          $aEmail1 = "blake@intechra.net";
          $aEmail2 = "johnv;
          $aEmail3 = "nobody@invalidhost.com";
          if ( $aValidator->is_email( $aEmail1 ) == True )
                    print( "'$aEmail1' is a valid email address<br>" );
          else
                    print( "'$aEmail1' is not a valid email address<br>" );
          if ( $aValidator->is_email( $aEmail2 ) == True )
                    print( "'$aEmail2' is a valid email address<br>" );
          else
                    print( "'$aEmail2' is not a valid email address<br>" );
          if ( $aValidator->is_email( $aEmail3 ) == True )
                    print( "'$aEmail3' is a valid email address<br>" );
          else
                    print( "'$aEmail3' is not a valid email address<br>" );
?>
```

The Validator class is a powerful set of methods that can speed your application development, but as with any third-party tool, you must test the code to make sure that it meets your specific requirements.

Cookies

Because of the ongoing debate about using cookies, most Web developers and users are familiar with the concept of a cookie. Because cookies are simply text files stored at the client, they are inherently innocuous. However, many end-users will not accept cookies sent to their browsers because of the hype surrounding their use. If your application relies on cookies to be successful, you may have some users that will not be able to use it properly. However, if you use cookies but do not require them, your application will be more successful with a larger audience.

PHP supports a single function for creating cookies, **setcookie()**. Because cookies are sent as part of the HTTP header, the **setcookie()** function must be called before any output data is sent to the browser, or you must enable PHP's output buffering to delay output to the browser until all the cookies have been defined. The **header()** function also has this limitation.

Any cookies sent to your application by the browser are automatically converted into PHP variables just like those from the GET and POST methods. Cookies can be scalar values or an array of values. The **setcookie()** function is defined as follows:

```
int setcookie (string name, string value, int expire, string path,
string domain, int secure)
```

All of the arguments to the function are optional except for the *name* argument. If the function is called with only a name, the cookie referenced by that name will be deleted. Any string value may be skipped by providing an empty string, (""). Any integer value may be skipped by providing the value zero (0). The *expire* time is a standard UNIX time integer as returned from **mktime()** or **time()**. The *secure* parameter indicates that the cookie should only be transmitted over a secure HTTPS connection.

Keep these caveats and common mistakes in mind when using cookies:

- Cookies will not be visible in the script until the page is reloaded.

- Browsers behave differently with respect to cookies. Test your application with as many browsers as you can.

- Each browser stores its cookies independently. That means if a user visits your site using one browser and you set a cookie, that cookie won't be available if the user returns using another browser.

For more information about cookies in general, see Netscape's cookie specification at http://www.netscape.com/newsref/std/cookie_spec.html.

The following two examples demonstrate the **setcookie()** function. Listing 9 displays setting and retrieving cookie values. Listing 10 shows how to use output buffering in conjunction with the **setcookie()** function.

Listing 9: Using cookies

```php
<?php
    // Check for the $LastTime cookie variable.
    if ( !empty( $LastTime ) )
    {
        $aMessage  = "The last time you visited was ";
        $aMessage .= date( "d F Y", $LastTime );
        $aMessage .= " at ";
        $aMessage .= date( "h:i:s a", $LastTime );
    }
    else
    {
        $aMessage  = "You have not visited in the past ";
        $aMessage .= "two weeks.";
    }
    // Set the $LastTime cookie that will be valid for
```

```php
    // two weeks
    $aTwoWeeks = time() + ( 60 * 60 * 24 * 14 );
    setcookie( "LastTime", time(), $aTwoWeeks );
    // check for the extremely important cookie array values
    $aValMessage = "";
    if ( !empty( $CookieArray ) )
    {
        $aValMessage  = "Values: " . $CookieArray[0];
        $aValMessage .= ", " . $CookieArray[1];
        $aStartValue = $CookieArray[1] + 1;
    }
    else
    {
        $aValMessage = "The Values are not available!";
        $aStartValue = 0;
    }
    // delete the extremely important cookie array values
    setcookie( "CookieArray[0]" );
    setcookie( "CookieArray[1]" );
    // add the extremely important cookie array values
    setcookie( "CookieArray[0]", $aStartValue, $aTwoWeeks );
    setcookie( "CookieArray[1]", $aStartValue + 1, $aTwoWeeks );
?>
<html>
<head>
    <title>Using Cookies</title>
</head>
<body>
<?php
    print( $aMessage . "<br><br>" . $aValMessage );
?>
</body>
</html>
```

Listing 10: Using setcookie() in conjunction with output buffering

```php
<?php
    /*
        start output buffering. if the ob_start() function
        is commented out, this script will result in an
        error.
    */
    ob_start();
?>
<html>
<head>
    <title>Using setcookie() in conjunction with output
buffering/<title>
</head>
<body>
<?php
setcookie( "anyname", "anyvalue", time() + 60 );
?>
This works just fine.
</body>
</html>
<?php ob_end_flush(); ?>
```

Last Note on Cookies

In previous versions of PHP, if you needed to set multiple cookies within a single script, you had to call **setcookie()** in reverse order of how you wanted to have the cookies handled. For example, if you wanted to delete a cookie and then create a new cookie with the same name, it was necessary to call **setcookie()** first to set the new value, and then to delete the original value. In PHP4, this is not the case. You must call the **setcookie()** function in the same order as you expect the cookies to be processed by the browser. Listing 9 shows this process.

Although the debate about whether to use cookies will certainly continue, implementing them using PHP is straightforward and simple. Some discussion of whether to use cookies can be found in Chapter 7, "Sessions and Application State."

Special Considerations in Web Development

For developers migrating from desktop software development to Web application development, this section outlines some considerations that must be made when processing and using information submitted through an HTML form.

Handling Bad Data

The first consideration is how to handle erroneous data. Often in traditional application data, user input can be validated in real time as the user provides the data. This means that the user can be notified of erroneous data on a field-by-field basis. In contrast, Web applications have no perfectly reliable ways to validate data on a field-by-field basis, so all the validation is usually deferred to the server. This means that if data errors exist, the user will not know until after an entire form is submitted. Therefore, you must consider how to respond to data errors while developing your application.

There are several ways to respond to data errors; I will discuss two. The first method is to simply list the error conditions or that an error occurred and then ask the user to return to the previous page to make corrections. In my opinion, this is the least desirable method, but it is simple to implement. If very little data (one or two fields) is collected in the form, this method may be acceptable. However, if you have created a large form, don't use this method because it may require the user to re-enter all of the data. Some browsers don't retain the form values when the Back button is used to return to a page.

The second way to handle bad data is to present the input page again with all of the data elements pre-populated and with the errors highlighted. You can create this display by posting the data collection script back to itself. This method requires more advanced planning, but it results in a more robust and usable application because the same script can be used to collect new data, edit existing data, and validate its data. Listing 11 shows how a single script can be used to collect and validate a simple form for collecting a person's e-mail address and phone number.

Listing 11: Handling erroneous data intelligently

```php
<?php
    error_reporting( 0 );
    // set up the form initially to collect new info.
    $aCurPhoneVal  = "";
    $aCurEmailVal  = "";
    $aPhoneTextCol = "black";
    $aEmailTextCol = "black";
    if ( !empty( $Submit ) )
    {
        /*
            if the $Submit variable is not empty, we are here
            because of a POST to this script. try to
            validate the form variables.
        */
        include( "../include/class.Validator.php3" );
        $aValidator = new Validator;
        $aValidPhone = $aValidator->is_phone( $Phone );
        $aValidEmail = $aValidator->is_email( $Email );
        if ( $aValidPhone && $aValidEmail )
        {
            // all data is valid, redirect to the appropriate page
            header( "Location: http://server.com/thanks.html\n" );
        }
        else
        {
            // some bad data, highlight it
            $aCurPhoneVal = $Phone;
            $aCurEmailVal = $Email;
            if ( $aValidPhone == False )
                $aPhoneTextCol = "red";
```

```
                        if ( $aValidEmail == False )
                            $aEmailTextCol = "red";
                    }
                }
        ?>
        <html>
            <head>
                <title>Handling Erroneous Data Intelligently</title>
            </head>
            <body>
        <?php
            if ( empty( $Submit ) ) {
        ?>
            Please enter your phone number and email address.
            <br>
        <?php
            } else { // if
        ?>
            There were some errors in the information you
            provided. Check the values highlighted in red.
        <?php
            } // end if
        ?>
        <form action="handle_errors.phtml" method="post">
            <font color="<?php print( $aPhoneTextCol );?>">
                Phone Number:</font>
            <input type="text" name="Phone"
                value="<?php echo $aCurPhoneVal;?>">
            <br>
            <font color="<?php print( $aEmailTextCol );?>">
                Email Address:</font>
            <input type="text" name="Email"
                value="<?php echo $aCurEmailVal;?>">
            <br>
            <input type="submit" name="Submit" value="Submit">
        </form>
        </body>
        </html>
```

In Listing 11, when the page is accessed directly, the value of the $Submit variable is empty, so the form is displayed with empty text boxes. When the user clicks the submit button, the page is accessed again, but this time the value of the $Submit variable is not empty, so the form is validated. If both fields validate properly, then the **header()** function is used to redirect the browser to a new page and thank the user for correct information. If either field fails validation, then the original form is displayed again, but this time the boxes are pre-populated with the data previously supplied. Additionally, the text color of the offending data items is changed to red to highlight the errors.

This method allows the user to quickly identify the information that needs to be changed, but it doesn't require that the entire form be completed again. If you are building a Web application that has a great deal of user input, consider using a similar method when handling data errors. If your application is cumbersome or requires the user to re-enter data, it will not be successful.

Again, the previous two methods are not the only two methods for handling erroneous data, but they illustrate some fundamentals in Web application development. Choosing an error handling method should be a key decision in your application design.

Handling and Reformatting Data for Display

In typical desktop application development, displaying data gathered from a user doesn't require much reformatting or processing. Occasionally numbers will be formatted to display currency values or thousands separators, but typically there is very little thought involved in displaying user-provided information. In Web application development, however, the redisplay of information gathered in a Web form is critical. This is because browsers are built to interpret and process all text retrieved from the Web server. If you provide a form to your user, and then display the data collected, some crafty users may include HTML tags in the fields just to see what will happen.

With that in mind, consider a form that collects feedback data from your visitors. Suppose you want to build a form that collects the user's name, e-mail address, and the body of the feedback message. After gathering the information, you display the message to allow for verification, and then you process the message. A creative or devious user may try to test your Web server by placing HTML tags or JavaScript code in the body of the message. This may not be particularly dangerous in all cases, but it will certainly result in some adverse side effects.

To protect yourself from this problem, always process form input before redisplaying it. PHP provides some functions to help you in this effort, including the **strip_tags()** and **htmlentities()** functions. The **strip_tags()** function removes all tags from a string and provides an optional parameter for specifying allowable tags to remain. The **htmlentities()** function converts HTML special characters into the equivalent HTML entities. For example the characters <and > are converted to **&lt**; and **&gt**;, respectively. The form and script in Listing 12 illustrate handling a basic form redisplay.

Listing 12: Handling data redisplay

```
<html>
<head>
    <title>Gathering Input for Redisplay</title>
</head>
```

```
<body>
    <form action="safedisplay.phtml" method="post">
        Enter some text:<br>
        <textarea cols="40" rows="6" name="TheText"></textarea>
        <br><br>
        Choose filtering method:
        <select name=""FilterType" size="1">
            <option value="0">none</option>
            <option value="1">strip_tags()</option>
            <option value="2">htmlentities()</option>
        </select>
        <br><br>
        <input type="submit" name="Submit" value="Submit">
    </form>
</body>
</html>
<!-- Begin Script, safedisplay.phtml -->
<?php
    error_reporting( 255 );
    switch ( $FilterType )
    {
        case 0 : // none
            $aDisplayText = $TheText;
            break;
        case 1 : // none
            $aDisplayText = strip_tags( $TheText );
            break;
        case 2 : // none
            $aDisplayText = htmlentities( $TheText );
            break;
    }
?>
<html>
<head>
    <title>Safely Redisplaying User Input</title>
</head>
<body>
<?php
    print( $aDisplayText );
?>
</body>
</html>
```

Figures 3.3 through 3.6 show the input form and the results of the script.
Figure 3.3 is the input form. Figure 3.4 shows what happens when there is
no filtering. Figures 3.5 and 3.6 show the results of the form information filtered with **strip_tags()** and **htmlentities()**, respectively.

If you look carefully at these figures, you'll see that there are some possibly unexpected results in the redisplay. For example, the single quote in
the word don't appeared on all of the display pages as an escaped single
quote (\'). Also, the hard returns entered in the text box didn't seem to
appear in the output.

The former condition is controlled by the **--enable-magic-quotes** configuration directive at compile time and by the **magic_quotes_gpc**, **magic_quotes_runtime**, and **magic_quotes_sybase** options in the PHP configuration file. When enabled, these options automatically escape the single quote, double quote, NUL, and backslash characters in strings coming from external sources, such as forms and databases. This functionality is enabled by default. It is particularly valuable when you are gathering information that will be stored in a database so that you don't have to manually escape the quotes in a SQL string. For display, call the **strip_slashes()** function to remove the escape characters from such strings.

As for the problem with hard returns, remember that HTML doesn't consider carriage return or newline characters to be hard breaks unless they occur within a <pre></pre> block. PHP provides the **nl2br()** function to convert all newline characters to <br> tags.

Listing 13 shows the same form and script as in Listing 12, but with additional options to conditionally call the **strip_slashes()** and **nl2br()** functions.

Figure 3.3
The input form

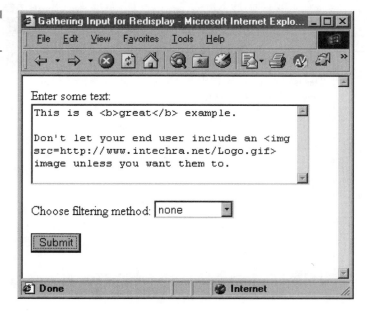

Figure 3.4
Display with no
filtering

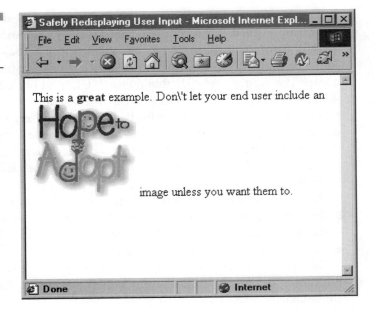

Figure 3.5
Display with
strip_tags()

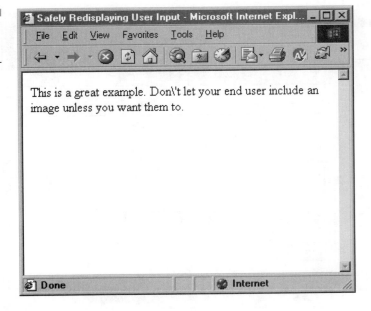

Figure 3.6
Display with
htmlentities()

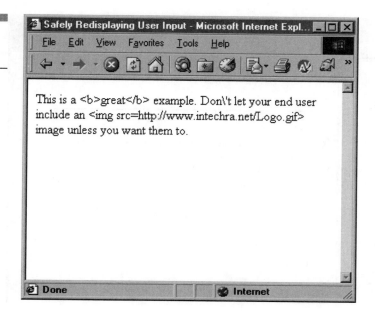

This is a great example. Don\'t let your end user include an <img src=http://www.intechra.net/Logo.gif> image unless you want them to.

Listing 13: Handling data redisplay revisited

```html
<html>
<head>
    <title>Gathering Input for Redisplay</title>
</head>
<body>
    <form action="safedisplay2.phtml" method="post">
        Enter some text:<br>
        <textarea cols="40" rows="6" name="TheText"></textarea>
        <br><br>
        Choose filtering method:
        <select name="FilterType" size="1">
            <option value="0">none</option>
            <option value="1">strip_tags()</option>
            <option value="2">htmlentities()</option>
        </select>
        <br><br>
        <input type="checkbox" name="DoSS"> Strip slashes<br>
        <input type="checkbox" name="DoNB"> nl2br<br><br>
        <input type="submit" name="Submit" value="Submit">
    </form>
</body>
</html>
<!-- Begin Script, safedisplay2.phtml -->
<?php
    error_reporting( 0 );
    switch ( $FilterType )
    {
        case 0 : // none
```

Figure 3.7
The input form

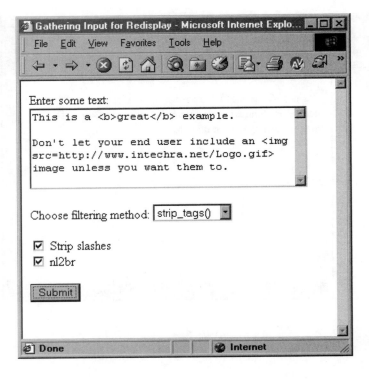

```
            $aDisplayText = $TheText;
            break;
        case 1 : // none
            $aDisplayText = strip_tags( $TheText );
            break;
        case 2 : // none
            $aDisplayText = htmlentities( $TheText );
            break;
    }
    if ( $DoSS == "on" )
        $aDisplayText = stripslashes( $aDisplayText );
    if ( $DoNB == "on" )
        $aDisplayText = nl2br( $aDisplayText );
?>
<html>
<head>
    <title>Safely Redisplaying User Input</title>
</head>
<body>
<?php
    print( $aDisplayText );
?>
</body>
</html>
```

Figure 3.8
Display with
strip_tags(),
strip_slashes(), and
nl2br()

With the changes in Listing 13, the input form and display form appear as in Figures 3.7 and 3.8, respectively.

If you are coming from a background in standard desktop application development, you must be mindful of the display caveats when using a browser for the application presentation layer. Besides being aware of the aforementioned situations, also consider that each browser will display your user interface slightly differently. For a detailed discussion of this issue, please see Chapter 9, "Browser Independence."

Summary

This chapter covered the basics of forms processing using PHP. Because PHP was developed specifically as a Web-based programming language, it simplifies the process of interacting with HTML forms considerably. More important than simply retrieving information from users is properly handling that information and protecting your application and servers from bad or harmful information. This chapter discussed some of the tools available to handle bad data and protect against harmful data. Lastly, this chapter gave an overview of storing and retrieving cookies at the client. Together these topics provide a framework for building the highly interactive Web applications that users are demanding.

CHAPTER 4

Working
with Files

Introduction

File handling is an expected role of any modern programming language. The ability to create, read, write, and otherwise manipulate files and other filesystem objects is critical for state management and serialization. PHP provides C-like functions for managing files and other filesystem objects. In the style of C, PHP uses file descriptors for all reading and writing functions and provides descriptors for the manipulation of other types of data streams, such as sockets and pipes. This facility makes writing to a file as simple as writing to a socket or sending output to another program through a pipe.

Reading and Writing Files

One of the major differences between writing Web-based applications and writing standard desktop applications is the management of the state of the application. In a typical desktop application, a user starts the application, invokes some series of commands, and then ends the application. During an instance of the application, it is simple to maintain its state in memory. In a Web-based application, the state must be maintained on the Web server, because the client is typically a generic Web browser. For a complete discussion of state management, see Chapter 7, "Sessions and Application State," but for now, suffice it to say that you can use files to maintain state and to provide other persistent data management needs in your application.

It is important to keep security in mind when using files on your Web server. Because your application will run in the context of a Web server, it will have the user permissions of the Web server. In the case of Apache, the default user is **nobody**, which limits the access your application will have to the filesystem. Take care when using files that you don't breach the overall security of your Web server. In many instances, using a database instead of files for most applications is safer and more practical. That said, there are cases when the overhead of a database or the needs of the application call for the use of files.

Listing 1 shows how to maintain an access count for the pages of your Web site. It uses the basic file operations to open, read, write, and close a simple log file. Note that this example doesn't use all of the available PHP file functions. Please see the reference at the end of this book for details on the other functions.

Listing 1: Using a file to maintain a count of Web accesses

```php
<?php
    /*
        This file can be included by any PHP script. It will
        automatically track page accesses.
        USAGE: Simply include this file. It will create a
        global variable, $aPageAccessCount, that will contain
        the current access count for the page that included
        the script.
    */
    error_reporting( 0 );
    $aLogFilePath = "/www/auto_logs/access.log";
    $aCountArray = array();
    // Check for the existence of the file
    if ( is_file( $aLogFilePath ) == True )
    {
        // open and read the file. The format is a simple
        // tab-delimted list of the form:
        //     script-path        count
        $aFile = fopen( $aLogFilePath, "r" );
        while( !feof( $aFile ) )
        {
            $aLine = fgets( $aFile, 1024 );
            $aTempArray = explode( "\t", $aLine );
            if ( count( $aTempArray ) == 2 )
            {
                $aCountArray[$aTempArray[0]] = $aTempArray[1];
            }
        }
        fclose( $aFile );
    }
    // set global page access count and update the temp array
    $aPageAccessCount = $aCountArray[$PATH_TRANSLATED] + 1;
    $aCountArray[$PATH_TRANSLATED] = $aPageAccessCount;
    // write the whole array back to the file
    $aFile = fopen( $aLogFilePath, "w" );
    foreach ( $aCountArray as $aKey => $aValue )
    {
        fputs( $aFile, "$aKey\t$aValue\n" );
    }
    fclose( $aFile );
?>
```

Listing 1 illustrates using a single file to maintain an access count for any number of pages in a Web site. It is not efficient, but it illustrates the idea. The script first checks for the existence of the log file using the **is_file**() function. If the file exists, then each line of the file is read and parsed. The format of each line is the full path name of a script, a tab character, and a count. The lines are parsed into the script name and count using the **explode**() function and are then stored in an associative array. If you want, you can use the associative array to display the access count for all of the files on your site, not just the current one. After the array is populated, the count of the current page (accessed by the PHP-provided global

$PATH_TRANSLATED) is updated, and the value is assigned to the **$aPageAccessCount** variable. Finally, the whole array is written back to the log file.

The Web page in Listing 2 shows how easily this script can be included and used. Again, if you are looking for this type of functionality on your Web site, note that this example is very inefficient. A more efficient implementation would only read and write the single value needed, not the entire file.

Listing 2: Using the script in Listing 1

```php
<?php
    include( "auto_counter.php" );
?>
<html>
<head>
    <title>Test Page 1</title>
</head>
<body>

    This page has been accessed <b>
    <?php
        print( $aPageAccessCount );
    ?>
    </b> times.
</body>
</html>
```

Using Sockets

PHP provides access to raw TCP/IP sockets so that you can communicate with other applications using any protocol you choose. Some of the more common TCP/IP protocols, such as HTTP, POP3, and SMTP, have PHP implementations so that you don't have to use raw sockets in those cases.

Listing 3 shows how to use sockets to access a *qotd* sever to get the quote of the day. The *qotd* protocol is extremely simple. Once a connection is made, the server sends out a text stream and then closes the connection. From the client perspective, all that must be done is to open a connection, read the data, and then close the connection.

Listing 3: Using sockets

```php
<html>
<head>
    <title>QOTD Example: Using Sockets with PHP</title>
</head>
```

```
<body>
<?php
    // open a socket to the qotd server
    $aFile = fsockopen( "208.129.36.164", 17 );
    // now read all of the data from the pipe
    while ( !feof( $aFile ) )
    {
        $aLine = fgets( $aFile, 1024 );
        print( "$aLine<br>" );
    }
    fclose( $aFile );
?>
</body>
</html>
```

Using Pipes

As with sockets, pipes in PHP are treated simply as another file descriptor. The only difference between a pipe and a file is that pipes are unidirectional streams. A pipe can be used to read the output of a program or script or to send data to a program or script. Listing 4 shows how to use a pipe to read the contents of a query to the **whois** command available on most Unix-based systems. This simple script and form allows the user to enter a **whois** query. The script shows a common practice of using the same code to display a form and process it.

Listing 4: Script for processing a whois query

```
<?php   /* whois */
    // path to the whois program
    $whois_prog = '/usr/bin/whois';
    if ( !is_file( $whois_prog ) )
    {
        // oops, we didn't find it there
        echo "Can't find $whois_prog!<br>";
        exit;
    }
?>
<html>
    <head>
        <title>Whois Example: Using Pipes with PHP</title>
    </head>
    <body>

    <?php
        if ( $REQUEST_METHOD == 'POST' )
        {
            // open a pipe to the whois command
            if ( $aFile = popen( "$whois_prog $WhoisQuery", "r" ) )
            {
```

```
                    // now read all of the data from the pipe
                    while ( !feof( $aFile ) )
                    {
                        $aLine = fgets( $aFile, 1024 );
                        print( "$aLine<br>" );
                    }
                    pclose( $aFile );
                }
                else
                {
                    echo "Unable to popen $whois for reading!<br>";
                }
                print( "<hr>" );
            }
    ?>
    <form action="<?php echo $PHP_SELF ?>" method="post">
        Enter <b>whois</b> query string: <input type="text"
name="WhoisQuery">
        <input type="submit" name="Submit" value="Submit">
    </form>
    </body>
</html>
```

File Class

As mentioned in the previous chapter, some great third-party tools are available for PHP. The File class, available from The WebMasters Net (http://www.theWebmasters.net), is a good tool if you are doing much work with files in your Web application. The class wraps many of the common PHP file functions and encapsulates error checking, so you can spend more time writing your application logic and less time writing basic error-handling functionality.

Listing 5 illustrates using the File class to display all the files in the current working directory of the Web server as links. When the links are clicked, the second script, Listing 6, uses the File class to read and display the contents of the file chosen.

Listing 5: Using the File class to display the contents of the current directory

```
<?php
    include( "class.File.php3" );
?>
<html>
<head>
    <title>Using the File class</title>
</head>
<body>
```

```
The following is the list of files in this directory.<br>
Click on a file name to view its contents.<br><br>
<?php
    $aFileClass = new File();
    $aDirContents = $aFileClass->get_files( "." );
    for ( $nIndex = 0; $nIndex < count( $aDirContents ); $nIndex++
)
    {
        $aCurFile = $aDirContents[$nIndex];
        print( "<a href=\"disp_file.phtml?fn=$aCurFile\">" );
        print( "$aCurFile</a><br>" );
    }
?>
</body>
</html>
```

Listing 6: Using the File class to display the contents of a file

```
<?php
    include( "class.File.php3" );
?>
<html>
<head>
    <title>Using the File class</title>
</head>
<body>
<?php
    print( "The file <b>$fn</b>:<br><br>" );
    $aFileClass = new File();
    $aFileCont  = $aFileClass->read_file( $fn );
    print( "<pre>" );
    print( nl2br( htmlentities( $aFileCont ) ) );
    print( "</pre>" );
?>
</body>
</html>
```

Summary

Deciding whether to use files in your Web-based application is a critical component of your application design. Not all applications will use files specifically, but an understanding of file descriptors and the file functions is needed when you use any type of data stream, including sockets and pipes. This chapter showed not only the basic PHP file and filesystem operations, but also a third-party wrapper class for manipulating files. This chapter's discussion of files and the previous chapter's discussion of forms is an appropriate introduction to the next chapter, "Forms and File Uploading."

Forms and File Uploading

## Chapter 5

Introduction

The previous two chapters provided the groundwork for this chapter, because uploading files requires an understanding of both HTML forms and the Web server filesystem. Handling incoming files in PHP is straightforward. PHP provides a built-in mechanism for receiving file uploads from any RFC 1867-compliant browser. Most modern browsers are now RFC 1867-compliant because this RFC was adopted as part of the HTML 3.2 standard.

When you allow your end-users to upload files as part of a form, take into consideration the type of files that you are requesting and their sizes. Using PHP's built-in mechanism to request small files works very well. However, if you expect to receive very large files, consider another mechanism, such as anonymous FTP. In either case, you may want to provide an alternate method for users to submit files if your application depends on those files.

Uploading a Single File

Providing a form for uploading files requires a few minor changes from the typical HTML form. The **<form>** element itself must have the **enctype** attribute set to "multipart/form-data" instead of the default, "application/x-www-form-urlencoded." You also must include an **<input>** tag of type **file**. Listing 1 shows a simple HTML form containing a single file input tag.

Listing 1: HTML form with a file input tag

```
<html>
<head>
    <title>Upload Form</title>
</head>
<body>
<form action="upload_single.phtml" method="post"
enctype="multipart/form-data">
    Upload a file: <input type="file" name="thefile"><br><br>
    <input type="submit" name="Submit" value="Submit">
</form>
</body>
</html>
```

When the form in Listing 1 is submitted, PHP automatically provides four global variables that describe the uploaded file:

■ **$thefile**—This variable is the temporary file name in which the uploaded file was stored on the server computer.

- **$thefile_name**—This variable is the original name of the file on the sender's computer.
- **$thefile_size**—This variable is the size of the uploaded file in bytes.
- **$thefile_type**—This variable is the MIME type of the file (if the browser provided this information).

The actual names of these variables are based on the name of the file input tag in the HTML form, as shown in Listing 1. When you write scripts to handle file uploads, note that PHP will automatically delete the temporary file at the end of the script, so if you don't explicitly move it, you won't be able to access it later.

The script in Listing 2 shows how to use the form in Listing 1 to move and display the file if it is an image file (either GIF or JPEG) that is less than 100 kilobytes. If the file received is not the right type or is too large, an error message is displayed.

Listing 2: Using an uploaded file

```php
<?php
    $aErrors = "";
    if ( !empty( $thefile_name ) ) // no file selected
    {
        if ( ( $thefile_type == "image/gif" ) ||
             ( $thefile_type == "image/pjpeg" ) ||
             ( $thefile_type == "image/jpeg" ) )
        {
            if ( $thefile_size < ( 1024 * 100 ) )
            {
                $aCurBasePath = dirname( $PATH_TRANSLATED );
                $aNewName = $aCurBasePath . "/uppics/" .
$thefile_name;
                copy( $thefile, $aNewName );
            }
            else
            {
                $aErrors .= "The file was too big";
            }
        }
        else
        {
            $aErrors .= "The file was neither a gif nor a jpeg";
        }
    }
    else
    {
        $aErrors .= "No file was selected";
    }
?>
<html>
<head>
    <title>Display an Uploaded Image</title>
```

```
    </head>
    <body>

    <?php
        if ( $aErrors != "" )
        {
            print( "<b>There were errors</b>: $aErrors<br>" );
        }
        else
        {
            print( "The picture you uploaded:<br><br>" );
            print( "<img src=\"uppics/$thefile_name\" border=\"0\">" );
        }
    ?>
    </body>
    </html>
```

The example in Listing 2 doesn't take into account the fact that some browsers don't send the MIME type of the file. Other error checking, such as the success of the copy function, is also omitted. The example does, however, demonstrate the simplicity of using the file upload feature with PHP.

In the example, the first thing checked is whether a file was selected for upload at all. If no file is selected, the **$thefile_name** variable is empty. The file is then checked for the correct MIME type and file size. If both are acceptable, the current directory of the Web server is determined using the dirname($PATH_TRANSLATED) expression. The **dirname()** function returns the directory name of a path. The **$PATH_TRANSLATED** variable is provided by PHP and contains the full server path of the current PHP script. A new file path is created by appending "/uppics/" and the original file name to the current working directory. Finally, the uploaded file is copied from its temporary location to the new path. Note that the target directory must have the appropriate permissions set so that the file can be copied there. On Linux using a default Apache installation, this requirement means that the target directory must allow files to be written by the user **nobody**.

PHP provides an internal mechanism for limiting the maximum file size that may be uploaded on a per-script basis. This is accomplished by including a hidden input field named **MAX_FILE_SIZE** in the upload form. Listing 3 shows the same input form as in Listing 1, but with the **MAX_FILE_SIZE** variable set to only allow files that are a maximum of 100 kilobytes.

Listing 3: Limiting file upload size with MAX_FILE_SIZE

```
<form action="upload_single.phtml" method="post"
enctype="multipart/form-data">
    <INPUT TYPE="hidden" name="MAX_FILE_SIZE" value="102400">
    Upload a file: <input type="file" name="thefile"><br><br>
    <input type="submit" name="Submit" value="Submit">
</form>
```

Caveats

PHP limits the overall maximum file size that can be uploaded using this mechanism to 2 megabytes by default. This maximum value supercedes the **MAX_FILE_SIZE** form variable. The overall maximum can be changed by setting the **upload_max_filesize** value in the php.ini file or by setting the directive in the Apache.conf file (see the chapter on configuration options at the end of this book). When the maximum file size is reached (whether it is the maximum from the form variable or the overall maximum), PHP generates a warning, stops the upload, and sets the file name to **none**.

Although this maximum file size setting exists to protect your Web server, it also wreaks some havoc on your application and your ability to provide a positive user experience. Because the maximum file size error occurs before any code in your script is executed, there is no way to trap the warnings generated by the upload handling mechanism. This means that if you have the **display_errors** configuration item set to **On** (the default), a warning message will appear on the browser.

If you don't want these warning messages to appear, you will have to set the **display_errors** configuration item to **Off** in your php.ini file. You can then set the **log_errors** item to **On** and the **error_log** item to an appropriate setting for your environment. If you are using Linux and Apache, setting **error_log** to **stderr** will cause all PHP errors to appear in the Apache error_log file. Your application can then check the file upload variables and handle the error appropriately. If a user tries unsuccessfully to upload a file, the **$thefile** variable will be set to **none**, but the **$thefile_name** will contain a value.

Another thing to consider when developing a file-upload script is that the file will be uploaded to at least the maximum file size before any portion of your script is executed. So if your application allows large files, but accepts only certain file types, your end-users might have to wait a very long time before they find out that their submission was rejected.

Uploading an Array of Files

If you need to upload multiple files on a single form, you can use a PHP array to specify the incoming file information. The following example shows how to use an array to retrieve four files.

Listing 4: Uploading four files

```
<html>
<head>
    <title>Upload Form</title>
</head>
<body>
Please specify four image files for uploading:
<form action="upload_multiple.phtml" method="post"
enctype="multipart/form-data">
    File 1: <input type="file" name="thefiles[]"><br><br>
    File 2: <input type="file" name="thefiles[]"><br><br>
    File 3: <input type="file" name="thefiles[]"><br><br>
    File 4: <input type="file" name="thefiles[]"><br><br>
    <input type="submit" name="Submit" value="Submit">
</form>
</body>
</html>
```

Listing 5: Handling four uploaded files

```
<?php
    $aBasePath = dirname( $PATH_TRANSLATED );
    // For each file uploaded, copy it, and store its
    // new path for later use
    for ( $nIndex = 0; $nIndex < count( $thefiles ); $nIndex++ )
    {
        if ( !empty( $thefiles_name[$nIndex] ) )
        {
            $aType = $thefiles_type[$nIndex];
            if ( ( $aType == "image/gif" ) ||
                  ( $aType == "image/pjpeg" ) ||
                  ( $aType == "image/jpeg" ) )
            {
                $aNewName = $aBasePath . "/uppics/" .
$thefiles_name[$nIndex];
                copy( $thefiles[$nIndex], $aNewName );
                $aNewNames[] = $thefiles_name[$nIndex];
            }
        }
    }
?>
<html>
<head>
    <title>Display an Uploaded Image</title>
</head>
<body>

<?php
    $aCount = count( $aNewNames );
    print( "The <b>$aCount</b> pictures you uploaded:<br><br>" );
    foreach( $aNewNames as $aNewName )
    {
        print( "<img src=\"uppics/$aNewName\"
border=\"0\"><br><br>" );
    }
```

```
?>
</body>
</html>
```

Security

You must consider any potential threat when allowing your visitors to provide any information to your application. If you are allowing files to be uploaded, be sure that you take precautions to ensure that these files are used properly on the server. For example, if you are creating a site where PHP developers can upload their own scripts, don't allow the scripts to be executed on your server. Simply upload them and display them as plain text, but don't assume they are all safe for immediate execution.

Even allowing the display of uploaded files may open your application to some potential threats. Listing 6 shows a contrived example of how a file display mechanism can open a security hole.

Listing 6: Security flaw when dealing with uploaded files

```php
<?php
    include( "class.File.php3" );
    // copy the incoming file
    $aCurBasePath = dirname( $PATH_TRANSLATED );
    $aNewName = $aCurBasePath . "/uploads/" . $thefile_name;
    copy( $thefile, $aNewName );
?>
<html>
<head>
    <title>Upload Security Flaw</title>
</head>
<body>
<?php
    // display the contents of the file
    print( "The file <b>$aNewName</b>:<br><br>" );
    $aFileClass = new File();
    $aFileCont  = $aFileClass->read_file( $thefile );
    print( "<pre>" );
    print( nl2br( htmlentities( $aFileCont ) ) );
    print( "</pre>" );
?>
</body>
</html>
```

Obviously, this example is contrived. In the example, the uploaded file is copied to a new location, but when the file is displayed, the temporary file is read and presented through the browser. In reality, you would probably read and display the file stored at the path, **$aNewName**. But for the purposes of this demonstration, the preceding file shows how a poorly written script can open a security hole.

To exploit the problem in the script, one could type the name of the script in his or her browser and provide the name of a file on the server. For example, entering the following URL displays the entire contents of the /etc/passwd file (assuming a *nix system):

```
http://yourserver.com/yourpath/upload_flaw.phtml?thefile=/etc/passwd
```

Testing this on my Linux server showed that the threat is real. Even though the Web server user is **nobody**, the /etc/passwd file allows reading for any user.

As I emphasized when discussing forms, you must not assume that everyone will use your application the way you intended it to be used. Some users will purposefully try to exploit weaknesses in your application, and others will unintentionally wreak havoc. Carefully consider any potential side effects of allowing files to be uploaded onto your Web servers before providing this facility.

Summary

This chapter showed how to retrieve and use files uploaded through an RFC 1867-compliant browser. Examples were provided for handling a single file and for handling an array of files. Lastly, a small section on security illustrated how a poorly written script may create a security hole on your Web server.

Allowing file uploads in your application is useful for many reasons, but remember that some users may not have the connection speed or the patience for this feature, so providing an alternate mechanism for receiving files may be a good idea.

6

Working with Databases

Introduction

Being able to access databases is arguably the most important feature of any modern language or development tool. This importance is due to the fact that a *Database Management System* (DBMS) provides so many powerful data management functions such as indexing, data relationships, transaction support, cascading data actions, and more. PHP provides functions to access data through a rich set of database-specific functions.

Overview

As evidenced by the online documentation, the authors of PHP consider its database support the strongest and most significant feature of PHP. The supported databases include the following:

Adabas D	InterBase	Solid
dBase	mSQL	Sybase
Empress	MySQL	Velocis
FilePro	Oracle	Unix dbm
Informix	PostgreSQL	Microsoft SQL Server
ODBC		

With the inclusion of ODBC, PHP probably can be used to access any available DBMS. Because PHP provides access to so many different databases, it is impossible to give a thorough discussion of all of them in this book. Additionally, the SQL language is in itself a rich and powerful tool that cannot be adequately documented in this book. I highly recommend using a SQL reference specific to the DBMS you are using. In this chapter, I have assumed that readers know enough SQL to follow the examples in the listings.

This chapter will focus on providing examples of using MySQL and ODBC. I chose MySQL because it is a powerful DBMS available under the GNU *General Public License* (GPL) and because it is one of the most commonly used databases with PHP. I chose ODBC because most databases provide ODBC drivers, so the related examples could be used with almost any database available. The examples themselves illustrate the PHP language, not the best practices of SQL or database development in general.

The Database Functions

Each of the supported DBMSs has a set of PHP functions. The MySQL functions are all prepended with mysql_, and similar prefixes are provided for each DBMS. (See the reference section at the end of the book for the listing of all the database-related functions.) Although each database has its own set of functions, there is typically a common model for using databases in PHP. The pseudocode for getting data from any type of database is shown in Listing 1.

Listing 1: Pseudocode for retrieving data from a database

```php
<?php
    connect_to_DBMS();
    select_db();
    send_sql_statement();
    retrieve_results();
    while ( rows_exist )
        get_row();
    close_connection();
?>
```

The following two sections provide details on setting up and using MySQL and ODBC.

MySQL

MySQL is a great DBMS for most projects. The official site for MySQL is http://www.mysql.com/. At this site, you can download the latest version of the MySQL DBMS and find documentation on installing and configuring MySQL in your environment.

Getting Started with MySQL

Depending on your specific needs and your server type, you can either download the full MySQL source, or you may choose a binary distribution or binary RPM. The quickest way to get started with MySQL on an Intel-based Linux system is to download the binary RPM and install it. This method will install all of the server components so that you can begin working. If you are using a Win32-based system, the quickest way to get started is to download the zipped binary distribution.

PHP4 provides MySQL support by default, so you should not need to recompile PHP in order to start using the mysql_ functions. However, if you use PHP's built-in support for MySQL, you cannot also use other modules that refer to MySQL, such as mod_auth_mysql and mod_perl. If you need server modules that use MySQL, you will have to rebuild PHP and specify --with-mysql=/path/to/mysql.

Using MySQL

Once you have MySQL installed and running, you can begin writing PHP scripts to access the data in your databases. The script in Listing 2 illustrates the simplicity of using MySQL to retrieve some information from a database. For reference, the table that I will be using in the next two examples was created using the following SQL:

```
CREATE TABLE employees
(
        id tinyint(4) DEFAULT '0' NOT NULL auto_increment,
        first varchar(20),
        last varchar(20),
        address varchar(255),
        position varchar(50),
        PRIMARY KEY (id),
        UNIQUE id (id)
);
```

Listing 2: Retrieving information from a MySQL database

```
<html>
<head>
    <title>Getting Data from a MySQL DB</title>
</head>
<body>
<?php
    // Suppress errors and handle them internally
    $aDBLink = @mysql_connect( "db.server.com", "user", "pwd" );
    if ( !empty( $aDBLink ) )
    {
        // select the MySQL database
        if ( mysql_select_db( "mydb", $aDBLink ) == True )
        {
            $aSQL = "select * from employees";
            // execute the SELECT query
            $aQResult = mysql_query( $aSQL, $aDBLink );
            if ( $aQResult == True )
            {
```

```
                              // fetch a row and print two fields
                              while ( $aRow = mysql_fetch_array( $aQResult ) )
                              {
                                    $aFName = $aRow["first"];
                                    $aPos    = $aRow["position"];
                                    print( "$aFName, $aPos<br>" );
                              }
                              mysql_free_result( $aQResult );
                        }
                        else
                        {
                              print( "Query failed<br>" );
                        }
                  }
                  else
                  {
                        print( "Unable to select DB<br>" );
                  }
            }
            else
            {
                  print( "Unable to connect to DB<br>" );
            }
      ?>
      </body>
      </html>
```

When run, the script in Listing 2 first attempts to connect to the MySQL database server running at the host **db.server.com** with the username and password as specified. The @ symbol is prepended to the **mysql_connect** call to suppress internal warnings and errors. You may want to omit the @ symbol while you are testing, but use it in production and write custom error handling code to manage a connection failure. The script then attempts to select a particular database, in this case, **mydb**. If the script is successful, the database is queried using the **mysql_query** function. In the example, the query is a SELECT query, which returns records from a database. It could just as well have been any type of query, such as an INSERT, UPDATE, ADD TABLE, or any other valid SQL query. The result of the **mysql_query** function is nonzero on success and zero on failure. Additionally, if the query is a SELECT query, the result is an identifier that can be passed to the **mysql_result**, **mysql_fetch_array**, **mysql_fetch_lengths**, **mysql_fetch_object**, and **mysql_fetch_row** functions for retrieving the resultant data. In the example, **mysql_fetch_array** is used to retrieve a row from the data set, and then the fields are displayed.

The **mysql_fetch_array** and **mysql_fetch_row** are similar functions that return an entire row from the result data set in an array. The **mysql_fetch_array** function returns an associative array indexed by the names of the data columns. The **mysql_fetch_row** returns a numerically indexed array. Calling either function returns the current row in the data set and advances the script to the next row. If no more data is available, the functions return false. A call to **mysql_fetch_array** is not significantly slower than a call to **mysql_fetch_row**, but it provides more information and value.

Using Listing 2 as a starting point, you can write any conceivable database–driven application. The MySQL functions in PHP also provide some functionality that is not available in all the databases supported by PHP. Native functions for creating and dropping databases are provided along with a rich set of database structure querying functions. For example, you can use the **mysql_list_tables** function to list all of the tables in a MySQL database.

One of my favorite functions when using MySQL is **mysql_insert_id**. When using an auto_increment field with MySQL, you can simply insert the data into the table and then use the **mysql_insert_id function** to retrieve its unique identifier. Listing 3 provides a form for entering a new employee record into the database used in Listing 2. It takes advantage of the **mysql_insert_id** function to provide feedback about the insert operation.

Listing 3: Inserting a record into a MySQL database

```php
<?php
/*
    InsertRecord function:
        Inserts a new record into the employees database.
        Returns the unique ID of the new record on success
        or a negative value for various failure conditions.
*/
function InsertRecord( $aFirstName, $aLastName, $aAddr, $aPos )
{
    // set up the SQL INSERT statement
    $aSQL  = "insert into employees ( first, last, address, ";
    $aSQL .= "position ) values ( '$aFirstName', '$aLastName', ";
    $aSQL .= "'$aAddr', '$aPos' )";
    // connect to the DBMS and execute the INSERT statement
    $aDBLink = @mysql_connect( "db.server.com", "root", "" );
    if ( !empty( $aDBLink ) )
    {
        if ( mysql_select_db( "mydb", $aDBLink ) == True )
        {
            $aQResult = mysql_query( $aSQL, $aDBLink );
            if ( $aQResult == True )
            {
                $aResult = mysql_insert_id( $aDBLink );
            }
            else
            {
                // print( "Query failed<br>" );
                $aResult = -1;
            }
        }
    }
```

```
            else
            {
                // print( "Unable to select DB<br>" );
                $aResult = -2;
            }
        }
        else
        {
            // print( "Unable to connect to DB<br>" );
            $aResult = -3;
        }
        return $aResult;
    }
?>
<html>
    <head>
        <title>MySQL Example: Inserting into a table</title>
    </head>
    <body>

    <?php
        if ( $REQUEST_METHOD == 'POST' )
        {
            // We're here because the form was submitted
            $aResult = InsertRecord( $FirstName, $LastName,
                                     $Address, $Position );
            if ( $aResult > 0 )
            {
                print( "New record added, ID = $aResult<br>" );
            }
            else
            {
                print( "InsertRecord failed.  Errcode =
$aResult<br>" );
            }
            print( "<hr>" );
        }
    ?>
    Please enter the new employee information:<br>
    <form action="<?php echo $PHP_SELF ?>" method="post">
        First Name: <input type="text" name="FirstName"
maxlength="20"><br>
        Last Name: <input type="text" name="LastName"
maxlength="20"><br>
        Address: <input type="text" name="Address"
maxlength="255"><br>
        Position: <input type="text" name="Position"
maxlength="50"><br><br>
        <input type="submit" name="Submit" value="Submit">
    </form>
    </body>
</html>
```

In Listing 3, the **InsertRecord** function encapsulates the logic for inserting a new record into the database. It returns the unique identifier (the value assigned by MySQL to the **id** column) of the new record or a negative value that indicates one of three failure conditions. Realistically, this type of application would contain more error-checking code, such as checking for empty fields, but for this discussion, this additional code has been purposely omitted. Because the **id** field in the **employees** table is an auto-increment field, MySQL automatically generates a unique value for the field each time a record is inserted. In the example, this value is returned by the call to **mysql_insert_id**.

The previous examples are intended to illustrate the simplicity of using databases in PHP. You can find more examples of using databases in your Web applications in Chapter 15, "Database-Driven Web Sites." These more complete examples include error handling and more complex queries.

MySQL is a powerful DBMS that provides the basic functionality for most types of Web applications. It is fast and robust and provides most of the features of the available non-GPL databases. However, at the time of this writing, MySQL does not support transactions. Some SQL features, such as subqueries, are also unavailable in MySQL. If you are still in the position to choose your DBMS, consider your long-term needs and look for reviews of the systems you are considering. Cost is not the only consideration in high-quality application development. If you or your company already has a DBMS other than MySQL in place, the next section provides information about ODBC that may provide the connectivity to your existing data.

ODBC

Open Database Connectivity (ODBC) is a widely used *application-programming interface* (API) for database access. It is based on the Call-Level Interface specifications from X/Open and ISO/IEC and uses SQL as its database access language. Several implementations of the ODBC API support *nix platforms. ODBC for Windows is typically part of a standard Windows installation.

Getting Started with ODBC

PHP supports essentially any ODBC implementation, but this support must be configured manually because ODBC is not currently a default option. The four configuration options related to ODBC support in PHP are --with-unixODBC, --with-custom-odbc, --with-iodbc, and --with-openlink. You can find more details about these options in the reference section at the end of this book. The examples in this chapter use the unixODBC implementation (http://www.unixodbc.org/). It is distributed under GPL or LGPL licensing and is easy to install and configure.

ODBC is different from MySQL and other direct database APIs in that ODBC relies on a database driver to make the calls to the underlying DBMS. This means that you must first obtain a driver manager, such as unixODBC, and then get the database driver specific to your DBMS. Figure 6.1 shows the relationship between the components of an ODBC-based PHP application. The PHP application makes calls such as **odbc_connect** to the driver manager. The driver manager is responsible for loading the required database driver and passing on the request. The database driver then makes database-specific calls to fulfill the request.

Because using ODBC requires a driver manager and specific database drivers, setup and configuration of ODBC is a bit more complex than setting up MySQL. Each driver manager has its own setup and installation procedures, and each specific driver also has to be installed and configured.

In this book, I show how to configure and install the unixODBC driver manager and the ODBC-ODBC Bridge (OOB) driver available from Easysoft Limited, http://www.easysoft.com/. The OOB driver adds a little more complexity to the equation, but it provides so much value that it is worth the effort. The OOB driver provides cross-platform access to databases through its own client-server model. Figure 6.2 illustrates how the OOB driver is used.

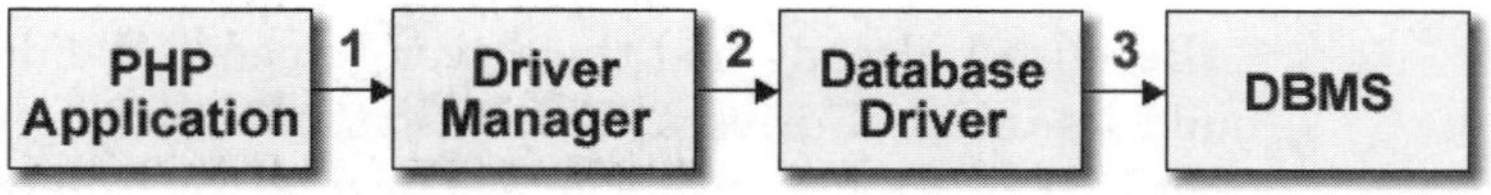

Figure 6.1
The components of a PHP application using ODBC

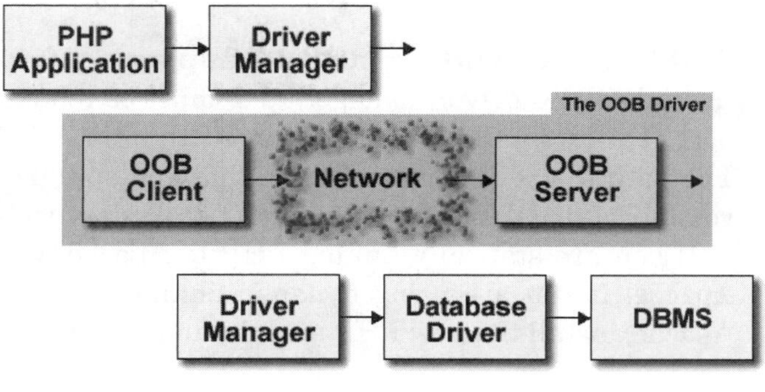

Figure 6.2
Adding the OOB driver

The advantage of the OOB driver is that you can easily use ODBC in an application on your Web server to access data from a DBMS running on another server (possibly running a different operating system). For example, in my test development, I installed Oracle 8i on a Windows NT server and created a simple database. I then used the OOB driver installed on my regular Linux Web server to access the database. You could use the same driver to access any ODBC-compliant database running on any platform anywhere.

The additional complexity with using OOB is that the OOB client and server software must be installed individually on separate machines. Fortunately, the Easysoft Web site makes identifying and downloading the appropriate software very easy.

The next three sections discuss installing the unixODBC driver manager, building PHP with unixODBC support, and installing the OOB driver, respectively. These sections are very Linux-specific and assume that you are familiar with building software on Linux and that you have the proper compilers and tools installed.

Installing and Building unixODBC   After downloading and extracting the unixODBC files, you need to build the driver manager. unixODBC provides the standard configure script for configuring the build environment. I used the following configure options to build unixODBC for my PHP configuration:

```
./configure --disable--drivers --disable-threads --
prefix=/usr/local/unixODBC --disable-gui
```

Because I already had the driver I needed, I didn't want unixODBC to build its internal drivers. The reason for disabling threads is that I have built PHP as a dynamically loaded module (--with-apxs) and Apache doesn't support threads by default. Building the module with thread support will cause Apache to fail when the module is loaded. Lastly, I disabled the graphical user interface features because I don't have X installed on my server.

Building PHP with unixODBC Support   After you build and install the unixODBC driver manager, PHP must be rebuilt with unixODBC support. The configuration option is --with-unixODBC=/path/to/unixODBC. The path to use is the same path that you specified as the --prefix when you built unixODBC. In my case, the path was /usr/local/unixODBC.

If you are statically linking PHP to Apache, you will have to rebuild Apache. If you are using dynamic linking, you will have to shut down Apache, install the new PHP module, and restart Apache.

Installing the OOB Driver   In my test case, I had to install the OOB server on my Windows NT machine and set it up to receive requests. I accomplished this by downloading the software, running the install program, and following the steps in the setup software that were provided. All of this worked without any problems. I then downloaded and installed the client software on my Linux server. This process was surprisingly easy because a step-by-step installation program was available for that, too. Based on your configuration, you will have to consult the Easysoft Web site for details on how to obtain and install the OOB client and server.

Configuring OOB   Once everything is installed, you must create *data source names* (DSNs) on both the client and server. Data source names are an ODBC-specific mechanism for describing information about a DBMS. On Windows, a DSN is created by using the "ODBC Data Sources" applet available from the Control Panel. OOB requires a System DSN rather than a User DSN. The applet provides help on how to create a System DSN.

To create a DSN on Linux, you must edit the odbcinst.ini and odbc.ini files either using the unixODBC graphical tools or your favorite text editor. The odbcinst.ini file is used to describe driver names and relate the names to driver files. Here is what mine looks like:

```
[OOB]
Driver = /usr/local/easysoft/oob/client/libesoobclient.so
Setup = /usr/local/easysoft/oob/client/libesoobsetup.so
FileUsage = 1
```

The odbc.ini file describes the DSNs. I configured mine in this way (contrived passwords and servers, obviously):

```
[localdsn]
Server=database.server.com
Driver=OOB
Port=8888
Transport=tcpip
LogonUser=prodplanner
LogonAuth=password
TargetDSN=LocalOracle
TargetUser=prodplanner
TargetAuth=password
```

Using ODBC

Once all of the components are installed and configured, using ODBC within PHP is much like using MySQL. Listing 4 is basically the ODBC equivalent of Listing 2. The table used in the example is equivalent to the one used in the previous examples.

Listing 4: Retrieving data from an ODBC database

```
<html>
<head>
     <title>Getting Data from an ODBC DB</title>
</head>
<body>
<?php
    putenv("ODBCINI=/usr/local/unixODBC/etc/odbc.ini");
    // Suppress errors and handle them internally
    $aDBLink = @odbc_connect( "localdsn", "user", "pwd" );
    if ( !empty( $aDBLink ) )
    {
        $aSQL = "select * from employees";
        $aQResult = @odbc_exec( $aDBLink, $aSQL );
        if ( $aQResult == True )
        {
            $aRow = array();
            $aRowNum = 1;
            while ( odbc_fetch_into( $aQResult, $aRowNum, &$aRow )
)
            {
                $aFName = $aRow[1];
                $aPos   = $aRow[4];
                print( "$aFName, $aPos<br>" );

                $aRowNum++;
            }
            odbc_free_result( $aQResult );
        }
        else
        {
            print( "Query failed<br>" );
        }
    }
    else
    {
        print( "Unable to connect to DB<br>" );
    }
?>
</body>
</html>
```

Listing 4 is very much the same as Listing 2. Although the function names are different, the concepts are nearly identical. One noticeable difference is the **putenv()** call at the beginning. This call provides the location of the ODBC initialization file to the environment. It is not necessary if you have set this value in the Web server environment some other way. Also, in Listing 4, the fields are referenced by position rather than by name for sim-

---

Note on Connecting to Databases

In the previous examples, the connection to databases has been made using the basic xxx_connect functions. PHP also provides the ability to create persistent connections through the xxx_pconnect functions. Using persistent connections can enhance the performance of your applications, because PHP internally maintains the database connections so they can be reused. Once a connection has been established for a particular hostname/username/password combination, PHP can instantly supply that same connection in a subsequent connection call. For databases that take a long time to create a connection (such as Oracle), using persistent connections can have a dramatic effect on the overall performance of your application.

---

plicity. ODBC functions are available in PHP for transaction support, cursors, and much more. You can find a full listing of ODBC functions with the functional reference at the end of this book.

PHPLIB

As mentioned in previous chapters, a large number of great libraries are available to the PHP programmer. The PHP Base Library (PHPLIB), available at http://phplib.netuse.de/, is one of the most commonly used PHP libraries. It provides database access classes, session management, authentication tools, and more.

The database access class in PHPLIB provides an abstraction layer to several of the databases supported by PHP. The abstraction layer provides a common interface to the underlying database functions so that a developer can easily transition from one database to another without needing to learn a new set of functions or change much code. At the time of this writing, PHPLIB supports MySQL, PostgreSQL, mSQL, Oracle 7 and Oracle 8, Sybase, Microsoft SQL Server, and ODBC databases.

The following listings illustrate the power of PHPLIB's database wrapper. Listing 5 shows how PHPLIB simplifies the code in Listing 2.

Listing 5: Using PHPLIB to reproduce the results of Listing 2

```php
<?php
    include ( "db_mysql.inc" );
    // Extend the DB_Sql class to use it with our
    // MySQL database instance
    class MySQLDBTest extends DB_Sql
    {
        var $Host       = "db.server.com";
        var $Database   = "mydb";
        var $User       = "user";
        var $Password   = "pwd";
    }
    // Create an instance of the new MySQLDBTest class
    $aDB = new MySQLDBTest;
    $aDB->query( "select * from employees" );
    while( $aDB->next_record() )
    {
        $aFName = $aDB->f( "first" );
        $aPos   = $aDB->f( "position" );
        print( "$aFName, $aPos<br>" );
    }
?>
```

The DB_Sql class provided by PHPLIB encapsulates all of the connection and database selection logic as well as all of the error-handling code. This results in a solution that is easier to read, maintain, and debug. The DB_Sql class is not intended to be used directly. Rather, it should always be subclassed so that the parameters specific to your environment can be overridden. If PHP supported abstract base classes, this class would be a perfect candidate for such an implementation. In Listing 5, the subclass **MySQLDBTest** is defined with the appropriate MySQL connection information. An instance of the class is then created and used.

The great value in using the PHPLIB database wrapper comes when the underlying DBMS changes. The following listing shows how easily the code in Listing 5 can be changed from a MySQL database access to an Oracle via ODBC database access.

Listing 6: Switching the code in Listing 5 to use Oracle/ODBC

```php
<?php
    putenv("ODBCINI=/usr/local/openlink/odbc.ini");
    include( "db_odbc.inc" );
    // Extend the DB_Sql class to use it with our
    // Oracle DBMS accessible via ODBC
    class OracleDBTest extends DB_Sql
    {
        var $Database   = "localdsn";
        var $User       = "user";
        var $Password   = "pwd";
    }
```

```
// Create an instance of the new OracleDBTest class
$aDB = new OracleDBTest;
$aDB->query( "select * from employees" );
while( $aDB->next_record() )
{
    $aFName = $aDB->f( "first" );
    $aPos   = $aDB->f( "position" );
    print( "$aFName, $aPos<br>" );
}
?>
```

The only material change between Listing 5 and Listing 6 is in the **include**() function, but the significance of this change cannot be overstated. In Listing 5, data was gathered from a MySQL database running on the same machine as the Web server. In Listing 6, the database was an Oracle instance running on an NT server.

Because of the simplicity of the PHPLIB design and implementation, it can be as useful to developers working in complex heterogeneous environments as it is to those in a single-server setup. It provides a common interface to several databases and promotes great code reuse. You can find more information about the other classes provided in the PHPLIB at http://phplib.netuse.de/.

Forms and Data Storage

A discussion of HTML forms is a necessity in a chapter dealing with databases because forms are the most common input mechanism in Web applications. As discussed in Chapter 3, "Forms and Cookies," PHP provides a great deal of functionality for handling forms. This section focuses on some of the caveats and security issues related to using forms and databases.

In its default configuration, PHP automatically escapes quotes, doublequotes, backslashes, and NUL characters for all GET, POST, and COOKIE variables. This means that by default, values passed from a form are automatically prepared to be used in a SQL query. If you have disabled this feature of PHP, you will have to call **addslashes**() before using form-gathered strings in SQL queries. Additionally, any values that will be displayed will have to be processed with the **stripslashes**() function before display.

As with any other application, you must validate the data provided in your HTML forms before attempting to store the data in the database. Chapter 3 discusses several mechanisms for performing data validation. The results of not checking the values can range from inconveniencing the end-user to breaching the security of your servers. For example, some error messages generated by the underlying database may include more information about your database than you would want to provide. Be prepared for instances where individuals may try to exploit the weaknesses of your application deliberately.

To protect against some types of attacks, always use the **maxlength** attribute in input fields (when available) and validate the type and contents of the data. As mentioned in Chapter 3, avoid validation as much as possible by providing input mechanisms that inherently avoid mistakes. List boxes, radio buttons, and similar input types provide a great deal of flexibility and inherently create less risk of input error.

When providing alternate input mechanisms, remember to use the database to create the input options initially. Creating these options in the database will result in a more maintainable application in the long run. For example, Listing 7 shows how to create a drop-down list box for selecting a U.S. state and a country. Obviously, one wouldn't select a state in the United States and then pick South Africa. This example simply demonstrates the concept. The database tables used are us_states and world_countries, respectively. Each table consists of a unique identifier and a name. The unique identifier is passed as the form value.

Listing 7: Using lookup tables to generate option lists

```php
<?php
    include ( "./db_mysql.inc" );
    class MySQLDBTest extends DB_Sql
    {
        var $Host        = "db.server.com";
        var $Database    = "mydb";
        var $User        = "root";
        var $Password    = "";
    }
    function GetGenOpts( $aTableName, $aCurSel = "" )
    {
        $aResult = "";
        $aDB = new MySQLDBTest;
        $aSQL = "select ID, Name from $aTableName order by Name";
        $aDB->query( $aSQL );
        while( $aDB->next_record() )
        {
            $aName      = $aDB->f( "Name" );
            $aID        = $aDB->f( "ID" );
            if ( $aID == $aCurSel )
            {
                $aResult .= "<option value=\"$aID\"
selected>$aName</option>";
            }
            else
            {
```

```
                            $aResult .= "<option
value=\"$aID\">$aName</option>";
                    }
            }
            return $aResult;
    }

?>
<html>
<head>
    <title>Form for selecting US state and world country</title>
</head>
<body>
<form action="some_place.phtml" method="post">
    <table>
        <tr>
            <td>
                Select US State:
            </td>
            <td>
                <select name="us_state" size="1">
                <?php
                    print( GetGenOpts( "us_states", "ID" ) );
                ?>
                </select>
            </td>
        </tr>
        <tr>
            <td>
                Select World Country:
            </td>
            <td>
                <select name="world_country" size="1">
                <?php
                    print( GetGenOpts( "world_countries", "ZA" ) );
                ?>
                </select>
            </td>
        </tr>
    </table>
</form>
</body>
</html>
```

Figure 6.3 shows the input form. The **GetGenOpts()** function can be used to create an option list for any table that has an **ID** and **Name** column. The optional parameter, **$aCurSel**, can be used to specify a current selection if the form is for editing existing data rather than gathering new data. Using database lookup tables also provides the opportunity to immediately update your application when needed. If you have a list of credit card types that you accept, storing this list in a database rather than statically defining it in your HTML pages means that when the list must be changed you don't have to hunt through your pages to find the references. You can simply change the values in the database table. Your application will be instantly updated without a single change in the code.

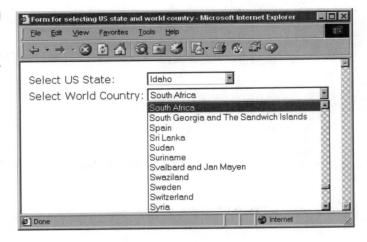

Again, the greatest defense against bad input is a good input mechanism. Any time that you provide text input forms, you need to verify the validity of the data before posting it to your database server.

From a security standpoint, most of the considerations are related to your particular database. Always secure your database so that it cannot be accessed except by your Web application. Obviously, your application should never provide a raw input box that allows your users to execute SQL against your database. Additionally, you should test your application for conditions that might cause errors. Try entering quotes and backslashes into your text fields. Also try entering semicolons and SQL statements to see what happens.

For example, consider a simple application that gathers a unique identifier and then executes the following SQL statement:

```
select * from table where ID = input_value
```

You expect **input_value** to contain a single value, so you embed the gathered value into your SQL statement. Although such an occurrence is highly unlikely, someone might enter the value **"1; drop database"** into the form. The resulting SQL statement becomes

```
select * from table where ID = 1; drop database
```

Although this example is unlikely to actually cause any damage, you may find similar examples that could breach security or cause database failure. Based on the type of application you are providing, you will know what level of security and validation to include.

Using the Power of the DBMS

This section is not directly related to using PHP with databases; it is an addendum to writing applications on the Web using databases. It could easily fall into a software-engineering chapter. For those with a background in client-server or multitier application development, much of the information in this section will be second nature. For those who haven't developed much software in a multitier environment, this material should be seriously considered when you are developing your database-driven Web applications.

Before developing applications for the Web, I developed mostly single-user applications for Windows. In all cases, the databases used were also single user and ran on the same box. This setup was convenient in the sense that no considerations had to be made for concurrency, and the DBMS was typically little more than an interface for data storage and retrieval.

In a multitier development environment, the DBMS becomes a much more significant part of the overall application. Typically, a modern DBMS is required to manage concurrency, user privileges, transactions, and more while handling multiple simultaneous requests. Besides these critical functions, most modern DBMSs also provide a vast number of internal functions that can aid in your application development. Whether your database server and Web server are located on the same physical hardware or on separate machines, you should exploit the power of the DBMS whenever possible.

In a recent contracting engagement, I came across a great example. The task was to duplicate several rows of existing data in a table, modifying some of the data columns in the new rows. The code I found looked something like the following:

```
select all of the rows to duplicate
for each row
    initialize a new string that will contain a sql INSERT
statement
    select a new primary key from the database
    for each field in the row
        if this field should be copied verbatim
            copy the existing data to the sql INSERT string
        else
            add the new data values to the sql INSERT string
    execute the sql INSERT string
next row
```

With no offense intended toward the original programmer, this routine illustrates a brute-force coding style common to young or inexperienced software developers. This routine requires 1 + (2 * number of rows) database calls. The first call is to retrieve all of the rows, then for each row there is one call to generate a new primary key for the data and one call for the insert statement. The entire routine can be reduced to a single SQL statement executed entirely at the database:

```
INSERT into table SELECT sequence.nextval as primary key,
other_data_fields from table
```

The preceding example relies on a DBMS that supports internal sequences to generate the primary keys, but it shows how some creative SQL can avoid a significant amount of code and improve the overall application performance. Whenever you find yourself building a lot of code to reformat, filter, or sort data that has been collected from a database, first reconsider your original SQL query. You may find that you can use built-in database functions or more complex SQL to achieve most of the desired results.

In another recent development project, I was required to sort personnel records based on the difference in age of the individual from a specific age. For example, I had to rank all of the people in the database based on how closely their age was to 30 years. Additionally, each person had to be given an integer score from 0 to 10 based on how closely they matched the age requirement. Anyone not within 10 years of the target age could be ranked the same. The following query used looks complex, but it provides all of the information without requiring any additional code to manipulate the results:

```
select concat( FIRSTNAME, ' ',  SURNAME ) as FULLNAME, ROUND( MAX(
0, ( 10 - ABS( ( 30 - ROUND( ( ( TO_DAYS( NOW() ) - TO_DAYS(
BIRTHDATE ) ) / 365 ) ) ) ) ) ) ) as AGE_DIFF from persons order
by AGE_DIFF desc
```

Each row in the result set contains the person's full name and an integer score. All that is required at this point is to loop through the results and display them. The top records are people that are closest to being 30 years old.

One of the most important considerations in Web application development is to use the right tools and the right people for each segment of the development process. The next major section of this book, "Project Management in Web Development," presents more information about software engineering in Web applications.

Summary

This chapter presented an overview of using databases with PHP. Because of the number of databases supported natively by PHP, this chapter focused on a discussion of MySQL and ODBC. A brief discussion of software engineering and using the DBMS was also included. Further database examples are provided in Chapters 15, 16, and 17. You can find the most comprehensive examples in Chapter 15, "Database-Driven Web Site."

Sessions and Application State

Introduction

Chapter 4, "Working with Files," provided a brief overview of maintaining application state using files, but it had little discussion of the general need for keeping state. In desktop software applications, state is maintained automatically in all of the application variables in memory, files, and databases used by the program. The state of the program is known because the execution model is so simple: the user starts the program, does some work, and then exits the application. If the user switches tasks temporarily and then returns, the application state will have remained the same. When the user exits the application, necessary information is serialized to a persistent storage device and the session ends.

In Web-based applications, session information management is more complex. This complexity is due to the fact that neither the browser nor the Web server was developed solely for the purpose of running your Web application. Because Web applications are inherently multiuser applications, state management is a task requiring both the client and the server. The client represents the individual user and provides user-specific information. The server uses the client-specific information to track and update session information each time a Web page is accessed.

PHP provides several methods for maintaining application state. PHP4 introduced built-in session functions, and third-party session management modules are also available. Another method is to use PHP to create your own session management implementation.

Understanding Session Basics

As mentioned in the introduction, session management in a Web environment requires cooperation between the client browser and the Web server. When a session starts, the Web server creates a unique session identifier (ID) and issues it to the client. Typically, the session ID is stored using a cookie on the client computer. Thereafter, the browser provides the session ID to the server each time a new page is requested. The server uses the session ID to restore all of the session information to the application when needed. When the session ends, the session data is removed from the server. Figure 7.1 shows the interaction between the client and Web server (in this case, a 1U server from Penguin Computing) when starting a session and using session variables.

Figure 7.1
Starting a session and
using session
variables

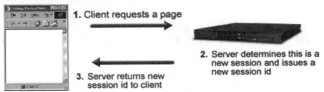

Session Start

1. Client requests a page

2. Server determines this is a
new session and issues a
new session id

3. Server returns new
session id to client

Session Use

1. Client requests a page and
includes current session id

2. Server restores all session
variables for use by
server-side scripts

Native PHP Session Management

Version 4 of PHP introduced session management. The session functions
are fully documented in the reference section at the end of this book. All of
the session functions are prepended with **session_**.

Using session variables in PHP involves these basic steps:

1. Start a session using **session_start()**.
2. Register the session variable names you will be using with
session_register().
3. Use the session variables.

PHP session management is very configurable. You can change how the
session ID is propagated through your application, where the session variables are stored on the server, and how often the server removes expired
sessions. Because a lot of options are available for using PHP sessions, this
section is subdivided to provide information in order of increasing implementation complexity.

Getting Started with PHP Sessions

Listings 1 and 2 show the simplicity of using sessions in PHP using the
default settings. Listing 1 sets up all of the session variables used in the

application and provides a link to Listing 2. Listing 2 displays the session variables that Listing 1 made available.

Listing 1: Starting a session and setting some variables

```php
<?php
    session_start();
    session_register( "aUser", "aAccount" );
    $aUser       = "Cidnie";
    $aAccount    = "1016";
?>
<html>
<head>
    <title>Getting Started With Sessions: Page 1</title>
</head>
<body>
<?php
    print( "Current User: $aUser<br>" );
    print( "Current Account: $aAccount<br>" );
?>
    <br><br>
    <a href="listing2.phtml">Go to page 2</a>
</body>
</html>
```

Listing 2: Using session variables from Listing 1

```php
<?php
    session_start();
?>
<html>
<head>
    <title>Getting Started With Sessions: Page 2</title>
</head>
<body>
<?php
    print( "Current User: $aUser<br>" );
    print( "Current Account: $aAccount<br>" );
?>
</body>
</html>
```

In Listing 1, the first step is to start the session with a call to **session_start()**. In the default session configuration, PHP uses cookies to store the session ID. As a result, calling **session_start()** has the same restrictions as calling **set_cookie()** or **header()**. Specifically, these functions must either be called before any information is sent to the browser or output buffering must be turned on in the script. Although you can change the way the session ID is propagated through the application, the simplest method is to use the default mechanism, cookies. The alternate methods are discussed later.

After the session is started, two variables are registered in the session, **aUser** and **aAccount**. When the end-user clicks the link to go to Page 2, the browser transparently sends along the session ID to the server. In Listing 2, PHP uses the session ID to restore all of the session variables when **session_start()** is called from that script. Figures 7.2 and 7.3 show the results of the pages in Listings 1 and 2, respectively.

Just by way of information, printing the current session identifier using the PHP variable **$PHPSESSID** is possible. Also, in the default configuration on Apache/Linux, the session information is stored in the **/tmp** directory in files of the form sess_$PHPSESSID. After I ran the previous example, I found the file sess_5bf8f6191efe8fb5dfadb7165b5142a2, which contained the data: **aUser|s:6:"Cidnie";aAccount|s:4:"1016";**.

Figure 7.2
The results of
Listing 1

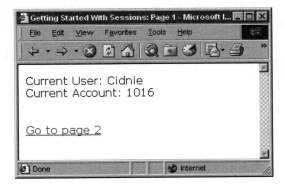

Figure 7.3
The results of
Listing 2

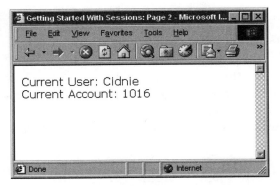

The defaults provided by PHP for managing sessions are simple to use and will meet the needs of most Web-based applications. In some instances, however, using cookies may not be the preferred method for propagating the session ID, and for some large Web applications, using files on the Web server will hinder the scalability of an application. The next two sections discuss methods for tackling these issues.

Propagating the Session ID Without Cookies

If your application absolutely requires the session variables, you may want to use a mechanism other than cookies to propagate the session ID. Don't forget that some users probably have disabled cookies in their browsers. PHP provides some alternatives for using cookies. The first is to manually pass the session ID as a GET or POST variable. The script in Listing 3 shows how to change the code from Listing 1 to propagate the session ID in a GET request.

Listing 3: Manually propagating the session ID using the HTTP GET method

```php
<?php
    session_start();
    session_register( "aUser", "aAccount" );
    $aUser      = "Cidnie";
    $aAccount   = "1016";
?>
<html>
<head>
    <title>Manually Propagating Session ID: Page 1</title>
</head>
<body>
<?php
    print( "Current User: $aUser<br>" );
    print( "Current Account: $aAccount<br>" );
?>
    <br><br>
    <a href="listing2.phtml?<?=SID?>">Go to next page</a>
</body>
</html>
```

Notice that the code is exactly the same as in Listing 1, except for the anchor tag on the third line from the end. In this case, the PHP constant **SID** is appended to the URL. The constant **SID** is defined as **Session Name=SessionID**. The following code is semantically identical to the line in Listing 3:

```php
<a href="listing4.phtml?<?php echo session_name() . "=" .
session_id() ?>">Go to next page</a>
```

Note that **SID** is a constant, not a variable, so if you try to print **$SID** rather than **SID**, you won't get the same results. Listing 3 showed the shortcut <?=SID?> notation. This notation is equivalent to writing <?php echo SID; ?>, assuming that --enable-short-tags was specified when you built PHP.

Listing 3 illustrates the mechanism for manually propagating a session ID through a program, but it doesn't show the extent to which this mechanism impacts your application development. With this mechanism, every link and every form in your application must include the session ID. If you fail to include the session ID in even a single link, the session ID will be lost, and your application will fail. Fortunately, PHP provides another feature, automatic URL rewriting, to handle this problem for you.

If you want to propagate the session ID through your application using GET and POST, you can enable the feature by building PHP with the **--enable-trans-sid** option. After PHP is rebuilt with this option, the code in Listing 3 can be changed to the slightly simpler code in Listing 4.

Listing 4: Letting PHP rewrite relative URLs for session ID propagation

```php
<?php
    session_start();
    session_register( "aUser", "aAccount" );
    $aUser      = "Cidnie";
    $aAccount   = "1016";
?>
<html>
<head>
    <title>Manually Propagating Session ID Automatically: Page 1</title>
</head>
<body>
<?php
    print( "Current User: $aUser<br>" );
    print( "Current Account: $aAccount<br>" );
?>
    <br><br>
    <a href="listing2.phtml">Go to next page</a>
</html>
```

This difference between Listing 3 and Listing 4 is that Listing 4 makes no reference to the **SID** constant in the anchor tag. As a note, Listing 4 is essentially identical to Listing 1, but the effect of the code is much different when executed because of the change in configuration. However, when the link is clicked, the URL contains the full **PHPSESSID=xxx** information, just like in Listing 3. This code works because PHP scans the page for relative URLs and adds the necessary session ID information automatically. To illustrate, the following listing contains some relative URLs and some absolute URLs. After the listing is a list of the URLs as they appeared after being processed by PHP.

Listing 5: Examples of PHP automatic URL rewriting

```
<?php
    session_start();
    session_register( "aUser", "aAccount" );
    $aUser      = "Cidnie";
    $aAccount   = "1016";
?>
<html>
<head>
    <title>URL Re-writing Examples</title>
</head>
<body>
<?php
    print( "Current User: $aUser<br>" );
    print( "Current Account: $aAccount<br>" );
?>
    <br><br>
    <a href="listing2.phtml">Link 1</a>
    <br><br>
    <a href="listing2.phtml?MyVar=1234">Link 2</a>
    <br><br>
    <a href="http://www.php.net/">Link 3</a>
    <br><br>
    <a href="http://mysvr.com/ch07/listing2.phtml">Link 4</a>
    <br><br>
    <form action="listing2.phtml" method="post">
        <input type="submit" name="Submit" value="Form Submit Button">
    </form>
</html>
```

When the code in Listing 5 is run, the following HTML is sent to the browser:

```
<html>
<head>
    <title>URL Re-writing Examples</title>
</head>
<body>
Current User: Cidnie<br>Current Account: 1016<br>     <br><br>
    <a
href="listing2.phtml?PHPSESSID=fda5227ef187a0bbb3d7d0ced1c5491a">Li
nk 1</a>
    <br><br>
    <a
href="listing2.phtml?MyVar=1234&PHPSESSID=fda5227ef187a0bbb3d7d0ced
1c5491a">Link 2</a>
    <br><br>
    <a href="http://www.php.net/">Link 3</a>
```

```
<br><br>
<a href="http://mysvr.com/ch07/listing2.phtml">Link 4</a>
<br><br>
<form action="listing2.phtml?PHPSESSID=fda5227ef187a0bbb3d7d0
ced1c5491a"
method="post">
        <input type="submit" name="Submit" value="Form Submit
Button">
    </form>
</html>
```

Because the first two links are relative links, the session information was correctly appended to the URL. Link 3 is obviously not a relative link, so the session ID was not appended. This behavior is expected. Link 4 illustrates that you need to be careful when using the automatic URL rewriting feature of PHP. In this case, the absolute URL was specified in the anchor tag even though the page was on the same server. PHP rewrites only URLs that use the standard notation for relative links.

The form in the example was included because PHP also rewrites the form's action attribute to include the session ID. This means that even forms in your application will work correctly. One caveat is that the form must use the POST method. If you try to use a form with the GET method and with URL rewriting, it doesn't work correctly. Although the action attribute is rewritten correctly, the browser doesn't include the PHPSES-SID variable in the query string when submitting the form. (This scenario was tested with the latest versions of Netscape and Internet Explorer.)

Propagating the session ID through the GET and POST methods enables you to avoid some of the problems with using cookies, and it can be simple to implement. If you are considering using the automatic URL rewriting feature of PHP, you should also consider the effect it will have on your application's performance. PHP will have to search all of the links in each page and rewrite the URLs as needed each time the page is processed.

To test the performance hit, I took a sample Web page and then built a script to request the page from the Web server and record the time required to retrieve it. The sample page contained 14 links, 12 of which were relative links, requiring URL rewriting. The total page size was 9.55 KB. I then used the script in Listing 6 to request the page 1,000 times consecutively. I ran the script with **--enable-trans-sid** enabled and then without.

I ran each test multiple times and then found an average difference in time. The average time savings was about 9 percent per page when **--enable-trans-sid** was disabled. Although this difference may not be significant in some sites, it may be important in very high-traffic sites. Before committing to any solution, you should run your own tests to determine the impact of using one solution over another.

Error Update

As discussed in this section, an error in PHP version 4.0.1 patch level 2 causes problems when using automatic URL rewriting. Version 4.0.2 of PHP has fixed this bug. Should you need this feature, make sure that you use version 4.0.2 or later of PHP.

Listing 6: Timing script

```php
<?php
    function getmicrotime()
    {
        $mtime = microtime();
        $mtime = explode( " ", $mtime );
        $mtime = $mtime[1] + $mtime[0];
        return ( $mtime );
    }
    $aStartTime = getmicrotime();
    $aFileName = "http://mysvr.com/h2atest.phtml";
    for ( $nIndex = 0; $nIndex < 1000; $nIndex++ )
    {
        $aData = file( $aFileName );
    }
    $aEndTime = getmicrotime();
    $aTotTime = $aEndTime - $aStartTime;
    print( "Total Time: $aTotTime\n" );
?>
```

Storing the Session Variables in a Database

Once you have determined where you are going to store the session ID, the next big decision is where to store the session variables themselves. PHP provides a mechanism for storing session variables however you like: Define six callback functions and register them with PHP to write any session management scheme you want. The six functions and their parameters are as follows:

■ **bool open(string save_path, string sess_name);** This function is executed on the initialization of a session. You can use it for any required initialization. The first argument is the path defined in the **session.save_path** configuration item in php.ini or the most recent value passed to the **session_save_path()** function. The second argument is the session's name defined in the **session.name** configuration item in php.ini or the most recent value passed to the **session_name()** function. The defaults are "/tmp" and "PHPSESSID," respectively.

- **bool close();** This function is executed on the shutdown of a session.

- **mixed read(string sess_id);** This function is used at startup to read the contents of the session. If no session data is available, the empty string ("") should be returned. If an error occurs, false should be returned. If data is available for the session, the return value should be the serialized session data. This data should be the exact same value as provided by PHP in the **write()** function.

- **bool write(string sess_id, string value);** When the session data needs to be saved, this function is invoked. The data in the **value** parameter is the serialized data that should be stored for the session.

- **bool destroy(string sess_id);** This function is executed when the **session_destroy()** function is called. It should destroy all data associated with the session.

- **bool gc(int max_lifetime);** This function is called when a session is started. It is called with a frequency equal to the value of the **session.gc_probability** configuration item. It is used for garbage collection. When called, this function should delete all session data for sessions that have not been updated within **max_lifetime** seconds. Session garbage collection is discussed in the next section of this chapter.

Once you have developed your callback functions, register them with the **session_set_save_handler()** function. PHP will then call your session management functions whenever needed. To illustrate the concept, Listing 7 contains a set of session management functions that just print out the fact that they were called by PHP. The **read()** function included in this listing returns two session variables just for testing.

Listing 7: User-defined session management: mysession.php

```php
<?php
function mysess_open( $aSavePath, $aSessionName )
{
    print( "mysess_open( $aSavePath, $aSessionName )<br>" );
    return True;
}
function mysess_close()
{
    print( "mysess_close()<br>" );
    return True;
}
```

```php
function mysess_read( $aKey )
{
    print( "mysess_read( $aKey )<br>" );
    return "aUser|s:6:\"Cidnie\";aAccount|s:4:\"1016\";";
}
function mysess_write( $aKey, $aVal )
{
    print( "Here I am!\n\nRight here!\n\n" );
    print( "mysess_write( $aKey, $aVal )<br>" );
    return True;
}
function mysess_destroy( $aKey )
{
    print( "mysess_destroy( $aKey )<br>" );
    return True;
}
function mysess_gc( $aMaxLifetime )
{
    print( "mysess_gc( $aMaxLifetime )<br>" );
    return True;
}
session_set_save_handler( "mysess_open", "mysess_close",
"mysess_read",
                        "mysess_write", "mysess_destroy",
"mysess_gc" );
?>
```

To show how PHP calls the functions in a practical example, I used the script in Listing 8 as a test. I also set the value of **session.gc_probability** to 100 so that the garbage collection routine would be called at the start of every session.

Listing 8: Testing mysession.php

```php
<?php
    include( "./mysession.php" );
    session_start();
?>
<html>
<head>
    <title>Custom Session Management</title>
</head>
<body>
<?php
    print( "Current User: $aUser<br>" );
    print( "Current Account: $aAccount<br>" );
    $aUser = "Katie";
    $aAccount = "2026";
    print( "Current User: $aUser<br>" );
    print( "Current Account: $aAccount<br>" );
?>
</body>
</html>
```

When the script was run, the output was not entirely what I expected. Figure 7.4 shows the entire output of the script. Note that there is no indi-

Figure 7.4
Output of
mysession.php

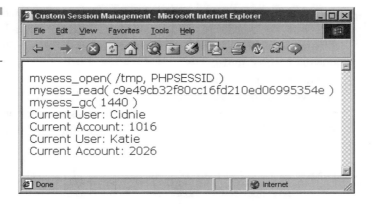

Figure 7.4
Output of
mysession.php

cation that the write or close functions were called. I expected to see them at the bottom of the page, but they were not there. As you can see in the body of the **mysess_write()** function, I even added a superfluous **print()** statement to double-check. Still, the output to the browser did not indicate that either the write or close callback functions were called. Upon further investigation, I found that all output from both of these functions was in my Apache error_log file. This result means that somewhere the output was redirected temporarily from stdout to stderr. The effect of this redirection is that you can't send output to the browser in the body of either the write or close function, but this problem is probably not a major concern for writing a real session management mechanism. As a note, this same effect may not be seen on other platform/server combinations depending on how standard output and errors are handled. For example, the Xitami server running on Windows shows all of the output text in the browser as expected.

After you understand how the basic mechanism works, building a real session management handler becomes easy. If you are going to use session variables, you should store them in a database rather than in a file. This idea may seem counterintuitive at first, but storing any application data on a specific Web server can limit the scalability of your application. If your application is ever distributed over more than one Web server with a load-balancing router redirecting client requests, using a file-based session system will cause your application to fail. This failure results from the fact that each request for a page may be redirected to a different server in the cluster. If the initial data is stored on server one and a subsequent request is redirected to server two, the session data will not be available. If all session data is stored on the back-end database server, your session variables will be available to every Web server in the cluster.

The following listing shows a basic example of how to store session data in a MySQL database. The example uses the PHPLIB DB_Sql class discussed in Chapter 6, "Working with Databases," to improve the readability of the code. The table used to store the session was defined as follows:

```
CREATE TABLE Sessions
(
    SessionID       char(32)      not null,
    LastUpdated     datetime      not null,
    DataValue       text,
    PRIMARY KEY ( SessionID ),
    INDEX ( LastUpdated )
);
```

This simple table consists of the session ID, a date/time field to track the last update, and the data itself as a MySQL text BLOB. The **LastUpdated** field is indexed to improve performance when doing garbage collection. The full source code for the session manager is in Listing 9.

Listing 9: Session management using MySQL DBMS: mysql_session.php

```php
<?php
    include ( "db_mysql.inc" );
    // Extend the DB_Sql class to use it with our
    // MySQL database instance
    class MySQLDB extends DB_Sql
    {
        var $Host       = "my.db.server";
        var $Database   = "mydb";
        var $User       = "user";
        var $Password   = "pwd";
    }
    function mysess_open( $aSavePath, $aSessionName )
    {
        // don't need to do anything here
        return True;
    }
    function mysess_close()
    {
        // don't need to do anything here
        return True;
    }
    function mysess_read( $aKey )
    {
        $aDB = new MySQLDB;
        $aSQL = "select DataValue from Sessions where
SessionID='$aKey'";
        $aDB->query( $aSQL );
```

```
            if ( $aDB->num_rows() = 1 )
            {
                $aDB->next_record();
                $aData = $aDB->f( "DataValue" );
                return $aData;
            }
            else
            {
                // Insert a row for this session to simplify write
function
                $aSQL  = "insert into Sessions values ( '$aKey', NOW(),
'' )";
                $aDB->query( $aSQL );
                return "";
            }
        }
        function mysess_write( $aKey, $aVal )
        {
            $aDB = new MySQLDB;
            $aData = addslashes( $aVal );
            $aSQL  = "update Sessions set DataValue='$aData', ";
            $aSQL .= "LastUpdated=NOW() where SessionID='$aKey'";
            $aDB->query( $aSQL );
            return True;
        }
        function mysess_destroy( $aKey )
        {
            $aDB = new MySQLDB;
            $aSQL  = "delete from Sessions where SessionID = '$aKey'";
            $aDB->query( $aSQL );
            return True;
        }
        function mysess_gc( $aMaxLifetime )
        {
            $aDB = new MySQLDB;
            $aSQL  = "delete from Sessions where UNIX_TIMESTAMP(NOW())
";
            $aSQL .= "- UNIX_TIMESTAMP(LastUpdated) > $aMaxLifetime";
            $aDB->query( $aSQL );
            return True;
        }
        session_set_save_handler( "mysess_open", "mysess_close",
"mysess_read",
                                  "mysess_write", "mysess_destroy",
"mysess_gc" );
        ?>
```

The code in Listing 9 is quite simple for such a powerful upgrade to session management. The functions **mysess_open()** and **mysess_close()** are not used because they're not necessary. All session data is stored in a single table, so the values passed to the **mysess_open()** function are irrelevant, and nothing is left to clean up at the end of a session.

The interesting functions are **mysess_read()**, **mysess_write()**, **mysess_destroy()**, and **mysess_gc()**. In **mysess_read()**, the database is queried to locate the data associated with the session ID. If the data is found, it is returned. If no record is currently in the database, one is created with an empty **DataValue** field, and the null string ("") is returned. The reason for this action is so that when the session variables are written later, checking for existing values in the database is unnecessary.

The **mysess_write()** function updates the **DataValue** and **LastUpdated** fields each time it is called. The **mysess_destroy()** function immediately deletes the record associated with the session ID. The **mysess_gc()** function deletes all rows in the session table that have a **LastUpdated** time that is more than **$aMaxLifetime** seconds old. The following code shows how the session manager and table are used in practice:

```php
<?php
    include( "./mysql_session.php" );
    session_start();
    session_register( "aUser", "aAccount" );
    $aUser      = "Cidnie";
    $aAccount   = "1016";
?>
<html>
<head>
    <title>MySQL Session Management: First Page</title>
</head>
<body>
<?php
    print( "Current User: $aUser<br>" );
    print( "Current Account: $aAccount<br>" );
?>
    <br><br>
    <a href="mysql_session_mgmt2.phtml?<?=SID?>">Go to next page</a>
</body>
</html>
```

The previous examples show how simply you can build and use a user-defined session storage mechanism in PHP. Some optimizations and features could be added to make the implementation more robust, but the examples present the general idea. If your application requires session variables, PHP provides enough customization to allow you to make all of the best decisions about a session-management implementation.

Other PHP Session Functions and Options

PHP provides a few additional functions for session management that have not yet been covered. The **session_name()**, **session_module_name()**, **session_save_path()**, and **session_id()** functions can be used to query or change the current session name, module name, save path, or ID, respectively. I have a difficult time envisioning a project where changing any of these values on the fly would be recommended. If your application has so many session variables that you are partitioning them using any of these functions, you may want to seriously consider the suggestions in the "Software Engineering and Sessions" section, later in this chapter.

The following options are provided in the php.ini file for configuring PHP sessions:

■ **session.save_handler:** This option defines the name of the handler that is used for storing and retrieving data associated with a session. The options are **files**, **user**, and **mm**. This option can be checked or modified at runtime using the **session_module_name()** function. Setting this option to **files** causes the session data to be saved on the server in a file. Setting it to **user** implies that your application will provide its own handling mechanism. Using the **mm** setting causes the session variables to be stored in shared memory on the Web server. If you call the **session_set_save_handler()** function, this value is implicitly set to **user**. This option defaults to **files**.

■ **session.save_path:** This option defines the argument that is passed to the save handler. If you choose the default files handler, this is the path where the files are created. This option defaults to **/tmp**.

■ **session.name:** This option specifies the name of the session, which is used as a cookie name. It should contain only alphanumeric characters. This option defaults to **PHPSESSID**.

■ **session.auto_start:** This option specifies whether the session module starts a session automatically on request at startup. It defaults to **0** (disabled).

■ **session.lifetime:** This option specifies the lifetime of the cookie in seconds, a value which is sent to the browser. The value 0 means "until the browser is closed." This option defaults to **0**.

■ **session.serialize_handler:** This option defines the name of the handler that is used to serialize/deserialize data. Currently, a PHP internal format (named **php**) and WDDX are supported (named **wddx**). WDDX is available only if PHP is compiled with WDDX support. This option defaults to **php**.

■ **session.gc_probability:** This option specifies the probability that the gc (garbage collection) routine is started on each request as a percentage. PHP uses this value to determine how often to call the garbage collection function. Garbage collection refers to deleting the session variables stored on the Web server. Because finding out when a session has ended is impossible, PHP calls the garbage collection function to remove session variables that have not been updated for a certain period of time (see the **session.gc_maxlifetime** item). This option defaults to **1**, meaning that 1 percent of the time a session is started, the garbage collection routine will be called. If you are using **GET** and **POST** to propagate session IDs, you should probably increase this value. The reason is because a user may bookmark a URL in your application that has an embedded session ID. You don't want your users coming back and picking up an old session.

- **session.gc_maxlifetime:** This option specifies the number of seconds after which data will be seen as "garbage" and cleaned up. The default is 1,440 seconds (24 minutes). Depending on your application, you may want sessions to expire sooner or later.

- **session.referer_check:** This option determines whether session IDs referred to by external sites will be eliminated. If session IDs are propagated using the URL method, users, not knowing about the impact, might publish session IDs. This situation can lead to security problems, which is what this check tries to prevent. This option defaults to **0**.

- **session.entropy_file:** This option gives a path to an external resource (file), which will be used as an additional entropy source in the session ID creation process. Examples are /dev/random or /dev/urandom, which are available on many Unix systems.

- **session.entropy_length:** This option specifies the number of bytes, which will be read from the file specified in the preceding option. This option defaults to **0** (disabled).

- **session.use_cookies:** This option specifies whether the module will use cookies to store the session ID on the client side. It defaults to **1** (enabled).

PHP provides a great deal of flexibility in implementing sessions. When you are planning an application that will use session variables, be sure to consider all of the available options. Although cookies may seem to be a simple implementation, they may cause significant problems because some users will disable cookies. The other methods of propagating session IDs require more work, but the additional planning will be worthwhile. I recommend propagating the session ID in the URL because this method requires you to make explicit decisions about which pages in the application will use session information. I also recommend using a template-based approach to Web design (see Chapter 12, "Separating HTML from PHP4 Code," for details) that makes manually propagating session IDs much simpler than the approaches shown in this chapter.

Using PHPLIB for Session Management

As mentioned in Chapter 6, "Working with Databases," PHPLIB is a great class library that provides some advanced features for developing PHP-based applications. PHPLIB was one of the first (and probably the best known) class libraries to provide session management in PHP. Conceptually, it is very similar to the implementation available natively in PHP4. The PHPLIB session support is implemented entirely in PHP code, so it is extensible and configurable through a simple extension of the base class. It also provides some initialization options that can be very valuable in real-world applications.

PHPLIB session management relies on a container class also implemented in PHPLIB. It uses a subclass of one of the CT_xxx classes to manage the physical persistence of session variables. This means that PHPLIB can also be extended to allow session variables to be stored in essentially any location. PHPLIB also requires that its page management functions be used to signal the beginning and end of a page and which of the PHPLIB "features" will be used on that page.

Listing 10 illustrates using PHPLIB to store session variables in a MySQL database. This example is essentially identical to Listing 9 except that it uses cookies to store the client-side session ID.

Listing 10: Session Management PHPLIB

```php
<?php
    include( "page.inc" );
    include( "ct_sql.inc" );
    include( "session.inc" );
    include( "db_mysql.inc" );
    // Extend the DB_Sql class to use it with our
    // MySQL database instance
    class MySQLDB extends DB_Sql
    {
        var $Host       = "db.server.com";
        var $Database   = "mydb";
        var $User       = "user";
        var $Password   = "pwd";
    }
    class MySQLCt extends CT_Sql
    {
        var $classname = "MySQLCt";
        var $database_table = "active_sessions";
        var $database_class = "MySQLDB";
    }
    class MySqlSession extends Session
```

```
    {
        var $classname = "MySqlSession"; // Persistence support
        var $mode      = "cookie";
        var $lifetime  = 0;               // use session cookies
        var $that_class = "MySQLCt";      // which container to use
    }
    page_open( array( "sess" => "MySqlSession" ) );
    $sess->register( "aUser" );
    $sess->register( "aAccount" );
    $aUser      = "Cidnie";
    $aAccount   = "1016";
?>
<html>
<head>
    <title>PHPLIB Session Management: First Page</title>
</head>
<body>
<?php
    print( "Current User: $aUser<br>" );
    print( "Current Account: $aAccount<br>" );
?>
    <br><br>
    <a href="phplib_session_mgmt2.phtml">Go to next page</a>
</body>
</html>
<?php
    page_close();
?>
```

PHPLIB is an extremely flexible solution for maintaining session information. Like PHP, it provides mechanisms for storing the session variables in a file, shared memory, and database tables. The code in Listing 10 is slightly more complex to read, but seasoned developers will see that the code inherently provides a great deal of extensibility by simply subclassing the base classes needed for session management. The first subclass, **MySQLDB**, is a simple subclass that provides access to a MySQL database instance. The next subclass, **MySQLCt**, is a subclass of the **CT_Sql** container class, a generic container class for storing information in a SQL database. It contains a reference to the **MySQLDB** class that accesses the database tables. Finally, the **MySQLSession** class extends the base **Session** class and specifies the **MySQLCt** class as the storage container for all session information.

The database table structure required for PHPLIB session management is as follows:

```
CREATE TABLE active_sessions (
    sid varchar(32) NOT NULL,
    name varchar(32) NOT NULL,
    val text,
    changed varchar(14) NOT NULL,
    PRIMARY KEY (name, sid),
    KEY changed (changed)
```

);

Once the subclasses are created, PHPLIB uses the **page_open()** function to add the session "feature" to the current page. Calling this function results in a global variable **$sess** being created for use in subsequent session management calls. The basic functionality of the **Session** class in PHPLIB is nearly identical to the native PHP implementation. After the class is created, session variables are registered and used by the application. The only additional requirement is that the script calls **page_close()** to signify the end of the script.

As with the native PHP session management, PHPLIB enables you to use cookies or GET/POST variables for session ID propagation. PHPLIB also provides the tools to develop a container class for storing session variables in any server location imaginable. One additional feature of the PHPLIB implementation is its capability to provide an initialization file for setting up standard session variables at the beginning of each session. The following code is an example of an initialization file:

```php
<?php
    global $lang;    // application language
    $lang = "de";    // german by default
    $sess->register("lang");
    global $cur;     // application currency
    $cur = "EUR";    // Euro by default
    $sess->register("cur");
    global $cart;
    $cart = new Shop_Cart; // Create a shopping cart object def'd
in local.inc
    $sess->register("cart"); // register it.
?>
```

Although PHP natively supports many of the same functions as the PHPLIB solution, it may be nice to have the entire PHP source code as provided by PHPLIB if you need to do some debugging or customization. You also can use PHPLIB as a solution with older versions of PHP that don't support sessions natively.

Developing Custom Session Management

In some situations, a fully functional session management system may not be required in your application. In many instances, the only information that needs to persist from page to page is a single primary key or identifier.

In these cases, it may be more efficient to propagate the identifier throughout the application using GET or POST variables. Then you can use your DBMS to look up relevant information on each page.

This solution is simple to implement and doesn't require any of the additional overhead consumed by any of the aforementioned session management tools. On the other hand, propagating the identifier requires a little more forethought and planning when developing the application itself. Additionally, propagating the ID in plain text may compromise the security of your application, so implementing an encryption scheme is recommended when using this method.

Again, as with any other aspect of your application design, use a thoughtful design process to identify the needs of your application before choosing a session management scheme. Choosing the wrong tool up front can be costly in terms of time and money and can lead to maintenance problems in the long term.

Software Engineering and Sessions

Session variables can be critically important in many Web-based applications. They are flexible and easy to use, but like any programming tool, they should be used carefully and by design. Because session variables are so easy to use, they are commonly overused in the same way that global variables can be overused in traditional software development.

When designing your Web application, you need to carefully evaluate any purpose for which session variables are being considered. Make your decision about using a session variable in the same way you would evaluate the use of a global variable. Steve McConnell, author of *Code Complete* (Microsoft Press, 1993), suggests the following as valid reasons to use global data:

- **Preservation of global values.** Global data, such as a mode (that is, trial, full), reflects the state of the entire application. It could also be a large data element, such as a lookup table, that is used throughout the application.
- **Substitution for named constants.** Because PHP provides named constants, this use is unlikely.
- **Streamlining use of extremely common data.** Occasionally a data element is used so frequently in an application that it appears in the parameter list of every routine.

■ **Eliminating tramp data.** Sometimes a value is passed to a routine simply to be passed to another routine. When the routine in the middle of the call chain doesn't use the data, the data is called *tramp data.*

This list identifies the main issues in evaluating the use of global data in generic application programming, but you can evaluate the use of session variables with the same set of criteria.

Be careful when considering a session variable because it seems to be used in every routine in your application or on every single page of your Web site. This issue seems to lead to the most frequent misuse of any global data and of session variables. Keep in mind that when you define session variables in your application, each page in the session has to load all the session variables defined, even those not used on the current page. Also, avoid using session variables if your only reason is that they provide a more convenient mechanism for accessing session-related data.

In a recent contracting engagement, I came across a very good example of poor use of session variables. In the application, each user can create a data profile and grant access to other users to view and modify some of that data. These secondary users are advisors and professionals that the primary user trusts. When the original user grants access to an advisor, the permissions information is stored in the DBMS. The permissions table contains the user ID of the primary user and of the advisor and the primary key ID of the data that is accessible by the secondary user. When an advisor logs into the application, he or she must first choose which client data to view. Session variables are then set in the application that define the account ID of the advisor and the account ID of the client data to view and edit.

If these ID variables were the only session variables, there would be no problem. The problem in the application is that someone decided to bypass using the database to check permissions by passing around a comma-separated list of permissible data IDs. So any time the advisor creates a data element in the program, the comma-separated list is updated (along with the permissions database table). Then, when any data element is selected from the database, its ID is checked against the session permissions list rather than being checked against the database.

The main problem with this approach is that it results in a data synchronization problem. If the primary user updates the permissions table while the advisor is online using the application, the advisor will have access to the data elements that were permissible at the beginning of her session. Additionally, developing new code under this model is frustrating because the developer does not know whether to use the permissions information in the database or in the session variables.

The unfortunate reality in this scenario is that the two goals of the original programmers weren't even met. First, the session variables were created to eliminate a database call (to speed page loading) at the beginning of each page to gather the permissions information. Second, session variables were used to simplify checking permissions within the body of the code.

The first goal wasn't met because although the programmer doesn't explicitly load session variables, they still have to be loaded from a persistent storage location. So for every page in the application, the permissions data is retrieved from a file on the Web server when the page is loaded and stored again to the file when the page is complete. This process means that even pages that don't use the permissions information have the overhead of loading all the application permissions information. Loading the permissions information from the database only on the pages that require it would have been much more efficient.

The second goal wasn't met because the programmers weren't using the power of the database to its fullest extent. On many of the pages, the code looked like the following:

```
select all needed data from the primary user's account
for each row
       if the primary id of this row is in the session permission list
              display or use the data
         otherwise
              ignore this row because this advisor shouldn't see it
```

As I mentioned in Chapter 6, "Working with Databases," you must use the DBMS to its fullest extent to improve the efficiency of any Web application. The preceding code could be eliminated if the database query joined the required data with the permissions table. Doing so would eliminate a tremendous amount of code and would entirely eliminate the need to keep a list of permissions in the session.

Session variables fill a great need in Web application development, but they should be used with care. Consider all the alternatives to using a session variable while designing your applications. Most Web-based applications need only a few session variables. Ask yourself these questions when considering using a session variable:

■ **Is this variable going to be used throughout the program?** If this value will be used on every page of the application, it is probably a great candidate for a session variable. For example, if your application requires some type of login mechanism, you may want to keep the ID of the user in a session variable.

- **Is this variable unique to this session?** If this information is really session-related information, then use a session variable. For example, if you are creating a shopping cart, then you probably want to store the ID of the cart in a session variable. However, if your application requires a more persistent shopping cart wherein users can continue shopping in a subsequent session, you probably don't need a session variable, but you do need a good database design.

- **Does this variable represent primary data?** This question goes along with the first question. If your application uses a session variable to keep the ID of the user, avoid keeping additional user-specific information in the session. Rather, use the primary ID to look up the required information when it is needed. For example, if your application allows the user to personalize her pages, don't keep the personalization variables in the session. Keep the primary ID in the session and write some functions to gather the personalization information when needed. Not only does this structure eliminate a data redundancy problem, but it also allows a user to change her preferences in one session and have them reflected in another concurrent session.

- **Does my application really need session variables?** This question may seem obvious, but it is often overlooked because of the simplicity of implementing session variables. Just because a user visits your site and performs some actions there does not necessarily imply that a session is needed. Session variables should not be used to just replace another storage mechanism.

If your answers to these questions oppose the suggested answers, consider an alternate method for storing your persistent data. Sessions are a great tool, but they can lead to buggy, hard-to-maintain applications if they are used incorrectly.

Summary

Several great solutions are available for implementing session management in PHP. Choose the implementation that best fits your needs and make the decision based on long-term needs rather than the short-term impact on coding. Sloppy session variable usage will result in an application that is hard to maintain and can produce bugs that are very difficult to identify.

Authentication

Introduction

The previous chapter, "Sessions and Application State," discussed tracking visitors through a Web site to provide continuity in the application. This chapter focuses on ensuring that visitors have the authority to view your applications.

Different types of authentication schemes exist to fill different needs. Most Web servers provide tools for authentication based on permissions and server-based files. I discuss server-based authentication schemes in this chapter, but focus on using Linux and Apache only. (Windows and IIS also provide options for authentication, but these options aren't discussed in this chapter.) A server- and platform-independent mechanism is also presented later in this chapter.

Basic Authentication Using Apache

This section starts by discussing the basic authentication scheme provided by the Apache Web server and the caveats to using this mechanism. For those familiar with the Apache authentication directives and .htaccess files and the other Apache configuration files, this discussion will not provide much new information.

A basic site may require that general access to pages is restricted. Using the Web server's authentication scheme is usually a quick and effective way to provide this functionality. For example, you may want to develop a set of administrative pages for your site through which you can view or update aspects of your site. You don't want outsiders viewing these administrative pages, but you want to be able to access them from any browser anywhere.

To accomplish this, you can move all of the administrative pages to a subdirectory under your site's root directory and add a configuration directive in Apache to require authentication for pages requested from that subdirectory. The configuration directive can appear in the httpd.conf file or in an **.htaccess** file in the subdirectory itself. If you have access to the Apache config files, use them instead of an .htaccess file. Using an .htaccess file is less efficient than using the regular Apache config files because the .htaccess file is read each time a page is requested from the directory containing the .htaccess file. However, if your site is hosted at a third-party hosting service, you probably won't be able to modify the Apache config files yourself, let alone restart the Web server to realize the changes.

Listing 1 shows the source to a simple HTML page that provides a link to an administrative page. The administrative page is in a subdirectory that requires basic authentication, so clicking the link will cause the browser to present its standard authentication dialog box, which is shown in Figure 8.1. Listing 2 shows the Apache authentication directives used to cause this dialog box to appear.

Listing 1: Simple HTML page linking to administrative pages

```
<html>
<head>
     <title>Basic Apache Authentication</title>
</head>
<body>
    <a href="admin/index.phtml">Go to Admin Pages</a>
</body>
</html>
```

Listing 2: Apache configuration directives for basic authentication

```
AuthUserFile /www/auth_users
AuthName Adminstrative
AuthType Basic
<Limit GET>
require valid-user
</Limit>
```

You can find more information about using Apache authentication online and in the many great Apache books available. This type of authentication requires cooperation between the browser and the Web server to implement. Internally, the Web server sends a 401 response to the browser when

Figure 8.1
Browser
Authentication
dialog box

the user needs to be authenticated. The browser queries the user and sends the information back to the Web server. If the Web server accepts the authentication, the requested resource is made available to the user. The browser continues to send the authentication information in each request to the server until the user closes the browser.

PHP provides global variables that you can use within your applications to query the authentication information. You can use the $PHP_AUTH_USER and $PHP_AUTH_PW variables to query the user and password, respectively. Listing 3 is a page that just displays the authentication information. Figure 8.2 shows the page after it is requested from the page in Listing 1.

Listing 3: Displaying the PHP authentication variables

```html
<html>
<head>
    <title>Admin Pages</title>
</head>
<body>
<h1>Welcome to the Admin Pages</h1>
<?php
    print( "PHP_AUTH_USER: $PHP_AUTH_USER<br>" );
    print( "PHP_AUTH_PW: $PHP_AUTH_PW<br>" );
?>
</body>
</html>
```

The Apache authentication scheme provides basic security for your site. It is particularly useful in situations where you need to protect all the pages and other resources in a part of your site's directory tree. The limitation to

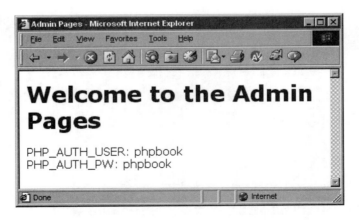

Figure 8.2
The PHP authentication variables

using this scheme exactly as outlined in this section is that you must manually add and remove users via commands on the server. The next section shows how you can use PHP to update your password file, so you can create a Web-based tool for adding and removing users.

Updating the .htaccess File with PHP

If basic Web server authentication will suffice for your application, you may want to create a PHP-based administrative tool to simplify the management of users. You may also want to provide a tool through which other trusted individuals can manage the users without having to give the individuals direct access to your Web server system.

The developers at The Webmasters Net (http://www.theWebmasters.net/) have created two classes for managing user and group files for basic authentication. You can use the **Htpasswd** class to manage a standard htpasswd file used by Apache for basic authentication. Listing 4 shows how the class can be used with very little code to authenticate a user. The example uses the same file as was used in the previous examples.

Listing 4: Checking for a valid user with the Htpasswd class

```
<html>
<head>
    <title>Quick Validate Using Htpasswd Class</title>
</head>
<body>
<?php
    include( "./class.Htpasswd.php3" );
    $aHTPasswd = new Htpasswd("/www/auth_users");
    if ( !$aHTPasswd->EXISTS )
    {
        print( "authentication error<br>" );
    }
    else
    {
        if ( $aHTPasswd->verifyuser( "phpbook", "phpbook" ) )
        {
            print( "phpbook is a valid user<br>" );
        }
        else
        {
            print( "phpbook is not a valid user<br>" );
        }
```

```
    }
?>
</body>
</html>
```

You can use the **Htpasswd** class to add a new user, delete a user, change a user's password, validate a user, and rename a user. With these tools, you can craft a comprehensive user management tool to aid in your overall authentication scheme. The scripts in Listing 5, Listing 6, and Listing 7 show how all of these features can be combined in a single form for quick user management.

The first part of the script, Listing 5, is used to initialize the script and determine whether this page is being viewed initially or whether it is being invoked as the result of a POST request. This script is similar to many of the examples in this book in that it posts information back to itself, so it is used for both displaying and updating functionality.

Listing 5: Using the Htpasswd class for user management

```php
<?php
    include( "./class.Htpasswd.php3" );
    $aHTPasswd = new Htpasswd("/www/auth_users");
    if ( !$aHTPasswd->EXISTS )
    {
        print( "fatal error<br>" );
        exit;
    }

    if (  $REQUEST_METHOD == 'POST' )
    {
        switch ( $acttype )
        {
            case 'none' :
                break;
            case 'add' :
                $aHTPasswd->addUser( $NewUserName, $NewUserPass );
                print( "<b>Added user, $NewUserName</b><br>" );
                break;
            case 'delete' :
                $aUserName = $aHTPasswd-
>USERS[$CurUserRow]["user"];
                $aHTPasswd->deleteUser( $aUserName );
                print( "<b>Deleted user, $aUserName</b><br>" );
                break;
            case 'rename' :
                $aUserName = $aHTPasswd-
>USERS[$CurUserRow]["user"];
                $aHTPasswd->renameUser( $aUserName, $RenameName );
                print( "<b>Renamed user from $aUserName to
$RenameName</b><br>" );
                break;
            case 'changepass' :
                $aUserName = $aHTPasswd-
>USERS[$CurUserRow]["user"];
```

```
                          $aHTPasswd->changePass( $aUserName, $ChangePass );
                          print( "<b>Changed user password for
        $aUserName</b><br>" );
                          break;
              }
          }
      ?>
```

If this script is invoked from a POST request, then the form variable,
$acttype, is checked to determine which action to take. The five possible
values are **none**, **add**, **delete**, **rename**, and **changepass**. Based on the
type of action requested by the user, an appropriate action is taken. The
script assumes that all inputs are valid and provided. Error checking would
obviously have to be added to complete this script for real-world usage.

The next section of the script shows how the **$acttype** variable is set. For
each button on the form, an associated action is defined. JavaScript is used
to set the hidden **$acttype** form variable and then to post the form.

Listing 6: Setting the $acttype variable

```
<html>
<head>
            <title>Simplistic User Manager</title>
      <script language="JavaScript">
      <!--
          function DoSubmit( aType )
          {
              document.mainform.acttype.value = aType;
              document.mainform.submit();
          }
      //-->
      </script>
</head>
```

The remainder of the page is shown in Listing 7. It is a fairly basic
HTML form page. The only PHP code in this section is used to add the existing user names to the SELECT list. Each button element contains an
onClick attribute that calls the preceding JavaScript function to submit
the form properly.

Listing 7: HTML form page

```
<body>
    <form action="<?=$PHP_SELF?>" method="post" name="mainform"
id="mainform">
    <input type="hidden" name="acttype" value="none">
    <h1>Simplistic User Manager</h1>
    <h2>Add a User</h2>
    New User Name: <input type="text" name="NewUserName"><br>
    New User Password: <input type="password"
name="NewUserPass"><br>
    <input type="button" value="Add User" onClick="DoSubmit( 'add'
```

```
);">
    <hr>
    <h2>Modify a User</h2>
    <table>
        <tr>
            <td>
                <select name="CurUserRow" size="10">
                <?php
                    $nIndex = 0;
                    foreach( $aHTPasswd->USERS as $aUser )
                    {
                        print( "<option
value=\"$nIndex\">$aUser[user]</option>" );
                        $nIndex++;
                    }
                ?>
                </select>
            </td>
            <td>
                Delete selected user: <input type="button"
value="Delete"
onClick="DoSubmit( 'delete' );"><br><br>
                Rename selected user: <input type="text"
name="RenameName">
<input type="button" value="Rename" onClick="DoSubmit( 'rename'
);"><br><br>
                Change password for selected user: <input
type="password"
name="ChangePass"><input type="button" value="Change Pass"
onClick="DoSubmit( 'changepass' );"><br><br>
            </td>
        </tr>
    </table>
    </form>
</body>
</html>
```

Figure 8.3 shows the page after the new user, **scott**, has just been added. As mentioned previously, this script is far from complete for a real user management tool, but it illustrates how you can use the **Htpasswd** class. You can use the **Htgroup** class, also from The Webmasters Net, to create and manage user groups.

Basic Authentication Using PHP

The previous two sections focused on using Apache's basic authentication for protecting segments of a Web site (usually a directory). In some cases, you may need to protect only some of the pages on your site, or you may not have access to modify files on the Web server at all. If this is the case, you can use PHP to send header information back to the server and request authentication directly.

Figure 8.3
The user manager
in action

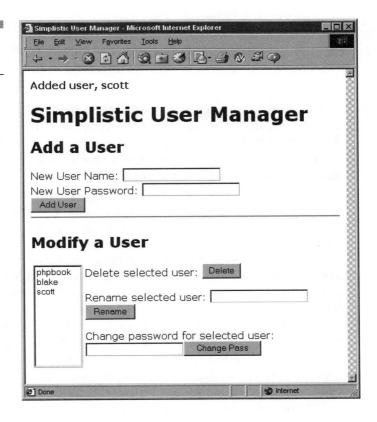

Figure 8.3
The user manager
in action

As is the case when sending any header information, you must either send all of the headers before any other data, or use output buffering. Listing 8 shows the very simplest script for requesting authentication in PHP. The script is an include file, auth_include.php, so it can be easily included in any page requiring authentication:

Listing 8: The auth_include.php script

```php
<?php
    $aDoAuth = True;
    if ( isset( $PHP_AUTH_USER ) )
    {
        if ( ( $PHP_AUTH_USER == "ryan" ) &&
            ( $PHP_AUTH_PW == "dentist" ) )
        {
            // valid user and password
            $aDoAuth = False;
        }
    }
    if( $aDoAuth == True )
    {
```

```
        Header( "WWW-Authenticate: Basic realm=\"My Realm\"" );
        Header( "HTTP/1.0 401 Unauthorized" );
        echo "You have not logged into this system.\n";
        exit;
    }
?>
```

This script first checks to see whether the **$PHP_AUTH_USER** variable is set. If so, it checks the values of **$PHP_AUTH_USER** and **$PHP_AUTH_PW** against the valid user and password for the application. If this check passes, the authentication header does not need to be sent. If the check fails, the script sends the HTTP 401 header to the browser, which causes the authentication dialog box to appear. The process is repeated until the user provides the correct credentials or chooses to cancel the operation. By simply including this file at the top of any other PHP script, authentication occurs.

A real authentication scheme would not embed all of the username/password combinations in the script itself. Rather, a database or a directory service (such as LDAP) or flat files would be used to store the authentication information.

One advantage to using this approach is that you can "unauthenticate" a user at any time by sending the HTTP 401 header again. You may want to do this to force users to log in again after a certain timeout period or to provide different authentication requirements for the different areas of your application.

PHP provides enough tools and flexibility for you to develop any type of authentication system you need. The preceding methods have relied on the browser's capability to handle the HTTP 401 response and the limitations thereof. The next method discusses a more platform-neutral and flexible approach to authentication.

Complete PHP-Based Authentication

Using the methods described in the preceding sections to implement authentication is straightforward and simple. Most Web developers have used an **htaccess** file to secure a directory before, so the concepts are usually well understood. This section focuses on an implementation that doesn't rely on the HTTP 401 response from the server to force the browser to request authentication. The main reason for using the following type of implementation is to provide more flexibility to your application.

The following implementation relies on the **Auth** class in PHPLIB. This implementation is extremely robust and flexible, and therefore requires a good deal of effort to start it. Once implemented, though, it is a fantastic replacement for the methods described in the preceding sections. It doesn't rely on the browser to provide an authentication dialog box, so any HTML form can be used to gather the specific information your application needs. Additionally, PHPLIB provides permissions-based authentication, so you can assign a permissions level to each user and each page.

The authentication scheme provided by PHPLIB is similar in many ways to its session management functions. It also requires a PHPLIB session to work. The PHPLIB authentication scheme is invoked by calling PHPLIB's **page_open()** function and requesting the **sess** feature. When this feature is requested, PHPLIB internally checks for an authenticated user. If authentication has not yet occurred, PHPLIB displays a user-defined page. This page gathers whatever information your application needs to properly complete the authentication. PHPLIB then calls a user-provided function to check the credentials of the user. If you accept the user, PHPLIB displays the page; otherwise, the authentication is attempted again. Figure 8.4 shows the interaction between the client, Web server (again a 1U server from Penguin Computing), and your PHP application.

Because of the flexibility available using PHPLIB, several steps are required to use its authentication class. First, Listing 9 shows the user-defined classes needed to implement the **Auth** class and its supporting classes. (The session and database classes in Listing 9 are the same as were used in Chapter 7.) In this case, the user is authenticated against a MySQL database table. The table used for authentication is defined as follows:

Figure 8.4
Interaction in a
PHPLIB
authentication
scheme

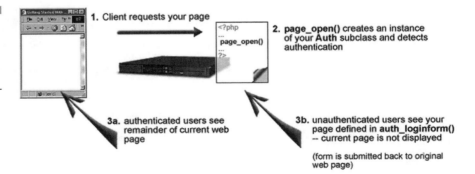

1. Client requests your page

2. **page_open()** creates an instance of your **Auth** subclass and detects authentication

3a. authenticated users see remainder of current web page

3b. unauthenticated users see your page defined in **auth_loginform()** -- current page is not displayed

(form is submitted back to original web page)

```
CREATE TABLE MyAuth (
    FirstName varchar(20) NOT NULL,
    SurName varchar(30) NOT NULL,
    Password varchar(20) NOT NULL,
    PRIMARY KEY (FirstName, SurName)
);
```

Listing 9: Setting up the classes for using the PHPLIB Auth class

```php
<?php
include( "page.inc" );
include( "ct_sql.inc" );
include( "session.inc" );
include( "db_mysql.inc" );
include( "auth.inc" );
class MySQLDB extends DB_Sql
{
    var $Host       = "db.server.com";
    var $Database   = "mydb";
    var $User       = "user";
    var $Password   = "pass";
}
class MySQLCt extends CT_Sql
{
    var $classname = "MySQLCt";
    var $database_table = "active_sessions";
    var $database_class = "MySQLDB";
}
class MySqlSession extends Session
{
    var $classname = "MySqlSession"; // Persistence support
    var $mode      = "cookie";
    var $lifetime  = 0;              // use session cookies
    var $that_class = "MySQLCt";     // which container to use
    var $allowcache_expire = 0;
}
class Sample_Auth extends Auth
{
    var $classname = "Sample_Auth";
    var $lifetime  = 20; // 20 minutes (0 == forever)
    function auth_loginform()
    {
        include( "./sample_lform.htinc" );
    }
    function auth_validatelogin()
    {
        global $FirstName, $SurName, $Password;
        $aDB  = new MySQLDB;
        $aSQL = "select * from MyAuth where ( FirstName = ";
        $aSQL .= "'$FirstName' ) and ( SurName = '$SurName' )";
        $aSQL .= "and ( Password = '$Password' )";
        $aDB->query( $aSQL );
        if ( $aDB->num_rows() > 0 )
        {
            return $FirstName;
        }
        else
```

```
                    {
                            return False;
                    }
            }
    }
?>
```

The **Sample_Auth** subclass extends the **Auth** base class to provide the specific functionality for this application. Specifically, the **auth_login-form()** and **auth_validatelogin()** functions are defined. The **auth_login-form()** function is called whenever the Auth class needs to authenticate a user. You could write PHP **print()** statements to provide the HTML for the login form, but including a file is typically easier. Listing 10 shows the file used in this example.

Listing 10: The sample login form (sample_lform.htinc)

```php
<?php
    global $FirstName;
    global $SurName;
    $aCurFirstName  = "";
    $aCurSurName    = "";
    if ( !empty( $FirstName ) )
    {
        $aCurFirstName = $FirstName;
    }
    if ( !empty( $SurName ) )
    {
        $aCurSurName = $SurName;
    }
?>
<html>
<head>
    <title>PHPLIB Auth Login Form</title>
</head>
<body>
<form action="<?=$this->url()?>" method="post">
<table>
    <tr>
        <td>
            First Name:
        </td>
        <td>
            <input type="text" name="FirstName"
value="<?=$aCurFirstName?>">
        </td>
    </tr>
    <tr>
        <td>
            Last Name:
        </td>
        <td>
            <input type="text" name="SurName"
value="<?=$aCurSurName?>">
        </td>
```

```
        </tr>
        <tr>
            <td>
                Password:
            </td>
            <td>
                <input type="password" name="Password">
            </td>
        </tr>
        <tr>
            <td colspan="2">
                <input type="submit" name="Submit" value="Log In">
            </td>
        </tr>
        <?php if ( !empty( $FirstName ) ) { ?>
            <tr>
                <td colspan="2">
                    <br><br>
                    The information you provided could not
                    be validated. Please try again.
                </td>
            </tr>
        <?php } ?>
    </table>
    </form>
    </body>
    </html>
```

This page is designed to be displayed only by the **Auth** class. It first checks to see whether the form variables are already set to some values. This could happen if the form were displayed and the credentials gathered from the user failed validation. In this case, the **Auth** class will present the login form again. The form variables are presented back to the user in the **FirstName** and **SurName** input boxes as a courtesy (so they don't have to be entered again).

Next, the page displays three input boxes to gather the user's first name, surname, and password. The form is set to post to the **$this->url**() location. In the context of the page, the **$this** variable refers to the current instance of your **Auth** subclass. The **url**() function returns the page that was originally requested by the user before the **Auth** class intervened and presented your login form. Finally, to provide feedback to the user, a warning is displayed on the form if the user previously provided authentication information that failed to validate.

When the form is posted back to the original page, **Auth** checks for authentication again. To do so, it calls your implementation of the **auth_validatelogin**() function. Listing 11 shows the implementation for this example.

Listing 11: The auth_validatelogin() function

```
function auth_validatelogin()
    {
        global $FirstName, $SurName, $Password;
        $aDB  = new MySQLDB;
        $aSQL = "select * from MyAuth where ( FirstName = ";
        $aSQL .= "'$FirstName' ) and ( SurName = '$SurName' )";
        $aSQL .= "and ( Password = '$Password' )";
        $aDB->query( $aSQL );
        if ( $aDB->num_rows() > 0 )
        {
            return $FirstName;
        }
        else
        {
            return False;
        }
    }
```

This function makes a reference to the global variables **$FirstName**, **$SurName**, and **$Password** that were defined in the login form. It then checks against a simple MySQL table that has three columns: **FirstName**, **SurName**, and **Password**. If a record in the table matches the values provided by the user, **auth_validatelogin()** returns the first name of the user. (Note that using the first name of a user as a unique user ID is probably a bad idea. This is just an example.) If there is no matching record, the return value is **False**.

Listing 12 shows how a typical Web page can use the **Auth** class for authentication. The example displays four links to other similar pages that require authentication. The last page in the list also performs a logout function that unauthenticates the current user.

Listing 12: A sample page using the Auth class

```php
<?php
    // No caching (from php.net site)
    include( "./auth_phplib.php" );
    page_open( array( "sess"    => "MySqlSession",
                      "auth"    => "Sample_Auth" ) );
    header ("Expires: Mon, 26 Jul 1997 05:00:00 GMT");
    header ("Last-Modified: " . gmdate("D, d M Y H:i:s") . " GMT");
    header ("Cache-Control: no-cache");
    header ("Pragma: no-cache");
?>
<html>
<head>
    <title>Sample Using PHPLIB Auth Class</title>
    <META HTTP-EQUIV="Expires" CONTENT="-1">
```

```
    <META HTTP-EQUIV="Pragma" CONTENT="no-cache">
</head>
<body>

<h2>Main Page</h2>
You are authenticated for this page!
<ul>
    <li><a href="test_auth_phplib.phtml">go to main page</a></li>
    <li><a href="test_auth_phplib2.phtml">go to second page</a></li>
    <li><a href="test_auth_phplib3.phtml">go to third page</a></li>
    <li><a href="test_auth_phplib_logout.phtml">log out</a></li>
</ul>

</body>
</html>
<?php
    page_close();
?>
```

The page first includes the sample authentication definition file, and then calls the PHPLIB **page_open()** function to request the session and authentication features. At the end of the page, the **page_close()** function is called to save the session information. PHPLIB relies on its session variables to retain authentication information between pages. The second and third pages are functionally identical to the first page. The "logout" page includes the following code at the bottom of the page to force a logout of the current user:

```
<?php
    $auth->logout();
    page_close();
?>
```

The **$auth->logout()** function may be called at any time, but it just forces reauthentication on the next page requested by the user.

Several lines in this example are not specifically related to the authentication mechanism. Specifically, the **header()** function calls and the **<META>** tags are to ensure that the browser doesn't cache the current page. This code is especially important because a cached page may confuse users as to whether they are logged in. Microsoft Internet Explorer is especially problematic in this area, so special care was taken to ensure this example worked. When these pages were tested, no problems occurred with IE 5.5, any version of Netscape, WebTV, or Opera.

As mentioned earlier, PHPLIB provides a great deal of flexibility when implementing its authentication scheme. You can create as complex or as simple a mechanism as your application requires. The advantages of this mechanism are the flexibility of creating your own authentication form, the ability to authenticate against any type of data store, and the option to unauthenticate a user easily in code. Also, providing an application-specific authentication scheme seems to be more effective, especially for novice users who may be confused by a generic popup dialog box.

Summary

This chapter discussed many of the facets of authenticating your users using PHP. The first few methods discussed are very platform-specific, but simple to implement. The last method, which requires the PHPLIB classes, is more complex to implement, but it is far more flexible and is entirely portable across Web servers and operating systems.

If your application requires some type of authentication, you should take time during your design phase to identify your specific authentication requirements. Some authentication mechanisms may not provide the level of flexibility that your application requires. Others may not provide the level of security required. Use this chapter to evaluate your needs against the available options.

Browser
Independence

Introduction

In standard application development, the user interface is custom-developed for the application, and is typically targeted to a single platform. The interface is not expected to change unexpectedly at runtime, based on which user is accessing the software. In Web development, however, the interface is not nearly so constant, because the interface may be rendered by different browsers on various platforms. Developing a browser-independent application requires the ability to detect the type of browser being used and its capabilities.

Although most modern browsers will display your application similarly, differences will always exist. If your application requires a particular browser feature, you will need to program your application to detect the browser being used, and respond accordingly. PHP provides multiple methods for browser detection, ranging from developing your own solution to using third-party tools. This chapter will provide examples of many of the methods so that you can determine which one your application requires.

Getting Started

At the most basic level, PHP provides access to the browser type through the **$HTTP_USER_AGENT** global variable. This user-agent string is sent from the browser on each request to the server. If you need to make just a simple determination of the browser type, you may be able to use the **$HTTP_USER_AGENT** variable directly. For example, using string comparison, you can detect a recent Internet Explorer browser as shown in Listing 1.

Listing 1: Displaying basic browser information

```
<html>
<head>
    <title>Quick Browser Check</title>
</head>
<body>
<?php
    $aPos = strpos( $HTTP_USER_AGENT, "MSIE" ) ;
    if ( $aPos === False ) // note 3 "=" to check value AND type
    {
        print( "<b>Not</b> MS Internet Explorer Browser!<br>" );
    }
    else
```

```
        {
                print( "MS Internet Explorer Browser!<br>" );
        }
?>
</body>
</html>
```

This example displays whether the client browser is an Internet Explorer browser. It relies on the user agent containing the **MSIE** substring, which is present in most user agent strings supplied by Internet Explorer. You may use the information in your application to display a message or to redirect your users to different sections of your Web site that are optimized for a particular browser. This method can work in some instances, but it is far too simplistic to handle the vast number of valid user agent strings. Several of the browsers have changed the format of their user agent strings over time, so detecting a particular browser type can be very problematic if you need accurate information about the browser. For example, some versions of Internet Explorer include the following user agent strings:

- Microsoft Internet Explorer/4.40.305beta (Windows 95)[en]

- Mozilla/2.0 (compatible; MSIE 3.02; Update a; AOL 3.0; Windows 95)[en]

- Mozilla/4.0 (compatible; MSIE 5.0; Windows NT 5.0)[en]

The variants of the user agent cause string-based checking to become unwieldy. So many combinations of browsers, versions, platforms, and languages exist that ensuring the accurate detection of even a single browser type becomes problematic.

In reality, just knowing the type of the browser typically isn't significant. Rather, you need to know whether the browser supports a specific capability such as JavaScript or frames. This kind of information isn't embedded in the user agent string. The next section discusses a PHP-based solution to this problem.

PHP Internal Functions

Knowing the capabilities of a browser is typically the goal of implementing any type of browser detection. However, with the huge number of combinations of browsers and platforms, it is difficult to implement a generic solution to the problem. Fortunately, PHP provides some methods for making a more accurate browser determination with the **get_browser()** function.

Additional Browscap Information

At the time of this writing, some additional tweaks had to be per-formed to get the **get_browser()** functionality working with PHP. I found that the browscap.ini file available from cyScape (listed previously) needed some edits to be used with PHP 4.0 patch level 2. First, a blank line needed to be added to the end of the file. Without the extra carriage-return, a parse error was generated when PHP started up.

The second and more complex problem was related to the structure of the file itself. Basically, browscap.ini is a standard initialization file with each section representing a specific user agent. Each section refers to a parent section, so a hierarchy is defined in the file. That way, a new browser defines new capabilities, and its parent record defines previous capabilities. The problem is that PHP internally converts all of the attributes to lower case when initially reading the file. This conversion causes PHP to be unable to find the parent sections because they are not defined in all lowercase. To solve the problem, I ran the browscap.ini file through the following simple PHP script to convert all the lines to lowercase:

```php
<?php
    $aArray = file( "./browscap.ini" );
    $aNewFile = fopen( "./browscap.new", "w" );
    foreach( $aArray as $aLine )
    {
        $aNewLine = strtolower( $aLine );
        fputs( $aNewFile, $aNewLine );
    }
    fclose( $aNewFile );
?>
```

The side effect of this change is that all calls to the **get_browser()** function need to include a call to **strtolower()**. However, once the changes were made, the **get_browser()** function behaved as expected.

To use the **get_browser()** function, you must download a copy of the browscap.ini file, which is available from a number of Web sites. At the time of this writing, the file is available from http://www.cyscape.com/browscap/ and can be downloaded for free. After downloading the file and installing it on your Web server, you will have to update the php.ini file. Edit the file so that the configuration entry for the **browscap** configuration item is set to the full path of your browscap.ini file. After restarting the Web server, you will be able to access the information contained in the file. At the time of this writing, the browscap file contained entries for over 2,100 user agent strings.

Using the **get_browser()** function in conjunction with the browscap.ini file simplifies the process of determining browser capabilities and expands its scope. Listing 2 shows an example of using the **get_browser()** function. As explained in the note, "Additional Browscap Information," the first step is to convert the **$HTTP_USER_AGENT** to lowercase. Then, using a technique from the documentation at http://www.php.net/, the user agent is massaged again to properly format it for the call to **get_browser()**. The **eregi_replace()** function is used to replace the language specification (for example, **[en]**) to a wildcard, as is found in the browscap.ini file.

Listing 2: Using get_browser()

```php
<?php
    function GetMassagedUA()
    {
        global $HTTP_USER_AGENT;
        $aUserAgent = strtolower( $HTTP_USER_AGENT );
        $aUserAgent = eregi_replace( "\[[a-z]{2,}\]", "*",
$aUserAgent );
        if ( strpos( $aUserAgent, '*' ) === False )
        {
            $aUserAgent .= '*';
        }
        return $aUserAgent;
    }
?>
<html>
<head>
    <title>Browser Capabilities</title>
</head>
<body>
<h1>Browser Capabilities</h1>
<?php
    $aUserAgent = GetMassagedUA();
    print( "<h2>$aUserAgent</h2>" );
    $array = (array) get_browser( $aUserAgent );
    if ( count( $array ) > 1 )
    {
        while ( list( $key, $value ) = each ($array) )
        {
            $aValue = stripslashes( $value );
            echo ("<b>$key=</b> $aValue<br>");
        }
    }
    else
    {
        print( "<i>no information for user agent</i><br>" );
```

```
    }
?>
</body>
</html>
```

Figure 9.1 shows the results of viewing this page in Netscape 2.02; Figure 9.2 shows the results in Netscape 4.7.

The listing of available capabilities shows the power of the **get_browser()** function. In the code in Listing 2, all of the capabilities are displayed by casting the returned object to an array and cycling through the returned array key/value pairs. Alternately, each value can be queried directly from the object using the syntax **$object->capability**. Listing 3 is an example of checking for frames support.

Listing 3: Using get_browser() to check for frames support

```php
<?php
    function GetMassagedUA()
    {
```

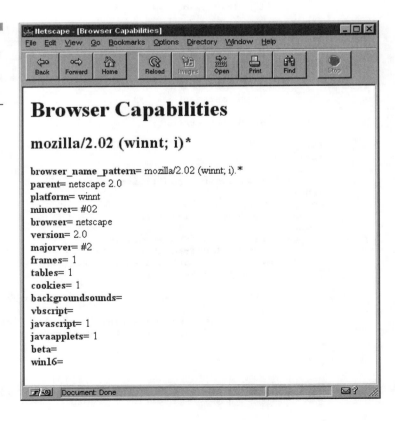

Figure 9.1
Results of Listing 1 when accessed by Netscape 2.02 browser

Figure 9.2
Results of Listing 1
when accessed by
Netscape 4.7
browser

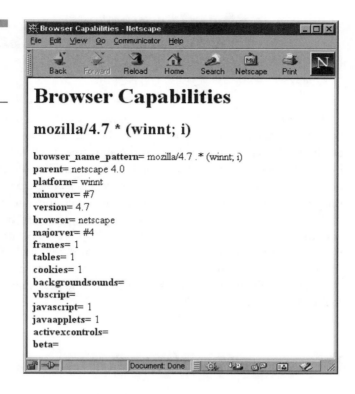

```
            global $HTTP_USER_AGENT;
            $aUserAgent = strtolower( $HTTP_USER_AGENT );
            $aUserAgent = eregi_replace( "\[[a-z]{2,}\]", "*",
    $aUserAgent );
            if ( strpos( $aUserAgent, '*' ) === False )
            {
                $aUserAgent .= '*';
            }
            return $aUserAgent;
        }
    ?>
    <html>
    <head>
        <title>Frame Support?</title>
    </head>
    <body>
    <?php
        $aUserAgent = GetMassagedUA();
        print( "<h2>$aUserAgent</h2>" );
        $aBrowsCap = get_browser( $aUserAgent );
        if ( $aBrowsCap->frames == 1 )
        {
            print( "This browser supports frames<br>" );
        }
```

```
    else
    {
        print( "This browser doesn't support frames<br>" );
    }
?>
</body>
</html>
```

The **get_browser()** function provides a great deal of information, and it is a good start if your application needs to determine browser capabilities on the fly. However, it does have some significant limitations. As mentioned in the discussion earlier, using the browscap.ini files available on the Internet has its quirks. Also, the functionality relies on the browscap.ini file to be updated frequently to deal with the constant changes in available browsers and capabilities. At the time of this writing, the **get_browser()** function was unable to correctly detect Internet Explorer 5.5 and Opera 4.02. This problem is due to the fact that updating and redistributing the browscap file takes time. If your application must be able to accurately detect the capabilities of the current browser, the next section describes a third-party tool that fits the bill.

BrowserHawk

The BrowserHawk® component available from cyScape is an incredible tool for detecting browser capabilities. It is available as a COM object if you happen to be using a Windows-based server, and as a Java bean if you are not. Java support is available with PHP 4, but it is not the default. In order to use a Java bean or other Java code on the server, PHP must be built with the **--with-java** configuration option. It is also necessary to have a Java Virtual Machine (JVM) available on the Web server. Many distributions of Linux provide a JVM, and in many instances, the JVM is installed by default.

Additionally, the BrowserHawk component requires some other third-party Java beans. One required bean is the Simple API for XML (SAX) bean, which is available at http://www.megginson.com/SAX/. The required servlet beans are available in many places, including the more recent JVMs available from major vendors. Specifically, your server will need access to the **javax.servlet.http.HttpServlet** Java class.

Once you have downloaded and installed the required Java classes, you can configure PHP to begin using BrowserHawk. As with any Java class, you must specify the exact location of the Java implementation file using the **java.class.path** in the php.ini file. The following is an example:

```
java.class.path=/usr/share/kaffe/Klasses.jar:/home/blake
/php4.0.1pl2/ext/java/php_java.jar:/home/blake/bhawk/lib/bhawk4j.jar
:/home
/blake/java/sax2.jar:/home/blake/java/servlet.jar:/home/blake/bhawk:
```

As this example shows, the required BrowserHawk classes are available to PHP in the .../bhawk4j.jar, .../sax2.jar, and .../servlet.jar paths. The path also includes a path with no file (/home/blake/bhawk) that specifies the location of the BrowserHawk license and data files. This path should be the location where BrowserHawk was installed.

After all the configuration items are set and PHP has been rebuilt with Java support, check the configuration using the **phpinfo()** function. Calling the **phpinfo()** function from a PHP script causes a great deal of HTML-formatted information to be displayed. Figure 9.3 shows a section of this information indicating that Java is available.

After you configure BrowserHawk and Java in PHP, using the Browser-Hawk components is straightforward. The code in Listing 4 shows how to create a BrowserHawk object and use it to gather some basic browser information.

Listing 4: Getting started with BrowserHawk

```
<html>
<head>
    <title>Getting Started with BrowserHawk</title>
</head>
<body>
    <h1>Getting Started with BrowserHawk</h1>
<?php
    print( "<h2>$HTTP_USER_AGENT</h2>" );
    $aBrowserHawk = new Java( "com.cyscape.browserhawk.BrowserHawk"
);
    $aBrowserInfo = $aBrowserHawk->getBrowserInfo(
```

Figure 9.3
The phpinfo()
function showing
Java availability

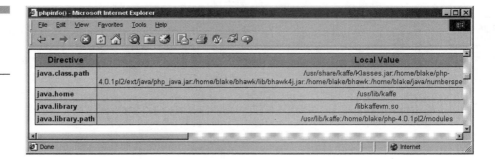

```
            "$HTTP_USER_AGENT" );
                // does this browser support ActiveX?
                if ( $aBrowserInfo->getActiveXControls() == True )
                {
                    print( "This browser supports ActiveX controls<br>" );
                }
                else
                {
                    print( "This browser doesn't support ActiveX controls<br>"
);
                }
            ?>
            </body>
            </html>
```

Listing 4 checks for ActiveX control support, but it could check for any of the BrowserHawk properties just as easily. Table 9.1 lists the methods that BrowserHawk provides to gather information about the browser capabilities.

Table 9.1

BrowserHawk methods

Type	Method	Purpose
Boolean	getActiveXControls()	Returns whether the browser supports ActiveX controls.
Boolean	getAOL()	Returns whether the visitor is accessing your site through an America Online (AOL)-branded browser (on the AOL network).
double	getAOLVersion()	Returns the AOL version number being used.
int	getAuthenticodeUpdate()	Returns the version of Authenticode that the browser supports.
Boolean	getBackgroundSounds()	Returns whether the browser supports playing background sounds.
Boolean	getBeta()	Returns whether the browser is a beta version.
java.lang.String	getBrowser()	Returns the common name associated with the browser, such as Netscape and IE (Internet Explorer).
Boolean	getCDF()	Returns whether the browser supports Channel Definition Format (CDF) for subscribing to Web content with optional auto-updates.
Boolean	getCompressGZip()	Returns whether the browser accepts compressed content in GZip format.

continues

Table 9.1 cont.	Type	Method	Purpose
BrowserHawk methods	Boolean	getCookies()	Returns whether the browser supports the capability to accept cookies.
	Boolean	getCrawler()	Returns whether the browser is a crawler, spider, or other agent used to index a site for searchable content.
	Boolean	getDHTML()	Returns whether the browser supports DHTML script.
	java.lang.String	getFileUpload()	Returns whether the browser supports the capability to have a user upload a file to your server from the browser (whether the browser supports RFC 1867).
	Boolean	getFontColor()	Returns whether the browser supports the display of colored text.
	Boolean	getFontSize()	Returns whether the browser supports the capability to display varying font sizes.
	Boolean	getFrames()	Returns whether the browser supports frames.
	java.lang.String	getFullversion()	Returns the entire version of the browser, including all major and minor numbers and letters, if any.
	Boolean	getGold()	Returns whether the browser is a Gold version of the Netscape browsers.
	Boolean	getHDML()	Returns true if the client device supports HDML (WAP's predecessor).
	java.lang.String	getIPAddr()	Returns the Internet Protocol (IP) address of the visitor.
	Boolean	getJavaApplets()	Returns whether the browser supports Java applets.
	Boolean	getJavaScript()	Returns whether the browser supports JavaScript.
	double	getJavaScriptVer()	Returns the version of JavaScript that the browser supports.
	java.lang.String	getLanguage()	Returns the most likely preference for the visitor's spoken language.
	int	getMajorver()	Returns the major version of the browser.

continues

	Type	Method	Purpose
Table 9.1 cont. BrowserHawk methods	double	getMinorver()	Returns the minor version of the browser.
	java.lang.String	getMinorverlet()	Returns the minor version letter of the browser, if any.
	Boolean	getMouseOver()	Returns whether the browser supports the capability to use JavaScript mouse-over effects.
	Boolean	getMSN()	Returns whether the user is on the Microsoft network (MSN).
	java.lang.String	getOSDetails()	Returns details on the operating system (OS) the visitor is using.
	Boolean	getPDA()	Returns true if the browser is a Personal Digital Assistant (PDA) device such as a Palm Pilot.
	java.lang.String	getPlatform()	Returns more general information (as compared to getOSDetails()) about the user's platform.
	Boolean	getPNG()	Returns whether the browser supports the Portable Network Graphic (PNG) image file format.
	Boolean	getProxy()	Returns whether the user is connecting through a proxy server.
	Boolean	getSSL()	Returns whether the browser supports the Secure Sockets Layer (SSL) protocol.
	Boolean	getSSLActive()	Returns whether the user is connected through an active SSL connection.
	java.lang.String	getSSLCipherSuite()	Returns the SSL cipher suite used for this SSL session; available only if the user is connected through an active SSL connection.
	int	getSSLKeySize()	Returns the SSL key size that the browser supports; available only if the user is connected through an active SSL connection.
	Boolean	getStyleSheets()	Returns whether the browser supports cascading style sheets (CSS).
	Boolean	getTableBGColor()	Returns whether the browser supports the capability to control the color of individual HTML table cells.

continues

Table 9.1 cont.	Type	Method	Purpose
BrowserHawk methods	Boolean	getTableBGImage()	Returns whether the browser supports the capability to display an image in the background of individual HTML table cells.
	Boolean	getTables()	Returns whether the browser supports the capability to display HTML tables.
	Boolean	getVBScript()	Returns whether the browser supports VBScript.
	double	getVersion()	Returns the version of the browser.
	int	getVersionpos()	Returns which position the browser's version number is in for a given user agent.
	Boolean	getWAP()	Returns true for devices that support WML and WAP (Wireless Application Protocol), such as wireless phones.
	java.lang.String	getWAPDeviceModel()	Contains the model of the WAP device if known.
	java.lang.String	getWAPGateway()	Shows details of the UP.Link gateway if it is being used.
	int	getWAPMaxDeckSize()	Contains the approximate maximum number of bytes that the wireless device will support in a deck.
	java.lang.String	getWAPSubscriberID()	Automatically set to the unique subscriber ID of the WAP visitor when available.
	Boolean	getWin16()	Returns whether the browser is running on a 16-bit Windows operating system, such as Windows 3.1.
	Boolean	getXML()	Returns whether the browser supports direct XML display.

The one disadvantage of using the BrowserHawk Java bean is that it is targeted toward JSP developers, so some of its methods are not directly accessible through PHP. Some of the advanced reporting functions cannot be used because they rely on JSP-specific objects. Nevertheless, the standard browser information object reports enough information for most needs and is constantly up-to-date with the latest browsers.

The advantages of using the BrowserHawk component over the other methods discussed in this chapter are its accuracy and flexibility. Browser-Hawk updates its database automatically as needed. From the documentation, BrowserHawk initially recognizes as many as nine times more user agents than the browscap method. BrowserHawk is also designed to test more browser capabilities than other methods typically do.

If your application relies on providing browser-specific information or requires very specific browser features to run, BrowserHawk will provide the best detection solution. Your application will continue to work correctly irrespective of the constant changes in browser technology.

Using Browser Information

Determining the capabilities of the browser is the first step in building a browser-independent application. The more important step is deciding how to use the information. As with all other design decisions, this decision will be specific to the needs of your application. Some browser capabilities and application features, such as animated demos and cascading style sheets support, will be noncritical. Other features may completely impede your application, such as the browser's capability to use SSL encryption or upload files.

Your application design should account for the required browser features and provide a graceful failure if the features aren't available. Listing 5 shows an example of how to provide a graceful failure. Additionally, you may want to conditionally provide some content based on the browser's capability to display it. Listing 6 shows an example of how you might provide such content.

Listing 5: Graceful failure of an application with a browser that doesn't support file uploading

```php
<?php
    $aBrowserHawk = new Java( "com.cyscape.browserhawk.BrowserHawk"
);
    $aBrowserInfo = $aBrowserHawk->getBrowserInfo(
"$HTTP_USER_AGENT" );
?>
<html>
<head>
    <title>Upload File</title>
</head>
<body>
<h1>Upload a file</h1>
```

```
<form action="someurl.phtml" method="post" enctype="multipart/form-
data">
<?php
    if ( $aBrowserInfo->getFileUpload() == True ) {
?>
    <input type="file" name="File"><br><br>
    <input type="submit" name="Submit" value="Submit">
<?php
    } else {
?>
    Your browser doesn't support file uploading.<br><br>
    Please e-mail the file to files@my.domain.com.
<?php
    }
?>
</form>
</body>
</html>
```

This example displays a file upload form if the browser provides the upload facility. If the browser does not support this facility, a message is displayed asking the user to e-mail the file. In a real-world application, failing gracefully is critical to provide a positive experience to the end-user. When choosing a fail-over mechanism, be considerate of the user and his ability to understand the meaning of the failure. Most people don't need to see a message such as "Your browser doesn't support RFC 1867." If your application can continue without the feature, don't display a message at all. Simply provide the highest level of functionality available.

Listing 6: Conditional content based on browser capabilities

```
<?php
    $aBrowserHawk = new Java( "com.cyscape.browserhawk.BrowserHawk"
);
    $aBrowserInfo = $aBrowserHawk->getBrowserInfo(
"$HTTP_USER_AGENT" );
    if ( $aBrowserInfo->getPNG() == True )
    {
        $aImage = "Logo.png";
    }
    else
    {
        $aImage = "Logo.gif";
    }
?>
<html>
<head>
    <title>Our Logo</title>
</head>
<body>
<h1>Our Logo</h1>
<img src="<?=$aImage?>" width="180" height="70" alt="" border="0">
</body>
</html>
```

This example displays a graphic in PNG format if the browser can display this format; otherwise, a GIF version of the graphic is sent. This example is simplistic, but it illustrates some basic options. Rather than using variables to provide optional content, your application could use browser capabilities information to display an entirely different section of the site. For example, you may want to build a site optimized for viewing on TV-based browsers. These systems have a restricted viewing size and generally fewer font options. Therefore, special design considerations are needed to enhance the viewing experience for these browsers. The following code is a basic example of how this might be implemented. The listing is assumed to be the site's index page.

```php
<?php
    $aBrowserHawk = new Java( "com.cyscape.browserhawk.BrowserHawk"
);
    $aBrowserInfo = $aBrowserHawk->getBrowserInfo(
"$HTTP_USER_AGENT" );
    if ( $aBrowserInfo->getBrowser() == "WebTV" )
    {
        // WebTV browser, redirect to WebTV optimized pages
        header( "Location: http://mysite.com/webtv/\n" );
    }
    else
    {
        // Not WebTV browser, redirect to standard pages
        header( "Location: http://mysite.com/main/\n" );
    }
?>
```

In the preceding example, visitors using a TV-based browser are redirected to specifically optimized pages. Other users go to a standard set of pages developed for other types of browsers. The example could be extended to detect PDA-based browsers or other specific types of browsers.

One disadvantage of using this mechanism is that if a person were to send a link to a friend using a different browser, the friend would see the page intended for a browser other than her own. Additionally, this mechanism requires that each page have multiple separate files based on the target browsers. Managing this type of design is unwieldy for large sites. A better solution for creating browser-specific pages is to identify the key differentiating elements and place them in separate files per browser. Then basic content can be merged with browser-specific pages when requested. This type of mechanism can be implemented using a template system such as the one discussed in Chapter 12 and Chapter 14. Examples of this scenario will be given in those chapters.

 ## Summary

Detecting the capabilities of the browser can be profoundly important to many Web-based applications. When designing your application, consider the limitations of the various browsers before committing to specific features. Then, based on design requirements, use the browser detection tools to enhance your users' experience. Avoid situations where the browser is allowed to present cryptic error messages because a particular feature is unavailable. Constantly work toward providing a consistent experience irrespective of the client browser being used.

Debugging

Introduction

Debugging Web applications is as critical as debugging any other type of application. The problem is that it can be difficult to perform debugging remotely, especially if you do not have sufficient access to the Web server. This chapter provides some hints and tools that you can use to increase your productivity while debugging applications. Additionally, some of this chapter serves as a software-engineering reminder, because debugging can be avoided to a great extent when projects are engineered well.

Because of the recent excitement surrounding Web application development, many new tools (PHP included) for creating Web applications have become available. These tools have sprouted from existing tools in some cases, such as ASP and JSP, and others have been developed for the sole purpose of developing interactive Web applications. Surprisingly, software engineering practices following these tools are few in number. Perhaps this lack of engineering practices is a result of the need to be first to market with an application or the fact that more experienced software developers weren't the early adopters of these technologies. Whatever the reason, all the software engineering knowledge needs to be applied to this new development environment. The first section of this chapter serves as a refresher on the topic of software engineering. It is included in this chapter because excessive debugging time is precipitated by a failure to properly plan a project.

Software Engineering and Debugging

Chapter 3, "Forms and Cookies," made the point that you can avoid unnecessary form validation tasks by providing better input mechanisms. In the same respect, developing better (more defensive) code up front prevents a great deal of debugging later.

Web development projects must be created with the same amount of careful preparation as any other application. Creating great applications requires proper design, adherence to defined development standards, software reviews, unit testing, and debugging. Debugging is necessarily last in the list because it implies that code has passed through all the other required steps. The following sections review each of these steps with the assumption that you have some background in software engineering.

Application Design

Identifying the prerequisites of an application before developing any code is critical in any project. In large projects, this planning can take weeks or months; in a small project, the planning can be scratched onto a sticky note in a few minutes. In either case, the key is to think through the requirements of the application and consider as many possible combinations of solutions before writing code. Data from TRW and IBM shows that making changes to an application early in the development process (before coding has started) is 10 to 200 times cheaper than making the same changes late in the process (McConnell, 1993).

Depending on the project, identifying the functional requirements may involve a great deal of work. Dividing the application into functional modules first can simplify this process. In a Web application, such modules can include database interaction, user authorization, state management, and so forth. Once the functional modules have been identified, each module can be subdivided as necessary, and requirements for each module can be written. In small applications, a good strategy may be to divide the functional modules into individual code files or OO classes.

In addition to identifying the functional requirements of the application, you must consider architecture issues. These issues include which server platform to use, which *database management system* (DBMS) to use, and other less obvious items, such as how to organize the code files, how to deal with changes, and whether to buy or build some components. Although PHP can run on a multitude of hardware/Web server combinations, each comes with its own personality. Take time to identify the reason for making a hardware/server decision. The amount of the initial monetary investment is rarely a good reason for choosing a platform. Choosing a DBMS is equally as important if your application is highly dynamic. Additionally, you need to decide whether the Web server and database server will run on the same hardware. Depending on the size and nature of your application, this issue is critical.

Next, take time to design the organization of code. Use a file- or directory-naming convention so that code identification is simplified. Build an alternate plan in any case where the probability of change is great. If you anticipate changes in advance, you can build the application to localize the changes to a few code modules and buffer the rest. This type of design is especially important if you are using any third-party tools or beta-level software in your development environment. Creating functional wrappers for such code is easy to implement and will result in a more manageable application in the long term.

Lastly, take time to decide which modules of your application will be developed using off-the-shelf tools from third-party vendors. The buy-versus-build decision is complex. Depending on the development schedule, you may not have time to adequately test a third-party tool. On the other hand, you may not have time to build it either. To buffer the effect of these decisions, use an in-house set of wrapper functions to hide the implementation.

Proper application design requires time. In a well-developed environment, 20 to 30 percent of the total development time is spent in design activities (McConnell, 1993). Note that this period of time is strictly for high-level design. Other detailed design time is also required.

Defining Development Standards

Defining standards for development increases the ease of long-term maintenance on projects of any size. Even small applications developed by a single programmer can benefit from a well-established set of development standards. A development standard includes such items as naming, commenting, and layout conventions. Some of these items, such as layout conventions, are less critical because modern editors can reformat code, but others, such as file and directory naming conventions, can have a great effect on maintenance.

Software Reviews

Software reviews provide an opportunity to accomplish several goals at one time. For example, code reviews provide the opportunity to validate the adherence to development standards. Reviews also enable the chance for less experienced developers to benefit from the knowledge of more experienced colleagues. Reviews are also the most effective mechanism for improving software quality. Case studies of software reviews in real-world applications have revealed that proper reviews have a defect-detection rate between 55 and 60 percent. This rate contrasts to only 25 percent for unit testing, 35 percent for function testing, and 45 percent for integration testing. Additionally, when used in large projects, reviews increase overall productivity. In some cases, reviews resulted in an 80 to 90 percent reduction in defects with a 10 to 25 percent increase in productivity (McConnell, 1993). Reviews should be conducted both during design and during construction. Design reviews provide an opportunity to identify flaws when they are the cheapest to correct.

You can use any one of several methods to complete a review. Some of the options are formal code inspections, walk-through reviews, and code readings. In a formal code inspection, several members of a team meet together to identify errors. A moderator keeps the meeting moving and ensures that the only topic is error identification. A formal code inspection should not include the discussion of solutions. In a walk-through review, a group of developers informally discusses the code in question. When errors are identified, solutions may be suggested, but the main purpose of the walk-through should still be error identification. Code readings focus more on the code and less on meetings. Typically, a section of code is distributed to two or more readers who work independently to identify errors. The results of the code reading are then returned to the original developer.

Based on the size of your organization and project, using one review method may have advantages over another. For example, if you work alone or on a small team, you may find it beneficial to hire a contractor to perform reviews via code readings. No matter which method you choose, performing software reviews is the most effective way to identify problems in a design or implementation.

Testing

Typically, testing is not overlooked, but occasionally testing is done in a haphazard way. As in any project, testing a Web application should involve testing at several levels, including function testing, module testing, and integration testing. Each unit of testing should be planned and deliberate. When a test plan is developed before the work begins, a set of expectations and requirements is related to the tests.

In small projects, testing may involve simply jotting down a few sample scenarios related to using the application and then checking each case. Larger projects may include people who are dedicated to testing, but each developer should be responsible for providing enough information to the testers so that they can be effective. Each code developer should also be responsible for unit testing on a function or page level.

Debugging

Debugging is one of the last steps in the application development process because at the point that debugging occurs, all of the design, development, and some testing should be complete. Debugging may occur during any phase of testing as part of the process. Any changes made to code during the debugging process should be retested through all testing levels because the changes could introduce new errors.

Debugging should be a thorough process aimed at identifying the root of problems. It should never be simply a patching process that temporarily fixes errant cases but provides no lasting solution. Everyone involved in debugging should understand the root of the problem when the bug is declared fixed. Understanding the root problem leads to developing complete solutions instead of simply working around the bug. Depending on the nature of the bug, some temporary fixes may be appropriate, and they should be documented. Resolving their underlying problems should be considered a priority.

This book can't possibly cover everything about proper software engineering practices. The essential points to remember are that software engineering is as critical in Web projects as in any other application and that proper software engineering reduces the amount of debugging that is required. The next sections cover some of the tools and techniques specific to debugging PHP applications.

Defensive Coding

Even before you begin debugging your code, you can take steps to write code that is less likely to contain errors. This kind of code is known as *defensive code.* Writing defensive code includes properly commenting routines and internally checking the state of the routines during development. Commenting is a personal issue with developers, but it should be guided by standards. At a minimum, developers should comment about the purpose of a routine, class, or include file and always comment on obscure sections of code.

As for checking the state of a routine, PHP provides the **assert()** function, just as many high-level languages do. The **assert()** function checks the assertion parameter and takes some action if its value is false. In PHP, the **assert()** function accepts either a string or Boolean parameter. If the parameter is a string, it is evaluated as PHP code. The assert options (**assert.active**, **assert.warning**, **assert.bail**, **assert.callback**, and **assert.quiet_eval**) in the php.ini file or the options specified when you use the **assert_options()** function define the action that the **assert()** function takes. Table 10.1 explains the various assert options.

The **assert()** function is intended to be used only during the development process and should not be used for normal run-time operations. Your

Debugging

Table 10.1

Assert Options and
Their Descriptions

Option	Default	Description
assert_active	1	Enables assert() evaluation
assert_warning	1	Issues a PHP warning for each failed assertion
assert_bail	0	Terminates execution on failed assertions
assert_quiet_eval	0	Disables error reporting during assertion expression evaluation
assert_callback	(null)	Is a user function to call on failed assertions

application should be written to function identically with and without the **assert()** function calls. Listing 1 shows an example of the **assert()** function validating input parameters.

Listing 1: Using the assert() Function to Validate Input Parameters

```php
<?php
    function ArrayAverage( $aArray )
    {
        $aTotal = 0;
        // single quote eval string so PHP doesn't expand the
variables
        assert( 'is_array( $aArray )' );
        foreach( $aArray as $aElement )
        {
            assert( 'is_numeric( $aElement )' );
            $aTotal += $aElement;
        }
        return ( $aTotal / count( $aArray ) );
    }
?>
```

The **ArrayAverage()** function in Listing 1 expects an array of numeric values (whether numbers or numeric strings) as its parameter and returns the average of the values in the array. The **assert()** statement is used to validate that the parameter passed is an array and later to validate that each array element is numeric. Note that the **assert()** function can take a string that is evaluated as PHP code, so if you use variables within the string, you should ensure that PHP doesn't expand the variables too soon. To avoid this problem, use single-quoted strings. A test script for the function in Listing 1 is in Listing 2.

Listing 2: Using the ArrayAverage() Function

```php
<?php
    include( "./arrayfunc.php" );
?>
<html>
<head>
    <title>Testing Assertions</title>
</head>
<body>
    <?php
        $aResult = ArrayAverage( array( 1, 2, 3, 4, 5 ) );
        print( "ArrayAverage( array( 1, 2, 3, 4, 5 ) ) =
$aResult<br>" );
        $aResult = ArrayAverage( array( 10.1, "5.5", 3, "4", 5 ) );
        print( "ArrayAverage( array( 10.1, \"5.5\", 3, \"4\", 5 ) )
= $aResult<br>" );
        $aResult = ArrayAverage( array( 1, 2, "cat", 4, 5 ) );
        print( "ArrayAverage( array( 1, 2, \"cat\", 4, 5 ) ) =
$aResult<br>" );
        $aResult = ArrayAverage( 1, 2 );
        print( "ArrayAverage( 1, 2 ) = $aResult<br>" );
    ?>
</body>
</html>
```

The test script calls the **ArrayAverage()** function four times. For the first two times, it passes valid parameters, while the last two times, it passes bad values. Figure 10.1 shows the output of the script. Note that

Figure 10.1
Testing the
ArrayAverage()
function

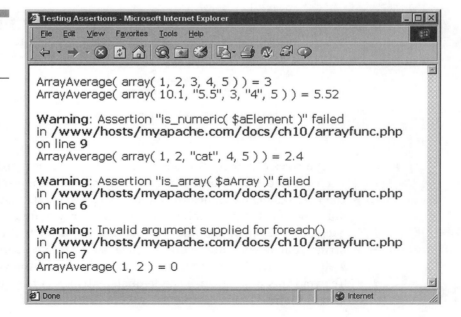

because PHP inherently coerces variable types, it enables the call to **ArrayAverage(array(1, 2, "cat", 4, 5))** to succeed without any complaints (other than the assertion warning).

The action taken by the **assert()** function varies according to the assert settings. The previous examples use the default assert settings. The nice thing about using the **assert()** function in an application is that it has no effect on the application when **assert.active** is set to false. To establish this setting in code, you can either call **assert_options (ASSERT_ACTIVE, false)** or set the configuration directive accordingly. By using the configuration directive, you can deploy an application in one environment so that all assertions are evaluated and in another environment where they are ignored.

PHP provides another defensive-coding function: **error_reporting()**. This function takes an integer argument that specifies the reporting level. The argument is a bitmask so that you can specify a specific set of errors. PHP specifies a set of named constants to use with this function, as shown in the following minitable:

Value	Internal name
1	E_ERROR
2	E_WARNING
4	E_PARSE
8	E_NOTICE
16	E_CORE_ERROR
32	E_CORE_WARNING
64	E_COMPILE_ERROR
128	E_COMPILE_WARNING
256	E_USER_ERROR
512	E_USER_WARNING
1024	E_USER_NOTICE

Additionally, the named constant **E_ALL** sets error reporting to include all error information. While building applications, you should set the error-reporting level to **E_ALL** so that you are aware of all the warnings and errors in your code. This setting is also important when you include third-party code in your application because it helps you identify potential errors in the third-party source code. Listing 3 is an example of code that generates a warning when the **error_reporting()** function is set to the maximum level but that generates no warnings in its default state.

Listing 3: An error_reporting() Example

```html
<html>
<head>
    <title>Error Reporting Levels</title>
</head>
<body>
<?php
    $aArray = array( "state" => "Idaho", "county" => "Madison",
                     "city" => "Rexburg", "country" => "US" );
    // default error reporting
    print( "aArray[state] = " . $aArray[state] . "<br>" );
    error_reporting( E_ALL );
    print( "aArray[state] = " . $aArray[state] . "<br>" );
?>
</body>
</html>
```

Figure 10.2 shows the results of this example. As you can see, setting a more stringent error-reporting level can uncover coding flaws that might create adverse effects as the application is developed. In this case, the problem may seem innocuous, but consider what would happen if a new named constant, **state,** which represents the run-time state of the application, were introduced. Listing 4 shows the script with this new constant. The results of running the script are in Figure 10.3.

Listing 4: Second error_reporting() Example with Named Constant

```php
<?php
    // the run-time state of the application
    define( state, 3 );
    // additional code uses the state constant
?>
<html>
<head>
    <title>Error Reporting Levels</title>
</head>
<body>
<?php
    $aArray = array( "state" => "Idaho", "county" => "Madison",
                     "city" => "Rexburg", "country" => "US" );
    // default error reporting
    print( "aArray[state] = " . $aArray[state] . "<br>" );
    error_reporting( E_ALL );
    print( "aArray[state] = " . $aArray[state] . "<br>" );
?>
</body>
</html>
```

In both of the previous samples, when the error-reporting level is set at its default level, no warning is generated, and the code executes seemingly

Figure 10.2
The results of the
error_reporting()
script

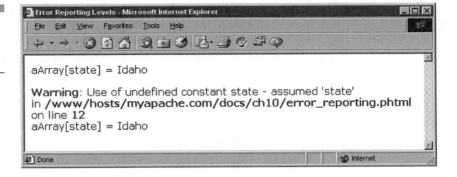

Figure 10.3
The results of the
second
error_reporting()
script

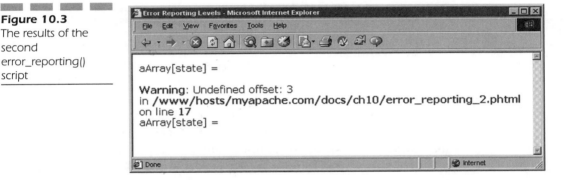

perfectly. However, after the named constant is introduced in the second case, the previously working code is broken. This problem would be even more difficult to find if the named constant were introduced in a shared include file. This example serves to illustrate the value of using PHP's error-reporting mechanism to its fullest. Any warnings in code should be fixed so that future errors are avoided.

Depending on your environment, you may set error reporting to its highest level during development and to its lowest level in production. This setting would prevent errors and warnings from appearing in the browser. However, I personally recommend keeping the error level set to its maximum level and changing the logging location instead. You can make this change by setting the configuration items **display_errors**, **log_errors**, and **error_log** to **Off**, **On**, and **stderr**, respectively. This causes PHP to forego displaying errors in the browser and to log the errors to the **stderr** file instead. If you are using Apache, the **stderr** file is the Apache error log file. If you want, you can use a different logging location.

When the script in Listing 3 is run with the aforementioned setting, the following lines are recorded in the Apache error log, and no errors are displayed in the browser:

```
[Wed Sep  6 08:52:42 2000] [error] PHP Warning:  Use of undefined
constant state
 - assumed 'state' in
/www/hosts/myapache.com/docs/ch10/error_reporting_2.phtml
on line 3
/www/hosts/myapache.com/docs/ch10/error_reporting_2.phtml(3) :
Warning - Use of
undefined constant state - assumed 'state'
[Wed Sep  6 08:52:42 2000] [error] PHP Warning:  Undefined offset:
3 in /www/ho
sts/myapache.com/docs/ch10/error_reporting_2.phtml on line 15
/www/hosts/myapache.com/docs/ch10/error_reporting_2.phtml(15) :
Warning - Undefined offset:  3
[Wed Sep  6 08:52:42 2000] [error] PHP Warning:  Undefined offset:
3 in /www/ho
sts/myapache.com/docs/ch10/error_reporting_2.phtml on line 17
/www/hosts/myapache.com/docs/ch10/error_reporting_2.phtml(17) :
Warning - Undefined offset:  3
```

The next step to be considered when writing defensive code is to build some logging into your application. At some point in your application, you may want to checkpoint some functionality or report an internal warning and then continue. PHP provides the **error_log()** function so that you can include custom logging in your application. The prototype for the **error_log** function is as follows:

```
int error_log (string message, int type [, string dest [, string
headers]])
```

The first parameter, **message,** is the information to be logged. The second parameter describes where the message should be logged. Table 10.2 lists the valid values for the **type** parameter.

As of this writing, **type** 2 is not available. The source code contains a comment noting that remote debugging is not available. The other type values work as described. Listing 5 shows how the **error_log()** function is used.

Listing 5: Using the error_log() Function

```
<html>
<head>
```

Value	Description
Table 10.2 *Type Parameter Values*	

Value	Description
0	The **message** parameter is sent to PHP's system logger through the use of the operating system's system logging mechanism or a file, depending on what the error_log configuration directive is set to.
1	The specified message is sent by e-mail to the address in the **dest** parameter. This message type is the only one to use the **headers** parameter. This message type uses the same internal function that the **mail()** function does.
2	The message is sent through the PHP debugging connection. This option is available only if remote debugging has been enabled. In this case, the **dest** parameter specifies the host name or IP address and, optionally, the port number of the socket receiving the debug information.
3	The message is appended to the **dest** file.

```
      <title>Logging Errors</title>
</head>
<body>
    <?php
        // log an error to the system log
        error_log( "MY ERROR: error occurred!", 0 );
        // log an error via e-mail
        error_log( "MY ERROR: error occurred!", 1,
"app_errors@intechra.net",
                   "From: error_logger@myhost.com\r\n" );
        // log an error to a specific file
        error_log( "MY ERROR: error occurred!", 3, "/tmp/error.log"
);
    ?>
    Some errors occurred.
</body>
</html>
```

The first call to the **error_log()** function in Listing 5 just logs an error to the system log. In this example, this error is sent to the Apache error log. The second call results in an e-mail message being sent to the recipient in the **dest** parameter. The header information uses the same syntax as the PHP **mail()** function. The last call appends the error to the application-specific file, /tmp/error.log.

Using the previous mechanisms is not debugging per se, but employing them can save debugging time by eliminating some errors and oversights during the development stage. As mentioned before, avoiding debugging by writing more correct code is far more valuable than the best debugging tools available.

User-Defined Error Handling

As in almost every other PHP feature, you can customize error handling to meet the needs of your application and organization. As shown at the end of the last section, the **error_log()** function provides a straightforward mechanism for logging custom application errors, but it doesn't handle the errors generated by PHP or other third-party code. It also doesn't account for messages generated by the **assert()** function. Fortunately, PHP provides a way to handle these cases.

The **set_error_handler()** function enables you to register a callback function with PHP that is called whenever an error message is generated within PHP. The **set_error_handler()** function accepts a single argument, which is the error-handling callback function name. The prototype for the callback function is as follows:

```
function ErrorCallback( int errorno, string errorstr, string
scriptname, int lineno, array context )
```

Listing 6 gives an example of setting an error-handling callback function and using it.

Listing 6: Using set_error_handler()

```php
<?php
    function myErrorHandler( $aErrorNo, $aErrorStr, $aFile, $aLine,
$aContext)
    {
        switch ( $aErrorNo )
        {
            case E_ERROR:
                $aErrorType = "E_ERROR"; // shouldn't occur
                break;
            case E_WARNING:
                $aErrorType = "E_WARNING";
                break;
            case E_PARSE:
                $aErrorType = "E_PARSE"; // shouldn't occur
                break;
            case E_NOTICE:
                $aErrorType = "E_NOTICE";
                break;
            case E_CORE_ERROR:
                $aErrorType = "E_CORE_ERROR"; // shouldn't occur
                break;
            case E_CORE_WARNING:
                $aErrorType = "E_CORE_WARNING"; // shouldn't occur
                break;
            case E_COMPILE_ERROR:
```

```
                            $aErrorType = "E_COMPILE_ERROR"; // shouldn't occur
                            break;
                        case E_COMPILE_WARNING:
                            $aErrorType = "E_COMPILE_WARNING"; // shouldn't
        occur
                            break;
                        case E_USER_ERROR:
                            $aErrorType = "E_USER_ERROR";
                            break;
                        case E_USER_WARNING:
                            $aErrorType = "E_USER_WARNING";
                            break;
                        case E_USER_NOTICE:
                            $aErrorType = "E_USER_NOTICE";
                            break;
                        default:
                            $aErrorType = "UNKNOWN ERROR TYPE";
                            break;
                    }
                    print( "<table border=\"1\"><tr><td>" );
                    print( "<b>$aErrorType</b>: <i>$aErrorStr</i><br>" );
                    print( "In file $aFile at line $aLine<br>" );
                    print( "</td></tr></table>" );
                }
                set_error_handler( "myErrorHandler" );
                error_reporting( E_ALL );
        ?>
        <html>
        <head>
            <title>User-Defined Error Handler</title>
        </head>
        <body>
            <?php
                trigger_error( "Test error", E_USER_ERROR );
                $aArray = array( "state" => "Idaho", "county" => "Madison",
                                 "city" => "Rexburg", "country" => "US" );
                print( "aArray[state] = " . $aArray[state] . "<br>" );
            ?>
        </body>
        </html>
```

In Listing 6, the user-defined error handler, **myErrorHandler(),** displays the error information in a single-cell table with a border to help offset the error from other HTML output. After the error handler is installed, the script causes two errors. The first is generated using the PHP **trigger_error()** function. The second error (a notice) is the same as the error in Listing 3. Figure 10.4 shows the output.

When you use the **set_error_handler()** function, note that PHP does not forward any errors of type **E_ERROR**, **E_PARSE**, **E_CORE_ERROR**, **E_CORE_WARNING**, **E_COMPILE_ERROR**, or **E_COMPILE_WARNING** to the user-defined callback function. Errors of these types may not be safe to handle in user space. For this reason, the "shouldn't occur" comments appear in the error handler in Listing 6.

Note on set_error_handler()

The **set_error_handler()** function is available starting with PHP version 4.0.1. Additionally, the callback function used in the examples in this chapter accepts five parameters, including the name of the script, line number, and context information. These parameters are available only in PHP 4.0.2 and higher. Earlier versions had only two parameters: the message type and message string.

Figure 10.4
The
set_error_handler()
function

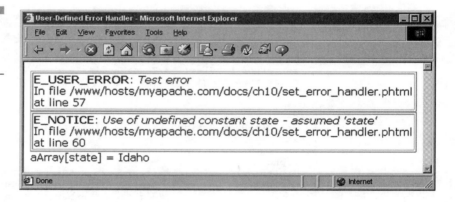

In Listing 6, the context information is not used. This will be discussed in the next section of this chapter. The context information contains the names and values of variables as they existed in the context of the script where the error occurred.

The **assert()** function also enables you to use a user-defined callback function. To accomplish this, use the **assert_options()** function to set the callback. The callback function for handling assertion failures is defined as follows:

```
function AssertCallback( $aFileName, $aLineNum, $aAssertion )
```

Listing 7 gives an example of setting and using the assert() callback function.

Note on assert_options()

A minor bug in the **assert_options()** function exists in versions of PHP up to and including version 4.0.2. The bug occurs when calling the function as **assert_options(ASSERT_CALLBACK)** in order to determine the name of the current callback function. Although the documentation states that calling the function this way should just return the current callback function name, it actually clears the current callback function after returning the name. Therefore, if you want to use **assert()** with a callback function, be sure not to call the **assert_options()** function to check that your callback function name is registered. This bug has been noted and corrected for a version of PHP beyond 4.0.2.

Listing 7: Using assert() with a User-Defined Callback Function

```php
<?php
    error_reporting( E_ALL );
    function MyACallback( $aFileName, $aLineNum, $aAssertion )
    {
        print( "<table border=\"1\"><tr><td>" );
        print( "<b>assert()</b> failure: <i>$aAssertion</i><br>" );
        print( "In file $aFileName at line $aLineNum<br>" );
        print( "</td></tr></table>" );
    }
    // set the callback function
    assert_options( ASSERT_CALLBACK, "MyACallback" );
    // turn off the normal warning messages
    assert_options( ASSERT_WARNING, 0 );
?>
<html>
<head>
    <title>Assert Callback</title>
</head>
<body>
    Cause an assert() failure.
    <?php
        assert( "1 == 2" );
    ?>
</body>
</html>
```

Listing 7 is similar to Listing 6. The assertion is displayed in a single-cell table. If the assert option **ASSERT_WARNING** is not disabled, the

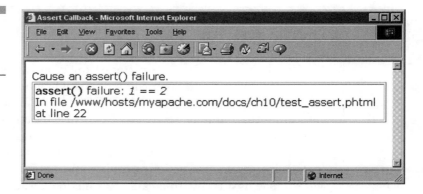

Figure 10.5
A user-defined
assert() function
callback

standard PHP output will be generated along with the user-defined information. Figure 10.5 shows the output of the script in Listing 7.

PHP provides a great deal of functionality to aid in the error-handling process. This flexibility in turn makes it possible to write code that is easier to debug and maintain. The next section combines all the techniques discussed to this point in a way that will help you in debugging throughout the development cycle.

Advanced Error Handling

Now that the techniques for error handling have been discussed, an overall error-handling tool can be developed. One motivation for this section is that the tools provided by PHP don't automatically aggregate the various types of error information. The other motivation is a personal one. PHP 3 has a remote debugging feature that has not been reintroduced in PHP 4. It enables you to send information over TCP/IP to a remote machine. This feature will probably appear again soon, but in the meantime, the basic error-handling technique in this section addresses the issue.

The example in this section is extremely large, so it will be discussed in sections. The module is in a single include file, MyDebug.php. The module will be referred to as the **MyDebug** module. It is built so that it can easily be included in any PHP script. When the file is included, the PHP code in Listing 8 is executed.

Listing 8: Including the MyDebug Module

```
ParseConfig( getenv( "MYDEBUG_CONFIG" ) );
if ( $aMyDebugType & MYDEBUG_DISPLAYFILE )
{
    // if we can't write to the log file, tell the user to
    // then disable file logging
    if ( CheckFileSanity( $aMyDebugFile ) == False )
    {
        error_log( "MyDebug failed to open file $aMyDebugFile",
0 );
        $aMyDebugType &= ~MYDEBUG_DISPLAYFILE;
    }
}
if ( $aMyDebugType & MYDEBUG_DISPLAYFILE )
{
    $aFileHandle = fopen( $aMyDebugFile, "a" );
}
if ( $aMyDebugType & MYDEBUG_DISPLAYIP )
{
    $aSocketHandle = fsockopen( "udp://$aMyDebugIP",
$aMyDebugPort );
}
// Now register the error-handling callbacks and cleanup
function
set_error_handler( "MyErrHandler" );
assert_options( ASSERT_CALLBACK, "MyAssertHandler" );
assert_options( ASSERT_WARNING, 0 );
register_shutdown_function( "MyDebugShutdown" );
```

The first line in Listing 8 parses the **MyDebug** configuration string that is available in the server environment. For example, an Apache configuration file could contain code similar to the following:

```
SetEnv MYDEBUG_CONFIGFILE=/tmp/mydebug.log;
MAIL=mydebug@intechra.net;IP=myserver.com:5400;
```

This configuration item is specific to the **MyDebug** module and is not available as a regular part of PHP or Apache. Note that you can also set environment variables via server configuration files that can be used in your PHP code. The **MYDEBUG_CONFIG** item defines where **MyDebug** logs the errors. In this example, the module logs an error to a log file (/tmp/mydebug.log), to an e-mail address (mydebug@intechra.net), and to a UDP socket (myserver.com:5400). In reality, you would probably choose only one of the logging methods at a time, but the **MyDebug** module is configurable to enable multiple simultaneous logging locations. The **ParseConfig()** function parses the configuration string and sets the appropriate global variables.

After the configuration string is parsed, any file that is being used for logging is checked to ensure that it can be written to. If the **MyDebug** module cannot write to the file, file logging is disabled. Next, the **MyDebug** module opens a file and socket for logging as needed. The socket is opened using UDP in case the listener is not available. This capability is useful especially if you want to leave the logging active on a production server but don't always have the listener running.

Next, the **MyDebug** module registers the callback functions for handling internal errors and assertion failures. Finally, a shutdown function is registered with PHP so that when the script ends, an opportunity to clean up the module exists. Listing 9 shows the shutdown function.

Listing 9: The Shutdown Function

```
function MyDebugShutdown( )
{
    global $aFileHandle, $aSocketHandle, $aMyDebugType;
    if ( $aMyDebugType & MYDEBUG_DISPLAYFILE )
    {
        fclose( $aFileHandle );
    }
    if ( $aMyDebugType & MYDEBUG_DISPLAYIP )
    {
        fclose( $aSocketHandle );
    }
}
```

The **shutdown** function closes the file and socket descriptors as needed. Any PHP script can register a shutdown function. PHP enables you to register multiple shutdown functions that are executed when the script ends. Although this fact is not mentioned in documentation, the shutdown functions are called in the same order they are registered. Because this order is undocumented, your scripts should not rely on the shutdown ordering or you should test the order yourself. You can also pass additional parameters to the **register_shutdown_function()** function. PHP then passes these parameters back to your shutdown function. Note that output cannot be sent to the browser in the body of a shutdown function. Once the **MyDebug** module has configured itself, it handles errors through the callback functions in Listing 10.

Listing 10: Error-handling Callback Functions

```
// The callback for set_error_handler() function
function MyErrHandler( $aErrorNo, $aErrorStr, $aFile, $aLine,
$aContext)
```

```
    {
        MyDebug( $aErrorStr, $aFile, $aLine, MYDEBUG_ERRCALLBACK,
                    $aErrorNo, $aContext );
    }
    //  The callback for assert_options() function
    function MyAssertHandler( $aFileName, $aLineNum, $aAssertion )
    {
        MyDebug( "assert( $aAssertion ) failed", $aFileName,
                    $aLineNum, MYDEBUG_ASSERTCALLBACK );
    }
```

Both callbacks pass the parameters on to the main error handler, which can also be called directly from a script. The main handler is the **MyDebug()** function in Listing 11.

Listing 11: The MyDebug() Function

```
    //  The MyDebug function is the main handler
    function MyDebug( $aMessage, $aFile, $aLine,
                    $aCallType = MY_DEBUG_INTERNAL, $aErrType =
0,
                    $aErrContext = array() )
    {
        global $aMyDebugType;
        for ( $aDisplayType = MYDEBUG_DISPLAYFILE;
              $aDisplayType <= MYDEBUG_DISPLAYIP;
              $aDisplayType++ )
        {
            if ( $aDisplayType & $aMyDebugType )
            {
                $aType      = FormatType( $aCallType, $aDisplayType
);
                $aMessage   = FormatMsg ( $aCallType, $aMessage,
$aErrType, $aDisplayType );
                if ( $aCallType == MYDEBUG_ERRCALLBACK )
                {
                    $aContext = FormatContext( $aErrContext,
$aDisplayType );
                }
                else
                {
                    $aContext = "";
                }
                MyDebugOutput( $aType, $aMessage, $aFile, $aLine,
$aContext, $aDisplayType );
            }
        }
    }
```

The **MyDebug()** function formats the various parameters based on the type of the display medium(file, e-mail, or TCP/IP). It then calls the **MyDebugOutput()** function in Listing 12 to send the information to the proper location. The formatting functions in Listing 11 will be discussed later.

Listing 12: The MyDebugOutput() Function

```
function MyDebugOutput( $aType, $aMessage, $aFile, $aLine,
$aContext, $aDisplayType )
    {
        global $aFileHandle, $aSocketHandle, $aMyDebugEmail;
        switch( $aDisplayType )
        {
            case MYDEBUG_DISPLAYFILE:
                $aMsg = "$aType: '$aMessage' occured in $aFile on
line $aLine.  ";
                if ( $aContext != "" )
                {
                    $aMsg .= "Context information
follows:\n{$aContext}\n";
                }
                else
                {
                    $aMsg .= "\n";
                }
                fputs( $aFileHandle, $aMsg );
                break;
            case MYDEBUG_DISPLAYEMAIL:
                $aMsg = "$aType: '$aMessage' occured in $aFile on
line $aLine.  ";
                if ( $aContext != "" )
                {
                    $aMsg .= "Context information
follows:\n{$aContext}\n";
                }
                else
                {
                    $aMsg .= "\n";
                }
                mail( $aMyDebugEmail, "MyDebug Report", $aMsg,
"From: mydebug@host.com\r\n" );
                break;
            case MYDEBUG_DISPLAYIP:
                $aMsg =
"$aType|$aMessage|$aFile|$aLine|$aContext^^";
                fputs( $aSocketHandle, $aMsg );
                break;
        }
    }
```

The **MyDebugOutput**() function sends the information to the proper location. This implementation is surprisingly simple considering that it has such a powerful set of options. Each of the formatting functions used in the **MyDebug** module provides a mechanism for translating the internal error codes into human-readable codes as needed. For example, the **Format-Type**() function in Listing 13 formats the error type code.

Listing 13: The FormatType() Function

```
/*  This function formats the message type based on where
        it is going to be displayed */
```

```
function FormatType( $aCallType, $aDisplayType )
{
    switch( $aDisplayType )
    {
        case MYDEBUG_DISPLAYFILE:
        case MYDEBUG_DISPLAYEMAIL:
            switch ( $aCallType )
            {
                case MYDEBUG_INTERNAL:
                    return "INTERNAL";
                    break;
                case MYDEBUG_ERRCALLBACK:
                    return "ERROR CALLBACK";
                    break;
                case MYDEBUG_ASSERTCALLBACK:
                    return "ASSERT CALLBACK";
                    break;
            }
            break;
        case MYDEBUG_DISPLAYIP:
            return $aCallType;
            break;
    }
}
```

If the display is TCP/IP, then no formatting is done. The type number itself is sent to the remote location. Otherwise, the type number is converted to a meaningful string. The other formatting functions used in **MyDebug** behave similarly. The one formatting function that is significantly different is the error-context formatting function, **FormatContext()**. This function is used only when the **set_error_handler()** callback function handles the error. The context information provided by PHP includes all the variables in the local scope where the error occurred. The format of the context information is an associative array of variable names and values. Parsing this information requires a recursive function to enable arrays within the context. The functions in Listing 14 parse the context information into a human-readable string.

Listing 14: Parsing the Context Information

```
/*  This function formats the message based on where
    it is going to be displayed. This function relies
    on the FormatContextR recursive function. */
function FormatContext( $aErrContext, $aDisplayType )
{
    // for now all display types receive the same context
string
    $aString = "";
    $aDelim  = "\n";
    FormatContextR( $aErrContext, $aString, $aDelim );
    return $aString;
}
function FormatContextR( $aErrContext, &$aString, $aDelim )
```

```
    {
        foreach( $aErrContext as $aVarName => $aVarValue )
        {
            if ( is_array( $aVarValue ) == True )
            {
                $aString .= "$aVarName = array( ";
                FormatContextR( $aVarValue, $aString, "," );
                $aString .= " )$aDelim";
            }
            else
            {
                $aString .= "$aVarName = {$aVarValue}{$aDelim}";
            }
        }
    }
```

The **FormatContext()** function sets some parameters and then calls the recursive function **FormatContextR()**. The recursive function then loops through the context variable array, writing each name/value to the output string. If an array is encountered, the **FormatContextR()** function is called recursively.

Depending on the location of the error, the local context may contain a great deal of information. If an error occurs in the main body of a script, all the global variables, including the environment and GET/POST variables, will have a local scope. These variables also will all be included in the context information. If an error occurs in a function, the context information will have only local function variables.

With the **MyDebug** module included in a test script (shown in Listing 15) and the configuration set to log to a file, the following error string is found at the end of the log file. The following isn't the entire output, just the output of the last error in the script:

```
ERROR CALLBACK: 'PHP error type: E_USER_ERROR - error in sum'
occurred in /www/hosts/myapache.com/docs/ch10/test_mydebug.phtml on
line 14.  Context information follows:
a = 1
b = 2
aArray = array( 0 = spring, 1 = summer, 2 = autumn, 3 = winter,  )
```

Listing 15: The Test Script

```php
<?php
    include_once( "./mydebug.php" );
?>
<html>
<head>
    <title>Test of the MyDebug Module</title>
</head>
<body>
<?php
```

```
            function sum( $a, $b )
            {
                $aArray = array( "spring", "summer", "autumn", "winter"
);
                trigger_error( "error in sum", E_USER_ERROR );
            }
            assert( "1 == 2" );
            trigger_error( "Test error", E_USER_ERROR );
            $aArray = array( "state" => "Idaho", "county" => "Madison",
                            "city" => "Rexburg", "country" => "US" );
            print( "<br><br>aArray[state] = " . $aArray[state] . "<br>"
);
            sum( 1, 2 );
        ?>
    </body>
    </html>
```

The test script in Listing 15 does nothing except generate errors. The **sum()** function included therein doesn't attempt to do anything but show how the function scope affects the context information provided by PHP. The error lines shown immediately before Listing 15 are the lines generated by calling the **sum()** function.

To illustrate the flexibility of this module, a Windows-based application has been built to be a listener for the TCP/IP display function. The listener is a simple Delphi application that listens for UDP packets on port 5400. It then formats the lines it receives and displays them. Figure 10.6 shows the application running after PHP generated some errors.

One of the main reasons that PHP is so attractive as a language is that it is so extensible. The **MyDebug** module is written entirely in PHP and adds a great deal of functionality to the language. (The full source for the MyDebug module is available on the Web site mentioned in the reference section at the end of this book.) The module is not complete and could be improved in many ways. For example, using e-mail to report errors is extremely inefficient, but if the configuration options enabled e-mailing

Figure 10.6
The MyDebug
listener

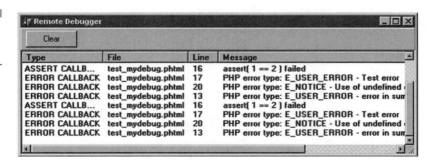

only critical errors while logging warnings and notices, the module could be used in a production environment. The exciting prospect is that with PHP all of these things can be accomplished natively. Not all Web-programming tools are so extensible.

Summary

This chapter focused on providing defensive coding techniques to avoid debugging tasks as much as possible, rather than on debugging specifically. Currently, PHP does not support a native script debugger similar to those available in other modern tools. However, by using some creativity and the extensibility of PHP, you can develop some great debugging techniques. This chapter highlighted one module that provides a flexible error-handling solution that can be extended and modified to meet the needs of almost any developer.

Bibliography

McConnell, Steve. *Code Complete*. Seattle: Microsoft Press, 1993.

11

Code Reuse

Introduction

Developing applications using reusable code modules should be a significant consideration in any software development project. The primary reason is that reusable code modules provide a basis for subsequent projects and can improve the efficiency of a development team over time.

Because PHP provides a means for including external files and creating object-oriented classes, code reuse is straightforward. This chapter briefly discusses reusing code from a software engineering perspective and provides some examples of reusable PHP code. The chapter also discusses reusing non-PHP code within PHP projects. This flexibility in PHP provides developers with the ability to port existing applications to the Web without a complete rewrite.

Software Engineering and Code Reuse

Reusing code is not just taking existing code and integrating it into a new product. New code is often created with reuse as a goal. When code reuse is planned, the long-term benefits can be significant, but developing reusable code is often more time-consuming and expensive than building stand-alone code. In fact, estimates suggest that developing reusable code is as much as two to three times more expensive than developing the same code for stand-alone use (McConnell, 1996). The benefits of reuse are not immediately available, but some companies have seen productivity increase as much as 58 percent per year for four years (McConnell, 1996).

These benefits are not manifested unless a well-designed and planned approach is developed. Some keys for planning code reuse are as follows:

- Develop a management commitment to reusing code
- Ensure that developing reusable code is integral to the entire development process and that all developers are committed to the idea
- Focus development efforts on small, precise, reusable code modules
- Develop reusable code with the highest development and documentation standards

When developing code, be sure to consider that you may need similar code in a future project. If you develop code with this in mind, you will be more likely to break functional groups out into separate reusable modules or classes. If you are sure that you can reuse a section of code, develop and document that code using your organization's best practices guidelines. Avoid using project-specific information or assumptions and build the reusable module in a way that simplifies your future reuse needs.

With PHP, reusable code can be implemented using several methods, such as creating separate source files (include files) and object-oriented classes. Whether you prefer to take the include-file approach or the object approach makes little difference. The key is to build your reusable code in an organized and well-documented fashion. Use encapsulation and information-hiding techniques in your efforts to maximize the effectiveness of your reusable code.

Reusing Existing Code

Because of the nature of Internet projects, not much code may exist in an organization. Therefore, code reuse may need to be simply a planned practice in anticipation of future projects. Some techniques that are available in PHP will be discussed to help you plan your projects with reuse in mind.

If your application is a port from a desktop application to a Web-based application, or if you are moving from another language to PHP, you may have some old code that you would like to reuse. Because PHP is so extensible, many methods exist for using non-PHP code within a PHP-base application. Some of these methods will be described in the following section.

PHP

PHP inherently provides several tools for promoting code reuse. Because of this, an established base of third-party tools has already been developed for PHP. Some of these have been mentioned in previous chapters and are listed in the Internet resources section at the end of the book.

The most obvious method for reusing code in PHP is to use the **include()** or **require()** function to include existing code. Used throughout the examples, these functions can be used to include pure PHP code, HTML, or a combination. Beginning with PHP version 4, the **include_once()** and **require_once()** functions are available to simplify the file inclusion process. These functions eliminate the problems that occur when files are included multiple times in a script. Listings 1 and 2 illustrate such problems and the solutions for them.

Listing 1: The include File, date_funcs.php

```php
<?php
    include_once( "./format_funcs.php" );
    // returns the number of days between to days
    // in a formatted string, dates in format mm-dd-yyyy
    function GetDateDiff( $aDateStr1, $aDateStr2 )
    {
        $aDateArray1 = explode( "-", $aDateStr1 );
        assert( 'count( $aDateArray1 ) == 3' );
        $aDateArray2 = explode( "-", $aDateStr2 );
        assert( 'count( $aDateArray2 ) == 3' );
        $aTime1 = mktime( 0, 0, 0, $aDateArray1[0],
$aDateArray1[1], $aDateArray1[2] );
        $aTime2 = mktime( 0, 0, 0, $aDateArray2[0],
$aDateArray2[1], $aDateArray2[2] );
        $aTimeDiff = abs( $aTime1 - $aTime2 );
        return GetFormattedNumber( $aTimeDiff / ( 60 * 60 * 24 ) );
    }
?>
```

Listing 2: The include File, format_funcs.php

```php
<?php
    function GetFormattedNumber( $aNum )
    {
        return number_format( $aNum, 0, '.', ' ' );
    }
?>
```

Listing 3 attempts to use functions in both of the preceding include files.

Listing 3: The Main Script Trying to Use Both include Files

```php
<?php
    include( "./date_funcs.php" );
    include( "./format_funcs.php" );
?>
<html>
<head>
    <title>Problem of multiple include()'s</title>
</head>
<body>
    <?php
        $aNumVisitors   = 14500;
        print( "There have been " );
        print( GetFormattedNumber( $aNumVisitors ) );
        print( " visitors to this site " );
        print( "in the last " );
        print( GetDateDiff( "9-21-2000", "8-15-1992" ) );
        print( " days." );
    ?>
</body>
</html>
```

The problem in Listing 3 is that one of the include files, date_funcs.php, also includes the format_funcs.php file itself. When the script in Listing 3 is run, the following error message is generated:

```
PHP Fatal error:  Cannot redeclare getformattednumber() in
/www/hosts/myapache.com/docs/ch11/format_funcs.php on line
2/www/hosts/myapache.com/docs/ch11/format_funcs.php(2) : Fatal
error - Cannot redeclare getformattednumber()
```

Listing 4 shows how this problem can be easily solved using the **include_once()** function.

Listing 4: The Main Script Using include_once()

```php
<?php
    include_once( "./date_funcs.php" );
    include_once( "./format_funcs.php" );
?>
<html>
<head>
<title>Problem of multiple include()'s</title>
</head>
<body>
    <?php
        $aNumVisitors  = 14500;
        print( "There have been " );
        print( GetFormattedNumber( $aNumVisitors ) );
        print( " visitors to this site " );
        print( "in the last " );
        print( GetDateDiff( "9-21-2000", "8-15-1992" ) );
        print( " days." );
    ?>
</body>
</html>
```

The **require()** and **require_once()** functions behave similarly. These inclusion mechanisms make it possible to develop an in-house library of commonly used routines and to use PHP code from other vendors. Additionally, PHP supports the creation of object-oriented classes that can be reused and extended. Several examples of extending third-party classes have been given in previous chapters. Because PHP supports include modules and OO, it is inherently capable of providing the tools required for developing reusable code. Beyond this, however, is the extensibility of PHP provided by being able to reuse other existing code.

C/C++

PHP is written in C and C++. Because of this, it is possible to integrate existing C/C++ code directly into PHP. In fact, many of the PHP extensions are direct ports from C/C++. For example, the CyberCash™ Merchant Control Kit is provided natively in C and its functions are available in PHP as the **cybercash_xxx()** functions.

If you have a base of existing C/C++ code for a project that is going to be ported to the Web, you should consider including that code in your PHP. Realize that this requires a great deal of effort and may be less efficient than simply rewriting the functionality in PHP.

This discussion is going to focus on creating built-in PHP functions based on existing C functions. If your code base is mostly C++, you can create native PHP objects that use the C++ implementation, but this will not be discussed here. Alternatively, you could provide a functional mapping to existing C++ object methods.

Assume that you have the three functions shown in Listing 5 and that you want to make native PHP function equivalents. These are functions used to calculate U.S. mortgage payments and amortization tables. The first two functions return a single value representing the monthly payment and total of all payments, respectively. The last function returns an array of values representing the monthly interest portion of the payment. Using this information, an amortization schedule can be generated.

Listing 5: The C Functions to be Converted to PHP

```
/*
    _fin_mpmt:
    calculate the monthly payment for a mortgage based
    on loan amount (p), interest (i) and term (l)
*/
double _fin_mpmt( double p, double i, double l )
{
    double j;
    double n;
    j = i / ( 12 * 100 );
    n = l * 12;
    return ( p * ( j / ( 1 - ( pow( ( 1 + j ), ( n * -1 ) ) ) ) )
);
}
/*
    _fin_total:
    calculate the total payment amount over the
    life of a mortgage for a mortgage based
    on loan amount (p), interest (i) and term (l)
*/
double _fin_total( double p, double i, double l )
{
    return _fin_mpmt( p, i, l ) * l * 12;
}
/*
    _fin_table:
    calculate interest paid per month using
```

```
          an amortization schedule for a mortgage based
          on loan amount (p), interest (i) and term (l)
*/
void _fin_table( double p, double i, double l, double* pIntPmt )
{
    double n, m, h, q, j, c;
    int    nIndex;
    j = i / ( 12 * 100 );
    n = l * 12;
    q = p;
    m = _fin_mpmt( p, i, l );
    for ( nIndex = 0; nIndex < n; nIndex++ )
    {
        h = q * j;
        c = m - h;
        q = q - c;
        pIntPmt[nIndex] = h;
    }
    return;
}
```

In the PHP distribution, a utility called **build_skel** creates a set of skeleton configuration files for your new PHP extension. The utility can be found in the ext subdirectory of the PHP source distribution. To add the financial functions to PHP, run the **build_skel** utility as shown here:

```
./build_skel --extname=fin_funcs --proto=/path/to/fin_funcs.proto -
--assign-params
```

The **extname** parameter is the name of the new PHP extension, while the **proto** parameter is a file containing the prototypes of the functions to create. The prototype file should consist of PHP function prototypes. The prototype file used for financial functions is shown here:

```
double fin_mpmt( double principle, double interest, double length )
double fin_total( double principle, double interest, double length
)
array fin_table( double principle, double interest, double length )
```

The **assign-params** parameter causes the skeleton source file to include correctly typed parameters, as will be shown later. Other parameters are available for controlling documentation output and other code-generation settings. For more details, run the **build_skel** script with no parameters. After running the script, as shown previously, a new directory is created, ext/fin_funcs, which contains the extension files required by PHP. The first change that must be made is to the config.m4 file. Instructions are included in the file, explaining which changes need to be made. The ext/fin_funcs/config.m4 file is shown here (all comments are removed from the file):

```
PHP_ARG_ENABLE(fin_funcs, whether to enable fin_funcs support,
[  --enable-fin_funcs              Enable fin_funcs support])
if test "$PHP_FIN_FUNCS" != "no"; then
  AC_DEFINE(HAVE_FIN_FUNCS, 1, [ ])
  PHP_EXTENSION(fin_funcs, $ext_shared)
fi
```

The **build_skel** function creates a C source file that includes the required functions and included header files so that immediately after running the utility and editing the config.m4 file, you can build PHP with support for your new extension. Realize that the actual functions will have to be developed before anything useful can be accomplished. To ensure that the skeleton and configuration files are correct, the following steps can be taken:

1. Run the **buildconf** script in the PHP base directory.
2. Run the **configure** script and add support for your new extension.
3. Make PHP.
4. Run the test script in your extension directory (extension_name.php) to check that the extension is enabled in PHP.

The test extension is enabled by the configuration directive, --enable-fin_funcs. The test script that detects whether an extension is enabled is similar to the following:

```php
<?php
    if ( extension_loaded( "fin_funcs" ) )
    {
        // call one of the functions
}
    else
    {
        print( "fin_funcs not available<br>" );
    }
?>
```

Once PHP is configured to use a new extension, the extension.c file must be updated to provide the implementation of each function. In many cases, this simply involves including the original function headers and then calling the original functions. In the financial functions example, the function bodies are defined as shown in Listing 6. Note that the **build_skel** script generated most of the code in the body of each function. Only the code in bold is code that has to be added manually.

Listing 6: The Financial Functions Added to PHP

```
/* {{{ proto double fin_mpmt(double principle, double interest,
double length)
    */
```

```
PHP_FUNCTION(fin_mpmt)
{
        zval **principle_arg, **interest_arg, **length_arg;
        double principle;
        double interest;
        double length;
        double aRetVal;
        if (ZEND_NUM_ARGS() != 3 || zend_get_parameters_ex(3,
&principle_arg, &interest_arg, &length_arg) == FAILURE){
                WRONG_PARAM_COUNT;
        }
        convert_to_double_ex(principle_arg);
        principle = Z_DVAL_PP(principle_arg);
        convert_to_double_ex(interest_arg);
        interest = Z_DVAL_PP(interest_arg);
        convert_to_double_ex(length_arg);
        length = Z_DVAL_PP(length_arg);
        aRetVal = _fin_mpmt( principle, interest, length );
        RETVAL_DOUBLE( aRetVal );
}
/* }}} */
/* {{{ proto double fin_total(double principle, double interest,
double length)
        */
PHP_FUNCTION(fin_total)
{
        zval **principle_arg, **interest_arg, **length_arg;
        double principle;
        double interest;
        double length;
        double aRetVal;
        if (ZEND_NUM_ARGS() != 3 || zend_get_parameters_ex(3,
&principle_arg, &interest_arg, &length_arg) == FAILURE){
                WRONG_PARAM_COUNT;
        }
        convert_to_double_ex(principle_arg);
        principle = Z_DVAL_PP(principle_arg);
        convert_to_double_ex(interest_arg);
        interest = Z_DVAL_PP(interest_arg);
        convert_to_double_ex(length_arg);
        length = Z_DVAL_PP(length_arg);
        aRetVal = _fin_total( principle, interest, length );
        RETVAL_DOUBLE( aRetVal );
}
/* }}} */
/* {{{ proto array fin_table(double principle, double interest,
double length)
    */
PHP_FUNCTION(fin_table)
{
        zval **principle_arg, **interest_arg, **length_arg;
        double principle;
        double interest;
        double length;
        double* pIntPmts;
        int n, nIndex;

        if (ZEND_NUM_ARGS() != 3 || zend_get_parameters_ex(3,
        &principle_arg, &interest_arg, &length_arg) == FAILURE){
```

```
                WRONG_PARAM_COUNT;
                }
                convert_to_double_ex(principle_arg);
                principle = Z_DVAL_PP(principle_arg);
                convert_to_double_ex(interest_arg);
                interest = Z_DVAL_PP(interest_arg);
                convert_to_double_ex(length_arg);
                length = Z_DVAL_PP(length_arg);
            n = (int)length * 12;
            pIntPmts = emalloc( sizeof( double ) * n );
            _fin_table( principle, interest, length, pIntPmts );
            if ( array_init( return_value ) == FAILURE )
            {
                php_error( E_ERROR, "fin_table: unable to allocate result
    array" );
            }
            else
            {
                for ( nIndex = 0; nIndex < n; nIndex++ )
                {
                    add_next_index_double( return_value, pIntPmts[nIndex]
    );
                }
            }
            efree( pIntPmts );
    }
    /* }}} */
```

In the first two functions, only three lines of new code are required to implement the extension. The first line is a variable declaration, the second is the call to the internal function for calculating the value, and the third sets the return value. The last function is implemented in such a way that it returns a PHP array. This requires a little more work than the first two functions, but the benefits are significant.

The implementation of the **fin_table()** function illustrates several techniques important to real-world PHP development. First, memory allocation must be managed through the **emalloc()** and **efree()** functions to ensure that PHP can perform normal garbage collections. In the **fin_table()** implementation, memory is allocated internally to store the temporary array of values generated by the **_fin_table()** internal C function. After calling the internal function, the return value is initialized as a PHP array using the **array_init()** function. Then the values are copied from the C-based array to the new PHP array by looping through the elements and calling the **add_next_index_double()** function. Finally, the temporary memory is freed and the function returns.

After building this implementation into PHP, the functions can be used as any other native PHP function. Listing 7 illustrates the new PHP extension.

Listing 7: Using the Financial Functions Added to PHP

```php
<html>
<head>
    <title>Mortgage Calculator</title>
</head>
<body>
<?php
    if ( $REQUEST_METHOD == 'POST' )
    {
        print( "Mortgage Amount: <b>$" . number_format( $Amount ) .
"</b><br>" );
        print( "Interest Rate: <b>{$Interest}%</b><br>" );
        print( "Term: <b>$Term years</b><br><hr>" );
        $aMontlyPayment = fin_mpmt( $Amount, $Interest, $Term );
        print( "Monthly Payment: <b>$" . number_format(
$aMontlyPayment, 2 ) . "</b><br>" );
        print( "Total of all Payments: <b>$" . number_format(
fin_total( $Amount, $Interest, $Term ), 2 ) . "</b><br><br>" );
        $aArray = fin_table( $Amount, $Interest, $Term );
    ?>
        <table border="1">
            <tr>
                <td>
                    Payment #
                </td>
                <td>
                    Principle
                </td>
                <td>
                    Interest
                </td>
            </tr>
    <?php
    $nIndex = 1;
    foreach( $aArray as $aIntPmt )
    {
        $aPrinciple = number_format( $aMontlyPayment -
$aIntPmt, 2 );
        $aIntPmt = number_format( $aIntPmt, 2 );
    ?>
            <tr>
                <td>
                    <?=$nIndex?>
                </td>
                <td>
                    $<?=$aPrinciple?>
                </td>
                <td>
                    $<?=$aIntPmt?>
                </td>
            </tr>
    <?php
    $nIndex++;
    }
    ?>
        </table>
```

```php
        <?php
    }
?>
<form action="<?=$PHP_SELF?>" method="post">
    <table>
        <tr>
            <td colspan="2">
                This is a simple mortgage payment calculator.
                Enter the mortgage amount, interest rate, and term
                below.
            </td>
        </tr>
        <tr>
            <td>
                Amount:
            </td>
            <td>
                <input type="text" name="Amount">
            </td>
        </tr>
        <tr>
            <td>
                Interest Rate ("7.5" == 7.5%):
            </td>
            <td>
                <input type="text" name="Interest">
            </td>
        </tr>
        <tr>
            <td>
                Term (years):
            </td>
            <td>
                <input type="text" name="Term">
            </td>
        </tr>
        <tr>
            <td colspan="2">
                <input type="submit" name="Submit" value="Submit">
            </td>
        </tr>
    </table>
</form>
</body>
</html>
```

The previous script displays a form for gathering the required mortgage information and then posts to itself. When called from an HTTP POST request, the financial functions are invoked and the information displayed. Figure 11.1 shows a portion of the output generated in a typical call.

As stated before, if you have an extensive library of C/C++ code from an existing application and need to move it to the Web, PHP provides a straightforward mechanism for integrating the existing code into the new code. The benefits of doing so include the ability to reuse mature code and the high performance of compiled code. Also, the functions developed in

Figure 11.1
Using the new
financial extension

C/C++ may provide functionality that cannot be developed using PHP alone. For example, a secure sockets implementation in C provides functionality that cannot currently be achieved using just PHP functions.

When considering integrating existing C/C++ code into PHP, understand that the cost of integration may be higher than the cost of rewriting the functions in PHP. The previous example could easily have been rewritten in PHP and would have been much less time-consuming. Furthermore, the integration steps would have to be replicated to some extent for each new version of PHP. This necessitates an ongoing maintenance over the life of a Web project if you plan to always stay current with the latest version of PHP.

Another option for reusing C/C++ code is to compile it and execute it on the Web server via PHP. This method is discussed later in this chapter.

Java

In Chapter 9, "Browser Independence," a brief discussion of using Java with PHP was provided. The capability to create and use Java classes is new to PHP version 4. Because of Java's popularity, many existing Java classes and beans are available through third-party vendors that can be included in your Web applications. Java support is not included by default in PHP, so you may need to rebuild PHP on your platform to take advantage of this powerful tool.

Building Java Support into PHP for *nix   If you are using PHP on a *nix platform, you need to rebuild PHP manually to include the Java support. From the PHP manual, the **--with-java** configuration option cannot be used if you have built Apache with PHP statically linked. The **--with-java** option only works if PHP is built as a cgi executable or as a dynamically loaded Apache module. For security reasons, the cgi executable version of PHP is not recommended. If you have not built Apache with support for dynamic modules previously, you may need to rebuild Apache before rebuilding PHP.

The following script rebuilds Apache with support for dynamic modules and creates a properly configured **apxs** script, which is needed later for the PHP build. It is assumed that the script will be run from the base Apache installation directory.

```
make clean
./configure --enable-module=so --enable-rule=SHARED_CORE --
prefix=/www
make
make install
```

Once Apache has been rebuilt, PHP can include Java support using the following script. It is assumed that the script will be run in the main PHP installation directory.

```
make clean
./configure --with-apxs=/www/bin/apxs --with-java ...
make
make install
```

The **--with-java** option may include a path indicating the base installation directory of your preferred JVM. Once this has finished, you can check your PHP configuration using the **phpinfo()** function. You also need to set some Java configuration items in the php.ini file. The first is a line to include the extension (**extension=libphp_java.so**). The other items will be discussed later.

Including Java Support with PHP for Windows   Rather than building the Windows version of PHP, the Java extensions are available to be downloaded from www.php.net. You should check which version of the *Java development kit* (JDK) you have installed on your Windows server using the command-line, **java -showversion**. Download the appropriate Java extensions binary and copy the php_java.dll into your system folder. On Windows 95, this is typically \windows\system, and on Windows NT, it is typically \winnt\system32.

Next, the php.ini file must be updated. First, a line must be added to include the Java extension (**extension=php_java.dll**). Then a section for the Java configuration options should be added appropriately, which is essential for any platform.

The Java Configuration Items No matter what your platform, if you have built Java support into PHP, you will need to add some configuration items to the php.ini file. Under Windows, the section should look similar to the following:

```
[java]
java.class.path="D:\php4\php_java.jar;D:\Intechra\PHP4 Book\Other
Supporting Materials\RTF2HTML\lib\Scrooge_09b7.jar"
java.home="D:\Program Files\JavaSoft\JRE\1.3"
java.library="D:\Program
Files\JavaSoft\JRE\1.3\bin\hotspot\jvm.dll"
```

Under *nix, the section should be like the following:

```
[java]
java.library.path=/usr/lib/kaffe:/home/blake/php-4.0.1pl2/modules
java.home=/usr/lib/kaffe
java.class.path=/usr/share/kaffe/Klasses.jar:/home/blake/php-
4.0.1pl2/ext/java/p
hp_java.jar:/home/blake/bhawk/lib/bhawk4j.jar:/home/blake/bhawk:/
home/blake/java
/numberspeller.jar:/home/blake/java/sax2.jar:/home/blake/java/
servlet.jar:/home/
blake/java/scrooge.jar
java.library=/www/libexec/libkaffevm.so
```

After you have configured Java support, you must specify the location of the Java classes or JAR files in the php.ini file. This must be done for each Java class you want to use. As can be seen in the previous configuration items, the **java.class.path** contains the full path of the actual Java implementation files.

As with any language that supports building components, Java provides a rich set of third-party tools that can be reused in any language that supports the *application programming interface* (API). One commercially available Java bean is the Scrooge RTF to HTML converter available at www.betabeans.de. This Java bean uses a simple API to convert *rich text files* (RTFs) to standard HTML. This functionality can be useful in any application where users are encouraged to post content. Because RTF supports various font and layout styles, using RTF enables the end-user to provide rich content files without the inherent danger of allowing your users to directly add HTML to your site. The Scrooge bean includes a sample RTF file (shown in Figure 11.2) that can be used to test the flexibility and power of the bean.

Using the Scrooge Java bean is simple and straightforward. The included documentation provides the Java class name to be used and the available properties and methods. To convert an RTF file to HTML, the **convert()** method is used. The script in Listing 8 shows how the Scrooge bean can be used in a real-world situation.

Listing 8: Using the Scrooge Java Bean

```
<html>
<head>
    <title>Using RTF to HTML</title>
</head>
<body>
<?php
    if ( $REQUEST_METHOD == 'POST' )
    {
        if ( ( $rtffile_type == "text/richtext" ) ||
             ( $rtffile_type == "application/rtf" ) )
        {
            // create an instance of the Scrooge Java bean
            $aR2H    = new Java( "de.betabeans.scrooge.Scrooge" );
            $aArray  = file( $rtffile );

            $aR2H->setOptWrapHTML( False );
            $aOutput = $aR2H->convert( implode( "", $aArray ) );
```

Figure 11.2

The Scrooge sample RTF file

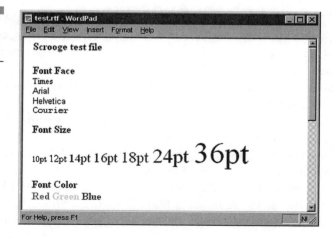

```
                    print( $aOutput );
            }
            else
            {
                    print( "The file you selected was not an <b>RTF</b>
file.<br>" );
            }
    }
?>
<form action="<?=$PHP_SELF?>" method="post"
enctype="multipart/form-data">
    Upload a file: <input type="file" name="rtffile"><br><br>
    <input type="submit" name="Submit" value="Submit">
</form>
</body>
</html>
```

This short script provides a file upload form through which a user can upload an RTF file. When the form is posted, the script first checks the file type and, if correct, creates an instance of the Scrooge bean. The uploaded file is then read into an array using the **file()** function. Next, the array is converted to a string using the **implode()** function, and the string is passed to the Scrooge bean. The return value from the bean is a single string containing the HTML representing the converted file. The HTML is printed for display in the browser. Figure 11.3 shows a portion of the output using the sample RTF file.

Java is just one language that supports the creation of third-party components that can be used in the PHP environment. The next section covers the use of COM objects with PHP.

Figure 11.3
The HTML output of the sample RTF file

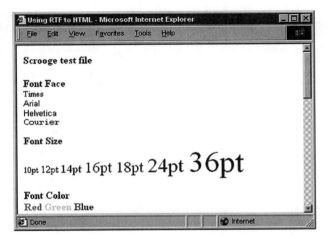

COM

COM is inherently Windows-based, so this discussion only applies to using PHP on a Windows server. The binary distribution of PHP for Windows is built with COM support, so no additional configuration is required. The COM implementation in PHP has evolved from a function-based API in version 3 of PHP to an object-oriented implementation in PHP 4. This makes using COM with PHP very natural.

The COM object that will be discussed here is the Cloanto Currency Server available at http://cloanto.com. This object provides exchange rate and currency conversion services. It updates its internal database of conversion rates automatically, so you can use it in an international e-commerce application to display prices in the local currency.

The object provides a rich API, but it is simple to use the basic functionality in a test environment. Listing 9 shows how the object can be used. Figures 11.4 and 11.5 show the output form using two different currencies.

Listing 9: Using the Cloanto Currency Server

```php
<?php
    $aWidBase1  = 10.50; // price of widget 1 in USD
    $aWidBase2  = 12.95; // price of widget 2 in USD
    $aWidBase3  = 59.95; // price of widget 3 in USD
    if ( empty( $ToCurr ) || ( trim( $ToCurr ) == "" ) )
    {
        $aCurSymbol = "USD";
    }
    else
    {
        $aCurSymbol = $ToCurr;
    }
    $objCurrServer = new COM( "CloantoCurrencyServer.Server" );
    $aWidPrice1 = $objCurrServer->ConvertToStr( "USD",
"$aCurSymbol", $aWidBase1, True, "., " );
    $aWidPrice2 = $objCurrServer->ConvertToStr( "USD",
"$aCurSymbol", $aWidBase2, True, "., " );
    $aWidPrice3 = $objCurrServer->ConvertToStr( "USD",
"$aCurSymbol", $aWidBase3, True, "., " );
?>
<html>
<head>
<title>Widget Price Table</title>
</head>
<body>
    <table border="1">
        <tr>
            <th><font size="1">Widget Item Number</font></th>
            <th><font size="1">Widget Description</font></th>
            <th><font size="1">Widget Price</font></th>
```

Figure 11.4
The Cloanto
Currency Server
example in U.S.
Dollars

Figure 11.5
The Cloanto
Currency Server
example in
Hungarian Forint

```
    </tr>
    <tr>
        <td>123</td>
        <td>Blue Widget</td>
        <td><?=$aCurSymbol?> <?=$aWidPrice1?></td>
    </tr>
    <tr>
        <td>124</td>
        <td>Chrome Widget</td>
        <td><?=$aCurSymbol?> <?=$aWidPrice2?></td>
```

```
            </tr>
            <tr>
                <td>125</td>
                <td>Invisible Widget</td>
                <td><?=$aCurSymbol?> <?=$aWidPrice3?></td>
            </tr>
        </table>
        <form action="<?=$PHP_SELF?>" method="post">
            <br><br>
            Select your local currency:
            <select name="ToCurr" size="1">
            <?php
                $aCurrCount = $objCurrServer->Currencies->Count;
                for ( $nIndex = 1; $nIndex <= $aCurrCount; $nIndex++ )
                {
                    $aCurrency = $objCurrServer->Currencies->Item(
$nIndex );

                    $aCurCode  = $aCurrency->Code;
                    $aCurName  = $aCurrency->Name;
                    $aSelected = "";
                    if ( $aCurCode == $aCurSymbol )
                    {
                        $aSelected = " selected";
                    }
                ?>
                    <option value="<?=$aCurCode?>"
<?=$aSelected?>><?=$aCurName?></option>
                    <?php
                }
            ?>
            </select>
            <input type="submit" name="Submit" value="Convert">
        </form>
    </body>
</html>
```

Listing 9 shows a simple price table for three different types of wid-
gets. It also provides a form for selecting the local currency type. When
the form is posted, the script uses the Cloanto Currency Server to localize the price into the most current value. The object can be used to list
all the currencies and their exchange rates, and also perform on-the-fly
conversions.

If you are building an e-commerce application, this object can add significant value to your end users in that it eliminates any confusion about
pricing. Using the Cloanto Currency Server along with browser detection
techniques, it may be possible to provide local prices without needing to
query the user for his or her currency type.

Because of the vast numbers of Windows developers and the maturity of
the COM object model, many COM objects are available for all types of projects. With COM support in PHP, you can easily leverage this existing code
base in your projects.

Other Uses

Perhaps you have an existing code base that can't be used with one of the aforementioned methods. If so, you still may be able to take advantage of the existing code with PHP. If the code is a script (such as a Perl script) or can be compiled into an executable, you will be able to use the code.

PHP provides several functions for executing server-side programs and scripts. Because the goal is integration, the best method for using server-side executables is probably to use the **popen()** function to execute the program or script and gather the output for PHP processing. This technique was introduced back in Chapter 4, "Working with Files," using the **whois** command available on many *nix systems. Listing 10 shows how to use PHP to determine the current amount of memory usage on a *nix system.

Listing 10: Using Pipes to Integrate PHP with Existing Scripts or Executables

```php
<html>
<head>
    <title>Untitled</title>
</head>
<body>
<?php
    $aFreeProg = '/usr/bin/free';
    if ( !is_file( $aFreeProg ) )
    {
        print( "Unable to locate necessary server program<br>" );
    }
    else
    {
        $aLines = array();
        if ( $aProgFile = popen( $aFreeProg . " -t", "r" ) )
        {
            $nIndex = 0;
            $aLines = array();
            while ( !feof( $aProgFile ) )
            {
                $aLine = fgets( $aProgFile, 1024 );
                $aLines[$nIndex++] = $aLine;
            }
            pclose( $aProgFile );
            $aCount = count( $aLines );
            $aTotal = $aLines[$aCount - 2];
            $aArray  = split( "[ ]+", $aTotal );
            $aTotalK = number_format( $aArray[1] );
            $aUsedK  = number_format( $aArray[2] );
            $aFreeK  = number_format( $aArray[3] );
            ?>
            The total amount of memory available is
<?=$aTotalK?> KB.<br>
```

```
              The amount of free memory is <?=$aFreeK?> KB.<br>
              The amount of used memory is <?=$aUsedK?> KB.<br>
         <?php
      }
      else
      {
         print ( "Unable to use required server program<br>" );
      }
   }
?>
</body>
</html>
```

Listing 10 simply opens a pipe to the standard *nix **free** command. This command returns information about the available memory for the platform. The script opens the pipe, which in turn executes the program. The script then reads each line of output from the pipe and stores it in an array. The pipe is then closed. Next, the script parses the relevant information from the output array and displays it in the browser. Depending on the output, more complex parsing may be required, but the basic idea is illustrated.

This technique can be used with any type of server script or program that returns information on a standard output file. For *nix systems, this means that almost any command can be used directly from PHP to provide a system status, feedback, or other processing. If you need to port some existing code to PHP, a quick prototyping solution could be to use the existing code in the manner described earlier. This will enable you to begin testing the feasibility of an online application while minimizing the amount of development required. However, it is important to note that invoking executables requires a significant amount of server resources, so using these techniques in production may result in a sluggish, hard-to-scale application.

Summary

PHP does not lack options for reusing code. Whether you plan to develop a reusable code library in PHP or you need to port existing code to a new Web-based application, you will find ample solutions. Also, because of the great availability of commercial third-party components (either COM objects or Java beans), you may find that significant portions of your planned application have already been developed. Using these resources can significantly reduce your application development time. Used wisely, they can also lead to a more maintainable, scalable application.

Bibliography

McConnell, Steve. *Rapid Development*. Seattle: Microsoft Press.1996.

12

Separating
HTML from
PHP

Introduction

In standard application development, the separation of user interface development from application development is not typically considered. This is due to the fact that standard applications use a common set of standard tools for interface development that most technical developers can use. The only items sent to separate designers are the logos, button images, and similar graphical aspects of the product.

Web development, however, provides an opportunity for a much richer interface and therefore often requires specialized designers who provide the application's look and feel. When the tasks of interface development and code development are divided between individuals or teams, the separation of HTML from code occurs naturally and integration becomes important. Even in small, single-person projects, separating the interface from the application logic makes maintaining the whole application simpler and more efficient.

Overview

Web development is often called multitier or n-tier application development because several logical tiers take place in any Web application. The commonly named tiers include the presentation or interface tier, the application or business tier, and the database tier. Each tier can be physically separate from the others. The most important facet of multitiered development is the logical separation, not the physical implementation.

The main advantages of a multitiered approach to Web application development include the following:

- The ability to separate the development tasks based on those most qualified to perform them. For example, graphic artists and designers prepare the presentation, software developers write the application logic, and database managers maintain and develop the database infrastructure.
- The ability to change aspects of an individual tier while leaving the others unaffected. In practice, this is still difficult, but many small changes can be localized to a single tier.
- The ability to move or replicate individual tiers to different physical hardware for scaling or redundancy requirements.

As with any application, in Web development projects, changes can be requested late in the development process. If these changes are localized to the interface, the coding effort may not be affected. Building an application that buffers the effect of late-hour changes is the motivation of this chapter. Additionally, separating the interface from the application logic is inherently a modular development technique that can increase the reusability of the application modules.

In traditional application design, modular design typically refers to creating modules of code that can be reused in other applications. In Web design, modules can include interface information, such as copyright notices, along with the code modules.

Modularity contributes more to software maintainability than structure does and is the most important factor in preventing corrective maintenance. In fact, 89 percent of code users reported improved maintainability with modular programming, and in a comprehension test, programmers scored 15 percent higher on a modular program than on a non-modular one (McConnell, 1993).

As mentioned in previous chapters, developing modular applications requires additional design and development considerations, but it results in easier-to-understand and more maintainable applications. In *A Methodology for Client/Server and Web Application Development*, Roger Fournier suggests that shared application components or modules should always be designed, coded, and tested first and then distributed to application developers at the enterprise level. These shared components should include not only shared code modules, but also database-stored procedures, triggers, and remote procedures (Fournier, 1998).

Several methods for implementing these concepts are detailed in the following section. Additionally, complete examples illustrating the techniques are included, as well as in Chapter 14, "Template-Based Web Site." Some examples of what not to do are also included in the following sections.

Separation and Integration Using PHP Built-in Functions

Because PHP inherently provides such a rich set of functions and tools, integrating separate code modules with interface modules can be accomplished directly in the language. This section covers some techniques for accomplishing this.

Motivation

The primary motivation for separating code from HTML design elements is to allow reusability and maintainability. In all the examples in this book thus far, HTML and PHP have been intermingled to provide quick, simple examples. In a real-world development, this technique is cumbersome and creates hard-to-read PHP scripts. For example, the script in Listing 1 shows a fragment of a Web page with PHP and HTML integrated together.

Listing 1: PHP and HTML Together

```php
<?php
if ( $aShowForm == true ) {
?>
<p>
<font face="Arial" size="3">
<b>
<?php
print( $aQuestion );
?>
</b>
<form action="response.php3" method="POST">
<?php if ( !empty( $UserID ) ) { ?>
<input type="Hidden" name="UserID" value="<?php print( $UserID );
?>">
<?php } ?>
<?php if ( $aQuestionID != -1 ) { ?>
<input type="Hidden" name="QuestionID" value="<?php print(
$aQuestionID ); ?>">
<?php } ?>
<ul>
<font face="Arial" size="2">
   <!--display possible answers-->
<?php
if ( $aQuestionID != -1 )
{
    if ( $aSortOrd == 0 ) // Sort alphabetically
    {
        $aSQL = "SELECT * from Answers where
(QuestionID=$aQuestionID) ORDER BY Text";
    }
    else
    {
        $aSQL = "SELECT * from Answers where
(QuestionID=$aQuestionID)";
    }
    $aDB->SetSQL( $aSQL );
```

Besides being hard to read because the sample is incomplete, Listing 1 shows how complex an HTML page with embedded PHP can become. Even with syntax-highlighting editors, locating code blocks within this page is difficult.

The maintenance problems with this type of development go beyond the basic problem of readability. It is also hard to make changes to either the code or the design without affecting the other. For example, suppose the graphic designers update the navigation images and they need to be reintegrated into the page. The question of who should perform the change is difficult to answer because the designer may not have the experience to update the page without breaking the code, and the software developer may have to rework sections of code just to integrate the new design. In any case, this results in wasted effort and delays to the schedule that could be circumvented by using better development practices.

If your organization is committed to delivering high-quality and easily maintainable Web applications, developing pages in the previous method does not work. Additionally, if you have made an investment in your interface design, don't jeopardize it by developing an application that won't enable simple changes to be made. Native PHP methods for integrating separate code and design modules are illustrated next.

Implementation

The simplest method for reintegrating separate code and design modules is to use the PHP **include()** and **require()** functions. This method involves separating the HTML design elements into separate files that can be used by the PHP code module at run time. For example, Listings 2 and 3 show a simple page design that is divided into a header and footer section. Listing 4 shows how the segments are integrated with some dynamic content.

Listing 2: The HTML Header Section

```
<!DOCTYPE HTML PUBLIC "-//W3C//DTD HTML 4.0 Transitional//EN">
<html>
<head>
      <title>Intechra LLC Company News Application</title>
</head>
<body>
<img src="logo.jpg" width="622" height="106" alt="" border="0">
<h1>Intechra LLC Company News</h1>
```

Listing 3: The HTML Footer Section

```
<br><br><br>
<hr>
<p>
    Copyright &copy; 2000 by Intechra LLC.  All rights reserved.
</p>
```

```
</body>
</html>
```

Listing 4: The PHP Script for Integrating Code and Interface

```
<?php
    include( "./header_1.html" );
    print( "Date: " . date( "Y-m-d" ) . "<br><br>" );
    print( "News Story information here..." );
    include( "./footer_1.html" );
?>
```

Although simplistic, this example shows how using the **include()** function to integrate HTML and code can result in a powerful and maintainable Web application. Figure 12.1 shows how the page looks in a browser. If nothing more, this example should show the value of separating code from HTML. If the header or footer section of the site requires a design change, only that HTML file must be updated. At the same time, if the code is reworked so real news stories are pulled from a database or file, nothing in the HTML needs to be changed.

As an alternative, you may use the standard file functions in PHP to read and include the HTML rather than using the **include()** or **require()** func-

Figure 12.1
Integrating HTML and PHP code using include()

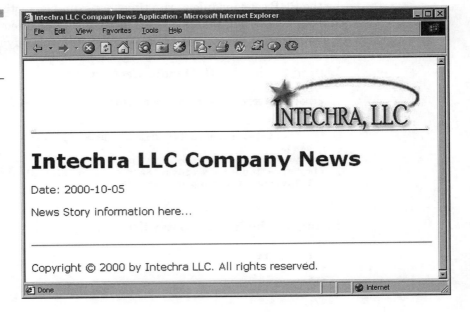

tions. This method provides more control over file handling, including the ability to search for the file and to handle error conditions. Also, using a custom file inclusion routine requires that no PHP code can be used in the HTML files.

The following listings show a more complete example using the previous technique with the PHP file functions, rather than the **include()** function. Additionally, *cascading style sheets* (CSSs) are used in the example to provide even more design customization. Listings 5 and 6 again show the header and footer HTML, and Listing 7 contains the application logic. Two separate CSSs also have been created for this illustration.

Listing 5: The HTML Header

```
<!DOCTYPE HTML PUBLIC "-//W3C//DTD HTML 4.0 Transitional//EN">
<html>
<head>
    <title>Intechra LLC Company News Application</title>
    <link rel="STYLESHEET" type="text/css" href="css1.css">
</head>
<body>
<img src="logo.jpg" width="622" height="106" alt="" border="0">
<h1>Intechra LLC Company News</h1>
```

Listing 6: The HTML Footer

```
<p class="copyright">
    Copyright &copy; 2000 by Intechra LLC.  All rights reserved.
</p>
</body>
</html>
```

Listing 7: The PHP Script for the Application

```
<?php
    function MyIncludeFile( $aFileName )
    {
        if ( !is_file( $aFileName ) )
        {
            // redirect to an error page
            exit;
        }
        $aFileArray = file( $aFileName );
        foreach( $aFileArray as $aLine )
        {
            print( "$aLine" );
        }
    }
    MyIncludeFile ( "./header_2.html" );
    include( "./db_mysql.inc" );
```

```
// create a news_db class for getting the stories
class news_db extends DB_Sql
{
    var $Host       = "db.server.com";
    var $Database   = "mydb";
    var $User        = "root";
    var $Password   = "";
}
// Create an instance of the new news_db class
$aDB = new news_db;
$aDB->query( "select * from news order by date desc limit 5" );
while( $aDB->next_record() )
{
    $aNewsID    = $aDB->f( "news_id" );
    $aAuthor    = $aDB->f( "author" );
    $aTitle     = $aDB->f( "title" );
    $aSynopsis = $aDB->f( "synopsis" );
    print( "<h2>$aTitle</h2>" );
    print( "<h4>by: $aAuthor</h4>" );
    print( "<p>$aSynopsis</p>" );
    print( "<a href=\"full_story.phtml?news_id=$aNewsID\">full
story...</a>" );
    print( "<br><br><hr>" );
}
    MyIncludeFile( "./footer_2.html" );
?>
```

This application actually uses a small database to store the news stories.
The PHPLIB database classes are used in the example, as in previous
examples. The actual content and structure of the database is not important, but the illustration of the code separation and integration techniques
is. Additionally, the flexibility of using this technique with CSSs is important. Although some basic HTML tags can be found in the body of the PHP
page, their use is restricted to a limited subset and their display properties
are controlled by CSS. The actual display of the application is shown in Figures 12.2 and 12.3.

What to Avoid

One should avoid mixing HTML and code when using this method. The
included HTML files should contain only HTML, and the included PHP
files should contain only PHP code. This makes it easier to separate the
responsibilities of the PHP programmers and the interface designers. Avoid
creating PHP code modules that generate HTML. Although this provides a
mechanism for writing pure PHP code without the inline HTML tags, it
makes design activities the sole responsibility of the PHP programmer. It
also increases the difficulty of making sweeping design changes over an
entire Web site.

Figure 12.2
The news application
with style sheet 1

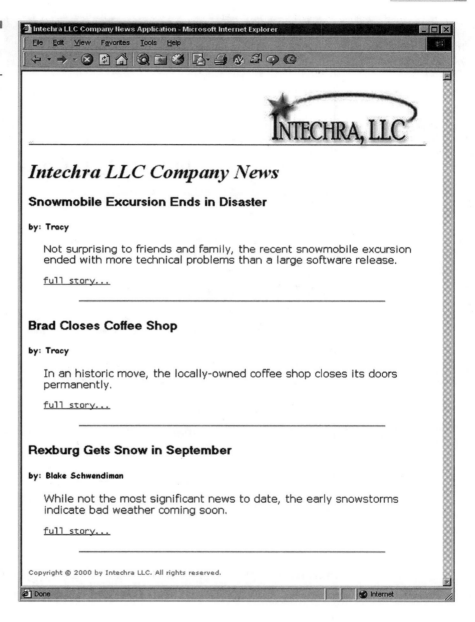

Figure 12.2
The news application
with style sheet 1

Figure 12.3
The news application
with style sheet 2

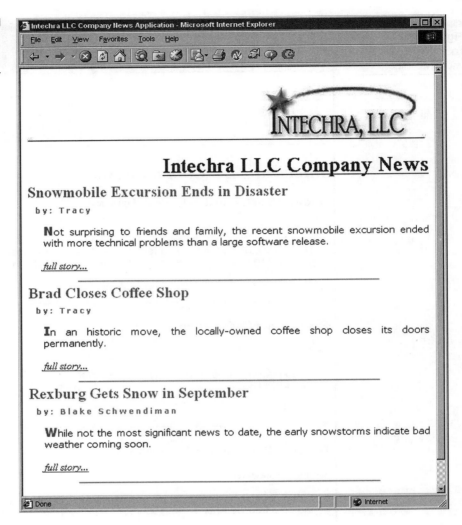

Summary: Separation and Integration Using PHP Built-in Functions

When developing a mechanism for separating PHP code from HTML, it is important to remember the driving reason for doing so. Occasionally, programmers become overzealous with their need to code and create mechanisms that don't address the real need. The purpose of separating HTML from PHP is to simplify the application, segregate the responsibilities of the designer and developer, and increase the maintainability of the application. The purpose is not to find ways to code around HTML or to create HTML output within PHP code.

In fact, the goal of separating HTML from PHP should be to completely separate the design from the application logic. Using the previous technique along with CSSs in the design, this goal can be met almost entirely. However, times will occur when some HTML tags need to be dynamically generated. For example, anchor tags often need to be generated dynamically. Also, if you are propagating a session id or another application-specific identifier through the application, you will need to dynamically generate all anchor tags. In these cases, if you choose to use the aforementioned method for integrating code and HTML, you will be forced to include some HTML tags in the PHP code.

The next section, "Using a Template System," provides details on a method that can completely separate all PHP code and HTML. This is the recommended method because *all* HTML becomes the responsibility of the designers.

Using a Template System

A template system is a mechanism for completely separating HTML design elements from PHP code. The obvious advantage of using templates is their capability to enable the skilled designers to have full control over all aspects of the design. When all HTML tags are removed from the code, the entire application design can be modified independently of the application logic.

As with all beneficial development practices, using templates requires additional design considerations and a commitment to the practice in order to be successful. The basic idea is that every page of a Web site is divided into one or more design templates that are merged with dynamic content by PHP code. In a simple application, a single template file may exist for all the pages in a site. In more complex applications, hundreds of template files may be available.

FastTemplate

Although one can create a custom template system, a fantastic third-party tool is available from www.thewebmasters.net called FastTemplate. The FastTemplate tool is easy to use and provides adequate documentation to get started. As an overview, the basic procedure for using FastTemplate is to first create the template files, typically with the **tpl** extension. Then in code, the basic steps are as follows:

1. Create an instance of the FastTemplate class.
2. Use the **define()** method to associate template files with a unique name.
3. Use the **assign()** method to assign values to template variables.
4. Use the **parse()** method to process a template file and assign values to its variables.
5. Use the **FastPrint()** or **fetch()** methods to print or retrieve the parsed template file.

The FastTemplate implementation delimits variables using curly braces ({}). A sample template file is shown in Listing 8.

Listing 8: The PHP Script for the Application

```
<!DOCTYPE HTML PUBLIC "-//W3C//DTD HTML 4.0 Transitional//EN">
<html>
<head>
    <title>{TITLE}</title>
</head>
<body bgcolor="{BODY_COLOR}">
    {BODY}
    <hr>
    <font size="1">
        {COPYRIGHT}
    </font>
</body>
</html>
```

The sample template in Listing 8 contains four FastTemplate variables: TITLE, BODY_COLOR, BODY, and COPYRIGHT. In the most simplistic case, these variables can be set directly in code, as shown in Listing 9.

Listing 9: The PHP Script for the Application

```
<?php
    include( "class.FastTemplate.php" );
    $aTemplate = new FastTemplate( "." );
    $aTemplate->define( array( 'basic' => 'sample_1.tpl' ) );
    $aBodyText = "This is a very simple page body.  ";
    for ( $nIndex = 1; $nIndex <= 10; $nIndex++ )
    {
        $aBodyText .= "$nIndex ";
    }
    $aTemplate->assign( array( 'TITLE'      => 'Simple Sample',
                               'BODY_COLOR' => 'white',
```

```
                                        'BODY'        => $aBodyText,
                                        'COPYRIGHT'   => 'Copyright 2000
Intechra LLC' ) );
    $aTemplate->parse( 'PAGE', 'basic' );
    $aTemplate->FastPrint( 'PAGE' );
?>
```

The first step is to create an instance of the FastTemplate class. The constructor takes a single argument indicating the path to the template files. In this example, the current directory "." is used. Next, the template file in Listing 8 is defined to have the name **basic**. The body text is generated and stored in a PHP variable on the next lines, and then the FastTemplate variables are assigned values using the **assign()** method. Finally, the template is parsed and stored in a new variable, **PAGE**, and then that variable is printed. The page output is shown in Figure 12.4.

When FastTemplate parses a template, the results are stored in a named variable that can be printed or fetched for other purposes, or that variable can be used in another template. This last option enables template files to be nested. Using the same basic template, the following listings show how to nest additional template files. The new files are the copyright template file and the body template file shown in Listings 10 and 11, respectively.

Listing 10: The Copyright Template File (copyright.tpl)

```
Copyright &copy; {YEARS} by Intechra LLC.
All rights reserved.  For additional copyright
and legal information, please
<a href="legal.phtml">click here</a>.
```

Figure 12.4
The simple
FastTemplate output

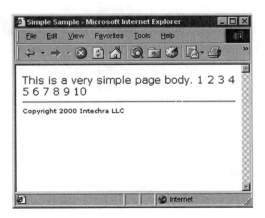

Listing 11: The Body Template File (body.tpl)

```
<table width="100%">
    <tr>
        <th colspan="3">
            {PAGE_HEADER}
        </th>
    </tr>
    <tr>
        <td colspan="3">
             
        </td>
    </tr>
    <tr>
        <td align="center" valign="top">
            <!-- Navigation -->
            <a href="index.phtml">home</a><br><br>
            <a href="about.phtml">about us</a><br><br>
            <a href="links.phtml">links</a><br><br>
        </td>
        <td width="90%">
            <!-- Main content section -->
            {PAGE_CONTENT}
        </td>
        <td width="125">
            <!-- Advertisers and other here -->
            <!-- TBD Later -->
        </td>
    </tr>
</table>
```

Each of the additional template files listed previously introduces additional FastTemplate variables that must be assigned values to be used properly. As a note, if you fail to assign a value to a particular FastTemplate variable, warnings like the following will be generated:

```
[Fri Oct  6 00:22:11 2000] [error] [FastTemplate] Warning: no
value found for variable: {PAGE_HEADER}
[Fri Oct  6 00:22:11 2000] [error] [FastTemplate] Warning: no value
found for variable: {PAGE_CONTENT}
[Fri Oct  6 00:22:11 2000] [error] [FastTemplate] Warning: no value
found for variable: {YEARS}
```

With the addition of the new template files, the main PHP file must be changed. Listing 12 shows the new PHP file that uses the nested templates.

Listing 12: Nested Template Files

```
<?php
    include( "class.FastTemplate.php" );
      function GetCurrentYear( )
      {
```

```
        $aNow           = getdate();
        $aNowYear       = $aNow["year"];
        return $aNowYear;
    }
    $aTemplate = new FastTemplate( "." );
    $aTemplate->define( array( 'basic'      => 'sample_1.tpl',
                               'copyright'  => 'copyright.tpl',
                               'body'       => 'body.tpl' ) );
    $aBodyText = "This is a very simple page body.  ";
    for ( $nIndex = 1; $nIndex <= 10; $nIndex++ )
    {
        $aBodyText .= "$nIndex ";
    }
    $aStartYear   = 1997;
    $aCurrentYear = GetCurrentYear();
    $aYears = "$aStartYear";
    for ( $nIndex = $aStartYear + 1; $nIndex <= $aCurrentYear;
$nIndex++ )
    {
        $aYears .= ", $nIndex";
    }
    $aTemplate->assign( array( 'TITLE'        => 'Better Sample',
                               'BODY_COLOR'   => 'white',
                               'YEARS'        => $aYears,
                               'PAGE_HEADER'  => 'A Better
Example',
                               'PAGE_CONTENT' => $aBodyText
                               ) );
    $aTemplate->parse( 'BODY', 'body' );
    $aTemplate->parse( 'COPYRIGHT', 'copyright' );
    $aTemplate->parse( 'PAGE', 'basic' );
    $aTemplate->FastPrint( 'PAGE' );
?>
```

The previous nested example defines the two added template files using the names **copyright** and **body**. Because these template files contain Fast-Template variables of their own, these variables must be assigned values. The **YEARS** variable is generated dynamically so that the copyright information is always current. The **PAGE_HEADER** and **PAGE_CONTENT** variables are set with a generic header and the **$aBodyText** variable, respectively. The **$aBodyText** variable is the same value as in the previous example. Note that the **BODY** and **COPYRIGHT** variables are not set in the **assign()** method in this example. Rather, these variables receive their values in the new **parse()** method calls at the bottom of the script. The output of this script is shown in Figure 12.5.

The FastTemplate class is a powerful tool that can be used to create extremely rich and complex designs. To illustrate more of the techniques of using the class, the following examples revisit the news application introduced earlier. Rather than using include files to build the pages, the following code exploits the power of the FastTemplate class.

Figure 12.5
The nested
FastTemplate output

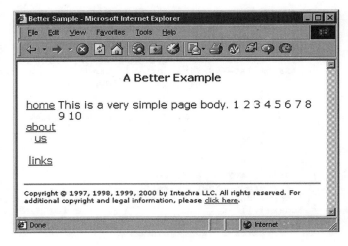

Listings 13, 14, and 15 contain the HTML templates for the base layout, body, and news item, respectively. The same copyright template from the last example is used in this example.

Listing 13: The Base Template for the News Application (ft_news_base.tpl)

```
<!DOCTYPE HTML PUBLIC "-//W3C//DTD HTML 4.0 Transitional//EN">
<html>
<head>
    <title>{TITLE}</title>
    <link rel="STYLESHEET" type="text/css" href="css2.css">
</head>
{NEWS_BODY}
</html>
```

Listing 14: The Body Template for the News Application (ft_news_body.tpl)

```
<body>
    <table width="640" border="0" align="center">
        <tr>
            <td>
                <img src="logo.jpg" width="622" height="106" alt=""
border="0">
                <h1>Intechra LLC Company News</h1>
            </td>
        </tr>
        <tr>
            <td>
```

```
                           <br><br>
                           {NEWS_ITEMS}
                      </td>
                 </tr>
                 <tr>
                      <td>
                           <br>
                           <p class="copyright">
                                {COPYRIGHT}
                           </p>
                      </td>
                 </tr>
            </table>
      </body>
```

Listing 15: The News Item Template for the News Application (ft_news_item.tpl)

```
<h2>{NEWS_TITLE}</h2>
<h4>by: {NEWS_AUTHOR}</h4>
<p>{NEWS_SYNOPSIS}</p>
<a href="{FULL_STORY_URL}">full story...</a>
<br><br><hr>
```

The script for generating the news page is shown in Listing 16. This script is more complex than the last example, but most of the code is borrowed from previous examples.

Listing 16: The Main News Application Script

```
<?php
    include( "class.FastTemplate.php" );
    include( "./db_mysql.inc" );
    error_reporting( E_ALL & ~E_NOTICE );
    function GetCurrentYear( )
    {
        $aNow          = getdate();
        $aNowYear      = $aNow["year"];
        return $aNowYear;
    }
    // create a news_db class for getting the stories
    class news_db extends DB_Sql
    {
        var $Host      = "db.server.com";
        var $Database  = "mydb";
        var $User      = "root";
        var $Password  = "";
    }
    $aTemplate = new FastTemplate( "." );
    $aTemplate->define( array( "base"      => "ft_news_base.tpl",
                               "body"      => "ft_news_body.tpl",
                               "item"      => "ft_news_item.tpl",
                               "copyright" => "copyright.tpl" ) );
    // generate the copyright years
```

```
    $aStartYear    = 1997;
    $aCurrentYear = GetCurrentYear();
    $aYears = "$aStartYear";
    for ( $nIndex = $aStartYear + 1; $nIndex <= $aCurrentYear;
$nIndex++ )
    {
        $aYears .= ", $nIndex";
    }
    $aTemplate->assign( array( "YEARS"    => $aYears,
                               "TITLE"    => "Intechra LLC News" )
);
    // Create an instance of the new news_db class
    // and generate the news items
    $aDB = new news_db;
    $aDB->query( "select * from news order by date desc limit 5" );
    while( $aDB->next_record() )
    {
        $aNewsID   = $aDB->f( "news_id" );
        $aAuthor   = $aDB->f( "author" );
        $aTitle    = $aDB->f( "title" );
        $aSynopsis = $aDB->f( "synopsis" );
        $aURL = "full_story.phtml?news_id=$aNewsID";
        $aTemplate->assign( array( "NEWS_TITLE"      => $aTitle,
                                   "NEWS_AUTHOR"     => $aAuthor,
                                   "NEWS_SYNOPSIS"   => $aSynopsis,
                                   "FULL_STORY_URL" => $aURL ) );
        $aTemplate->parse( "NEWS_ITEMS", ".item" );
    }
    $aTemplate->parse( "COPYRIGHT", "copyright" );
    $aTemplate->parse( "NEWS_BODY", "body" );
    $aTemplate->parse( "BASE", "base" );
    $aTemplate->FastPrint( "BASE" );
?>
```

This example borrows the copyright year functions from the previous example and the news database functionality from the previous news example. Note that PHP warnings are suppressed at the beginning of this script because of a warning generated by FastTemplate that will be explained later.

This script defines four template files, as listed. The two main FastTemplate variables assigned at the top of the script are **YEARS** and **TITLE**, representing the copyright years and page title, respectively.

The next major function of the script is to dynamically add the news items. This is done by selecting the five most recent items from the database and looping through them. In each iteration of the loop, the **item** template is parsed and appended to the **NEWS_ITEMS** FastTemplate variable. The append function is accomplished by prepending the name of the template with a period (.). It is during the first iteration of this loop that FastTemplate generates a warning indicating that the **NEWS_ITEMS** variable is not currently set. After the **NEWS_ITEMS** variable is set in the loop, the rest of the template files are parsed and the page is printed.

The previous example shows how to use the FastTemplate class to generate repeating elements such as the news items. Similar constructs can be used to create table rows or lists of links. Once the basic concepts are understood, using the FastTemplate class becomes second nature.

The clear advantage of the FastTemplate class or any template system is that all design elements can be developed and maintained independently of the application code. Although using a template system requires some shifts in thinking about design, the value added is definitely worth the investment in change.

Advanced Techniques Using FastTemplate

In previous chapters, two items were deferred specifically to this chapter. The first was in Chapter 7, "Sessions and Application State," where better way to propagate session identifiers through an application was mentioned. The second was in Chapter 9, "Browser Independence," where the suggestion was made that a template system be used as an alternate method of providing browser-specific content. This section focuses on these two ideas.

The first concept, propagating session identifiers, should be obvious at this point. Using templates, the design can include variable URL references that are generated by PHP code. A basic example of a navigation template is given in Listing 17.

Listing 17: The Navigation Template (navi.tpl)

```
<a href="{HREF_INDEX}">home</a>
<a href="{HREF_NEWS}">news</a>
<a href="{HREF_LINKS}">links</a>
```

The actual URLs for the links can then be generated on the fly to contain session information or other application-specific details. Another advantage to using variable URLs is that page locations can be more easily modified throughout an application. Listing 18 shows a script that generates the dynamic URLs for the previous template.

Listing 18: The Navigation Template

```php
<?php
    include( "./class.FastTemplate.php" );
    session_start();
    function MyGenURL( $aLinkName )
    {
        switch( $aLinkName )
```

```
        {
            case 'HREF_INDEX' :
                $aBaseURL = 'index.phtml';
                break;
            case 'HREF_NEWS' :
                $aBaseURL = 'news.phtml';
                break;
            case 'HREF_LINKS' :
                $aBaseURL = 'links.phtml';
                break;
            default :
                $aBaseURL = 'badlink.phtml';
                break;
        }
        return $aBaseURL . "?". session_name() . "=" .
session_id();
    }
    $aTemplate = new FastTemplate( "." );
    $aTemplate->define( array( 'navi' => 'navi.tpl' ) );
    $aTemplate->assign( array( 'HREF_INDEX' => MyGenURL(
'HREF_INDEX' ),
                               'HREF_NEWS'  => MyGenURL(
'HREF_NEWS' ),
                               'HREF_LINKS' => MyGenURL(
'HREF_LINKS' ) ) );
    $aTemplate->parse( 'NAVI', 'navi' );
    $aTemplate->FastPrint( 'NAVI' );
?>
```

The **MyGenURL()** function defined previously is the core of this script. It takes a symbolic link name and returns a real page location with the session information appended to it. Using a function like this one has the additional benefit of handling unknown link names. This can provide a way to avoid the dreaded "**HTTP 404: Page Not Found**" errors that plague large Web applications.

Using templates to provide browser-specific content is also advantageous. The methods that were suggested in Chapter 9 for providing browser-specific content were to conditionally include content or to redirect the user to a browser-specific directory. The first method is preferred if templates are used. The problem with redirection is that a user can bookmark a page or send a link to a friend and then visit the link with a different browser from the one used to initially locate the page. The example in Listings 19, 20, 21, and 22 show how browser-specific content can be integrated using templates. Listing 19 is the base page template. Listings 20 and 21 are the capability-specific pages and Listing 22 is the PHP script.

Listing 19: The Base Page Template (base_basic.tpl)

```
<!DOCTYPE HTML PUBLIC "-//W3C//DTD HTML 4.0 Transitional//EN">
<html>
<head>
```

```
        <title>{TITLE}</title>
    </head>
    <body>
    {NAVI}
    </body>
    </html>
```

Listing 20: The Flash-Based Menu (flash_menu.tpl)

```
<OBJECT classid="clsid:D27CDB6E-AE6D-11cf-96B8-444553540000"
codebase="http://download.macromedia.com/pub/shockwave/cabs/flash/s
wflash.cab#version=5,0,0,0" WIDTH=320 HEIGHT=240> <PARAM NAME=movie
VALUE="flash_menu.swf"> <PARAM NAME=quality VALUE=high> <PARAM
NAME=bgcolor VALUE=#FFFFFF> <EMBED src="flash_menu.swf"
quality=high bgcolor=#FFFFFF  WIDTH=320 HEIGHT=240
TYPE="application/x-shockwave-flash"
PLUGINSPAGE="http://www.macromedia.com/shockwave/download/index.cgi
?P1_Prod_Version=ShockwaveFlash"></EMBED>
```

Listing 21: The html Menu (html_menu.tpl)

```
<a href="index.phtml">home</a>
<a href="news.phtml">news</a>
<a href="links.phtml">links</a>
```

Listing 22: The Script

```php
<?php
    include( "./class.FastTemplate.php" );
    // assume $aHasFlash is set using a real Flash detection
technique
    $aHasFlash = False;
    if ( $aHasFlash == True )
    {
        $aNaviFile = "flash_menu.tpl";
    }
    else
    {
        $aNaviFile = "html_menu.tpl";
    }
    $aTemplate = new FastTemplate( "." );
    $aTemplate->define( array( "navi" => $aNaviFile,
                               "base" => "base_basic.tpl" ) );
    $aTemplate->assign( array( "TITLE" => "Keen browser-specific
example" ) );
    $aTemplate->parse( "NAVI", "navi" );
    $aTemplate->parse( "BASE", "base" );
    $aTemplate->FastPrint( "BASE" );
?>
```

The previous example illustrates how you might provide a Macromedia Flash™ menu when the target browser supports it and a regular HTML menu for other browsers. Obviously, a real capability detection technique such as those listed on the Macromedia® Web site would be used.

Based on the specific needs of your site, you could conceivably subdivide many aspects of the design based on browser capabilities and use a template system to provide the best content for each browser.

Summary

Separating the design elements of a Web application from the business logic, promotes a modular design and therefore increases reusability and maintainability. Because of the flexibility of PHP, the goal of modular Web site development can be achieved in multiple ways. The preferred method described here is to use a template system to fully separate all the design elements from code.

As an aside, behind this chapter is a personal motivation. I realized quite some time ago that I'm never going to be a graphic designer or artist, so I've gone to great lengths in my company to find ways to integrate professionally created designs into my applications. This results in an overall improvement in the site because the presentation layer is high quality and I don't have to develop or maintain it personally. I use the FastTemplate class in nearly all of my Web projects now. It is easy for my designer to develop site template files using the curly brace notation and it enables me to take fully functional designs and quickly apply application logic.

Bibliography

Fournier, Roger. *A Methodology for Client/Server and Web Application Development.* New Jersey: Prentice Hall PTR. 1998.

McConnell, Steve. *Code Complete.* Seattle: Microsoft Press. 1993.

Cool PHP

Chapter 13

Introduction

With a language as powerful and extensible as PHP, it is difficult to categorize all of the cool things that can be done with it. This chapter provides
a look at some of these. The subjects discussed here are either things that I
have needed in the past or questions that are often posed in PHP news-
groups or mailing lists. This chapter cannot possibly cover all of the extensions and features of PHP, but it does cover some that are not specifically
discussed elsewhere in this book.

Sending Non-HTML Files to a Browser

Generally speaking, PHP is used to send HTML files to a Web browser, but
PHP can be used to automate file downloads or provide other types of files
to the browser. For example, you may want to provide a method for your
users to download a section of an online database in a text format such as
comma-separated values (CSV). The following example illustrates how to
enable a user to download a section of a database table. Listing 1 is the
script that gathers the information from the database, formats it, and sends
it to the browser.

Listing 1: Sending a CSV file to a Browser

```php
<?php
    // I renamed db_mysql.inc to db_mysql.php for my environment
    include_once( "db_mysql.php" );
    // create a new DB subclass for gathering the employee data
    class employee_db extends DB_Sql
    {
        var $Host        = "db.server.com";
        var $Database    = "mydb";
        var $User        = "root";
        var $Password    = "";
    }
    $aSQL   = "select * from employees";
    $aDB = new employee_db();
    $aDB->query( $aSQL );
    /* the metadata() method is very dependent on the MySQL
versions of MySQL */
    $aMetaData = $aDB->metadata();
    $aData = "";
    $aNumFields = count( $aMetaData );
```

```
        for ( $nIndex = 0; $nIndex < $aNumFields; $nIndex++ )
        {
            $aData .= "\"" . $aMetaData[$nIndex]["name"] . "\",";
        }
        // trim off the last character of the string (,) and end the
 line (\n)
        $aData = substr( $aData, 0, strlen( $aData ) - 1 ) . "\n";
        while ( $aDB->next_record() )
        {
            $aLine = "";
            for ( $nIndex = 0; $nIndex < $aNumFields; $nIndex++ )
            {
                $aLine .= "\"" . $aDB->f( $nIndex ) . "\",";
            }
            // trim off the last character of the string (,) and end
 the line (\n)
            $aLine = substr( $aLine, 0, strlen( $aLine ) - 1 );
            $aLine .= "\n";
            $aData .= $aLine;
        }
        header( "Content-length: " . strlen( $aData ) );
        header( "Content-type: application/octetstream" );
        header( "Content-disposition: inline;
 filename=\"employees.csv\"" );
        print( $aData );
    ?>
```

The first step in the script is to define a subclass of the PHPLIB DB_Sql class that is used to query the database. Refer to Chapter 6, "Working with Databases," for more information about this. Next, the query is issued and metadata is gathered about the query. The metadata contains the number of fields and the name of each field returned. This is used to construct the first line of the CSV file. Typically, CSV files contain a header row that names the columns, followed by the actual data lines. Each field in a CSV file is enclosed in quotes and separated by commas. Each line is terminated by the newline character.

After the header line is added, the script loops through all of the records and constructs CSV-formatted lines for each. Then three header lines are sent to the browser. The first line represents the length of the content being sent. The next line provides a content or media type of the data. This is important because the browser uses this information to determine how to display the content. If this line were set to text/html, the browser would attempt to display the information as HTML. Because the type is set to application/octetstream, the browser will not try to interpret the data, but rather provide a mechanism for downloading the content to disk. The last line tells the browser that the content will be sent inline with the headers and provides a suggested name for the file. Figure 13.1 shows the dialog box that Internet Explorer displays when this script is executed.

The first two lines of the file are shown in Listing 2. Figure 13.2 shows the file as it appears in Microsoft Excel.

Figure 13.1
The Save As dialog

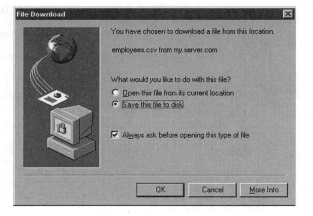

Figure 13.2
The CSV file in Excel

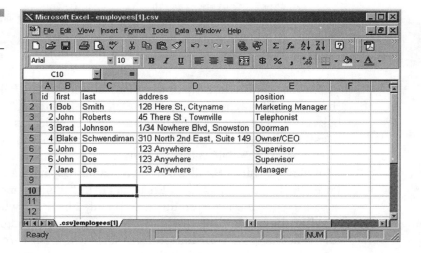

Listing 2: The Raw CSV Output

```
"id","first","last","address","position"
"1","Bob","Smith","128 Here St, Cityname","Marketing Manager"
```

Another common use for sending non-HTML content to the browser is to send image files. For example, you may have an application that stores small images in a database. You can then use PHP to store and retrieve the images and present them. The following listings show how to collect an image from an HTML form, store it in a database, and then display that image in another page. Listing 3 shows the HTML form for uploading the image, and Listing 4 is the script that saves the image information into the database. The MySQL table for storing the images is defined in the following way:

```
CREATE TABLE pictures (
    picture_id int(11) DEFAULT '0' NOT NULL,
    name varchar(30) NOT NULL,
    date datetime DEFAULT '0000-00-00 00:00:00' NOT NULL,
    pic_data mediumblob NOT NULL,
    pic_size int(11) DEFAULT '0' NOT NULL,
    pic_type varchar(30) NOT NULL,
    PRIMARY KEY (picture_id)
);
```

Listing 3: The Image Upload Form

```
<html>
<head>
     <title>Picture Upload</title>
</head>
<body>
    <form action="upload_pic.phtml" method="post"
enctype="multipart/form-data">
        <table>
            <tr>
                <td colspan="2">
                    Please select a picture (jpeg or gif) file
                    to upload and provide a name for the
                    picture.
                </td>
            </tr>
            <tr>
                <td>
                    Picture File:
                </td>
                <td>
                    <input type="file" name="PicFile">
                </td>
            </tr>
            <tr>
                <td>
                    Picture Name:
                </td>
                <td>
                    <input type="text" name="PicName"
maxlength="30">
                </td>
            </tr>
            <tr>
                <td colspan="2">
                    <input type="submit" name="Submit"
value="Submit">
                </td>
            </tr>
```

```
        </table>
    </form>
</body>
</html>
```

Listing 4: Storing an Uploaded Image in a Database

```php
<?php
    include_once( "db_mysql.php" );  // db_mysql.inc renamed
    // create a new DB subclass for saving/retrieving picture data
    class pictures_db extends DB_Sql
    {
        var $Host       = "db.server.com";
        var $Database   = "mydb";
        var $User       = "root";
        var $Password   = "";
    }
    $aErrors = False;
    if ( !empty( $PicFile_name ) ) // no file selected
    {
        if ( ( $PicFile_type == "image/gif" ) ||
              ( $PicFile_type == "image/pjpeg" ) ||
              ( $PicFile_type == "image/jpeg" ) )
        {
            $aFile = fopen( $PicFile, "rb" );
            $aFileContents = addslashes( fread( $aFile, filesize(
$PicFile ) ) );
            fclose( $aFile );
            $aDB = new pictures_db();
            $aSQL = "select ( max( picture_id ) + 1 ) as new_id
from pictures";
            $aDB->query( $aSQL );
            if ( $aDB->next_record() )
            {
                $aNewID = $aDB->f( "new_id" );
            }
            if ( empty( $aNewID ) == True )
            {
                $aNewID = 1;
            }
            $aSQL  = "insert into pictures ( picture_id, name,
date, pic_data, ";
            $aSQL .= "pic_size, pic_type ) values ( $aNewID,
'$PicName', ";
            $aSQL .= "NOW(), '$aFileContents', '$PicFile_size',
'$PicFile_type' )";
            print( $aSQL );
            $aDB->query( $aSQL );
            if ( $aDB->Errno != 0 )
            {
                $aErrors = True;
            }
        }
        else
        {
            $aErrors = True;
        }
```

```
    }
    else
    {
        $aErrors = True;
    }
    if ( $aErrors == False )
    {
        header( "Location: upload_ok.html\n" );
    }
    else
    {
        header( "Location: upload_failed.html\n" );
    }
?>
```

The previous script again uses the PHPLIB database wrapper to manage all the database calls. The script first checks to ensure that the file is of a correct type. Then, the file is read into a single variable and prepared for database use with the **addslashes()** function. Next, a new unique identifier is obtained from the table and the data is stored. At the end of the script, the browser is redirected based on success or failure.

To display the images, the code in Listings 5 and 6 are used. Listing 5 is a simple HTML page that displays a single, hard-coded image. Listing 6 is the actual image display script.

Listing 5: The HTML Page Displaying an Image from a Database

```
<html>
<head>
    <title>Display Picture</title>
</head>
<body>
<img src="show_pic.phtml?ID=1" border="0" alt="">
</body>
</html>
```

Listing 6: The Image Display Script

```
<?php
    include_once( "db_mysql.php" );  // db_mysql.inc renamed
    // create a new DB subclass for saving/retrieving picture data
    class pictures_db extends DB_Sql
    {
        var $Host      = "db.server.com";
        var $Database  = "mydb";
        var $User      = "root";
        var $Password  = "";
    }
    $aDB = new pictures_db();
    $aSQL = "select * from pictures where ( picture_id = $ID )";
    $aDB->query( $aSQL );
```

```
    if ( $aDB->next_record() )
    {
        header( "Content-length: " . $aDB->f( "pic_size" ) );
        header( "Content-type: " . $aDB->f( "pic_type" ) );
        print( $aDB->f( "pic_data" ) );
    }
    else
    {
        // picture with given ID not found, handle error!
        Header( "HTTP/1.0 404 Not Found" );
    }
?>
```

Although it may appear odd to have an <img> tag referencing a PHP script, it makes no difference. The important code is in the PHP script itself where the content-type is set to the correct media type for the image in the database. The script simply selects the correct image from the database and sends the data. If the picture identifier (**$ID**) is not found in the database, the script returns the standard HTTP 404 error code.

Because PHP makes it possible to set any of the HTTP headers, any type of content may be provided using PHP scripts. This flexibility makes developing rich applications simple and straightforward.

Automation Scripts

PHP is not just a Web programming language reliant on a Web server, but it is a full scripting language that can be used for any programming task. Because it is so feature-rich, it can be used to automate tasks that would be difficult in standard shell programming languages or batch files. Additionally, because PHP is available on so many platforms, the same scripts can be used to automate tasks on different platforms.

Using PHP as a standalone scripting tool requires that you build the CGI version of PHP. This is discussed in Chapter 1, "Building and Installing PHP 4." Once you have a CGI binary available, you can run any PHP script from a command line. The following example shows how to use PHP to generate *domain name system* (DNS) zone files for maintaining a large number of zones.

Figure 13.3 shows the data model for a simple DNS management database. The actual implementation of the tables is given in Listing 7.

Listing 7: The DNS Management Database

```
CREATE TABLE Domains (
    domain_id int(11) NOT NULL,
```

Figure 13.3
The DNS
management
database

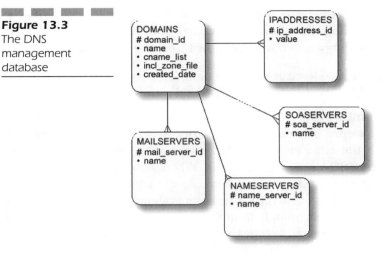

```
    name varchar(250) NOT NULL,
    soa_server_id int(11) DEFAULT '1' NOT NULL,
    cname_list varchar(250) NOT NULL,
    mail_server_id int(11) DEFAULT '1' NOT NULL,
    ip_address_id int(11) DEFAULT '1' NOT NULL,
    incl_zone_file tinyint(4) DEFAULT '1' NOT NULL,
    created_date datetime DEFAULT '0000-00-00 00:00:00' NOT NULL,
    PRIMARY KEY (domain_id),
    KEY name (name),
    UNIQUE name_2 (name),
    KEY created_date (created_date)
);
CREATE TABLE IPAddresses (
    ip_address_id int(11) NOT NULL,
    value varchar(15) NOT NULL,
    PRIMARY KEY (ip_address_id),
    KEY value (value)
);
CREATE TABLE MailServers (
    mail_server_id int(11) NOT NULL,
    name varchar(250) NOT NULL,
    PRIMARY KEY (mail_server_id),
    KEY name (name)
);
CREATE TABLE NameServers (
    name_server_id int(11) NOT NULL,
    name varchar(250) NOT NULL,
    PRIMARY KEY (name_server_id),
    KEY name (name)
);
CREATE TABLE SOAServers (
    soa_server_id int(11) NOT NULL,
    name varchar(250) NOT NULL,
    PRIMARY KEY (soa_server_id),
    KEY name (name)
);
```

The previous database is used to store all the information required to create zone files and the other configuration files for maintaining a DNS server. The following code shows one record from the Domains table:

```
INSERT INTO Domains VALUES( '4', 'intechra.net', '1', 'www,
secure, mail', '1', '1', '1', '2000-08-25 13:29:37');
```

This row contains the DNS information for the *intechra.net* domain. Although this record information isn't particularly useful by itself, when it is joined with the other related tables, information about its IP address, mail server, and SOA server is available. When using all this information and a PHP script to manage it, the process of updating a DNS server is greatly simplified. The following seven listings show the components of the main script. Listings 8 through 13 are the template files used to generate the output files. This example relies on the FastTemplate class discussed in Chapter 12, "Separating HTML from PHP."

Listing 8: The Primary Template for a DNS Zone File (dns_primary.tpl)

```
$TTL 86400
{DOMAIN}. IN SOA      {SOA_SERVER}. {ADMINISTRATOR}. (
              {SERIAL}    ; serial
              10800       ; refresh
              3600        ; retry
              604800      ; expire
              86400       ; default_ttl
              )
{NAMESERVERS}
{DOMAIN}.    IN A    {IPADDRESS}
{CNAME_RECORDS}
{DOMAIN}.    IN MX 10    {MAIL_SERVER}.
{DOMAIN}.    LOC 43 49 57.551 N 111 46 38.071 W 1480.7m
```

Listing 9: The DNS Host Name Template (replaces CNAME_RECORDS in Listing 8) (dns_secondary.tpl)

```
{CNAME} IN      CNAME   {DOMAIN}.{CRLF}
```

Listing 10: The DNS Name Server Template (replaces NAMESERVERS in Listing 8) (dns_nservers.tpl)

```
{DOMAIN}.    IN NS   {NAMESERVER}.{CRLF}
```

Listing 11: The Primary Template for the named.conf File (named_primary.tpl)

```
acl trustedslaves { ns1.nameserver.com;ns2.nameserver.com; };
options {
     directory "/var/named";
     recursion yes;
     fetch-glue no;
     allow-query { any; };
};
zone "." { type hint; file "cache.db"; };
{ZONES}
```

Listing 12: The Secondary Template for the named.conf File (replaces ZONES in Listing 11) (named_secondary.tpl)

```
zone "{DOMAIN}" { type master; file "{DOMAIN_FILE}"; notify yes;
allow-transfer { trustedslaves; }; };
```

Listing 13: The Template for the DNS Slave File (named_slaves.tpl)

```
zone "{DOMAIN}" { type slave; file "{DOMAIN_FILE}"; masters {
master.com; }; };
```

The previous templates provide the framework for creating all the configuration files needed for use with a BIND name server. The first three generate the individual zone files that may have a variable number of name servers and host name definitions. The other templates are used to create the **named.conf** file and the slave file for use on a slave name server.

The script in Listing 14 is used to query the database for the DNS information and generate all the DNS configuration files.

Listing 14: The DNS Script

```php
<?php
    include( "./class.FastTemplate.php" );
    include( "./db_mysql.php" );  // db_mysql.inc renamed
    // create the application database class
    class genapps_db extends DB_Sql
    {
        var $Host      = "db.server.com";
        var $Database  = "GenApps";
        var $User      = "root";
        var $Password  = "pwd";
    }
    // path for the output files
    $aPath = "./dns_output";
```

```
$tpl    = new FastTemplate( "." );
$tpl->define( array( named_main      => "named_primary.tpl",
                     named_zones     => "named_secondary.tpl",
                     named_slaves    => "named_slaves.tpl",
                     dns_main        => "dns_primary.tpl",
                     dns_cnames      => "dns_secondary.tpl",
                     dns_nservers    => "dns_nservers.tpl" ) );
// get a list of all known nameservers and keep it for later
$aNSDB = new genapps_db();
$aSQL  = "select * from NameServers";
$aNSDB->query( $aSQL );
// select all of the zone information
$aDB   = new genapps_db();
$aSQL  = "select A.name, A.cname_list, A.incl_zone_file, B.name
as soa_server, C.name as ";
$aSQL .= "mail_server, D.value as ip_address from Domains A,
SOAServers B, ";
$aSQL .= "MailServers C, IPAddresses D where ( A.soa_server_id
= B.soa_server_id ) ";
$aSQL .= "and ( A.mail_server_id = C.mail_server_id ) and ";
$aSQL .= "( A.ip_address_id = D.ip_address_id )";
$aDB->query( $aSQL );
while ( $aDB->next_record() )
{
    $aDomainName    = strtolower( $aDB->f( "name" ) );
    $aCNames        = $aDB->f( "cname_list" );
    $aSoaServer     = $aDB->f( "soa_server" );
    $aMailServer    = $aDB->f( "mail_server" );
    $aIPAddress     = $aDB->f( "ip_address" );
    $aInclZoneFile  = $aDB->f( "incl_zone_file" );
    $tpl->assign( array( DOMAIN          => $aDomainName,
                         ADMINISTRATOR   => "admin." .
$aSoaServer,
                         SERIAL          => date( "Ymd" ) .
"00",
                         MAIL_SERVER     => $aMailServer,
                         SOA_SERVER      => $aSoaServer,
                         IPADDRESS       => $aIPAddress,
                         CRLF            => "\n" ) );
    /* the host names (CNAME records) are stored in a comma-
       separated list in the database.  expand the list and
       create a line for each entry */
    $tpl->clear( CNAME_RECORDS );
    $aCNameList     = explode( ",", $aCNames );
    foreach( $aCNameList as $aCName )
    {
        $aCName = trim( $aCName );
        $tpl->assign( array( CNAME => $aCName ) );
        $tpl->parse( CNAME_RECORDS, ".dns_cnames" );
    }
    // add the name servers lines to the zone file
    $tpl->clear( NAMESERVERS );
    $aNSDB->seek( 0 );
    while ( $aNSDB->next_record() )
    {
        $tpl->assign( array( NAMESERVER => $aNSDB->f( "name" )
) );
        $tpl->parse( NAMESERVERS, ".dns_nservers" );
    }
```

```
            $aDomainFile = $aDomainName . ".db";
            /*  the zone file is only written if the 'incl_zone_file'
                field in the database is set to '1'
            */
            if ( $aInclZoneFile == "1" )
            {
                $tpl->parse( DNS_MAIN, "dns_main" );
                $aFile = fopen( "$aPath/$aDomainFile", "w" );
                fwrite( $aFile, $tpl->fetch( DNS_MAIN ) );
                fclose( $aFile );
                print( "Domain file '$aDomainFile' created\n" );
            }
            /* add the current domain name to the master and slave
              configuration files */
            $tpl->assign( array( DOMAIN_FILE => $aDomainFile ) );
            $tpl->parse( ZONES, '.named_zones' );
            $tpl->parse( SLAVES, '.named_slaves' );
        }
        $tpl->parse( NAMED_CONF, 'named_main' );
        $aFile = fopen( "$aPath/named.conf", "w" );
        fwrite( $aFile, $tpl->fetch( NAMED_CONF ) );
        fclose( $aFile );
        print( "Master file 'named.conf' created\n" );
        $aFile = fopen( "$aPath/named.slave", "w" );
        fwrite( $aFile, $tpl->fetch( SLAVES ) );
        fclose( $aFile );
        print( "Domain file 'named.slave' created\n" );
?>
```

The previous script opens loops through each entry in the Domains table and creates a zone file. The zone file is constructed by using the templates in Listings 8, 9, and 10. A sample zone file is shown in Figure 13.4.

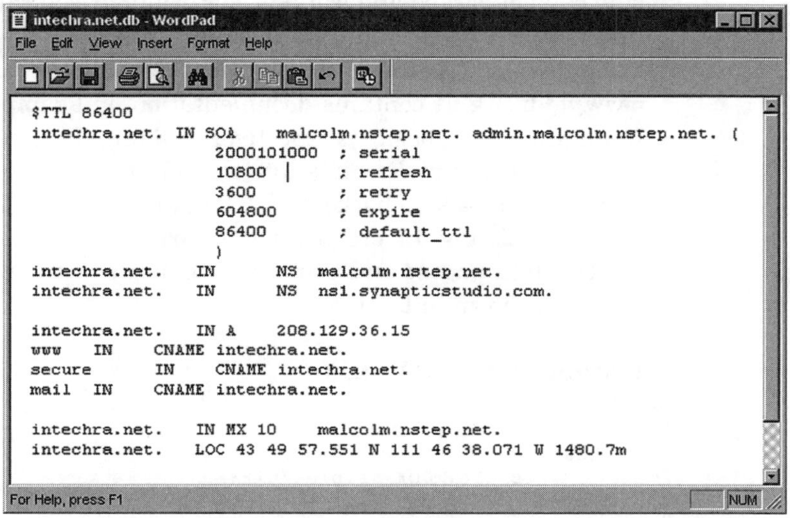


```
$TTL 86400
intechra.net. IN SOA     malcolm.nstep.net. admin.malcolm.nstep.net. (
                   2000101000  ; serial
                   10800       ; refresh
                   3600        ; retry
                   604800      ; expire
                   86400       ; default_ttl
                   )
intechra.net.   IN      NS  malcolm.nstep.net.
intechra.net.   IN      NS  ns1.synapticstudio.com.

intechra.net.   IN A    208.129.36.15
www    IN     CNAME intechra.net.
secure        IN     CNAME intechra.net.
mail   IN     CNAME intechra.net.

intechra.net.   IN MX 10    malcolm.nstep.net.
intechra.net.   LOC 43 49 57.551 N 111 46 38.071 W 1480.7m
```

Figure 13.4
Sample DNS zone file

In addition, the properly formatted **named.conf** file is created simultaneously. To write the files, the FastTemplate **fetch()** method is used to retrieve the stored text.

To run this script on either Windows or *nix, simply use the **php create_dns.php** command. The progress of the script is printed to standard output and the files are created in the directory specified at the top of the script.

Because PHP is a full scripting language, powerful tools can be written to automate complex tasks. Used in conjunction with automated scheduling services such as **cron**, PHP can be used to perform a multitude of complex tasks. Creating template-based configuration files for any program or service is easily accomplished using PHP along with the FastTemplate package. Because PHP is so extensible, it can easily be used to script tasks such as mass mailings, database backups and updates, network and application monitoring, and much more.

WDDX

The *Web Distributed Data Exchange* (WDDX) is a free, open XML-based technology that enables Web applications created with any platform to easily exchange data with one another over the Web. WDDX support can be built into PHP by specifying the **--enable-wddx** configuration option. The goal of WDDX is to provide a consistent data interface for sharing content between networked applications. For example, you can use WDDX to share information in your database with partners.

The WDDX *software development kit* (SDK) can be obtained from www.wddx.org. It contains documentation and samples for using WDDX. From the most basic perspective, building PHP with WDDX support enables you to *serialize* data into the WDDX packet format and *deserialize* WDDX data packets back into PHP data structures. To illustrate, the PHP script in Listing 15 creates some variables and serializes them into a WDDX data packet and prints the contents of the packet. The serialized output is shown in Listing 16.

Listing 15: Using WDDX

```
<html>
<head>
    <title>WDDX Sample</title>
</head>
```

```
<body>
<?php
    $aFirstName  = "Arian";
    $aAge        = 25;
    $aArray      = array( "red", "green", "blue" );
    $aPacketID   = wddx_packet_start( "products" );
    wddx_add_vars( $aPacketID, "aFirstName" );
    wddx_add_vars( $aPacketID, "aAge" );
    wddx_add_vars( $aPacketID, "aArray" );
    $aWDDXPacket = wddx_packet_end( $aPacketID );
    print( $aWDDXPacket );
?>
</body>
</html>
```

Listing 16: WDDX Output

```
<wddxPacket
version='1.0'><header><comment>products</comment></header><data><st
ruct><var name='aFirstName'><string>Arian</string></var><var
name='aAge'><number>25</number></var><var name='aArray'><array
length='3'><string>red</string><string>green</string><string>blue</
string></array></var></struct></data></wddxPacket>
```

In the previous example, the **wddx_packet_start()** function creates a new WDDX packet. Then three PHP variables are added to the packet and it is closed. The WDDX data packet is shown in Listing 16 and contains all the information needed to restore the variables using the **wddx_deserialize()** function.

To show how WDDX can be used in a multiple language scenario, the following example sends a WDDX data packet to a Web page where it is used by JavaScript. The WDDX data represents product information including product name, price, and weight. When the product name is selected from a list, its price and weight are updated in the browser using read-only form elements. This example demonstrates how data sets can be used on the client with JavaScript and either form elements or DHTML to provide quick access to data. Listing 17 shows the HTML template, and Listing 18 shows the PHP script that uses it.

Listing 17: Using WDDX to Manipulate Client-Side Data

```
<html>
<head>
    <title>{TITLE}</title>
    <link rel="STYLESHEET" type="text/css" href="css2.css">
    <!--- Include Core WDDX / Javascript support --->
    <SCRIPT SRC="wddx.js" LANGUAGE="JavaScript"></SCRIPT>
    <!--- Include WddxDeserializer object support --->
    <SCRIPT SRC="wddxDes.js" LANGUAGE="JavaScript"></SCRIPT>
    <script language="JavaScript">
```

```
<!--
    function show_props(obj, obj_name)
    {
        var result = "";
        for (var i in obj)
        {
            result += obj_name + "." + i + " = " + obj[i] +
"\n";
        }
        return result;
    }
    function SetupProductsList()
    {
        MyDeser   = new WddxDeserializer;
        aProducts = MyDeser.deserialize( '{PRODUCTS_WDDX}' );
    }
    function Initialize()
    {
        SetupProductsList();
        aNumProds = aProducts.ARECORDS.length;
        // clear the products list

        // add products to the list
        for ( var nIndex = 0; nIndex < aNumProds; nIndex++ )
        {
            aValue = aProducts.ARECORDS[nIndex].PRODUCT_ID;
            aName  = aProducts.ARECORDS[nIndex].DESCRIPTION;
            // create a new option
            NewOpt = new Option( aName, aValue, false, true );
            // Add the new object to the SELECT list
            document.MainForm.Product_List.options[nIndex] =
NewOpt;
        }
        SetInfo();
    }
    function SetInfo()
    {
        // set price and weight based on selected product
        var RowNum =
document.MainForm.Product_List.selectedIndex;
        if ( RowNum > -1 )
        {
            document.MainForm.Price.value =
aProducts.ARECORDS[RowNum].PRICE;
            document.MainForm.Weight.value =
aProducts.ARECORDS[RowNum].WEIGHT;
        }
    }
    //-->
    </script>
</head>
<body onload="Initialize()">
<form action="" name="MainForm" id="MainForm">
    <table>
        <tr>
            <td colspan="3">
                Select a product from the list below to view
                its price and weight.
```

```
                    </td>
                </tr>
                <tr>
                    <td colspan="3">
                         
                    </td>
                </tr>
                <tr>
                    <th>
                        Product
                    </th>
                    <th>
                        Price
                    </th>
                    <th>
                        Weight (lbs)
                    </th>
                </tr>
                <tr>
                    <td>
                        <select name="Product_List" size="1"
onChange="SetInfo();">
                        <option></option>
                        <option></option>
                        </select>
                    </td>
                    <td>
                        <input type="text" name="Price" readonly>
                    </td>
                    <td>
                        <input type="text" name="Weight" readonly>
                    </td>
                </tr>
        </table>
    </form>
    </body>
    </html>
```

The previous HTML template relies heavily on JavaScript for its implementation. The first function **show_props()** is simply a testing function for
displaying the properties of a given object. The **SetupProductsList()** function is used to deserialize the products data provided from the database via
PHP. It relies on the **WddxDeserializer** object available in the WDDX
SDK available from www.wddx.org. When the WDDX data packet is deserialized, the JavaScript object, **aProducts**, contains all the production
information.

The **Initialize()** function initializes the page and is therefore called
automatically in the page's **onLoad** event. It in turn calls the **SetupProd-
uctsList()** function and then adds the product names and identifiers to the
product drop-down list. The **SetInfo()** function is called whenever the
selected item in the product list is changed by the user. When this happens,
the values displayed in the price and yield boxes are updated.

Listing 18: Setting up the WDDX Data Set

```php
<?php
    include( "class.FastTemplate.php" );
    include( "db_mysql.inc" );
    error_reporting( E_ALL & ~E_NOTICE );
    class products_db extends DB_Sql
    {
        var $Host       = "db.server.com";
        var $Database   = "mydb";
        var $User       = "root";
        var $Password   = "";
    }
    $aTemplate = new FastTemplate( "." );
    $aTemplate->define( array( "base"      => "products_wddx.tpl" )
);
    $aTemplate->assign( array( "TITLE"      => "Products Page" ) );
    $aPacketID = wddx_packet_start( "products" );
    $aRecords = array();
    $nIndex    = 0;
    $aDB = new products_db;
    $aDB->query( "select * from Products" );
    while( $aDB->next_record() )
    {
        $aRecord = $aDB->Record;
        foreach( $aRecord as $aName => $aValue )
        {
            if ( !is_numeric( $aName ) )
            {
                $aRecords[$nIndex][$aName] = $aValue;
            }
        }
        $nIndex++;
    }
    wddx_add_vars( $aPacketID, "aRecords" );
    $aWDDXPacket = wddx_packet_end( $aPacketID );
    $aTemplate->assign( array( "PRODUCTS_WDDX"     => addslashes(
$aWDDXPacket ) ) );
    $aTemplate->parse( "BASE", "base" );
    $aTemplate->FastPrint( "BASE" );
?>
```

The main PHP script uses the FastTemplate class to build the full HTML page. The main work of the script is to read the contents of the **Products** table and create a WDDX packet containing the relevant information. This is done by looping through the available records and adding the data to a new array, **$aRecords**. This array is a two-dimensional array with the first index being numeric representing the row number. The second dimension is an associative array with the name of the column and its value.

As a note on this code, the line that calls the **is_numeric()** function is used to remove redundant information returned by the **mysql_fetch_array()** function that is called internally. The **mysql_fetch_array()** function returns a row from a recordset in the form of an array. In addition to storing the data in the numeric indices of the result array, it also stores the data in associative indices, using the field names as keys. The previous check removes the numerically indexed data from the array, leaving only the associative array information.

Figure 13.5 shows the page displayed in a browser. Whenever a new product is selected, the price and weight are updated automatically.

Although WDDX can be used as shown in the previous example to provide client-side data, it has many other significant uses. For server-to-server data transfers, WDDX can provide syndicated content and other data that can be shared easily between platforms and development tools. If you have plans to syndicate your application's content, WDDX provides the tools to quickly deliver the content in a platform and language neutral fashion.

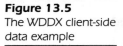

Network Monitoring

Because PHP supports sockets and network protocols intrinsically, developing a network monitoring utility in PHP is straightforward. The following example uses pipes and sockets to perform some simple network monitoring functions. Much more could be done including checking the status of a name server, mail server, and so on. This example serves as a framework for building more functionality.

Listing 19 contains three functions, **phpPing()**, **phpTrace()**, and **php PageCheck()**. The first two rely on system commands to perform a ping

Figure 13.5
The WDDX client-side data example

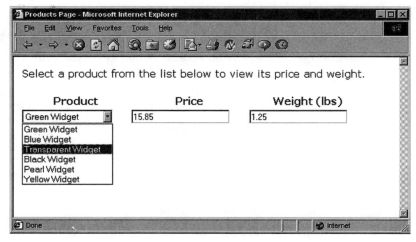

and traceroute, respectively. The last uses sockets to request an HTTP HEAD for a page to check Web server and page availability.

Listing 19: The Network Functions

```php
<?php
    $aPingCmd  = '/bin/ping -c 4';            // *nix
    $aTraceCmd = '/usr/sbin/traceroute -n';   // *nix
    // returns the average ping time
    function phpPing( $aAddress )
    {
        global $aPingCmd;
        $aTotalTime = 0.0;
        $aPingCount = 0;
        if ( $aFile = popen( "$aPingCmd $aAddress", "r" ) )
        {
            // now read all of the data from the pipe
            while ( !feof( $aFile ) )
            {
                $aLine = fgets ( $aFile, 1024 );
                // locate the time information
                $aPos  = strpos( $aLine, "time=" );
                if ( $aPos > 0 )
                {
                    // use PHP's variable coersion to convert the
time to a number
                    $aTime = substr( $aLine, $aPos + 5 ) * 1.0;
                    $aTotalTime += $aTime;
                    $aPingCount++;
                }
            }
            pclose( $aFile );
        }
        return $aTotalTime / $aPingCount;
    }
    function phpTrace( $aAddress )
    {
        global $aTraceCmd;
        $aTraceResults = "";
        if ( $aFile = popen( "$aTraceCmd $aAddress", "r" ) )
        {
            // now read all of the data from the pipe
            while ( !feof( $aFile ) )
            {
                $aLine = fgets ( $aFile, 1024 );
                $aTraceResults .= $aLine . "<br>";
            }
            pclose( $aFile );
        }
        return $aTraceResults;
    }
    function phpPageCheck( $aWebPage )
    {
        $aURL = parse_url( $aWebPage );
        $aResult = False;
        if ( $aURL["scheme"] == "http" )
```

```
                    {
                        // request header information for a web page
                        $aRequest  = "HEAD {$aURL['path']} HTTP/1.0\r\n\r\n";
                        $aSocket = fsockopen( $aURL["host"], 80 );
                        if ( $aSocket )
                        {
                            fputs( $aSocket, $aRequest );
                            while( !feof( $aSocket ) )
                            {
                                $aLine = fgets( $aSocket, 1024 );
                                // find the HTTP response line
                                if ( substr( $aLine, 0, 4 ) == "HTTP" )
                                {
                                    $aArray = explode( " ", $aLine );
                                    // if the HTTP response code >= 200 and <
300, ok!
                                    if ( ( $aArray[1] >= 200 ) && ( $aArray[1]
< 300 ) )
                                    {
                                        $aResult = True;
                                    }
                                }
                            }
                        }
                    }
                    return $aResult;
            }
        ?>
```

The previous functions can be used by an automation script to record periodic information to a database or file, or they can be used directly in a Web page. The script in Listing 20 shows how to use the previous functions, and the output is shown in Figure 13.6.

Listing 20: Using the Network Functions

```
<?php
    include( "./net_funcs.php" );
?>
<html>
<head>
    <title>Network Tools Test</title>
</head>
<body>
<?php
    print( "phpPing: " . phpPing ( 'www.php.net' ) . "<br><br>" );
    print( "phpTrace: <ul>" . phptrace ( 'www.php.net' ) .
"</ul><br>" );
    print( "phpPageCheck: " );
    print( phpPageCheck( 'http://www.php.net/' ) ? "OK" : "NOT OK"
);
    print( "<br>" );
?>
</body>
</html>
```

Figure 13.6
The network test
output

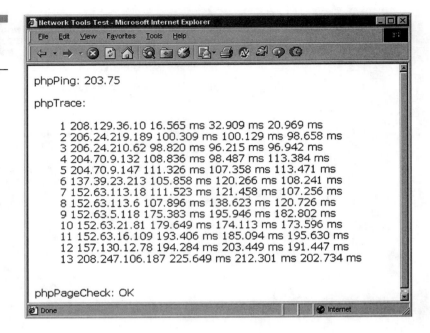

```
phpPing: 203.75

phpTrace:

    1 208.129.36.10 16.565 ms 32.909 ms 20.969 ms
    2 206.24.219.189 100.309 ms 100.129 ms 98.658 ms
    3 206.24.210.62 98.820 ms 96.215 ms 96.942 ms
    4 204.70.9.132 108.836 ms 98.487 ms 113.384 ms
    5 204.70.9.147 111.326 ms 107.358 ms 113.471 ms
    6 137.39.23.213 105.858 ms 120.266 ms 108.241 ms
    7 152.63.113.18 111.523 ms 121.458 ms 107.256 ms
    8 152.63.113.6 107.896 ms 138.623 ms 120.726 ms
    9 152.63.5.118 175.383 ms 195.946 ms 182.802 ms
   10 152.63.21.81 179.649 ms 174.113 ms 173.596 ms
   11 152.63.16.109 193.406 ms 185.094 ms 195.630 ms
   12 157.130.12.78 194.284 ms 203.449 ms 191.447 ms
   13 208.247.106.187 225.649 ms 212.301 ms 202.734 ms

phpPageCheck: OK
```

This example shows how easy it is to use PHP as a language for performing basic network monitoring. PHP supports additional network protocols such as IMAP, SNMP, NNTP, and POP3 that can be used to extend the previous examples to check the availability of all kinds of network servers and components.

Summary

This chapter discussed a variety of subjects to show the power and flexibility of PHP. Other extensions exist for tasks such as image file creation, XML parsing, PDF file creation, and more. Because PHP is so inherently extensible and powered by a large group of open-source developers, expect to see functionality and flexibility continually expanding.

Template-Based Web Site

Introduction

In Chapter 12, "Separating HTML from PHP," using template systems was introduced. This chapter focuses on presenting a full discussion of using Web templates. Using templates in your application design does more than provide a facility for separating application code from design. Templates can be used to provide co-branding facilities, a personalized user experience, browser independence, and internationalization capabilities. The examples in this chapter use the FastTemplate class from http://www.thewebmasters.net/. Other template systems exist, but this implementation is powerful, flexible, and easy to learn.

Templates Basics

Building Web applications that take advantage of a template system requires more up-front design than building the same applications without templates. However, the benefits of using a well-designed template system pay for the effort very quickly. Figure 14.1 shows how a typical Web page may be deconstructed into several separate template files.

Figure 14.1
Web pages consist of several template files

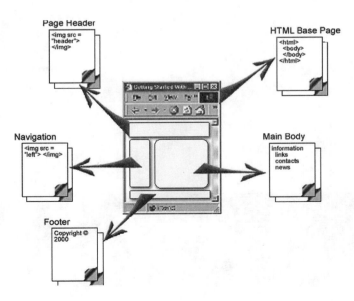

In Figure 14.1, the page displayed in the browser consists of one or more template files that provide HTML for the different logical sections of the page. On some Web sites, only one template may be available for all pages on the site. In others, each page may be constructed from several template files. In order to design a site using templates, the needs of the site and the elements of each page on the site must be assessed.

As an example, consider a site providing an online merchandise catalog. The catalog is divided into product categories such as apparel, gifts, toys, and so on. Each page of the catalog must display common navigation elements and an overall site logo. When shopping within a specific product category, the site displays category-specific images and information. Each product page also provides product-specific information such as cost, weight, available colors, and so on. To design a template-based system for this site, the following templates are defined:

1. **merch_base.tpl**: The base file that includes general layout HTML

2. **merch_header.tpl**: The main header common across all pages in the site

3. **merch_catXXX_header.tpl**: The category-specific header files for each category (XXX replaced by category name)

4. **merch_navi.tpl**: The navigation for the catalog pages

5. **merch_body.tpl**: The body for each page

6. **merch_footer.tpl:** The footer information for each page

The actual HTML file for each of the previous template pages is shown in this section to illustrate how these files are actually created. Listings 1 through 6 represent the files mentioned previously. Listing 3 is the **merch_catapparel_header.tpl** file for the *apparel* product category. Other category files are not shown because they are essentially the same.

Listing 1: merch_base.tpl

```
<html>
<head>
    <title>{TITLE}</title>
</head>
<body bgcolor="White">
    <table width="630" border="0" cellspacing="0" cellpadding="0"
align="center">
        <tr>
            <td colspan="2">{PAGE_HEADER}</td>
        </tr>
        <tr>
            <td colspan="2" align="center">{CAT_HEADER}</td>
        </tr>
```

```
        <tr>
            <td valign="top">{LEFT_NAVI}</td>
            <td valign="top">
                {BODY}
            </td>
        </tr>
        <tr>
            <td colspan="2">
                {PAGE_FOOTER}
            </td>
        </tr>
    </table>
</body>
</html>
```

Listing 2: merch_header.tpl

```
<img src="merch_layout_r1_c1.gif" width="630" height="61" border="0">
```

Listing 3: merch_catapparel_header.tpl

```
<img name="merch_layout_r2_c1" src="merch_layout_r2_c1.gif" width="630"
    height="37" border="0"><br>
    <div align="center"><p>{CATEGORY_SPECIALS}</p></div>
```

Listing 4: merch_navi.tpl

```
<img src="merch_layout_r3_c1.gif" width="104" height="382" border="0"
    usemap="#merch_layout_r3_c1">
    <map name="merch_layout_r3_c1">
    <area shape="rect" coords="5,180,97,221" href="{HREF_COMPANY_INFO}"
    >
    <area shape="rect" coords="7,143,86,166" href="{HREF_CONTACT}" >
    <area shape="rect" coords="12,90,84,132" href="{HREF_CART}" >
    <area shape="rect" coords="18,56,73,80" href="{HREF_HOME}" >
    </map>
```

Listing 5: merch_body.tpl

```
<p>
         
    </p>
    <h3>
        {PRODUCT_NAME}
    </h3>
    <p>
        {PRODUCT_DESCRIPTION}
    </p>
    <p>
        {PRODUCT_PRICE}
    </p>
```

Listing 6: merch_footer.tpl

```
<hr>
<p>
    Copyright &copy {COPYRIGHT_YEARS} by Intechra LLC. All rights
reserved.
</p>
```

The previous files show how little it takes to develop a fairly sophisticated template-based Web application. Some of the files, such as the main header simply contain an image. Others, like the navigation template, contain both the navigation image and the client-side image map for implementing the navigation. Notice that the navigation template does not contain actual URLs, but only template variables. This enables the application to provide dynamic information in the URL itself such as a session identifier. The PHP script in Listing 7 shows how to bring these template files together.

Listing 7: Putting the above templates together

```php
<?php
    include( "class.FastTemplate.php" );
    // assume we know the merchandise category is apparel
    $aCategoryHeader = 'merch_catapparel_header.tpl';
    $aTPL = new FastTemplate( "." );
    $aTPL->define( array( 'base'       => 'merch_base.tpl',
                          'header'     => 'merch_header.tpl',
                          'navi'       => 'merch_navi.tplv',
                          'footer'     => 'merch_footer.tpl',
                          'cat_header' => $aCategoryHeader,
                          'body'       => 'merch_body.tpl'
                  ) );
    $aTPL->assign( array( 'TITLE'               => 'Merchandise
Catalog: Apparel',
                          'CATEGORY_SPECIALS'   => 'Intechra T-
Shirts on Sale!',
                          'PRODUCT_NAME'        => 'Intechra T-
Shirt',
                          'PRODUCT_DESCRIPTION' => 'A really keen
t-shirt with the Intechra LLC logo!',
                          'PRODUCT_PRICE'       => '$14.95',
                          'COPYRIGHT_YEARS'     => '2000',
                          'HREF_HOME'           => 'index.phtml',
                          'HREF_CART'           => 'cart.phtml',
                          'HREF_CONTACT'        => 'contact.phtml',
                          'HREF_COMPANY_INFO'   => 'company.phtml'
                          ) );
    $aTPL->parse( 'PAGE_HEADER', 'header' );
    $aTPL->parse( 'CAT_HEADER',  'cat_header' );
    $aTPL->parse( 'LEFT_NAVI',   'navi' );
    $aTPL->parse( 'BODY',        'body' );
    $aTPL->parse( 'PAGE_FOOTER', 'footer' );
    $aTPL->parse( 'BASE',        'base' );
    $aTPL->FastPrint( 'BASE' );
```

```
?>
```

The previous script uses the FastTemplate class to parse and merge all of the template files for the merchandise catalog. This example hard codes all of the values to simplify this discussion. In a real application, information about which product category and product to display would be provided through forms or other dynamic methods. This script simply assigns values to each of the variables that are needed for each of the template pages.

To understand how FastTemplate parses pages, note that some Fast-Template variables are set specifically using the **assign()** method. For example, the **COPYRIGHT_YEARS** variable used in the **merch_footer.tpl** template is set to the value 2000 using the **assign()** method. Additionally, some FastTemplate variables are set using the **parse()** method. For example, the **PAGE_HEADER** variable is set by parsing the page named 'header.' This makes the value of **PAGE_HEADER** available when needed to parse the **merch_base.tpl** file, named 'base' in this example. Remember that when you are nesting template files, you must assign all of the variables required for a template before parsing that template. Also, you must parse templates in the right order. For example, if you were to parse the 'base' page first, most of the required variables (such as **PAGE_HEADER** and **BODY**) would not be available.

The power of using templates is the ability it provides to make sweeping design changes to a Web site. Figure 14.2 shows how the page generated in Listing 6 looks. By changing the 'base' template file from that shown in Listing 1 to the one shown in Listing 8, the site looks entirely different. The effect of changing the 'base' template file is shown in Figure 14.3.

Listing 8: The New 'base' Template File

```html
<html>
<head>
     <title>{TITLE}</title>
    <link rel="STYLESHEET" type="text/css" href="new_base.css">
</head>
<body bgcolor="White">
    <table width="630" border="0" cellspacing="0" cellpadding="0"
align="center">
        <tr>
            <td colspan="2">{PAGE_HEADER}</td>
        </tr>
        <tr>
            <td colspan="2" align="center">{CAT_HEADER}</td>
        </tr>
        <tr>
```

Figure 14.2
The page generated
by Listing 6

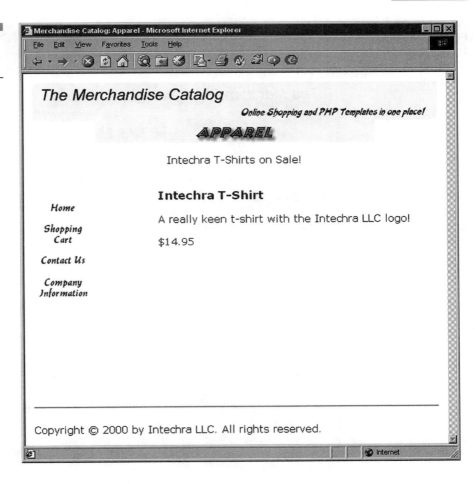

```
        <td width="526" valign="top">
            {BODY}
        </td>
        <td valign="top">{LEFT_NAVI}</td>
    </tr>
    <tr>
        <td colspan="2">
            {PAGE_FOOTER}
        </td>
    </tr>
    </table>
</body>
</html>
```

The power of using a template system cannot be overstated. With the

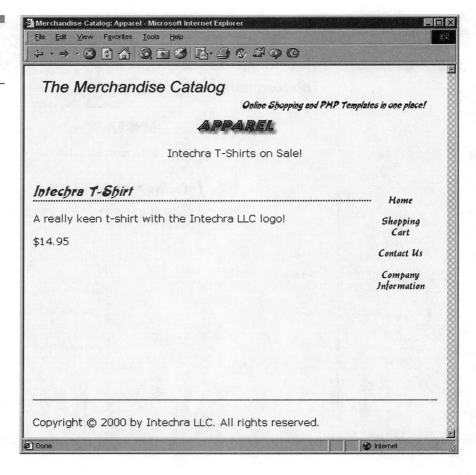

change of 'base' template files shown previously, the look and feel of the Web application were changed significantly, but the effect on the PHP code was precisely nothing. This flexibility enables designers to create and maintain rich application interfaces while application coders simultaneously develop and maintain the business logic. Obviously, some required interaction occurs between the coders and designers, but once a set of defined template file names and template variables is established, the work of either group can move forward in parallel. Additionally, using templates enables the coding team to begin development using a set of prototype interface files while the designers fine-tune their templates.

In thez previous example, one significant change to the 'base' template is the inclusion of a *Cascading Style Sheet* (CSS) file. CSS is a valuable addition to any Web development effort as it is the ultimate *template* system for HTML. Using CSS, the attributes of all HTML elements can be changed. For example, using CSS, the <h3> tag can be defined to have a very particular look in the context of your site. Figures 14.4 and 14.5 show screenshots of a commercial CSS editor called TopStyle by Bradbury Software, LLC (http://www.bradsoft.com/). The editor simplifies the process of creating CSS files and provides an inline display of the styles that are updated as changes are made.

Using CSS in conjunction with a template-based system maximizes your ability to change the look of a site while minimizing the impact to code development. In fact, CSS files can even be applied dynamically as a variable in the template. Although this may not be optimal for all types of sites, it does provide another level of configurability to the display of your Web applications.

The previous examples provide a basic framework for developing a template based Web application. However, no examples of providing repeating elements have been given. For example, you may need to provide a table containing all of the products or a list of all the categories in your database.

Figure 14.4
A style sheet showing how the <body>, <td> and <h3> tags can be modified

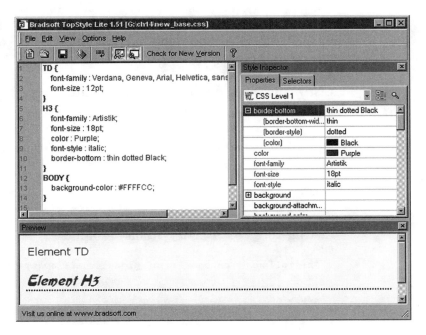

Figure 14.5

Another style sheet
showing how the
<body>, <td>, and
<h3> tags can be
modified

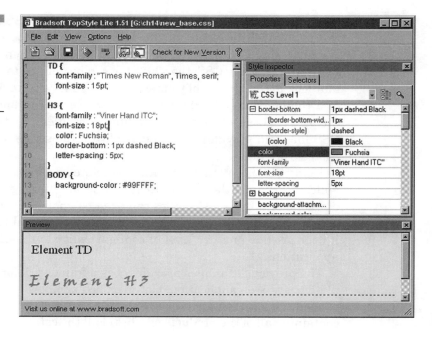

The following example shows how to include repeating elements using the
FastTemplate class. Listing 9 is the base template file. Listing 10 contains
the 'items' template and Listing 11 is the template for each individual item.
Listing 12 is the script that puts it all together.

Listing 9: The Category 'base' Template

```
<html>
<head>
    <title>{TITLE}</title>
</head>
<body>
   {ITEMS}
</body>
</html>
```

Listing 10: The Category 'items' Template

```
The following categories of products are available:
<ul>
    {ITEM_LIST}
</ul>
```

Listing 11: The Category Template for a Single Category Item

```
<li><a
href="show_category.phtml?cat_id={CAT_ID}">{CAT_NAME}</a></li>
```

Listing 12: The Script to Generate the Category List Page

```php
<?php
    include( "class.FastTemplate.php" );

    $aTPL = new FastTemplate( "." );
    $aTPL->define( array( 'base'  => 'cat_base.tpl',
                          'items' => 'cat_items.tpl',
                          'item'  => 'cat_item.tpl' ) );

    $aCategories = array( "apparel", "gifts", "toys", "books" );

    foreach( $aCategories as $aID => $aName )
    {
        $aTPL->assign( array( 'CAT_ID'   => $aID,
                              'CAT_NAME' => $aName ) );

        // parse the item template and append it to the
        // ITEM_LIST template variable
        $aTPL->parse( 'ITEM_LIST', '.item' );
    }

    $aTPL->assign( array( 'TITLE'  => 'Category List' ) );
    $aTPL->parse( 'ITEMS', 'items' );
    $aTPL->parse( 'BASE', 'base' );
    $aTPL->FastPrint( 'BASE' );
?>
```

The previous code uses a hard-coded array of categories to generate the category list page. The output is shown in Figure 14.6. Again, suppose that the design department decides to change the display format from a bulleted

Figure 14.6
The category list

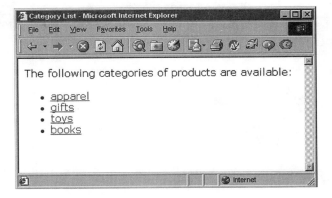

list to a table. The changes are localized to the 'items' and 'item' files. Using this example, the templates need to be changed to those shown in Listings 13 and 14, respectively. The effect is shown in Figure 14.7.

Listing 13: The New 'items' Template

```
The following categories of products are available:
<br><br>
<table border="1">
    {ITEM_LIST}
</table>
```

Listing 14: The New 'item' Template

```
<tr>
    <td>
        Category #{CAT_ID}
    </td>
    <td>
        <a
href="show_category.phtml?cat_id={CAT_ID}">{CAT_NAME}</a>
    </td>
</tr>
```

The previous examples show the basic steps to generate lists of repeating elements using FastTemplate. Another mechanism is available in FastTemplate to eliminate the additional file required to provide the template for the individual elements. To do this requires changes to the 'items' template file and the main PHP script. Listings 15 and 16 show the changes. The output of using this mechanism is exactly the same as shown in Figure 14.7.

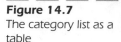

Figure 14.7
The category list as a table

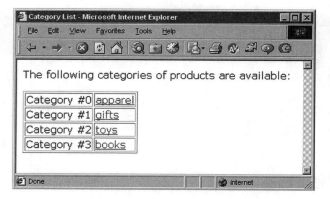

Listing 15: The New 'items' Template Using Dynamic Blocks

```
The following categories of products are available:
<br><br>
<table border="1">
    <!-- BEGIN DYNAMIC BLOCK: item -->
    <tr>
        <td>
            Category #{CAT_ID}
        </td>
        <td>
            <a
href="show_category.phtml?cat_id={CAT_ID}">{CAT_NAME}</a>
        </td>
    </tr>
    <!-- END DYNAMIC BLOCK: item -->
</table>
```

This template defines within itself a sub-template or dynamic block named 'item.' This is essentially the same as creating a separate file to contain the 'item' template. The advantage of this syntax is maintaining the flow of the template file. Also, the total number of files required for using this syntax is reduced. Using this format does require some changes to the usage of the FastTemplate class, as shown in Listing 16.

Listing 16: The New PHP Script

```php
<?php
    include( "class.FastTemplate.php" );

    $aTPL = new FastTemplate( "." );
    $aTPL->define( array( 'base'  => 'cat_base.tpl',
                          'items' => 'cat_items_dyn.tpl') );

    $aTPL->define_dynamic( 'item', 'items' );

    $aCategories = array( "apparel", "gifts", "toys", "books" );

    foreach( $aCategories as $aID => $aName )
    {
        $aTPL->assign( array( 'CAT_ID'   => $aID,
                              'CAT_NAME' => $aName ) );

        // parse the item template and append it to the
        // ITEM_LIST template variable
        $aTPL->parse( 'ITEM_LIST', '.item' );
    }

    $aTPL->assign( array( 'TITLE'   => 'Category List' ) );
    $aTPL->parse( 'ITEMS', 'items' );
    $aTPL->parse( 'BASE', 'base' );
    $aTPL->FastPrint( 'BASE' );
?>
```

Two changes in this script are evident from the one in Listing 12. First, the call to the **define()** method has one less element. Second, the **define_dynamic()** method is used to tell FastTemplate that within the 'items' template, a dynamic block with the label 'item' exists. FastTemplate then treats that dynamic block in the same way it would a separate file.

When using this mechanism, it is imperative that the dynamic block is syntactically correct. The syntax of your BEGIN and END lines needs to be exact; it is case sensitive. The code block begins on a new line all by itself. No other text can appear on the line with the BEGIN or END statement, although you can have any amount of whitespace before or after. It must be in the format shown in the following line of code. The line must be exact, right down to the spacing of the characters. The same is true for your END line. The BEGIN and END lines cannot span multiple lines.

```
<!- BEGIN DYNAMIC BLOCK: handle_name ->
```

All of the previous examples serve to provide a framework for building maintainable Web applications using templates. The next sections of this chapter provide some additional examples in real-world scenarios.

Co-Branding

Co-branding is a great application for a template-based Web site. Co-branding a site in this context is taken to mean providing a partner company's site design as a framework for your application. For example, using the merchandise catalog discussed previously, it is possible to have several distributor Web sites, each with a unique look and feel, that want to include your application as one of their services. There are several ways to accomplish this with PHP, but by using templates it can be completed very quickly.

The method for creating a co-branded site is essentially the same as creating any other template-based site. However, because your application relies on the interface from another company, integration and testing must be performed by both parties to ensure that all of the features work as expected. When developing an application that may be co-branded, more care is also needed to decide how customizable your site will be. In some cases, partners may provide additional copyright verbiage, request terminology changes and more. In a simple case, you may only be provided with a few logos to integrate.

To illustrate, the following template files are used with the merchandise application discussed earlier. In this scenario, just the copyright statement and base template files are changed. Listings 17 and 18 show the partner's copyright/footer template and the base file.

Listing 17: The Partner's Copyright/footer Template

```
<hr>
<p>
    Some portions of this site are copyright 2000 by Keen Partner
Company.
    Copyright &copy {COPYRIGHT_YEARS} by Intechra LLC. All rights
reserved.
</p>
```

Listing 18: The Partner's Base Template

```
<html>
  <head>
      <title>{TITLE}</title>
      <link rel="STYLESHEET" type="text/css" href="new_base.css">
  </head>
  <body bgcolor="White">
      <table width="630" border="0" cellspacing="0" cellpadding="0"
align="center">
          <tr>
              Keen Partner Company Uses "The Merchandise Catalog"
              <td colspan="2">{PAGE_HEADER}</td>
          </tr>
          <tr>
              <td colspan="2" align="center">{CAT_HEADER}</td>
          </tr>
          <tr>
              <td width="526" valign="top">
                  {BODY}
              </td>
              <td valign="top">{LEFT_NAVI}</td>
          </tr>
          <tr>
              <td colspan="2">
                  {PAGE_FOOTER}
              </td>
          </tr>
      </table>
  </body>
</html>
```

The main script to merge the templates and create the output page is also modified to determine the proper view of the site, based on the appropriate partner. For this example, the main, non-branded Web site is accessed by using the URL http://www.merchcatalog.com/, and the partner site is accessed using http://cobrand.merchcatalog.com/. Note that these names are only used for testing and are not intended to represent real-world Web sites. When the main script is executed, it checks the host name of the requested URL and displays the appropriate page. Listing 19 shows the script.

Listing 19: The Main Co-Branding Script

```php
<?php
    include( "class.FastTemplate.php" );
    $aHostArray = explode( ".", $HTTP_HOST );
    $aPartner = $aHostArray[0];
    switch ( $aPartner )
    {
        case "cobrand" :
            $aPartnerBase   = "partner_base.tpl";
            $aPartnerFooter = "partner_footer.tpl";
            break;
        default :
            $aPartnerBase   = "merch_base2.tpl";
            $aPartnerFooter = "merch_footer.tpl";
            break;
    }
    // assume we know the merchandise category is apparel
    $aCategoryHeader = 'merch_catapparel_header.tpl';
    $aTPL = new FastTemplate( "." );
    $aTPL->define( array( 'base'       => $aPartnerBase,
                          'header'     => 'merch_header.tpl',
                          'navi'       => 'merch_navi.tpl',
                          'footer'     => $aPartnerFooter,
                          'cat_header' => $aCategoryHeader,
                          'body'       => 'merch_body.tpl'
               ) );
    $aTPL->assign( array( 'TITLE'               => 'Merchandise
Catalog: Apparel',
                          'CATEGORY_SPECIALS'   => 'Intechra T-
Shirts on Sale!',
                          'PRODUCT_NAME'        => 'Intechra T-
Shirt',
                          'PRODUCT_DESCRIPTION' => 'A really keen
t-shirt with the Intechra LLC logo!',
                          'PRODUCT_PRICE'       => '$14.95',
                          'COPYRIGHT_YEARS'     => '2000',
                          'HREF_HOME'           => 'index.phtml',
                          'HREF_CART'           => 'cart.phtml',
                          'HREF_CONTACT'        => 'contact.phtml',
                          'HREF_COMPANY_INFO'   => 'company.phtml'
               ) );
    $aTPL->parse( 'PAGE_HEADER', 'header' );
    $aTPL->parse( 'CAT_HEADER',  'cat_header' );
    $aTPL->parse( 'LEFT_NAVI',   'navi' );
    $aTPL->parse( 'BODY',        'body' );
    $aTPL->parse( 'PAGE_FOOTER', 'footer' );
    $aTPL->parse( 'BASE',        'base' );
    $aTPL->FastPrint( 'BASE' );
?>
```

When the previous script is executed, the **$HTTP_HOST** variable is checked to see which specific host was requested. If the host is "cobrand," the partner templates are used. Otherwise, the non-branded templates are used. When the previous page is accessed using the http://www.merchcatalog.com/ URL, the output is exactly the same as shown in Figure 14.3. Figure 14.8 shows the output of the page when accessed using the co-brand URL.

Figure 14.8
The co-branded
merchandise catalog

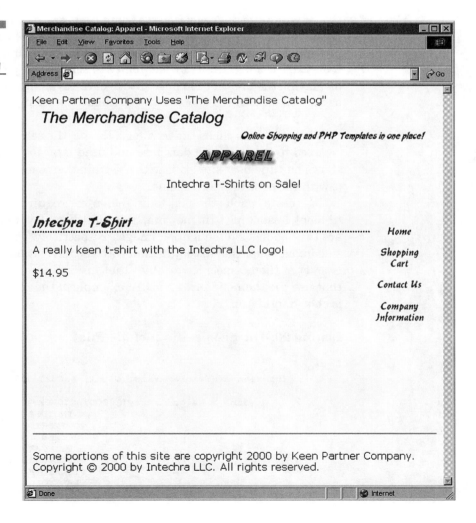

Merchandise Catalog: Apparel - Microsoft Internet Explorer

File   Edit   View   Favorites   Tools   Help

Address

Keen Partner Company Uses "The Merchandise Catalog"

The Merchandise Catalog

Online Shopping and PHP Templates in one place!

APPAREL

Intechra T-Shirts on Sale!

Intechra T-Shirt

A really keen t-shirt with the Intechra LLC logo!

$14.95

Home

*Shopping
Cart*

Contact Us

*Company
Information*

Some portions of this site are copyright 2000 by Keen Partner Company. Copyright © 2000 by Intechra LLC. All rights reserved.

Done   Internet

User Personalization

Personalization seems to be one of the biggest trends in Web site development lately. Every portal and many large sites offer a method for personalizing the site to your wants and needs. In many cases, the personalization offered is limited to content types and some basic colors. Using templates, far more customization is possible. Rather than contrive some examples for this section of the book, I shall reference some work that I have already done on user customization. My intent here is not to advertise the services of the site, but to show how completely a site can be customized using a good template system.

The site is http://www.HopeToAdopt.com/ and is an online service for adoptive families. The site enables users to create a custom online profile by providing answers to basic questions and making simple selections. The coolest part of the site is in the ability to select a very personal theme for displaying the information pages. Each of the available themes is presented as an icon on a page. A portion of the theme selection page is shown in Figure 14.9.

When the user clicks the icon for a theme, the selected theme identifier is saved to the back-end database and used later for display. Figure 14.10 shows how the user site looks with the train theme and Figure 14.11 shows it with the southwestern theme.

To create each theme, four files are required: {theme}_navi.jpg, {theme}_header.jpg, {theme}_map.tpl and {theme}_vars.php. The first two are the header and navigation images, respectively. The third is the client-side image map used in conjunction with the navigation image. The last file is a set of theme-specific variables that are included into the PHP scripts that use the theme information. An example of the information in this file is shown in Listing 20.

Listing 20: Theme-specific Include File

```php
<?php
    function AddTemplateVars( &$tpl, $aCurTemplate )
    {
        $tpl->assign( array(   BODYBGCOLOR        => "#FFFFFF",
                               MAINWIDTH          => 584,
                               TOPIMGWIDTH        => 584,
                               TOPIMGHEIGHT       => 128,
                               LEFTIMGWIDTH       => 137,
                               LEFTIMGHEIGHT      => 312,
                               FILLWIDTH          => 584 - 137,
                               TABLECOLOR         =>
"#ffadad" ) );
```

Figure 14.9
Selecting a custom
theme for a Web site

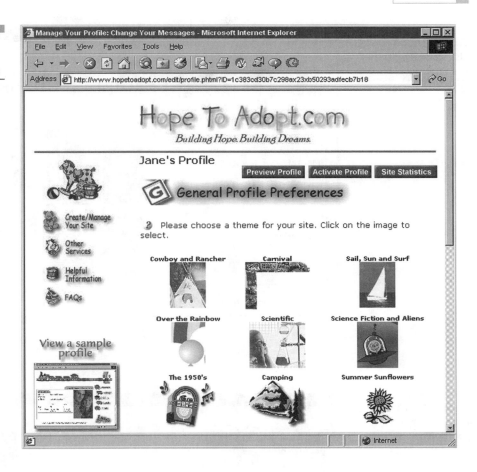

```
        }
        function GetTemplateValue( $aValName )
        {
                switch ( $aValName )
                {
                        case "NavSide" : return "left";
                        case "HasOvr"  : return False;
                }
        }
?>
```

The previous file provides information about the colors to use with the
theme and the widths and heights of the various images used in the theme.
Also, a function is available that provides information back to the main
scripts about the layout of the theme.

Figure 14.10
User profile with the
train theme

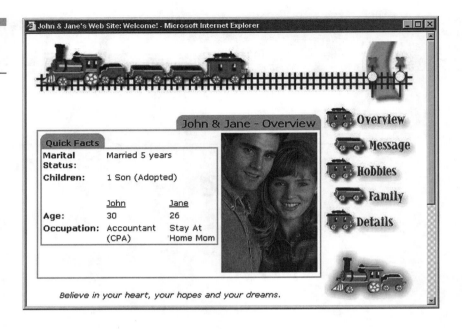

Figure 14.10
User profile with the
train theme

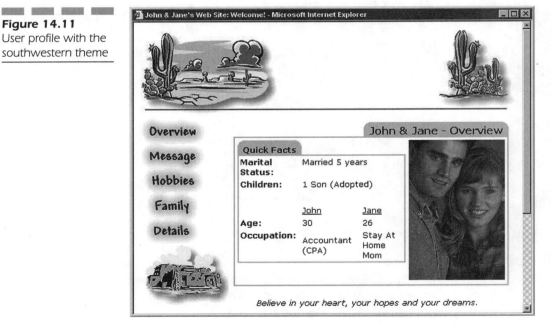

Figure 14.11
User profile with the
southwestern theme

The previous examples are very specific to the HopeToAdopt.com application, but they serve to illustrate the flexibility of using a template system in Web development. Again, the HopeToAdopt.com site is used as an example to show the power of templates in a real-world scenario rather than using another contrived example. While the full code of the HopeToAdopt.com application cannot possibly be included here, the previous examples are a sufficient framework for creating such a site.

Internationalization

Providing localized versions of Web applications is becoming more and more frequent. Using a template system to manage Internationalization enables you to deploy an application in a single language and then easily add languages later. Again, developing this kind of complex application requires a great deal of planning up front, but the effort is well rewarded. One of the main decisions is to decide how locale-specific elements are partitioned and identified. One method is to create directories for each locale. Another is to embed locale identifiers in the names of the template files. The latter method is used in the examples.

For each language or locale in the example, four files were required: a header image, a navigation image, an image map, and a body file. Rather than show all of the files here, only the main script and the output are shown. Listing 21 is the main script that generates a single page of the Internationalized template site.

Listing 21: The Main Script of the Internationalized Template Site

```php
<?php
    include( "class.FastTemplate.php" );
    $aTPL = new FastTemplate( "." );
    if ( empty( $Lang ) )
    {
        $Lang = 'enu';
    }
    $aHeaderImg = "intl_head_{$Lang}.gif";
    $aNaviImg   = "intl_nav_{$Lang}.gif";
    $aNaviMap   = "intl_map_{$Lang}.tpl";
    $aBodyTpl   = "body_{$Lang}.tpl";
    $aTPL->define( array( 'base'    => 'intl_base.tpl',
                          'body'    => $aBodyTpl,
                          'navimapv => $aNaviMap ) );
    $aTPL->assign( array( 'HREF_HOME'      =>
"intl.phtml?Lang=$Lang",
                          'HREF_LINKS'     =>
```

```
                "links.phtml?Lang=$Lang",
                                        'HREF_ABOUT'        =>
                "about.phtml?Lang=$Lang",
                                        'HREF_CONTACT'      =>
                "contact.phtml?Lang=$Lang",
                                        'HEADER_IMG'        => $aHeaderImg,
                                        'NAV_IMG'           => $aNaviImg,
                                        'HREF_ENU'          => $PHP_SELF .
                "?Lang=enu",
                                        'HREF_AFK'          => $PHP_SELF .
                "?Lang=afk",
                                        'HREF_DEU'          => $PHP_SELF .
                "?Lang=deu" ) );
        $aTPL->parse( 'NAV_MAP', 'navimap' );
        $aTPL->parse( 'BODY', 'body' );
        $aTPL->parse( 'BASE', 'base' );
        $aTPL->FastPrint( 'BASE' );
?>
```

The only significant difference in this script from the others in this chapter is the section at the top that determines the current language and uses that information to determine the proper file names to use. In this scheme, the language identifier is passed on the URL, so each link and form in the site must be constructed to pass this information along to the next page. In a large application, the above method of defining all possible links in every script becomes unwieldy. In practice, the code to generate links would probably be stored in a separate include file. Notwithstanding the simplicity of the example above, the flexibility and power is fantastic. Figures 12, 13, and 14 show the main page in English, Afrikaans, and German, respectively.

Figure 14.12
The Internationalized template site in English

Figure 14.13
The Internationalized template site in Afrikaans

Figure 14.14
The Internationalized
template site in
German

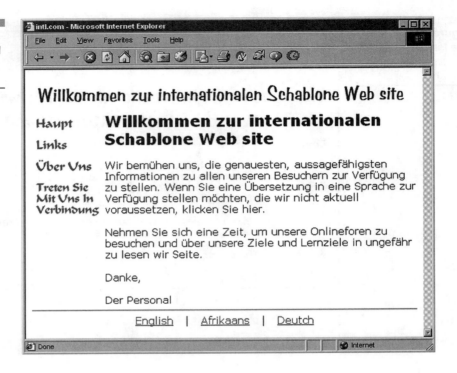

Summary

This chapter shows how using a template system improves the flexibility and maintainability of a Web application. Examples were provided showing how templates can be used to provide co-branding, user personalization, and internationalization.

The template system discussed here is the FastTemplate class available from http://www.thewebmasters.net/. Whether you choose to use this template system or another, it is highly recommended that you investigate using templates to manage your Web-based applications.

15

Database-Driven Web Sites

Introduction

Chapter 6, "Working with Databases," introduced the PHP tools that provide access to database information. In the last chapter, a detailed discussion of using template systems to separate interface from application code is provided. These chapters together provide the framework for this chapter. This chapter focuses on design and implement details at a high level, so the low-level database functions are not discussed. More information about these can be found in Chapter 6 and in the function reference at the end of the book.

Database Design

As with any aspect of software development, a good product is the result of a good design. Failing to design your database well typically leads to problems in integration, maintenance, and production. Proper database design is the subject of many fantastic books and is too large and complex to be handled here, but some basic information is provided as a starting point.

The first database design decision determines which *database management system* (DBMS) to use. Because PHP supports so many of the popular DBMSs, the decision can be made with respect to cost, functionality, scalability, and other key aspects of the DBMS rather than language support.

For many PHP applications, MySQL is a great choice for a DBMS because MySQL support is built into PHP by default. MySQL is available under the GNU *General Public License* (GPL). It provides extensive SQL support and a rich API. A detailed discussion of installing and using MySQL can be found in Chapter 6. The examples in this chapter are developed with a MySQL database.

Other DBMSs are available and have their own strengths. If you are planning to deploy a very high-traffic Web application or if you need transaction support, you may investigate Oracle or Microsoft SQL Server as your DBMS. Again, choosing the right DBMS for your application requires you to consider the tradeoffs between DBMS price, support, scalability, and functionality. Choosing the wrong DBMS can result in applications that perform poorly under stress or fail altogether. If you expect that your DBMS may change during your application's lifecycle, use a generic API to buffer your application from the DBMS-specific functions and use standard SQL. Also be aware of the differences in SQL support between the various DBMSs. Oracle, for example, supports subqueries such as the following:

```
select * from table1 where id in ( select id from table2 )
```

At the time of this writing, MySQL did not support such constructs. Developing DBMS-neutral SQL can be a challenge in itself, so changing from one DBMS to another may be impractical even for relatively small applications.

Once you have decided on a DBMS, the next step is to carefully create the actual data model. As an illustration, consider an online merchandise catalog for multiple merchants or "stores." This chapter details the design and implementation of this type of database and provides the framework for the next two chapters. The goal of the online catalog is to provide a single database that partitions data into various merchants with each merchant having multiple merchandise categories. From a very high level, the model is shown in Figure 15.1.

From the model in Figure 15.1, each merchant may provide one or more merchandise categories and each category may contain one or more products. From this basic level of detail, the entire data model can be formed. Figure 15.2 shows the fully developed data model for the merchant catalog. The actual implementation of the model is given in Listing 1.

Listing 1: The Merchandise Catalog Data Model—Implementation

```
CREATE TABLE mcMerchants
(
    merchant_id     int                      not null,
    name            varchar(50)              not null,
    created_date    datetime                 not null,
```

Figure 15.1
The Merchandise
Catalog data
model—basic

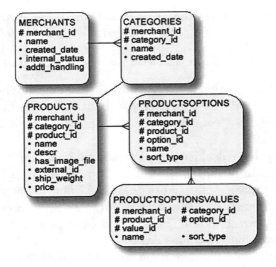

Figure 15.2
The Merchandise
Catalog data
model—full

```
    internal_status int                        not null,
    addtl_handling  float           default 0.0 not null,
    primary key ( merchant_id ),
    index( name )
);
CREATE TABLE mcCategories
(
    merchant_id     int                        not null,
    category_id     int                        not null,
    name            varchar(50)                not null,
    created_date    datetime                   not null,
    primary key ( merchant_id, category_id ),
    index( name )
);
CREATE TABLE mcProducts
(
    merchant_id     int                        not null,
    category_id     int                        not null,
    product_id      int                        not null,
    name            varchar(200)               not null,
    descr           text                       not null,
    has_image_file  tinyint        default 0   not null,
    external_id     varchar(100)               not null,
    ship_weight     float                      not null,
    price           float                      not null,
    primary key ( merchant_id, category_id, product_id ),
    index( name )
);
CREATE TABLE mcProductsOptions
(
    merchant_id     int                        not null,
    category_id     int                        not null,
    product_id      int                        not null,
```

```
    option_id         int                              not null,
    name              varchar(100)                     not null,
    sort_type         tinyint        default 0         not null,
    primary key ( merchant_id, category_id, product_id, option_id
),
    index( name )
);
CREATE TABLE mcProductsOptionsValues
(
    merchant_id       int                              not null,
    category_id       int                              not null,
    product_id        int                              not null,
    option_id         int                              not null,
    value_id          int                              not null,
    name              varchar(100)                     not null,
    primary key ( merchant_id, category_id, product_id, option_id,
value_id ),
    index( name )
);
```

Once the model has been developed and reviewed, the implementation of the application can begin. The primary goals of the merchant catalog application are as follows:

■ Display product information in a logical and easy-to-use format.

■ Enable the merchant to update information about products at any time from any Internet-connected location.

■ Enable the merchant to manage product categories and assign products to categories at any time from any Internet-connected location.

Basically, the goals are to provide an Internet-based method for adding, deleting, editing, and displaying any of the merchant catalog information. The ability to manage the data is discussed in depth in the following section.

Data Management Application

Once the database is designed and implemented in a DBMS, application logic can be created to manage the actual database records. The basic actions required on any type of data are the ability to add, edit, and delete. In this application, the ability to manage a hierarchy of data is also required. To manage this requirement, one business rule that is assumed is that at least one product category must exist for a merchant before any products are added.

With that business rule in place, the logical starting point is to allow a merchant to manage category information. The assumption for this application is that the merchant is able to log into a section of the site for management. The login process sets a merchant ID session variable used throughout the management application. Using the previously discussed template system, FastTemplate, the template files in Listings 2 through 4 are needed as a basis for the data management application.

Listing 2: Data Management Application Template—Base (mgmt_app_base.tpl)

```
<html>
<head>
<title>{TITLE}</title>
    <link rel="STYLESHEET" type="text/css" href="mgmt.css">
</head>
<body bgcolor="White">
    {BODY}
</body>
</html>
```

Listing 3: Data Management Application Template—Body (mgmt_body.tpl)

```
<table width="630" align="center">
    <tr>
        <td align="center" class="title">
            {MERCHANT_NAME}
        </td>
    </tr>
    <tr>
        <td>
            {PAGE_BODY}
        </td>
    </tr>
    <tr>
        <td>
             
        </td>
    </tr>
    <tr>
        <td>
            {FOOTER}
        </td>
    </tr>
</table>
```

Listing 4: Data Management Application Template—Footer (mgmt_footer.tpl)

```
<hr>
<p class="footer">
    Copyright &copy; 2000 by Intechra LLC.  All rights reserved.
```

```
</p>
```

The templates in Listings 2 through 4 provide the basic framework for the data management application. For the category-specific management page, the template files are shown in Listings 5 through 7. Listing 8 then shows the script used to bring the templates together with the database information.

Listing 5: Data Management Application Template—Category Main (mgmt_cats_ovr.tpl)

```
<h1>
    Product Category Management
</h1>
<p>
    Use the tools below to add, edit and delete product
    categories.
</p>
<p>
    <a href="mgmt_cat_add.phtml">Click here</a> to add a new
category.
</p>
{EXISTING_CATEGORIES}
```

Listing 6: Data Management Application Template—Current Category Table (mgmt_cats_table.tpl)

```
<h2>
    Existing Product Categories:
</h2>
<table cellspacing="0" cellpadding="0">
    <tr>
        <th>
              Category ID  
        </th>
        <th>
              Category Name  
        </th>
        <th>
              Actions  
        </th>
    </tr>
    {CATEGORY_LIST}
</table>
```

Listing 7: Data Management Application Template—Current Category Item (mgmt_cats_item.tpl)

```
<tr>
    <td>
        {CAT_ID}
    </td>
    <td>
```

```
                    {CAT_NAME}
            </td>
            <td class="small">
                <a href="mgmt_cat_edit.phtml?cat_id={CAT_ID}">EDIT</a>
                <a href="mgmt_cat_del.phtml?cat_id={CAT_ID}">DELETE</a>
            </td>
        </tr>
```

Listing 8: Data Management Application—Category Management (mgmt_cats.phtml)

```php
<?php
    session_start(); // implicitly sets the $aMerchantID session
variable
    if ( empty( $aMerchantID ) == True )
    {
        header( "Location: login.phtml?retpage=" . urlencode(
$REQUEST_URI ) . "\n" );
        exit;
    }
    include( "class.FastTemplate.php" );
    include( "./mgmt_db.php" );
    include( "./mgmt_funcs.php" );
    $aTPL = new FastTemplate( "." );
    $aDB  = new mgmt_db();
    $aTPL->define( array(    "base"       =>  "mgmt_app_base.tpl",
                             "body"       =>  "mgmt_body.tpl",
                             "footer"     =>  "mgmt_footer.tpl",
                             "page_body"  =>  "mgmt_cats_ovr.tpl",
                             "cat_table"  =>  "mgmt_cats_table.tpl",
                             "cat_item"   =>  "mgmt_cats_item.tpl" )
);

    $aSQL = "select category_id, name from mcCategories where (
merchant_id = $aMerchantID )";
    $aDB->query( $aSQL );
    if ( $aDB->num_rows() > 0 )
    {
        while ( $aDB->next_record() )
        {
            $aCatID   = $aDB->f( "category_id" );
            $aCatName = $aDB->f( "name" );
            $aTPL->assign( array( "CAT_ID"      => $aCatID,
                                  "CAT_NAME"    => $aCatName ) );
            $aTPL->parse( "CATEGORY_LIST", ".cat_item" );
        }
        $aTPL->parse( "EXISTING_CATEGORIES", "cat_table" );
    }
    else
    {
        $aTPL->assign( array(    "EXISTING_CATEGORIES" =>  "" ) );
    }

    $aTPL->assign( array(    "TITLE"         =>  "Merchandise
Catalog Management",
                             "MERCHANT_NAME" =>  GetMerchantName(
$aDB, $aMerchantID )
                    ) );
```

```
        $aTPL->parse( "PAGE_BODY", "page_body" );
        $aTPL->parse( "FOOTER", "footer" );
        $aTPL->parse( "BODY", "body" );
        $aTPL->parse( "PAGE", "base" );
        $aTPL->FastPrint( "PAGE" );
    ?>
```

The first thing this script does is start a session and check for the merchant identifier, **$aMerchantID**. If the merchant id is not set, then the user is forced to a login page. The login page checks the credentials of the visitor and if successful, sets the merchant id in the aforementioned session variable. Next, using the merchant id as a filter, the script checks for existing categories in the database. If there is at least one category, the script loops through the data and generates a table of existing categories. Figure 15.3 shows the main page as it looks for a merchant with two categories.

The script provides a mechanism for adding product categories through a single link. If categories exist, each category has its own edit and delete link as shown in Figure 15.2. The Add Category template and script are shown in Listings 9 and 10, respectively.

Figure 15.3
The Merchandise Catalog category management page

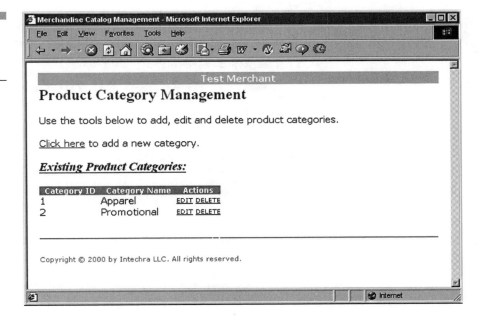

Listing 9: Data Management Application Template—Add Category (mgmt_cat_add.tpl)

```html
<h1>
    Add Product Category
</h1>
<form action="{FORM_ACTION}" method="post">
    <table>
        <tr>
            <td colspan="2">
                {ERRORS}
            </td>
        </tr>
        <tr>
            <td>
                Category Name:
            </td>
            <td>
                <input type="text" name="CategoryName">
            </td>
        </tr>
        <tr>
            <td colspan="2">
                <input type="submit" name="Submit" value="Submit">
            </td>
        </tr>
    </table>
</form>
```

Listing 10: Data Management Application—Add Category (mgmt_cat_add.phtml)

```php
<?php
    session_start(); // implicitly sets the $aMerchantID session
variable
    if ( empty( $aMerchantID ) == True )
    {
        header( "Location: login.phtml?retpage=" . urlencode(
$REQUEST_URI ) . "\n" );
        exit;
    }
    include( "class.FastTemplate.php" );
    include( "./mgmt_db.php" );
    include( "./mgmt_funcs.php" );
    $aTPL = new FastTemplate( "." );
    $aDB  = new mgmt_db();
    $aErrors = "";
    if ( $REQUEST_METHOD == 'POST' ) // we're here from posting the
form
    {
        if ( IsValidCategory( $aDB, $aMerchantID, $CategoryName )
== True )
        {
            SaveCategory( $aDB, $aMerchantID, $CategoryName );
            header( "Location: mgmt_cats.phtml\n" );
            exit;
```

```
        }
        else
        {
            $aErrors  = "The category name is already being used.
";
            $aErrors .= "Please use a different name for the new
category.";
        }
    }
    $aTPL->define( array(    "base"      => "mgmt_app_base.tpl",
                             "body"      => "mgmt_body.tpl",
                             "footer"    => "mgmt_footer.tpl",
                             "page_body" => "mgmt_cat_add.tpl" ) );
    $aTPL->assign( array(    "TITLE"        => "Merchandise
Catalog Management",
                             "MERCHANT_NAME" => GetMerchantName(
$aDB, $aMerchantID ),
                             "FORM_ACTION"   => $PHP_SELF,
                             "ERRORS"        => $aErrors
                        ) );
    $aTPL->parse( "PAGE_BODY", "page_body" );
    $aTPL->parse( "FOOTER", "footer" );
    $aTPL->parse( "BODY", "body" );
    $aTPL->parse( "PAGE", "base" );
    $aTPL->FastPrint( "PAGE" );
?>
```

The script in Listing 10 is similar to many other data gathering and validation scripts described in this book in that the same script is used to render the form initially, handle the form, and validate the posted data. In this case, the logic for checking the validity and storing the new category are wrapped in the functions, **IsValidCategory()** and **SaveCategory()** respectively. These utility functions are shown later in a listing of the complete *mgmt_funcs.php* file. The validation routine simply checks for a category of the same name.

The edit and delete functions for the category management are very similar to other scripts shown throughout the book. By studying Listing 8, you can see that the edit and delete links for each category include the category id. For example, the full URL for deleting the *Apparel* category is **http://testserver.com/ch15/mgmt_cat_del.phtml?cat_id=1**. The category id is passed to the script so that a simple SQL delete statement can be constructed. For editing, the same mechanism is used to initially populate the name in an edit box. The full source for these functions is not shown because of their similarity to the code in Listings 9 and 10. The delete and update category functions are shown in the listing for the *mgmt_funcs.php* file (Listing 12).

The business rule for editing a category is that the new category name must not be the same as any existing category name. For deleting a category, the rule is that the category must not contain any products. If products were in the category, deleting the category itself would result in orphan product records and potential application errors. When building database driven Web applications, capturing the business rules in the application code is critical for success. Some rules can be enforced by DBMS features such as enforced relationship rules and cascading data actions. Other rules can be enforced by the DBMS through the use of triggers or stored procedures. Additionally, application code is often used to enforce business rules.

When relying on code for business rule management, the best practice is to always provide functions for managing all aspects of the business rules. For example, use a function called **DeleteEntity()** rather than building the delete SQL inline. Doing so enables quick changes to be made to business rules that have immediate effect throughout the application. The **DeleteEntity()** function can encapsulate all of the logic required for checking database integrity constraints and other business rules inline and return error codes relative to any failures. This promotes code reuse and simplifies the deployment of new logic application-wide.

Returning to the merchandise catalog application, the next step is to create the data management pages for the actual products. These pages are logically identical to the category management pages. The management page is shown in Figure 15.4 and the main script for generating the page is shown in Listing 11.

Figure 15.4
The Product
Management screen

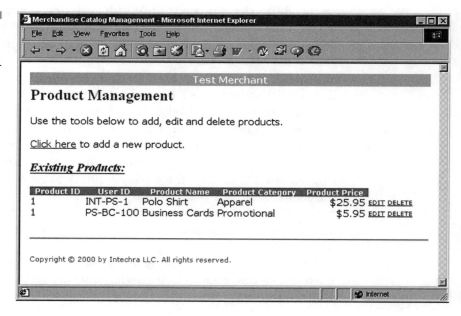

Listing 11: Data Management Application—Product Management (mgmt_prods.phtml)

```php
<?php
    error_reporting( E_ALL & ~E_NOTICE );
    session_start(); // implicitly sets the $aMerchantID session
variable
    if ( empty( $aMerchantID ) == True )
    {
        header( "Location: login.phtml?retpage=" . urlencode(
$REQUEST_URI ) . "\n" );
        exit;
    }
    include( "class.FastTemplate.php" );
    include( "./mgmt_db.php" );
    include( "./mgmt_funcs.php" );
    $aTPL = new FastTemplate( "." );
    $aDB  = new mgmt_db();
    $aTPL->define( array(    "base"      => "mgmt_app_base.tpl",
                             "body"      => "mgmt_body.tpl",
                             "footer"    => "mgmt_footer.tpl",
                             "page_body" => "mgmt_prods_ovr.tpl",
                             "prod_table" =>
"mgmt_prods_table.tpl",
                             "prod_item" => "mgmt_prods_item.tpl"
) );
    $aSQL = "select a.category_id, a.product_id, a.name,
a.external_id, a.price, ";
    $aSQL .= "b.name as cat_name from mcProducts a, mcCategories b
where ( a.merchant_id ";
    $aSQL .= "= $aMerchantID ) and ( a.category_id = b.category_id
)";
    $aDB->query( $aSQL );
    if ( $aDB->num_rows() > 0 )
    {
        while ( $aDB->next_record() )
        {
            $aCatID     = $aDB->f( "category_id" );
            $aCatName   = $aDB->f( "cat_name" );
            $aProdID    = $aDB->f( "product_id" );
            $aProdName  = $aDB->f( "name" );
            $aProdEID   = $aDB->f( "external_id" );
            $aProdPrice = $aDB->f( "price" );
            $aTPL->assign( array( "PROD_ID"    => $aProdID,
                                  "PROD_EID"   => $aProdEID,
                                  "PROD_NAME"  => $aProdName,
                                  "PROD_CAT"   => $aCatName,
                                  "PROD_PRICE" => '$' .
number_format( $aProdPrice, 2 ) ) );
            $aTPL->parse( "PRODUCT_LIST", ".prod_item" );
        }
        $aTPL->parse( "EXISTING_PRODUCTS", "prod_table" );
    }
    else
    {
        $aTPL->assign( array(   "EXISTING_PRODUCTS" => "" ) );
    }
```

```php
    $aTPL->assign( array(    "TITLE"        => "Merchandise
Catalog Management",
                             "MERCHANT_NAME" => GetMerchantName(
$aDB, $aMerchantID )
                        ) );
    $aTPL->parse( "PAGE_BODY", "page_body" );
    $aTPL->parse( "FOOTER", "footer" );
    $aTPL->parse( "BODY", "body" );
    $aTPL->parse( "PAGE", "base" );
    $aTPL->FastPrint( "PAGE" );
?>
```

The add, delete, and edit pages for the product management section are not listed in detail here but are available at the Web site listed in the reference section at the end of this book. The business rules for adding a new product are as follows:

■ The product must be assigned to a single category.

■ Within its category, the product name must be unique.

■ The price of the product must be zero or greater than zero.

■ The shipping weight of the product must be zero or greater than zero.

Currently, no restrictions apply to deleting a product. When a product is edited, the same business rules for adding a new product must be maintained. A segment of the *mgmt_funcs.php* file is shown in Listing 12, which lists some of the database access functions and business rules functions used throughout the application.

Listing 12: Data Management Application—Utility Functions (mgmt_funcs.php)

```php
<?php
    function GetMerchantName( $aDB, $aMerchantID )
    {
        $aResult = "";
        $aSQL    = "select name from mcMerchants where ";
        $aSQL   .= "( merchant_id = $aMerchantID )";
        $aDB->query( $aSQL );
        if ( $aDB->next_record() == True )
        {
            $aResult = $aDB->f( "name" );
        }
        return $aResult;
    }
    function NewCategoryID( $aDB, $aMerchantID )
    {
        $aSQL  = "select ( max( category_id ) + 1 ) as new_id ";
        $aSQL .= "from mcCategories where ( merchant_id =
$aMerchantID )";
        $aDB->query( $aSQL );
        if ( $aDB->next_record() )
```

```
            {
                $aResult = $aDB->f( "new_id" );
            }
            if ( empty( $aResult ) == True )
            {
                $aResult = 1;
            }
            return $aResult;
        }
        function IsValidCategory( $aDB, $aMerchantID, $aCategoryName )
        {
            $aSQL  = "select category_id from mcCategories where ";
            $aSQL .= "( merchant_id = $aMerchantID ) and ";
            $aSQL .= "( upper( name ) = upper( '$aCategoryName' ) )";
            $aDB->query( $aSQL );
            // if there is a record with the same category name, then
            // return false
            return ( $aDB->num_rows() == 0 );
        }
        function SaveCategory( $aDB, $aMerchantID, $aCategoryName )
        {
            $aNewID = NewCategoryID( $aDB, $aMerchantID );
            $aSQL  = "insert into mcCategories ( merchant_id, ";
            $aSQL .= "category_id, name, created_date ) values ";
            $aSQL .= "( $aMerchantID, $aNewID, '$aCategoryName', ";
            $aSQL .= " NOW() )";
            $aDB->query( $aSQL );
            return ( $aDB->Errno == 0 );
        }
        function DeleteCategory( $aDB, $aMerchantID, $aCategoryID )
        {
            $aSQL  = "delete from mcCategories where ( merchant_id = ";
            $aSQL .= "$aMerchantID ) and ( category_id = $aCategoryID
)";
            $aDB->query( $aSQL );
            return ( $aDB->Errno == 0 );
        }
        function UpdateCategory( $aDB, $aMerchantID, $aCategoryID,
$aCategoryName )
        {
            $aSQL  = "update mcCategories set name='$aCategoryName' ";
            $aSQL .= "where ( merchant_id = $aMerchantID ) and ";
            $aSQL .= "( category_id = $aCategoryID )";
            $aDB->query( $aSQL );
            return ( $aDB->Errno == 0 );
        }
        ... (more) ...
    ?>
```

The data management application is just a small part of the whole product catalog application. It provides the Web interface for maintaining and managing the catalog items. The other major aspect of the product catalog is the ability to display items, search for items, and get detailed information about the items in the catalog. The next section of this chapter provides information on this.

Data Display

The data display logic for the product database consists of providing a categorical display, an alphabetic product list, and a search facility for finding specific products. To segregate the products and categories by merchant, again a session variable is used to identify the current merchant data to be viewed. This session variable is set before the visitor first enters the product display area.

The main page of the product catalog is shown in Figure 15.5. This page provides immediate access to category information and the search facility. If no categories exist (implying no products), the page displays that no products are available from the merchant. The main script for generating this page is shown in Listing 13.

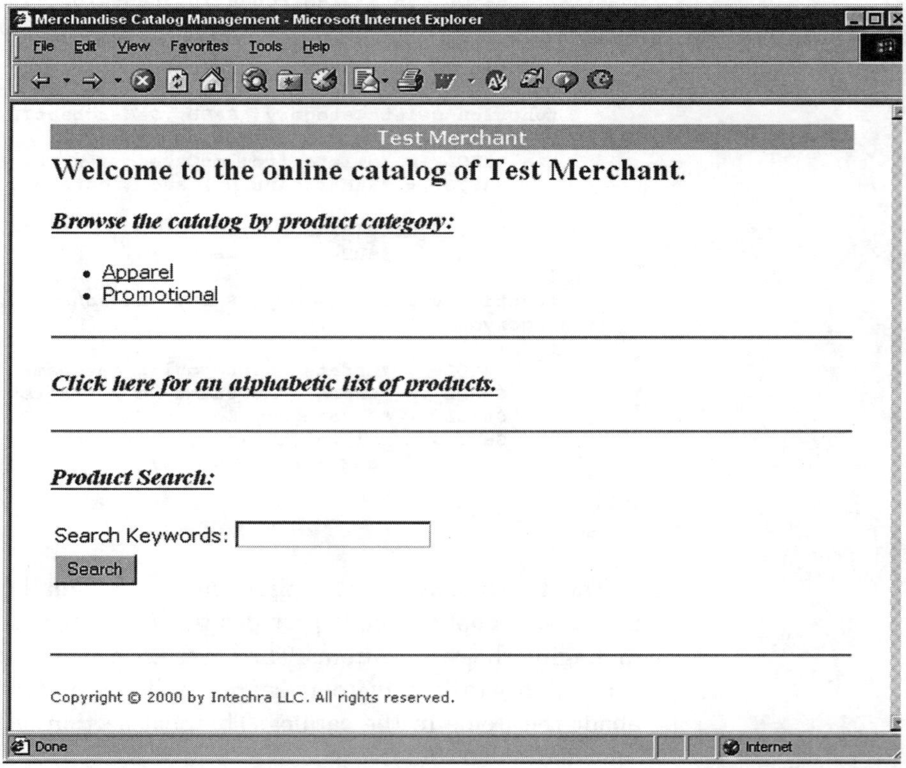

Figure 15.5
Main page of the
Merchandise Catalog

Listing 13: Data Management Application—Utility Functions (mgmt_funcs.php)

```php
<?php
    error_reporting( E_ALL & ~E_NOTICE );
    session_start(); // implicitly sets the $aMerchantID session
variable
    if ( empty( $aMerchantID ) == True )
    {
        print( "Internal application error.  No merchant id." );
        exit;
    }
    include( "class.FastTemplate.php" );
    include( "./mgmt_db.php" );
    include( "./mgmt_funcs.php" );
    $aTPL = new FastTemplate( "." );
    $aDB  = new mgmt_db();
    $aTPL->define( array(  "base"      => "mgmt_app_base.tpl",
                           "body"      => "mgmt_body.tpl",
                           "footer"    => "mgmt_footer.tpl",
                           "page_body" => "mgmt_main.tpl",
                           "cat_body"  => "mgmt_main_body.tpl",
                           "cat_item"  =>
"mgmt_main_cat_item.tpl" ) );
    $aSQL = "select category_id, name from mcCategories where (
merchant_id = $aMerchantID )";
    $aDB->query( $aSQL );
    if ( $aDB->num_rows() > 0 )
    {
        while ( $aDB->next_record() )
        {
            $aCatID   = $aDB->f( "category_id" );
            $aCatName = $aDB->f( "name" );
            $aTPL->assign( array( "CAT_HREF"    => GetCategoryHREF(
$aCatID ),
                                  "CAT_NAME"    => $aCatName ) );
            $aTPL->parse( "CATEGORY_LIST", ".cat_item" );
        }
        $aTPL->parse( "CATALOG_MAIN_BODY", "cat_body" );
    }
    else
    {
        $aTPL->assign( array(  "CATALOG_MAIN_BODY" =>  "There are
no products available." ) );
    }
    $aTPL->assign( array(  "TITLE"         =>  "Merchandise
Catalog Management",
                           "MERCHANT_NAME" =>  GetMerchantName(
$aDB, $aMerchantID )
                              ) );
    $aTPL->parse( "PAGE_BODY", "page_body" );
    $aTPL->parse( "FOOTER", "footer" );
    $aTPL->parse( "BODY", "body" );
    $aTPL->parse( "PAGE", "base" );
    $aTPL->FastPrint( "PAGE" );
?>
```

The template files used to generate the main page are very similar to the ones used with the category management script described in the previous listing. One interesting note in the previous listing is the **GetCategoryHREF()** function that generates the URL when clicking on one of the category names. The function is included as part of the *mgmt_funcs.php* file and is shown in Listing 14. The reason for this function is to provide a method for using this same script to generate a set of static pages from the dynamic data. This is discussed in detail in the next chapter.

Listing 14: GetCategoryHREF()

```php
function GetCategoryHREF( $aCatID, $aDynamic = True )
    {
        if ( $aDynamic == True )
        {
            return "mgmt_prod_list.phtml?cat_id=$aCatID";
        }
        else
        {
            return "mgmg_cat_{$aCatID}.html";
        }
    }
```

The product listing script is shown in Listing 15. This single script is used to display the categorical listing, the alphabetical listing, and the search results.

Listing 15: Product Listing Example

```php
<?php
    error_reporting( E_ALL & ~E_NOTICE );
    session_start(); // implicitly sets the $aMerchantID session
variable
    if ( empty( $aMerchantID ) == True )
    {
        print( "Internal application error.  No merchant id." );
        exit;
    }
    include( "class.FastTemplate.php" );
    include( "./mgmt_db.php" );
    include( "./mgmt_funcs.php" );
    if ( $REQUEST_METHOD == 'POST' ) // we're here from posting the
search form
    {
        $aSQL  = "select a.category_id, a.product_id, a.name,
a.external_id, a.price, ";
        $aSQL .= "a.ship_weight, a.has_image_file, a.descr, b.name
as cat_name from ";
        $aSQL .= "mcProducts a, mcCategories b where (
a.merchant_id = $aMerchantID ) ";
        $aSQL .= "and ( a.category_id = b.category_id ) and ( (
upper( a.name ) like ";
```

```
            $aSQL .= "upper( '%{$SearchTerms}%' ) ) or ( upper( a.descr
) like ";
            $aSQL .= "upper( '%{$SearchTerms}%' ) ) ) order by a.name";
    }
    else
    {
        if ( empty( $cat_id ) == False ) // categorical listing
        {
            $aSQL  = "select a.category_id, a.product_id, a.name,
a.external_id, ";
            $aSQL .= "a.price, a.ship_weight, a.has_image_file,
a.descr, b.name as ";
            $aSQL .= "cat_name from mcProducts a, mcCategories b
where ";
            $aSQL .= "( a.merchant_id = $aMerchantID ) and
( a.category_id = b.category_id ) ";
            $aSQL .= "and ( a.category_id = $cat_id ) order by
a.name";
        }
        else // alphabetical listing
        {
            $aSQL  = "select a.category_id, a.product_id, a.name,
a.external_id, a.price, ";
            $aSQL .= "a.ship_weight, a.has_image_file, a.descr,
b.name as cat_name from ";
            $aSQL .= "mcProducts a, mcCategories b where
( a.merchant_id = $aMerchantID ) ";
            $aSQL .= "and ( a.category_id = b.category_id ) order
by a.name";
        }
    }
    $aTPL = new FastTemplate( "." );
    $aDB  = new mgmt_db();
    $aTPL->define( array(   "base"      =>   "mgmt_app_base.tpl",
                            "body"      =>   "mgmt_body.tpl",
                            "footer"    =>   "mgmt_footer.tpl",
                            "page_body" =>   "mgmt_prod_main.tpl",
                            "prod_item" =>   "mgmt_prod_item.tpl" )
);
    $aDB->query( $aSQL );
    if ( $aDB->num_rows() > 0 )
    {
        while ( $aDB->next_record() )
        {
            $aProdName     = $aDB->f( "name" );
            $aProdEID      = $aDB->f( "external_id" );
            $aProdPrice    = $aDB->f( "price" );
            $aProdWeight   = $aDB->f( "ship_weight" );
            $aHasImage     = $aDB->f( "has_image_file" );
            $aProdDescr    = $aDB->f( "descr" );
            $aCatName      = $aDB->f( "cat_name" );
            $aCatID        = $aDB->f( "category_id" );
            $aProdID       = $aDB->f( "product_id" );
            $aImageFile = "images/default.jpg";
            if ( $aHasImage == True )
            {
                $aImageFile =
"images/{$aMerchID}_{$aCatID}_{$aProdID}.jpg";
            }
```

```
                    $aTPL->assign( array( "PROD_NAME"      => $aProdName,
                                          "CAT_NAME"       => $aCatName,
                                          "PROD_EID"       => $aProdEID,
                                          "PROD_PRICE"     => '$' .
number_format( $aProdPrice, 2 ),
                                          "PROD_DESCR"     => $aProdDescr,
                                          "IMAGE_FILE"     => $aImageFile
                                        ) );
                    $aTPL->parse( "ITEM_LIST", ".prod_item" );
            }
        }
        else
        {
            $aTPL->assign( array(  "ITEM_LIST" =>  "There are no
products available for the criteria you selected." ) );
        }
        $aTPL->assign( array(  "TITLE"         =>  "Merchandise
Catalog Management",
                               "MERCHANT_NAME" =>  GetMerchantName
( $aDB, $aMerchantID )
                             ) );
        $aTPL->parse( "PAGE_BODY", "page_body" );
        $aTPL->parse( "FOOTER", "footer" );
        $aTPL->parse( "BODY", "body" );
        $aTPL->parse( "PAGE", "base" );
        $aTPL->FastPrint( "PAGE" );
?>
```

The first step taken by the script is to determine how to select the correct data subset. If the script is activated as the result of an HTTP POST, then it is being used by the search feature. Otherwise, it is either a categorical listing or alphabetic listing. If the variable **$cat_id** is set, then the request is for a categorical listing. Based on the type of request, a SQL statement is generated. Based on the results of the SQL statement, the output page either contains a list of products or a message indicating that no products match the criteria. For each record, the *has_image_file* flag is checked. If true, then the standardized image name is generated and used; otherwise, a default image is displayed.

The output of the categorical, alphabetical, and search-based listings are in Figures 15.6, 15.7, and 15.8, respectively. The search term used for the page was "knit."

This section has focused on the display side of a database-driven Web site. Typically, displaying database information is much simpler than managing the data because fewer conditions and less opportunities exist for user error. The next two chapters build on the information and examples presented here.

Figure 15.6
Categorical product
listing (Apparel
category)

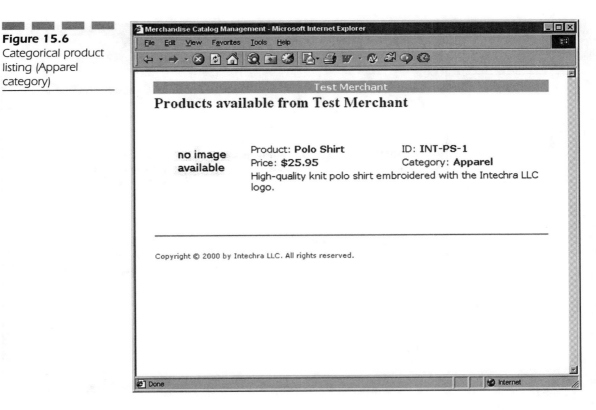

Figure 15.7
Alphabetical product
listing

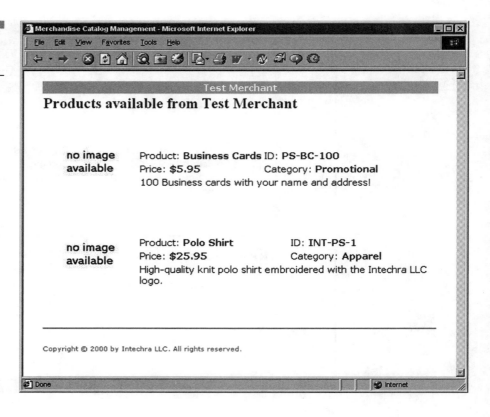

Figure 15.8
Search-based product
listing (term = "knit")

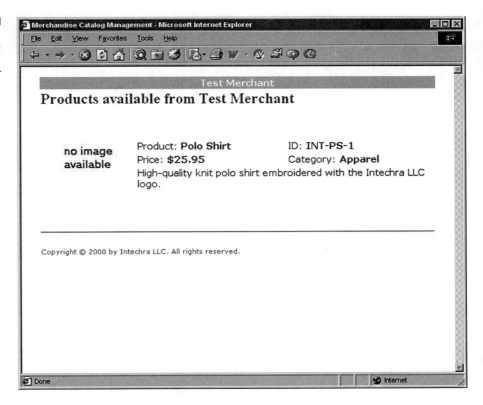

Summary

Building database-driven Web applications requires a great deal of planning and development, but the goal is worth the effort. Once a data management system is in place, the application can be updated at any time from any location resulting in a highly dynamic, manageable Web application. The critical steps are to carefully design the database and to capture the business rules of the application using modular programming. If these items are carefully designed and implemented, the management and maintenance of the application will be greatly simplified.

Generating Static HTML Pages from Dynamic Data

## Chapter 16

Introduction

The primary purpose for using PHP is typically to create Web pages with dynamic content. This content ranges from the simplest visitor tracking information to database-generated and personalized content. In some cases, however, fully dynamic content is not required and can be detrimental to the overall performance of a site. In many cases, site content is only semi-dynamic.

For example, the merchandise catalog in the previous chapter is only dynamic in the sense that the products can be changed, but every visitor should see the same content for every product and category. In situations like these, it is more efficient to generate static HTML pages once (any time the underlying data is changed) and display the static page on each request. Fortunately, PHP can easily be used to generate the pages, so no additional tools are needed to transition your fully dynamic site to a semidynamic one.

Concepts

Conceptually, the method for creating static pages is to send HTML to a file rather than sending it out to the browser. This can easily be accomplished by simply writing to a file using the standard PHP file functions. However, this method requires you to rewrite your pages so that all of the HTML is included in the PHP code. This is impractical for most sites. A better method would have to work for all existing scripts and pages with only minor changes. These concepts are discussed in the section titled "Generating Static Pages."

Another method for improving server performance is to temporarily cache pages so that the time-consuming aspects of the script are not run for every request, but only occasionally. This method is described in the section titled "Caching Techniques."

Generating Static Pages

Because PHP is so flexible, there are at least two ways to generate static pages from existing PHP scripts requiring only minor changes. The first is to use PHP's output buffering functions, and the second is to use the Fast-Template class that has been discussed in other chapters.

Using Output Buffering

Depending on the size and complexity of your site, you may be able to use PHP's output buffering functions to capture the HTML output and store it to a file. The script in Listing 1 is the same logically as the Listing 7 of Chapter 6, "Working with Databases." The script generates an HTML for choosing a US state and world country. It generates the lists from a database. This is a good candidate for creating a static page because the list of US states and world countries is fairly static. If performance is an issue in your application, it makes little sense to gather these elements from the database each time a user visits the page. It does make sense, however, to store the values in the database and to generate the list dynamically when the values change.

Listing 1: Using Output Buffering to Create a Static HTML Page from PHP

```php
<?php
    ob_start();
    include ( "db_mysql.php" );
    class MySQLDBTest extends DB_Sql
    {
        var $Host       = "db.server.com";
        var $Database   = "mydb";
        var $User        = "root";
        var $Password    = "";
    }
    function GetGenOpts( $aTableName, $aCurSel = "" )
    {
        $aResult = "";
        $aDB = new MySQLDBTest;
        $aSQL = "select ID, Name from $aTableName order by Name";
        $aDB->query( $aSQL );
        while( $aDB->next_record() )
        {
            $aName      = $aDB->f( "Name" );
            $aID        = $aDB->f( "ID" );
            if ( $aID == $aCurSel )
            {
                $aResult .= "<option value=\"$aID\"
selected>$aName</option>";
            }
            else
            {
                $aResult .= "<option
value=\"$aID\">$aName</option>";
            }
        }
        return $aResult;
    }
```

```
?>
<html>
<head>
    <title>Form for selecting US state and world country</title>
</head>
<body>
<form action="some_place.phtml" method="post">
    <table>
        <tr>
            <td>
                Select US State:
            </td>
            <td>
                <select name="us_state" size="1">
                <?php
                    print( GetGenOpts( "us_states", "ID" ) );
                ?>
                </select>
            </td>
        </tr>
        <tr>
            <td>
                Select World Country:
            </td>
            <td>
                <select name="world_country" size="1">
                <?php
                    print( GetGenOpts( "world_countries", "ZA" ) );
                ?>
                </select>
            </td>
        </tr>
</form>
</body>
</html>
<?php
    $aFileName = ereg_replace( 'phtml', 'html', $PATH_TRANSLATED );
    $aFile = fopen( $aFileName, "w" );
    fwrite( $aFile, ob_get_contents() );
    fclose( $aFile );
    ob_end_clean();
    print( "File <i>$aFileName</i> successfully created<br>" );
?>
```

The first step in this script is to enable output buffering using the
ob_start() function. While output buffering is enabled, no output is sent to
the browser by the script, but all output is stored in an internal buffer. At
the end of the script, a new file name is generated by converting the existing server filename extension for the current script from *phtml* to *html*. The
file is then written, the output buffer is cleared, and a status line is sent to
the browser. The new file can then be accessed from the browser by changing the extension of the request to *html*.

This method works great for many types of pages. In practice, it is likely
that you would want to keep the actual page-generating scripts in a pass-

word-protected location on your server so that only valid users are able to access them. Then it becomes possible to build pages to manage the dynamic data and generate static pages all from a Web interface.

Using FastTemplate

In the last chapter, a merchandise catalog site was introduced. This is another example of a site where the actual page information isn't likely to change very often. The categories and products offered by a company may change once a month or once a week. However, the catalog is intended to be viewed daily and must always contain up-to-date information. The Fast-Template class was used in the previous chapter to develop the merchandise catalog site. This chapter discusses the changes that must be made to the scripts in order to create the static pages.

First, the file structure for the catalog must be defined. For the category pages, each category page is named using the convention, *mgmt_cat_{ $aCatID}.html*. The script in Listing 2 is the script that creates the categorical product listings for all categories. It is similar to the script in Listing 15 of Chapter 15, "Database-Driven Web Sites." In this case, it provides a categorical listing for **all** categories and saves each listing page to a separate file using the aforementioned naming convention.

Listing 2: Using FastTemplate to Create a Static HTML Page from PHP

```php
<?php
    error_reporting( E_ALL & ~E_NOTICE );
    session_start(); // implicitly sets the $aMerchantID session
variable
    if ( empty( $aMerchantID ) == True )
    {
        print( "Internal application error.  No merchant id." );
        exit;
    }
    include( "class.FastTemplate.php" );
    include( "./mgmt_db.php" );
    include( "./mgmt_funcs.php" );
    $aTPL    = new FastTemplate( "." );
    $aDB     = new mgmt_db();
    $aCatDB  = new mgmt_db();
    $aTPL->define( array(   "base"      => "mgmt_app_base.tpl",
                            "body"      => "mgmt_body.tpl",
                            "footer"    => "mgmt_footer.tpl",
                            "page_body" => "mgmt_prod_main.tpl",
                            "prod_item" => "mgmt_prod_item.tpl" )
    );
```

```php
    $aSQL = "select category_id from mcCategories";
    $aCatDB->query( $aSQL );
    while( $aCatDB->next_record() )
    {
        $cat_id = $aCatDB->f( "category_id" );
        //print( "$cat_id<br>" );
        $aSQL  = "select a.category_id, a.product_id, a.name,
a.external_id, ";
        $aSQL .= "a.price, a.ship_weight, a.has_image_file,
a.descr, b.name as ";
        $aSQL .= "cat_name from mcProducts a, mcCategories b where
";
        $aSQL .= "( a.merchant_id = $aMerchantID ) and
( a.category_id = b.category_id ) ";
        $aSQL .= "and ( a.category_id = $cat_id ) order by a.name";
        $aDB->query( $aSQL );
        if ( $aDB->num_rows() > 0 )
        {
            while ( $aDB->next_record() )
            {
                $aProdName    = $aDB->f( "name" );
                $aProdEID     = $aDB->f( "external_id" );
                $aProdPrice   = $aDB->f( "price" );
                $aProdWeight  = $aDB->f( "ship_weight" );
                $aHasImage    = $aDB->f( "has_image_file" );
                $aProdDescr   = $aDB->f( "descr" );
                $aCatName     = $aDB->f( "cat_name" );
                $aCatID       = $aDB->f( "category_id" );
                $aProdID      = $aDB->f( "product_id" );
                $aImageFile = "images/default.jpg";
                if ( $aHasImage == True )
                {
                    $aImageFile =
"images/{$aMerchID}_{$aCatID}_{$aProdID}.jpg";
                }
                $aTPL->assign( array( "PROD_NAME"         =>
$aProdName,
                                      "CAT_NAME"          =>
$aCatName,
                                      "PROD_EID"          =>
$aProdEID,
                                      "PROD_PRICE"        => '$' .
number_format( $aProdPrice, 2 ),
                                      "PROD_DESCR"        =>
$aProdDescr,
                                      "IMAGE_FILE"        =>
$aImageFile
                                    ) );
                $aTPL->parse( "ITEM_LIST", ".prod_item" );
            }
        }
        else
        {
            $aTPL->assign( array(   "ITEM_LIST" =>  "There are no
products available for the category <i>$aCatName</i>." ) );
        }
        $aTPL->assign( array(   "TITLE"           =>  "Merchandise
Catalog Management: Category - $aCatName",
```

```
                                 "MERCHANT_NAME" =>
        GetMerchantName( $aDB, $aMerchantID )
                                       ) );
            $aTPL->parse( "PAGE_BODY", "page_body" );
            $aTPL->parse( "FOOTER", "footer" );
            $aTPL->parse( "BODY", "body" );
            $aTPL->parse( "PAGE", "base" );
            $aFileName = "mgmt_cat_{$aCatID}.html";
            $aFile = fopen( $aFileName, "w" );
            fwrite( $aFile, $aTPL->fetch( "PAGE" ) );
            fclose( $aFile );
            print( "Category, <i>$aCatName</i>, written to file:
        <b>$aFileName</b><br>" );
            $aTPL->Clear();
        }
    ?>
```

Again, this script assumes that the merchant id is available in a session variable. FastTemplate internally stores all of the page information in internal buffers while performing its tasks. FastTemplate provides the **fetch()** method to get the contents of any variable used to generate the page. In the previous sample, the **fetch()** method is used to get the value of **PAGE**, which represents the entire HTML page. This value is then saved to the output file, and a confirmation message is displayed in the browser. The **Clear()** method is used to clear all of the FastTemplate buffers and variables for the next iteration of the loop.

In the previous chapter, a specific URL function, **GetCategoryHREF()** was mentioned that is used in the catalog management application. It is shown again in Listing 3. This function is used to gather the actual URL to a category page. In its default mode, it returns a dynamic page URL, but by setting the **$aDynamic** flag to false, it returns a static page URL.

Listing 3: The GetCategoryHREF() Function

```
function GetCategoryHREF( $aCatID, $aDynamic = True )
    {
        if ( $aDynamic == True )
        {
            return "mgmt_prod_list.phtml?cat_id=$aCatID";
        }
        else
        {
            return "mgmt_cat_{$aCatID}.html";
        }
    }
```

Depending on how you are using your site, you may want to develop this type of method so that you can view the pages dynamically while editing data and generate the static pages later.

For many types of sites, generating static pages from dynamic data is practical and increases overall server efficiency. If your application is one where the changes to data are relatively infrequent, you may want to consider generating static pages. For high-traffic sites, the increase in efficiency can easily outweigh the additional complexity required to develop the page generation scripts. Using server daemons such as **cron**, the page generation even can be scheduled to occur at regular intervals.

Caching Techniques

Generating completely static pages is efficient for many types of sites, but it does require additional planning and development to be effective. For some applications, a middle-ground technique of caching pages may be sufficient. Conceptually, caching is very similar to generating static pages, but the implementation still requires that each page be a PHP script. When the script is requested, it first checks for a valid cached page. If one exists, its contents are sent to the browser. If not, the page is generated and cached for the next request.

Whether a page is valid depends on the nature of the page. For example, you may have a welcome page that displays the current date. If the page has nothing more dynamic, it really only needs to be dynamically generated once per day. The cached page is valid for 24 hours. Other pages may be news pages that are updated hourly. In this case, a cached page is valid for one hour.

The implementation of cached pages is very simple. Either output buffering or templates can be used; output buffering is used for the examples given in Listings 4 and 5. Listing 4 contains the caching logic functions that can be included on any page. Listing 5 is the main page. It provides the current weather information by using a third-party script called **MWeather** available at *http://sourceforge.net/projects/mweather/*.

Listing 4: Caching Functions (cache.php)

```php
<?php
    function GetCacheFileName( $aFileName )
    {
        return $aFileName . ".cache";
    }
    function DumpCacheFile( $aFileName, $aExpire = 3600 )
    {
        $aCacheFile = GetCacheFileName( $aFileName );
        if ( is_file( $aCacheFile ) == True )
```

```
        {
            $aModTime = filemtime( $aCacheFile );
            $aCurTime = time();
            if ( ( $aCurTime - $aModTime ) > $aExpire )
            {
                return False;
            }
            else
            {
                readfile( $aCacheFile );
                return True;
            }
        }
    }
    function SaveCacheFile( $aFileName, $aContents )
    {
        $aCacheFile = GetCacheFileName( $aFileName );
        $aFile = fopen( $aCacheFile, "w" );
        fwrite( $aFile, $aContents );
        fclose( $aFile );
    }
?>
```

Listing 5: Using the Caching Functions

```
<?php
    error_reporting( E_ALL & ~E_NOTICE );
    include( "./cache.php" );
    if ( $aResult = DumpCacheFile( $PATH_TRANSLATED, 60 * 60 ) )
    {
        // there was a valid cache file, exit script
        exit;
    }
    ob_start();
    // page data
    $aOldIncludePath = ini_get( 'include_path' );
    ini_set( 'include_path', $aOldIncludePath . ":./mweather" );
    include( "mweather.php" );
    ini_restore( 'include_path' );
    SaveCacheFile( $PATH_TRANSLATED, ob_get_contents() );
?>
```

The script in Listing 5 uses the caching functions in Listing 4 to provide a one-hour cache file for the weather page. The call to **DumpCacheFile()** performs several important functions. First, it checks the last-modified date of the cache file and compares it to the current time. If the difference between these times is greater than the **expire** value, the function returns False. If not, the function reads and outputs the cache file and returns True. On return, the main script checks the return value. If True, the main script exits because the cache file is valid and has been sent. If False, the script continues as normal, using output buffering to store the output file. At the end of the script, the **SaveCacheFile()** function is called to cache the current page contents.

The page in this example is generated entirely by including the *mweather.php* file. The only other functions in the main script are used to add some information to the value of PHP's **include_path** variable. This is used simply for the **MWeather** functionality and has nothing to do with caching.

The *cache.php* include file could conceivably be used with any PHP script to help manage on-demand page caching. However, it is critical to understand what types of scripts are good candidates for this type of caching. This method only works if the page or script is not requested as the result of an HTTP GET or POST. In other words, this type of caching is impractical for caching pages that are dependent on user-specific values functioning properly. In the previous example, the page is intended to show the current weather for Rexburg, Idaho, no matter who is visiting. If the script were written to display the weather for the visitor, the caching technique would not work. Imagine if the page were cached for a visitor from London and the next visitor were from Cape Town. The cached page would obviously be invalid for the visitor from Cape Town.

Caching of the previous type is useful, but it cannot be used in all cases. If your application contains pages providing information that varies over time, but it is not based on the visitor, then this type of caching is very useful and can significantly improve performance. In the example, the time required to query the actual weather source is about one to two seconds. When cached, the page returns instantly.

Summary

Although PHP is primarily built to provide dynamic Web pages, it is important to consider cases where fully dynamic pages are not required. By generating static pages or by caching pages, you can significantly improve the performance of your Web site. Web application developers should balance the speed of static pages with the flexibility of dynamic pages in a way that provides the most usability and performance for the enduser.

E-Commerce Web Sites

Introduction

It goes without saying that e-commerce is one of the largest motivators for most companies to develop an online presence. Therefore, it is critical to understand how PHP can be used to facilitate all facets of e-commerce development. Much of this chapter is dedicated to the concepts and design considerations surrounding e-commerce development. The actual coding and integration of e-commerce tools is trivial; building a secure, stable, and scalable e-commerce application is the real challenge.

Security

Security is the primary concern when building e-commerce applications. It is critical that you design your applications to protect the collected information about your customers or you won't have any. Several steps must be taken to ensure the highest level of security possible. These steps are not made as a recommendation, but are requirements for most credit card merchant accounts.

Using SSL

The first step is to determine which sections of your Web site require a secure server using the *secure sockets layer* (SSL). Most applications have basically two segments of an e-commerce site. The first is the product/service description area that includes all of the public-accessible pages related to the products or services offered by the site. This typically includes other pages such as company contact information, terms of services, and other non-commerce information. The second segment consists of the actual buying/shopping application. Here, critical private information such as buyer identification and credit card numbers is gathered. For the most part, this chapter is dedicated to the latter segment of the site.

Using SSL with PHP is the same as using PHP with a non-SSL server. Several secure Web server options are available, including Stronghold (http://www.c2.net/products/sh3/). Stronghold is an Apache-based secure

Web server. RedHat (http://www.redhat.com/) also provides a version of its server product that includes OpenSSL that can be used to build a secure Apache Web server. Once you have obtained and installed an Apache-based secure Web server, you can easily incorporate PHP as a shared module using the methods described in Chapter 1, "Building and Installing PHP 4." Also, if you prefer, you may re-build the secure Apache with PHP statically linked.

Certificates

The next step required to deploy a secure server is to install a security certificate. A certificate is a server-based file that is transmitted by the Web server to the client browser along with the server request pages. Several companies provide security certificates that are recognized by most modern browsers. One such company is Thawte Consulting (http://www.thawte. com/). The Thawte site contains all of the information required to evaluate, test, and ultimately buy your security certificate. A few of the documents needed to obtain a certificate are as follows:

1. Proof of Organization Name, such as articles of incorporation
2. Proof of Right to use Domain Name

If the name in number 1 matches the name obtained from a *whois* query to the requested domain, then number 2 doesn't require any additional documentation.

You can get up and running with a test certificate that is available at the Thawte Web site. The test certificate causes the browser to display a warning message when used, but it enables you to test your implementation before purchasing an actual certificate.

If you are using Apache, you must install your certificate on the Web server machine and edit the *httpd.conf* file to use the certificate files. A sample configuration for a name-based virtual hosting system is shown in Listing 1.

Listing 1: httpd.conf with Certificate Directives

```
SSLCertificateFile /apache/conf/ssl.crt/server.crt
SSLCertificateKeyFile /apache/conf/ssl.key/server.key
NameVirtualHost 129.129.1.1:443
<VirtualHost 129.129.1.1:443>
  SSLEnable
```

```
    ServerAdmin webmaster@server.com
    DocumentRoot /home/server/secure
    ServerName secure.server.com
    DirectoryIndex index.phtml index.html
</VirtualHost>
```

Instructions for obtaining and installing your certificate are available from the Thawte Web site. Additional instructions regarding the use of the certificate with your Web server are typically documented with the Web server. If you choose Red Hat, the documentation is clear and easy to follow.

Database Security

One of the discoveries in some of the recent credit card thefts on the Internet is that in many of the cases, the sites were storing credit card information unencrypted in Web-accessible databases. Even sites that were using SSL encryption to gather information were still storing the private information in insecure ways. Recently, some merchant account agreements have required that data be stored encrypted, behind firewalls, or both. This is just common sense. Your application should encrypt the transmission *and storage* of all private information.

Many modern database management systems provide methods for encrypting data. For example, the MySQL DBMS provides **ENCODE()** and **DECODE()** as a part of its language. Although these functions may not be rigorous enough for this critical information, the point is that they are available. Use them or something similar to provide a level of protection on the data you collect. Ultimately, you and your company are liable for any breaches in security that lead to critical data being used wrongly.

Payment Processing

After building and testing the secure Web server, the next step is to choose a payment processing method. PHP provides native interfaces to several payment processing systems including CyberCash, VeriSign, and CCVS. To understand the interaction between the enduser, the secure Web server, and the payment processing tools, see Figure 17.1.

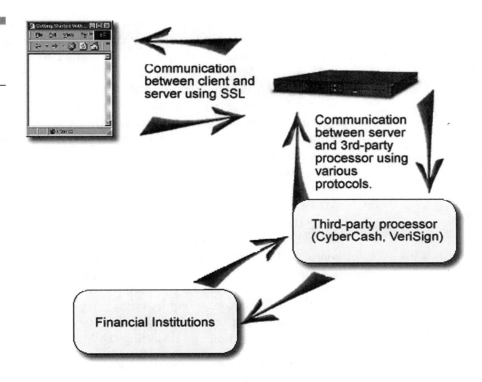

Communication
between client and
server using SSL

Communication
between server
and 3rd-party
processor using
various
protocols.

Third-party processor
(CyberCash, VeriSign)

Financial Institutions

Four primary entities are shown in Figure 17.1, the client or enduser, the server, the third-party processor, and the financial institutions. The client and server communicate via SSL, providing encrypted two-way data transmission. The server (again a 1U server from Penguin computing) also communicates with the third-party processor using a protocol determined by the processor. The third-party processor communicates directly with the financial institutions to determine whether to approve a credit card or other payment transaction. If you are using CCVS, it is possible to bypass the third-party processor and communicate directly with the financial clearinghouses.

One reason for choosing CyberCash as a third-party processor is that the protocol used to communicate between the server and CyberCash is built into the CyberCash programming interface. Other third-party processors require that the applications use secure sockets to communicate with them. It is important to realize that although you may have a secure server that is capable of using SSL, PHP does not provide an SSL implementation. In other words, if you open a socket using PHP, it will not use SSL just because your Web server uses SSL. Until PHP provides a method for directly using SSL sockets natively, some third-party processing options will not be available. CyberCash provides its own Triple DES encryption algorithm to ensure security between the Web server and its processing center. The remainder of this section focuses on using CyberCash as a payment processor.

CyberCash (http://www.cybercash.com/) is a third-party processor that provides *application programming interfaces* (APIs) for developers using C/C++ and Java. The C/C++ version of the API can be built into PHP using the PHP configuration option, **--with-cybercash**. To do this, first obtain the CyberCash *Merchant Connection Kit* (MCK) from the CyberCash Web site. In conjunction with this, you must be sure that your merchant account can be used with CyberCash. If you do not already have a merchant account, you can register for one online with one of the CyberCash partner merchants. This process requires that you provide detailed financial information, but it can be completed in as little as 24 hours. The major steps required for obtaining and installing the MCK are as follows:

1. Establish a relationship with a CyberCash-affiliated acquiring financial institution (merchant account).

2. Register as a CyberCash merchant at http://amps.cybercash.com/.

3. Download the MCK.

4. Decompress and install the MCK.

5. Build PHP with CyberCash support (**--with-cybercash**).

Detailed instructions for downloading and installing the MCK are available at the CyberCash Web site. The MCK may be installed on *nix or Windows-based servers. The installation procedure on *nix is very simple. Here are the basic steps:

1. Decompress the installer: *uncompress install-mck-3.2.0.6-<operating_system>.Z.*

2. Edit the permissions of the installer so that it can be executed: *chmod +x install-mck-3.2.0.6-<operating system>.*

3. Run the install program: *./install-mck-3.2-<operating system>*.

4. Run the configuration program: *./configure*.

At steps 3 and 4, text prompts appear that require you to provide information about your company, your online store, and other relevant data. Once these steps have been completed, PHP can be rebuilt using the **--with-cybercash=/path/to/mck** option. The full path to the location where you installed the MCK must be provided. After rebuilding PHP with CyberCash support, you can begin performing test transactions.

One of the very nice things about using the MCK with PHP is that much of the configuration of the MCK, as detailed in the user guides, can be bypassed. Using PHP to communicate with CyberCash is as simple as including a single script. The sample script for using CyberCash is found in the source distribution in the *<php>/ext/cybercash/* directory. This test script (*test.php*) is shown in Listing 2.

Listing 2: test.php (CyberCash test script)

```php
<?php
require "cyberlib.php";
$merchant=""; /* Your merchant ID goes here. */
$merchant_key=""; /* Your merchant key goes here. */
$payment_url="http://cr.cybercash.com/cgi-bin/";
$auth_type="mauthonly";
$response=SendCC2_1Server($merchant,$merchant_key,$payment_url,
                $auth_type,array("Order-ID" => "2342322",
                "Amount" => "usd 11.50",
                "Card-Number" => "4111111111111111",
                "Card-Address" => "1600 Pennsylvania Avenue",
                "Card-City" => "Washington",
                "Card-State" => "DC",
                "Card-Zip" => "20500",
                "Card-Country" => "USA",
                "Card-Exp" => "12/99",
                "Card-Name" => "Bill Clinton"));
while(list($key,$val)=each($response))
{
   echo $key."=".$val."<br>";
}
?>
```

The test script illustrates how easily payment processing can be accomplished with CyberCash and PHP. The variables, **$merchant** and **$merchant_key** must contain the merchant ID and key that you were assigned by CyberCash. Then, using a simple associative array to set the required

CyberCash variables, the payment is processed by calling the **SendCC2_1Server()** function defined in the *cyberlib.php* include file. It is not necessary to directly use any of the **cybercash_xxx** functions available in PHP. The **SendCC2_1Server()** function encapsulates these functions and manages the socket-based communication with CyberCash.

The information sent to CyberCash is provided via an associative array in PHP. This array is the last parameter sent to the **SendCC2_1Server()** function. The elements of this array are determined by the value of the **$auth_type** variable. The **$auth_type** variable specifies the type of action to perform or the type of message sent to CyberCash. The available Cyber-Cash messages are shown in Table 17.1.

The CyberCash documentation provides details about each of the messages and their purpose. For many stores, the first message (and possibly the only message) that needs to be implemented is the **mauthonly** message. This message is used to authorize credit card sales. Depending on the product or service you offer, you may configure CyberCash to automatically mark and settle all transactions that are authorized.

The fields used with the **mauthonly** message are described in Table 17.2. The mandatory fields are marked with a check.

The return value from the **SendCC2_1Server()** is also an associative array containing information about the transaction from CyberCash. The response from a **mauthonly** message includes fields shown in Table 17.3.

An example of using CyberCash in a real-world scenario is shown in Listing 3. This example includes error handling and user feedback that is not present in the basic test case in Listing 2.

Listing 3: Using CyberCash

```php
<?php
    include "cyberlib.php"; // CyberCash processing functions
    include "dbclass.php";  // Database class for this application
    include "class.FastTemplate.php"; // FastTemplate
    // utility function for turning an associative array
    // into a single semicolon-separated string
    function ArrayCrunch( $aArray )
    {
        $aResult = "";
        foreach( $aArray as $aKey => $aValue )
        {
            $aResult .= "$aKey=$aValue;";
        }
        return $aResult;
```

Table 17.1

Available
CyberCash
Messages and
Their Functions

Use This Message	To Perform This Function
batch-commit	Commit transactions assembled in a batch.
batch-prep	Query for transactions that are marked as ready to be sent to the processor in a batch.
batch-query	Query for a batch.
batch-retry	Retry a batch in pending state.
batch-unroll	Query for transactions that were sent in a batch.
card-query	Request credit card data from the Gateway for a given order.
checkauth	Validate and authorize a merchant-initiated check payment. This message is available only for the Paymentech processor (using the *Electronic Check Payment* (ECP) option).
checkreturn	Return money to a consumer's checking account.
mauthcapture	Authorize and capture a merchant-originated credit card sale. This message is for host capture processors only.
mauthonly	Authorize a merchant-originated credit card sale. This message is for terminal capture processors only.
postauth	Capture a credit card payment previously authorized with mauthonly or checkauth.
query	Query the transaction's database.
retry	Retry a pending transaction for a given order.
return	Return money to the consumer's credit card.
void	Void a transaction.
merchant-check-payment	Validate and authorize a merchant initiated PayNow check transaction.
check-query	Query the PayNow check transactions database for information about particular checks.
check-update-status	Update the check server database with changes from the last check update at the Gateway.
check-query-order-status	Query for the current status of orders.

Table 17.2

mauthonly Fields
and Their
Descriptions

Field	Description	Mandatory
order-id	The unique order ID for this transaction.	☑
amount	The amount to authorize (that is, the amount to be charged) for this transaction. Use the format currency dollar.cents (for example, usd 12.50).	☑
card-number	The card number for the credit card used for this transaction.	☑
card-exp	The expiration date of the credit card used for this transaction. Use the format mm/yy (for example, 02/00 for February 2000). This field is required.	☑
card-name	The name of the credit card owner.	
card-address	The street address where the credit card owner resides. NOTE: This field is required for AVS and for Discover cards.	
card-city	The city where the credit card owner resides. NOTE: This field is required for Discover cards.	
card-zip	The postal zip code where the credit card owner resides. The following examples are all valid entries: "22091," "20191-1448," "NW3 5RJ," and "113 192" NOTE: This field is required for AVS and Discover cards.	
card-state	The state where the credit card owner resides. NOTE: This field is required for Discover cards.	
card-country	The country where the credit card owner resides.	

```
}
$tpl = new FastTemplate( "." );
// get customer id from encrypted ID form field
$aCustomerID   = UnhideID( $ID );
$merchant      = ""; /* Your merchant ID goes here. */
$merchant_key  = ""; /* Your merchant key goes here. */
$payment_url   = "http://cr.cybercash.com/cgi-bin/";
$auth_type     = "mauthonly";
$aDB = new dbAccess;
$aDB->Init();
// check to make sure this customer hasn't already paid
$aSQL = "select ISPAID from orders where ( ID = $aCustomerID
)";
$aDB->SetSQL( $aSQL );
if ( $aDB->RecordCount() == 1 )
{
```

Table 17.3

mauthonly
Response Fields
and Their
Descriptions

Field	Description
MStatus	The returned status code of the command issued. This field is always present. It can assume the following values: ■ **success**-successful transaction. ■ **success-duplicate**—result of a previously successful transaction. ■ **partial success**—batch with failed transactions. ■ **failure-hard**—failed transaction; subsequent retry will not help. ■ **failure-q-or-cancel**, **failure-q-or-discard**—failed transaction due to a communication failure; this may be retried. ■ **failure-swversion**—failed transaction because of old or non-existent software (version) being used. ■ **failure-bad-money**—failed transaction because of a credit problem with the financial institution.
MErrLoc	The location of the error that occurred in the transaction. This field is present only if the transaction did not succeed (in other words, MStatus was not "success"). The following values can be returned: ■ **smps**—failure occurred at the CashRegister. ■ **ccsp**—failure occurred at the Gateway. ■ **financial institution**—failure occurred at the payment processor. ■ **CCMckDirectLib3_2**—failure occurred at the MCK.
MErrMsg	The text message of the error that occurred in the transaction. This field is present only if the transaction did not succeed (in other words, MStatus was not "success").
MErrCode	A number code that corresponds to the error message sent in the MErrMsg field.
merch-txn	The number that the Gateway uses to refer to a transaction that was performed or attempted. This field is always present.
order-id	The order ID of the order whose transaction was just processed. This field is always present.
cust-txn	The transaction number used by a CyberCash wallet to identify a transaction. For non-wallet transactions, it is the same as merch-txn.
aux-msg	The Gateway merchant message contains additional verbiage from the Gateway or payment server.
MSWErrMsg	The error message when an outdated version of the Wallet or the payment server is being used. This field may not always be present.
addnl-response-data	Additional transaction data returned from the Gateway. NOTE: If no additional data exists, this field will be empty.

```
        $aRow           = $aDB->GetData( 0 );
        $aIsPaid        = $aRow["ISPAID"];
    }
    else
    {
        $aIsPaid        = 0;
    }
    // If the customer has already paid, indicate that information
    // and exit this script
    if ( $aIsPaid == 1 )
    {
        mail( "blake@intechra.net", "Payment Retry ($aCustomerID)",
"Tried To Pay Again??", "From: support@intechra.net\r\n" );
        $tpl->define( array(     base            => "a_base.tpl",
                                 footer          =>
"c_footer.tpl",
                                 body            =>
"s_paid_already.tpl"
                         ) );
        $tpl->assign( array(     TITLE           => "Intechra.Net
Payment",
                                 URL             => $aInternalURL,
                                 THEDATE         => date( "l, j F Y"
),
                                 ORDERID         => $aOrderID,
                                 HIDDENID        => $ID
                         ) );
        AddSiteVars( $tpl, $aHiddenID );
        $tpl->parse( FOOTER, "footer" );
        $tpl->parse( BODY, "body" );
        $tpl->parse( PAGE, "base" );
        $tpl->FastPrint( PAGE );
        exit;
    }
    // get a new MCK_ID for this customer
    $aSQL = "select MAX( MCK_ID ) as MAX_ID from customers_to_mcks
where ( ID = $aCustomerID )";
    $aDB->SetSQL( $aSQL );
    if ( $aDB->RecordCount() == 1 )
    {
        $aRow           = $aDB->GetData( 1 );
        $aMaxID         = $aRow["MAX_ID"];
    }
    else
    {
        $aMaxID         = 0;
    }
    $aCurID        = $aMaxID + 1;
    $aOrderID      = "INT-" . date( "Ymd" ) . "-" . sprintf( "%06d",
$aCustomerID ) . "-" . sprintf( "%04d", $aCurID );
    $aOrderDetails = array( "Order-ID"      => $aOrderID,
                            "Amount"        => "usd 39.00",
                            "Card-Number"   => $CCNum,
                            "Card-Address"  => $CCAddr,
                            "Card-City"     => $CCCity,
```

```
                                        "Card-State"      => $CCState,
                                        "Card-Zip"        => $CCZip,
                                        "Card-Exp"        => $CCExpDate,
                                        "Card-Name"       => $CCName );
            $response = SendCC2_1Server( $merchant, $merchant_key,
        $payment_url, $auth_type, $aOrderDetails );
            $aRawRequest  = ArrayCrunch( $aOrderDetails );
            $aRawResponse = ArrayCrunch( $response );
            $aSQL = "insert into customers_to_mcks values ( $aCustomerID,
        $aCurID, 0, NOW(), ENCODE( \"$aRawRequest\", \"good_password\" ),
        ENCODE( \"$aRawResponse\", \"good_password\" ) )";
            $aDB->SetSQL( $aSQL );
            if ( $response["MStatus"] == "success" )
            {
                mail( "blake@intechra.net", "Intechra Account Paid: Success
        ($aCustomerID)", "Paid Successfully", "From:
        support@intechra.net\r\n" );
                $aSQL = "update orders set ISPAID = 1 where ( ID =
        $aCustomerID )";
                $aDB->SetSQL( $aSQL );
                $tpl->define( array(    base              => "a_base.tpl",
                                        footer            =>
        "c_footer.tpl",
                                        body              => "s_paid_ok.tpl"
                                ) );
                $tpl->assign( array(    TITLE             => "Intechra.net
        Payment",
                                        URL               => $aInternalURL,
                                        THEDATE           => date( "l, j F Y"
        ),
                                        ORDERID           => $aOrderID,
                                        HIDDENID          => $ID
                                ) );
                AddSiteVars( $tpl, $aHiddenID );
                $tpl->parse( FOOTER, "footer" );
                $tpl->parse( BODY, "body" );
                $tpl->parse( PAGE, "base" );
                $tpl->FastPrint( PAGE );
            }
            else
            {
                mail( "blake@intechra.net", "Intechra Account Paid: Fail
        ($aCustomerID)", "Failure in Payment", "From:
        support@intechra.net\r\n" );
                $tpl->define( array(    base              => "a_base.tpl",
                                        footer            =>
        "c_footer.tpl",
                                        body              =>
        "s_paid_fail.tpl"
                                ) );
                $tpl->assign( array(    TITLE             => "Intechra.net
        Payment",
                                        HIDDENID          => $ID
                                ) );
                $tpl->parse( FOOTER, "footer" );
```

```
        $tpl->parse( BODY, "body" );
        $tpl->parse( PAGE, "base" );
        $tpl->FastPrint( PAGE );
    }
?>
```

The script in Listing 3 shows how a real payment processing system can be built around the code in Listing 2. This script is used as the action of a form that gathers the relevant credit card information. First, this script obtains the customer ID from a field in the form. Next, it sets the Cyber-Cash variables including setting the message type to **mauthonly** as previously described. Then the database is checked to ensure that this customer has not already made a payment. In this application, each customer makes a single payment for services rendered. If the customer has already paid, the script mails the administrator an informational message and then displays a page indicating to the user that payment has already been made. The script then exits.

If the payment has not been made previously, then a new id is gathered from the database that will be used to generate a unique order number. According to the CyberCash documentation, the order ID must be 25 characters or fewer, and it must be unique; use letters, numbers, periods, dashes, and underscores. The script generates a unique order ID of the format **INT-YYYYMMDD-CCCCC-OOOO** where **YYYYMMDD** is the current date, **CCCCC** is the customer id, and **OOOO** is the id that was gathered from the database.

The payment information is then set in the **$aOrderDetails** array and the **SendCC2_1Server()** function is called. The request and response are stored into the database with basic encryption applied to both the request and the response. Then the status of the response is checked. If successful, a message indicating success is displayed, and the customer's payment record is updated. If a failure occurs, the customer is notified. In either case, an email is sent to the administrator for notification.

As illustrated in the examples, the implementation of the CyberCash API in PHP is actually trivial, but developing a secure, stable e-commerce system takes a significant amount of planning and thought. When dealing with actual money transactions, your customers expect the very best service. If your application allows for accidental multiple payments or fails to provide adequate feedback, your customers will be dissatisfied. Take time to read the documentation provided by your third-party processor. A great deal of information is available, and it is again your responsibility to understand it and implement it correctly.

Product Delivery

Another aspect of e-commerce that requires planning is managing shipment of physical goods to the customer. If your product must be shipped, then additional steps are required in conjunction with those previously described. The reason is that most credit card merchants require that the customer's card may not be charged until goods have been delivered. It is acceptable to request authorization before the goods are shipped, but the payment transaction may not be settled until the goods have been shipped. Also, providing real shipping costs as a part of the ordering process is important both for your business and the customer.

If you are shipping goods, then your payment processing application will be more complex than the ones shown in this chapter. However, all of the necessary steps can be performed using PHP. A recommended scenario is to provide an additional application to record shipment status so that when an order actually ships, the credit card payment is finalized and a message is sent to the customer.

Several online options are available to provide real-time shipping options and costs. Both UPS (http://www.ups.com/) and Federal Express (http://www.fedex.com/) provide tools for integrating shipping options into a Web application. The UPS tools are flexible and powerful and can be easily integrated into PHP applications with very little code. Unfortunately, I was not able to receive permission to document either of these systems before this chapter had to be finished. When I receive authorization, I will provide the information at the Web site listed in the Internet Resources section in the appendices. Let it suffice to say that using the UPS online tools provides a mechanism by which you can provide real shipping costs from any origin to any destination using any service rate. The data is maintained at the UPS site; your application queries their servers for the data at the time of the sale.

Summary

Developing e-commerce applications is not particularly challenging from a pure coding perspective. The challenge comes in developing an e-commerce application that is secure and simple for the user and integrates all the necessary technologies. When deploying e-commerce applications, take the necessary time to understand all of the components and test the system thoroughly. Provide your customers with peace of mind by securely storing all data and using SSL for all client-to-server data requests.

APPENDIX A

abs

Returns the absolute value of a number. If the argument number is float, then return type is also float; otherwise it is int.

   mixed **abs**(mixed number)

accept_connect

After the socket **$socket** has been created using **socket()**, bound to a name with **bind()**, and told to listen for connections with **listen()**, this function will accept incoming connections on that socket. Once a successful connection is made, a new socket descriptor is returned, which may be used for communication. If multiple connections are queued on the socket, the first will be used. If no connections are pending, **accept_connect()** will block until a connection becomes present. If **$socket** has been made non-blocking using **socket_set_blocking()** or **set_nonblock()**, an error code will be returned.

   int **accept_connect**(int socket)

   The socket descriptor returned by **accept_connect()** may not be used to accept new connections. The original listening socket **$socket**, however, remains open and may be reused.

   Returns a new socket descriptor on success, or a negative error code on failure. This code may be passed to **strerror()** to get a textual explanation of the error. See also **bind()**, **connect()**, **listen()**, **socket()**, **socket_get_status()**, and **strerror()**.

acos

Returns the arc cosine of **arg** in radians. See also **asin()** and **atan()**.

   float **acos**(float arg)

AddCSlashes

Returns a string with backslashes before characters that are listed in **$charlist** parameter. It escapes \n, \r, and so on in C-like style, and characters with ASCII code lower than 32 and higher than 126 are converted to octal representation. Be careful when escaping alphanumeric characters. You can specify a range in **$charlist** such as "\0..\37", which would escape all characters with ASCII code between 0 and 31.

   string **AddCSlashes**(string str, string charlist)

   Example: Addcslashes()

```
$escaped = addcslashes ($not_escaped, "\0..\37!@\177..\377");
```

Note: Added in PHP4b3-dev. See also **stripcslashes()**, **stripslashes()**, **htmlspecialchars()**, **htmlspecialchars()**, and **quotemeta()**.

AddSlashes

Returns a string with backslashes before characters that need to be quoted in database queries and so on. These characters are single quote ('), double quote ("), backslash (\ ) and NUL (the null byte). See also **stripslashes()**, **htmlspecialchars()**, and **quotemeta()**.

    string **AddSlashes**(string str)

apache_lookup_uri

This performs a partial request for a URI. It goes just far enough to obtain all the important information about the given resource and returns this information in a class. The properties of the returned class are:

status	the_request	status_line
method	content_type	handler
uri	filename	path_info
args	boundary	no_cache
no_local_copy	allowed	send_bodyct
bytes_sent	byterange	clength
unparsed_uri	mtime	request_time

    class **apache_lookup_uri**(string filename)

    Note: Apache_lookup_uri() only works when PHP is installed as an Apache module.

apache_note

This is an Apache-specific function, which gets and sets values in a request's *notes* table. If called with one argument, it returns the current value of note *note_name*. If called with two arguments, it sets the value of note *note_name* to *note_value* and returns the previous value of note *note_name*.

    string **apache_note**(string note_name, [string note_value])

array

Returns an array of the parameters. The parameters can be given an index with the => operator.

    array **array**([mixed . . .])

    Array() is a language construct used to represent literal arrays, and is not a regular function. The following example demonstrates how to create a two-dimensional array, how to specify keys for associative arrays, and how to skip-and-continue numeric indices in normal arrays. See also **list()**.

Example: Array()

```
$fruits = array (
    "fruits"  => array ("a"=>"orange", "b"=>"banana", "c"=>"apple"),
    "numbers" => array (1, 2, 3, 4, 5, 6),
    "holes"   => array ("first", 5 => "second", "third")
);
```

array_count_values

This function returns an array using the values of the **$input** array as keys, and their frequency in **$input** as values.

array **array_count_values**(array input)

Example: Array_count_values()

```
$array = array (1, "hello", 1, "world", "hello");
array_count_values ($array); // returns array (1=>2, "hello"=>2, "world"=>1)
```

array_diff

Returns an array containing all the values of **$array1** that are not present in any of the other arguments. Note that keys are preserved. See also **array_intersect()**.

array **array_diff**(array array1, array array2, [array . . .])

Example: Array_diff()

```
$array1 = array ("a" => "green", "red", "blue");
$array2 = array ("b" => "green", "yellow", "red");
$result = array_diff ($array1, $array2);
```

This makes *$result* have array *("blue")*;.

array_flip

This function returns an array in flip order.

array **array_flip**(array trans)

Example: Array_flip()

```
$trans = array_flip ($trans);
$original = strtr ($str, $trans);
```

array_intersect

Returns an array containing all the values of $array1 that are present in all the arguments. Note that keys are preserved. See also **array_diff()**.

array **array_intersect**(array array1, array array2, [array . . .])

Example: Array_intersect()

```
$array1 = array ("a" => "green", "red", "blue");
$array2 = array ("b" => "green", "yellow", "red");
$result = array_intersect ($array1, $array2);
```

This makes *$result* have array ("a" => "green", "red");.

array_keys Returns the keys, numeric and string, from the **$input** array. If the optional **$search_value** is specified, then only the keys for that value are returned. Otherwise, all the keys from the **$input** are returned. See also **array_values()**.

array **array_keys**(array input, [mixed search_value])

Example: Array_keys()

```
$array = array (0 => 100, "color" => "red");
array_keys ($array);        // returns array (0, "color")
$array = array ("blue", "red", "green", "blue", "blue");
array_keys ($array, "blue");  //  returns array (0, 3, 4)
```

This function was added to PHP 4; the following is an implementation for those still using PHP 3.

Example: Implementation of **array_keys()** for PHP 3 users

```
function array_keys ($arr, $term="") {
    $t = array();
    while (list($k,$v) = each($arr)) {
        if ($term && $v != $term)
            continue;
            $t[] = $k;
        }
        return $t;
}
```

array_merge

This function merges the elements of two or more arrays together so that the values of one are appended to the end of the previous one. It returns the resulting array.

If the input arrays have the same string keys, then the later value for that key will overwrite the previous one. If, however, the arrays have the same numeric key, the later value will not overwrite the original value, but will be appended.

array **array_merge**(array array1, array array2, [array . . .])

Example: array_merge()

```
$array1 = array ("color" => "red", 2, 4);
$array2 = array ("a", "b", "color" => "green", "shape" => "trapezoid", 4);
array_merge ($array1, $array2);
```

Resulting array will be array("color" => "green", 2, 4, "a", "b", "shape" => "trapezoid", 4). See also **array_merge_recursive()**.

array_merge_recursive

Merges the elements of two or more arrays together so that the values of one are appended to the end of the previous one. It returns the resulting array.

If the input arrays have the same string keys, then the values for these keys are merged together into an array. This is done recursively so that if one of the values is an array itself, the function will merge it with a corresponding entry in another array too. If, however, the arrays have the same numeric key, the later value will not overwrite the original value, but will be appended.

array **array_merge_recursive**(array array1, array array2, [array . . .])

Example: Array_merge_recursive()

```
$ar1 = array ("color" => array ("favorite" => "red"), 5);
$ar2 = array (10, "color" => array ("favorite" => "green", "blue"));
$result = array_merge_recursive ($ar1, $ar2);
```

Resulting array will be array ("color" => array *("favorite"* => array ("red", "green"), "blue"), 5, 10). See also **array_merge()**.

array_multisort

This function can be used to sort several arrays at once or a multi-dimensional array accordingly by one or more dimensions. It maintains key association when sorting.

bool **array_multisort**(array ar1, [mixed arg], [mixed . . .], [array . . .])

The input arrays are treated as columns of a table to be sorted by rows—this resembles the functionality of SQL ORDER BY clause. The first array is the primary one by which to sort. The rows (values) in that array that compare the same are sorted by the next input array, and so on.

The argument structure of this function is somewhat unusual, but flexible. The very first argument has to be an array. Subsequently, each argument can be either an array or a sorting flag from the following lists.

Sorting order flags:

- SORT_ASC—sort in ascending order
- SORT_DESC—sort in descending order

  Sorting type flags:

- SORT_REGULAR—compare items normally
- SORT_NUMERIC—compare items numerically
- SORT_STRING—compare items as strings

No two sorting flags of the same type can be specified after each array. The sorting flags specified after an array argument apply only to that array. They are reset to default SORT_ASC and SORT_REGULAR after each new array argument.

Returns true on success, false on failure.

Example: Sorting multiple arrays

```
$ar1 = array ("10", 100, 100, "a");
$ar2 = array (1, 3, "2", 1);
array_multisort ($ar1, $ar2);
```

In this example, after sorting, the first array will contain 10, "a", 100, 100. The second array will contain 1, 1, 2, "3". The entries in the second array, corresponding to the identical entries in the first array (100 and 100), were sorted as well.

Example: Sorting multi-dimensional array

```
$ar = array (array ("10", 100, 100, "a"), array (1, 3, "2", 1));
array_multisort ($ar[0], SORT_ASC, SORT_STRING,
                 $ar[1], SORT_NUMERIC, SORT_DESC);
```

In this example, after sorting, the first array will contain 10, 100, 100, "a" (it was sorted as strings in ascending order), and the second one will contain 1, 3, "2", 1 (sorted as numbers, in descending order).

array_pad

Returns a copy of the **$input** padded to size specified by **$pad_size** with value **$pad_value**. If **$pad_size** is positive, then the array is padded on the right; if it's negative, then the array is padded on the left. If the absolute value of **$pad_size** is less than or equal to the length of the **$input**, then no padding takes place.

array **array_pad**(array input, int pad_size, mixed pad_value)

Example: Array_pad()

```
$input = array (12, 10, 9);
$result = array_pad ($input, 5, 0);
// result is array (12, 10, 9, 0, 0)
$result = array_pad ($input, -7, -1);
// result is array (-1, -1, -1, -1, 12, 10, 9)
$result = array_pad ($input, 2, "noop");
// not padded
```

array_pop

This function pops and returns the last value of the **$array**, shortening the **$array** by one element.

mixed **array_pop**(array array)

Example: Array_pop()

```
$stack = array ("orange", "apple", "raspberry");
$fruit = array_pop ($stack);
```

After this, *$stack* has only 2 elements: "orange" and "apple", and *$fruit* has "raspberry". See also **array_push()**, **array_shift()**, and **array_unshift()**.

array_push

Treats **$array** as a stack, and pushes the passed variables onto the end of **$array**.

int **array_push**(array array, mixed var, [mixed . . .])

The length of **$array** increases by the number of variables pushed. It has the same effect as the following:

```
$array[] = $var;
```

repeated for each **$var**.
Returns the new number of elements in the array.
Example: Array_push()

```
$stack = array (1, 2);
array_push ($stack, "+", 3);
```

This example would result in *$stack* having 4 elements: 1, 2, "+", and 3. See also: **array_pop()**, **array_shift()**, and **array_unshift()**.
array_rand   This function is rather useful when you want to pick one or more random entries out of an array. It takes an $input array and an optional argument $num_req, which specifies how many entries you want to pick—if not specified, it defaults to 1.

mixed **array_rand**(array input, [int num_req])

If you are picking only one entry, **array_rand()** returns the key for a random entry. Otherwise, it returns an array of keys for the random entries. This is done so that you can pick random keys as well as values out of the array.
Don't forget to call **srand()** to seed the random number generator.
Example: Array_rand()

```
srand ((double) microtime() * 10000000);
$input = array ("Neo", "Morpheus", "Trinity", "Cypher", "Tank");
$rand_keys = array_rand ($input, 2);
print $input[$rand_keys[0]]."\n";
print $input[$rand_keys[1]]."\n";
```

array_reverse

Takes input **$array** and returns a new array with the order of the elements reversed.

array **array_reverse**(array array)

Example: Array_reverse()

```
$input = array ("php", 4.0, array ("green", "red"));
$result = array_reverse ($input);
```

This makes *$result* have array (*array* (*"green"*, *"red"*), *4.0*, *"php"*) .

array_shift

Shifts the first value of the **$array** off and returns it, shortening the **$array** by one element and moving everything down.

> mixed **array_shift**(array array)

> **Example: Array_shift()**

```
$args = array ("-v", "-f");
$opt = array_shift ($args);
```

This would result in *$args* having one element "-f" left, and *$opt* being "-v". See also **array_unshift()**, **array_push()**, and **array_pop()**.

array_slice

Returns a sequence of elements from the **$array**, specified by the **$offset** and **$length** parameters. See also **array_splice()**.

> array **array_slice**(array array, int offset, [int length])

If **$offset** is positive, the sequence will start at that offset in the **$array**. If **$offset** is negative, the sequence will start that far from the end of the **$array**.

If **$length** is given and is positive, then the sequence will have that many elements in it. If **$length** is given and is negative, then the sequence will stop that many elements from the end of the array. If it is omitted, then the sequence will have everything from **$offset** up until the end of the **$array**.

> **Example: Array_slice()**

```
$input = array ("a", "b", "c", "d", "e");
$output = array_slice ($input, 2);       // returns "c", "d", and "e"
$output = array_slice ($input, 2, -1);   // returns "c", "d"
$output = array_slice ($input, -2, 1);   // returns "d"
$output = array_slice ($input, 0, 3);    // returns "a", "b", and "c"
```

array_splice

Removes the elements designated by **$offset** and **$length** from the **$input** array, and replaces them with the elements of the **$replacement** array, if supplied. See also **array_slice()**.

> array **array_splice**(array input, int offset, [int length], [array replacement])

If **$offset** is positive, then the start of removed portion is at that offset from the beginning of the **$input** array. If **$offset** is negative, then it starts that far from the end of the **$input** array.

If **$length** is omitted, it removes everything from **$offset** to the end of the array. If **$length** is specified and is positive, then that many elements will be removed. If **$length** is specified and is negative, then the end of the removed portion will be that many elements from the end of the array. Tip: To remove everything from **$offset** to the end of the array when **$replacement** is also specified, use *count($input)* for **$length**.

If **$replacement** array is specified, then the removed elements are replaced with elements from this array. If **$offset** and **$length** are such that nothing is removed, then the elements from the **$replacement** array are inserted in the place specified by the **$offset**.

Tip: If the replacement is just one element, it is unnecessary to put *array()* around it, unless the element is an array itself.

The following equivalencies hold:

```
array_push ($input, $x, $y)      array_splice ($input, count ($input), 0,
                                               array ($x, $y))
array_pop ($input)               array_splice ($input, -1)
array_shift ($input)             array_splice ($input, 0, 1)
array_unshift ($input, $x, $y)   array_splice ($input, 0, 0, array ($x, $y))
$a[$x] = $y                      array_splice ($input, $x, 1, $y)
```

Returns the array consisting of removed elements.

Example: Array_splice()

```
$input = array ("red", "green", "blue", "yellow");
array_splice ($input, 2);       // $input is now array ("red", "green")
array_splice ($input, 1, -1);   // $input is now array ("red", "yellow")
array_splice ($input, 1, count($input), "orange");
                                // $input is now array ("red", "orange")
array_splice ($input, -1, 1, array("black", "maroon"));
                                // $input is now array ("red", "green",
                                //           "blue", "black", "maroon")
```

array_unique

Takes input $array and returns a new array without duplicate values. Note that keys are preserved.

array **array_unique**(array array)

Example: Array_unique() example

```
$input = array ("a" => "green", "red", "b" => "green", "blue", "red");
$result = array_unique ($input);
```

This makes *$result* have array ("a" => *"green", "red", "blue");*.

array_unshift

This function prepends passed elements to the front of the **$array** . Note that the list of elements is prepended as a whole, so that the prepended elements stay in the same order. This function returns the new number of elements in the **$array** .

int **array_unshift**(array array, mixed var, [mixed . . .])

Example: Array_unshift()

```
$queue = array ("p1", "p3");
array_unshift ($queue, "p4", "p5", "p6");
```

This would result in *$queue* having 5 elements: "p4", "p5", "p6", "p1", and "p3". See also **array_shift()**, **array_push()**, and **array_pop()**.

array_values

Returns all the values from the **$input** array.

array **array_values**(array input)

Example: Array_values()

```
$array = array ("size" => "XL", "color" => "gold");
array_values ($array);    // returns array ("XL", "gold")
```

Note: This function was added to PHP 4; the following is an implementation for those still using PHP 3.

Example: Implementation of **array_values()** for PHP 3 users

```
function array_values ($arr) {
    $t = array();
    while (list($k, $v) = each ($arr)) {
        $t[] = $v;
        return $t;
    }
}
```

array_walk

Applies the function named by **$func** to each element of **$arr**. **$func** will be passed array value as the first parameter and array key as the second parameter. If **$userdata** is supplied, it will be passed as the third parameter to the user function.

int **array_walk**(array arr, string func, mixed userdata)

If **$func** requires more than two or three arguments, depending on **$userdata**, a warning will be generated each time **array_walk()** calls **$func**. These warnings may be suppressed by prepending the '@' sign to the **array_walk()** call, or by using **error_reporting()**.

Note: If **$func** needs to be working with the actual values of the array, specify that the first parameter of **$func** should be passed by reference. Then any changes made to those elements will be made in the array itself.

Passing the key and userdata to **$func** was added in 4.0.

In PHP 4, **reset()** needs to be called as necessary because **array_walk()** does not reset the array by default.

Example: Array_walk()

```
$fruits = array ("d"=>"lemon", "a"=>"orange", "b"=>"banana", "c"=>"apple");
function test_alter (&$item1, $key, $prefix) {
    $item1 = "$prefix: $item1";
}
function test_print ($item2, $key) {
    echo "$key. $item2<br>\n";
}
```

```
array_walk ($fruits, 'test_print');
reset ($fruits);
array_walk ($fruits, 'test_alter', 'fruit');
reset ($fruits);
array_walk ($fruits, 'test_print');
```

See also **each()** and **list()**.

arsort

This function sorts an array such that array indices maintain their correlation with the array elements they are associated with. This is used mainly when sorting associative arrays, where the actual element order is significant.

void **arsort**(array array, [int sort_flags])

Example: Arsort()

```
$fruits = array ("d"=>"lemon", "a"=>"orange", "b"=>"banana", "c"=>"apple");
arsort ($fruits);
reset ($fruits);
while (list ($key, $val) = each ($fruits)) {
    echo "$key = $val\n";
}
```

This example would display the following:

```
fruits[a] = orange
fruits[d] = lemon
fruits[b] = banana
fruits[c] = apple
```

The fruits have been sorted in reverse alphabetical order, and the index associated with each element has been maintained.

You may modify the behavior of the sort using the optional parameter **$sort_flags**, for details see **sort()**. See also: **asort()**, **rsort()**, **ksort()**, and **sort()**.

asin

Returns the arc sine of arg in radians. See also **acos()** and **atan()**.

float **asin**(float arg)

asort

This function sorts an array such that array indices maintain their correlation with the array elements they are associated with. This is used mainly when sorting associative arrays, where the actual element order is significant.

void **asort**(array array, [int sort_flags])

Example: Asort()

```
$fruits = array ("d"=>"lemon", "a"=>"orange", "b"=>"banana", "c"=>"apple");
asort ($fruits);
reset ($fruits);
while (list ($key, $val) = each ($fruits)) {
    echo "$key = $val\n";
}
```

This example would display the following:

```
fruits[c] = apple
fruits[b] = banana
fruits[d] = lemon
fruits[a] = orange
```

The fruits have been sorted in alphabetical order, and the index associated with each element has been maintained.

You may modify the behavior of the sort using the optional parameter **$sort_flags**, for details see **sort()**. See also **arsort()**, **rsort()**, **ksort()**, and **sort()**.

aspell_check

Checks the spelling of a word and returns true if the spelling is correct, false if not.

boolean **aspell_check**(int dictionary_link, string word)

Example: Aspell_check()

```
$aspell_link=aspell_new ("english");
if (aspell_check ($aspell_link, "testt")) {
    echo "This is a valid spelling";
} else {
    echo "Sorry, wrong spelling";
}
```

aspell_check_raw

Checks the spelling of a word, without changing its case or trying to trim it in any way and returns true if the spelling is correct, false if not.

boolean **aspell_check_raw**(int dictionary_link, string word)

Example: Aspell_check_raw()

```
$aspell_link=aspell_new ("english");
if (aspell_check_raw ($aspell_link, "test")) {
    echo "This is a valid spelling";
} else {
    echo "Sorry, wrong spelling";
}
```

aspell_new

Opens up a new dictionary and returns the dictionary link identifier for use in other aspell functions.

int **aspell_new**(string master, string personal)

Example: Aspell_new()

```
$aspell_link=aspell_new ("english");
```

aspell_suggest

Returns an array of possible spellings for the given word.

array **aspell_suggest**(int dictionary_link, string word)

Example: Aspell_suggest()

```
$aspell_link=aspell_new ("english");
if (!aspell_check ($aspell_link, "test")) {
    $suggestions=aspell_suggest ($aspell_link, "test");
    for ($i=0; $i < count ($suggestions); $i++) {
        echo "Possible spelling: " . $suggestions[$i] . "<br>";
    }
}
```

assert

Checks the given **$assertion** and takes appropriate action if the result is false.

int **assert**(string | bool assertion)

If the **$assertion** is given as a string, it will be evaluated as PHP code by **assert()**. The advantages of a string **$assertion** are less overhead when assertion checking is off and messages containing the **$assertion** expression when an assertion fails.

Assertion should be used as a debugging feature only. You may use them for sanity-checks that test for conditions that should always be true but indicate some programming errors if not. Assertion can also be used to check for the presence of certain features like extension functions or certain system limits and features.

Assertions should not be used for normal runtime operations such as input parameter checks. As a rule of thumb, your code should always be able to work correctly if assertion checking is not activated.

The behavior of **assert()** may be configured by **assert_options()** or by .ini-settings described in that function's manual page.

assert_options

When using this function, you may set the various assert() control options or just query their current settings.

mixed **assert_options**(int what, [mixed value])

assert options

Option		Ini-parameter	Default	Description
ASSERT_ACTIVE		assert.active	1	Enable **assert**() evaluation.
ASSERT_WARNING		assert.warning	1	Issue a PHP warning for each failed assertion.
ASSERT_BAIL		assert.bail	0	Terminate execution on failed assertions.
ASSERT_QUIET_EVAL		assert.quiet_eval	0	Disable error_reporting during assertion expression evaluation.
ASSERT_CALLBACK		assert_callback	(null)	Use function to call on failed assertions. **assert_options**() will return the original setting of any option or *false* on errors.

atan

Returns the arc tangent of arg in radians. See also **asin**() and **acos**().

float **atan**(float arg)

atan2

Calculates the arc tangent of the two variables **$x** and **$y**. It is similar to calculating the arc tangent of **$y / $x** , except that the signs of both arguments are used to determine the quadrant of the result. The function returns the result in radians, which is between -PI and PI, inclusively. See also **acos**() and **atan**().

float **atan2**(float y, float x)

base64_decode

Decodes **$encoded_data** and returns the original data. The returned data may be binary. See also **base64_encode**(), *RFC-2045* section 6.8.

string **base64_decode**(string encoded_data)

base64_encode

Returns **$data** encoded with base64. This encoding is designed to make binary data survive transport through transport layers that are not 8-bit clean, such as mail bodies. Base64-encoded data takes about 33 percent more space than the original data. See also **base64_decode()**, **chunk_split()**, RFC-2045 section 6.8.

string **base64_encode**(string data)

basename

Given a string containing a path to a file, this function will return the base name of the file. See also **dirname()**.

string **basename**(string path)

In Windows, both slash (/) and backslash (\ ) are used as path separator characters. In other environments, the forward slash (/) is used.
Example: basename()

```
$path = "/home/httpd/html/index.php3";
$file = basename ($path); // $file is set to "index.php3"
```

base_convert

Returns a string containing **$number** represented in base **$tobase**. The base in which **$number** is given is specified in **$frombase**. Both **$frombase** and **$tobase** have to be between 2 and 36, inclusively. Digits in numbers with a base higher than 10 will be represented with the letters a-z, with a meaning 10, b meaning 11, and z meaning 35.

string **base_convert**(string number, int frombase, int tobase)

Example: base_convert()

```
$binary = base_convert ($hexadecimal, 16, 2);
```

bcadd

Adds the $left operand to the $right operand and returns the sum in a string. The optional **$scale** parameter is used to set the number of digits after the decimal place in the result. See also **bcsub()**.

string **bcadd**(string left operand, string right operand, [int scale])

bccomp

Compares the $left operand to the $right operand and returns the result as an integer. The optional **$scale** parameter is used to set the number of digits after the decimal place, which will be used in the comparison. The return value is 0 if the two operands are equal. If the $left operand is larger than the $right operand, the return value is +1. If the $left operand is less than the $right operand, the return value is -1.

> int **bccomp**(string left operand, string right operand, [int scale])

bcdiv

Divides the $left operand by the $right operand and returns the result. The optional **$scale** sets the number of digits after the decimal place in the result. See also **bcmul()**.

> string **bcdiv**(string left operand, string right operand, [int scale])

bcmod

Get the modulus of the **$left operand** using **$modulus**. See also **bcdiv()**.

> string **bcmod**(string left operand, string modulus)

bcmul

Multiplies the **$left** operand by the **$right** operand and returns the result. The optional **$scale** sets the number of digits after the decimal place in the result. See also **bcdiv()**.

> string **bcmul**(string left operand, string right operand, [int scale])

bcpow

Raises **$x** to the power **$y**. The optional **$scale** can be used to set the number of digits after the decimal place in the result. See also **bcsqrt()**.

> string **bcpow**(string x, string y, [int scale])

bcscale

Sets the default scale parameter for all subsequent bc math functions that do not explicitly specify a scale parameter.

> string **bcscale**(int scale)

bcsqrt

Returns the square root of the **$operand**. The optional **$scale** parameter sets the number of digits after the decimal place in the result. See also **bcpow()**.

> string **bcsqrt**(string operand, int scale)

bcsub

Subtracts the **$right** operand from the **$left** operand and returns the result in a string. The optional **$scale** parameter is used to set the number of digits after the decimal place in the result. See also **bcadd()**.

>   string **bcsub**(string left operand, string right operand, [int scale])

bin2hex

Returns an ASCII string containing the hexadecimal representation of **$str**. The conversion is done byte-wise with the high-nibble first.

>   string **bin2hex**(string str)

bind

Binds the name given in **$address** to the socket described by **$socket**, which must be a valid socket descriptor created with **socket()**.

>   int **bind**(int socket, string address, [int port])

The **$address** parameter is either an IP address in dotted-quad notation (for example, *127.0.0.1*), if the socket is of the AF_INET family; or the pathname of a Unix-domain socket, if the socket family is AF_UNIX.

The **$port** parameter is only used when connecting to an AF_INET socket, and it designates the port on the remote host to which a connection should be made.

Returns zero on success, or a negative error code on failure. This code may be passed to **strerror()** to get a textual explanation of the error. See also **accept_connect()**, **connect()**, **listen()**, **socket()**, **socket_get_status()**, and **strerror()**.

bindec

Returns the decimal equivalent of the binary number represented by the binary_string argument. **Octdec** converts a binary number to a decimal number. The largest number that can be converted is 31 bits of 1's or 2147483647 in decimal. See also the **decbin()** function.

>   int **bindec**(string binary_string)

bindtextdomain

This function sets the path for a domain.

>   string **bindtextdomain**(string domain, string directory)

call_user_func

Calls a user defined function given by the **$function_name** parameter.

> mixed **call_user_func**(string function_name, [mixed parameter], [mixed . . .])

Example: call_user_func

```
function barber ($type) {
    print "You wanted a $type haircut, no problem";
}
call_user_func ('barber', "mushroom");
call_user_func ('barber', "shave");
```

call_user_method

Calls the method referred by **$method_name** from the user defined **$obj** object. The following is an example of usage, where we define a class, instantiate an object, and use **call_user_method**() to call indirectly its **print_info** method. See also **call_user_func**().

> mixed **call_user_method**(string method_name, object obj, [mixed parameter], [mixed . . .])

Example: call_user_method

```
<?php
class Country {
    var $NAME;
    var $TLD;
    function Country($name, $tld) {
        $this->NAME = $name;
        $this->TLD = $tld;
    }
    function print_info($prestr="") {
        echo $prestr."Country: ".$this->NAME."\n";
        echo $prestr."Top Level Domain: ".$this->TLD."\n";
    }
}
$cntry = new Country("Peru","pe");
echo "* Calling the object method directly\n";
$cntry->print_info();
echo "\n* Calling the same method indirectly\n";
call_user_method ("print_info", $cntry, "\t");
?>
```

ceil

Returns the next highest integer value from **$number**. Using **ceil**() on integers is absolutely a waste of time.

> int **ceil**(float number)

Note: PHP/FI 2's **ceil**() returned a float. Use: *$new = (double)ceil($number)*; to get the old behavior. See also **floor**() and **round**().

chdir

Changes PHP's current directory to **$directory**. Returns false if unable to change directory, true otherwise.

    int **chdir**(string directory)

checkdate

Returns true if the date given is valid; otherwise, returns false. Checks the validity of the date formed by the arguments. A date is considered valid if the year is between 1 and 32767, inclusively, and month is between 1 and 12, inclusively.

    int **checkdate**(int month, int day, int year)

$Day is within the allowed number of days for the given **$month**. Leap years are taken into consideration.

checkdnsrr

Searches DNS for records of type **$type** corresponding to **$host**. Returns true if any records are found; returns false if no records were found or if an error occurred.

    int **checkdnsrr**(string host, [string type])

$type may be any one of the following: A, MX, NS, SOA, PTR, CNAME, or ANY. The default is MX. **$Host** may either be the IP address in dotted-quad notation or the host name. See also **get-mxrr()**, **gethostbyaddr()**, **gethostbyname()**, **gethostbynamel()**, and the named(8) manual page.

chgrp

Attempts to change the group of the file **$filename** to **$group**. Only the superuser may change the group of a file arbitrarily; other users may change the group of a file to any group of which that user is a member. Returns true on success; otherwise, returns false. See also **chown()** and **chmod()**. This function does not work on Windows' systems.

    int **chgrp**(string filename, mixed group)

chmod

Attempts to change the mode of the file specified by **$filename** to that given in **$mode**.

    int **chmod**(string filename, int mode)

Note that **$mode** is not automatically assumed to be an octal value, so strings (such as "g+w") will not work properly. To ensure the expected operation, you need to prefix **$mode** with a zero (0):

```
chmod ("/somedir/somefile", 755);    // decimal; probably incorrect
chmod ("/somedir/somefile", "u+rwx,go+rx"); // string; incorrect
chmod ("/somedir/somefile", 0755);   // octal; correct value of mode
```

Returns true on success and false otherwise. See also **chown()** and **chgrp()**.
Note: This function does not work on Windows' systems.

Chop

Returns the argument string without trailing whitespace, including newlines.

string **Chop**(string str)

Example: Chop()

```
$trimmed = chop ($line);
```

Note: chop() is different than the Perl **chop** function, which removes the last character in the string. See also **trim()**, **ltrim()**, **rtrim()**, and **chop()**.

chown

Attempts to change the owner of the file filename to user user. Only the superuser may change the owner of a file. Returns true on success; otherwise returns false. See also **chown()** and **chmod()**.

int **chown**(string filename, mixed user)

Note: This function does not work on Windows' systems.

Chr

Returns a one-character string containing the character specified by **$ascii**.

string **Chr**(int ascii)

Example: Chr()

```
$str .= chr (27); /* add an escape character at the end of $str */
/* Often this is more useful */
$str = sprintf ("The string ends in escape: %c", 27);
```

This function complements **ord()**. See also **sprintf()** with a format string of *%c*.

chunk_split

Can be used to split a string into smaller chunks, which is useful for converting **base64_encode()** output to match RFC 2045 semantics, for example. It inserts every **$chunklen** (defaults to 76) chars the string **$end** (defaults to "\r\n"). It returns the new string, leaving the original string untouched.

string **chunk_split**(string string, [int chunklen], [string end])

Example: chunk_split()

```
# format $data using RFC 2045 semantics
$new_string = chunk_split (base64_encode($data));
```

This function is significantly faster than **ereg_replace()**. This function was added in 3.0.6.

class_exists

This function returns true if the class given by **$class_name** has been defined; otherwise, it returns false.

bool **class_exists**(string class_name)

clearstatcache

Invoking the **stat** or **lstat** system call on most systems is quite expensive. Therefore, the result of the last call to any of the status functions is stored for use on the next such call using the same filename. If you wish to force a new status check, for instance if the file is being checked many times and may change or disappear, use this function to clear the results of the last call from memory.

void **clearstatcache**(void)

This value is only cached for the lifetime of a single request.

Affected functions include **stat()**, **lstat()**, **file_exists()**, **is_writeable()**, **is_readable()**, **is_executable()**, **is_file()**, **is_dir()**, **is_link()**, **filectime()**, **fileatime()**, **filemtime()**, **fileinode()**, **filegroup()**, **fileowner()**, **filesize()**, **filetype()**, and **fileperms()**.

close

Closes the file (or socket) descriptor given by **$socket**.

bool **close**(int socket)

Note that **close()** should not be used on PHP file descriptors created with **fopen()**, **popen()**, **fsockopen()**, or **psockopen()**; it is meant for sockets created with **socket()** or **accept_connect()**.

Returns true on success, or false if an error occurs (that is, **$socket** is invalid). See also **bind()**, **listen()**, **socket()**, **socket_get_status()**, and **strerror()**.

closedir

Closes the directory stream indicated by **$dir_handle**. The stream must have previously been opened by **opendir()**.

void **closedir**(int dir_handle)

closelog

Closes the descriptor being used to write to the system logger. The use of closelog() is optional. See also **define_syslog_variables()**, **syslog()**, and **openlog()**.

int **closelog**(void)

compact()

Takes a variable number of parameters. Each parameter can be either a string containing the name of the variable, or an array of variable names. The array can contain other arrays of variable names inside it; **compact()** handles it recursively. See also **extract()**.

> array **compact**(mixed varname, [mixed . . .])

For each of these, **compact()** looks for a variable with that name in the current symbol table. The variable is then added to the output array so that the variable name becomes the key, and the contents of the variable becomes the value for that key. In short, it does the opposite of **extract()**; it returns the output array with all the variables added to it.

Example: compact()

```
$city = "San Francisco";
$state = "CA";
$event = "SIGGRAPH";
$location_vars = array ("city", "state");
$result = compact ("event", $location_vars);
```

After this, *$result* will be array ("event" => "SIGGRAPH", "city" => "San Francisco", "state" => "CA").

com_get

Returns the value of the **$property** of the COM component referenced by **$com_object**. Returns false on error.

> mixed **com_get**(resource com_object, string property)

com_invoke

Invokes a method of the COM component referenced by $com_object. Returns false on error, returns the $function_name's return value on success.

> mixed **com_invoke**(resource com_object, string function_name, [mixed function parameters, . . .])

com_load

Creates a new COM component and returns a reference to it. Returns false on failure.

> string **com_load**(string module name, [string server name])

com_propget

This function is an alias for **com_get()**.

> mixed **com_propget**(resource com_object, string property)

com_propput

This function is an alias for **com_set()**.

> void **com_propput**(resource com_object, string property, mixed value)

com_propset

This function is an alias for **com_set()**.

> void **com_propset**(resource com_object, string property, mixed value)

com_set

Sets the value of the **$property** of the COM component referenced by **$com_object**. Returns true if **$property** is set. Returns false on error.

> void **com_set**(resource com_object, string property, mixed value)

connect

Initiates a connection using the socket descriptor **$socket**, which must be a valid socket descriptor created with **socket()**.

> int **connect**(int socket, string address, [int port])

The **$address** parameter is either an IP address in dotted-quad notation (for example, *127.0.0.1*), if the socket is of the AF_INET family; or the pathname of a Unix-domain socket, if the socket family is AF_UNIX .

The **$port** parameter is only used when connecting to an AF_INET socket, and it designates the port on the remote host to which a connection should be made.

Returns zero on success, or a negative error code on failure. This code may be passed to **strerror()** to get a textual explanation of the error. See also **bind()**, **listen()**, **socket()**, **socket_get_status()**, and **strerror()**.

connection_aborted

Returns true if client is disconnected. See the Connection **Handling()** description in the **Features()** chapter for a complete explanation.

> int connection_aborted(void)

connection_status

Returns the connection status bit field. See the Connection **Handling()** description in the **Features()** chapter for a complete explanation.

> int connection_status(void)

connection_timeout

Returns true if the script is timed out. See the Connection **Handling()** description in the **Features()** chapter for a complete explanation.

int connection_timeout(*void*)

convert_cyr_string

Converts the given string from one Cyrillic character set to another. The **$from** and **$to** arguments are single characters that represent the source and target Cyrillic character sets. The supported types are as follows:

- k—koi8-r
- w—windows-1251
- i—iso8859-5
- a—x-cp866
- d—x-cp866
- m—x-mac-cyrillic

string **convert_cyr_string**(string str, string from, string to)

copy

Makes a copy of a file. Returns true if the copy succeeds, false otherwise. See also **rename()**.

int **copy**(string source, string dest)

Example: Copy()

```
if (!copy($file, $file.'.bak')) {
    print ("failed to copy $file...<br>\n");
}
```

cos

Returns the cosine of arg in radians. See also **sin()** and **tan()**.

float **cos**(float arg)

count

Returns the number of elements in **$var**, which is typically an array (since anything else will have one element).

int **count**(mixed var)

Returns **1** if the variable is not an array.

Returns **0** if the variable is not set. **Count()** may return 0 for a variable that isn't set, but it may also return **0** for a variable that has been initialized with an empty array. Use **isset()** to test if a variable is set. See also **sizeof()**, **isset()**, and **is_array()**.

count_chars

Counts the number of occurrences of every byte-value (0..255) in **$string** and returns it in various ways. The optional parameter **$Mode** defaults to 0. Depending on **$mode count_chars()**, it returns one of the following: 0, an array with the byte-value as key, and the frequency of every byte as value.

mixed **count_chars**(string string, [string mode])

1—same as 0, but only byte-values with a frequency greater than zero are listed.
2—same as 0, but only byte-values with a frequency equal to zero are listed.
3—a string containing all used byte-values is returned.
4—a string containing all not used byte-values is returned.
Note: This function was added in PHP 4.0.

cpdf_add_annotation

Adds a note with the lower left corner at (**$llx**, **$lly**) and the upper right corner at (**$urx**, **$ury**).

void **cpdf_add_annotation**(int pdf document, double llx, double lly, double urx, double ury, string title, string content, [int mode])

The optional parameter **$mode** determines the unit length. If it is 0 or omitted, the default unit, as specified for the page, is used. Otherwise, the coordinates are measured in postscript points disregarding the current unit.

cpdf_add_outline

Adds a bookmark with text $text that points to the current page.

void **cpdf_add_outline**(int pdf document, string text)

Example: Adding a page outline

```
<?php
$cpdf = cpdf_open(0);
cpdf_page_init($cpdf, 1, 0, 595, 842);
cpdf_add_outline($cpdf, 0, 0, 0, 1, "Page 1");
// ...
// some drawing
// ...
cpdf_finalize($cpdf);
Header("Content-type: application/pdf");
cpdf_output_buffer($cpdf);
cpdf_close($cpdf);
?>
```

cpdf_arc

Draws an arc with center at point (**$x-coor**, **$y-coor**) and radius **$radius**, starting at angle **$start** and ending at angle **$end**.

The optional parameter **$mode** determines the unit length. If it is 0 or omitted, the default unit, as specified for the page, is used. Otherwise, the coordinates are measured in postscript points disregarding the current unit. See also **cpdf_circle()**.

> void **cpdf_arc**(int pdf document, double x-coor, double y-coor, double radius, double start, double end, [int mode])

cpdf_begin_text

Starts a text section. It must end with **cpdf_end_text()**.

> void **cpdf_begin_text**(int pdf document)

> **Example: Text output**

```php
<?php
cpdf_begin_text($pdf);
cpdf_set_font($pdf, 16, "Helvetica", "WinAnsiEncoding");
cpdf_text($pdf, 100, 100, "Some text");
cpdf_end_text($pdf)
?>
```

> See also **cpdf_end_text()**.

cpdf_circle

Draws a circle with center at point (**$x-coor**, **$y-coor**) and radius **$radius**.

> void **cpdf_circle**(int pdf document, double x-coor, double y-coor, double radius, [int mode])

The optional parameter **$mode** determines the unit length. If it is 0 or omitted, the default unit, as specified for the page, is used. Otherwise, the coordinates are measured in postscript points disregarding the current unit. See also **cpdf_arc()**.

cpdf_clip

Clips all drawing to the current path.

> void **cpdf_clip**(int pdf document)

cpdf_close

Closes the pdf document. This should be the last function, even after **cpdf_finalize()**, **cpdf_output_buffer()**, and **cpdf_save_to_file()**. See also **cpdf_open()**.

> void **cpdf_close**(int pdf document)

cpdf_closepath

Closes the current path.

> void **cpdf_closepath**(int pdf document)

cpdf_closepath_fill_stroke

Closes and fills the interior of the current path with the current fill color and draws current path. See also **cpdf_closepath()**, **cpdf_stroke()**, **cpdf_fill()**, **cpdf_setgray_fill()**, **cpdf_setgray()**, **cpdf_setrgbcolor_fill()**, **cpdf_setrgbcolor()**.

> void **cpdf_closepath_fill_stroke**(int pdf document)

cpdf_closepath_stroke

This function is a combination of **cpdf_closepath()** and **cpdf_stroke()**. Then, it clears the path. See also **cpdf_closepath()**, **cpdf_stroke()**.

> void **cpdf_closepath_stroke**(int pdf document)

cpdf_continue_text

Outputs the string in **$text** in the next line. See also **cpdf_show_xy()**, **cpdf_text()**, **cpdf_set_leading()**, **cpdf_set_text_pos()**.

> void **cpdf_continue_text**(int pdf document, string text)

cpdf_curveto

Draws a Bezier curve from the current point to the point (**$x3, $y3**), using (**$x1, $y1**) and (**$x2, $y2**) as control points.

> void **cpdf_curveto**(int pdf document, double x1, double y1, double x2, double y2, double x3, double y3, [int mode])

The optional parameter **$mode** determines the unit length. If it is 0 or omitted, the default unit, as specified for the page, is used. Otherwise, the coordinates are measured in postscript points disregarding the current unit. See also **cpdf_moveto()**, **cpdf_rmoveto()**, **cpdf_rlineto()**, **cpdf_lineto()**.

cpdf_end_text

The **cpdf_end_text()** function ends a text section which was started with **cpdf_begin_text()**. See also **cpdf_begin_text()**.

> void **cpdf_end_text**(int pdf document)

Example: Text output

```php
<?php
cpdf_begin_text($pdf);
```

```
cpdf_set_font($pdf, 16, "Helvetica", "WinAnsiEncoding");
cpdf_text($pdf, 100, 100, "Some text");
cpdf_end_text($pdf)
?>
```

cpdf_fill

Fills the interior of the current path with the current fill color. See also **cpdf_closepath()**, **cpdf_stroke()**, **cpdf_setgray_fill()**, **cpdf_setgray()**, **cpdf_setrgbcolor_fill()**, **cpdf_setrgbcolor()**.

void **cpdf_fill**(int pdf document)

cpdf_fill_stroke

Fills the interior of the current path with the current fill color and draws current path. See also **cpdf_closepath()**, **cpdf_stroke()**, **cpdf_fill()**, **cpdf_setgray_fill()**, **cpdf_setgray()**, **cpdf_setrgbcolor_fill()**, **cpdf_setrgbcolor()**.

void **cpdf_fill_stroke**(int pdf document)

cpdf_finalize

This function ends the document. You still have to call **cpdf_close()**. See also **cpdf_close()**.

void **cpdf_finalize**(int pdf document)

cpdf_finalize_page

Ends the page with page number **$page** number. This function is only for saving memory. A finalized page takes less memory but cannot be modified anymore. See also **cpdf_page_init()**.

void **cpdf_finalize_page**(int pdf document, int page number)

cpdf_global_set_document_limits

Sets several document limits. This function has to be called before **cpdf_open()** to take effect. It sets the limits for any document open afterwards. See also **cpdf_open()**.

void **cpdf_global_set_document_limits**(int maxpages, int maxfonts, int maximages, int maxannotations, int maxobjects)

cpdf_import_jpeg

Opens an image stored in the file with the name **$file name**. The format of the image has to be jpeg. The image is placed on the current page at position (**$x-coor**, **$y-coor**). The image is rotated by **$angle** degrees.

int **cpdf_import_jpeg**(int pdf document, string file name, double x-coor, double y-coor, double angle, double width, double height, double x-scale, double y-scale, [int mode])

The optional parameter **$mode** determines the unit length. If it is 0 or omitted, the default unit, as specified for the page, is used. Otherwise, the coordinates are measured in postscript points disregarding the current unit. See also **cpdf_place_inline_image()**.

cpdf_lineto

Draws a line from the current point to the point with coordinates (**$x-coor**, **$y-coor**).

void **cpdf_lineto**(int pdf document, double x-coor, double y-coor, [int mode])

The optional parameter **$mode** determines the unit length. If it is 0 or omitted, the default unit, as specified for the page, is used. Otherwise, the coordinates are measured in postscript points disregarding the current unit. See also **cpdf_moveto()**, **cpdf_rmoveto()**, **cpdf_curveto()**.

cpdf_moveto

Sets the current point to the coordinates **$x-coor** and **$y-coor**.

void **cpdf_moveto**(int pdf document, double x-coor, double y-coor, [int mode])

The optional parameter **$mode** determines the unit length. If it is 0 or omitted, the default unit, as specified for the page, is used. Otherwise, the coordinates are measured in postscript points disregarding the current unit.

cpdf_newpath

Starts a new path on the document given by the **$pdf_document** parameter.

void **cpdf_newpath**(int pdf_document)

cpdf_open

Opens a new pdf document. The first parameter turns document compression on if it is unequal to 0. The second optional parameter sets the file in which the document is written. If it is omitted, the document is created in memory and can either be written into a file with the **cpdf_save_to_file()** or written to standard output with **cpdf_output_buffer()**.

int **cpdf_open**(int compression, [string filename])

Note: The return value will be needed in further versions of ClibPDF as the first parameter in all other functions which are writing to the pdf document.

The ClibPDF library takes the filename "-" as a synonym for **stdout**. If PHP is compiled as an apache module, this will not work due to the way **ClibPDF** outputs to **stdout** do not work with apache. You can solve this problem by skipping the filename and using **cpdf_output_buffer()** to output the pdf document. See also **cpdf_close()**, **cpdf_output_buffer()**.

cpdf_output_buffer

Outputs the pdf document to **stdout**. The document has to be created in memory, which is the case if **cpdf_open()** has been called with no filename parameter. See also **cpdf_open()**.

void **cpdf_output_buffer**(int pdf document)

cpdf_page_init

Starts a new page with height **$height** and width **$width** . The page has number **$page number** and orientation **$orientation**. **$orientation** can be 0 for portrait and 1 for landscape. The last optional parameter **$unit** sets the unit for the coordinate system. The value should be the number of postscript points per unit. Since one inch is equal to 72 points, a value of 72 would set the unit to one inch. The default is also 72. See also **cpdf_set_current_page()**.

void **cpdf_page_init**(int pdf document, int page number, int orientation, double height, double width, [double unit])

cpdf_place_inline_image

Places an image created with the php image functions on the page at position (**$x-coor**, **$y-coor**). The image can be scaled at the same time.

void **cpdf_place_inline_image**(int pdf document, int image, double x-coor, double y-coor, double angle, double width, double height, [int mode])

The optional parameter **$mode** determines the unit length. If it is 0 or omitted, the default unit, as specified for the page, is used. Otherwise, the coordinates are measured in postscript points disregarding the current unit. See also **cpdf_import_jpeg()**.

cpdf_rect

The **cpdf_rect()** function draws a rectangle with its lower left corner at point (**$x-coor**, **$y-coor**). This width is set to **$width**. This height is set to **$height**.

void **cpdf_rect**(int pdf document, double x-coor, double y-coor, double width, double height, [int mode])

The optional parameter **$mode** determines the unit length. If it is 0 or omitted, the default unit, as specified for the page, is used. Otherwise, the coordinates are measured in postscript points disregarding the current unit.

cpdf_restore

Restores the environment saved with **cpdf_save()**. It works like the postscript command **grestore**. This is very useful if you want to translate or rotate an object without effecting other objects.

void **cpdf_restore**(int pdf document)

Example: Save/Restore

```
<?php
cpdf_save($pdf);
// do all kinds of rotations, transformations, ...
cpdf_restore($pdf)
?>
```

See also **cpdf_save**().

cpdf_rlineto

Draws a line from the current point to the relative point with coordinates (**$x-coor**, **$y-coor**).

    void **cpdf_rlineto**(int pdf document, double x-coor, double y-coor, [int mode])

The optional parameter **$mode** determines the unit length. If it is 0 or omitted, the default unit, as specified for the page, is used. Otherwise, the coordinates are measured in postscript points disregarding the current unit. See also **cpdf_moveto**(), **cpdf_rmoveto**(), **cpdf_curveto**().

cpdf_rmoveto

Sets the current point relative to the coordinates **$x-coor** and **$y-coor**.

    void **cpdf_rmoveto**(int pdf document, double x-coor, double y-coor, [int mode])

The optional parameter **$mode** determines the unit length. If it is 0 or omitted, the default unit, as specified for the page, is used. Otherwise, the coordinates are measured in postscript points disregarding the current unit. See also **cpdf_moveto**().

cpdf_rotate

Sets the rotation in degrees to **$angle**.

    void **cpdf_rotate**(int pdf document, double angle)

cpdf_save

Saves the current environment. It works like the postscript command gsave. This is very useful if you want to translate or rotate an object without effecting other objects. See also **cpdf_restore**().

    void **cpdf_save**(int pdf document)

cpdf_save_to_file

Outputs the pdf document into a file if it has been created in memory.

    void **cpdf_save_to_file**(int pdf document, string filename)

This function is not needed if the pdf document has been opened by specifying a filename as a parameter of **cpdf_open**(). See also **cpdf_output_buffer**(), **cpdf_open**().

cpdf_scale

Sets the scaling factor in both directions.

> void **cpdf_scale**(int pdf document, double x-scale, double y-scale)

cpdf_setdash

Sets the dash pattern **$white** white units and **$black** black units. If both are 0, a solid line is set.

> void **cpdf_setdash**(int pdf document, double white, double black)

cpdf_setflat

Sets the flatness to a value between 0 and 100.

> void **cpdf_setflat**(int pdf document, double value)

cpdf_setgray

Sets the current drawing and filling color to the given gray value. See also **cpdf_setrgbcolor_stroke(), cpdf_setrgbcolor_fill().**

> void **cpdf_setgray**(int pdf document, double gray value)

cpdf_setgray_fill

Sets the current gray value to fill a path. See also **cpdf_setrgbcolor_fill()**.

> void **cpdf_setgray_fill**(int pdf document, double value)

cpdf_setgray_stroke

Sets the current drawing color to the given gray value. See also **cpdf_setrgbcolor_stroke()**.

> void **cpdf_setgray_stroke**(int pdf document, double gray value)

cpdf_setlinecap

Sets the **linecap** parameter between a value of 0 and 2. 0 = butt end, 1 = round, 2 = projecting square.

> void **cpdf_setlinecap**(int pdf document, int value)

cpdf_setlinejoin

Sets the **linejoin** parameter between a value of 0 and 2. 0 = miter, 1 = round, 2 = bevel.

> void **cpdf_setlinejoin**(int pdf document, long value)

cpdf_setlinewidth

Sets the line width to **$width**.

void **cpdf_setlinewidth**(int pdf document, double width)

cpdf_setmiterlimit

Sets the miter limit to a value greater or equal than 1.

void **cpdf_setmiterlimit**(int pdf document, double value)

cpdf_setrgbcolor

Sets the current drawing and filling color to the given rgb color value. See also **cpdf_setrgbcolor_stroke()**, **cpdf_setrgbcolor_fill()**.

void **cpdf_setrgbcolor**(int pdf document, double red value, double green value, double blue value)

cpdf_setrgbcolor_fill

Sets the current rgb color value to fill a path. See also **cpdf_setrgbcolor_stroke()**, **cpdf_setrgbcolor()**.

void **cpdf_setrgbcolor_fill**(int pdf document, double red value, double green value, double blue value)

cpdf_setrgbcolor_stroke

Sets the current drawing color to the given rgb color value. See also **cpdf_setrgbcolor_fill()**, **cpdf_setrgbcolor()**.

void **cpdf_setrgbcolor_stroke**(int pdf document, double red value, double green value, double blue value)

cpdf_set_char_spacing

Sets the spacing between characters. See also **cpdf_set_word_spacing()**, **cpdf_set_leading()**.

void **cpdf_set_char_spacing**(int pdf document, double space)

cpdf_set_creator

Sets the creator of a pdf document. See also **cpdf_set_subject()**, **cpdf_set_title()**, **cpdf_set_keywords()**.

void **cpdf_set_creator**(string creator)

cpdf_set_current_page

Sets the page on which all operations are performed. One can switch between pages until a page is finished with **cpdf_finalize_page()**. See also **cpdf_finalize_page()**.

void **cpdf_set_current_page**(int pdf document, int page number)

cpdf_set_font

Sets the current font face, font size, and encoding. Currently, only the standard postscript fonts are supported.

> void **cpdf_set_font**(int pdf document, string font name, double size, string encoding)

The last parameter **$encoding** can take the following values: "MacRomanEncoding," "Mac-ExpertEncoding," "WinAnsiEncoding," and "NULL." "NULL" stands for the font's built-in encoding. See the ClibPDF Manual for more information, especially for how to support Asian fonts.

cpdf_set_horiz_scaling

Sets the horizontal scaling to **$scale** percent.

> void **cpdf_set_horiz_scaling**(int pdf document, double scale)

cpdf_set_keywords

Sets the keywords of a pdf document. See also **cpdf_set_title()**, **cpdf_set_creator()**, **cpdf_set_subject()**.

> void **cpdf_set_keywords**(string keywords)

cpdf_set_leading

Sets the distance between text lines. This will be used if text is output by **cpdf_continue_text()**. See also **cpdf_continue_text()**.

> void **cpdf_set_leading**(int pdf document, double distance)

cpdf_set_page_animation

The **cpdf_set_page_animation()** function set the transition between following pages.
The value of **$transition** can be as follows:

0 for none,

1 for two lines sweeping across the screen reveal the page,

2 for multiple lines sweeping across the screen reveal the page,

3 for a box reveals the page,

4 for a single line sweeping across the screen reveals the page,

5 for the old page dissolves to reveal the page,

6 for the dissolve effect moves from one screen edge to another,

7 for the old page is simply replaced by the new page (default)

The value of **$duration** is the number of seconds between page flipping.

> void **cpdf_set_page_animation**(int pdf document, int transition, double duration)

cpdf_set_subject

Sets the subject of a pdf document. See also **cpdf_set_title()**, **cpdf_set_creator()**, **cpdf_set_keywords()**.

> void **cpdf_set_subject**(string subject)

cpdf_set_text_matrix

Sets a matrix, which describes a transformation applied on the current text font.

> void **cpdf_set_text_matrix**(int pdf document, array matrix)

cpdf_set_text_pos

Sets the position of text for the next **cpdf_show()** function call.

> void **cpdf_set_text_pos**(int pdf document, double x-coor, double y-coor, [int mode])

The optional parameter **$mode** determines the unit length. If it is 0 or omitted, the default unit, as specified for the page, is used. Otherwise, the coordinates are measured in postscript points disregarding the current unit. See also **cpdf_show()**, **cpdf_text()**.

cpdf_set_text_rendering

Determines how text is rendered.

> void **cpdf_set_text_rendering**(int pdf document, int mode)

The possible values for **$mode** are 0=fill text, 1=stroke text, 2=fill and stroke text, 3=invisible, 4=fill text and add it to clipping path, 5=stroke text and add it to clipping path, 6=fill and stroke text and add it to clipping path, 7=add it to clipping path.

cpdf_set_text_rise

Sets the text rising to $value units.

> void **cpdf_set_text_rise**(int pdf document, double value)

cpdf_set_title

Sets the title of a pdf document. See also **cpdf_set_subject()**, **cpdf_set_creator()**, **cpdf_set_keywords()**.

> void **cpdf_set_title**(string title)

cpdf_set_word_spacing

Sets the spacing between words. See also **cpdf_set_char_spacing()**, **cpdf_set_leading()**.

> void **cpdf_set_word_spacing**(int pdf document, double space)

cpdf_show

Outputs the string in **$text** at the current position. See also **cpdf_text()**, **cpdf_begin_text()**, **cpdf_end_text()**.

> void **cpdf_show**(int pdf document, string text)

cpdf_show_xy

Outputs the string **$text** at position with coordinates (**$x-coor** , **$y-coor**).

> void **cpdf_show_xy**(int pdf document, string text, double x-coor, double y-coor, [int mode])

The optional parameter **$mode** determines the unit length. If it is 0 or omitted, the default unit, as specified for the page, is used. Otherwise, the coordinates are measured in postscript points disregarding the current unit.

Note: The function **cpdf_show_xy()** is identical to **cpdf_text()** without the optional parameters. See also **cpdf_text()**.

cpdf_stringwidth

Returns the width of the string in **$text**. It requires a font to be set first. See also **cpdf_set_font()**.

> double **cpdf_stringwidth**(int pdf document, string text)

cpdf_stroke

Draws a line along current path. See also **cpdf_closepath()**, **cpdf_closepath_stroke()**.

> void **cpdf_stroke**(int pdf document)

cpdf_text

Outputs the string **$text** at position with coordinates (**$x-coor, $y-coor**).

> void **cpdf_text**(int pdf document, string text, double x-coor, double y-coor, [int mode], [double orientation], [int alignmode])

The optional parameter **$mode** determines the unit length. If it is 0 or omitted, the default unit, as specified for the page, is used. Otherwise, the coordinates are measured in postscript points disregarding the current unit. The optional parameter **$orientation** is the rotation of the text in degree. The optional parameter **$alignmode** determines how the text is aligned.

See the ClibPDF documentation for possible values. See also **cpdf_show_xy()**.

cpdf_translate

Sets the origin of coordinate system to the point (**$x-coor, $y-coor**).

> void **cpdf_translate**(int pdf document, double x-coor, double y-coor, [int mode])

The optional parameter **$mode** determines the unit length. If it is 0 or omitted, the default unit, as specified for the page, is used. Otherwise, the coordinates are measured in postscript points disregarding the current unit.

crc32

Generates the cyclic redundancy checksum polynomial of 32-bit lengths of the **$str**. This is usually used to validate the integrity of data being transmitted. See also **md5()**.

int **crc32**(string str)

create_function

Creates an anonymous function from the parameters passed, and returns a unique name for it. Usually the **$args** will be passed as a single quote delimited string, and this is also recommended for the **$code** . The reason for using single quoted strings,is to protect the variable names from parsing; otherwise, if you use double quotes, you will need to escape the variable names, such as \\$avar.

string **create_function**(string args, string code)

You can use this function to create a function from information gathered at run time, for example:

Example: Creating an anonymous function with **create_function()**.

```
$newfunc = create_function('$a,$b','return "ln($a) + ln($b) = ".log($a * $b);');
echo "New anonymous function: $newfunc\n";
echo $newfunc(2,M_E)."\n";
// outputs
// New anonymous function: lambda_1
// ln(2) + ln(2.718281828459) = 1.6931471805599
```

Or, perhaps to have a general handler function that can apply a set of operations to a list of parameters, you can do the following:

Example: Making a general processing function with **create_function()**

```
function process($var1, $var2, $farr) {
    for ($f=0; $f < count($farr); $f++)
    echo $farr[$f]($var1,$var2)."\n";
}
// create a bunch of math functions
$f1 = 'if ($a >=0) {return "b*a^2 = ".$b*sqrt($a);} else {return false;}';
$f2 = "return \"min(b^2+a, a^2,b) = \".min(\$a*\$a+\$b,\$b*\$b+\$a);";
$f3 = 'if ($a > 0 && $b != 0) {return "ln(a)/b = ".log($a)/$b;} else {return false;}';
$farr = array(
    create_function('$x,$y', 'return "some trig: ".(sin($x) + $x*cos($y));'),
    create_function('$x,$y', 'return "a hypotenuse: ".sqrt($x*$x + $y*$y);'),
    create_function('$a,$b', $f1),
    create_function('$a,$b', $f2),
    create_function('$a,$b', $f3)
    );
echo "\nUsing the first array of anonymous functions\n";
echo "parameters: 2.3445, M_PI\n";
```

```
process(2.3445, M_PI, $farr);
// now make a bunch of string processing functions
$garr = array(
    create_function('$b,$a','if (strncmp($a,$b,3) == 0) return "** \"$a\" '.
    'and \"$b\"\n** Look the same to me! (looking at the first 3 chars)";'),
    create_function('$a,$b,'; return "CRCs: ".crc32($a)." , ".crc32(b);'),
    create_function('$a,$b,'; return "similar(a,b) =
".similar_text($a,$b,&$p)."($p%)";')
    );
echo "\nUsing the second array of anonymous functions\n";
process("Twas brilling and the slithy toves", "Twas the night", $garr);
```

and when you run the code above, the output will be as follows:

```
Using the first array of anonymous functions
parameters: 2.3445, M_PI
some trig: -1.6291725057799
a hypotenuse: 3.9199852871011
b*a^2 = 4.8103313314525
min(b^2+a, a^2,b) = 8.6382729035898
ln(a/b) = 0.27122299212594

Using the second array of anonymous functions
** "Twas the night" and "Twas brilling and the slithy toves"
** Look the same to me! (looking at the first 3 chars)
CRCs: -725381282 , 1908338681
similar(a,b) = 11(45.833333333333%)
```

But perhaps the most common use for of lambda-style (anonymous) functions is to create callback functions, for example, when using **array_walk()** or **usort()**:

Example: Using anonymous functions as callback functions

```
$av = array("the ","a ","that ","this ");
array_walk($av, create_function('&$v,$k','$v = $v."mango";'));
print_r($av);  // for PHP 3 use var_dump()
// outputs:
// Array
// (
//    [0] => the mango
//    [1] => a mango
//    [2] => that mango
//    [3] => this mango
// )
// an array of strings ordered from shorter to longer
$sv = array("small","larger","a big string","it is a string thing");
print_r($sv);
// outputs:
// Array
// (
//    [0] => small
//    [1] => larger
//    [2] => a big string
//    [3] => it is a string thing
// )
// sort it from longer to shorter
usort($sv, create_function('$a,$b','return strlen($b) - strlen($a);'));
print_r($sv);
// outputs:
```

```
// Array
// (
//    [0] => it is a string thing
//    [1] => a big string
//    [2] => larger
//    [3] => small
// )
```

crypt

Encrypts a string using the standard Unix DES encryption method. Arguments are a string to be encrypted and an optional two-character salt string on which to base the encryption. For more information, see the Unix man page for your crypt function. If the salt argument is not provided, one will be randomly generated by PHP.

string **crypt**(string str, [string salt])

Some operating systems support more than one type of encryption. In fact, sometimes the standard DES encryption is replaced by an MD5-based encryption algorithm. The encryption type is triggered by the salt argument. At installation time, PHP determines the capabilities of the crypt function and will accept salts for other encryption types. If no salt is provided, PHP will auto-generate a standard two-character DES salt by default. This will occur unless the default encryption type on the system is MD5, in which case a random MD5-compatible salt is generated. PHP sets a constant named CRYPT_SALT_LENGTH, which informs you whether a regular two-character salt applies to your system or the longer 12-character MD5 salt is applicable.

If you are using the supplied salt, you should be aware that the salt is generated once. If you are calling this function recursively, this may impact both appearance and, to a certain extent, security.

The standard DES encryption **crypt()** contains the salt as the first two characters of the output.

On systems where the **crypt()** function supports multiple encryption types, the following constants are set to 0 or 1 depending on whether the given type is available:

CRYPT_STD_DES—Standard DES encryption with a two-character SALT

CRYPT_EXT_DES—Extended DES encryption with a nine-character SALT

CRYPT_MD5—MD5 encryption with a 12-character SALT starting with 1

CRYPT_BLOWFISH—Extended DES encryption with a 16-charcter SALT starting with 2

A decrypt function is not available because **crypt()** uses a one-way algorithm. See also **md5()**.

curl_close

Closes a CURL session and frees all resources. The CURL handle, **$ch**, is also deleted.

void **curl_close**(int ch)

curl_exec

This function should be called after you initialize a CURL session and all the options for the session are set. Its purpose is simply to execute the predefined CURL session given by the **$ch**.

    bool **curl_exec**(int ch)

curl_init

Initializes a new session and returns a CURL handle for use with the **curl_setopt()**, **curl_exec()**, and **curl_close()** functions. If the optional **$url** parameter is supplied, then the CURLOPT_URL option will be set to the value of the parameter. You can manually set this using the **curl_setopt()** function. See also **curl_close(), curl_setopt()**.

    int **curl_init**([string url])

Example: Initializing a new CURL session and fetching a web page

```php
<?php
$ch = curl_init();
curl_setopt ($ch, CURLOPT_URL, "http://www.zend.com/");curl_setopt ($ch,
CURLOPT_HEADER, 0);
curl_exec ($ch);
curl_close ($ch);
?>
```

curl_setopt

Sets options for a CURL session identified by the **$ch** parameter. The **$option** parameter is the option you want to set, and the **$value** is the value of the option given by the **$option**.

    bool **curl_setopt**(int ch, string option, mixed value)

The **$value** should be along for the following options (specified in the **$option** parameter):

CURLOPT_INFILESIZE: When you are uploading a file to a remote site, this option should be used to tell PHP what the expected size of the infile will be.

CURLOPT_VERBOSE: Set this option to a non-zero value if you want CURL to report everything that is happening.

CURLOPT_HEADER: Set this option to a non-zero value if you want the header to be included in the output.

CURLOPT_NOPROGRESS: Set this option to a non-zero value if you don't want PHP to display a progress meter for CURL transfers **Note:** PHP automatically sets this option to a non-zero parameter; this should only be changed for debugging purposes.

CURLOPT_NOBODY: Set this option to a non-zero value if you don't want the body included with the output.

CURLOPT_FAILONERROR: If the HTTP code returned is greater than 300, set this option to a non-zero value if you want PHP to fail silently. The default behavior is to return the page normally, ignoring the code.

CURLOPT_UPLOAD: Set this option to a non-zero value if you want PHP to prepare for an upload.

CURLOPT_POST: Set this option to a non-zero value if you want PHP to do a regular HTTP POST. This POST is a normal application/x-www-from-urlencoded kind, most commonly used by HTML forms.

CURLOPT_FTPLISTONLY: Set this option to a non-zero value and PHP will just list the names of an FTP directory.

CURLOPT_FTPAPPEND: Set this option to a non-zero value and PHP will append to the remote file instead of overwriting it.

CURLOPT_NETRC: Set this option to a non-zero value and PHP will scan your $\sim$./netrc file to find your username and password for the remote site with which you are establishing a connection.

CURLOPT_FOLLOWLOCATION: Set this option to a non-zero value to follow any "Location:" header that the server sends as a part of the HTTP header.

Note: This is recursive; PHP will follow as many "Location:" headers that it is sent.

CURLOPT_PUT: Set this option a non-zero value to HTTP PUT a file. The file to PUT must be set with the CURLOPT_INFILE and CURLOPT_INFILESIZE.

CURLOPT_MUTE: Set this option to a non-zero value and PHP will be completely silent with regards to the CURL functions.

CURLOPT_TIMEOUT: Pass a long as a parameter that contains the maximum time, in seconds, that you will allow the curl functions to take.

CURLOPT_LOW_SPEED_LIMIT: Pass a long as a parameter containing the transfer speed in bytes per second below which the transfer should be during CURLOPT_LOW_SPEED_TIME seconds in order for PHP to consider it too slow and abort.

CURLOPT_LOW_SPEED_TIME: Pass along as a parameter containing the time in seconds that the transfer should be below the CURLOPT_LOW_SPEED_LIMIT in order for PHP to consider it too slow and abort.

CURLOPT_RESUME_FROM: Pass along as a parameter containing the offset, in bytes, from where you want the transfer to start.

CURLOPT_SSLVERSION: Pass a long as a parameter containing the SSL version (2 or 3) to use. By default, PHP will try to determine this by itself. In some cases, however, you must set this manually.

CURLOPT_TIMECONDITION: Pass along as a parameter defining how the CURLOPT_TIMEVALUE is treated. You can set this parameter to TIMECOND_IFMODSINCE or TIMECOND_ISUNMODSINCE. This is a HTTP-only feature.

CURLOPT_TIMEVALUE : Pass along as a parameter that is the time in seconds since January 1st, 1970. The time will be used as specified by the CURLOPT_TIMEVALUE option, or by default, the TIMECOND_IFMODSINCE will be used.

The **$value** parameter should be a string for the following values of the **$option** parameter:

CURLOPT_URL : This is the URL that you want PHP to fetch. You can also set this option when initializing a session with the **curl_init()** function.

CURLOPT_USERPWD : Pass a string formatted in the [username]:[password] manner, for PHP to use for the connection.

CURLOPT_PROXYUSERPWD : Pass a string formatted in the [username]:[password] format, for connection to the HTTP proxy.

CURLOPT_RANGE : Pass the specified range you want. It should be in the "X-Y" format, where X or Y may be left out. The HTTP transfers also support several intervals, separated with commas as in X-Y,N-M.

CURLOPT_POSTFIELDS : Pass a string containing the full data to post in an HTTP "POST" operation.

CURLOPT_REFERER : Pass a string containing the "referer" header to be used in an HTTP request.

CURLOPT_USERAGENT : Pass a string containing the "user-agent" header to be used in an HTTP request.

CURLOPT_FTPPORT : Pass a string containing that which will be used to get the IP address to use for the ftp "PORT" instruction. The POST instruction tells the remote server to connect to our specified IP address. The string may be a plain IP address, a hostname, a network interface name (under UNIX), or just a plain '-' to use the systems default IP address.

CURLOPT_COOKIE : Pass a string containing the content of the cookie to be set in the HTTP header.

CURLOPT_SSLCERT : Pass a string containing the filename of PEM formatted certificate.

CURLOPT_SSLCERTPASSWD : Pass a string containing the password required to use the CURLOPT_SSLCERT certificate.

CURLOPT_COOKIEFILE : Pass a string containing the name of the file containing the cookie data. The cookie file can be in Netscape format or just in plain HTTP-style headers dumped into a file.

CURLOPT_CUSTOMREQUEST : Pass a string to be used instead of GET or HEAD when doing an HTTP request. This is useful for doing DELETE or another, more obscure, HTTP request.

Note: Don't do this without making sure your server supports the command first.

The following options expect a file descriptor that is obtained by using the **fopen()** function:

CURLOPT_FILE : The file where the output of your transfer should be placed, the default is STDOUT.

CURLOPT_INFILE : The file from where the input of your transfer comes.

CURLOPT_WRITEHEADER : The file where you write the header part of the output.

CURLOPT_STDERR : The file to write errors to instead of stderr.

curl_version

Returns a string containing the current CURL version.

string **curl_version**(void)

current

Every array has an internal pointer to its "current" element, which is initialized to the first element inserted into the array. This function simply returns the array element that's currently being pointed by the internal pointer. It does not move the pointer in any way.

mixed **current**(array array)

If the internal pointer points beyond the end of the elements list, **current()** returns false. If the array contains empty elements (0 or "", the empty string), then this function will return false for these elements as well. This makes it impossible to determine if you are really at the end of the list in such an array using **current().** To properly traverse an array that may contain empty elements, use the **each()** function. See also **end(), next(), prev(),** and **reset().**

cybercash_base64_decode

string **cybercash_base64_decode**(string inbuff)

cybercash_base64_encode

string **cybercash_base64_encode**(string inbuff)

cybercash_decr

Returns an associative array with the elements "errcode" and, if "errcode" is false, "outbuff" (string), "outLth" (long) and "macbuff" (string).

array **cybercash_decr**(string wmk, string sk, string inbuff)

cybercash_encr

Returns an associative array with the elements "errcode" and, if "errcode" is false, "outbuff" (string), "outLth" (long) and "macbuff" (string).

array **cybercash_encr**(string wmk, string sk, string inbuff)

date

Returns a string formatted according to the given format string using the given $timestamp or the current local time if no timestamp is given.

string **date**(string format, [int timestamp])

The following characters are recognized in the format string: an - "am" or "pm":

A—"AM" or "PM"

B—Swatch Internet time

d —day of the month, 2 digits with leading zeros; for example, "01" to "31"

D—day of the week, textual, 3 letters; for example, "Fri"

F—month, textual, long; for example, "January"

g—hour, 12-hour format without leading zeros; for example, "1" to "12"

G—hour, 24-hour format without leading zeros; for example, "0" to "23"

h—hour, 12-hour format; for example, "01" to "12"

H—hour, 24-hour format; for example, "00" to "23"

i—minutes; for example, "00" to "59"

I (capital i)—"1" if Daylight Savings Time, "0" otherwise.

j—day of the month without leading zeros; for example, "1" to "31"

l (lowercase 'L')—day of the week, textual, long; for example, "Friday"

L—Boolean for whether it is a leap year; for example, "0" or "1"

m—month; for example, "01" to "12"

M—month, textual, 3 letters; for example, "Jan"

n—month without leading zeros; for example, "1" to "12"

s—seconds; for example, "00" to "59"

S—English ordinal suffix, textual, 2 characters; for example, "th", "nd"

t—number of days in the given month; for example, "28" to "31"

T—Timezone setting of this machine; for example, "MDT"

U—seconds since the epoch

w—day of the week, numeric, for example, "0" (Sunday) to "6" (Saturday)

Y—year, 4 digits; for example, "1999"

y—year, 2 digits; for example, "99"

z—day of the year; for example, "0" to "365"

Z—timezone offset in seconds; for example, "-43200" to "43200")

Unrecognized characters in the format string will be printed as is. The "Z" format will always return "0" when using **gmdate()**.

Example: Date()

```
print (date ("l dS of F Y h:i:s A"));
print ("July 1, 2000 is on a " . date ("l", mktime(0,0,0,7,1,2000)));
```

It is possible to use **date()** and **mktime()** together to find dates in the future or in the past.
Example: Date() and mktime()

```
$tomorrow  = mktime (0,0,0,date("m")  ,date("d")+1,date("Y"));
$lastmonth = mktime (0,0,0,date("m")-1,date("d"),  date("Y"));
$nextyear  = mktime (0,0,0,date("m"),  date("d"),  date("Y")+1);
```

To format dates in other languages, you should use the **setlocale()** and **strftime()** functions.
See also **gmdate()** and **mktime()**.

dbase_add_record

Adds the data in the **$record** to the database. If the number of items in the supplied record isn't
equal to the number of fields in the database, the operation will fail and false will be returned.

bool **dbase_add_record**(int dbase_identifier, array record)

dbase_close

Closes the database associated with **$dbase_identifier**.

bool **dbase_close**(int dbase_identifier)

dbase_create

The **$fields** parameter is an array of arrays, each array describing the format of one field in the
database. Each field consists of a name, a character indicating the field type, a length, and a
precision.

int **dbase_create**(string filename, array fields)

The types of fields available are as follows:

L Boolean—These do not have a length or precision.

M Memo—These do not have a length or precision. **Note:** These aren't supported by PHP.

D Date (stored as YYYYMMDD))—These do not have a length or precision.

N Number—These have both a length and a precision (the number of digits after the
decimal point).

C String

If the database is successfully created, a dbase_identifier is returned; otherwise, false is
returned.

Example: Creating a dBase database file

```
// "database" name
$dbname = "/tmp/test.dbf";
// database "definition"
$def =
    array(
        array("date",     "D"),
        array("name",     "C",  50),
        array("age",      "N",   3, 0),
        array("email",    "C", 128),
        array("ismember", "L")
    );
// creation
if (!dbase_create($dbname, $def))
    print "<strong>Error!</strong>";
```

dbase_delete_record

Marks **$record** to be deleted from the database. To actually remove the record from the database, you must also call **dbase_pack()**.

bool **dbase_delete_record**(int dbase_identifier, int record)

dbase_get_record

Returns the data from **$record** in an array. The array is indexed starting at 0, and includes an associative member named "deleted," which is set to 1 if the record has been marked for deletion (see **dbase_delete_record()**). Each field is converted to the appropriate PHP type. (Dates are left as strings.)

array **dbase_get_record**(int dbase_identifier, int record)

dbase_get_record_with_names

Returns the data from **$record** in an associative array. The array also includes an associative member named "deleted," which is set to 1 if the record has been marked for deletion (see **dbase_delete_record()**). Each field is converted to the appropriate PHP type. (Dates are left as strings.)

array **dbase_get_record_with_names**(int dbase_identifier, int record)

dbase_numfields

Returns the number of fields (columns) in the specified database. Field numbers are between 0 and **dbase_numfields($db)-1**, and record numbers are between 1 and **dbase_numrecords ($db)**.

int **dbase_numfields**(int dbase_identifier)

Example: Using **dbase_numfields()**

```
$rec = dbase_get_record($db, $recno);
$nf  = dbase_numfields($db);
```

```
for ($i=0; $i < $nf; $i++) {
    print $rec[$i]."<br>\n";
}
```

dbase_numrecords

Returns the number of records (rows) in the specified database. Record numbers are between 1 and **dbase_numrecords($db)**, and field numbers are between 0 and **dbase_numfields($db)1**.

int **dbase_numrecords**(int dbase_identifier)

dbase_open

The flags correspond to those for the open() system call. (Typically 0 means read-only, 1 means write-only, and 2 means read and write.) Returns a **dbase_identifier** for the opened database, or false if the database couldn't be opened.

int **dbase_open**(string filename, int flags)

dbase_pack

Packs the specified database (permanently deleting all records marked for deletion using **dbase_delete_record()**).

bool **dbase_pack**(int dbase_identifier)

dbase_replace_record

Replaces the data associated with the record **$record_number** with the data in the $record in the database. If the number of items in the supplied record is not equal to the number of fields in the database, the operation will fail and false will be returned. **$dbase_record_number** is an integer, which spans from one to the number of records in the database (as returned by **dbase_numrecords()**).

bool **dbase_replace_record**(int dbase_identifier, array record, int dbase_record_number)

dba_close()

Closes the established database and frees all resources specified by **$handle**. **$handle** is a database handle returned by **dba_open()**. **Dba_close()** does not return any value. See also **dba_open()** and **dba_popen()**.

void **dba_close**(int handle)

dba_delete

Deletes the entry specified by **$key** from the database specified with **$handle**. **$key** is the key of the entry which is deleted. **$handle** is a database handle returned by **dba_open()**.

dba_delete() returns true or false, if the entry is deleted or not deleted, respectively. See also **dba_exists()**, **dba_fetch()**, **dba_insert()**, and **dba_replace()**.

    string **dba_delete**(string key, int handle)

dba_exists

Checks whether the specified **$key** exists in the database specified by **$handle**. **$Key** is the key the check is performed for. **$Handle** is a database handle returned by **dba_open()**. **Dba_exists()** returns true or false, if the key is found or not found, respectively. See also **dba_fetch()**, **dba_delete()**, **dba_insert()**, and **dba_replace()**.

    bool **dba_exists**(string key, int handle)

dba_fetch

Fetches the data specified by **$key** from the database specified with **$handle**. **$Key** is the key the data is specified by. **$Handle** is a database handle returned by **dba_open()**. **Dba_fetch()** returns the associated string true or false, if the key/data pair is found or not found, respectively. See also **dba_exists()**, **dba_delete()**, **dba_insert()**, and **dba_replace()**.

    string **dba_fetch**(string key, int handle)

dba_firstkey

Returns the first key of the database specified by **$handle** and resets the internal key pointer. This permits a linear search through the whole database. **$Handle** is a database handle returned by **dba_open()**. **Dba_firstkey()** returns the key true or false depending on whether it succeeds or fails, respectively. See also **Dba_nextkey()**.

    string **dba_firstkey**(int handle)

dba_insert

Inserts the entry described with **$key** and **$value** into the database specified by **$handle**. It fails if an entry with the same **$key** already exists. **$key** is the key of the entry to be inserted. **$value** is the value to be inserted. **$handle** is a database handle returned by **dba_open()**. **dba_insert()** returns true or false, depending on whether it succeeds or fails, respectively. See also **dba_exists()**, **dba_delete()**, **dba_fetch()**, **dba_replace()**.

    bool **dba_insert**(string key, string value, int handle)

dba_nextkey

Returns the next key of the database specified by **$handle** and increments the internal key pointer. **$handle** is a database handle returned by **dba_open()**. **dba_nextkey()** returns the key true or false depending on whether it succeeds or fails, respectively. See also **dba_firstkey()**.

    string **dba_nextkey**(int handle)

dba_open

Establishes a database instance for **$path** with **$mode** using **$handler**. **$path** is commonly a regular path in your filesystem. **$mode** is "r" for read access; "w" for read/write access to an already existing database; "c" for read/write access and database creation if it doesn't currently exist; and "n" for create, truncate, and read/write access. **$handler** is the name of the handler that shall be used for accessing **$path**. It is passed all optional parameters given to **dba_open()** and can act on behalf of them. **dba_open()** returns a positive handler id or false, depending on whether the open is successful or fails, respectively. See also **dba_popen()**, **dba_close()**.

   int **dba_open**(string path, string mode, string handler, [string . . .])

dba_optimize

Optimizes the underlying database specified by **$handle**. **$handle** is a database handle returned by **dba_open()**. **dba_optimize()** returns true or false, if the optimization succeeds or fails, respectively. See also **dba_sync()**.

   bool **dba_optimize**(int handle)

dba_popen

Establishes a persistent database instance for **$path** with **$mode** using **$handler**. **$path** is commonly a regular path in your filesystem. **$mode** is "r" for read access; "w" for read/write access to an already existing database; "c" for read/write access and database creation if it doesn't currently exist; and "n" for create, truncate, and read/write access. **$handler** is the name of the handler that shall be used for accessing **$path**. It is passed all optional parameters given to **dba_popen()** and can act on behalf of them. **dba_popen()** returns a positive handler id or false, depending on whether the open is successful or fails, respectively. See also **dba_open()**, **dba_close()**.

   int **dba_popen**(string path, string mode, string handler, [string . . .])

dba_replace

Replaces or inserts the entry described with **$key** and **$value** into the database specified by **$handle**. **$key** is the key of the entry to be inserted. **$value** is the value to be inserted. **$handle** is a database handle returned by **dba_open()**. **dba_replace()** returns true or false, depending on whether it succeeds or fails, respectively. See also **dba_exists()**, **dba_delete()**, **dba_fetch()**, and **dba_insert()**.

   bool **dba_replace**(string key, string value, int handle)

dba_sync

Synchronizes the database specified by **$handle**. This will probably trigger a physical write-to disk, if supported. **$handle** is a database handle returned by **dba_open()**. **dba_sync()** returns true or false, if the synchronization succeeds or fails, respectively. See also **dba_optimize()**.

bool **dba_sync**(int handle)

dblist

string **dblist**(void)

dbmclose

Unlocks and closes the specified database.

bool **dbmclose**(int dbm_identifier)

dbmdelete

Deletes the value for **$key** in the database. Returns false if the key didn't exist in the database.

bool **dbmdelete**(int dbm_identifier, string key)

dbmexists

Returns true if a value is present that is associated with the **$key**.

bool **dbmexists**(int dbm_identifier, string key)

dbmfetch

Returns the value associated with **$key**.

string **dbmfetch**(int dbm_identifier, string key)

dbmfirstkey

Returns the first key in the database. Note that no particular order is guaranteed since the database may be built using a hash-table, which doesn't guarantee any ordering.

string **dbmfirstkey**(*int* dbm_identifier)

dbminsert

Adds the value to the database with the specified key. Returns -1 if the database was opened read-only, 0 if the insert was successful, and 1 if the specified key already exists. (To replace the value, use **dbmreplace()**.)

int **dbminsert**(*int* dbm_identifier, *string* key, *string* value)

dbmnextkey

Returns the next key after **$key**. By calling **dbmfirstkey()** followed by successive calls to **dbmnextkey(),** it is possible to visit every key/value pair in the dbm database.

string **dbmnextkey**(*int* dbm_identifier, *string* key)

Example: Visiting every key/value pair in a DBM database

```
$key = dbmfirstkey ($dbm_id);
while ($key) {
    echo "$key = " . dbmfetch ($dbm_id, $key) . "\n";
    $key = dbmnextkey ($dbm_id, $key);
}
```

dbmopen

The first argument is the full-path filename of the DBM file to be opened, and the second is the file open mode which is one of the following: "r", "n", "c," or "w," standing for read-only, new (implies read-write, and most likely will truncate an already-existing database of the same name), create (implies read-write, and will not truncate an already-existing database of the same name), and read-write, respectively. Returns an identifier to be passed to the other DBM functions on success, or false on failure.

int **dbmopen**(*string* filename, *string* flags)

If NDBM support is used, NDBM will actually create filename.dir and filename.pag files. GDBM only uses one file, as does the internal flat-file support, and Berkeley DB creates a filename.db file. Note that PHP does its own file locking in addition to any file locking that may be done by the DBM library itself. PHP does not delete the .lck files it creates. It uses these files simply as fixed inodes on which to do the file locking. For more information on DBM files, see your Unix man pages, or obtain GNU's GDBM *(ftp://ftp.gnu.org/pub/gnu/gdbm/).*

dbmreplace

Replaces the value for the specified key in the database. This will also add the key to the database if it didn't already exist.

bool **dbmreplace**(*int* dbm_identifier, *string* key, *string* value)

dcgettext

This function enables you to override the current domain for a single message lookup. It also enables you to specify a category.

string **dcgettext**(*string* domain, *string* message, *int* category)

debugger_off

Disables the internal PHP debugger. The debugger is still under development.

int **debugger_off**(*void*)

debugger_on

Enables the internal PHP debugger, connecting it to **$address**. The debugger is still under development.

int **debugger_on**(*string* address)

decbin

Returns a string containing a binary representation of the given number argument. The largest number that can be converted is 2147483647 in decimal, resulting to a string of 31 1's. See also the **bindec()** function.

string **decbin**(*int* number)

dechex

Returns a string containing a hexadecimal representation of the given number argument. The largest number that can be converted is 2147483647 in decimal, resulting to "7ffffff". See also the **hexdec()** function.

string **dechex**(*int* number)

decoct

Returns a string containing an octal representation of the given number argument. The largest number that can be converted is 2147483647 in decimal, resulting to "17777777777". See also **octdec()**.

string **decoct**(*int* number)

define

Defines a named constant. This is similar to a variable, except that constants do not have a dollar sign '$' before them;

- Constants may be accessed anywhere without regard to variable scoping rules.

- Constants may not be redefined or undefined once they have been set.

- Constants may only evaluate to scalar values.

The name of the constant is given by **$name**; the value is given by **$value**. The optional third parameter **$case_insensitive** is also available. If the value 1 is given, then the constant will be defined case-insensitive. The default behavior is case-sensitive; for example, CONSTANT and Constant represent different values.

int **define**(*string* name, *mixed* value, [*int* case_insensitive])

Example: Defining Constants

```
<?php
define ("CONSTANT", "Hello world.");
echo CONSTANT; // outputs "Hello world."
?>
```

Define() returns true on success and false if an error occurs. See also **defined()** and the section on **Constants()**.

defined

Returns true if the named constant given by **$name** has been defined, false otherwise. See also **define()** and the section on **Constants()**.

int **defined**(*string* name)

define_syslog_variables

Initializes all constants used in the syslog functions. See also **openlog()**, **syslog()**, and **closelog()**.

void define_syslog_variables(*void*)

deg2rad

This function converts **$number** from degrees to the radian equivalent. See also **rad2deg()**.

double **deg2rad**(*double* number)

delete

This is a dummy manual entry to satisfy those people who are looking for **unlink()** or **unset()** in the wrong place. See also **unlink()** to delete files and **unset()** to delete variables.

void **delete**(*string* file)

dgettext

The **dgettext()** function enables you to override the current domain for a single message lookup.

string **dgettext**(*string* domain, *string* message)

die

This language construct outputs a message and terminates parsing of the script. It does not return anything. See also **exit()**.

void **die**(*string* message)

Example: die

```php
<?php
$filename = '/path/to/data-file';
$file = fopen ($filename, 'r')
    or die("unable to open file ($filename)");
?>
```

dir

A pseudo-object oriented mechanism for reading a directory. The given **$directory** is opened. Two properties are available once the directory has been opened. The handle property can be used with other directory functions such as **readdir()**, **rewinddir().** and **closedir()**. The path property is set to path the directory that was opened. Three methods are available: read, rewind, and close.

new **dir**(*string* directory)

Example: Dir()

```
$d = dir("/etc");
echo "Handle: ".$d->handle."<br>\n";
echo "Path: ".$d->path."<br>\n";
while($entry=$d->read()) {
    echo $entry."<br>\n";
}
$d->close();
```

dirname

Given a string containing a path to a file, this function will return the name of the directory. On Windows, both slash (/) and backslash (\ ) are used as path separator character. In other environments, the forward slash (/) is used. See also **basename()**.

string **dirname**(*string* path)

Example: Dirname()

```
$path = "/etc/passwd";
$file = dirname ($path); // $file is set to "/etc"
```

diskfreespace

Given a string containing a directory, this function will return the number of bytes available on the corresponding filesystem or disk partition.

float **diskfreespace**(*string* directory)

Example: diskfreespace()

```
$df = diskfreespace("/"); // $df contains the number of bytes
                          // available on "/"
```

dl

Loads the PHP extension defined in **$library**. See also the **extension_dir()** configuration directive.

int **dl**(*string* library)

doubleval

Returns the double (floating point) value of **$var**.

double **doubleval**(*mixed* var)

```
$Var may be any scalar type. You cannot use doubleval() on arrays or objects.
$var = '122.34343The';
$double_value_of_var = doubleval ($var);
print $double_value_of_var; // prints 122.34343
```

See also **intval()**, **strval()**, **settype()**, and Type juggling.

each

Returns the current key and value pair from the array **$array** and advances the array cursor. This pair is returned in a four-element array, with the keys 0, 1, key, and value. Elements 0 and key contain the key name of the array element, and 1 and value contain the data. If the internal pointer for the array points past the end of the array contents, **each()** returns false.

array **each**(*array* array)

Example: Each()

```
$foo = array ("bob", "fred", "jussi", "jouni", "egon", "marliese");
$bar = each ($foo);
```

$bar now contains the following key/value pairs:

```
0 => 0
1 => 'bob'
 key => 0
 value => 'bob'
$foo = array ("Robert" => "Bob", "Seppo" => "Sepi");
$bar = each ($foo);
```

$bar now contains the following key/value pairs:

0 => 'Robert'

1 => 'Bob'

key => 'Robert'

value => 'Bob'

Each() is typically used in conjunction with **list()** to traverse an array, for instance, *$HTTP_POST_VARS* :

Example: Traversing *$HTTP_POST_VARS* with **each()**

```
echo "Values submitted via POST method:<br>";
reset ($HTTP_POST_VARS);
while (list ($key, $val) = each ($HTTP_POST_VARS)) {
    echo "$key => $val<br>";
}
```

After **each()** has executed, the array cursor will be left on the next element of the array, or on the last element if it hits the end of the array. See also **key()**, **list()**, **current()**, **reset()**, **next()**, and **prev()**.

easter_date

Returns the UNIX timestamp corresponding to midnight on Easter of the given year. If no year is specified, the current year is assumed.

Warning: This function will generate a warning if the year is outside of the range for UNIX timestamps (that is, before 1970 or after 2037).

int **easter_date**(*int* year)

Example: easter_date()

```
echo date ("M-d-Y", easter_date(1999));     /* "Apr-04-1999" */
echo date ("M-d-Y", easter_date(2000));     /* "Apr-23-2000" */
echo date ("M-d-Y", easter_date(2001));     /* "Apr-15-2001" */
```

The date of Easter Day was defined by the Council of Nicaea in AD325 as the Sunday after the first full moon that falls on or after the Spring Equinox. The Equinox is assumed to always fall on March 21, so the calculation reduces to determining the date of the full moon and the date of the following Sunday. The algorithm used here was introduced around the year 532 by Dionysius Exiguus. Under the Julian Calendar (for years before 1753), a simple 19-year cycle is used to track the phases of the Moon. Under the Gregorian Calendar (for years after 1753—devised by Clavius and Lilius, and introduced by Pope Gregory XIII in October 1582 and into Britain and then its colonies in September 1752), two correction factors are added to make the cycle more accurate. (The code is based on a C program by Simon Kershaw, <webmaster@ely.anglican.org>) See **easter_days()** for calculating Easter before 1970 or after 2037.

easter_days

Returns the number of days between March 21 and the date on which Easter falls for a given year. If no year is specified, the current year is assumed. This function can be used instead of **easter_date()** to calculate Easter for years that fall outside the range of UNIX timestamps (that is, before 1970 or after 2037).

int **easter_days**(*int* year)

Example: Easter_date()

```
echo easter_days (1999);      /* 14, i.e. April 4   */
echo easter_days (1492);      /* 32, i.e. April 22  */
echo easter_days (1913);      /*  2, i.e. March 23  */
```

The date of Easter Day was defined by the Council of Nicaea in AD325 as the Sunday after the first full moon that falls on or after the Spring Equinox. The Equinox is assumed to always fall on March 21, so the calculation reduces to determining the date of the full moon and the date of the following Sunday. The algorithm used here was introduced around the year 532 by Dionysius Exiguus. Under the Julian Calendar (for years before 1753), a simple 19-year cycle is used to track the phases of the Moon. Under the Gregorian Calendar (for years after 1753—devised by Clavius and Lilius, and introduced by Pope Gregory XIII in October 1582, and into Britain and then its colonies in September 1752), two correction factors are added to make the cycle more accurate. (The code is based on a C program by Simon Kershaw, <webmaster@ely.anglican.org>) See **easter_days()** for calculating Easter before 1970 or after 2037.

echo

Outputs all parameters. **Echo()** is not actually a function (it is a language construct), so you are not required to use parentheses with it.

echo(*string* arg1, *string* ... **)**

Example: Echo()

```
echo "Hello World";
echo "This spans
multiple lines. The newlines will be
output as well";
echo "This spans\nmultiple lines. The newlines will be\noutput as well.";
```

Note: In fact, if you want to pass more than one parameter to echo, you must not enclose the parameters within parentheses. See also **print()**, **printf()**, and **flush()**.

empty

Returns false if **$var** is set and has a non-empty or non-zero value; otherwise, it returns true.

int **empty(** *mixed* var**)**

```
$var = 0;
if (empty($var)) {  // evaluates true
    echo '$var is either 0 or not set at all';
}
if (!isset($var)) { // evaluates false
    echo '$var is not set at all';
}
```

Note that this is meaningless when used on anything that isn't a variable. For example, empty (addslashes ($name)) has no meaning because it would be checking whether something that isn't a variable is a variable with a false value. See also **isset()** and **unset()**.

end

Advances **$array**'s internal pointer to the last element, and then returns that element. See also **current()**, **each()**, **end()**, **next()**, and **reset()**.

mixed **end**(*array* array)

ereg

Searches a **$string** for matches to the regular expression given in **$pattern**. If matches are found for parenthesized substrings of **$pattern** and the function is called with the third argument **$regs** , the matches will be stored in the elements of the array **$regs**. $regs[1] will contain the substring which starts at the first left parenthesis; $regs[2] will contain the substring starting at the second, and so on. $regs[0] will contain a copy of **$string**.

int **ereg**(*string* pattern, *string* string, [*array* regs])

If **ereg()** finds any matches at all, $regs will be filled with exactly ten elements, even though more or fewer than ten parenthesized substrings actually may have matched. This has no effect on the ability of **ereg()** to match more substrings. If no matches are found, $regs will not be altered by **ereg()**. Searching is case sensitive. It returns true if a match for **$pattern** was found in **$string**, or false if no matches were found or an error occurred. The following code snippet takes a date in ISO format (YYYY-MM-DD) and prints it in DD.MM.YYYY format:

Example: Ereg()

```
if (ereg ("([0-9]{4})-([0-9]{1,2})-([0-9]{1,2})", $date, $regs)) {
    echo "$regs[3].$regs[2].$regs[1]";
} else {
    echo "Invalid date format: $date";
}
```

See also **eregi()**, **ereg_replace()**, **and eregi_replace()**.

eregi

This function is identical to **ereg()**, except that this ignores case distinction when matching alphabetic characters. See also **ereg()**, **ereg_replace()**, and **eregi_replace()**.

int **eregi**(*string* pattern, *string* string, [*array* regs])

eregi_replace

This function is identical to **ereg_replace()**, except that this ignores case distinction when matching alphabetic characters. See also **ereg()**, **eregi()**, and **ereg_replace()**.

string **eregi_replace**(*string* pattern, *string* replacement, *string* string)

ereg_replace

This function scans **$string** for matches to **$pattern**, then replaces the matched text with **$replacement**. The modified string is returned, which may mean that the original string is returned if no matches exist to be replaced.) If **$pattern** contains parenthesized substrings,

$replacement may contain substrings of the form \ \ digit, which will be replaced by the text matching the digit'th parenthesized substring; \ \0 will produce the entire contents of string. Up to nine substrings may be used. Parentheses may be nested, in which case they are counted by the opening parenthesis.

string **ereg_replace**(*string* pattern, *string* replacement, *string* string)

If no matches are found in **$string**, then **$string** will be returned unchanged. For example, the following code snippet prints "This was a test" three times:

Example: Ereg_replace()

```
$string = "This is a test";
echo ereg_replace (" is", " was", $string);
echo ereg_replace ("( )is", "\\1was", $string);
echo ereg_replace ("(( )is)", "\\2was", $string);
```

One thing to take note of is that if you use an integer value as the **$replacement** parameter, you may not get the results you expect. This is because **ereg_replace()** will interpret the number as the ordinal value of a character, and apply that.

Example: ereg_replace()

```
<?php
/* This will not work as expected. */
$num = 4;
$string = "This string has four words.";
$string = ereg_replace('four', $num, $string);
echo $string;    /* Output: 'This string has  words.' */
/* This will work. */
$num = '4';
$string = "This string has four words.";
$string = ereg_replace('four', $num, $string);
echo $string;    /* Output: 'This string has 4 words.' */
?>
```

See also **ereg()**, **eregi()**, and **eregi_replace()**.

error_log

Sends an error message to the Web server's error log and a TCP port or to a file. The first parameter, **$message**, is the error message that should be logged. The second parameter, **$message_type** says where the message should go:

int **error_log**(*string* message, *int* message_type, [*string* destination], [*string* extra_headers])

0   **$message** is sent to PHP's system logger, using the Operating System's system logging mechanism or a file, depending on what the **error_log()** configuration directive is set to.

1   **$message** is sent via email to the address in the **$destination** parameter. This is the only message type where the fourth parameter, **$extra_headers**, is used. This message type uses the same internal function as **Mail()** does.

2   **$message** is sent through the PHP debugging connection. This option is only available if remote debugging has **been enabled()**. In this case, the **$destination** parameter specifies the host name or IP address and optionally, the port number of the socket receiving the debug information.

3   **$message** is appended to the file **$destination**.

Example: error_log()

```
// Send notification through the server log if we can not
// connect to the database.
if (!Ora_Logon ($username, $password)) {
    error_log ("Oracle database not available!", 0);
}
// Notify administrator by email if we run out of FOO
if (!($foo = allocate_new_foo())) {
    error_log ("Big trouble, we're all out of FOOs!", 1,
               "operator@mydomain.com");
}
// other ways of calling error_log():
error_log ("You messed up!", 2, "127.0.0.1:7000");
error_log ("You messed up!", 2, "loghost");
error_log ("You messed up!", 3, "/var/tmp/my-errors.log");
```

error_reporting

Sets PHP's error reporting level and returns the old level. The error reporting level is either a bit mask or named constant. Using named constants is strongly encouraged to ensure compatibility for future versions. As error levels are added, the range of integers increases, so older integer-based error levels will not always behave as expected.

int **error_reporting**([*int* level])

Example: Error Integer changes

```
error_reporting (55);   // PHP 3 equivalent to E_ALL ^ E_NOTICE
/* ...in PHP 4, '55' would mean (E_ERROR | E_WARNING | E_PARSE |
E_CORE_ERROR | E_CORE_WARNING) */
error_reporting (2039); // PHP 4 equivalent to E_ALL ^ E_NOTICE
error_reporting (E_ALL ^ E_NOTICE); // The same in both PHP 3
and 4
```

constant	value
1	E_ERROR()
2	E_WARNING()
4	E_PARSE()
8	E_NOTICE()
16	E_CORE_ERROR()
32	E_CORE_WARNING()

64	E_COMPILE_ERROR()
128	E_COMPILE_WARNING()
256	E_USER_ERROR()
512	E_USER_WARNING()
1024	E_USER_NOTICE()

Example: error_reporting()

```
error_reporting(0);
/* Turn off all reporting */
error_reporting (7); // Old syntax, PHP 2/3
error_reporting  (E_ERROR | E_WARNING | E_PARSE); // New syntax for PHP 3/4
/* Good to use for simple running errors  */
error_reporting  (15); // Old syntax, PHP 2/3
error_reporting (E_ERROR | E_WARNING | E_PARSE | E_NOTICE); // New syntax for PHP 3/4
/*   good for code authoring to report uninitialized or (possibly mis-spelled) variables
*/
error_reporting (63); // Old syntax, PHP 2/3
error_reporting (E_ALL); // New syntax for PHP 3/4
/* report all PHP errors */
```

escapeshellarg

Adds single quotes around a string and quotes/escapes any existing single quotes, enabling you to pass a string directly to a shell function and having it be treated as a single safe argument. This function should be used to escape individual arguments to shell functions coming from user input. The shell functions include **exec()**, **system()**, and the **backtick operator()**. A standard use would be as follows:

string **escapeshellarg**(*string* arg)

```
system("ls ".EscapeShellArg($dir))
```

See also **exec()**, **popen()**, **system()**, and the **backtick operator()**.

escapeshellcmd

Escapes any characters in a string that might be used to trick a shell command into executing arbitrary commands. This function should be used to make sure that any data coming from user input is escaped before this data is passed to the **exec()** or **system()** functions, or to the backtick **operator()**.

string **escapeshellcmd**(*string* command)

A standard use would be as follows:

```
$e = EscapeShellCmd($userinput);
system("echo $e"); // here we don't care if $e has spaces
$f = EscapeShellCmd($filename);
```

```
system("touch \"/tmp/$f\"; ls -l \"/tmp/$f\""); // and here we do, so we use quotes
```

See also **escapeshellarg()**, **exec()**, **popen()**, **system()**, and the **backtick operator()**.

eval()

Evaluates the string given in **$code_str** as PHP code. Among other things, this can be useful for storing code in a database text field for later execution. Some factors should be kept in mind when using **eval()**. Remember that the string passed must be valid PHP code, including things like terminating statements with a semicolon so the parser doesn't die on the line after the **eval()**, and properly escaping things in **$code_str**. Also remember that variables given values under **eval()** will retain these values in the main script afterwards. A *return* statement will terminate the evaluation of the string immediately. In PHP 4, you may use *return* to return a value that will become the result of the **eval()** function. In PHP 3, **eval()** was of type *void* and never did return anything.

mixed **eval**(*string* code_str)

Example: Eval() example - simple text merge

```php
<?php
$string = 'cup';
$name = 'coffee';
$str = 'This is a $string with my $name in it.<br>';
echo $str;
eval ("\$str = \"$str\";");
echo $str;
?>
```

The previous example will show the following:

```
This is a $string with my $name in it.
This is a cup with my coffee in it.
```

exec()

Executes the given **$command**; however, it does not output anything. It simply returns the last line from the result of the command. If you need to execute a command and have all the data from the command passed directly back without any interference, use the **PassThru()** function. If the **$array** argument is present, then the specified array will be filled with every line of output from the command. Note that if the array already contains some elements, **exec()** will append to the end of the array. If you do not want the function to append elements, call **unset()** on the array before passing it to **exec()**. If the **$return_var** argument is present along with the **$array** argument, then the return status of the executed command will be written to this variable.

string **exec**(*string* command, [*string* array], [*int* return_var])

Note that if you are going to allow data coming from user input to be passed to this function, then you should be using **EscapeShellCmd()** to make sure that users cannot trick the system into executing arbitrary commands. Note also that if you start a program using this function and want to leave it running in the background, you have to make sure that the output of that program is redirected to a file or some other output stream; otherwise, PHP will hang until the execution of the program ends. See also **system()**, **PassThru()**, **popen()**, **EscapeShellCmd()**, and the **backtick operator()**.

exit

This language construct terminates parsing of the script. It does not return. See also **die()**.

> void **exit**(void)

exp

Returns e raised to the power of **$arg**. See also **pow()**.

> *float* **exp**(*float* arg)

explode

Returns an array of strings, each of which is a substring of **$string** formed by splitting it on boundaries formed by the string **$delim**. If **$limit** is set, the returned array will contain a maximum of **$limit** elements with the last element containing the whole rest of **$string**.

> *array* **explode**(*string* separator, *string* string, [*int* limit])

Example: Explode()

```
$pizza = "piece1 piece2 piece3 piece4 piece5 piece6";
$pieces = explode (" ", $pizza);
```

Note: Although **implode()** can for historical reasons accept its parameters in either order, **explode()** cannot. You must ensure that the **$separator** argument comes before the **$string** argument. See also **split()** and **implode()**.

extension_loaded

Returns true if the extension identified by **$name** is loaded. You can see the names of various extensions by using **phpinfo()**. See also **phpinfo()**. **Note:** This function was added in 3.0.10.

> *bool* **extension_loaded**(*string* name)

extract

This function is used to import variables from an array into the current symbol table. It takes associative array **$var_array** and treats keys as variable names and values as variable values. For each key/value pair, it will create a variable in the current symbol table, subject to **$extract_type** and **$prefix** parameters.

> *void* **extract**(*array* var_array, [*int* extract_type], [*string* prefix])

Extract() checks for collisions with existing variables. The way collisions are treated is determined by **$extract_type**. It can be one of the following values:

EXTR_OVERWRITE   If there is a collision, overwrite the existing variable.
EXTR_SKIP   If there is a collision, don't overwrite the existing variable.
EXTR_PREFIX_SAME   If there is a collision, prefix the new variable with **$prefix**.
EXTR_PREFIX_ALL   Prefix all variables with **$prefix**.

If **$extract_type** is not specified, it is assumed to be EXTR_OVERWRITE. Note that **$prefix** is only required if **$extract_type** is EXTR_PREFIX_SAME or EXTR_PREFIX_ALL. **Extract()** checks each key to see if it constitutes a valid variable name. If it does, only then does it proceed to import it. A possible use for extract is to import into symbol table variables contained in an associative array returned by **wddx_deserialize()**.

Example: Extract()

```
<php?
/* Suppose that $var_array is an array returned from
   wddx_deserialize */
$size = "large";
$var_array = array ("color" => "blue",
                    "size" => "medium",
                    "shape" => "sphere");
extract ($var_array, EXTR_PREFIX_SAME, "wddx");
print "$color, $size, $shape, $wddx_size\n";
?>
```

The above example will produce:

```
blue, large, sphere, medium
```

The *$size* wasn't overwritten because we specified EXTR_PREFIX_SAME, which resulted in *$wddx_size* being created. If EXTR_SKIP was specified, then even $wddx_size wouldn't have been created. EXTR_OVERWRITE would have cause *$size* to have value "medium", and EXTR_PREFIX_ALL would result in new variables being named *$wddx_color*, *$wddx_size*, and *$wddx_shape*.

ezmlm_hash ezmlm_hash()

Calculates the hash value needed when keeping EZMLM mailing lists in a MySQL database.

int **ezmlm_hash**(*string* addr)

Example: Calculating the hash and subscribing a user

```
$user = "kris@koehntopp.de";
$hash = ezmlm_hash ($user);
$query = sprintf ("INSERT INTO sample VALUES (%s, '%s')", $hash, $user);
$db->query($query); // using PHPLIB db interface
```

fclose

The file pointed to by fp is closed. Returns true on success and false on failure. The file pointer must be valid and must point to a file successfully opened by fopen() or fsockopen().

int **fclose**(*int* fp)

fdf_close

Closes the FDF document. See also **fdf_open()**.

boolean **fdf_close**(*int* fdf_document)

fdf_create

Creates a new FDF document. This function is needed if one would like to populate input fields in a PDF document with data.

int **fdf_create**(*void*)

Example: Populating a PDF document

```php
<?php
$outfdf = fdf_create();
fdf_set_value($outfdf, "volume", $volume, 0);
fdf_set_file($outfdf, "http:/testfdf/resultlabel.pdf");
fdf_save($outfdf, "outtest.fdf");
fdf_close($outfdf);
Header("Content-type: application/vnd.fdf");
$fp = fopen("outtest.fdf", "r");
fpassthru($fp);
unlink("outtest.fdf");
?>
```

See also **fdf_close()**, **fdf_save()**, and **fdf_open()**.

fdf_get_file

Returns the value of the /F key. See also **fdf_set_file()**.

string **fdf_get_file**(*int* fdf_document)

fdf_get_status

Returns the value of the /STATUS key. See also **fdf_set_status()**.

string **fdf_get_status**(*int* fdf_document)

fdf_get_value

Returns the value of a field. See also **fdf_set_value()**.

string **fdf_get_value**(*int* fdf_document, *string* fieldname)

fdf_next_field_name

Returns the name of the field after the field in **$fieldname** or the field name of the first field if the second parameter is NULL. See also **fdf_set_field()**, **fdf_get_field()**.

> *string* **fdf_next_field_name**(*int* fdf_document, *string* fieldname)

fdf_open

Opens a file with form data. This file must contain the data as returned from a PDF form. Currently, the file has to be created manually by using **fopen()** and writing the content of HTTP_FDF_DATA with **fwrite()** into it. A mechanism such as one for HTML form data where for each input field a variable is created does not exist. See also **fdf_close()**.

> *int* **fdf_open**(*string* filename)

Example: Accessing the form data

```php
<?php
// Save the FDF data into a temp file
$fdffp = fopen("test.fdf", "w");
fwrite($fdffp, $HTTP_FDF_DATA, strlen($HTTP_FDF_DATA));
fclose($fdffp);
// Open temp file and evaluate data
$fdf = fdf_open("test.fdf");
...
fdf_close($fdf);
?>
```

fdf_save

Saves a FDF document. The FDF Toolkit provides a way to output the document to stdout if the parameter **$filename** is '.'. This does not work if PHP is used as an apache module. In such a case, one will have to write to a file and use, for example, **fpassthru().** to output it. See also **fdf_close()** and example for **fdf_create()**.

> *int* **fdf_save**(*string* filename)

fdf_set_ap

Sets the appearance of a field (that is, the value of the /AP key). The possible values of **$face** are 1=FDFNormalAP, 2=FDFRolloverAP, and 3=FDFDownAP.

> *boolean* **fdf_set_ap**(*int* fdf_document, *string* field_name, *int* face, *string* filename, *int* page_number)

fdf_set_file

Sets the value of the /F key. The /F key is just a reference to a PDF form that is to be populated with data. In a Web environment, it is a URL (for example, *http:/testfdf/resultlabel.pdf*). See also **fdf_get_file()** and example for **fdf_create()**.

> *boolean* **fdf_set_file**(*int* fdf_document, *string* filename)

fdf_set_flags
Sets certain flags of the given field **$fieldname**. See also **fdf_set_opt()**.

boolean **fdf_set_flags**(*int* fdf_document, *string* fieldname, *int* whichFlags, *int* newFlags)

fdf_set_javascript_action
Sets a JavaScript action for the given field **$fieldname**. See also **fdf_set_submit_form_action()**.

boolean **fdf_set_javascript_action**(*int* fdf_document, *string* fieldname, *int* trigger, *string* script)

fdf_set_opt
Sets options of the given field **$fieldname**. See also **fdf_set_flags()**.

boolean **fdf_set_opt**(*int* fdf_document, *string* fieldname, *int* element, *string* str1, *string* str2)

fdf_set_status
Sets the value of the /STATUS key. See also **fdf_get_status()**.

boolean **fdf_set_status**(*int* fdf_document, *string* status)

fdf_set_submit_form_action
Sets a submit form action for the given field **$fieldname**. See also **fdf_set_javascript_action()**.

boolean **fdf_set_submit_form_action**(*int* fdf_document, *string* fieldname, *int* trigger, *string* script, *int* flags)

fdf_set_value
Sets the value of a field. The last parameter determines if the field value is to be converted to a PDF Name (**$isName** = 1) or set to a PDF String (**$isName** = 0). See also **fdf_get_value()**.

boolean **fdf_set_value**(*int* fdf_document, *string* fieldname, *string* value, *int* isName)

feof
Returns true if the file pointer is at EOF; otherwise an error occurs, and it returns false. The file pointer must be valid and must point to a file successfully opened by **fopen()**, **popen()**, or **fsockopen()**.

int **feof**(*int* fp)

fgetc

Returns a string containing a single character read from the file pointed to by fp. Returns false on EOF. The file pointer must be valid and must point to a file successfully opened by **fopen()**, **popen()**, or **fsockopen()**. See also **fread()**, **fopen()**, **popen()**, **fsockopen()**, and **fgets()**.

string **fgetc**(*int* fp)

fgetcsv

Similar to **fgets()**, except that **fgetcsv()** parses the line, it reads for fields in CSV format and returns an array containing the fields read. The field delimiter is a comma, unless you specify another delimiter with the optional third parameter. **$Fp** must be a valid file pointer to a file successfully opened by **fopen()**, **popen()**, or **fsockopen()**. The length must be greater than the longest line to be found in the CSV file (allowing for trailing line-end characters). **Fgetcsv()** returns false on error, including end of file. N.B. A blank line in a CSV file will be returned as an array, comprising a single null field, and will not be treated as an error.

array **fgetcsv**(*int* fp, *int* length, [*string* delimiter])

Example: Fgetcsv() example - Read and print entire contents of a CSV file

```
$row = 1;
$fp = fopen ("test.csv","r");
while ($data = fgetcsv ($fp, 1000, ",")) {
    $num = count ($data);
    print "<p> $num fields in line $row: <br>";
    $row++;
    for ($c=0; $c<$num; $c++) {
        print $data[$c] . "<br>";
    }
}
fclose ($fp);
```

fgets

Returns a string of up to length - 1 bytes read from the file pointed to by fp. Reading ends when length - 1 bytes have been read, on a newline (which is included in the return value), or on EOF (whichever comes first). If an error occurs, it returns false.

string **fgets**(*int* fp, *int* length)

A few common pitfalls are as follows:

■ People used to the 'C' semantics of fgets should note the difference in how EOF is returned.

■ The file pointer must be valid and must point to a file successfully opened by **fopen()**, **popen()**, or **fsockopen()**.

Example: Reading a file line by line

```
$fd = fopen ("/tmp/inputfile.txt", "r");
while (!feof ($fd)) {
    $buffer = fgets($fd, 4096);
    echo $buffer;
}
fclose ($fd);
```

See also **fread()**, **fopen()**, **popen()**, **fgetc()**, **fsockopen()**, and **socket_set_timeout()**.

fgetss

Identical to **fgets()**, except that fgetss attempts to strip any HTML and PHP tags from the text it reads. You can use the optional third parameter to specify tags that should not be stripped. **Note: $allowable_tags** was added in PHP 3.0.13, PHP4B3. See also **fgets()**, **fopen()**, **fsockopen()**, **popen()**, and **strip_tags()**.

string **fgetss**(*int* fp, *int* length, [*string* allowable_tags])

file

Identical to **readfile()**, except that **file()** returns the file in an array. Each element of the array corresponds to a line in the file, with the newline still attached. You can use the optional second parameter and set it to "1," if you want to search for the file in the **include_path**, as well.

array **file**(*string* filename, [*int* use_include_path])

```php
<?php
// get a web page into an array and print it out
$fcontents = file ('http://www.php.net');
while (list ($line_num, $line) = each ($fcontents)) {
    echo "<b>Line $line_num:</b> " . htmlspecialchars ($line) . "<br>\n";
}
// get a web page into a string
$fcontents = join ('', file ('http://www.php.net'));
?>
```

See also **readfile()**, **fopen()**, **fsockopen()**, and **popen()**.

fileatime

Returns the time the file was last accessed, or false in case of an error. The time is returned as a Unix timestamp. The results of this function are cached. See **clearstatcache()** for more details.

int **fileatime**(*string* filename)

Note: The atime of a file is supposed to change whenever the data blocks of a file are being read. This can be costly performance-wise when an application regularly accesses a very large number of files or directories. Some Unix filesystems can be mounted with atime updates disabled to increase the performance of such applications; USENET news spools are a common example. On such filesystems, this function will be useless.

filectime

Returns the time the file was last changed, or false in case of an error. The time is returned as a Unix timestamp. The results of this function are cached. See **clearstatcache()** for more details.

int **filectime**(*string* filename)

Note: In most Unix filesystems, a file is considered changed when its Inode data is changed. In other words, when the permissions, the owner, the group, or other metadata from the Inode is written to, the file is considered changed. See also **filemtime()** (use this when creating "Last Modified" footers on Web pages) and **fileatime()**.

Note: In some Unix texts, the ctime of a file is being referred to as the creation time of the file; this is wrong. Creation time does not exist for Unix files in most Unix filesystems.

filegroup

Returns the group ID of the owner of the file, or false in case of an error. The group ID is returned in numerical format. Use **posix_getgrgid()** to resolve it to a group name. The results of this function are cached. See **clearstatcache()** for more details.

Note: This function does not work on Windows' systems.

int **filegroup**(*string* filename)

fileinode

Returns the inode number of the file, or false in case of an error. The results of this function are cached. See **clearstatcache()** for more details.

Note: This function does not work on Windows' systems.

int **fileinode**(*string* filename)

filemtime

Returns the time the file was last modified, or false in case of an error. The time is returned as a Unix timestamp. The results of this function are cached. See **clearstatcache()** for more details.

Note: This function returns the time to when the data blocks of a file were being written, that is, the time when the content of the file was changed. Use **date()** on the result of this function to get a printable modification date for use in page footers.

int **filemtime**(*string* filename)

fileowner

Returns the file owner's user ID, or false in case of an error. The user ID is returned in numerical format. Use **posix_getpwuid()** to resolve it to a username. The results of this function are cached. See **clearstatcache()** for more details.

Note: This function does not work on Windows' systems.

int **fileowner**(*string* filename)

fileperms
Returns the permissions on the file, or false in case of an error. The results of this function are cached. See **clearstatcache()** for more details.

int **fileperms**(*string* filename)

filepro
This reads and verifies the map file, storing the field count and info. No locking is done, so you should avoid modifying your filePro database while it may be opened in PHP.

bool **filepro**(*string* directory)

filepro_fieldcount
Returns the number of fields (columns) in the opened filePro database. See also **filepro()**.

int filepro_fieldcount(*void*)

filepro_fieldname
Returns the name of the field corresponding to **$field_number**.

string **filepro_fieldname**(*int* field_number)

filepro_fieldtype
Returns the edit type of the field corresponding to **$field_number**.

string **filepro_fieldtype**(*int* field_number)

filepro_fieldwidth
Returns the width of the field corresponding to **$field_number**.

int **filepro_fieldwidth**(*int* field_number)

filepro_retrieve
Returns the data from the specified location in the database.

string **filepro_retrieve**(*int* row_number, *int* field_number)

filepro_rowcount
Returns the number of rows in the opened filePro database. See also **filepro()**.

int filepro_rowcount(*void*)

filesize

Returns the size of the file, or false in case of an error. The results of this function are cached. See **clearstatcache()** for more details.

> *int* **filesize**(*string* filename)

filetype

Returns the type of the file. Possible values are fifo, char, dir, block, link, file, and unknown. Returns false if an error occurs. The results of this function are cached. See **clearstatcache()** for more details.

> *string* **filetype**(*string* filename)

file_exists

Returns true if the file specified by **$filename** exists; otherwise, returns false. **file_exists()** will not work on remote files; the file to be examined must be accessible via the server's filesystem. The results of this function are cached. See **clearstatcache()** for more details.

> *bool* **file_exists**(*string* filename)

flock

PHP supports a portable way of locking complete files in an advisory way, which means all accessing programs have to use the same way of locking or it will not work. **flock()** operates on **$fp**, which must be an open file pointer. **$operation** is one of the following values:

- To acquire a shared lock (reader), set **$operation** to LOCK_SH (set to 1 prior to PHP 4.0.1).
- To acquire an exclusive lock (writer), set **$operation** to LOCK_EX (set to 2 prior to PHP 4.0.1).
- To release a lock (shared or exclusive), set **$operation** to LOCK_UN (set to 3 prior to PHP 4.0.1).
- If you don't want **flock()** to block while locking, add LOCK_NB (4 prior to PHP 4.0.1) to **$operation**.

> *bool* **flock**(*int* fp, *int* operation, [*int* wouldblock])

Flock() enables you to perform a simple reader/writer model, which can be used on virtually every platform (including most Unices and even Windows). The optional third argument is set to true if the lock would block (EWOULDBLOCK errno condition). **Flock()** returns true on success and false on error, for example, when a lock could not be acquired.

floor

Returns the next lowest integer value from **$number**. Using **floor()** on integers is absolutely a waste of time.

Note: PHP/FI 2's **floor()** returned a float. Use: *$new = (double) floor($number)*; to get the old behavior. See also **ceil()** and **round()**.

int **floor**(*float* number)

flush

Flushes the output buffers of PHP and whatever backend PHP is using (CGI, a Web server, and so on). This effectively tries to push all the output so far to the user's browser.

void **flush**(*void*)

fopen

If **$filename** begins with "http://" (not case sensitive), an HTTP 1.0 connection is opened to the specified server and a file pointer is returned to the beginning of the text of the response. A 'Host:' header is sent with the request in order to handle name-based virtual hosts. It does not handle HTTP redirects, so you must include trailing slashes on directories. If **$filename** begins with "ftp://" (not case sensitive), an ftp connection to the specified server is opened and a pointer to the requested file is returned. If the server does not support passive mode ftp, this will fail. You can open files for either reading or writing via ftp but not both simultaneously. If **$filename** is one of "php://stdin", "php://stdout", or "php://stderr", the corresponding stdio stream will be opened. (This was introduced in PHP 3.0.13; in earlier versions, a filename such as "/dev/stdin" or "/dev/fd/0" must be used to access the stdio streams.) If **$filename** begins with anything else, the file will be opened from the filesystem, and a file pointer to the file opened is returned. If the open fails, the function returns false.

int **fopen**(*string* filename, *string* mode, [*int* use_include_path])

$mode may be any of the following:

- 'r'—Open for reading only; place the file pointer at the beginning of the file.
- 'r+'—Open for reading and writing; place the file pointer at the beginning of the file.
- 'w'—Open for writing only; place the file pointer at the beginning of the file and truncate the file to zero length. If the file does not exist, attempt to create it.
- 'w+'—Open for reading and writing; place the file pointer at the beginning of the file and truncate the file to zero length. If the file does not exist, attempt to create it.
- 'a'—Open for writing only; place the file pointer at the end of the file. If the file does not exist, attempt to create it.
- 'a+'—Open for reading and writing; place the file pointer at the end of the file. If the file does not exist, attempt to create it.

The **$mode** may contain the letter 'b'. This is useful only on systems that differentiate between binary and text files (that is, it's useless on Unix). If not needed, this will be ignored.

You can use the optional third parameter and set it to "1", if you want to search for the file in the **include_path()**, as well.

Example: Fopen()

```
$fp = fopen ("/home/rasmus/file.txt", "r");
$fp = fopen ("/home/rasmus/file.gif", "wb");
$fp = fopen ("http://www.php.net/", "r");
$fp = fopen ("ftp://user:password@example.com/", "w");
```

If you are experiencing problems with reading and writing to files and you are using the server module version of PHP, remember to make sure that the files and directories you are using are accessible to the server process.

On the Windows platform, be careful to escape any backslashes used in the path to the file, or use forward slashes.

```
$fp = fopen ("c:\\data\\info.txt", "r");
```

See also **fclose()**, **fsockopen()**, **socket_set_timeout()**, and **popen()**.

fpassthru

Reads to EOF on the given file pointer and writes the results to standard output. If an error occurs, **fpassthru()** returns false. The file pointer must be valid and must point to a file successfully opened by **fopen()**, **popen()**, or **fsockopen()**. The file is closed when **fpassthru()** is done reading it (leaving **$fp** useless). If you just want to dump the contents of a file to stdout, you may want to use the **readfile()**, which saves you the **fopen()** call. See also **readfile()**, **fopen()**, **popen()**, and **fsockopen()**.

int **fpassthru**(*int* fp)

fputs()

An alias to **fwrite()**, and is identical in every way. Note that the **$length** parameter is optional, and if not specified, the entire string will be written.

int **fputs**(*int* fp, *string* str, [*int* length])

fread()

Reads up to **$length** bytes from the file pointer referenced by **$fp**. Reading stops when **$length** bytes have been read or EOF is reached, whichever comes first.

string **fread**(*int* fp, *int* length)

```
// get contents of a file into a string
$filename = "/usr/local/something.txt";
$fd = fopen ($filename, "r");
$contents = fread ($fd, filesize ($filename));
fclose ($fd);
```

See also **fwrite()**, **fopen()**, **fsockopen()**, **popen()**, **fgets()**, **fgetss()**, **fscanf()**, **file()**, and **fpassthru()**.

FrenchToJD

Converts a date from the French Republican Calendar to a Julian Day Count. These routines only convert dates in years 1 through 14 (Gregorian dates 22 September 1792 through 22 September 1806). This more than covers the period when the calendar was in use.

int **FrenchToJD**(*int* month, *int* day, *int* year)

fscanf

Similar to **sscanf()**, but it takes its input from a file associated with **$handle** and interprets the input according to the specified **$format**. If only two parameters were passed to this function, the values parsed would be returned as an array. Otherwise, if optional parameters are passed, the function will return the number of assigned values. The optional parameters must be passed by reference.

mixed **fscanf**(*int* handle, *string* format, [*string* var1])

Example: Fscanf()

```
$fp = fopen ("users.txt","r");
while ($userinfo = fscanf ($fp, "%s\t%s\t%s\n")) {
    list ($name, $profession, $countrycode) = $userinfo;
    //... do something with the values
}
fclose($fp);
```

Example: users.txt

```
javier   argonaut       pe
hiroshi  sculptor       jp
robert   slacker  us
luigi    florist  it
```

See also **fread()**, **fgets()**, **fgetss()**, **sscanf()**, **printf()**, and **sprintf()**.

fseek

Sets the file position indicator for the file referenced by **$fp**. The new position, measured in bytes from the beginning of the file, is obtained by adding **$offset** to the position specified by **$whence**, whose values are defined as follows:

- SEEK_SET—Set position equal to **$offset** bytes.
- SEEK_CUR—Set position to current location plus **$offset**.
- SEEK_END—Set position to end-of-file plus **$offset**.

int **fseek**(*int* fp, *int* offset, [*int* whence])

If $whence is not specified, it is assumed to be **SEEK_SET**. Upon success, returns 0; otherwise, returns -1. Note that seeking past EOF is not considered an error. This may not be used on file pointers returned by **fopen()** if they use the "http://" or "ftp://" formats.

Note: The $whence argument was added after PHP 4.0 RC1. See also **ftell()** and **rewind()**.

fsockopen

Initiates a stream connection in the Internet (AF_INET, using TCP or UDP) or Unix (AF_UNIX) domain. For the Internet domain, it will open a TCP socket connection to **$hostname** on port **$port**. **$hostname** may, in this case, be either a fully qualified domain name or an IP address. For UDP connections, you need to explicitly specify the protocol: **$udp://hostname**. For the Unix domain, **$hostname** will be used as the path to the socket, **$port** must be set to 0 in this case. The optional **$timeout** can be used to set a timeout in seconds for the connect system call.

int **fsockopen**(*string* hostname, *int* port, [*int* errno], [*string* errstr], [*double* timeout])

Fsockopen() returns a file pointer, which may be used together with the other file functions (such as **fgets()**, **fgetss()**, **fputs()**, **fclose()**, and **feof()**). If the call fails, it will return false. If the optional **$errno** and **$errstr** arguments are present, they will be set to indicate the actual system level error that occurred on the system-level *connect()* call. If the returned errno is 0 and the function returned false, it is an indication that the error occurred before the *connect()* call. This is most likely due to a problem initializing the socket. Note that the **$errno** and **$errstr** arguments must be passed by reference.

Depending on the environment, the Unix domain or the optional connect timeout may not be available. The socket will, by default, be opened in blocking mode. You can switch it to non-blocking mode by using **socket_set_blocking()**.

Example: Fsockopen()

```
$fp = fsockopen ("www.php.net", 80, &$errno, &$errstr, 30);
if (!$fp) {
    echo "$errstr ($errno)<br>\n";
} else {
    fputs ($fp, "GET / HTTP/1.0\r\n\r\n");
    while (!feof($fp)) {
        echo fgets ($fp,128);
    }
    fclose ($fp);
}
```

The following example shows how to retrieve the day and time from the UDP service "day-time" (port 13) in your own machine.

Example: Using UDP connection

```
<?php
$fp = fsockopen("udp://127.0.0.1", 13, &$errno, &$errstr);
if (!$fp) {
    echo "ERROR: $errno - $errstr<br>\n";
} else {
    fwrite($fp,"\n");
```

```
        echo fread($fp, 26);
        fclose($fp);
    }
    ?>
```

See also **pfsockopen()**, **socket_set_blocking()**, **socket_set_timeout()**, **fgets()**, **fgetss()**, **fputs()**, **fclose()**, and **feof()**).

fstat

Gathers the statistics of the file opened by the file pointer fp. This function is similar to the **stat()** function, except that it operates on an open file pointer instead of a filename.

array **fstat**(*int* fp)

Returns an array with the statistics of the file with the following elements:

device	inode	number of links
user id of owner	group id owner	device type if inode device*
size in bytes	time of last access	time of last modification
time of last change	blocksize for filesystem I/O *	number of blocks allocated

*Only valid on systems supporting the st_blksize type—other systems (Windows, for example) return -1. The results of this function are cached. See **clearstatcache()** for more details.

ftell

Returns the position of the file pointer referenced by fp, for example, its offset into the file stream. If an error occurs, returns false. The file pointer must be valid and must point to a file successfully opened by **fopen()** or **popen()**. See also **fopen()**, **popen()**, **fseek()**, and **rewind()**.

int **ftell**(*int* fp)

ftp_cdup

Returns true on success, false on error. Changes to the parent directory.

int **ftp_cdup**(*int* ftp_stream)

ftp_chdir

Returns true on success, false on error. Changes to the specified **$directory**.

int **ftp_chdir**(*int* ftp_stream, *string* directory)

ftp_connect

Returns an FTP stream on success, false on error. **ftp_connect()** opens up a FTP connection to the specified **$host**. The **$port** parameter specifies an alternate port to which it can connect. If it is omitted or zero, then the default FTP port 21 will be used.

int **ftp_connect**(*string* host, [*int* port])

ftp_delete

Returns true on success, false on error. **ftp_delete()** deletes the file specified by **$path** from the FTP server.

int **ftp_delete**(*int* ftp_stream, *string* path)

ftp_fget

Returns true on success, false on error. **ftp_fget()** retrieves **$remote_file** from the FTP server, and writes it to the given file pointer, **$fp**. The transfer **$mode** specified must be either FTP_ASCII or FTP_BINARY.

int **ftp_fget**(*int* ftp_stream, *int* fp, *string* remote_file, *int* mode)

ftp_fput

Returns true on success, false on error. **ftp_fput()** uploads the data from the file pointer **$fp** until end of file. The results are stored in **$remote_file** on the FTP server. The transfer **$mode** specified must be either FTP_ASCII or FTP_BINARY.

int **ftp_fput**(*int* ftp_stream, *string* remote_file, *int* fp, *int* mode)

ftp_get

Returns true on success, false on error. **ftp_get()** retrieves **$remote_file** from the FTP server, and saves it to **$local_file** locally. The transfer **$mode** specified must be either FTP_ASCII or FTP_BINARY.

int **ftp_get**(*int* ftp_stream, *string* local_file, *string* remote_file, *int* mode)

ftp_login

Returns true on success, false on error. Logs in the given FTP stream.

int **ftp_login**(*int* ftp_stream, *string* username, *string* password)

ftp_mdtm

Returns a UNIX timestamp on success, or -1 on error. **ftp_mdtm()** checks the last modified time for a file, and returns it as a UNIX timestamp. If an error occurs, or the file does not exist, -1 is returned. Note that not all servers support this feature, and **ftp_mdtm()** does not work with directories.

    int **ftp_mdtm**(*int* ftp_stream, *string* remote_file)

ftp_mkdir

Returns the newly created directory name on success, false on error. Creates the specified **$directory**.

    string **ftp_mkdir**(*int* ftp_stream, *string* directory)

ftp_nlist

Returns an array of filenames on success, false on error.

    array **ftp_nlist**(*int* ftp_stream, *string* directory)

ftp_pasv

Returns true on success, false on error. **ftp_pasv()** turns on passive mode if the **$pasv** parameter is true and turns off passive mode if **$pasv** is false. In passive mode, data connections are initiated by the client, rather than by the server.

    int **ftp_pasv**(*int* ftp_stream, *int* pasv)

ftp_put

Returns true on success, false on error. **ftp_put()** stores **$local_file** on the FTP server, as **$remote_file**. The transfer **$mode** specified must be either FTP_ASCII or FTP_BINARY.

    int **ftp_put**(*int* ftp_stream, *string* remote_file, *string* local_file, *int* mode)

    Example: Ftp_put()

```
$upload = ftp_put ($conn_id, "$destination_file", "$source_file", FTP_ASCII);
```

ftp_pwd

Returns the current directory or false on error.

    string **ftp_pwd**(*int* ftp_stream)

ftp_quit ftp_connect()

Closes **$ftp_stream**.

    int **ftp_quit**(*int* ftp_stream)

ftp_rawlist ftp_rawlist()

Executes the FTP LIST command and returns the result as an array. Each array element corresponds to one line of text. The output is not parsed in any way. The system type identifier returned by **ftp_systype()** can be used to determine how the results should be interpreted.

int **ftp_rawlist**(*int* ftp_stream, *string* directory)

ftp_rename

Returns true on success, false on error. **ftp_rename()** renames the file specified by **$from** to the new name **$to**.

int **ftp_rename**(*int* ftp_stream, *string* from, *string* to)

ftp_rmdir

Returns true on success, false on error. Removes the specified **$directory**.

int **ftp_rmdir**(*int* ftp_stream, *string* directory)

ftp_site

Returns true on success, false on error. **ftp_site()** sends the command specified by **$cmd** to the FTP server. SITE commands are not standardized and vary from server to server. They are useful for handling such things as file permissions and group membership.

int **ftp_site**(*int* ftp_stream, *string* cmd)

ftp_size

Returns the file size on success, or -1 on error. **ftp_size()** returns the size of a file. If an error occurs, or if the file does not exist, -1 is returned. Not all servers support this feature.

int **ftp_size**(*int* ftp_stream, *string* remote_file)

ftp_systype

Returns the remote system type, or false on error.

string **ftp_systype**(*int* ftp_stream)

ftruncate

Takes the file pointer, fp, and truncates the file to length, size. This function returns true on success and false on failure.

int **ftruncate**(*int* fp, *int* size)

function_exists

Checks the list of defined functions for **$function_name**. Returns true if the given function name were found, false otherwise.

int **function_exists**(*string* function_name)

func_get_arg

Returns the argument, which is at the **$arg_num** 'th offset, into a user-defined function's argument list. Function arguments are counted starting from zero. **Func_get_arg()** will generate a warning if called from outside of a function definition. If **$arg_num** is greater than the number of arguments actually passed, a warning will be generated and **func_get_arg()** will return false.

mixed **func_get_arg**(*int* arg_num)

```php
<?php
function foo () {
    $numargs = func_num_args();
    echo "Number of arguments: $numargs<br>\n";
    if ($numargs >= 2) {
    echo "Second argument is: " . func_get_arg (1) . "<br>\n";
    }
}
foo (1, 2, 3);
?>
```

Func_get_arg() may be used in conjunction with **func_num_args()** and **func_get_args()** to enable user-defined functions to accept variable-length argument lists. This function was added in PHP 4.

func_get_args

Returns an array in which each element is the corresponding member of the current user-defined function's argument list. **Func_get_args()** will generate a warning if called from outside of a function definition.

array **func_get_args**(*void*)

```php
<?php
function foo () {
    $numargs = func_num_args();
    echo "Number of arguments: $numargs<br>\n";
    if ($numargs >= 2) {
    echo "Second argument is: " . func_get_arg (1) . "<br>\n";
    }
    $arg_list = func_get_args();
    for ($i = 0; $i < $numargs; $i++) {
    echo "Argument $i is: " . $arg_list[$i] . "<br>\n";
    }
}
foo (1, 2, 3);
?>
```

Func_get_args() may be used in conjunction with **func_num_args()** and **func_get_arg()** to enable user-defined functions to accept variable-length argument lists. This function was added in PHP 4.

func_num_args

Returns the number of arguments passed into the current user-defined function. **Func_num_args()** will generate a warning if called from outside of a function definition.

int **func_num_args**(*void*)

```php
<?php
function foo() {
    $numargs = func_num_args();
    echo "Number of arguments: $numargs\n";
}
foo (1, 2, 3);    // Prints 'Number of arguments: 3'
?>
```

Func_num_args() may be used in conjunction with **func_get_arg()** and **func_get_args()** to enable user-defined functions to accept variable-length argument lists. This function was added in PHP 4.

fwrite()

Writes the contents of **$string** to the file stream pointed to by **$fp**. If the **$length** argument is given, writing will stop after **$length** bytes have been written or the end of **$string** is reached, whichever comes first. Note that if the **$length** argument is given, then the **magic_quotes_run-time()** configuration option will be ignored and no slashes will be stripped from **$string**. See also **fread()**, **fopen()**, **fsockopen()**, **popen()**, and **fputs()**.

int **fwrite**(*int* fp, *string* string, [*int* length])

getallheaders

Returns an associative array of all the HTTP headers in the current request.

Note: You can also get at the value of the common CGI variables by reading them from the environment, which works whether or not you are using PHP as an Apache module. Use **phpinfo()** to see a list of all of the environment variables defined this way.

array **getallheaders**(*void*)

Example: getallheaders()

```php
$headers = getallheaders();
while (list ($header, $value) = each ($headers)) {
    echo "$header: $value<br>\n";
}
```

This example will display all the request headers for the current request. **Getallheaders()** is currently only supported when PHP runs as an Apache module.

getcwd

Returns the current working directory.

string **getcwd**(void)

getdate

Returns an associative array containing the date information of the $timestamp as the following array elements:

- "seconds"—seconds
- "minutes"—minutes
- "hours"—hours
- "mday"—day of the month
- "wday"—day of the week, numeric
- "mon"—month, numeric
- "year"—year, numeric
- "yday"—day of the year, numeric; for example, "299"
- "weekday"—day of the week, textual, full; for example, "Friday"
- "month"—month, textual, full; for example, "January"

array **getdate**(*int* timestamp)

getenv

Returns the value of the environment variable **$varname**, or false on an error.

string **getenv**(*string* varname)

```
$ip = getenv ("REMOTE_ADDR"); // get the ip number of the user
```

You can see a list of all the environmental variables by using phpinfo(). You can find out what many of them mean by taking a look at the CGI specification (http://hoohoo.ncsa.uiuc.edu/cgi/), specifically the page on environmental variables (http://hoohoo.ncsa.uiuc.edu/cgi/env.html). **Note:** This function does not work in ISAPI mode.

gethostbyaddr

Returns the host name of the Internet host specified by **$ip_address**. If an error occurs, returns **$ip_address**. See also **gethostbyname()**.

string **gethostbyaddr**(*string* ip_address)

gethostbyname

Returns the IP address of the Internet host specified by $hostname. See also **gethostbyaddr()**.

string **gethostbyname**(*string* hostname)

gethostbynamel

Returns a list of IP addresses to which the Internet host specified by **$hostname** resolves. See also **gethostbyname()**, **gethostbyaddr()**, **checkdnsrr()**, **getmxrr()**, and the named(8) manual page.

array **gethostbynamel**(*string* hostname)

GetImageSize

Determines the size of any GIF, JPG, PNG, or SWF image file and return the dimensions along with the file type and a height/width text string to be used inside a normal HTML IMG tag. Returns an array with 4 elements. Index 0 contains the width of the image in pixels. Index 1 contains the height. Index 2 contains a flag indicating the type of the image. 1 = GIF, 2 = JPG, 3 = PNG, 4 = SWF. Index 3 is a text string with the correct "height=xxx width=xxx" string that can be used directly in an IMG tag.

array **GetImageSize**(*string* filename, [*array* imageinfo])

Example: GetImageSize

```
<?php $size = GetImageSize ("img/flag.jpg"); ?>
<IMG SRC="img/flag.jpg" <?php echo $size[3]; ?>
```

The optional **$imageinfo** parameter enables you to extract some extended information from the image file. Currently, this will return the different JPG APP markers in an associative array. Some programs use these APP markers to embed text information in images. A very common one to embed IPTC *http://www.xe.net/iptc/* information in the APP13 marker. You can use the **iptcparse()** function to parse the binary APP13 marker into something readable.

Example: GetImageSize returning IPTC

```
<?php
    $size = GetImageSize ("testimg.jpg",&$info);
    if (isset ($info["APP13"])) {
        $iptc = iptcparse ($info["APP13"]);
        var_dump ($iptc);
    }
?>
```

Note: This function does not require the GD image library.

getlastmod

Returns the time of the last modification of the current page. The value returned is a Unix time-stamp, suitable for feeding to **date()**. Returns false on error.

int **getlastmod**(*void*)

Example: getlastmod()

```
// outputs e.g. 'Last modified: March 04 1998 20:43:59.'
echo "Last modified: ".date ("F d Y H:i:s.", getlastmod());
```

See also **date()**, **getmyuid()**, **get_current_user()**, **getmyinode()**, and **getmypid()**.

getmxrr

Searches DNS for MX records corresponding to **$hostname**. Returns true if any records are found; returns false if no records are found or if an error occurred. A list of the MX records found is placed into the array **$mxhosts**. If the **$weight** array is given, it will be filled with the weight information gathered. See also **checkdnsrr()**, **gethostbyname()**, **gethostbynamel()**, **gethostbyaddr()**, and the named(8) manual page.

int **getmxrr**(*string* hostname, *array* mxhosts, [*array* weight])

getmyinode

Returns the current script's inode, or false on error. See also **getmyuid()**, **get_current_user()**, **getmypid()**, and **getlastmod()**. **Note:** This function is not supported on Windows' systems.

int **getmyinode**(*void*)

getmypid

Returns the current PHP process ID, or false on error. **Note:** When running as a server module, separate invocations of the script are not guaranteed to have distinct pids. See also **getmyuid()**, **get_current_user()**, **getmyinode()**, and **getlastmod()**.

int **getmypid**(*void*)

getmyuid

Returns the user ID of the current script, or false on error. See also **getmypid()**, **get_current_user()**, **getmyinode()**, and **getlastmod()**.

int **getmyuid**(*void*)

getprotobyname

Returns the protocol number associated with the protocol **$name** as per /etc/protocols. See also **getprotobynumber()**.

int **getprotobyname**(*string* name)

getprotobynumber

Returns the protocol name associated with protocol **$number** as per /etc/protocols. See also **getprotobyname()**.

> *string* **getprotobynumber**(*int* number)

getrandmax

Returns the maximum value that can be returned by a call to **rand()**. See also **rand()**, **srand()**, **mt_rand()**, **mt_srand()**, and **mt_getrandmax()**.

> *int* **getrandmax**(*void*)

getrusage

This is an interface to getrusage(2). It returns an associative array containing the data returned from the system call. If who is 1, getrusage will be called with RUSAGE_CHILDREN.

> *array* **getrusage**([*int* who])

Example: Getrusage

```
$dat = getrusage();
echo $dat["ru_nswap"];        # number of swaps
echo $dat["ru_majflt"];       # number of page faults
echo $dat["ru_utime.tv_sec"]; # user time used (seconds)
echo $dat["ru_utime.tv_usec"]; # user time used (microseconds)
```

See your system's man page on getrusage(2) for more details.

getservbyname

Returns the Internet port, which corresponds to **$service** for the specified **$protocol** as per /etc/services. **$protocol** is either *TCP* or *UDP*. See also **getservbyport()**.

> *int* **getservbyname**(*string* service, *string* protocol)

getservbyport

Returns the Internet service associated with **$port** for the specified **$protocol** as per /etc/services. **$protocol** is either TCP or UDP. See also **getservbyname()**.

> *string* **getservbyport**(*int* port, *string* protocol)

gettext

This function returns a translated string if one is found in the translation table, or it returns the submitted message if not found. You may use an underscore character as an alias to this function.

> *string* **gettext**(*string* message)

Example: Gettext() -check

```php
<?php
// Set language to German
putenv ("LANG=de");
// Specify location of translation tables
bindtextdomain ("myPHPApp", "./locale");
// Choose domain
textdomain ("myPHPApp");
// Print a test message
print (gettext ("Welcome to My PHP Application"));
?>
```

gettimeofday

This is an interface to gettimeofday(2). It returns an associative array containing the data returned from the system call.

- "sec"—seconds

- "usec"—microseconds

- "minuteswest"—minutes west of Greenwich

- "dsttime"—type of dst correction

array **gettimeofday**(*void*)

gettype

Returns the type of the PHP variable **$var**. Possible values for the returned string are shown in the following table:

boolean	integer	double	string
array	object	resource	user function
unknown type			

string **gettype**(*mixed* var)

See also **settype()**.

get_browser

Attempts to determine the capabilities of the user's browser. This is done by looking up the browser's information in the browscap.ini file. By default, the value of $HTTP_USER_AGENT is used; however, you can alter this (for example, look up another browser's info) by passing the optional **$user_agent** parameter to **get_browser()**. The information is returned in an object, which will contain various data elements representing, for instance, the browser's major and minor version numbers and ID string; true/false values for features such as frames, JavaScript, and cookies, and so forth. Although browscap.ini contains information on many browsers, it relies on user updates to keep the database current. The format of the file is fairly self-explanatory. The following example shows how one might list all available information retrieved about the user's browser:

object **get_browser**([*string* user_agent])

Example: Get_browser()

```php
<?php
function list_array ($array) {
    while (list ($key, $value) = each ($array)) {
    $str .= "<b>$key:</b> $value<br>\n";
    }
    return $str;
}
echo "$HTTP_USER_AGENT<hr>\n";
$browser = get_browser();
echo list_array ((array) $browser);
?>
```

The output of the previous script would look something like this:

```
Mozilla/4.5 [en] (X11; U; Linux 2.2.9 i586)<hr>
<b>browser_name_pattern:</b> Mozilla/4\.5.*<br>
<b>parent:</b> Netscape 4.0<br>
<b>platform:</b> Unknown<br>
<b>majorver:</b> 4<br>
<b>minorver:</b> 5<br>
<b>browser:</b> Netscape<br>
<b>version:</b> 4<br>
<b>frames:</b> 1<br>
<b>tables:</b> 1<br>
<b>cookies:</b> 1<br>
<b>backgroundsounds:</b> <br>
<b>vbscript:</b> <br>
<b>javascript:</b> 1<br>
<b>javaapplets:</b> 1<br>
<b>activexcontrols:</b> <br>
<b>beta:</b> <br>
<b>crawler:</b> <br>
<b>authenticodeupdate:</b> <br>
<b>msn:</b> <br>
```

In order for this to work, your **browscap()** configuration file setting must point to the correct location of the browscap.ini file. For more information (including locations from which you may obtain a browscap.ini file), check the PHP FAQ at *http://www.php.net/FAQ.php*.

get_cfg_var

Returns the current value of the PHP configuration variable specified by **$varname**, or false if an error occurs. It will not return configuration information set when the PHP was compiled, nor read from an Apache configuration file (using the php3_configuration_option directives). To check whether the system is using a configuration **file()**, try retrieving the value of the cfg_file_path configuration setting. If this is available, a configuration file is being used.

string **get_cfg_var**(string varname)

get_class

Returns the name of the class of which the object $obj is an instance. See also **get_parent_class()**, **is_subclass_of()**.

string **get_class**(object obj)

get_class_methods

Returns an array of method names defined for the class specified by **$class_name**. See also **get_class_vars()**, **get_object_vars()**.

array get_class_methods(string class_name)

get_class_vars

Returns an array of default properties of the class. See also **get_class_methods()**, **get_object_vars()**.

array **get_class_vars**(string class_name)

get_current_user

Returns the name of the owner of the current PHP script. See also **getmyuid()**, **getmypid()**, **getmyinode()**, and **getlastmod()**.

string **get_current_user**(void)

get_declared_classes

Returns an array of the names of the declared classes in the current script. In PHP 4.0.1pl2, three extra classes are returned at the beginning of the array: stdClass (defined in Zend/zend.c), OverloadedTestClass (defined in ext/standard/basic_functions.c), and Directory (defined in ext/standard/dir.c).

array **get_declared_classes**(*void*)

get_extension_funcs

Returns the names of all the functions defined in the module indicated by **$module_name**.

array **get_extension_funcs**(string module_name)

Example: get_extension_funcs

```
print_r (get_extension_funcs ("xml"));
print_r (get_extension_funcs ("gd"));
```

will print a list of the functions in the modules *xml* and *gd* respectively. See also **get_loaded_extensions()**.

get_html_translation_table

Returns the translation table that is used internally for **htmlspecialchars()** and **htmlentities()**. Two new defines (**HTML_ENTITIES, HTML_SPECIALCHARS**) enable you to specify the table you want. As in the **htmlspecialchars()** and **htmlentities()** functions, you can optionally specify the quote_style with which you are working. The default is ENT_COMPAT mode. See the description of these modes in **htmlspecialchars()**.

string **get_html_translation_table**(int table, [int quote_style])

Example: Translation Table

```
$trans = get_html_translation_table (HTML_ENTITIES);
$str = "Hallo & <Frau> & Krämer";
$encoded = strtr ($str, $trans);
```

The $encoded variable will now contain: "Hallo & <Frau> & Krämer". The cool thing is using **array_flip()** to change the direction of the translation.

```
$trans = array_flip ($trans);
$original = strtr ($str, $trans);
```

The content of $original would be: "Hallo & <Frau> & Krämer". **Note:** This function was added in PHP 4.0. See also **htmlspecialchars()**, **htmlentities()**, **strtr()**, and **array_flip()**.

get_included_files

This function returns an associative array of the names of all the files that have been loaded into a script using **include_once()**. The indexes of the array are the file names as used in the **include_once()** without the ".php" extension. As of PHP 4.0.1pl2, this function assumes that the include_once files end in the extension ".php", other extensions do not work. See also **require_once()**, **include_once()**, **get_required_files()**.

array get_included_files(void)

get_loaded_extensions

Returns the names of all the modules compiled and loaded in the PHP interpreter.

array get_loaded_extensions(*void*)

Example: get_loaded_extensions

```
print_r (get_loaded_extensions());
```

will print a list like this:

```
Array
(
    [0] => xml
    [1] => wddx
    [2] => standard
    [3] => session
    [4] => posix
    [5] => pgsql
    [6] => pcre
    [7] => gd
    [8] => ftp
    [9] => db
    [10] => Calendar
    [11] => bcmath
)
```

See also **get_extension_funcs()**.

get_magic_quotes_gpc

Returns the current active configuration setting of **magic_quotes_gpc()** (0 for off, 1 for on). See also **get_magic_quotes_runtime()**, **set_magic_quotes_runtime()**.

long get_magic_quotes_gpc(void)

get_magic_quotes_runtime

Returns the current active configuration setting of **magic_quotes_runtime()** (0 for off, 1 for on). See also **get_magic_quotes_gpc()**, **set_magic_quotes_runtime()**.

long get_magic_quotes_runtime(void)

get_meta_tags

Opens **$filename** and parses it line by line for tags of the form.

array **get_meta_tags**(string filename, [int use_include_path])

Example: Meta Tags

```
<meta name="author" content="name">
<meta name="tags" content="php3 documentation">
</head> <!-- parsing stops here -->
```

Note: Pay attention to line endings—PHP uses a native function to parse the input, so a Mac file won't work on Unix.

The value of the name property becomes the key, and the value of the content property becomes the value of the returned array. Therefore, you can easily use standard array functions to traverse it or access single values. Special characters in the value of the name property are substituted with '_', the rest is converted to lower case. Setting *use_include_path* to 1 will result in PHP trying to open the file along the standard include path.

get_object_vars

Returns an associative array of defined object properties for the specified object **$obj**. If variables declared in the class of which the **$obj** is an instance have not been assigned a value, those will not be returned in the array.

array **get_object_vars**(object obj)

Example: Use of **get_object_vars()**

```php
<?php
class Point2D {
    var $x, $y;
    var $label;
    function Point2D($x, $y) {
        $this->x = $x;
        $this->y = $y;
    }
    function setLabel($label) {
        $this->label = $label;
    }
    function getPoint() {
        return array("x" => $this->x,
                     "y" => $this->y,
                     "label" => $this->label);
    }
}
$p1 = new Point2D(1.233, 3.445);
print_r(get_object_vars($p1));
// "$label" is declared but not defined
// Array
// (
//     [x] => 1.233
//     [y] => 3.445
// )
$p1->setLabel("point #1");
print_r(get_object_vars($p1));
// Array
// (
//     [x] => 1.233
//     [y] => 3.445
//     [label] => point #1
// )
?>
```

See also **get_class_methods()**, **get_class_vars()**.

get_parent_class

Returns the name of the parent class to the class of which the object **$obj** is an instance. See also **get_class()**, **is_subclass_of()**.

string **get_parent_class**(object obj)

get_required_files

Returns an associative array of the names of all the files that have been loaded into a script using **require_once()**. The indexes of the array are the file names as used in the **require_once()** without the ".php" extension.

array get_required_files(void)

Example: Printing the required and included files

```
<?php
require_once ("local.php");
require_once ("../inc/global.php");
for ($i=1; $i<5; $i++)
    include "util".$i."php";
echo "Required_once files\n";
print_r (get_required_files());
echo "Included_once files\n";
print_r (get_included_files());
?>
```

will generate the following output:

```
Required_once files
Array
(
    [local] => local.php
    [../inc/global] => /full/path/to/inc/global.php
)
Included_once files
Array
(
    [util1] => util1.php
    [util2] => util2.php
    [util3] => util3.php
    [util4] => util4.php
)
```

Note: As of PHP 4.0.1pl2, this function assumes that the *required_once* files end in the extension ".php", other extensions do not work. See also **require_once()**, **include_once()**, **get_included_files()**.

gmdate

Identical to the **date()** function, except that the time returned is *Greenwich Mean Time* (GMT). For example, when run in Finland (GMT +0200), the following first line prints "Jan 01 1998 00:00:00," and the second prints "Dec 31 1997 22:00:00."

string **gmdate**(string format, int timestamp)

Example: Gmdate()

```
echo date ("M d Y H:i:s", mktime (0,0,0,1,1,1998));
echo gmdate ("M d Y H:i:s", mktime (0,0,0,1,1,1998));
```

See also **date()**, **mktime()**, and **gmmktime()**.

gmmktime

Identical to **mktime(),** except the passed parameters represents a GMT date.

int **gmmktime**(int hour, int minute, int second, int month, int day, int year, [int is_dst])

gmstrftime

Behaves the same as **strftime()**, except that the time returned is GMT. For example, when run in Eastern Standard Time (GMT -0500), the first line below prints "Dec 31 1998 20:00:00," and the second prints "Jan 01 1999 01:00:00."

string **gmstrftime**(string format, int timestamp)

Example: Gmstrftime()

```
setlocale ('LC_TIME', 'en_US');
echo strftime ("%b %d %Y %H:%M:%S", mktime (20,0,0,12,31,98))."\n";
echo gmstrftime ("%b %d %Y %H:%M:%S", mktime (20,0,0,12,31,98))."\n";
```

See also **strftime()**.

GregorianToJD

Valid Range for Gregorian Calendar 4714 B.C. to 9999 A.D. Although this software can handle dates all the way back to 4714 B.C., such use may not be meaningful. The Gregorian calendar was not instituted until October 15, 1582 (or October 5, 1582 in the Julian calendar). Some countries did not accept it until much later. For example, Britain converted in 1752, the USSR in 1918, and Greece in 1923. Most European countries used the Julian calendar prior to the Gregorian.

int **GregorianToJD**(int month, int day, int year)

Example: Calendar functions

```
<?php
$jd = GregorianToJD (10,11,1970);
echo "$jd\n";
$gregorian = JDToGregorian ($jd);
echo "$gregorian\n";
?>
```

gzclose

The gz-file pointed to by zp is closed. Returns true on success and false on failure. The gz-file pointer must be valid and must point to a file successfully opened by gzopen().

int **gzclose**(int zp)

gzcompress

Returns a gzip-compressed version of the input **$data** or false on errors. The optional parameter **$level** can be given as 0 for no compression and up to 9 for maximum compression. See also **gzuncompress()**.

> string **gzcompress**(string data, [int level])

gzeof

Returns true if the gz-file pointer is at EOF or an error occurs; otherwise, returns false. The gz-file pointer must be valid and must point to a file successfully opened by **gzopen()**.

> int **gzeof**(int zp)

gzfile

Identical to **readgzfile()**, except that **gzfile()** returns the file in an array. You can use the optional second parameter and set it to "1," if you want to search for the file in the **include_path()** as well. See also **readgzfile()**, **and gzopen()**.

> array **gzfile**(string filename, [int use_include_path])

gzgetc

Returns a string containing a single (uncompressed) character read from the file pointed to by zp. Returns false on EOF (as does **gzeof()**). The gz-file pointer must be valid and must point to a file successfully opened by **gzopen()**. See also **gzopen()**, and **gzgets()**.

> string **gzgetc**(int zp)

gzgets

Returns a (uncompressed) string of up to length -1 bytes read from the file pointed to by fp. Reading ends when length -1 bytes have been read, on a newline or on EOF (whichever comes first). If an error occurs, returns false. The file pointer must be valid and must point to a file successfully opened by **gzopen()**. See also **gzopen()**, **gzgetc()**, and **fgets()**.

> string **gzgets**(int zp, int length)

gzgetss

Identical to **gzgets()**, except that **gzgetss()** attempts to strip any HTML and PHP tags from the text it reads. You can use the optional third parameter to specify tags that should not be stripped. **$Allowable_tags** was added in PHP 3.0.13, PHP4B3. See also **gzgets()**, **gzopen()**, and **strip_tags()**.

> string **gzgetss**(int zp, int length, [string allowable_tags])

gzopen

Opens a gzip (.gz) file for reading or writing. The mode parameter is as in **fopen()** ("rb" or "wb") but can also include a compression level ("wb9") or a strategy: 'f' for filtered data as in "wb6f", 'h' for Huffman only compression as in "wb1h". (See the description of deflateInit2 in zlib.h for more information about the strategy parameter). **Gzopen()** can be used to read a file, which is not in gzip format. In this case, **gzread()** will directly read from the file without decompression. **Gzopen()** returns a file pointer to the file opened. After that, everything you read from this file descriptor will be transparently decompressed and what you write gets compressed. If the open fails, the function returns false. You can use the optional third parameter and set it to "1," if you want to search for the file in the **include_path()** as well.

int **gzopen**(string filename, string mode, [int use_include_path])

Example: Gzopen()

```
$fp = gzopen ("/tmp/file.gz", "r");
```

See also **gzclose()**.

gzpassthru

Reads to EOF on the given gz-file pointer and writes the (uncompressed) results to standard output. If an error occurs, returns false. The file pointer must be valid and must point to a file successfully opened by **gzopen()**. The gz-file is closed when **gzpassthru()** is done reading it (leaving **$zp** useless).

int **gzpassthru**(int zp)

gzputs

An alias to **gzwrite()**, and it is identical in every way.

int **gzputs**(int zp, string str, [int length])

gzread

Reads up to **$length** bytes from the gz-file pointer referenced by **$zp**. Reading stops when **$length** (uncompressed) bytes have been read or EOF is reached, whichever comes first.

string **gzread**(int zp, int length)

```
// get contents of a gz-file into a string
$filename = "/usr/local/something.txt.gz";
$zd = gzopen ($filename, "r");
$contents = gzread ($zd, 10000);
gzclose ($zd);
```

See also **gzwrite()**, **gzopen()**, **gzgets()**, **gzgetss()**, **gzfile()**, and **gzpassthru()**.

gzrewind

Sets the file position indicator for zp to the beginning of the file stream. If an error occurs, returns 0. The file pointer must be valid and must point to a file successfully opened by **gzopen()**. See also **gzseek()gztell()**.

int **gzrewind**(int zp)

gzseek

Sets the file position indicator for the file referenced by zp to offset bytes into the file stream. Equivalent to calling (in C) **gzseek(zp, offset, SEEK_SET)**. If the file is opened for reading, this function is emulated but can be extremely slow. If the file is opened for writing, only forward seeks are supported; gzseek then compresses a sequence of zeroes up to the new starting position. Upon success, returns 0; otherwise, returns -1.

Note: Seeking past EOF is not considered an error. See also **gztell()** and **gzrewind()**.

int **gzseek**(int zp, int offset)

gztell

Returns the position of the file pointer referenced by **$zp**; that is, its offset into the file stream. If an error occurs, returns false. The file pointer must be valid and must point to a file successfully opened by **gzopen()**. See also **gzopen()**, **gzseek()**, and **gzrewind()**.

int **gztell**(int zp)

gzuncompress

Takes **$data** compressed by **gzcompress()** and returns the original uncompressed data or false on error. The function will return an error if the uncompressed data is more than 256 times the length of the compressed input **$data** or more than the optional parameter **$length**. See also **gzcompress()**.

string **gzuncompress**(string data, [int length])

gzwrite

Writes the contents of **$string** to the gz-file stream pointed to by **$zp**. If the **$length** argument is given, writing will stop after **$length** (uncompressed) bytes have been written or the end of **$string** is reached, whichever comes first. **Note:** If the **$length** argument is given, then the **magic_quotes_runtime()** configuration option will be ignored and no slashes will be stripped from **$string**. See also **gzread()**, **gzopen()**, and **gzputs()**.

int **gzwrite**(int zp, string string, [int length])

header

Used at the top of an HTML file to send raw HTTP header strings. See the HTTP 1.1 Specification (*http://www.w3.org/Protocols/rfc2616/rfc2616*) for more information on raw http headers.

Note: Remember that the **Header()** function must be called before any actual output is sent either by normal HTML tags or from PHP. It is a very common error to read code with **include()** or with **auto_prepend** and have spaces or empty lines in this code that force output before **header()** is called. Two special-case header calls exist. The first is the "Location" header. Not only does it send this header back to the browser, it also returns a REDIRECT status code to Apache. From a script writer's point of view this should not be important, but for people who understand Apache internals, it is important to understand.

int **header**(string string)

```
header ("Location: http://www.php.net"); /* Redirect browser
                                             to PHP web site */
exit;                    /* Make sure that code below does
                            not get executed when we redirect. */
```

The second special-case is any header that starts with the string, "HTTP/" (case is not significant). For example, if you have your ErrorDocument 404 Apache directive pointed to a PHP script, it would be a good idea to make sure that your PHP script is actually generating a 404. The following is the first thing you should do in your script:

```
header ("HTTP/1.0 404 Not Found");
```

PHP scripts often generate dynamic HTML that must not be cached by the client browser or any proxy caches between the server and the client browser. Many proxies and clients can be forced to disable caching with the following:

```
header ("Expires: Mon, 26 Jul 1997 05:00:00 GMT");    // Date in the past
header ("Last-Modified: " . gmdate("D, d M Y H:i:s") . " GMT");
                                                       // always modified
header ("Cache-Control: no-cache, must-revalidate");  // HTTP/1.1
header ("Pragma: no-cache");                           // HTTP/1.0
```

See also **headers_sent()**.

headers_sent

Returns true if the HTTP headers have already been sent, false otherwise. See also **header()**.

boolean **headers_sent**(string void)

hebrev

The optional parameter **$max_chars_per_line** indicates maximum number of characters per line will be output. The function tries to avoid breaking words. See also **hebrevc()**.

string **hebrev**(string hebrew_text, [int max_chars_per_line])

hebrevc

This function is similar to **hebrev()** with the difference that it converts newlines (\n) to "
\n". The optional parameter max_chars_per_line indicates maximum number of characters per line will be output. The function tries to avoid breaking words. See also **hebrev()**.

string **hebrevc**(string hebrew_text, [int max_chars_per_line])

hexdec

Returns the decimal equivalent of the hexadecimal number represented by the hex_string argument. HexDec converts a hexadecimal string to a decimal number. The largest number that can be converted is 7ffffff or 2147483647 in decimal. See also the **dechex()** function.

int **hexdec**(string hex_string)

highlight_file

Prints out a syntax highlighted version of the code contained in **$filename** using the colors defined in the built-in syntax highlighter for PHP.

void **highlight_file**(string filename)

Example: Creating a source highlighting URL

To setup a URL that can code highlight any script that you pass to it, we will make use of the "ForceType" directive in Apache to generate a nice URL pattern, and use the function **highlight_file()** to show a nice looking code list. In your httpd.conf, you can add the following:

```
<Location /source>
    ForceType application/x-httpd-php
</Location>
```

Then make a file named "source" and put it in your Web root directory:

```
<HTML>
<HEAD>
<TITLE>Source Display</TITLE>
</HEAD>
<BODY BGCOLOR="white">
<?php
    $script = getenv ("PATH_TRANSLATED");
    if(!$script) {
    echo "<BR><B>ERROR: Script Name needed</B><BR>";
    } else {
    if (ereg("(\.php|\.inc)$",$script)) {
    echo "<H1>Source of: $PATH_INFO</H1>\n<HR>\n";
    highlight_file($script);
    } else {
    echo "<H1>ERROR: Only PHP or include script names are allowed</H1>";
    }
    }
    echo "<HR>Processed: ".date("Y/M/d H:i:s",time());
?>
```

```
</BODY>
</HTML>
```

Then you can use an URL like the one following in order to display a colorized version of a script located in "/path/to/script.php" in your Web site.

```
http://your.server.com/source/path/to/script.php
```

See also **highlight_string()** and **show_source()**.

highlight_string

Prints out a syntax highlighted version of **$str** using the colors defined in the built-in syntax highlighter for PHP. See also **highlight_file()** and **show_source()**.

void **highlight_string**(string str)

htmlentities

This function is identical to **htmlspecialchars()** in all ways, except that all characters that have HTML character entity equivalents are translated into these entities. Like **htmlspecialchars()**, it takes an optional second argument that indicates what should be done with single and double quotes. **ENT_COMPAT** (the default) will only convert double-quotes and leave single-quotes alone. **ENT_QUOTES** will convert both double and single quotes, and **ENT_NOQUOTES** will leave both double and single quotes unconverted. At present, the ISO-8859-1 character set is used. Note that the optional second argument was added in PHP 3.0.17 and PHP 4.0.3. See also **htmlspecialchars()** and **nl2br()**.

string **htmlentities**(string string, [int quote_style])

htmlspecialchars

Certain characters have special significance in HTML and should be represented by HTML entities if they are to preserve their meanings. This function returns a string with some of these conversions made; the translations made are those most useful for everyday Web programming. If you require all HTML character entities to be translated, use **htmlentities()** instead. This function is useful in preventing user-supplied text from containing HTML markup, such as in a message board or guest book application. The optional second argument, quote_style, tells the function what to do with single and double quote characters. The default mode, **ENT_COMPAT**, is the backwards compatible mode, which only translates the double-quote character and leaves the single-quote untranslated. If **ENT_QUOTES** is set, both single and double quotes are translated, and if **ENT_NOQUOTES** is set, neither single nor double quotes are translated.

string **htmlspecialchars**(string string, [int quote_style])

The translations performed are as follows:

- '&' (ampersand) becomes '&'
- '"' (double quote) becomes '"' when ENT_NOQUOTES is not set.

■ '"' (single quote) becomes ''' only when ENT_QUOTES is set.

■ '<' (less than) becomes '<'

■ '>' (greater than) becomes '>'

Note: This function does not translate anything beyond what is listed. For full entity translation, see **htmlentities()**. Also note that the optional second argument was added in PHP 3.0.17 and PHP 4.0.3. See also **htmlentities()** and **nl2br()**.

hw_Array2Objrec

Converts an **$object_array** into an object record. Multiple attributes, such as 'Title,' in different languages are treated properly. See also **hw_objrec2array()**.

string **hw_Array2Objrec**(array object_array)

hw_Children

Returns an array of object ids. Each id belongs to a child of the collection with ID **$objectID**. The array contains all children, both documents and collections.

array **hw_Children**(int connection, int objectID)

hw_ChildrenObj

Returns an array of object records. Each object record belongs to a child of the collection with ID **$objectID**. The array contains all children, both documents and collections.

array **hw_ChildrenObj**(int connection, int objectID)

hw_Close

Returns false if connection is not a valid connection index, otherwise true. Closes down the connection to a Hyperwave server with the given connection index.

int **hw_Close**(int connection)

hw_Connect

Opens a connection to a Hyperwave server and returns a connection index on success, or false if the connection could not be made. Each of the arguments should be a quoted string, except for the port number. The **$username** and **$password** arguments are optional and can be left out. In such a case, no identification with the server will be done. It is similar to identify as user anonymous. This function returns a connection index that is needed by other Hyperwave functions. You can have multiple connections open at once. Keep in mind, that the password is not encrypted. See also **hw_pConnect()**.

int **hw_Connect**(string host, int port, string username, string password)

hw_Cp

Copies the objects with object ids, as specified in the second paramete,r to the collection with the id **$destination** id. The value return is the number of copied objects. See also **hw_mv()**.

int **hw_Cp**(int connection, array object_id_array, int destination id)

hw_Deleteobject

Deletes the object with the given object id in the second parameter. It will delete all instances of the object. Returns true if no error occurs, otherwise false. See also **hw_mv()**.

int **hw_Deleteobject**(*int* connection, *int* object_to_delete)

hw_DocByAnchor

Returns a th object id of the document to which **$anchorID** belongs.

int **hw_DocByAnchor**(*int* connection, *int* anchorID)

hw_DocByAnchorObj

Returns an object record of the document to which **$anchorID** belongs.

string **hw_DocByAnchorObj**(*int* connection, *int* anchorID)

hw_Document_Attributes

Returns the object record of the document. For backward compatibility, **hw_DocumentAttributes()** is also accepted. This is deprecated, however. See also **hw_Document_BodyTag()** and **hw_Document_Size()**.

string **hw_Document_Attributes**(*int* hw_document)

hw_Document_BodyTag

Returns the BODY tag of the document. If the document is an HTML document, the BODY tag should be printed before the document. See also **hw_Document_Attributes()** and **hw_Document_Size()**. For backward compatibility, **hw_DocumentBodyTag()** is also accepted. This is deprecated, however.

string **hw_Document_BodyTag**(*int* hw_document)

hw_Document_Content

Returns the content of the document. If the document is an HTML document, the content is everything after the BODY tag. Information from the HEAD and BODY tag is in the stored in the object record. See also **hw_Document_Attributes()**, **hw_Document_Size()**, and **hw_DocumentSetContent()**.

string **hw_Document_Content**(*int* hw_document)

hw_Document_SetContent

Sets or replaces the content of the document. If the document is an HTML document, the content is everything after the BODY tag. Information from the HEAD and BODY tag is stored in the object record. If you also provide this information in the content of the document, the Hyperwave server will change the object record accordingly when the document is inserted; probably not a very good idea. If this function fails, the document will retain its old content. See also **hw_Document_Attributes()**, **hw_Document_Size()**, and **hw_Document_Content()**.

string **hw_Document_SetContent**(*int* hw_document, *string* content)

hw_Document_Size

Returns the size in bytes of the document. See also **hw_Document_BodyTag()** and **hw_Document_Attributes()**. For backward compatibility, **hw_DocumentSize()** is also accepted. This is deprecated, however.

int **hw_Document_Size**(*int* hw_document)

hw_EditText

Uploads the text document to the server. The object record of the document may not be modified while the document is edited. This function will only work for pure text documents. It will not open a special data connection; therefore, it blocks the control connection during the transfer. See also **hw_PipeDocument()**, **hw_FreeDocument()**, **hw_Document_BodyTag()**, **hw_Document_Size()**, **hw_Output_Document()**, and **hw_GetText()**.

int **hw_EditText**(*int* connection, *int* hw_document)

hw_Error

Returns the last error number. If the return value is 0, no error has occurred. The error relates to the last command.

int **hw_Error**(*int* connection)

hw_ErrorMsg

Returns a string containing the last error message or 'No Error'. If false is returned, this function failed. The message relates to the last command.

string **hw_ErrorMsg**(*int* connection)

hw_Free_Document

Frees the memory occupied by the Hyperwave document.

int **hw_Free_Document**(*int* hw_document)

hw_GetAnchors

Returns an array of object ids with anchors of the document with object ID **$objectID**.

array **hw_GetAnchors**(*int* connection, *int* objectID)

hw_GetAnchorsObj

Returns an array of object records with anchors of the document with object ID **$objectID**.

array **hw_GetAnchorsObj**(*int* connection, *int* objectID)

hw_GetAndLock

Returns the object record for the object with ID **$objectID**. It will also lock the object, so other users cannot access it until it is unlocked. See also **hw_Unlock**(), and **hw_GetObject**().

string **hw_GetAndLock**(*int* connection, *int* objectID)

hw_GetChildColl

Returns an array of object ids. Each object ID belongs to a child collection of the collection with ID **$objectID**. The function will not return child documents. See also **hw_GetChildren**(), and **hw_GetChildDocColl**().

array **hw_GetChildColl**(*int* connection, *int* objectID)

hw_GetChildCollObj

Returns an array of object records. Each object record belongs to a child collection of the collection with ID **$objectID**. The function will not return child documents. See also **hw_ChildrenObj**() and **hw_GetChildDocCollObj**().

array **hw_GetChildCollObj**(*int* connection, *int* objectID)

hw_GetChildDocColl

Returns array of object ids for child documents of a collection. See also **hw_GetChildren**() and **hw_GetChildColl**().

array **hw_GetChildDocColl**(*int* connection, *int* objectID)

hw_GetChildDocCollObj

Returns an array of object records for child documents of a collection. See also **hw_ChildrenObj**() and **hw_GetChildCollObj**().

array **hw_GetChildDocCollObj**(*int* connection, *int* objectID)

hw_GetObject

Returns the object record for the object with ID **$objectID** if the second parameter is an integer. If the second parameter is an array of integers, the function will return an array of object records. In such a case, the last parameter is also evaluated, which is a query string.

array **hw_GetObject**(*int* connection, *[int | array]* objectID, *string* query)

The query string has the following syntax:

```
<expr> ::= "(" <expr> ")" |
"!" <expr> | /* NOT */
<expr> "||" <expr> | /* OR */
<expr> "&&" <expr> | /* AND */
<attribute> <operator> <value>
<attribute> ::= /* any attribute name (Title, Author, DocumentType ...) */
<operator> ::= "=" | /* equal */
"<" | /* less than (string compare) */
">" | /* greater than (string compare) */
"~" /* regular expression matching */
```

The query enables one to further select certain objects from the list of given objects. Unlike the other query functions, this query may use unindexed attributes. The number of object records returned depends on the query and if access to the object is allowed. See also **hw_GetAndLock()** and **hw_GetObjectByQuery()**.

hw_GetObjectByQuery

Searches for objects on the whole server and returns an array of object ids. The maximum number of matches is limited to **$max_hits**. If **$max_hits** is set to -1, the maximum number of matches is unlimited. The query will only work with indexed attributes. See also **hw_GetObjectByQueryObj()**.

array **hw_GetObjectByQuery**(*int* connection, *string* query, *int* max_hits)

hw_GetObjectByQueryColl

Searches for objects in collection with ID **$objectID** and returns an array of object ids. The maximum number of matches is limited to **$max_hits**. If **$max_hits** is set to -1, the maximum number of matches is unlimited. The query will only work with indexed attributes. See also **hw_GetObjectByQueryCollObj()**.

array **hw_GetObjectByQueryColl**(*int* connection, *int* objectID, *string* query, *int* max_hits)

hw_GetObjectByQueryCollObj

Searches for objects in collection with ID **$objectID** and returns an array of object records. The maximum number of matches is limited to **$max_hits**. If **$max_hits** is set to -1, the maximum number of matches is unlimited. The query will only work with indexed attributes. See also **hw_GetObjectByQueryColl()**.

array **hw_GetObjectByQueryCollObj**(*int* connection, *int* objectID, *string* query, *int* max_hits)

hw_GetObjectByQueryObj

Searches for objects on the whole server and returns an array of object records. The maximum number of matches is limited to **$max_hits**. If **$max_hits** is set to -1, the maximum number of matches is unlimited. The query will only work with indexed attributes. See also **hw_GetObjectByQuery()**.

array **hw_GetObjectByQueryObj**(*int* connection, *string* query, *int* max_hits)

hw_GetParent

Returns an indexed array of object ids. Each object id belongs to a parent of the object with ID **$objectID**.

array **hw_GetParents**(*int* connection, *int* objectID)

hw_GetParentsObj

Returns an indexed array of object records plus an associated array with statistical information about the object records. The associated array is the last entry of the returned array. Each object record belongs to a parent of the object with ID **$objectID**.

array **hw_GetParentsObj**(*int* connection, *int* objectID)

hw_GetRemote

Returns a remote document. Remote documents in Hyperwave notation are documents retrieved from an external source. Common remote documents are. for example. external Web pages or queries in a database. In order to be able to access external sources through remote documents, Hyperwave introduces the *Hyperwave Gateway Interface* (HGI), which is similar to the CGI. Currently, only ftp, http-servers, and some databases can be accessed by the HGI. Calling **hw_GetRemote()** returns the document from the external source. If you want to use this function, you should be very familiar with HGIs. You should also consider to use PHP instead of Hyperwave to access external sources. Adding database support by a Hyperwave gateway should be more difficult than doing it in PHP. See also **hw_GetRemoteChildren()**.

int **hw_GetRemote**(*int* connection, *int* objectID)

hw_GetRemoteChildren

Returns the children of a remote document. Children of a remote document are a remote document itself. This makes sense if a database query has to be narrowed and is explained in Hyperwave Programmers' Guide. If the number of children is 1, the function will return the document itself formatted by the HGI. If the number of children is greater than 1, it will return an array of object records with each maybe the input value for another call to **hw_GetRemoteChildren()**. Those object records are virtual and do not exist in the Hyperwave server, therefore they do not have a valid object ID. The way in which such an object record looks is up to the HGI. If you want to use this function, you should be very familiar with HGIs. You should also consider to use PHP instead of Hyperwave to access external sources. Adding database support by a Hyperwave gateway should be more difficult than doing it in PHP. See also **hw_GetRemote()**.

> *int* **hw_GetRemoteChildren**(*int* connection, *string* object record)

hw_GetSrcByDestObj

Returns the object records of all anchors pointing to the object with ID **$objectID**. The object can either be a document or an anchor of type destination. See also **hw_GetAnchors()**.

> *array* **hw_GetSrcByDestObj**(*int* connection, *int* objectID)

hw_GetText

Returns the document with object ID objectID. If the document has anchors that can be inserted, they will be inserted already. The optional parameter rootID/prefix can be a string or an integer. If it is an integer, it determines how links are inserted into the document. The default is 0 and will result in links that are constructed from the name of the link's destination object. This is useful for Web applications. If a link points to an object with name 'internet_movie', the HTML link will be <A HREF="/internet_movie">. The actual location of the source and destination object in the document hierarchy is disregarded. You will have to set up your Web browser to rewrite that URL to, for example, '/my_script.php3/internet_movie'. 'my_script.php3' will have to evaluate **$PATH_INFO** and retrieve the document. All links will have the prefix '/my_script.php3/'. If you do not want this, you can set the optional parameter rootID/prefix to any prefix, which is used instead. In this case, it has to be a string.

> *int* **hw_GetText**(*int* connection, *int* objectID, [*mixed* rootID/prefix])

If *rootID/prefix* is an integer and unequal to 0, the link is constructed from all the names starting at the object with the id *rootID/prefix*, separated by a slash relative to the current object. If, for example, the previous document, 'internet_movie', is located at 'a-b-c-internet_movie', with '-' being the separator between hierarchy levels on the Hyperwave server and the source document is located at 'a-b-d-source', the resulting HTML link would be: <A HREF="../c/internet_movie">. This is useful if you want to download the whole server content onto a disk and map the document hierarchy onto the file system. This function will only work for pure text documents. It will not open a special data connection; therefore, it blocks the control connection during the transfer.

See also **hw_PipeDocument()**, **hw_FreeDocument()**, **hw_Document_BodyTag()**, **hw_Document_Size()**, and **hw_Output_Document()**.

hw_getusername

Returns the username of the connection.

> *string* **hw_getusername**(*int* connection)

hw_Identify

Identifies as user with **$username** and **$password**. Identification is only valid for the current session. This function will not be needed very often. In most cases, it will be easier to identify with the opening of the connection. See also **hw_Connect()**.

int **hw_Identify**(*string* username, *string* password)

hw_InCollections

Checks whether a set of objects (documents or collections) specified by the **$object_id_array** is part of the collections listed in **$collection_id_array**. When the fourth parameter **$return_collections** is 0, the subset of object ids that is part of the collections (for example, the documents or collections that are children of one or more collections of collection ids or their subcollections, recursively) is returned as an array. When the fourth parameter is 1, however, the set of collections that have one or more objects of this subset as children are returned as an array. This option enables a client, for example, to highlight the part of the collection hierarchy that contains the matches of a previous query, in a graphical overview.

array **hw_InCollections**(*int* connection, *array* object_id_array, *array* collection_id_array, *int* return_collections)

hw_Info

Returns information about the current connection. The returned string has the following format: <Serverstring>, <Host>, <Port>, <Username>, <Port of Client>, <Byte swapping>.

string **hw_Info**(*int* connection)

hw_InsColl

Inserts a new collection with attributes as in **$object_array** into collection with object ID **$objectID**.

int **hw_InsColl**(*int* connection, *int* objectID, *array* object_array)

hw_InsDoc

Inserts a new document with attributes, as in **$object_record**, into collection with object ID **$parentID**. This function inserts either an object record only or an object record and a pure ascii text in **$text** if **$text** is given. If you want to insert a general document of any kind, use **hw_insertdocument()** instead. See also **hw_InsertDocument()** and **hw_InsColl()**.

int **hw_InsDoc**(*int* connection, *int* parentID, *string* object_record, *string* text)

hw_InsertDocument

Uploads a document into the collection with **$parent_id**. The document has to be created before with **hw_NewDocument()**. Make sure that the object record of the new document contains at least the following attributes: Type, DocumentType, Title, and Name. Possibly you also want to set the MimeType. The function returns the object id of the new document or false. See also **hw_PipeDocument()**.

> *int* **hw_InsertDocument**(*int* connection, *int* parent_id, *int* hw_document)

hw_InsertObject

Inserts an object into the server. The object can be any valid Hyperwave object. See the HG-CSP documentation for a detailed information on how the parameters have to be. **Note:** If you want to insert an anchor, the attribute position has always been set either to a start/end value or to 'invisible'. Invisible positions are needed if the annotation has no corresponding link in the annotation text. See also **hw_PipeDocument()**, **hw_InsertDocument()**, **hw_InsDoc()**, and **hw_InsColl()**.

> *int* **hw_InsertObject**(*int* connection, *string* object rec, *string* parameter)

hw_mapid

Maps a global object id on any Hyperwave server, even those you did not connect to with **hw_connect()**, onto a virtual object id. This virtual object id can then be used as any other object id, for example, to obtain the object record with **hw_getobject()**. The server id is the first part of the *global object id* (GOid) of the object, which is actually the IP number as an integer.

> **Note:** In order to use this function, you will have to set the F_DISTRIBUTED flag, which can currently only be set at compile time in hg_comm.c. It is not set by default. Read the comment at the beginning of **hg_comm.c**.

> *int* **hw_mapid**(*int* connection, *int* server id, *int* object id)

hw_Modifyobject

This command enables one to remove, add, or modify individual attributes of an object record. The object is specified by the Object ID **$object_to_change**. The first array **$remove** is a list of attributes to remove. The second array **$add** is a list of attributes to add. In order to modify an attribute, one will have to remove the old one and add a new one. **hw_modifyobject()** will always remove the attributes before it adds attributes, unless the value of the attribute to remove is not a string or array. The last parameter determines if the modification is performed recursively. 1 means recursive modification. If some of the objects cannot be modified, they will be skipped without notice. **hw_error()** may not indicate an error though some of the objects could not be modified.

> *int* **hw_Modifyobject**(*int* connection, *int* object_to_change, *array* remove, *array* add, *int* mode)

The keys of both arrays are the attributes' name. The value of each array element can either be an array, a string, or anything else. If it is an array, each attribute value is constructed by the key of each element plus a colon and the value of each element. If it is a string, it is taken as the attribute value. An empty string will result in a complete removal of that attribute. If the value is neither a string nor an array, but something else, for example, an integer, no operation at all will be performed on the attribute. This is necessary if you want to add a completely new attribute not just a new value for an existing attribute. If the remove array contained an empty string for that attribute, the attribute would try to be removed, which would fail because it doesn't exist. The following addition of a new value for that attribute would also fail. Setting the value for that attribute to 0, for example, would not even attempt to remove it, and the addition will work. If you would like to change the attribute 'Name' with the current value 'books' into 'articles', you will have to create two arrays and call **hw_modifyobject()**.

Example: modifying an attribute

```
// $connect is an existing connection to the Hyperwave server
// $objid is the ID of the object to modify
$remarr = array("Name" => "books");
$addarr = array("Name" => "articles");
$hw_modifyobject($connect, $objid, $remarr, $addarr);
```

In order to delete/add a name=value pair from/to, the object record just passes the remove/add array and sets the last/third parameter to an empty array. If the attribute is the first one with that name to add, set attribute value in the remove array to an integer.

Example: adding a completely new attribute

```
// $connect is an existing connection to the Hyperwave server
// $objid is the ID of the object to modify
$remarr = array("Name" => 0);
$addarr = array("Name" => "articles");
$hw_modifyobject($connect, $objid, $remarr, $addarr);
```

Note: Multilingual attributes, such as 'Title', can be modified in two ways; one can either provide the attribute's value in its native form 'language':'title' or provide an array with elements for each language as previously described. The previous example would then be as follows:

Example: modifying Title attribute

```
$remarr = array("Title" => "en:Books");
$addarr = array("Title" => "en:Articles");
$hw_modifyobject($connect, $objid, $remarr, $addarr);
```

or

Example: modifying Title attribute

```
$remarr = array("Title" => array("en" => "Books"));
$addarr = array("Title" => array("en" => "Articles", "ge"=>"Artikel"));
$hw_modifyobject($connect, $objid, $remarr, $addarr);
```

This removes the English title, 'Books', and adds the English title, 'Articles', and the German title, 'Artikel'.

Example: removing attribute

```
$remarr = array("Title" => "");
$addarr = array("Title" => "en:Articles");
$hw_modifyobject($connect, $objid, $remarr, $addarr);
```

Note: This will remove all attributes with the name 'Title' and adds a new 'Title' attribute. This comes in handy if you want to remove attributes recursively. If you need to delete all attributes with a certain name, you will have to pass an empty string as the attribute value. Only the attributes Title, Description, and Keyword will properly handle the language prefix. If those attributes do not carry a language prefix, the prefix 'xx' will be assigned. The Name attribute is somewhat special; in some cases, it cannot be complete removed. You will get an error message 'Change of base attribute' (not clear when this happens). Therefore, you will always have to add a new Name first and then remove the old one.

Note: You may not surround this function by calls to **hw_getandlock()** and **hw_unlock()**. **hw_modifyobject()** does this internally. Returns true if no error occurs, otherwise false.

hw_Mv

Moves the objects with object ids, as specified in the second parameter, from the collection with id **$source** id to the collection with the id **$destination** id. If the destination id is 0, the objects will be unlinked from the source collection. If this is the last instance of that object, it will be deleted. If you want to delete all instances at once, use **hw_deleteobject()**. The value return is the number of moved objects. See also **hw_cp()** and **hw_deleteobject()**.

int **hw_Mv**(*int* connection, *array* object id array, *int* source id, *int* destination id)

hw_New_Document

Returns a new Hyperwave document with document data set to **$document_data** and object record set to **$object_record**. The length of the **$document_data** has to passed in **$document_size**. This function does not insert the document into the Hyperwave server. See also **hw_FreeDocument()**, **hw_Document_Size()**, **hw_Document_BodyTag()**, **hw_Output_Document()**, and **hw_InsertDocument()**.

int **hw_New_Document**(*string* object_record, *string* document_data, *int* document_size)

hw_Objrec2Array

Converts an **$object_record** into an object array. The keys of the resulting array are the attributes' names. Multi-value attributes like 'Title' in different languages form its own array. The keys of this array are the left part to the colon of the attribute value. This left part must be two characters long. Other multi-value attributes without a prefix form an indexed array. If the optional parameter is missing, the attributes Title, Description, and Keyword' are treated as language attributes, and the attributes Group, Parent, and HtmlAttr are treated as non-prefixed multi-value attributes. By passing an array by holding the type for each attribute, you can alter this behavior. The array is an associated array with the attribute name as its key and the value being one of HW_ATTR_LANG or HW_ATTR_NONE. See also **hw_array2objrec()**.

array **hw_Objrec2Array**(*string* object_record, [*array* format])

hw_Output_Document

Prints the document without the BODY tag. For backward compatibility, **hw_Output Document()** is also accepted. This is deprecated, however.

int **hw_Output_Document**(*int* hw_document)

hw_pConnect

Returns a connection index on success, or false if the connection could not be made. Opens a persistent connection to a Hyperwave server. Each of the arguments should be a quoted string, except for the port number. The **$username** and **$password** arguments are optional. In such a case, no identification with the server will be done. It is similar to identify as user anonymous. This function returns a connection index that is needed by other Hyperwave functions. You can have multiple persistent connections open at once. See also **hw_Connect()**.

int **hw_pConnect**(*string* host, *int* port, *string* username, *string* password)

hw_PipeDocument

Returns the Hyperwave document with object ID **$objectID**. If the document has anchors that can be inserted, they will have been inserted already. The document will be transferred via a special data connection that does not block the control connection. See also **hw_GetText()**. For more on link insertion, see **hw_FreeDocument()**, **hw_Document_Size()**, **hw_Document_BodyTag()**, and **hw_Output_Document()**.

int **hw_PipeDocument**(*int* connection, *int* objectID)

hw_Root

Returns the object ID of the hyperroot collection; currently, this is always 0. The child collection of the hyperroot is the root collection of the connected server.

int **hw_Root**( )

hw_Unlock

Unlocks a document, so other users regain access. See also **hw_GetAndLock()**.

int **hw_Unlock**(*int* connection, *int* objectID)

hw_Who

Returns an array of users currently logged into the Hyperwave server. Each entry in this array is an array itself containing the elements id, name, system, onSinceDate, onSinceTime, TotalTime, and self. 'self' is 1, if this entry belongs to the user who initiated the request.

int **hw_Who**(*int* connection)

ibase_close

Closes the link to an InterBase database that is associated with a connection id returned from **ibase_connect()**. If the connection id is omitted, the last opened link is assumed. Default transaction on link is committed, other transactions are rolled back.

int **ibase_close**([*int* connection_id])

ibase_connect

Establishes a connection to an InterBase server. The $database argument has to be a valid path to database file on the server on which it resides. If the server is not local, it must be prefixed with either 'hostname:' (TCP/IP), '//hostname/' (NetBEUI), or 'hostname@' (IPX/SPX), depending on the connection protocol used. **$username** and **$password** can also be specified with PHP configuration directives ibase.default_user and ibase.default_password. **$charset** is the default character set for a database. **$buffers** is the number of database buffers to allocate for the server-side cache. If 0 or omitted, server chooses its own default. **$dialect** selects the default SQL dialect for any statement executed within a connection, and it defaults to the highest one supported by client libraries. In case a second call is made to **ibase_connect()** with the same arguments, no new link will be established. Instead, the link identifier of the already opened link will be returned. The link to the server will be closed as soon as the execution of the script ends, unless it's closed earlier by explicitly calling **ibase_close()**.

int **ibase_connect**(*string* database, [*string* username], [*string* password], [*string* charset], [*int* buffers], [*int* dialect], [*string* role])

Example: Ibase_connect()

```php
<?php
    $dbh = ibase_connect ($host, $username, $password);
    $stmt = 'SELECT * FROM tblname';
    $sth = ibase_query ($dbh, $stmt);
    while ($row = ibase_fetch_object ($sth)) {
        print $row->email . "\n";
    }
    ibase_close ($dbh);
?>
```

Note: $buffers was added in PHP4-RC2, and **$dialect** was added in PHP4-RC2. It is functional only with InterBase 6 and versions higher than that. **$role** was added in PHP4-RC2. It is functional only with InterBase 5 and versions higher than that.

See also **ibase_pconnect()**.

ibase_execute

Executes a query prepared by **ibase_prepare()**. This is much more effective than using **ibase_query()** if you are repeating the same kind of query several times with only some parameters changing.

int **ibase_execute**(*int* query, [*int* bind_args])

```php
<?php
    $updates = array(
        1 => 'Eric',
        5 => 'Filip',
        7 => 'Larry'
    );
    $query = ibase_prepare("UPDATE FOO SET BAR = ? WHERE BAZ = ?");
    while (list($baz, $bar) = each($updates)) {
        ibase_execute($query, $bar, $baz);
    }
?>
```

ibase_fetch_object

Fetches a row as a pseudo-object from a **$result_id** obtained either by **ibase_query()** or **ibase_execute()**.

object **ibase_fetch_object**(*int* result_id)

```php
<php
    $dbh = ibase_connect ($host, $username, $password);
    $stmt = 'SELECT * FROM tblname';
    $sth = ibase_query ($dbh, $stmt);
    while ($row = ibase_fetch_object ($sth)) {
        print $row->email . "\n";
    }
    ibase_close ($dbh);
?>
```

See also **ibase_fetch_row()**.

ibase_fetch_row

Returns the next row specified by the result identifier, which is obtained using the **ibase_query()**.

array **ibase_fetch_row**(*int* result_identifier)

ibase_free_query

Frees a query prepared by **ibase_prepare().**

int **ibase_free_query**(*int* query)

ibase_free_result

Frees a result set the has been created by ibase_query().

int **ibase_free_result**(*int* result_identifier)

ibase_num_fields

Returns an integer containing the number of fields in a result set. See also **ibase_field_info()**. **Note: Ibase_num_fields()** is currently not functional in PHP 4.

int **ibase_num_fields**(*int* result_id)

```php
<?php
    $dbh = ibase_connect ($host, $username, $password);
    $stmt = 'SELECT * FROM tblname';
    $sth = ibase_query ($dbh, $stmt);
    if (ibase_num_fields($sth) > 0) {
        while ($row = ibase_fetch_object ($sth)) {
            print $row->email . "\n";
        }
    } else {
        die ("No Results were found for your query");
    }

    ibase_close ($dbh);
?>
```

ibase_pconnect

Acts very much like ibase_connect() with two major differences. First, when connecting, the function will first try to find a (persistent) link that's already opened with the same parameters. If one is found, an identifier for it will be returned instead of opening a new connection. Second, the connection to the InterBase server will not be closed when the execution of the script ends. Instead, the link will remain open for future use (**ibase_close()** will not close links established by **ibase_pconnect()**). This type of link is therefore called 'persistent'. See also **ibase_connect()** for the meaning of parameters passed to this function; they are exactly the same.

int **ibase_pconnect**(*string* database, [*string* username], [*string* password], [*string* charset], [*string* role])

ibase_prepare

Prepares a query for later binding of parameter placeholders and execution via **ibase_execute()**.

int **ibase_prepare**([*int* link_identifier], *string* query)

ibase_query

Performs a query on an InterBase database, returning a result identifier for use with **ibase_fetch_row()**, **ibase_fetch_object()**, **ibase_free_result()**, and **ibase_free_query()**. Although this function supports variable binding to parameter placeholders, using this capability with it does not have very much meaning. For real life use and an example, see **ibase_prepare()** and **ibase_execute()**.

int **ibase_query**([*int* link_identifier], *string* query, [*int* bind_args])

ibase_timefmt

Sets the format of timestamp, date, or time type columns returned from queries. Internally, the columns are formatted by c-function **strftime()**, so refer to its documentation regarding to the format of the string. **$columntype** is one of the constants IBASE_TIMESTAMP, IBASE_DATE, and IBASE_TIME. If omitted, it defaults to IBASE_TIMESTAMP for backwards compatibility.

int **ibase_timefmt**(*string* format, [*int* columntype])

```php
<?php
    // InterBase 6 TIME-type columns will be returned in
    // the form '05 hours 37 minutes'.
    ibase_timefmt("%H hours %M minutes", IBASE_TIME);
?>
```

You can also set defaults for these formats with PHP configuration directives ibase.timestampformat, ibase.dateformat, and ibase.timeformat. **$columntype** was added in PHP 4.0. It only has meaning with InterBase version 6 and higher.

Note: A backwards incompatible change happened in PHP 4.0 when PHP configuration directive ibase.timeformat was renamed to ibase.timestampformat, and directives ibase.dateformat and ibase.timeformat were added so that the names would match their functionality better.

icap_close

Closes the given icap stream.

int **icap_close**(*int* icap_stream, [*int* flags])

icap_delete_event

Deletes the calendar event specified by the **$uid**. Returns true.

string **icap_delete_event**(*int* stream_id, *int* uid)

icap_fetch_event

Fetches an event from the calendar stream specified by **$event_id**.

int **icap_fetch_event**(*int* stream_id, *int* event_id, [*int* options])

Returns an event object consisting of the following:

- int id—ID of that event.
- int public—True if the event is public, false if it is private.
- string category—Category string of the event.
- string title—Title string of the event.
- string description—Description string of the event.
- int alarm—Number of minutes before the event to send an alarm/reminder.

- object start—Object containing a datetime entry.
- object end—Object containing a datetime entry.

  All datetime entries consist of an object that contains the following:

- int year—year
- int month—month
- int mday—day of month
- int hour—hour
- int min—minutes
- int sec—seconds

icap_list_alarms

Returns an array of event IDs that has an alarm going off at the given datetime. **Icap_list_alarms()** function takes in a datetime for a calendar stream. An array of event ids that has an alarm should be going off at the datetime are returned.

> *int* **icap_list_alarms**(*int* stream_id, *array* date, *array* time)

All datetime entries consist of an object that contains the following:

- int year—year
- int month—month
- int mday—day of month
- int hour—hour
- int min—minutes
- int sec—seconds

icap_list_events

Returns an array of event IDs between the two given datetimes. **Icap_list_events()** function takes in a beginning datetime and an end datetime for a calendar stream. An array of event ids between the given datetimes are returned.

> *array* **icap_list_events**(*int* stream_id, *int* begin_date, [*int* end_date])

All datetime entries consist of an object that contains the following:

- int year—year
- int month—month
- int mday—day of month
- int hour—hour

- int min—minutes
- int sec—seconds

icap_open

Returns an ICAP stream on success, false on error. **icap_open()** opens up an ICAP connection to the specified **$calendar** store. If the optional $options is specified, the **$options** is passed to that mailbox also.

stream **icap_open**(*string* calendar, *string* username, *string* password, *string* options)

icap_snooze

Turns on an alarm for a calendar event specified by the **$uid**. Returns true.

string **icap_snooze**(*int* stream_id, *int* uid)

icap_store_event

Stores an event into an ICAP calendar.

string **icap_store_event**(*int* stream_id, *object* event)

An event object consists of the following:

- int public—1 if public, 0 if private.
- string category —Category string of the event.
- string title—Title string of the event.
- string description—Description string of the event.
- int alarm—Number of minutes before the event to send out an alarm.
- datetime start—Datetime object of the start of the event.
- datetime end —Datetime object of the end of the event.

All datetime entries consist of an object that contains the following:

- int year—year
- int month—month
- int mday—day of month
- int hour—hour
- int min—minutes
- int sec —seconds

Returns true on success and false on error.

ifxus_close_slob

Deletes the slob object on the given slob object-id **$bid**. Returns false on error, otherwise true.

  int ifxus_close_slob(*int* bid)

ifxus_create_slob

Creates an slob object and opens it. Modes: 1 = LO_RDONLY, 2 = LO_WRONLY, 4 = LO_APPEND, 8 = LO_RDWR, 16 = LO_BUFFER, 32 = LO_NOBUFFER -> or-mask. You can also use constants named IFX_LO_RDONLY, IFX_LO_WRONLY, and so on. Returns false on error, otherwise the new slob object-id.

  int ifxus_create_slob(*int* mode)

ifxus_free_slob

Deletes the slob object. **$bid** is the id of the slob object. Returns false on error, otherwise true.

  int **ifxus_free_slob**(*int* bid)

ifxus_open_slob

Opens an slob object. **$bid** should be an existing slob id. Modes: 1 = LO_RDONLY, 2 = LO_WRONLY, 4 = LO_APPEND, 8 = LO_RDWR, 16 = LO_BUFFER, 32 = LO_NOBUFFER -> or-mask. Returns false on error, otherwise the new slob object-id.

  int **ifxus_open_slob**(*long* bid, *int* mode)

ifxus_read_slob

Reads nbytes of the slob object. **$bid** is a existing slob id, and $nbytes is the number of bytes to read. Return false on error, otherwise returns the string.

  int **ifxus_read_slob**(*long* bid, *long* nbytes)

ifxus_seek_slob

Sets the current file or seeks position of an open slob object. **$bid** should be an existing slob id. Modes: 0 = LO_SEEK_SET, 1 = LO_SEEK_CUR, 2 = LO_SEEK_END and **$offset** is an byte offset. Return false on error, otherwise the seek position.

  int **ifxus_seek_slob**(*long* bid, *int* mode, *long* offset)

ifxus_tell_slob

Returns the current file or seek position of an open slob object **$bid** should be an existing slob id. Return false on error, otherwise the seek position.

  int **ifxus_tell_slob**(*long* bid)

ifxus_write_slob

Writes a string into the slob object. **$bid** is a existing slob id and **$content** the content to write. Return false on error, otherwise bytes written.

   int **ifxus_write_slob**(*long* bid, *string* content)

ifx_affected_rows

$result_id is a valid result id returned by **ifx_query()** or **ifx_prepare()**. Returns the number of rows affected by a query associated with **$result_id**. For inserts, updates and deletes the number is the real number (sqlerrd[2]) of affected rows. For selects, it is an estimate (sqlerrd[0]); don't rely on it. The database server can never return the actual number of rows that will be returned by a SELECT because it has not even begun fetching them at this stage (just after the "PRE-PARE" when the optimizer has determined the query plan). It is useful to limit queries to reasonable result sets after **ifx_prepare()**. See also **ifx_num_rows()**.

   int **ifx_affected_rows**(*int* result_id)

Example: Informix affected rows

```
$rid = ifx_prepare ("select * from emp
                     where name like " . $name, $connid);
if (! $rid) {
    ... error ...
}
$rowcount = ifx_affected_rows ($rid);
if ($rowcount > 1000) {
    printf ("Too many rows in result set (%d)\n<br>", $rowcount);
    die ("Please restrict your query<br>\n");
}
```

ifx_blobinfile_mode

Sets the default blob mode for all select queries. Mode "0" means save Byte-Blobs in memory, and mode "1" means save Byte-Blobs in a file.

   void ifx_blobinfile_mode(*int* mode)

ifx_byteasvarchar

Sets the default byte mode for all select-queries. Mode "0" will return a blob id, and mode "1" will return a varchar with text content.

   void **ifx_byteasvarchar**(*int* mode)

ifx_close

Returns always true. **ifx_close()** closes the link to an Informix database associated with the specified link identifier. If the link identifier isn't specified, the last opened link is assumed.

   Note: This isn't usually necessary because non-persistent open links are automatically closed at the end of the script's execution. **ifx_close()** will not close persistent links generated by ifx_pconnect(). See also **ifx_connect()** and **ifx_pconnect()**.

int **ifx_close**([*int* link_identifier])

Example: Closing an Informix connection

```
$conn_id = ifx_connect ("mydb@ol_srv", "itsme", "mypassword");
... some queries and stuff ...
ifx_close($conn_id);
```

ifx_connect

Returns a connection identifier on success, or false on error. **ifx_connect()** establishes a connection to an Informix server. All of the arguments are optional, and if they're missing, defaults are taken from values supplied in configuration **file()**, ifx.default_host for the host (Informix libraries will use INFORMIXSERVER environment value if not defined), ifx.default_user for user, ifx.default_password for the password (none if not defined). In case a second call is made to **ifx_connect()** with the same arguments, no new link will be established. Instead, the link identifier of the already opened link will be returned. The link to the server will be closed as soon as the execution of the script ends, unless it's closed earlier by explicitly calling **ifx_close()**. See also **ifx_pconnect()** and **ifx_close()**.

int **ifx_connect**([*string* database], [*string* userid], [*string* password])

Example: Connect to a Informix database

```
$conn_id = ifx_connect ("mydb@ol_srv1", "imyself", "mypassword");
```

ifx_copy_blob

Duplicates the given blob object. **$bid** is the ID of the blob object. Returns false on error, otherwise the new blob object-id.

int **ifx_copy_blob**(*int* bid)

ifx_create_blob

Creates a blob object. Return false on error, otherwise the new blob object-id.

int **ifx_create_blob**(*int* type, *int* mode, *string* param)

- type: 1 = TEXT, 0 = BYTE
- mode: 0 = blob-object holds the content in memory, 1 = blob-object holds the content in file.
- param: if mode = 0: pointer to the content, if mode = 1: pointer to the filestring.

ifx_create_char

Creates an char object. **$param** should be the char content.

> *int* **ifx_create_char**(*string* param)

ifx_do

Returns true on success, false on error. Executes a previously prepared query or opens a cursor for it. Does not free **$result_id** on error. Also sets the real number of **ifx_affected_rows()** for non-select statements for retrieval by **ifx_affected_rows()** See also **ifx_prepare()**. Here is an example:

> *int* **ifx_do**(*int* result_id)

ifx_error

The Informix error codes (SQLSTATE & SQLCODE) formatted as follows:

> x [SQLSTATE = aa bbb SQLCODE=cccc]
>
> where x = space : no error
>
> E : error
>
> N : no more data
>
> W : warning
>
> ? : undefined

> *string* **ifx_error**(*void*)

If the "x" character is anything other than space, SQLSTATE and SQLCODE describe the error in more detail. See the Informix manual for the description of SQLSTATE and SQLCODE. Returns in a string one character describing the general results of a statement and both SQLSTATE and SQLCODE associated with the most recent SQL statement executed. The format of the string is "(char) [SQLSTATE=(two digits) (three digits) SQLCODE=(one digit)]". The first character can be ' ' (space) (success), 'W' (the statement caused some warning), 'E' (an error happened when executing the statement) or 'N' (the statement didn't return any data). See also **ifx_errormsg()**.

ifx_errormsg

Returns the Informix error message associated with the most recent Informix error, or when the optional "**$errorcode**" param is present, the error message corresponding to "**$errorcode**". See also **ifx_error()**.

> string **ifx_errormsg**([int errorcode])

```
printf("%s\n<br>", ifx_errormsg(-201));
```

ifx_fetch_row

Returns an associative array that corresponds to the fetched row, or false if no more rows exist. Blob columns are returned as integer blob id values for use in **ifx_get_blob**() unless you have used ifx_textasvarchar(1) or ifx_byteasvarchar(1), in which case blobs are returned as string values. Returns false on error. $result_id is a valid resultid returned by **ifx_query**() or **ifx_prepare**() (select type queries only). $position is an optional parameter for a "fetch" operation on scroll cursors: "NEXT," "PREVIOUS," "CURRENT," "FIRST," "LAST," or a number. If you specify a number, an absolute row fetch is executed. This parameter is optional, and only valid for scroll cursors.

array **ifx_fetch_row**(int result_id, [mixed position])

ifx_fetch_row() fetches one row of data from the result associated with the specified result identifier. The row is returned as an array. Each result column is stored in an array offset, starting at offset 0, with the column name as key. Subsequent calls to **ifx_fetch_row**() would return the next row in the result set, or false if no more rows exist.

Example: Informix fetch rows

```
$rid = ifx_prepare ("select * from emp where name like " . $name,
                    $connid, IFX_SCROLL);
if (! $rid) {
    ... error ...
}
$rowcount = ifx_affected_rows ($rid);
if ($rowcount > 1000) {
    printf ("Too many rows in result set (%d)\n<br>", $rowcount);
    die ("Please restrict your query<br>\n");
}
if (! ifx_do ($rid)) {
    ... error ...
}
$row = ifx_fetch_row ($rid, "NEXT");
while (is_array($row)) {
    for(reset($row); $fieldname=key($row); next($row)) {
        $fieldvalue = $row[$fieldname];
        printf ("%s = %s,", $fieldname, $fieldvalue);
    }
    printf("\n<br>");
    $row = ifx_fetch_row ($rid, "NEXT");
}
ifx_free_result ($rid);
```

ifx_fieldproperties

Returns an associative array with fieldnames as key and the SQL fieldproperties as data for a query with **$result_id**. Returns false on error. Returns the Informix SQL fieldproperies of every field in the query as an associative array. Properties are encoded as: "SQLTYPE;length; precision;scale;ISNULLABLE" where SQLTYPE = the Informix type like "SQLVCHAR" and ISNULLABLE = "Y" or "N".

array **ifx_fieldproperties**(int result_id)

Example: Informix SQL fieldproperties

```
$properties = ifx_fieldproperties ($resultid);
if (! isset($properties)) {
  ... error ...
}
for ($i = 0; $i < count($properties); $i++) {
    $fname = key ($properties);
    printf ("%s:\t type = %s\n", $fname, $properties[$fname]);
    next ($properties);
}
```

ifx_fieldtypes

Returns an associative array with fieldnames as key, and the SQL fieldtypes as data, for query with **$result_id**. Returns false on error.

array **ifx_fieldtypes**(int result_id)

Example: Fieldnames and SQL fieldtypes

```
$types = ifx_fieldtypes ($resultid);
if (! isset ($types)) {
  ... error ...
}
for ($i = 0; $i < count($types); $i++) {
    $fname = key($types);
    printf("%s :\t type = %s\n", $fname, $types[$fname]);
    next($types);
}
```

ifx_free_blob

Deletes the blobobject for the given blob object-id **$bid**. Returns false on error, otherwise true.

int **ifx_free_blob**(int bid)

ifx_free_char

Deletes the charobject for the given char object-id **$bid**. Returns false on error, otherwise true.

int **ifx_free_char**(int bid)

ifx_free_result

Releases resources for the query associated with **$result_id**. Returns false on error.

int **ifx_free_result**(int result_id)

ifx_getsqlca

Returns a pseudo-row (associative array) with sqlca.sqlerrd[0] ... sqlca.sqlerrd[5] after the query associated with **$result_id**. **$result_id** is a valid result id returned by **ifx_query()** or **ifx_prepare()**.

    array **ifx_getsqlca**(int result_id)

For inserts, updates, and deletes, the values returned are those as set by the server after executing the query. This gives access to the number of affected rows and the serial insert value. For SELECTs, the values are those saved after the PREPARE statement. This gives access to the *estimated* number of affected rows. The use of this function saves the overhead of executing a "select dbinfo('sqlca.sqlerrdx')" query, as it retrieves the values that were saved by the ifx driver at the appropriate moment.

Example: Retrieve Informix sqlca.sqlerrd[x] values

```
/* assume the first column of 'sometable' is a serial */
$qid = ifx_query("insert into sometable
                values (0, '2nd column', 'another column') ", $connid);
if (! $qid) {
    ... error ...
}
$sqlca = ifx_getsqlca ($qid);
$serial_value = $sqlca["sqlerrd1"];
echo "The serial value of the inserted row is : " . $serial_value<br>\n";
```

ifx_get_blob

Returns the content of the blob object for the given blob object-id **$bid**.

    int **ifx_get_blob**(*int* bid)

ifx_get_char

Returns the content of the char object for the given char object-id **$bid**.

    int **ifx_get_char**(*int* bid)

ifx_htmltbl_result

Returns the number of rows fetched or false on error. Formats all rows of the result_id query into a html table. The optional second argument is a string of <table> tag options.

    int **ifx_htmltbl_result**(*int* result_id, [*string* html_table_options])

ifx_nullformat

Sets the default return value of a NULL-value on a fetch row. Mode "0" returns "", and mode "1" returns "NULL".

    void **ifx_nullformat**(*int* mode)

ifx_num_fields

Returns the number of columns in query for $result_id or false on error. After preparing or executing a query, this call gives you the number of columns in the query.

int **ifx_num_fields**(*int* result_id)

ifx_num_rows

Gives the number of rows fetched so far for a query with **$result_id** after a **ifx_query()** or **ifx_do()** query.

int **ifx_num_rows**(*int* result_id)

ifx_pconnect

Returns a positive Informix persistent link identifier on success, or false on error. i**fx_pconnect()** acts very much like **ifx_connect()** with two major differences. This function behaves exactly like **ifx_connect()** when PHP is not running as an Apache module. First, when connecting, the function would first try to find a (persistent) link that's already open with the same host, username, and password. If one is found, an identifier for it will be returned instead of opening a new connection. Secondly, the connection to the SQL server will not be closed when the execution of the script ends. Instead, the link will remain open for future use (**ifx_close()** will not close links established by **ifx_pconnect()**). This type of links is therefore called 'persistent.' See also **ifx_connect()**.

int **ifx_pconnect**([*string* database], [*string* userid], [*string* password])

ifx_prepare

Returns a integer **$result_id** for use by **ifx_do()**. Sets **$affected_rows** for retrieval by the ifx_affected_rows() function. Prepares **$query** on connection **$conn_id**. For "select-type" queries, a cursor is declared and opened. The optional **$cursor_type** parameter enables you to make this a scroll and/or hold cursor. It's a bit mask and can be either IFX_SCROLL, IFX_HOLD, or both together. For either query type, the estimated number of affected rows is saved for retrieval by **ifx_affected_rows()**. If you have BLOB (BYTE or TEXT) columns in the query, you can add a **$blobidarray** parameter containing the corresponding blob ids, and you should replace those columns with a "?" in the query text.

int **ifx_prepare**(*string* query, *int* conn_id, [*int* cursor_def], *mixed* blobidarray)

If the contents of the TEXT (or BYTE) column allow it, you can also use "ifx_textasvarchar(1)" and "ifx_byteasvarchar(1)". This enables you to treat TEXT (or BYTE) columns just as if they were ordinary (but long) VARCHAR columns for select queries, and you don't need to bother with blob ids. With ifx_textasvarchar(0) or ifx_byteasvarchar(0) (the default situation), select queries will return BLOB columns as blob ids (integer value). You can get the value of the blob as a string or file with the blob functions. See also **ifx_do()**.

ifx_query

Returns a positive Informix result identifier on success, or false on error. A result_id resource used by other functions to retrieve the query results. Sets affected_rows for retrieval by the **ifx_affected_rows()** function. **ifx_query()** sends a query to the currently active database on the server that is associated with the specified link identifier. If the link identifier isn't specified, the last opened link is assumed. If no link is open, the function tries to establish a link as if **ifx_connect()** was called, and then uses it. Executes **$query** on connection **$conn_id** . For select-type queries a cursor is declared and opened. The optional **$cursor_type** parameter enables you to make this a scroll and/or hold cursor. It's a bit mask and can be either IFX_SCROLL, IFX_HOLD, or both together. Non-select queries are "execute immediate." IFX_SCROLL and IFX_HOLD are symbolic constants, and as such, should not be between quotes. If you omit this parameter, the cursor is a normal sequential cursor. For either query type, the number of (estimated or real) affected rows is saved for retrieval by **ifx_affected_rows()**.

int **ifx_query**(*string* query, [*int* link_identifier], [*int* cursor_type], [*mixed* blobidarray])

If you have BLOB (BYTE or TEXT) column in an update query, you can add a **$blobidarray** parameter containing the corresponding blob ids, and you should replace those columns with a "?" in the query text. If the contents of the TEXT (or BYTE) column allow it, you can also use "ifx_textasvarchar(1)" and "ifx_byteasvarchar(1)". This enables you to treat TEXT (or BYTE) columns just as if they were ordinary (but long) VARCHAR columns for select queries, and you don't need to bother with blob ids. With ifx_textasvarchar(0) or ifx_byteasvarchar(0) (the default situation), select queries will return BLOB columns as blob ids (integer value). You can get the value of the blob as a string or file with the blob functions. See also **ifx_connect()**.

Example: Show all rows of the orders table as a html table.

```
ifx_textasvarchar(1);        // use "text mode" for blobs
$res_id = ifx_query("select * from orders", $conn_id);
if (! $res_id) {
    printf("Can't select orders : %s\n<br>%s<br>\n", ifx_error());
    ifx_errormsg();
    die;
}
ifx_htmltbl_result($res_id, "border=\"1\"");
ifx_free_result($res_id);
```

Example: Insert some values into the catalog table

```
                        // create blob id's for a byte and text column
$textid = ifx_create_blob(0, 0, "Text column in memory");
$byteid = ifx_create_blob(1, 0, "Byte column in memory");
                        // store blob id's in a blobid array
$blobidarray[] = $textid;
$blobidarray[] = $byteid;
                        // launch query
$query = "insert into catalog (stock_num, manu_code, " .
        "cat_descr,cat_picture) values(1,'HRO',?,?)";
$res_id = ifx_query($query, $conn_id, $blobidarray);
if (! $res_id) {
```

```
    ... error ...
}
                        // free result id
ifx_free_result($res_id);
```

ifx_textasvarchar

Sets the default text mode for all select-queries. Mode "0" will return a blob id, and mode "1" will return a varchar with text content.

> *void* **ifx_textasvarchar**(*int* mode)

ifx_update_blob

Updates the content of the blob object for the given blob object **$bid**. **$content** is a string with new data. Returns false on error, otherwise true.

> **ifx_update_blob**(*int* bid, *string* content)

ifx_update_char

Updates the content of the char object for the given char object **$bid**. **$content** is a string with new data. Returns false on error, otherwise true.

> *int* **ifx_update_char**(*int* bid, *string* content)

ignore_user_abort

This function sets whether a client disconnect should cause a script to be aborted. It will return the previous setting and can be called without an argument to not change the current setting and only return the current setting. See the Connection **Handling()** section in the **Features()** chapter for a complete description of connection handling in PHP.

> *int* **ignore_user_abort**([*int* setting])

ImageArc

Draws a partial ellipse centered at **$cx** , **$cy** (top left is 0, 0) in the image represented by im. **$W** and **$h** specifies the ellipse's width and height, respectively, and the start and end points are specified in degrees indicated by the **$s** and **$e** arguments.

> *int* **ImageArc**(*int* im, *int* cx, *int* cy, *int* w, *int* h, *int* s, *int* e, *int* col)

ImageChar

Draws the first character of **$c** in the image identified by **$id** with its upper-left at **$x** , **$y** (top left is 0, 0) with the color **$col**. If font is 1, 2, 3, 4, or 5, a built-in font is used (with higher numbers corresponding to larger fonts). See also **imageloadfont()**.

> *int* **ImageChar**(*int* im, *int* font, *int* x, *int* y, *string* c, *int* col)

ImageCharUp

Draws the character **$c** vertically in the image identified by **$im** at coordinates **$x , $y** (top left is 0, 0) with the color **$col** . If font is 1, 2, 3, 4, or 5, a built-in font is used. See also **imageload-font()**.

int **ImageCharUp**(*int* im, *int* font, *int* x, *int* y, *string* c, *int* col)

ImageColorAllocate

Returns a color identifier representing the color composed of the given RGB components. The **$im** argument is the return from the **imagecreate()** function. **ImageColorAllocate()** must be called to create each color that is to be used in the image represented by **$im**.

int **ImageColorAllocate**(*int* im, *int* red, *int* green, *int* blue)

```
$white = ImageColorAllocate ($im, 255, 255, 255);
$black = ImageColorAllocate ($im, 0, 0, 0);
```

ImageColorAt

Returns the index of the color of the pixel at the specified location in the image. See also **image-colorset()** and **imagecolorsforindex()**.

int **ImageColorAt**(*int* im, *int* x, *int* y)

ImageColorClose

Returns the index of the color in the palette of the image that is closest to the specified RGB value. The distance between the desired color and each color in the palette is calculated as if the RGB values represented points in three-dimensional space. See also **imagecolorexact()**.

int **ImageColorClosest**(*int* im, *int* red, *int* green, *int* blue)

ImageColorDeAllocate

De-allocates a color previously allocated with the **ImageColorAllocate()** function.

int **ImageColorDeAllocate**(*int* im, *int* index)

```
$white = ImageColorAllocate($im, 255, 255, 255);
ImageColorDeAllocate($im, $white);
```

ImageColorExact

Returns the index of the specified color in the palette of the image. If the color does not exist in the image's palette, -1 is returned. See also **imagecolorclosest()**.

int **ImageColorExact**(*int* im, *int* red, *int* green, *int* blue)

ImageColorResolve

This function is guaranteed to return a color index for a requested color, either the exact color or the closest possible alternative. See also **imagecolorclosest()**.

> *int* **ImageColorResolve**(*int* im, *int* red, *int* green, *int* blue)

ImageColorSet

Sets the specified index in the palette to the specified color. This is useful for creating flood-fill-like effects in paletted images without the overhead of performing the actual flood-fill. See also **imagecolorat()**.

> *bool* **ImageColorSet**(*int* im, *int* index, *int* red, *int* green, *int* blue)

ImageColorsForIndex

Returns an associative array with red, green, and blue keys that contain the appropriate values for the specified color index. See also **imagecolorat()** and **imagecolorexact()**.

> *array* **ImageColorsForIndex**(*int* im, *int* index)

ImageColorsTotal

Returns the number of colors in the specified image's palette. See also **imagecolorat()** and **imagecolorsforindex()**.

> *int* ImageColorsTotal(*int* im)

ImageColorTransparent

Sets the transparent color in the **$im** image to **$col**. **$Im** is the image identifier returned by **ImageCreate()** and **$col** is a color identifier returned by ImageColorAllocate(). The identifier of the new (or current, if none is specified) transparent color is returned.

> *int* **ImageColorTransparent**(*int* im, [*int* col])

ImageCopy

Copies a part of **$src_im** onto **$dst_im** starting at the x,y coordinates **$src_x, $src_y** with a width of **$src_w** and a height of **$src_h**. The portion defined will be copied onto the x,y coordinates, **$dst_x** and **$dst_y**.

> *int* **ImageCopy**(*int* dst_im, *int* src_im, *int* dst_x, *int* dst_y, *int* src_x, *int* src_y, *int* src_w, *int* src_h)

ImageCopyResized

Copies a rectangular portion of one image to another image. **$Dst_im** is the destination image, **$src_im** is the source image identifier. If the source and destination coordinates and width and heights differ, appropriate stretching or shrinking of the image fragment will be performed. The coordinates refer to the upper left corner. This function can be used to copy regions within the same image (if **$dst_im** is the same as **$src_im**), but if the regions overlap, the results will be unpredictable.

int **ImageCopyResized**(*int* dst_im, *int* src_im, *int* dstX, *int* dstY, *int* srcX, *int* srcY, *int* dstW, *int* dstH, *int* srcW, *int* srcH)

ImageCreate

Returns an image identifier representing a blank image of size **$x_size** by **$y_size**.

int **ImageCreate**(*int* x_size, *int* y_size)

Example: Creating a new GD image stream and outputting an image.

```
<?php
header ("Content-type: image/png");
$im = @ImageCreate (50, 100)
    or die ("Cannot Initialize new GD image stream");
$background_color = ImageColorAllocate ($im, 255, 255, 255);
$text_color = ImageColorAllocate ($im, 233, 14, 91);
ImageString ($im, 1, 5, 5,  "A Simple Text String", $text_color);
ImagePng ($im);
?>
```

ImageCreateFromGIF

Returns an image identifier representing the image obtained from the given filename. **Image-CreateFromGif()** returns an empty string on failure. It also outputs an error message, which unfortunately displays as a broken link in a browser. To ease debugging, the following example will produce an error GIF:

int **ImageCreateFromGIF**(*string* filename)

Example: Example to handle an error during creation (courtesy vic@zymsys.com)

```
function LoadGif ($imgname) {
    $im = @ImageCreateFromGIF ($imgname); /* Attempt to open */
    if (!$im) { /* See if it failed */
        $im = ImageCreate (150, 30); /* Create a blank image */
        $bgc = ImageColorAllocate ($im, 255, 255, 255);
        $tc  = ImageColorAllocate ($im, 0, 0, 0);
        ImageFilledRectangle ($im, 0, 0, 150, 30, $bgc);
        /* Output an errmsg */
        ImageString($im, 1, 5, 5, "Error loading $imgname", $tc);
    }
    return $im;
}
```

Note: Because all GIF support was removed from the GD library in version 1.6, this function is not available if you are using that version of the GD library.

ImageCreateFromJPEG

Returns an image identifier representing the image obtained from the given filename. **ImagecreateFromJPEG()** returns an empty string on failure. It also outputs an error message, which unfortunately displays as a broken link in a browser. To ease debugging, the following example will produce an error JPEG:

> *int* **ImageCreateFromJPEG**(*string* filename)

Example: Example to handle an error during creation (courtesy vic@zymsys.com)

```
function LoadJpeg ($imgname) {
    $im = @ImageCreateFromJPEG ($imgname); /* Attempt to open */
    if (!$im) { /* See if it failed */
        $im = ImageCreate (150, 30); /* Create a blank image */
        $bgc = ImageColorAllocate ($im, 255, 255, 255);
        $tc  = ImageColorAllocate ($im, 0, 0, 0);
        ImageFilledRectangle ($im, 0, 0, 150, 30, $bgc);
        /* Output an errmsg */
        ImageString ($im, 1, 5, 5, "Error loading $imgname", $tc);
    }
    return $im;
}
```

ImageCreateFromPNG

Returns an image identifier representing the image obtained from the given filename. **ImageCreateFromPNG()** returns an empty string on failure. It also outputs an error message, which unfortunately displays as a broken link in a browser. To ease debugging, the following example will produce an error PNG:

> *int* **ImageCreateFromPNG**(*string* filename)

Example: Example to handle an error during creation (courtesy vic@zymsys.com)

```
function LoadPNG ($imgname) {
    $im = @ImageCreateFromPNG ($imgname); /* Attempt to open */
    if (!$im) { /* See if it failed */
        $im  = ImageCreate (150, 30); /* Create a blank image */
        $bgc = ImageColorAllocate ($im, 255, 255, 255);
        $tc  = ImageColorAllocate ($im, 0, 0, 0);
        ImageFilledRectangle ($im, 0, 0, 150, 30, $bgc);
        /* Output an errmsg */
        ImageString ($im, 1, 5, 5, "Error loading $imgname", $tc);
    }
    return $im;
}
```

ImageDashedLine

Draws a dashed line from **$x1, $y1** to **$x2, $y2** (top left is 0, 0) in image **$im** of color **$col**. See also **ImageLine()**.

> *int* **ImageDashedLine**(*int* im, *int* x1, *int* y1, *int* x2, *int* y2, *int* col)

ImageDestroy

Frees any memory associated with image **$im**. **$Im** is the image identifier returned by the **ImageCreate()** function.

int **ImageDestroy**(*int* im)

ImageFill

Performs a flood-fill starting at coordinate **$x, $y** (top left is 0, 0) with color **$col** in the image **$im**.

int **ImageFill**(*int* im, *int* x, *int* y, *int* col)

ImageFilledPolygon

Creates a filled polygon in image **$im**. **$Points** is a PHP array containing the polygon's vertices, that is, points[0] = x0, points[1] = y0, points[2] = x1, points[3] = y1, and so on. **$Num_points** is the total number of vertices.

int **ImageFilledPolygon**(*int* im, *array* points, *int* num_points, *int* col)

ImageFilledRectangle

Creates a filled rectangle of color **col()** in image **$im** starting at upper left coordinates **$x1 , $y1** and ending at bottom right coordinates **$x2, $y2**. 0, 0 is the top left corner of the image.

int **ImageFilledRectangle**(*int* im, *int* x1, *int* y1, *int* x2, *int* y2, *int* col)

ImageFillToBorder

Performs a flood-fill whose border color is defined by **$border**. The starting point for the fill is **$x , $y** (top left is 0, 0), and the region is filled with color **$col**.

int **ImageFillToBorder**(*int* im, *int* x, *int* y, *int* border, *int* col)

ImageFontHeight

Returns the pixel height of a character in the specified font. See also **ImageFontWidth()** and **ImageLoadFont()**.

int **ImageFontHeight**(*int* font)

ImageFontWidth

Returns the pixel width of a character in font. See also **ImageFontHeight()** and **ImageLoad-Font()**.

int **ImageFontWidth**(*int* font)

ImageGammaCorrect

Applies gamma correction to a gd image stream (**$im**) given an input gamma, the parameter **$inputgamma** and an output gamma, and the parameter **$outputgamma**.

int **ImageGammaCorrect**(*int* im, *double* inputgamma, *double* outputgamma)

ImageGIF

Creates the GIF file in filename from the image **$im**. The **$im** argument is the return from the **imagecreate()** function. The image format will be GIF87a unless the image has been made transparent with **ImageColorTransparent()**, in which case the image format will be GIF89a . The filename argument is optional, and if left off, the raw image stream will be output directly. By sending an image/gif content-type using **header()**, you can create a PHP script that outputs GIF images directly.

Note: Because all GIF support was removed from the GD library in version 1.6, this function is not available if you are using that version of the GD library.

int **ImageGIF**(*int* im, [*string* filename])

ImageInterlace

Turns the interlace bit on or off. If interlace is 1, the im image will be interlaced. If interlace is 0, the interlace bit is turned off. This functions returns whether the interlace bit is set for the image.

int **ImageInterlace**(*int* im, [*int* interlace])

ImageJPEG

Creates the JPEG file in filename from the image **$im**. The **$im** argument is the return from the **ImageCreate()** function. The filename argument is optional, and if left off, the raw image stream will be output directly. To skip the filename argument in order to provide a quality argument, just use an empty string ("). By sending an image/jpeg content-type using header(), you can create a PHP script that outputs JPEG images directly.

Note: JPEG support is only available in PHP if PHP was compiled against GD-1.8 or later.

int **ImageJPEG**(*int* im, [*string* filename], [*int* quality])

ImageLine

Draws a line from **$x1, $y1** to **$x2, $y2** (top left is 0, 0) in image im of color **$col**. See also **ImageCreate()** and **ImageColorAllocate()**.

int **ImageLine**(*int* im, *int* x1, *int* y1, *int* x2, *int* y2, *int* col)

ImageLoadFont

Loads a user-defined bitmap font and returns an identifier for the font (that is always greater than 5, so it will not conflict with the built-in fonts). The font file format is currently binary and architecture dependent. This means you should generate the font files on the same type of CPU as the machine on which you are running PHP. The font file format is as follows: byte position C data type description byte 0-3 int number of characters in the font byte 4-7 int value of first character in the font (often 32 for space) byte 8-11 int pixel width of each character byte 12-15 int pixel height of each character byte 16- char array with character data, one byte per pixel in each character, for a total of (nchars*width*height) bytes. See also **ImageFontWidth()** and **ImageFontHeight()**.

int **ImageLoadFont**(*string* file)

ImagePNG

Outputs a GD image stream (**$im**) in PNG format to standard output (usually the browser) or, if a filename is given by the **$filename**, it outputs the image to the file.

int **ImagePNG**(*int* im, [*string* filename])

```php
<?php
$im = ImageCreateFromPng("test.png");
ImagePng($im);
?>
```

ImagePolygon

Creates a polygon in image id. **$Points** is a PHP array containing the polygon's vertices, that is, points[0] = x0, points[1] = y0, points[2] = x1, points[3] = y1, and so on. **$Num_points** is the total number of vertices. See also **imagecreate()**.

int **ImagePolygon**(*int* im, *array* points, *int* num_points, *int* col)

ImagePSBBox

$Size is expressed in pixels. **$Space** enables you to change the default value of a space in a font. This amount is added to the normal value and can also be negative. **$Tightness** enables you to control the amount of white space between characters. This amount is added to the normal character width and can also be negative. **$Angle** is in degrees. Parameters **$space** and **$tightness** are expressed in character space units, where 1 unit is 1/1000 th of an em-square. Parameters **$space**, **$tightness**, and **$angle** are optional. The bounding box is calculated using information available from character metrics, and unfortunately tends to differ slightly from the results achieved by actually rasterizing the text. If the angle is 0 degrees, you can expect the text to need 1 pixel more in every direction. This function returns an array containing the following elements: 0 lower left x-coordinate, 1 lower left y-coordinate, 2 upper right x-coordinate, and 3 upper right y-coordinate. See also **imagepstext()**.

array **ImagePSBBox**(*string* text, *int* font, *int* size, [*int* space], [*int* tightness], [*float* angle])

ImagePSEncodeFont

Loads a character encoding vector from a file and changes the fonts encoding vector to it. Because a PostScript fonts default vector lacks most of the character positions above 127, you'll definitely want to change this if you use a language other than English. The exact format of this file is described in T1libs documentation. T1lib comes with two ready-to-use files, IsoLatin1.enc and IsoLatin2.enc. If you find yourself using this function all the time, a much better way to define the encoding is to set ps.default_encoding in the configuration **file()** to point to the right encoding file. All fonts you load will automatically have the right encoding.

    int **ImagePSEncodeFont**(*string* encodingfile)

ImagePsExtendFont

Extends or condenses a font (**$font_index**), if the value of the **$extend** parameter is less than the one that will be condensing the font.

    bool **ImagePsExtendFont**(*int* font_index, *double* extend)

ImagePSFreeFont

See also **ImagePSLoadFont()**.

    void **ImagePSFreeFont**(*int* fontindex)

ImagePSLoadFont

In the case where everything goes right, a valid font index will be returned and can be used for further purposes. Otherwise, the function returns false and prints a message describing what went wrong. See also **ImagePSFreeFont()**.

    int **ImagePSLoadFont**(*string* filename)

ImagePsSlantFont

Slants a font given by the **$font_index** parameter with a slant of the value of the **$slant** parameter.

    bool **ImagePsSlantFont**(*int* font_index, *double* slant)

ImagePSText

$Size is expressed in pixels. **$Foreground** is the color in which the text will be painted. **$Background** is the color to which the text will try to fade in with antialiasing. No pixels with the color **$background** are actually painted, so the background image does not need to be of solid color. The coordinates given by **$x, $y** will define the origin (or reference point) of the first character (roughly the lower-left corner of the character). This is different from the **ImageString()**, where **$x, $y** define the upper-right corner of the first character. Refer to PostScipt documentation about fonts and their measuring system if you have trouble understanding how this works.

array **ImagePSText**(*int* image, *string* text, *int* font, *int* size, *int* foreground, *int* background, *int* x, *int* y, [*int* space], [*int* tightness], [*float* angle], [*int* antialias_steps])

$Space enables you to change the default value of a space in a font. This amount is added to the normal value and can also be negative. **$Tightness** enables you to control the amount of white space between characters. This amount is added to the normal character width and can also be negative. **$Angle** is in degrees. **$Antialias_steps** enables you to control the number of colors used for antialiasing text. Allowed values are 4 and 16. The higher value is recommended for text sizes lower than 20, where the effect in text quality is quite visible. With bigger sizes, use 4; it is less computationally intensive. Parameters **$space** and **$tightness** are expressed in character space units, where 1 unit is $\frac{1}{1000}$ th of an em-square. Parameters **$space**, **$tightness**, **$angle**, and **$antialias** are optional. This function returns an array containing the following elements: 0 lower left x-coordinate, 1 lower left y-coordinate, 2 upper right x-coordinate, and 3 upper right y-coordinate. See also **imagepsbbox()**.

ImageRectangle

Creates a rectangle of color col in image im starting at upper left coordinate x1, y1 and ending at bottom right coordinate x2, y2. 0, 0 is the top left corner of the image.

int **ImageRectangle**(*int* im, *int* x1, *int* y1, *int* x2, *int* y2, *int* col)

ImageSetPixel

Draws a pixel at **$x, $y** (top left is 0, 0) in image **$im** of color **$col**. See also **ImageCreate()** and **ImageColorAllocate()**.

int **ImageSetPixel**(*int* im, *int* x, *int* y, *int* col)

ImageString

Draws the string **$s** in the image identified by **$im** at coordinates **$x, $y** (top left is 0, 0) in color **$col**. If font is 1, 2, 3, 4, or 5, a built-in font is used. See also **ImageLoadFont()**.

int **ImageString**(*int* im, *int* font, *int* x, *int* y, *string* s, *int* col)

ImageStringUp

Draws the string **$s** vertically in the image identified by **$im** at coordinates **$x, $y** (top left is 0, 0) in color **$col**. If font is 1, 2, 3, 4, or 5, a built-in font is used. See also **ImageLoadFont()**.

int **ImageStringUp**(*int* im, *int* font, *int* x, *int* y, *string* s, *int* col)

ImageSX

Returns the width of the image identified by **$im**. See also **ImageCreate()** and **ImageSY()**.

int **ImageSX**(*int* im)

ImageSY

Returns the height of the image identified by **$im**. See also **ImageCreate()** and **ImageSX()**.

int **ImageSY**(*int* im)

ImageTTFBBox

This function calculates and returns the bounding box in pixels for a TrueType text. **$text** is the string to be measured. **$size** is the font size. **$fontfile** is the name of the TrueType font file (can also be an URL). **$angle** is an angle in degrees in which **$text** will be measured. **ImageTTFB-Box()** returns an array with 8 elements representing four points making the bounding box of the text: 0 lower left corner, X position 1 lower left corner, Y position 2 lower right corner, X position 3 lower right corner, Y position 4 upper right corner, X position 5 upper right corner, Y position 6 upper left corner, X position 7 upper left corner, Y position. The points are relative to the text regardless of the angle, so "upper left" means in the top left-hand corner, seeing the text horizontally. This function requires both the GD library and the FreeType library. See also **Image TTFText()**.

array **ImageTTFBBox**(*int* size, *int* angle, *string* fontfile, *string* text)

ImageTTFText

Draws the string $text in the image identified by **$im**, starting at coordinates **$x , $y** (top left is 0, 0), at an angle of **$angle** in color **$col**, using the TrueType font file identified by **$fontfile**. The coordinates given by **$x, $y** will define the base point of the first character (roughly the lower-left corner of the character). This is different from the **ImageString()**, where x, y define the upper-right corner of the first character. **$Angle** is in degrees, with 0 degrees being left-to-right reading text (3:00 direction), and higher values representing a counter-clockwise rotation (that is, a value of 90 would result in bottom-to-top reading text). **$Fontfile** is the path to the TrueType font you wish to use. **$Text** is the text string, which may include UTF-8 character sequences (of the form:{) to access characters in a font beyond the first 255. **$Col** is the color index. Using the negative of a color index has the effect of turning off antialiasing. **ImageTTFText()** returns an array with 8 elements representing four points making the bounding box of the text. The order of the points is upper left, upper right, lower right, lower left. The points are relative to the text regardless of the angle, so "upper left" means in the top left-hand corner when you see the text horizontally.

array **ImageTTFText**(*int* im, *int* size, *int* angle, *int* x, *int* y, *int* col, *string* fontfile, *string* text)

This example script will produce a black GIF 400x30 pixels, with the words "Testing . . ." in white in the Arial font.

Example: ImageTTFText

```php
<?php
Header ("Content-type: image/gif");
$im = imagecreate (400, 30);
$black = ImageColorAllocate ($im, 0, 0, 0);
$white = ImageColorAllocate ($im, 255, 255, 255);
ImageTTFText ($im, 20, 0, 10, 20, $white, "/path/arial.ttf",
```

```
                    "Testing... Omega: &#937;");
ImageGif ($im);
ImageDestroy ($im);
?>
```

This function requires both the GD library and the *FreeType(URL)* library. See also **Image TTFBBox()**.

ImageTypes

This function returns a bit field corresponding to the image formats supported by the version of GD linked into PHP. The following bits are returned: IMG_GIF | IMG_JPG | IMG_PNG | IMG_WBMP.

int **ImageTypes**(*void*)

To check for PNG support, for example, do this:
Example: ImageTypes

```
<?php
if (ImageTypes() & IMG_PNG) {
    echo "PNG Support is enabled";
}
?>
```

imap_8bit

Converts an 8-bit string to a quoted-printable string (according to RFC2045(URL), section 6.7). Returns a quoted-printable string. See also **imap_qprint()**.

string **imap_8bit**(*string* string)

imap_alerts

Returns an array of all of the IMAP alert messages generated since the last **imap_alerts()** call, or the beginning of the page. When **imap_alerts()** is called, the alert stack is subsequently cleared. The IMAP specification requires that these messages be passed to the user.

array **imap_alerts**(*void*)

imap_append

Returns true on success, false on error. **imap_append()** appends a string message to the specified mailbox **$mbox**. If the optional $flags is specified, this function writes the $flags to that mailbox also. When talking to the Cyrus IMAP server, you must use "\r\n" as your end-of-line terminator, instead of "\n", or the operation will fail.

int **imap_append**(*int* imap_stream, *string* mbox, *string* message, [*string* flags])

Example: imap_append()

```
$stream = imap_open("{your.imap.host}INBOX.Drafts","username", "password");
$check = imap_check($stream);
print "Msg Count before append: ". $check->Nmsgs."\n";
imap_append($stream,"{your.imap.host}INBOX.Drafts"
                ,"From: me@my.host\r\n"
                ."To: you@your.host\r\n"
                ."Subject: test\r\n"
                ."\r\n"
                ."this is a test message, please ignore\r\n"
                );
$check = imap_check($stream);
print "Msg Count after append : ". $check->Nmsgs."\n";
imap_close($stream);
```

imap_base64

Decodes BASE-64 encoded text (see RFC2045(URL), Section 6.8). The decoded message is returned as a string. See also **imap_binary()**.

string **imap_base64(** *string* text)

imap_binary

Converts an 8-bit string to a base64 string (according to RFC2045(URL), Section 6.8). Returns a base64 string. See also **imap_base64()**.

string **imap_binary(** *string* string)

imap_body

Returns the body of the message, numbered **$msg_number** in the current mailbox. The optional **$flags** are a bit mask with one or more of the following:

- FT_UID—The **$msgno** is a UID.

- FT_PEEK—Do not set the \Seen flag if not already set.

- FT_INTERNAL—The return string is in internal format and will not canonicalize to CRLF.

   imap_body() will only return a verbatim copy of the message body. To extract single parts of a multipart MIME-encoded message, you have to use **imap_fetch_structure()** to analyze its structure and **imap_fetch_body()** to extract a copy of a single body component.

string **imap_body(** *int* imap_stream, *int* msg_number, [*int* flags])

imap_check

Returns information about the current mailbox. Returns false on failure. The **imap_check()** function checks the current mailbox status on the server and returns the information in an object with the following properties:

- Date—last change of mailbox contents
- Driver—protocol used to access this mailbox: POP3, IMAP, NNTP
- Mailbox—the mailbox name
- Nmsgs—number of messages in the mailbox
- Recent—number of recent messages in the mailbox

object **imap_check**(*int* imap_stream)

imap_clearflag_full

This function causes a store to delete the specified flag to the flags set for the messages in the specified sequence. The flags which you can unset are "\\Seen", "\\Answered", "\\Flagged", "\\Deleted", "\\Draft", and "\\Recent" (as defined by RFC2060). The options are a bit mask with one or more of the following: ST_UID. The sequence argument contains UIDs instead of sequence numbers.

string **imap_clearflag_full**(*int* stream, *string* sequence, *string* flag, *string* options)

imap_close

Closes the imap stream. Takes an optional **$flag** CL_EXPUNGE, which will silently expunge the mailbox before closing, removing all messages marked for deletion.

int **imap_close**(*int* imap_stream, [*int* flags])

imap_createmailbox

Creates a new mailbox specified by **$mbox**. Names containing international characters should be encoded by **imap_utf7_encode**(). Returns true on success and false on error. See also **imap_renamemailbox**(), **imap_deletemailbox**() and **imap_open**() for the format of **$mbox** names.

int **imap_createmailbox**(*int* imap_stream, *string* mbox)

Example: imap_createmailbox()

```
$mbox = imap_open("{your.imap.host}","username","password",OP_HALFOPEN)
    || die("can't connect: ".imap_last_error());
$name1 = "phpnewbox";
$name2 = imap_utf7_encode("phpnewbox");
$newname = $name1;
echo "Newname will be '$name1'<br>\n";
# we will now create a new mailbox "phptestbox" in your inbox folder,
# check its status after creation and finally remove it to restore
# your inbox to its initial state
if(@imap_createmailbox($mbox,imap_utf7_encode("{your.imap.host}
INBOX.$newname"))) {
  $status = @imap_status($mbox,"{your.imap.host}INBOX.$newname",SA_ALL);
  if($status) {
```

```
        print("your new mailbox '$name1' has the following status:<br>\n");
        print("Messages:    ". $status->messages   )."<br>\n";
        print("Recent:      ". $status->recent     )."<br>\n";
        print("Unseen:      ". $status->unseen     )."<br>\n";
        print("UIDnext:     ". $status->uidnext    )."<br>\n";
        print("UIDvalidity:". $status->uidvalidity)."<br>\n";
    if(imap_renamemailbox($mbox,"{your.imap.host}INBOX.$newname","{your.imap.host}INBOX.$na
me2")) {
        echo "renamed new mailbox from '$name1' to '$name2'<br>\n";
        $newname=$name2;
    } else {
        print "imap_renamemailbox on new mailbox failed: ".imap_last_error()."<br>\n";
    }
    } else {
        print  "imap_status on new mailbox failed: ".imap_last_error()."<br>\n";
    }
    if(@imap_deletemailbox($mbox,"{your.imap.host}INBOX.$newname")) {
        print "new mailbox removed to restore initial state<br>\n";
    } else {
        print  "imap_deletemailbox on new mailbox failed:
".implode("<br>\n",imap_errors())."<br>\n";
    }
} else {
    print  "could not create new mailbox: ".implode("<br>\n",imap_errors())."<br>\n";
}
imap_close($mbox);
```

imap_delete

Returns true. **imap_delete()** function marks messages pointed by **$msg_number** for deletion. The optional **$flags** parameter only has a single option, **$FT_UID**, which tells the function to treat the **$msg_number** argument as a **$UID**. Messages marked for deletion will stay in the mailbox until either **imap_expunge()** is called or **imap_close()** is called with the optional parameter CL_EXPUNGE.

int **imap_delete**(*int* imap_stream, *int* msg_number, [*int* flags])

Example: Imap_delete()

```
$mbox = imap_open ("{your.imap.host}INBOX", "username", "password")
    || die ("can't connect: " . imap_last_error());

$check = imap_mailboxmsginfo ($mbox);
print "Messages before delete: " . $check->Nmsgs . "<br>\n" ;
imap_delete ($mbox, 1);
$check = imap_mailboxmsginfo ($mbox);
print "Messages after  delete: " . $check->Nmsgs . "<br>\n" ;
imap_expunge ($mbox);
$check = imap_mailboxmsginfo ($mbox);
print "Messages after expunge: " . $check->Nmsgs . "<br>\n" ;
imap_close ($mbox);
```

imap_deletemailbox

Deletes the specified mailbox (see **imap_open()** for the format of **$mbox** names). Returns true on success and false on error. See also **imap_createmailbox()**, **imap_renamemailbox()**, and **imap_open()** for the format of **$mbox**.

> *int* **imap_deletemailbox**(*int* imap_stream, *string* mbox)

imap_errors

Returns an array of all of the IMAP error messages generated since the last **imap_errors()** call, or the beginning of the page. When **imap_errors()** is called, the error stack is subsequently cleared.

> *array* **imap_errors**(*void*)

imap_expunge

Deletes all the messages marked for deletion by **imap_delete()**, **imap_mail_move()**, or **imap_setflag_full()**. Returns true.

> *int* **imap_expunge**(*int* imap_stream)

imap_fetchbody

This function causes a fetch of a particular section of the body of the specified messages as a text string, and it returns that text string. The section specification is a string of integers delimited by periods, which index into a body part list as per the IMAP4 specification. Body parts are not decoded by this function. The options for **imap_fetchbody()** is a bit mask with one or more of the following:

- FT_UID—The **$msg_number** is a UID.
- FT_PEEK—Do not set the \Seen flag if not already set.
- FT_INTERNAL—The return string is in internal format, without any attempt to canonicalize CRLF.

> *string* **imap_fetchbody**(*int* imap_stream, *int* msg_number, *string* part_number, [*flags* flags])

imap_fetchheader

Causes a fetch of the complete, unfiltered *RFC822(URL)* format header of the specified message as a text string, and it returns that text string. The options are as follows:

- FT_UID—The msgno argument is a UID.
- FT_INTERNALL—The return string is in internal format, without any attempt to canonicalize to CRLF newlines.
- FT_PREFETCHTEXT—The RFC822.TEXT should be pre-fetched at the same time. This

avoids an extra RTT on an IMAP connection if a full message text is desired (for example, in a "save to local file" operation).

string **imap_fetchheader**(*int* imap_stream, *int* msgno, *int* flags)

imap_fetchstructure

This function fetches all the structured information for a given message. The optional **$flags** parameter only has a single option, **$FT_UID**, which tells the function to treat the **$msg_number** argument as a **$UID**. The returned object includes the envelope, internal date, size, flags, and body structure along with a similar object for each mime attachment.

object **imap_fetchstructure**(*int* imap_stream, *int* msg_number, [*int* flags])

The structure of the returned objects is as follows: Returned Objects for **imap_fetch structure**().

type	Primary body type
encoding	Body transfer encoding
ifsubtype	True, if a subtype string exists
subtype	MIME subtype
ifdescription	True, if a description string exists
description	Content description string
ifid	True, if an identification string exists
id	Identification string
lines	Number of lines
bytes	Number of bytes
ifdisposition	True, if a disposition string exists
disposition	Disposition string
ifdparameters	True, if the dparameters array exists
dparameters	Disposition parameter array
ifparameters	True, if the parameters array exists parameters MIME parameters array
parts	Array of objects describing each message part

Note: dparameters is an array of objects where each object has an attribute and a value property. Parameter is an array of objects where each object has an attribute and a value property. Parts is an array of objects identical in structure to the top-level object, with the limitation that it cannot contain further "parts" objects.

Primary body type
0: text, 1: multipart, 2: message, 3: application, 4: audio, 5: image, 6: video, 7: other
Transfer encodings
0: 7BIT, 1: 8BIT, 2: BINARY, 3: BASE64, 4: QUOTED-PRINTABLE; 5: OTHER

imap_fetch_overview

Fetches mail headers for the given **$sequence** and returns an overview of their contents. **$sequence** will contain a sequence of message indices or UIDs, if **$flags** contains FT_UID. The returned value is an array of objects describing one message header each:

- subject—The message subject.

- from—Who sent the message.

- date—When the message was sent.

- message_id—Message-ID.

- references—A reference to this message id.

- size—Size in bytes.

- uid—UID the message has in the mailbox.

- msgno—Message sequence number in the mailbox.

- recent—This message is flagged as recent.

- flagged—This message is flagged.

- answered—This message is flagged as answered.

- deleted—This message is flagged for deletion.

- seen—This message is flagged as already read.

- draft—This message is flagged as being a draft.

array **imap_fetch_overview**(*int* imap_stream, *string* sequence, [*int* flags])

Example: imap_fetch_overview()

```
$mbox = imap_open("{your.imap.host:143}","username","password")
     || die("can't connect: ".imap_last_error());
$overview = imap_fetch_overview($mbox,"2,4:6",0);
if(is_array($overview)) {
       reset($overview);
       while( list($key,$val) = each($overview)) {
               print      $val->msgno
               . " - " . $val->date
               . " - " . $val->subject
               . "\n";
       }
}
imap_close($mbox)
```

imap_getmailboxes

Returns an array of objects containing mailbox information. Each object has the following attributes: **$name**, specifying the full name of the mailbox; **$delimiter**, which is the hierarchy delimiter for the part of the hierarchy this mailbox is in; and **$attributes**, a bit mask that can be tested against:

■ LATT_NOINFERIORS—This mailbox has no "children" (no mailboxes exist below this one).

■ LATT_NOSELECT—This is only a container, not a mailbox; it cannot be opened .

■ LATT_MARKED—This mailbox is marked and used only by UW-IMAPD.

■ LATT_UNMARKED—This mailbox is not marked and only used by UW-IMAPD.

array **imap_getmailboxes**(*int* imap_stream, *string* ref, *string* pattern)

Mailbox names containing international characters outside the printable ASCII range will be encoded and may be decoded by **imap_utf7_decode()**. Normally, **$ref** should just be the server specification as described in **imap_open()**, and **$pattern** specifies where to start searching in the mailbox hierarchy . If you want all mailboxes, pass '*' for **$pattern**. Two special characters can be passed as part of the **$pattern** : '*' and '%'. '*', which means to return all mailboxes. If you pass **$pattern** as '*', you will get a list of the entire mailbox hierarchy. '%' means to return the current level only. '%' as the **$pattern** parameter will return only the top level mailboxes; '~/mail/%' on UW_IMAPD will return every mailbox in the ~/mail directory, but none in subfolders of that directory.

Example: imap_getmailboxes()

```
$mbox = imap_open("{your.imap.host}","username","password",OP_HALFOPEN)
     || die("can't connect: ".imap_last_error());
$list = imap_getmailboxes($mbox,"{your.imap.host}","*");
if(is_array($list)) {
  reset($list);
  while (list($key, $val) = each($list))
  {
    print "($key) ";
    print imap_utf7_decode($val->name).",";
    print "'".$val->delimiter."',";
    print $val->attributes."<br>\n";
  }
} else
  print "imap_getmailboxes failed: ".imap_last_error()."\n";
imap_close($mbox);
```

See also **imap_getsubscribed()**.

imap_getsubscribed

Identical to **imap_getmailboxes()**, except that it only returns mailboxes to which the user is subscribed.

array **imap_getsubscribed**(*int* imap_stream, *string* ref, *string* pattern)

imap_header

An alias to **imap_headerinfo()** and is identical to this in every way.

imap_header(*void*)

imap_headerinfo

Returns an object of various header elements: **remail**, **date**, **Date**, **subject**, **Subject**, **in_reply_to**, **message_id**, **newsgroups**, **followup_to**, **references**.

imap_headerinfo(*void*)

The message flags are as follows:

■ Recent—'R' if recent and seen, 'N' if recent and not seen, ' ' if not recent

■ Unseen—'U' if not seen AND not recent, ' ' if seen OR not seen and recent

■ Answered—'A' if answered, ' ' if unanswered

■ Deleted—'D' if deleted, ' ' if not deleted

■ Draft—'X' if draft, ' ' if not draft

■ Flagged—'F' if flagged, ' ' if not flagged

Note: The Recent/Unseen behavior is a little odd. If you want to know if a message is Unseen, you must check for Unseen == 'U' || Recent == 'N'.

■ toaddress (full to: line, up to 1024 characters)

■ to[] (returns an array of objects from the To line, containing): personal adl mailbox host

■ fromaddress (full from: line, up to 1024 characters)

■ from[] (returns an array of objects from the From line, containing): personal adl mailbox host

■ ccaddress (full cc: line, up to 1024 characters)

■ cc[] (returns an array of objects from the Cc line, containing): personal adl mailbox host

■ bccaddress (full bcc line, up to 1024 characters)

■ bcc[] (returns an array of objects from the Bcc line, containing): personal adl mailbox host

■ reply_toaddress (full reply_to: line, up to 1024 characters)

■ reply_to[] (returns an array of objects from the Reply_to line, containing): personal adl mailbox host

■ senderaddress (full sender: line, up to 1024 characters)

■ sender[] (returns an array of objects from the sender line, containing): personal adl mailbox host

■ return_path (full return-path: line, up to 1024 characters)

■ return_path[] (returns an array of objects from the return_path line, containing): personal adl mailbox host

■ udate (mail message date in unix time)

■ fetchfrom (from line formatted to fit **$fromlength** characters)

■ fetchsubject (subject line formatted to fit **$subjectlength** characters)

imap_headers

Returns an array of string formatted with header info. Allows one element per mail message.

array **imap_headers**(*int* imap_stream)

imap_last_error

Returns the full text of the last IMAP error message that occurred on the current page. The error stack is untouched. Calling **imap_last_error()** subsequently, with no intervening errors, will return the same error.

string **imap_last_error**(*void*)

imap_listmailbox

Returns an array containing the names of the mailboxes. See **imap_getmailboxes()** for a description of **$ref** and **$pattern**.

array **imap_listmailbox**(*int* imap_stream, *string* ref, *string* pattern)

Example: imap_listmailbox()

```
$mbox = imap_open("{your.imap.host}","username","password",OP_HALFOPEN)
     || die("can't connect: ".imap_last_error());
$list = imap_listmailbox($mbox,"{your.imap.host}","*");
if(is_array($list)) {
  reset($list);
  while (list($key, $val) = each($list))
    print imap_utf7_decode($val)."<br>\n";
} else
  print "imap_listmailbox failed: ".imap_last_error()."\n";
imap_close($mbox);
```

imap_listsubscribed

Returns an array of all the mailboxes that you have subscribed. This is almost identical to **imap_listmailbox()**, but it will only return mailboxes that the user you logged in as has subscribed.

array **imap_listsubscribed**(*int* imap_stream, *string* ref, *string* pattern)

imap_mail

This function is currently only available in PHP 3.

string **imap_mail**(*string* to, *string* subject, *string* message, [*string* additional_headers], [*string* cc], [*string* bcc], [*string* rpath])

imap_mailboxmsginfo

Returns information about the current mailbox. Returns false on failure. The **imap_mailboxmsginfo()** function checks the current mailbox status on the server. It is similar to **imap_status()** but will additionally sum up the size of all messages in the mailbox, which will take some additional time to execute. It returns the information in an object with the following properties:

object **imap_mailboxmsginfo**(*int* imap_stream)

Mailbox properties

- Date—Date of last change

- Driver—Driver

- Mailbox—Name of the mailbox

- Nmsgs—Number of messages

- Recent—Number of recent messages

- Unread—Number of unread messages

- Deleted—Number of deleted messages

- Size—Mailbox size

Example: imap_mailboxmsginfo()

```php
<?php
$mbox = imap_open("{your.imap.host}INBOX","username", "password")
     || die("can't connect: ".imap_last_error());
$check = imap_mailboxmsginfo($mbox);
if($check) {
    print "Date: "    . $check->Date    ."<br>\n" ;
    print "Driver: "  . $check->Driver  ."<br>\n" ;
    print "Mailbox: " . $check->Mailbox ."<br>\n" ;
    print "Messages: ". $check->Nmsgs   ."<br>\n" ;
    print "Recent: "  . $check->Recent  ."<br>\n" ;
    print "Unread: "  . $check->Unread  ."<br>\n" ;
    print "Deleted: " . $check->Deleted ."<br>\n" ;
    print "Size: "    . $check->Size    ."<br>\n" ;
} else {
    print "imap_check() failed: ".imap_lasterror(). "<br>\n";
}
imap_close($mbox);
?>
```

imap_mail_compose

string **imap_mail_compose**(*array* envelope, *array* body)

Example: imap_mail_compose()

```php
<?php
$envelope["from"]="musone@afterfive.com";
$envelope["to"]="musone@darkstar";
$envelope["cc"]="musone@edgeglobal.com";
$part1["type"]=TYPEMULTIPART;
$part1["subtype"]="mixed";
$filename="/tmp/imap.c.gz";
$fp=fopen($filename,"r");
$contents=fread($fp,filesize($filename));
fclose($fp);
$part2["type"]=TYPEAPPLICATION;
$part2["encoding"]=ENCBINARY;
$part2["subtype"]="octet-stream";
$part2["description"]=basename($filename);
$part2["contents.data"]=$contents;
$part3["type"]=TYPETEXT;
$part3["subtype"]="plain";
$part3["description"]="description3";
$part3["contents.data"]="contents.data3\n\n\n\t";
$body[1]=$part1;
$body[2]=$part2;
$body[3]=$part3;
echo nl2br(imap_mail_compose($envelope,$body));
?>
```

imap_mail_copy

Returns true on success and false on error. Copies mail messages specified by **$msglist** to specified mailbox. **$msglist** is a range, not just message numbers as described in RFC2060 (*http://www.faqs.org/rfcs/rfc2060.html*). Flags is a bit mask of one or more of CP_UID—the sequence numbers contain UIDS. CP_MOVE. Delete the messages from the current mailbox after copying.

int **imap_mail_copy**(*int* imap_stream, *string* msglist, *string* mbox, [*int* flags])

imap_mail_move

Moves mail messages specified by **$msglist** to specified mailbox. **$msglist** is a range, not just message numbers as described in RFC2060 (*http://www.faqs.org/rfcs/rfc2060.html*). Flags is a bit mask and may contain the single option CP_UID—the sequence numbers contain UIDS. Returns true on success and false on error.

int **imap_mail_move**(*int* imap_stream, *string* msglist, *string* mbox, [*int* flags])

imap_mime_header_decode

Decodes MIME message header extensions that are non ASCII text (see RFC2047 (*http://www.faqs.org/rfcs/rfc2047.html*)). The decoded elements are returned in an array of objects, where each object has two properties, charset and text. If the element hasn't been encoded, and in other words is in plain US-ASCII,the charset property of that element is set to default.

array imap_mime_header_decode(*string* text)

Example: imap_mime_header_decode()

```
$text="=?ISO-8859-1?Q?Keld_J=F8rn_Simonsen?= <keld@dkuug.dk>";
$elements=imap_mime_header_decode($text);
for($i=0;$i<count($elements);$i++) {
echo "Charset: {$elements[$i]->charset}\n";
echo "Text: {$elements[$i]->text}\n\n";
}
```

In the previous example, we would have two elements; whereas the first element had previously been encoded with ISO-8859-1, and the second element would be plain US-ASCII.

imap_msgno

Returns the message sequence number for the given UID. It is the inverse of **imap_uid()**.

int **imap_msgno**(*int* imap_stream, *int* uid)

imap_num_msg

Returns the number of messages in the current mailbox.

int **imap_num_msg**(*int* imap_stream)

imap_num_recent

Returns the number of recent messages in the current mailbox.

int **imap_num_recent**(*int* imap_stream)

imap_open

Returns an IMAP stream on success and false on error. This function can also be used to open streams to POP3 and NNTP servers, but some functions and features are not available on IMAP servers. A mailbox name consists of a server part and a mailbox path on this server. The special name INBOX stands for the current users personal mailbox. The server part, which is enclosed in '{' and '}', consists of the server's name or ip address, a protocol specification (beginning with '/'), and an optional port specifier beginning with ':'. The server part is mandatory in all mailbox parameters. Mailbox names that contain international characters besides those in the printable ASCII space have to be encoded with **imap_utf7_encode()**.

int **imap_open**(*string* mailbox, *string* username, *string* password, [*int* flags])

The options are a bit mask with one or more of the following:

- OP_READONLY—Open mailbox read-only.
- OP_ANONYMOUS—Don't use or update a .newsrc for news (NNTP only).
- OP_HALFOPEN—For IMAP and NNTP names, open a connection but don't open a mailbox.
- CL_EXPUNGE—Expunge mailbox automatically upon mailbox close.

To connect to an IMAP server running on port 143 on the local machine, do the following:

```
$mbox = imap_open ("{localhost:143}INBOX", "user_id", "password");
        To connect to a POP3 server on port 110 on the local server, use:
$mbox = imap_open ("{localhost/pop3:110}INBOX", "user_id", "password");
        To connect to an NNTP server on port 119 on the local server, use:
$nntp = imap_open ("{localhost/nntp:119}comp.test", "", "");
```

To connect to a remote server, replace "localhost" with the name or the IP address of the server to which you want to connect.

Example: imap_open()

```
$mbox = imap_open ("{your.imap.host:143}", "username", "password");
echo "<p><h1>Mailboxes</h1>\n";
$folders = imap_listmailbox ($mbox, "{your.imap.host:143}", "*");
if ($folders == false) {
    echo "Call failed<br>\n";
} else {
    while (list ($key, $val) = each ($folders)) {
        echo $val."<br>\n";
    }
}
echo "<p><h1>Headers in INBOX</h1>\n";
$headers = imap_headers ($mbox);
if ($headers == false) {
    echo "Call failed<br>\n";
} else {
    while (list ($key,$val) = each ($headers)) {
        echo $val."<br>\n";
    }
}
imap_close($mbox);
```

imap_ping

Returns true if the stream is still alive, false otherwise. **imap_ping()** function pings the stream to see if it is still active. It may discover new mail; this is the preferred method for a periodic "new mail check" as well as a "keep alive" for servers that have inactivity timeout. (As PHP scripts do not tend to run that long, this function probably will not be useful to anyone.)

int **imap_ping**(*int* imap_stream)

imap_qprint

Converts a quoted-printable string to an 8-bit string, according to RFC2045 (*http://www.faqs.org/rfcs/rfc2045.html*), section 6.7. Returns an 8-bit (binary) string. See also **imap_8bit()**.

string **imap_qprint**(*string* string)

imap_renamemailbox

Renames on old mailbox to new mailbox (see **imap_open()** for the format of **$mbox** names). Returns true on success and false on error. See also **imap_createmailbox()**, **imap_deletemail-box()**, and **imap_open()** for the format of **$mbox**.

    int **imap_renamemailbox**(*int* imap_stream, *string* old_mbox, *string* new_mbox)

imap_reopen

Reopens the specified stream to a new mailbox on an IMAP or NNTP server. The options are a bit mask with one or more of the following:

- OP_READONLY—Open mailbox read-only.

- OP_ANONYMOUS—Don't use or update a .newsrc for news (NNTP only).

- OP_HALFOPEN—For IMAP and NNTP names, open a connection but don't open a mailbox.

- CL_EXPUNGE—Expunge mailbox automatically upon mailbox close (see also **imap_delete()** and **imap_expunge()**).

Returns true on success and false on error.

    int **imap_reopen**(*int* imap_stream, *string* mailbox, [*string* flags])

imap_rfc822_parse_adrlist

Parses the address string as defined in RFC822 *(http://www.faqs.org/rfcs/rfc822.html)*. For each address, it returns an array of objects. The objects properties are as follows:

- mailbox—the mailbox name (username)

- host—the host name

- personal—the personal name

- adl—at domain source route

    array **imap_rfc822_parse_adrlist**(*string* address, *string* default_host)

    Example: imap_rfc822_parse_adrlist()

```
$address_string = "Hartmut Holzgraefe <hartmut@cvs.php.net>, postmaster@somedomain.net,
root";
$address_array  = imap_rfc822_parse_adrlist($address_string,"somedomain.net");
if(! is_array($address_array)) die("somethings wrong\n");
reset($address_array);
while(list($key,$val)=each($address_array)){
  print "mailbox : ".$val->mailbox."<br>\n";
  print "host    : ".$val->host."<br>\n";
  print "personal: ".$val->personal."<br>\n";
  print "adl     : ".$val->adl."<p>\n";
}
```

imap_rfc822_parse_headers

Returns an object of various header elements, similar to **imap_header()**, except without the flags and other elements that come from the IMAP server.

> *object* **imap_rfc822_parse_headers**(*string* headers, [*string* defaulthost])

imap_rfc822_write_address

Returns a properly formatted email address, as defined in RFC822 (*http://www.faqs.org/rfcs/rfc822.html*), given the mailbox, host, and personal info.

> *string* **imap_rfc822_write_address**(*string* mailbox, *string* host, *string* personal)

> **Example: imap_rfc822_write_address() example**

```
print imap_rfc822_write_address("hartmut","cvs.php.net","Hartmut Holzgraefe")."\n";
```

imap_scanmailbox

Returns an array containing the names of the mailboxes that have **$string** in the text of the mailbox. This function is similar to imap_listmailbox(), but it will additionally check for the presence of the string **$content** inside the mailbox data. See **imap_getmailboxes()** for a description of **$ref** and **$pattern**.

> *array* **imap_scanmailbox**(*int* imap_stream, *string* ref, *string* pattern, *string* content)

imap_search

Performs a search on the mailbox currently opened in the given imap stream. **$criteria** is a string, delimited by spaces, in which the following keywords are allowed. Any multi-word arguments, for example, FROM "joey smith", must be quoted.

> *array* **imap_search**(*int* imap_stream, *string* criteria, *int* flags)

- ALL—Return all messages matching the rest of the criteria.
- ANSWERED—Match messages with the \\ANSWERED flag set.
- BCC "string"—Match messages with "string" in the Bcc: field.
- BEFORE "date"—Match messages with Date: before "date."
- BODY "string"—Match messages with "string" in the body of the message.
- CC "string"—Match messages with "string" in the Cc: field.
- DELETED—Match deleted messages.
- FLAGGED—Match messages with the \\FLAGGED (sometimes referred to as Important or Urgent) flag set.
- FROM "string"—Match messages with "string" in the From: field.

- KEYWORD "string"—Match messages with "string" as a keyword.
- NEW—Match new messages.
- OLD—Match old messages.
- ON "date"—Match messages with Date: matching "date."
- RECENT—Match messages with the \\RECENT flag set.
- SEEN—Match messages that have been read (the \\SEEN flag is set).
- SINCE "date"—Match messages with Date: after "date."
- SUBJECT "string"—Match messages with "string" in the Subject:.
- TEXT "string"—Match messages with text "string."
- TO "string"—Match messages with "string" in the To: .
- UNANSWERED—Match messages that have not been answered.
- UNDELETED—Match messages that are not deleted.
- UNFLAGGED—Match messages that are not flagged.
- UNKEYWORD "string"—Match messages that do not have the keyword "string."
- UNSEEN—Match messages that have not been read yet.

For example, to match all unanswered messages sent by Mom, you would use "UNAN-SWERED FROM mom". Searches appear to be case insensitive. This list of criteria is from a reading of the UW c-client source code and may be incomplete or inaccurate (see also RFC2060, section 6.4.4). Valid values for flags are SE_UID, which causes the returned array to contain UIDs instead of messages sequence numbers.

imap_setflag_full

Causes a store to add the specified flag to the flags set for the messages in the specified sequence. The flags that you can set are "\\Seen", "\\Answered", "\\Flagged", "\\Deleted", "\\Draft", and "\\Recent" (as defined by RFC2060). The options are a bit mask with one or more of the following: ST_UID. The sequence argument contains UIDs instead of sequence numbers.

string **imap_setflag_full**(*int* stream, *string* sequence, *string* flag, *string* options)

Example: imap_setflag_full()

```
$mbox = imap_open("{your.imap.host:143}","username","password")
    || die("can't connect: ".imap_last_error());
$status = imap_setflag_full($mbox,"2,5","\\Seen \\Flagged");
print gettype($status)."\n";
print $status."\n";
imap_close($mbox);
```

imap_sort

Returns an array of message numbers sorted by the given parameters. **$Reverse** is 1 for reverse-sorting.

> *array* **imap_sort**(*int* stream, *int* criteria, *int* reverse, *int* options)

> Criteria can be one (and only one) of the following:

- SORTDATE—message Date
- SORTARRIVAL—arrival date
- SORTFROM—mailbox in first From address
- SORTSUBJECT—message Subject
- SORTTO—mailbox in first To address
- SORTCC—mailbox in first cc address
- SORTSIZE—size of message in octets

> The flags are a bit mask of one or more of the following:

- SE_UID—Return UIDs instead of sequence numbers.
- SE_NOPREFETCH—Don't prefetch searched messages.

imap_status

Returns an object containing status information.

> *object* **imap_status**(*int* imap_stream, *string* mailbox, *int* options)

> Valid flags are as follows:

- SA_MESSAGES—set status->messages to the number of messages in the mailbox.
- SA_RECENT—set status->recent to the number of recent messages in the mailbox.
- SA_UNSEEN—set status->unseen to the number of unseen (new) messages in the mailbox.
- SA_UIDNEXT—set status->uidnext to the next uid to be used in the mailbox.
- SA_UIDVALIDITY—set status->uidvalidity to a constant that changes when uids for the mailbox may no longer be valid.
- SA_ALL—set all of the above.

status->flags is also set, which contains a bit mask that can be checked against any of the above constants.

Example: imap_status()

```
$mbox = imap_open("{your.imap.host}","username","password",OP_HALFOPEN)
    || die("can't connect: ".imap_last_error());
$status = imap_status($mbox,"{your.imap.host}INBOX",SA_ALL);
if($status) {
```

```
    print("Messages:    ". $status->messages   )."<br>\n";
    print("Recent:      ". $status->recent     )."<br>\n";
    print("Unseen:      ". $status->unseen     )."<br>\n";
    print("UIDnext:     ". $status->uidnext    )."<br>\n";
    print("UIDvalidity:". $status->uidvalidity)."<br>\n";
} else
    print "imap_status failed: ".imap_lasterror()."\n";
imap_close($mbox);
```

imap_subscribe

Subscribes to a new mailbox. Returns true on success and false on error.

int **imap_subscribe**(*int* imap_stream, *string* mbox)

imap_uid

Returns the UID for the given message sequence number. An UID is an unique identifier that will not change over time, but a message sequence number may change whenever the content of the mailbox changes. This function is the inverse of **imap_msgno()**.

int **imap_uid**(*int* imap_stream, *int* msgno)

imap_undelete

Removes the deletion flag for a specified message, which is set by **imap_delete()** or **imap_mail_move()**. Returns true on success and false on error.

int **imap_undelete**(*int* imap_stream, *int* msg_number)

imap_unsubscribe

Unsubscribes from a specified mailbox. Returns true on success and false on error.

int **imap_unsubscribe**(*int* imap_stream, *string* mbox)

imap_utf7_decode

Decodes modified UTF-7 $text into 8-bit data. Returns the decoded 8-bit data, or false if the input string was not a valid modified UTF-7. This function is needed to decode mailbox names that contain international characters outside of the printable ASCII range. The modified UTF-7 encoding is defined in RFC 2060 (*http://www.faqs.org/rfcs/rfc2060.html*) , section 5.1.3 [original UTF-7 was defined in RFC1642 (*http://www.faqs.org/rfcs/rfc1642.html*)].

string **imap_utf7_decode**(*string* text)

imap_utf7_encode

Converts 8-bit $data to modified UTF-7 text. This is needed to encode mailbox names that contain international characters outside of the printable ASCII range. The modified UTF-7 encoding is defined in RFC 2060(URL), section 5.1.3 [original UTF-7 was defined in RFC1642(URL)]. Returns the modified UTF-7 text.

string **imap_utf7_encode**(*string* data)

imap_utf8

Converts the given $text to UTF8, as defined in RFC2044(URL).

string **imap_utf8**(*string* text)

implode

Returns a string containing a string representation of all the array elements in the same order, with the glue string between each element. **Note: implode()** can, for historical reasons, accept its parameters in either order. For consistency with **explode()**, however, it may be less confusing to use the documented order of arguments. See also **explode()**, **join()**, and **split()**.

string **implode**(*string* glue, *array* pieces)

Example: Implode()

```
$colon_separated = implode (":", $array);
```

ini_alter

Changes the value of a configuration option. Returns false on failure, and the previous value of the configuration option on success. **Note:** This is an alias of **ini_set()**. See also **ini_get()**, **ini_restore()**, and **ini_set()**.

string **ini_alter**(*string* varname, *string* newvalue)

ini_get

Returns the value of the configuration option on success, false on failure. See also **ini_alter()**, **ini_restore()**, and **ini_set()**.

string **ini_get**(*string* varname)

ini_restore

Restores a given configuration option to its original value. See also **ini_alter()**, **ini_get()**, and **ini_set()**.

string **ini_restore**(*string* varname)

ini_set

Sets the value of the given configuration option. Returns the old value on success, false on failure. See also **ini_alter()**, **ini_get()**, and **ini_restore()**.

string **ini_set**(*string* varname, *string* newvalue)

intval

Returns the integer value of **$var**, using the specified base for the conversion (the default is base 10). **$Var** may be any scalar type. You cannot use **intval()** on arrays or objects. See also **doubleval()**, **strval()**, and **settype()**.

int **intval**(*mixed* var, [*int* base])

in_array

Searches **$haystack** for **$needle**. Returns true if it is found in the array, false otherwise.

bool in_array **in_array**(*mixed* needle, *array* haystack)

Example: In_array()

```
$os = array ("Mac", "NT", "Irix", "Linux");
if (in_array ("Irix", $os))
    print "Got Irix";
```

ip2long

Generates an IPv4 Internet network address from its Internet standard format (dotted string) representation.

int **ip2long**(*string* ip_address)

Example: Ip2long()

```
<?
$ip = gethostbyname("www.php.net");
$out = "The following URLs are equivalent:<br>\n";
$out .= "http://www.php.net/, http://".$ip."/, and http://".ip2long($ip)."/<br>\n";
echo $out;
?>
```

See also **long2ip()**.

iptcparse

Parses a binary IPTC block into its single tags. It returns an array using the tagmarker as an index and the value as the value. It returns false on error or if no IPTC data was found. See **GetImageSize()** for a sample.

array **iptcparse**(*string* iptcblock)

isset

Returns true if **$var** exists; false otherwise. If a variable has been unset with **unset()**, it will no longer be **isset()**.

int **isset**(*mixed* var)

```
$a = "test";
echo isset ($a); // true
unset ($a);
echo isset ($a); // false
```

See also **empty()** and **unset()**.

is_array

Returns true if **$var** is an array, false otherwise. See also **is_double()**, **is_float()**, **is_int()**, **is_integer()**, **is_real()**, **is_string()**, **is_long()**, and **is_object()**.

int **is_array**(*mixed* var)

is_bool

Returns true if the **$var** parameter is a boolean. See also **is_array()**, **is_double()**, **is_float()**, **is_int()**, **is_integer()**, **is_real()**, **is_string()**, **is_long()**, and **is_object()**.

int **is_bool**(*mixed* var)

is_dir

Returns true if the filename exists and is a directory. The results of this function are cached. See **clearstatcache()** for more details. See also **is_file()** and **is_link()**.

bool **is_dir**(*string* filename)

is_double

Returns true if **$var** is a double, false otherwise. See also **is_array()**, **is_bool()**, **is_float()**, **is_int()**, **is_integer()**, **is_real()**, **is_string()**, **is_long()**, and **is_object()**.

int **is_double**(*mixed* var)

is_executable

Returns true if the filename exists and is executable. The results of this function are cached. See **clearstatcache()** for more details. See also **is_file()** and **is_link()**.

bool **is_executable**(*string* filename)

is_file

Returns true if the filename exists and is a regular file. The results of this function are cached. See **clearstatcache()** for more details. See also **is_dir()** and **is_link()**.

bool **is_file**(*string* filename)

is_float

An alias for is_**double()**. See also **is_double()**, **is_bool()**, **is_real()**, **is_int()**, **is_integer()**, **is_string()**, **is_object()**, **is_array()**, and **is_long()**.

int **is_float**(*mixed* var)

is_int

An alias for is_**long()**. See also **is_bool()**, **is_double()**, **is_float()**, **is_integer()**, **is_string()**, **is_real()**, **is_object()**, **is_array()**, and **is_long()**.

int **is_int**(*mixed* var)

is_integer

An alias for **is_long()**. See also **is_bool()**, **is_double()**, **is_float()**, **is_int()**, **is_string()**, **is_real()**, **is_object()**, **is_array()**, and **is_long()**.

int **is_integer**(*mixed* var)

is_link

Returns true if the filename exists and is a symbolic link. The results of this function are cached. See **clearstatcache()** for more details. See also **is_dir()** and **is_file()**. This function does not work on Windows' systems.

bool **is_link**(*string* filename)

is_long

Returns true if **$var** is an integer (long), false otherwise. See also **is_bool()**, **is_double()**, **is_float()**, **is_int()**, **is_real()**, **is_string()**, **is_object()**, **is_array()**, and **is_integer()**.

int **is_long**(*mixed* var)

is_numeric

Returns true if **$var** is a number or a numeric string, false otherwise. See also **is_bool()**, **is_double()**, **is_float()**, **is_int()**, **is_real()**, **is_string()**, **is_object()**, **is_array()**, and **is_integer()**.

int **is_numeric**(*mixed* var)

is_object

Returns true if **$var** is an object, false otherwise. See also **is_bool()**, **is_long()**, **is_int()**, **is_integer()**, **is_float()**, **is_double()**, **is_real()**, **is_string()**, and **is_array()**.

> *int* **is_object**(*mixed* var)

is_readable

Returns true if the filename exists and is readable. Keep in mind that PHP may be accessing the file as the user id that the Web server runs as (often 'nobody'). Safe mode limitations are not taken into account. The results of this function are cached. See **clearstatcache()** for more details. See also **is_writeable()**.

> *bool* **is_readable**(*string* filename)

is_real

An alias for **is_double()**. See also **is_bool()**, **is_long()**, **is_int()**, **is_integer()**, **is_float()**, **is_double()**, **is_object()**, **is_string()**, and **is_array()**.

> *int* **is_real**(*mixed* var)

is_resource

Returns true if the variable given by the **$var** parameter is a resource, otherwise it returns false. Resources are things like file or database result handles that are allocated and freed by internal PHP functions. They may need some cleanup when they are no longer in use but have not been freed by user code.

> *int* **is_resource**(*mixed* var)

is_string

Returns true if **$var** is a string, false otherwise. See also **is_bool()**, **is_long()**, **is_int()**, **is_integer()**, **is_float()**, **is_double()**, **is_real()**, **is_object()**, and **is_array()**.

> *int* **is_string**(*mixed* var)

is_subclass_of

Returns true if the object **$obj**, belongs to a class which is a subclass of **$superclass**, false otherwise. See also **get_class()** and **get_parent_class()**.

> *bool* **is_subclass_of**(*object* obj, *string* superclass)

is_uploaded_file

This function is available only in versions of PHP 3 after PHP 3.0.16 and versions of PHP 4 after 4.0.2. Returns true if the file named by filename was uploaded via HTTP POST. This is useful to help ensure that a malicious user hasn't tried to trick the script into working on files upon which it should not be working, for instance, /etc/passwd. This sort of check is especially important if there is any chance that anything done with uploaded files could reveal their contents to the user, or even to other users on the same system. See also **move_uploaded_file()**.

bool **is_uploaded_file**(*string* filename)

is_writeable

Returns true if the filename exists and is writeable. The filename argument may be a directory name enabling you to check if a directory is writeable. Keep in mind that PHP may be accessing the file as the user id that the Web server runs as (often 'nobody'). Safe mode limitations are not taken into account. The results of this function are cached. See **clearstatcache()** for more details. See also **is_readable()**.

bool **is_writeable**(*string* filename)

JDDayOfWeek

Returns the day of the week. Can return a string or an int depending on the mode.

mixed **JDDayOfWeek**(*int* julianday, *int* mode)

Calendar week modes

Mode	Meaning
0	Returns the day number as an int (0=sunday, 1=monday, and so on).
1	Returns string containing the day of week (English-Gregorian).
2	Returns a string containing the abbreviated day of week (English-Gregorian).

JDMonthName

Returns a string containing a month name. **$mode** tells this function to which calendar to convert the Julian Day Count, and what type of month names are to be returned.

string **JDMonthName**(*int* julianday, *int* mode)

Calendar modes

Mode	Meaning
0	Gregorian - abbreviated
1	Gregorian

Calendar modes (continued)

Mode	Meaning
2	Julian - abbreviated
3	Julian
4	Jewish
5	French Republican

JDToFrench

Converts a Julian Day Count to the French Republican Calendar.

> *string* **JDToFrench**(*int* month, *int* day, *int* year)

JDToGregorian

Converts Julian Day Count to a string containing the Gregorian date in the format of "month/day/year".

> *string* **JDToGregorian**(*int* julianday)

JDToJewish

Converts a Julian Day Count the Jewish Calendar.

> *string* **JDToJewish**(*int* julianday)

JDToJulian

Converts Julian Day Count to a string containing the Julian Calendar Date in the format of "month/day/year".

> *string* **JDToJulian**(*int* julianday)

jdtounix

Returns a UNIX timestamp corresponding to the Julian Day given in jday, or false if jday is not inside the UNIX epoch (Gregorian years between 1970 and 2037 or 2440588 <= jday <= 2465342). See also **jdtounix()**. **Note:** This function is only available in PHP versions after PHP4RC1.

> *int* **jdtounix**(*int* jday)

JewishToJD

Although this software can handle dates all the way back to the year 1 (3761 B.C.), such use may not be meaningful. The Jewish calendar has been in use for several thousand years, but in the early days there was no formula to determine the start of a month. A new month was started when the new moon was first observed.

int **JewishToJD**(*int* month, *int* day, *int* year)

join

An alias to **implode()** and is identical in every way. See also **explode()**, **implode()**, and **split()**.

string **join**(*string* glue, *array* pieces)

JulianToJD

Valid Range for Julian Calendar 4713 B.C. to 9999 A.D. Although this software can handle dates all the way back to 4713 B.C., such use may not be meaningful. The calendar was created in 46 B.C., but the details did not stabilize until at least 8 A.D., and perhaps as late in the 4th century. Also, the beginning of a year varied from one culture to another—not all accepted January as the first month.

int **JulianToJD**(*int* month, *int* day, *int* year)

key

Returns the index element of the current array position. See also **current()** and **next()**.

mixed **key**(array array)

krsort

Sorts an array by key in reverse order, maintaining key to data correlation. This is useful mainly for associative arrays.

int **krsort**(array array, [int sort_flags])

Example: Krsort()

```
$fruits = array ("d"=>"lemon", "a"=>"orange", "b"=>"banana", "c"=>"apple");
krsort ($fruits);
reset ($fruits);
while (list ($key, $val) = each ($fruits)) {
    echo "$key -> $val\n";
}
This example would display:
fruits[d] = lemon
fruits[c] = apple
fruits[b] = banana
fruits[a] = orange
```

You may modify the behavior of the sort using the optional parameter **$sort_flags**, see **sort()**for details. See also **asort()**, **arsort()**, **ksort()** **sort()**, **natsort()**, and **rsort()**.

ksort

Sorts an array by key, maintaining key to data correlation. This is useful mainly for associative arrays.

> int **ksort**(array array, [int sort_flags])

> **Example: Ksort()**

```
$fruits = array ("d"=>"lemon", "a"=>"orange", "b"=>"banana", "c"=>"apple");
ksort ($fruits);
reset ($fruits);
while (list ($key, $val) = each ($fruits)) {
    echo "$key -> $val\n";
}
This example would display:
fruits[a] = orange
fruits[b] = banana
fruits[c] = apple
fruits[d] = lemon
```

You may modify the behavior of the sort using the optional parameter **$sort_flags**, for details see **sort()**. See also **asort()**, **arsort()**, **sort()**, **natsort()**, and **rsort()**.

lcg_value

Returns a pseudo random number in the range of (0, 1). The function combines two CGs with periods of $2^{31} - 85$ and $2^{31} - 249$. The period of this function is equal to the product of both primes.

> double **lcg_value**(void)

ldap_add

Returns true on success and false on error. The **ldap_add()** function is used to add entries in the LDAP directory. The DN of the entry to be added is specified by dn. Array entries specify the information about the entry. The values in the entries are indexed by individual attributes. In case of multiple values for an attribute, they are indexed using integers starting with 0. entry["attribute1"] = value entry["attribute2"][0] = value1 entry["attribute2"][1] = value2.

> int **ldap_add**(int link_identifier, string dn, array entry)

> **Example: Complete example with authenticated bind**

```php
<?php
$ds=ldap_connect("localhost");  // assuming the LDAP server is on this host
if ($ds) {
    // bind with appropriate dn to give update access
    $r=ldap_bind($ds,"cn=root, o=My Company, c=US", "secret");
    // prepare data
    $info["cn"]="John Jones";
    $info["sn"]="Jones";
    $info["mail"]="jonj@here.and.now";
    $info["objectclass"]="person";
    // add data to directory
```

```
        $r=ldap_add($ds, "cn=John Jones, o=My Company, c=US", $info);
        ldap_close($ds);
    } else {
        echo "Unable to connect to LDAP server";
    }
    ?>
```

ldap_bind

Binds to the LDAP directory with specified RDN and password. Returns true on success and false on error. **ldap_bind()** does a bind operation on the directory. bind_rdn and bind_password are optional. If not specified, anonymous bind is attempted.

int **ldap_bind**(int link_identifier, [string bind_rdn], [string bind_password])

ldap_close

Returns true on success, false on error. **ldap_close()** closes the link to the LDAP server that's associated with the specified **$link_identifier**. This call is internally identical to **ldap_unbind()**. The LDAP API uses the call **ldap_unbind()**, so perhaps you should use this in preference to **ldap_close()**.

int **ldap_close**(int link_identifier)

ldap_compare

Returns true if **$value** matches, otherwise returns false. Returns -1 on error. **ldap_compare()** is used to compare **$value** of **$attribute** to value of same attribute in LDAP directory entry specified with **$dn** . The following example demonstrates how to check whether or not a given password matches the one defined in DN specified entry.

int **ldap_compare**(int link_identifier, string dn, string attribute, string value)

Example: Complete example of password check

```php
<?php
$ds=ldap_connect("localhost");  // assuming the LDAP server is on this host
if ($ds) {
    // bind
    if(ldap_bind($ds)) {
        // prepare data
        $dn = "cn=Matti Meikku, ou=My Unit, o=My Company, c=FI";
        $value = "secretpassword";
        $attr = "password";
        // compare value
        $r=ldap_compare($ds, $dn, $attr, $value);
        if ($r === -1) {
            echo "Error: ".ldap_error($ds);
        } elseif ($r === TRUE) {
            echo "Password correct.";
        } elseif ($r === FALSE) {
            echo "Wrong guess! Password incorrect.";
        }
```

```
    } else {
        echo "Unable to bind to LDAP server.";
    }
    ldap_close($ds);
} else {
    echo "Unable to connect to LDAP server.";
}
?>
```

Note: ldap_compare() cannot be used to compare BINARY values! This function was added in 4.0.2.

ldap_connect

Returns a positive LDAP link identifier on success, false on error. **ldap_connect()** establishes a connection to a LDAP server on a specified **$hostname** and **$port**. Both arguments are optional. If no arguments are specified, then the link identifier of the already opened link will be returned. If only $hostname is specified, then the port defaults to 389.

> int **ldap_connect**([string hostname], [int port])

ldap_count_entries

Returns number of entries in the result or false on error. **ldap_count_entries()** returns the number of entries stored in the result of previous search operations. **$result_identifier** identifies the internal ldap result.

> int **ldap_count_entries**(int link_identifier, int result_identifier)

ldap_delete

Returns true on success and false on error. **ldap_delete()** function deletes a particular entry in LDAP directory specified by dn.

> int **ldap_delete**(int link_identifier, string dn)

ldap_dn2ufn

Used to turn a DN into a more user-friendly form, stripping off type names.

> string **ldap_dn2ufn**(string dn)

ldap_err2str

Returns string error message. This function returns the string error message explaining the error number errno. Although LDAP errno numbers are standardized, different libraries return different or even localized textual error messages. Never check for a specific error message text, but always use an error number to check. See also **ldap_errno()** and **ldap_error()**.

> string **ldap_err2str**(int errno)

Example: Enumerating all LDAP error messages

```
<?php
  for($i=0; $i<100; $i++) {
    printf("Error $i: %s<br>\n", ldap_err2str($i));
  }
?>
```

ldap_errno

Returns the LDAP error number of the last LDAP command for this link. This function returns the standardized error number returned by the last LDAP command for the given link identifier. This number can be converted into a textual error message using **ldap_err2str()**. Unless you lower your warning level in your php3.ini sufficiently or prefix your LDAP commands with @ (at) characters to suppress warning output, the errors generated will also show up in your HTML output.

int **ldap_errno**(int link_id)

Example: Generating and catching an error

```
<?php
// This example contains an error, which we will catch.
$ld = ldap_connect("localhost");
$bind = ldap_bind($ld);
// syntax error in filter expression (errno 87),
// must be "objectclass=*" to work.
$res =  @ldap_search($ld, "o=Myorg, c=DE", "objectclass");
if (!$res) {
    printf("LDAP-Errno: %s<br>\n", ldap_errno($ld));
    printf("LDAP-Error: %s<br>\n", ldap_error($ld));
    die("Argh!<br>\n");
}
$info = ldap_get_entries($ld, $res);
printf("%d matching entries.<br>\n", $info["count"]);
?>
```

See also **ldap_err2str()** and **ldap_error()**.

ldap_error

Returns string error messages. This function returns the string error message explaining the error generated by the last LDAP command for the given link identifier. Although LDAP errno numbers are standardized, different libraries return different or even localized textual error messages. Never check for a specific error message text, but always use an error number to check. Unless you lower your warning level in your php3.ini sufficiently or prefix your LDAP commands with @ (at) characters to suppress warning output, the errors generated will also show up in your HTML output. See also **ldap_err2str()** and **ldap_errno()**.

string **ldap_error**(int link_id)

ldap_explode_dn

Used to split the DN returned by **ldap_get_dn()** and breaks it up into its component parts. Each part is known as *Relative Distinguished Name* (RDN). **ldap_explode_dn()** returns an array of all those components. **$with_attrib** is used to request if the RDNs are returned with only values or their attributes as well. To get RDNs with the attributes (that is, in attribute=value format) set **$with_attrib** to 0. To get only values, set it to 1.

array **ldap_explode_dn**(string dn, int with_attrib)

ldap_first_attribute

Returns the first attribute in the entry on success and false on error. Similar to reading entries, attributes are also read one by one from a particular entry. **ldap_first_attribute()** returns the first attribute in the entry pointed by the entry identifier. Remaining attributes are retrieved by calling **ldap_next_attribute()** successively. **$ber_identifier** is the identifier to internal memory location pointer. It is passed by reference. The same **$ber_identifier** is passed to the **ldap_next_attribute()** function, which modifies that pointer. See also **ldap_get_attributes()**.

string **ldap_first_attribute**(int link_identifier, int result_entry_identifier, int ber_identifier)

ldap_first_entry

Returns the result entry identifier for the first entry on success and false on error. Entries in the LDAP result are read sequentially using the **ldap_first_entry()** and **ldap_next_entry()** functions. **ldap_first_entry()** returns the entry identifier for first entry in the result. This entry identifier is then supplied to **lap_next_entry()** routine to get successive entries from the result. See also **ldap_get_entries()**.

int **ldap_first_entry**(int link_identifier, int result_identifier)

ldap_free_result

Returns true on success and false on error. **ldap_free_result()** frees up the memory allocated internally to store the result and pointed by the **$result_identifier**. All result memory will be automatically freed when the script terminates. Typically, all the memory allocated for the ldap result gets freed at the end of the script. In case the script is making successive searches that return large result sets, **ldap_free_result()** could be called to keep the runtime memory usage by the script low.

int **ldap_free_result**(int result_identifier)

ldap_get_attributes

Returns complete entry information in a multi-dimensional array on success and false on error. **ldap_get_attributes()** function is used to simplify reading the attributes and values from an entry in the search result. The return value is a multi-dimensional array of attributes and values. Having located a specific entry in the directory, you can find out what information is held for that entry by using this call. You would use this call for an application that "browses" directory entries and/or where you do not know the structure of the directory entries. In many applications, you will be searching for a specific attribute, such as an email address or a surname, and will not care what other data is held. The structure of the array is as follows: return_value["count"] =

number of attributes in the entry return_value[0] = first attribute return_value[n] = nth attribute return_value["attribute"]["count"] = number of values for attribute return_value["attribute"][0] = first value of the attribute return_value["attribute"][i] = ith value of the attribute.

> array **ldap_get_attributes**(int link_identifier, int result_entry_identifier)

Example: Show the list of attributes held for a particular directory **entry**.

```
// $ds is the link identifier for the directory
// $sr is a valid search result from a prior call to
// one of the ldap directory search calls
$entry = ldap_first_entry($ds, $sr);
$attrs = ldap_get_attributes($ds, $entry);
echo $attrs["count"]." attributes held for this entry:<p>";
for ($i=0; $i<$attrs["count"]; $i++)
    echo $attrs[$i]."<br>";
```

See also **ldap_first_attribute()** and **ldap_next_attribute()**.

ldap_get_dn

Returns the DN of the result entry and false on error. **ldap_get_dn()** function is used to find out the DN of an entry in the result.

> string **ldap_get_dn**(int link_identifier, int result_entry_identifier)

ldap_get_entries

Returns complete result information in a multi-dimensional array on success and false on error. **ldap_get_entries()** function is used to simplify reading multiple entries from the result and then reading the attributes and multiple values. The entire information is returned by one function call in a multi-dimensional array.

The structure of the array is as follows. The attribute index is converted to lowercase. (Attributes are case-insensitive for directory servers, but not when used as array indices) return_value["count"] = number of entries in the result return_value[0] : refers to the details of first entry return_value[i]["dn"] = DN of the ith entry in the result return_value[i]["count"] = number of attributes in ith entry return_value[i][j] = jth attribute in the ith entry in the result return_value[i]["attribute"]["count"] = number of values for attribute in ith entry return_value[i]["attribute"][j] = jth value of attribute in ith entry. See also **ldap_first_entry()** and **ldap_next_entry()**.

> array **ldap_get_entries**(int link_identifier, int result_identifier)

ldap_get_values

Returns an array of values for the attribute on success and false on error. **ldap_get_values()** function is used to read all the values of the attribute in the entry in the result. entry is specified by the **$result_entry_identifier**. The number of values can be found by indexing "count" in the resultant array. Individual values are accessed by integer index in the array. The first index is 0.

This call needs a **$result_entry_identifier**, so it needs to be preceded by one of the ldap search calls and one of the calls to get an individual entry. Your application will be either hard coded to look for certain attributes (such as "surname" or "mail") or you will have to use the **ldap_get_attributes()** call to work out what attributes exist for a given entry. LDAP allows more than one entry for an attribute, so it can, for example, store a number of email addresses for one person's directory entry,labeled with the attribute "mail" return_value["count"] = number of values for attribute return_value[0] = first value of attribute return_value[i] = ith value of attribute.

array **ldap_get_values**(int link_identifier, int result_entry_identifier, string attribute)

Example: List all values of the "mail" attribute for a **directory entry**.

```
// $ds is a valid link identifier for a directory server
// $sr is a valid search result from a prior call to
//      one of the ldap directory search calls
// $entry is a valid entry identifier from a prior call to
//         one of the calls that returns a directory entry
$values = ldap_get_values($ds, $entry,"mail");

echo $values["count"]." email addresses for this entry.<p>";
for ($i=0; $i < $values["count"]; $i++)
    echo $values[$i]."<br>";
```

ldap_get_values_len

Returns an array of values for the attribute on success and false on error. **ldap_get_values_len()** function is used to read all the values of the attribute in the entry in the result. entry is specified by the **$result_entry_identifier**. The number of values can be found by indexing "count" in the resultant array. Individual values are accessed by integer index in the array. The first index is 0. This function is used exactly like **ldap_get_values()** except that it handles binary data and not string data. **Note:** This function was added in 4.0.

array **ldap_get_values_len**(int link_identifier, int result_entry_identifier, string attribute)

ldap_list

Returns a search result identifier or false on error. **ldap_list()** performs the search for a specified filter on the directory with the scope LDAP_SCOPE_ONELEVEL. LDAP_SCOPE_ONELEVEL means that the search should only return information that is at the level immediately following the base dn given in the call. (Equivalent to typing "ls" and getting a list of files and folders in the current working directory.) This call takes 5 optional parameters. See **ldap_search()** notes. **Note:** These optional parameters were added in 4.0.2: **$attrsonly**, **$sizelimit**, **$timelimit**, and **$deref**.

int **ldap_list**(int link_identifier, string base_dn, string filter, [array attributes], [int attrsonly], [int sizelimit], [int timelimit], [int deref])

Example: Produce a list of all organizational units of an organization

```
// $ds is a valid link identifier for a directory server
$basedn = "o=My Company, c=US";
$justthese = array("ou");
$sr=ldap_list($ds, $basedn, "ou=*", $justthese);
$info = ldap_get_entries($ds, $sr);
for ($i=0; $i<$info["count"]; $i++)
    echo $info[$i]["ou"][0] ;
```

ldap_modify

Returns true on success and false on error. **ldap_modify()** function is used to modify the existing entries in the LDAP directory. The structure of the entry is same as in **ldap_add()**.

int **ldap_modify**(int link_identifier, string dn, array entry)

ldap_mod_add

Returns true on success and false on error. This function adds attribute(s) to the specified dn. It performs the modification at the attribute level as opposed to the object level. Object-level additions are done by the **ldap_add()** function.

int **ldap_mod_add**(int link_identifier, string dn, array entry)

ldap_mod_del

Returns true on success and false on error. This function removes attribute(s) from the specified dn. It performs the modification at the attribute level as opposed to the object level. Object-level deletions are done by the **ldap_del()** function.

int **ldap_mod_del**(int link_identifier, string dn, array entry)

ldap_mod_replace

Returns true on success and false on error. This function replaces attribute(s) from the specified dn. It performs the modification at the attribute level as opposed to the object level. Object-level modifications are done by the **ldap_modify()** function.

int **ldap_mod_replace**(int link_identifier, string dn, array entry)

ldap_next_attribute

Returns the next attribute in an entry on success and false on error. **ldap_next_attribute()** is called to retrieve the attributes in an entry. The internal state of the pointer is maintained by the **$ber_identifier**. It is passed by reference to the function. The first call to **ldap_next_attribute()** is made with the **$result_entry_identifier** returned from **ldap_first_attribute()**. See also **ldap_get_attributes()**.

string **ldap_next_attribute**(int link_identifier, int result_entry_identifier, int ber_identifier)

ldap_next_entry

Returns entry identifier for the next entry in the result whose entries are being read starting with **ldap_first_entry()**. If no more entries exist in the result, then it returns false. **ldap_next_entry()** function is used to retrieve the entries stored in the result. Successive calls to the **ldap_next_entry()** return entries one by one until no more entries are left. The first call to **ldap_next_entry()** is made after the call to **ldap_first_entry()** with the result_identifier as returned from the **ldap_first_entry()**. See also **ldap_get_entries()**.

int **ldap_next_entry**(int link_identifier, int result_entry_identifier)

ldap_read

Returns a search result identifier or false on error. **ldap_read()** performs the search for a specified filter on the directory with the scope LDAP_SCOPE_BASE, so it is equivalent to reading an entry from the directory. An empty filter is not allowed. If you want to retrieve absolutely all information for this entry, use a filter of "objectClass=*". If you know which entry types are used on the directory server, you might use an appropriate filter such as "objectClass=inetOrgPerson". This call takes five optional parameters. See **ldap_search()** notes. **Note:** These optional parameters were added in 4.0.2: **$attrsonly**, **$sizelimit**, **$timelimit**, and **$deref**.

int **ldap_read**(int link_identifier, string base_dn, string filter, [array attributes], [int attrsonly], [int sizelimit], [int timelimit], [int deref]

ldap_search

Returns a search result identifier or false on error. **ldap_search()** performs the search for a specified filter on the directory with the scope of LDAP_SCOPE_SUBTREE. This is equivalent to searching the entire directory. **$base_dn** specifies the base DN for the directory. An optional fourth parameter is available that can be added to restrict the attributes and values returned by the server to just those required. This is much more efficient than the default action, which is to return all attributes and their associated values. The use of the fourth parameter should therefore be considered good practice. The fourth parameter is a standard PHP string array of the required attributes, for example, array("mail","sn","cn").

Note: The dn is always returned irrespective of which attribute types are requested. Note also that some directory server hosts will be configured to return no more than a preset number of entries. If this occurs, the server will indicate that it has only returned a partial results set. This occurs also if the sixth parameter **$sizelimit** has been used to limit the count of fetched entries.

int **ldap_search**(int link_identifier, string base_dn, string filter, [array attributes], [int attrsonly], [int sizelimit], [int timelimit], [int deref])

The fifth parameter **$attrsonly** should be set to 1 if only attribute types are wanted. If set to 0, both attributes types and attribute values are fetched, which is the default behavior. With the sixth parameter **$sizelimit,** it is possible to limit the count of entries fetched. Setting this to 0 means no limit. **Note:** This parameter cannot override server-side preset sizelimit, however, you can set it lower. The seventh parameter **$timelimit** sets the number of seconds spent on the search. Setting this to 0 means no limit.

Note: This parameter cannot override server-side preset timelimit, however, you can set it lower. The eighth parameter **$deref** specifies how aliases should be handled during the search. It can be one of the following:

- LDAP_DEREF_NEVER—(Default) Aliases are never dereferenced.
- LDAP_DEREF_SEARCHING—Aliases should be dereferenced during the search but not when locating the base object of the search.
- LDAP_DEREF_FINDING—Aliases should be dereferenced when locating the base object but not during the search.
- LDAP_DEREF_ALWAYS—Aliases should be dereferenced always.

These optional parameters were added in 4.0.2: **$attrsonly**, **$sizelimit**, **$timelimit**, and **$deref**. The search filter can be simple or advanced, using boolean operators in the format described in the LDAP documentation (see the Netscape Directory SDK *(http: //developer.netscape.com/docs/manuals/directory/41/ag/find.htm)* for full information on filters). The example below retrieves the organizational unit, surname, given name, and email address for all people in "My Company" where the surname or given name contains the substring $person. This example uses a boolean filter to tell the server to look for information in more than one attribute.

Example: LDAP search

```
// $ds is a valid link identifier for a directory server
// $person is all or part of a person's name, e.g. "Jo"
$dn = "o=My Company, c=US";
$filter="(|(sn=$person*)(givenname=$person*))";
$justthese = array( "ou", "sn", "givenname", "mail");
$sr=ldap_search($ds, $dn, $filter, $justthese);
$info = ldap_get_entries($ds, $sr);
print $info["count"]." entries returned<p>";
```

ldap_unbind

Returns true on success and false on error. **ldap_unbind()** function unbinds from the LDAP directory.

int **ldap_unbind**(int link_identifier)

leak

Leaks the specified amount of memory. This is useful when debugging the memory manager, which automatically cleans up "leaked" memory when each request is completed.

void **leak**(int bytes)

levenshtein

Returns the Levenshtein-Distance between the two argument strings or -1, if one of the argument strings is longer than the limit of 255 characters (255 should be more than enough for name or dictionary comparison, and nobody serious would be doing genetic analysis with PHP). The Levenshtein distance is defined as the minimum number of characters you have to replace, insert, or delete to transform **$str1** into **$str2**. The complexity of the algorithm is O(m*n), where n and m are the lengths of **$str1** and **$str2** (rather good when compared to **similar_text()**, which is O(max(n,m)**3), but still expensive).

> int *levenshtein* (string *str1*, string *str2*)
> int **levenshtein** (string str1, string str2, int cost_ins, int cost_rep, int cost_del)
> int *levenshtein* (string *str1*, string *str2*, function *cost*)

In its simplest form, the function will take only the two strings as parameter and will calculate just the number of insert, replace, and delete operations needed to transform **$str1** into **$str2**. A second variant will take three additional parameters that define the cost of insert, replace, and delete operations. This is more general and adaptive than variant one, but not as efficient. The third variant (which is not implemented yet) will be the most general and adaptive but also the slowest alternative. It will call a user-supplied function that will determine the cost for every possible operation. The user-supplied function will be called with the following arguments:

- operation to apply: 'I', 'R', or 'D'
- actual character in string 1
- actual character in string 2
- position in string 1
- position in string 2
- remaining characters in string 1
- remaining characters in string 2

The user-supplied function has to return a positive integer describing the cost for this particular operation, but it may decide to use only some of the supplied arguments. The user-supplied function approach offers the possibility to take into account the relevance of and/or difference between certain symbols (characters) or even the context those symbols to determine the cost of insert, replace, and delete operations; however, this function performs this operation at the cost of loosing all optimizations done regarding CPU register utilization and cache misses that have been worked into the other two variants. See also **soundex()**, **similar_text()** and **metaphone()**.

link

Creates a hard link. See also the **symlink()** to create soft links, as well as **readlink()** along with **linkinfo()**.

Note: This function does not work on Windows' systems.

> int **link**(string target, string link)

linkinfo

Returns the st_dev field of the UNIX C stat structure returned by the lstat system call. This function is used to verify if a link (pointed to by **$path**) really exists (using the same method as the

S_ISLNK macro defined in stat.h). Returns 0 or false in case of error. See also **symlink**(), **link**(), and **readlink**().

Note: This function does not work on Windows' systems.

int **linkinfo**(string path)

list

Like **array**(), this is not really a function, but a language construct. **list**() is used to assign a list of variables in one operation.

void **list**(void)

Example: List()

```
<table>
 <tr>
  <th>Employee name</th>
  <th>Salary</th>
 </tr>
<?php
$result = mysql ($conn, "SELECT id, name, salary FROM employees");
while (list ($id, $name, $salary) = mysql_fetch_row ($result)) {
    print (" <tr>\n".
           "  <td><a href=\"info.php3?id=$id\">$name</a></td>\n".
           "  <td>$salary</td>\n".
           " </tr>\n");
}
?>
</table>
```

See also **each**() and **array**().

listen

After the socket **$socket** has been created using **socket**() and bound to a name with **bind**(), it may be told to listen for incoming connections on **$socket**. A maximum of **$backlog** incoming connections will be queued for processing. **listen**() is applicable only to sockets with type SOCK_STREAM or SOCK_SEQPACKET. Returns zero on success, or a negative error code on failure. This code may be passed to **strerror**() to get a textual explanation of the error. See also **accept_connect**(), **bind**(), **connect**(), **socket**(), **socket_get_status**(), and **strerror**().

int **listen**(int socket, int backlog)

localtime

Returns an array identical to that of the structure returned by the C function call. The first argument to **localtime**() is the timestamp. If this is not given, the current time is used. The second argument to the **localtime**() is the **$is_associative**. If this is set to 0 or not supplied, then the array is returned as a regular, numerically indexed array. If the argument is set to 1, then **localtime**() is an associative array containing all the different elements of the structure returned by the C function call to localtime.

array **localtime**([int timestamp], [bool is_associative])

The names of the different keys of the associative array are as follows:

- "tm_sec"—seconds
- "tm_min"—minutes
- "tm_hour"—hour
- "tm_mday"—day of the month
- "tm_mon"—month of the year
- "tm_year"—year, not y2k compliant
- "tm_wday"—day of the week
- "tm_yday"—day of the year
- "tm_isdst"—is daylight savings time in effect

log

Returns the natural logarithm of **arg**.

float **log**(float arg)

log10

Returns the base-10 logarithm of **$arg**.

float **log10**(float arg)

long2ip

Generates an Internet address in dotted format (that is, aaa.bbb.ccc.ddd) from the proper address representation. See also **ip2long()**.

string **long2ip**(int proper_address)

lstat

Gathers the statistics of the file or symbolic link named by filename. This function is identical to the **stat()** function except that if the **$filename** parameter is a symbolic link, the status of the symbolic link is returned, not the status of the file pointed to by the symbolic link.

array **lstat**(string filename)

Returns an array with the statistics of the file with the following elements:

device	inode	inode protection mode
number of links	user id of owner	group id owner
device type if inode device *	size in bytes	time of last access

time of last modification	time of last change	blocksize for filesystem I/O *
number of blocks allocated		

*Only valid on systems supporting the st_blksize type—other systems (such as Windows) return -1. The results of this function are cached. See **clearstatcache()** for more details.

ltrim

Strips whitespace from the start of a string and returns the stripped string. The whitespace characters it currently strips are "\n", "\r", "\t", "\v", "\0", and a plain space. See also **chop()**, **rtrim()**, and **trim()**.

    string **ltrim**(string str)

mail

Automatically mails the message specified in **$message** to the receiver specified in **$to**. Multiple recipients can be specified by putting a comma between each address in **$to**.

    bool **mail**(*string* to, *string* subject, *string* message, [*string* additional_headers])

Example: Sending mail.

```
mail("rasmus@lerdorf.on.ca", "My Subject", "Line 1\nLine
2\nLine 3");
```

If a fourth string argument is passed, this string is inserted at the end of the header. This is typically used to add extra headers. Multiple extra headers are separated with a newline.

Example: Sending mail with extra headers.

```
mail("nobody@aol.com", "the subject", $message,
    "From: webmaster@$SERVER_NAME\nReply-To: webmaster@$SERVER_NAME\nX-Mailer: PHP/" .
phpversion());
```

You can also use fairly simple string building techniques to build complex email messages.
Example: Sending complex email.

```
/* recipients */
$recipient .= "Mary <mary@u.college.edu>" . ", " ; //note the comma
$recipient .= "Kelly <kelly@u.college.edu> . ", ";
$recipient .= "ronabop@php.net";
/* subject */
$subject = "Birthday Reminders for August";
/* message */
$message .= "The following email includes a formatted ASCII table\n";
$message .= "Day \t\tMonth \t\tYear\n";
$message .= "3rd \t\tAug \t\t1970\n";
$message .= "17rd\t\tAug \t\t1973\n";
/* you can add a stock signature */
$message .= "--\r\n"; //Signature delimiter
$message .= "Birthday reminder copylefted by public domain";
/* additional header pieces for errors, From cc's, bcc's, etc */
```

```
$headers .= "From: Birthday Reminder <birthday@php.net>\n";
$headers .= "X-Sender: <birthday@php.net>\n";
$headers .= "X-Mailer: PHP\n"; // mailer
$headers .= "X-Priority: 1\n"; // Urgent message!
$headers .= "Return-Path: <birthday@php.net>\n";  // Return path for errors
$headers .= "Content-Type: text/html; charset=iso-8859-1\n" // Mime type
$headers .= "cc:birthdayarchive@php.net\n"; // CC to
$headers .= "bcc:birthdaycheck@php.net, birthdaygifts@php.net\n"; // BCCs to
/* and now mail it */
mail($recipient, $subject, $message, $headers);
```

max

Returns the numerically highest parameter value. If the first parameter is an array, **max()** returns the highest value in that array. If the first parameter is an integer, string or double, you need at least two parameters, and **max()** returns the biggest of these values. You can compare an unlimited number of values. If one or more of the values is a double, all the values will be treated as doubles, and a double is returned. If none of the values is a double, all of them will be treated as integers, and an integer is returned.

> *mixed* **max**(*mixed* arg1, *mixed* arg2, *mixed* argn)

mcal_append_event

Stores the global event into an MCAL calendar for the given stream. Returns the id of the newly inserted event.

> *int* **mcal_append_event**(*int* mcal_stream)

mcal_close

Closes the given mcal stream.

> *int* **mcal_close**(*int* mcal_stream, *int* flags)

mcal_create_calendar

Creates a new calendar named **$calendar**.

> *int* **mcal_create_calendar**(*string* calendar)

mcal_date_compare

Compares the two given dates. Returns <0, 0, >0 if a<b, a==b, a>b, respectively.

> *int* **mcal_date_compare**(*int* a_year, *int* a_month, *int* a_day, *int* b_year, *int* b_month, *int* b_day)

mcal_date_valid

Returns true if the given year, month, and day is a valid date, false if not.

> *int* **mcal_date_valid**(*int* year, *int* month, *int* day)

mcal_days_in_month

Returns the number of days in the given month, taking into account if the given year is a leap year or not.

int **mcal_days_in_month**(*int* month, *int* leap year)

mcal_day_of_week

Returns the day of the week of the given date.

int **mcal_day_of_week**(*int* year, *int* month, *int* day)

mcal_day_of_year

Returns the day of the year of the given date.

int **mcal_day_of_year**(*int* year, *int* month, *int* day)

mcal_delete_calendar

Deletes the calendar named **$calendar**.

int **mcal_delete_calendar**(*string* calendar)

mcal_delete_event

Deletes the calendar event specified by the event_id. Returns true.

int **mcal_delete_event**(*int* mcal_stream, [*int* event_id])

mcal_event_add_attribute

Adds an attribute to the stream's global event structure with the value given by "value."

void **mcal_event_add_attribute**(*int* stream, *string* attribute, *string* value)

mcal_event_init

Initializes a stream's global event structure. This effectively sets all elements of the structure to 0, or the default settings. Returns true.

int **mcal_event_init**(*int* stream)

mcal_event_set_alarm

Sets the streams global event structure's alarm to the given minutes before the event. Returns true.

int **mcal_event_set_alarm**(*int* stream, *int* alarm)

mcal_event_set_category

Sets the streams global event structure's category to the given string. Returns true.

   int **mcal_event_set_category**(*int* stream, *string* category)

mcal_event_set_class

Sets the streams global event structure's class to the given value. The class is either 1 for public, or 0 for private. Returns true.

   int **mcal_event_set_class**(*int* stream, *int* class)

mcal_event_set_description

Sets the streams global event structure's description to the given string. Returns true.

   int **mcal_event_set_description**(*int* stream, *string* description)

mcal_event_set_end

Sets the streams global event structure's end date and time to the given values. Returns true.

   int **mcal_event_set_end**(*int* stream, *int* year, *int* month, [*int* day], [*int* hour], [*int* min], [*int* sec])

mcal_event_set_recur_daily

Sets the streams global event structure's recurrence to the given value to be recurring on a daily basis, ending at the given date.

   int **mcal_event_set_recur_daily**(*int* stream, *int* year, *int* month, *int* day, *int* interval)

mcal_event_set_recur_monthly_mday

Sets the streams global event structure's recurrence to the given value to be recurring on a monthly by month day basis, ending at the given date.

   int **mcal_event_set_recur_monthly_mday**(*int* stream, *int* year, *int* month, *int* day, *int* interval)

mcal_event_set_recur_monthly_wday

Sets the streams global event structure's recurrence to the given value to be recurring on a monthly by week basis, ending at the given date.

   int **mcal_event_set_recur_monthly_wday**(*int* stream, *int* year, *int* month, *int* day, *int* interval)

mcal_event_set_recur_none

Sets the streams global event structure to not recur (event->recur_type is set to MCAL_RECUR_NONE).

   int **mcal_event_set_recur_none**(*int* stream)

mcal_event_set_recur_weekly

Sets the streams global event structure's recurrence to the given value to be recurring on a weekly basis, ending at the given date.

int **mcal_event_set_recur_weekly**(*int* stream, *int* year, *int* month, *int* day, *int* interval, *int* weekdays)

mcal_event_set_recur_yearly

Sets the streams global event structure's recurrence to the given value to be recurring on a yearly basis, ending at the given date.

int **mcal_event_set_recur_yearly**(*int* stream, *int* year, *int* month, *int* day, *int* interval)

mcal_event_set_start

Sets the streams global event structure's start date and time to the given values. Returns true.

int **mcal_event_set_start**(*int* stream, *int* year, *int* month, [*int* day], [*int* hour], [*int* min], [*int* sec])

mcal_event_set_title

Sets the streams global event structure's title to the given string. Returns true.

int **mcal_event_set_title**(*int* stream, *string* title)

mcal_expunge

Deletes all events which have been previously marked for deletion.

int **mcal_expunge**(*int* stream)

mcal_fetch_current_stream_event

int mcal_fetch_current_stream_event(*int* stream)

Returns the current stream's event structure as an object containing the following:

- int id—ID of that event.
- int public   True if the event if public, false if it is private.
- string category   Category string of the event.
- string title   Title string of the event.
- string description   Description string of the event.
- int alarm   Number of minutes before the event to send an alarm/reminder.
- object start   Object containing a datetime entry.
- object end   Object containing a datetime entry.

- int recur_type   Recurrence type.
- int recur_interval   Recurrence interval.
- datetime recur_enddate   Recurrence end date.
- int recur_data   Recurrence data.

  All datetime entries consist of an object that contains the following:

- int year—year
- int month—month
- int mday—day of month
- int hour—hour
- int min—minutes
- int sec—seconds
- int alarm—minutes before event to send an alarm

mcal_fetch_event

Fetches an event from the calendar stream specified by $id.

> *object* **mcal_fetch_event**(*int* mcal_stream, *int* event_id, [*int* options])

Returns an event object consisting of the following:

- int id—ID of that event.
- int public—True if the event if public, false if it is private.
- string category—Category string of the event.
- string title—Title string of the event.
- string description—Description string of the event.
- int alarm—Number of minutes before the event to send an alarm/reminder.
- object start—Object containing a datetime entry.
- object end—Object containing a datetime entry.
- int recur_type—Recurrence type.
- int recur_interval—Recurrence interval.
- datetime recur_enddate—Recurrence end date.
- int recur_data—Recurrence data.

  All datetime entries consist of an object that contains the following:

- int year—year
- int month—month

- int mday—day of month
- int hour—hour
- int min—minutes
- int sec—seconds
- int alarm—minutes before event to send an alarm

mcal_is_leap_year

Returns 1 if the given year is a leap year, 0 if not.

> *int* **mcal_is_leap_year**(*int* year)

mcal_list_alarms

Returns an array of event id's that has an alarm going off between the start and end dates, or if just a stream is given, uses the start and end dates in the global event structure. **mcal_list_events()** function takes in an optional beginning date and an end date for a calendar stream. An array of event ids that are between the given dates or the internal event dates are returned.

> *array* **mcal_list_alarms**(*int* mcal_stream, [*int* begin_year], [*int* begin_month], [*int* begin_day], [*int* end_year], [*int* end_month], [*int* end_day])

mcal_list_events

Returns an array of id's that are between the start and end dates, or if just a stream is given, uses the start and end dates in the global event structure. **mcal_list_events()** function takes in a beginning date and an optional end date for a calendar stream. An array of event id's that are between the given dates or the internal event dates are returned.

> *array* **mcal_list_events**(*int* mcal_stream, *object* begin_date, [*object* end_date])

mcal_next_recurrence

Returns an object filled with the next date the event occurs, on or after the supplied date. Returns empty date field if event does not occur or something is invalid. Uses weekstart to determine what day is considered the beginning of the week.

> *int* **mcal_next_recurrence**(*int* stream, *int* weekstart, *array* next)

mcal_open

Returns an MCAL stream on success, false on error. **mcal_open()** opens up an MCAL connection to the specified $calendar store. If the optional **$options** is specified, this function passes the **$options** to that mailbox also. The streams internal event structure is also initialized upon connection.

> *int* **mcal_open**(*string* calendar, *string* username, *string* password, *int* options)

mcal_popen

Returns an MCAL stream on success, false on error. **mcal_popen()** opens up an MCAL connection to the specified **$calendar** store. If the optional **$options** is specified, this function passes the **$options** to that mailbox also. The streams internal event structure is also initialized upon connection.

int **mcal_popen**(*string* calendar, *string* username, *string* password, *int* options)

mcal_rename_calendar

Renames the calendar **$old_name** to **$new_name**.

int **mcal_rename_calendar**(*string* old_name, *string* new_name)

mcal_reopen

Reopens an MCAL stream to a new calendar. **mcal_reopen()** reopens an MCAL connection to the specified **$calendar** store. If the optional **$options** is specified, it passes the **$options** to that mailbox also.

int **mcal_reopen**(*string* calendar, *int* options)

mcal_snooze

Turns off an alarm for a calendar event specified by the id. Returns true.

int **mcal_snooze**(*int* id)

mcal_store_event

Stores the modifications to the current global event for the given stream. Returns true on success and false on error.

int **mcal_store_event**(*int* mcal_stream)

mcal_time_valid

Returns true if the given hour, minutes, and seconds is a valid time, false if not.

int **mcal_time_valid**(*int* hour, *int* minutes, *int* seconds)

mcrypt_cbc

The first prototype is when linked against libmcrypt 2.2.x, the second when linked against libmcrypt 2.4.x. **Mcrypt_cbc()** encrypts or decrypts (depending on **$mode**) the **$data** with **$cipher** and **$key** in CBC cipher mode and returns the resulting string. See also **mcrypt_cfb()**, **mcrypt_ecb()**, and **mcrypt_ofb()**.

string **mcrypt_cbc** (int cipher, string key, string data, int mode [, string iv])
string **mcrypt_cbc** (string cipher, string key, string data, int mode [, string iv])

- **$Cipher** is one of the MCRYPT_ciphername constants.
- **$Key** is the key supplied to the algorithm. It must be kept secret.
- **$Data** is the data which shall be encrypted/decrypted.
- **$Mode** is MCRYPT_ENCRYPT or MCRYPT_DECRYPT.
- **$IV** is the optional initialization vector.

mcrypt_cfb

The first prototype is when linked against libmcrypt 2.2.x, the second when linked against libmcrypt 2.4.x. **Mcrypt_cfb()** encrypts or decrypts (depending on **$mode**) the **$data** with **$cipher** and **$key** in CFB cipher mode and returns the resulting string. See also **mcrypt_cbc()**, **mcrypt_ecb()**, and **mcrypt_ofb()**.

stringstring **mcrypt_cfb**(*int* cipher, *string* key, *string* data, *int* mode, *string* iv, *string* cipher, *string* key, *string* data, *int* mode, [*string* iv])

- **$Cipher** is one of the MCRYPT_ciphername constants.
- **$Key** is the key supplied to the algorithm. It must be kept secret.
- **$Data** is the data which shall be encrypted/decrypted.
- **$Mode** is MCRYPT_ENCRYPT or MCRYPT_DECRYPT.
- **$IV** is the initialization vector.

mcrypt_create_iv

Used to create an IV; takes two arguments, **$size** determines the size of the IV, **$source** specifies the source of the IV. The source can be MCRYPT_RAND (system random number generator), MCRYPT_DEV_RANDOM (read data from /dev/random), and MCRYPT_DEV_URANDOM (read data from /dev/urandom). If you use MCRYPT_RAND, make sure to call srand() before initializing the random number generator.

string **mcrypt_create_iv**(*int* size, *int* source)

Example: Mcrypt_create_iv()

```php
<?php
$cipher = MCRYPT_TripleDES;
$block_size = mcrypt_get_block_size ($cipher);
$iv = mcrypt_create_iv ($block_size, MCRYPT_DEV_RANDOM);
?>
```

mcrypt_decrypt

Decrypts the data and returns the unencrypted data.

string **mcrypt_decrypt**(*string* cipher, *string* key, *string* data, *string* mode, [*string* iv])

- **$Cipher** is one of the MCRYPT_ciphername constants of the name of the algorithm as string.
- **$Key** is the key with which the data is encrypted. If it's smaller than the required keysize, it is padded with '\0'.
- **$Data** is the data that will be decrypted with the given cipher and mode. If the size of the data is not n * blocksize, the data will be padded with '\0'.
- **$Mode** is one of the MCRYPT_MODE_modename constants of one of "ecb", "cbc", "cfb", "ofb", "nofb", or "stream".
- The **$IV** parameter is used for the initialization in CBC, CFB, OFB modes, and in some algorithms in STREAM mode. If you do not supply an IV while it is needed for an algorithm, the function issues a warning and uses an IV with all bytes set to '\0'.

mcrypt_ecb

The first prototype is when linked against libmcrypt 2.2.x, the second when linked against libmcrypt 2.4.x.

stringstring **mcrypt_ecb**(*int* cipher, *string* key, *string* data, *int* mode, *string* cipher, *string* key, *string* data, *int* mode, [*string* iv])

- **Mcrypt_ecb()** encrypts or decrypts (depending on **$mode**) the **$data** with **$cipher** and **$key** in ECB cipher mode and returns the resulting string.
- **$Cipher** is one of the MCRYPT_ciphername constants.
- **$Key** is the key supplied to the algorithm. It must be kept secret.
- **$Data** is the data which shall be encrypted/decrypted.
- **$Mode** is MCRYPT_ENCRYPT or MCRYPT_DECRYPT.

  See also **mcrypt_cbc()**, **mcrypt_cfb()**, and **mcrypt_ofb()**.

mcrypt_encrypt

Encrypts the data and returns the encrypted data.

string **mcrypt_encrypt**(*string* cipher, *string* key, *string* data, *string* mode, [*string* iv])

- **$Cipher** is one of the MCRYPT_ciphername constants of the name of the algorithm as string.
- **$Key** is the key with which the data will be encrypted. If it's smaller than the required keysize, it is padded with '\0'.
- **$Data** is the data that will be encrypted with the given cipher and mode. If the size of the data is not n * blocksize, the data will be padded with '\0'. The returned crypttext can be larger than the size of the data that is given by **$data** .

- **$Mode** is one of the MCRYPT_MODE_modename constants of one of "ecb", "cbc", "cfb", "ofb", "nofb", or "stream".

- The **$IV** parameter is used for the initialization in CBC, CFB, OFB modes, and in some algorithms in STREAM mode. If you do not supply an IV while it is needed for an algorithm, the function issues a warning and uses an IV with all bytes set to '\0'.

Example: Mcrypt_encrypt() Example

```php
<?php
$iv = mcrypt_create_iv (mcrypt_get_iv_size (MCRYPT_RIJNDAEL_256, MCRYPT_MODE_ECB),
MCRYPT_RAND);
$key = "This is a very secret key";
$text = "Meet me at 11 o'clock behind the monument.";
echo strlen ($text)."\n";
$crypttext = mcrypt_encrypt (MCRYPT_RIJNDAEL_256, $key, $text, MCRYPT_MODE_ECB, $iv);
echo strlen ($crypttext)."\n";
?>
```

The previous example will print out the following:

```
42
64
```

mcrypt_enc_get_algorithms_name
Returns the name of the algorithm.

string mcrypt_enc_get_algorithms_name(*resource* td)

mcrypt_enc_get_block_size
Returns the block size of the algorithm specified by the encryption descriptor td in bytes.

int mcrypt_enc_get_block_size(*resource* td)

mcrypt_enc_get_iv_size
Returns the size of the iv of the algorithm specified by the encryption descriptor in bytes. If it returns 0, then the IV is ignored in the algorithm. An IV is used in cbc, cfb, and ofb modes, and in some algorithms in stream mode.

int **mcrypt_enc_get_iv_size**(*resource* td)

mcrypt_enc_get_key_size
Returns the maximum supported key size of the algorithm specified by the encryption descriptor td in bytes.

int **mcrypt_enc_get_key_size**(*resource* td)

mcrypt_enc_get_modes_name

Returns the name of the mode.

string **mcrypt_enc_get_modes_name**(*resource* td)

mcrypt_enc_get_supported_key_sizes

Returns an array with the key sizes supported by the algorithm specified by the encryption descriptor. If it returns an empty array, then all key sizes between 1 and **mcrypt_enc_get_key_size()** are supported by the algorithm.

array **mcrypt_enc_get_supported_key_sizes**(*resource* td)

mcrypt_enc_is_block_algorithm

Returns 1 if the algorithm is a block algorithm, or 0 if it is a stream algorithm.

int **mcrypt_enc_is_block_algorithm**(*resource* td)

mcrypt_enc_is_block_algorithm_mode

Returns 1 if the mode is for use with block algorithms, otherwise it returns 0 (for example, 0 for stream, and 1 for cbc, cfb, ofb).

int **mcrypt_enc_is_block_algorithm_mode**(*resource* td)

mcrypt_enc_is_block_mode

Returns 1 if the mode outputs blocks of bytes, or 0 if it outputs bytes (for example, 1 for cbc and ecb, and 0 for cfb and stream).

int **mcrypt_enc_is_block_mode**(*resource* td)

mcrypt_enc_self_test

Runs the self test on the algorithm specified by the descriptor td. If the self test succeeds, it returns zero. In case of an error, it returns 1.

int **mcrypt_enc_self_test**(*resource* td)

mcrypt_generic

Encrypts data. The data is padded with "\0" to make sure the length of the data is n * blocksize. This function returns the encrypted data. **Note:** The length of the returned string can in fact be longer then the input, due to the padding of the data.

string **mcrypt_generic**(*resource* td, *string* data)

mcrypt_generic_end

Terminates encryption specified by the encryption descriptor (td). Actually it clears all buffers, and closes all the modules used. Returns false on error, or true on success.

bool **mcrypt_generic_end**(*resource* td)

mcrypt_generic_init

The maximum length of the key should be the one obtained by calling **mcrypt_enc_get_key_size**(), and every value smaller than this is legal. The IV should normally have the size of the algorithms block size, but you must obtain the size by calling **mcrypt_enc_get_iv_size**(). IV is ignored in ECB. IV MUST exist in CFB, CBC, STREAM, nOFB, and OFB modes. It needs to be random and unique, but not secret. The same IV must be used for encryption/decryption. If you do not want to use it, you should set it to zeros, but this is not recommended. The function returns -1 on error. You need to call this function before every **mcrypt_generic**() or **mdecrypt_generic**().

int **mcrypt_generic_init**(*resource* td, *string* key, *string* iv)

mcrypt_get_block_size

The first prototype is when linked against libmcrypt 2.2.x, the second when linked against libmcrypt 2.4.x. **Mcrypt_get_block_size**() is used to get the size of a block of the specified **$cipher**. **Mcrypt_get_block_size**() takes one or two arguments, the **$cipher** and **$module**, and returns the size in bytes. See also **mcrypt_get_key_size**().

int **mcrypt_get_block_size** (int cipher)
int **mcrypt_get_block_size** (string cipher, string module)

mcrypt_get_cipher_name

Used to get the name of the specified cipher. **Mcrypt_get_cipher_name**() takes the cipher number as an argument (libmcrypt 2.2.x) or takes the cipher name as an argument (libmcrypt 2.4.x) and returns the name of the cipher or false, if the cipher does not exist.

string **mcrypt_get_cipher_name** (int cipher)
string **mcrypt_get_cipher_name** (string cipher)

Example: Mcrypt_get_cipher_name()

```php
<?php
$cipher = MCRYPT_TripleDES;
print mcrypt_get_cipher_name ($cipher);
?>
```

The previous example will produce the following:

```
TripleDES
```

mcrypt_get_iv_size

The first prototype is when linked against libmcrypt 2.2.x, the second when linked against libmcrypt 2.4.x. **Mcrypt_get_iv_size()** returns the size of the *Initialization Vector* (IV) in bytes. On error, the function returns false. If the IV is ignored in the specified cipher/mode combination, zero is returned.

> *intint* **mcrypt_get_iv_size**(*string* cipher, *string* mode, *resource* td)

- **$Cipher** is one of the MCRYPT_ciphername constants of the name of the algorithm as string.
- **$Mode** is one of the MCRYPT_MODE_modename constants of one of "ecb", "cbc", "cfb", "ofb", "nofb", or "stream".
- **$Td** is the algorithm specified.

mcrypt_get_key_size

The first prototype is when linked against libmcrypt 2.2.x, the second when linked against libmcrypt 2.4.x. Used to get the size of a key of the specified **$cipher**. **Mcrypt_get_key_size()** takes one or two arguments, the **$cipher** and **$module**, and returns the size in bytes. See also **mcrypt_get_block_size()**.

> *intint* **mcrypt_get_key_size**(*int* cipher, *string* cipher, *string* module)

mcrypt_list_algorithms

Used to get an array of all supported algorithms in the **$lib_dir**. Takes an optional parameter a directory that specifies the directory where all algorithms are located. If not specified, the value of the mcrypt.algorithms_dir php.ini directive is used.

> *array* **mcrypt_list_algorithms**([*string* lib_dir])

Example: Mcrypt_list_algorithms()

```php
<?php
$algorithms = mcrypt_list_algorithms ("/usr/local/lib/libmcrypt");
foreach ($algorithms as $cipher) {
echo $cipher."/n";
}
?>
```

The previous example will produce a list with all supported algorithms in the "/usr/local/lib/libmcrypt" directory.

mcrypt_list_modes

Used to get an array of all supported modes in the **$lib_dir**. Takes an optional parameter a directory that specifies the directory where all modes are located. If not specified, the value of the mcrypt.modes_dir php.ini directive is used.

array **mcrypt_list_modes**([*string* lib_dir]

Example: Mcrypt_list_modes()

```php
<?php
$modes = mcrypt_list_modes ();
foreach ($modes as $mode) {
echo $mode."/n";
}
?>
```

The previous example will produce a list with all supported algorithms in the default mode directory. If it is not set with the ini directive mcrypt.modes_dir, the default directory of mcrypt is used (/usr/local/lib/libmcrypt).

mcrypt_module_get_algo_block_size

Returns the block size of the algorithm specified in bytes. The optional **$lib_dir** parameter can contain the location where the mode module is on the system.

int **mcrypt_module_get_algo_block_size**(*string* algorithm, [*string* lib_dir])

mcrypt_module_get_algo_key_size

Returns the maximum supported key size of the algorithm specified in bytes. The optional **$lib_dir** parameter can contain the location where the mode module is on the system.

int **mcrypt_module_get_algo_key_size**(*string* algorithm, [*string* lib_dir])

mcrypt_module_get_algo_supported_key_sizes

Returns an array with the key sizes supported by the specified algorithm. If it returns an empty array, then all key sizes between 1 and **mcrypt_module_get_algo_key_size()** are supported by the algorithm. The optional **$lib_dir** parameter can contain the location where the mode module is on the system.

array **mcrypt_module_get_algo_supported_key_sizes**(*string* algorithm, [*string* lib_dir])

mcrypt_module_is_block_algorithm

Returns true if the specified algorithm is a block algorithm, or false if it is a stream algorithm. The optional **$lib_dir** parameter can contain the location where the algorithm module is on the system.

bool **mcrypt_module_is_block_algorithm**(*string* algorithm, [*string* lib_dir])

mcrypt_module_is_block_algorithm_mode

Returns true if the mode is for use with block algorithms, otherwise it returns 0 (for example, 0 for stream, and 1 for cbc, cfb, ofb). The optional **$lib_dir** parameter can contain the location where the mode module is on the system.

bool **mcrypt_module_is_block_algorithm_mode**(*string* mode, [*string* lib_dir])

mcrypt_module_is_block_mode

Returns true if the mode outputs blocks of bytes or false if it outputs just bytes (for example, 1 for cbc and ecb, and 0 for cfb and stream). The optional **$lib_dir** parameter can contain the location where the mode module is on the system.

bool **mcrypt_module_is_block_mode**(*string* mode, [*string* lib_dir])

mcrypt_module_open

Opens the module of the algorithm and the mode to be used. The name of the algorithm is specified in algorithm, for example, "twofish" is one of the MCRYPT_ciphername constants. The library is closed by calling **mcrypt_module_close()**, but to call that function is unnecessary if **mcrypt_generic_end()** is called. Normally, it returns an encryption descriptor, or false on error.

The **$algorithm_directory** and **$mode_directory** are used to locate the encryption modules. When you supply a directory name, it is used. When you set one of these to the empty string (""), the value is set by the $mcrypt.algorithms_dir or **$mcrypt**. modes_dir ini-directive is used. When these are not set, the default directories are used that are compiled into libmcrypt (*usually /usr/local/lib/libmcrypt*).

resource **mcrypt_module_open**(*string* algorithm, *string* algorithm_directory, *string* mode, *string* mode_directory)

Example: Mcrypt_module_open()

```
<?php
$td = mcrypt_module_open (MCRYPT_DES, "", MCRYPT_MODE_ECB, "/usr/lib/mcrypt-modes");
?>
```

The previous example will try to open the DES cipher from the default directory and the EBC mode from the directory /usr/lib/mcrypt-modes.

mcrypt_module_self_test

Runs the self test on the algorithm specified. The optional **$lib_dir** parameter can contain the location of where the algorithm module is on the system. The function returns true if the self test succeeds, or false when if fails.

bool **mcrypt_module_self_test**(*string* algorithm, [*string* lib_dir])

mcrypt_ofb

The first prototype is when linked against libmcrypt 2.2.x, the second when linked against libmcrypt 2.4.x. **Mcrypt_ofb()** encrypts or decrypts (depending on **$mode**) the **$data** with **$cipher** and **$key** in OFB cipher mode and returns the resulting string.

stringstring **mcrypt_ofb**(*int* cipher, *string* key, *string* data, *int* mode, *string* iv, *string* cipher, *string* key, *string* data, *int* mode, [*string* iv])

- **$Cipher** is one of the MCRYPT_ciphername constants.
- **$Key** is the key supplied to the algorithm. It must be kept secret.
- **$Data** is the data which shall be encrypted/decrypted.
- **$Mode** is MCRYPT_ENCRYPT or MCRYPT_DECRYPT.
- **$IV** is the initialization vector.

  See also **mcrypt_cbc()**, **mcrypt_cfb()**, and **mcrypt_ecb()**.

md5

Calculates the MD5 hash of **$str** using the RSA Data Security, Inc. MD5 Message-Digest Algorithm(URL) . See also **crc32()**.

string **md5**(*string* str)

mdecrypt_generic

Decrypts data. **Note:** The length of the returned string can in fact be longer then the unencrypted string, due to the padding of the data.

string **mdecrypt_generic**(*resource* td, *string* data)

Example: Mdecrypt_generic()

```php
<?php
$iv_size = mcrypt_enc_get_iv_size ($td));
$iv = @mcrypt_create_iv ($iv_size, MCRYPT_RAND);
if (@mcrypt_generic_init ($td, $key, $iv) != -1)
{
    $c_t = mcrypt_generic ($td, $plain_text);
    @mcrypt_generic_init ($td, $key, $iv);
    $p_t = mdecrypt_generic ($td, $c_t);
}
if (strncmp ($p_t, $plain_text, strlen($plain_text)) == 0)
    echo "ok";
else
    echo "error";
?>
```

The previous example shows how to check if the data before the encryption is the same as the data after the decryption.

Metaphone

Calculates the metaphone key of **$str**. Similar to **soundex()** metaphone creates the same key for similar sounding words. It's more accurate than soundex(), as it knows the basic rules of English pronunciation. The metaphone-generated keys are of variable length. Metaphone was developed by Lawrence Philips <lphilips@verity.com>. It is described in ["Practical Algorithms for Programmers," Binstock & Rex, Addison Wesley, 1995].

Note: This function was added in PHP 4.0.

string **Metaphone**(*string* str)

method_exists

This function returns true if the method given by **$method_name** has been defined for the given **$object**, false otherwise.

bool **method_exists**(*object* object, *string* method_name)

mhash

Applies a hash function specified by **$hash** to the **$data** and returns the resulting hash (also called digest).

string **mhash**(*int* hash, *string* data)

mhash_count

Returns the highest available hash id. Hashes are numbered from 0 to this hash id.

int **mhash_count**(*void*)

Example: Traversing all hashes

```php
<?php
$nr = mhash_count();
for ($i = 0; $i <= $nr; $i++) {
    echo sprintf ("The blocksize of %s is %d\n",
        mhash_get_hash_name ($i),
        mhash_get_block_size ($i));
}
?>
```

mhash_get_block_size

Used to get the size of a block of the specified **$hash**. Takes one argument, the **$hash**, and returns the size in bytes or false, if the $hash does not exist.

int **mhash_get_block_size**(*int* hash)

mhash_get_hash_name

Used to get the name of the specified hash. Takes the hash id as an argument and returns the name of the hash or false, if the hash does not exist.

string **mhash_get_hash_name**(*int* hash)

Example: Mhash_get_hash_name()

```php
<?php
$hash = MHASH_MD5;
print mhash_get_hash_name ($hash);
?>
```

The previous example will print out the following:

```
MD5
```

microtime

Returns the string "msec sec" where sec is the current time measured in the number of seconds since the Unix Epoch (0:00:00 January 1, 1970 GMT), and msec is the microseconds part. This function is only available on operating systems that support the **gettimeofday**() system call. See also **time**().

string **microtime**(*void*)

min

Returns the numerically lowest parameter value. If the first parameter is an array, **min**() returns the lowest value in that array. If the first parameter is an integer, string or double, you need at least two parameters, and **min**() returns the lowest of these values. You can compare an unlimited number of values. If one or more of the values is a double, all the values will be treated as doubles, and a double is returned. If none of the values is a double, all of them will be treated as integers, and an integer is returned.

mixed **min**(*mixed* arg1, *mixed* arg2, *mixed* argn)

mkdir

Attempts to create the directory specified by pathname.

Note: You probably want to specify the mode as an octal number, which means it should have a leading zero.

int **mkdir**(*string* pathname, *int* mode)

```
mkdir ("/path/to/my/dir", 0700);
```

Returns true on success and false on failure. See also **rmdir**().

mktime

Warning: Note the strange order of arguments, which differs from the order of arguments in a regular UNIX mktime() call and which does not lend itself well to leaving out parameters from right to left. It is a common error to mix up these values in a script. Returns the Unix timestamp corresponding to the arguments given. This timestamp is a long integer containing the number of seconds between the Unix Epoch (January 1 1970) and the time specified. Arguments may be left out in order from right to left; any arguments thus omitted will be set to the current value according to the local date and time.

int **mktime**(*int* hour, *int* minute, *int* second, *int* month, *int* day, *int* year, [*int* is_dst])

$Is_dst can be set to 1 if the time is during daylight savings time, 0 if it is not, or -1 (the default) if it is unknown whether the time is within daylight savings time or not.

Note: $Is_dst was added in 3.0.10. **Mktime()** is useful for doing date arithmetic and validation because it will automatically calculate the correct value for out-of-range input. For example, each of the following lines produces the string "Jan-01-1998".

Example: Mktime()

```
echo date ("M-d-Y", mktime (0,0,0,12,32,1997));
echo date ("M-d-Y", mktime (0,0,0,13,1,1997));
echo date ("M-d-Y", mktime (0,0,0,1,1,1998));
echo date ("M-d-Y", mktime (0,0,0,1,1,98));
```

$Year may be a two or four digit value, with values between 0-69 mapping to 2000-2069 and 70-99 to 1970-1999 (on systems where time_t is a 32bit signed integer, as most common today, the valid range for **$year** is somewhere between 1902 and 2037). The last day of any given month can be expressed as the 0 day of the next month, not the -1 day. Both of the following examples will produce the string "The last day in Feb 2000 is: 29".

Example: Last day of next month

```
$lastday = mktime (0,0,0,3,0,2000);
echo strftime ("Last day in Feb 2000 is: %d", $lastday);
$lastday = mktime (0,0,0,4,-31,2000);
echo strftime ("Last day in Feb 2000 is: %d", $lastday);
```

Date with year, month, and day equal to zero is considered illegal. Otherwise it would be regarded as 30.11.1999, which would be strange behavior. See also **date()** and **time()**.

move_uploaded_file

Available only in versions of PHP 3 after PHP 3.0.16, and in versions of PHP 4 after 4.0.2. This function checks to ensure that the file designated by **$filename** is a valid upload file (meaning that it was uploaded via PHP's HTTP POST upload mechanism). If the file is valid, it will be moved to the filename given by **$destination**. If **$filename** is not a valid upload file, then no action will occur, and **move_uploaded_file()** will return false. If **$filename** is a valid upload file but cannot be moved for some reason, no action will occur, and **move_uploaded_file()** will return false. Additionally, a warning will be issued. This sort of check is especially important if there is any chance that anything done with uploaded files could reveal their contents to the user, or even to other users on the same system. See also **is_uploaded_file**(), and the section Handling file **uploads**() for a simple usage example.

bool **move_uploaded_file**(string filename, string destination)

msql

Returns a positive mSQL query identifier to the query result, or false on error. **msql**() selects a database and executes a query on it. If the optional link identifier isn't specified, the function will try to find an open link to the mSQL server. If no such link is found, it'll try to create one as if **msql_connect**() was called with no arguments (see **msql_connect**()).

int **msql**(string database, string query, int link_identifier)

msql_affected_rows

Returns number of affected ("touched") rows by a specific query (that is, the number of rows returned by a SELECT, the number of rows modified by an update, or the number of rows removed by a delete). See also **msql_query**().

int **msql_affected_rows**(int query_identifier)

msql_close

Returns true on success, false on error. **msql_close**() closes the link to a mSQL database that's associated with the specified link identifier. If the link identifier isn't specified, the last opened link is assumed.

Note: This isn't usually necessary, as non-persistent open links are automatically closed at the end of the script's execution. **msql_close**() will not close persistent links generated by **msql_pconnect**(). See also **msql_connect**() and **msql_pconnect**().

int **msql_close**(int link_identifier)

msql_connect

Returns a positive mSQL link identifier on success, or false on error. **msql_connect**() establishes a connection to a mSQL server. The hostname argument is optional, and if it's missing, localhost is assumed. In case a second call is made to **msql_connect**() with the same arguments, no new link will be established. Instead, the link identifier of the already opened link will be returned. The link to the server will be closed as soon as the execution of the script ends, unless it's closed earlier by explicitly calling **msql_close**(). See also **msql_pconnect**(), and **msql_close**().

int **msql_connect**([string hostname], [string :port], [string username], [string password])

msql_createdb

Identical to **msql_create_db**().

int **msql_createdb**(string database name, [int link_identifier])

msql_create_db

Attempts to create a new database on the server associated with the specified link identifier. See also **msql_drop_db()**.

> int **msql_create_db**(string database name, [int link_identifier])

msql_data_seek

Returns true on success, false on failure. Moves the internal row pointer of the mSQL result associated with the specified query identifier to point to the specified row number. The next call to **msql_fetch_row()** would return that row. See also **msql_fetch_row()**.

> int **msql_data_seek**(int query_identifier, int row_number)

msql_dbname

Returns the database name stored in position **$i** of the result pointer returned from the **msql_listdbs()** function. The **msql_numrows()** function can be used to determine how many database names are available.

> string **msql_dbname**(int query_identifier, int i)

msql_dropdb

See **msql_drop_db()**.

> **msql_dropdb**(void)

msql_drop_db

Returns true on success, false on failure. **msql_drop_db()** attempts to drop (remove) an entire database from the server associated with the specified link identifier. See also **msql_create_db()**.

> int **msql_drop_db**(string database_name, int link_identifier)

msql_error

Errors coming back from the mSQL database backend no longer issue warnings. Instead, use these functions to retrieve the error string.

> string **msql_error**( )

msql_fetch_array

Returns an array that corresponds to the fetched row, or false if no more rows exist. **msql_fetch_array()** is an extended version of **msql_fetch_row()**. In addition to storing the data in the numeric indices of the result array, it also stores the data in associative indices, using the field names as keys. The second optional argument **$result_type in msql_fetch_array()** is a constant and can take the following values: MSQL_ASSOC, MSQL_NUM, and MYSQL_BOTH. Be careful if you are retrieving results from a query that may return a record that contains only one field that has a value of 0 (or an empty string, or NULL).

Note: Using **msql_fetch_array()** is NOT significantly slower than using **msql_fetch_row()**, it actually provides a significant added value. For further details, also see **msql_fetch_row()**.

int **msql_fetch_array**(int query_identifier, [int result_type])

msql_fetch_field

Returns an object containing field information. **msql_fetch_field()** can be used in order to obtain information about fields in a certain query result. If the field offset isn't specified, the next field that wasn't yet retrieved by **msql_fetch_field()** is retrieved.

object **msql_fetch_field**(int query_identifier, int field_offset)

The properties of the object are as follows:

- name—column name
- table—name of the table to whichthe column belongs
- not_null—1 if the column cannot be null
- primary_key—1 if the column is a primary key
- unique—1 if the column is a unique key
- type—the type of column

See also **msql_field_seek()**.

msql_fetch_object

Returns an object with properties that correspond to the fetched row, or false if no more rows exist. **msql_fetch_object()** is similar to **msql_fetch_array()**, with one difference—an object is returned, instead of an array. Indirectly, that means that you can only access the data by the field names, not by their offsets (numbers are illegal property names). The optional second argument **$result_type** in **msql_fetch_array()** is a constant and can take the following values: MSQL_ASSOC, MSQL_NUM, and MSQL_BOTH. Speed-wise, the function is identical to **msql_fetch_array()**, and almost as quick as **msql_fetch_row()**; the difference is insignificant. See also **msql_fetch_array()** and **msql_fetch_row()**.

int **msql_fetch_object**(int query_identifier, [int result_type])

msql_fetch_row

Returns an array that corresponds to the fetched row, or false if no more rows exist. msql_fetch_row() fetches one row of data from the result associated with the specified query identifier. The row is returned as an array. Each result column is stored in an array offset, starting at offset 0. Subsequent call to msql_fetch_row() would return the next row in the result set, or false if no more rows exist. See also msql_fetch_array(), msql_fetch_object(), msql_data_seek(), and msql_result().

> array **msql_fetch_row**(int query_identifier)

msql_fieldflags

Returns the field flags of the specified field. Currently, this is either, "not null", "primary key", a combination of the two or "" (an empty string).

> string **msql_fieldflags**(int query_identifier, int i)

msql_fieldlen

Returns the length of the specified field.

> int **msql_fieldlen**(int query_identifier, int i)

msql_fieldname

Returns the name of the specified field. **$query_identifier** is the query identifier, and **$field** is the field index. msql_fieldname(**$result**, 2) will return the name of the second field in the result associated with the result identifier.

> *string* **msql_fieldname**(*int* query_identifier, *int* field)

msql_fieldtable

Returns the name of the table **$field** was fetched from.

> int **msql_fieldtable**(int query_identifier, int field)

msql_fieldtype

Similar to the **msql_fieldname()** function. The arguments are identical, but the field type is returned. This will be one of "int", "char", or "real".

> string **msql_fieldtype**(int query_identifier, int i)

msql_field_seek

Seeks to the specified field offset. If the next call to **msql_fetch_field()** won't include a field offset, this field would be returned. See also **msql_fetch_field()**.

> int **msql_field_seek**(int query_identifier, int field_offset)

msql_freeresult

See **msql_free_result()**.

> msql_freeresult(void)

msql_free_result

Frees the memory associated with **$query_identifier**. When PHP completes a request, this memory is freed automatically. So you only need to call this function when you want to make sure you don't use too much memory while the script is running.

int **msql_free_result**(int query_identifier)

msql_listdbs

See **msql_list_dbs()**.

msql_listdbs(*void*)

msql_listfields

See **msql_list_fields()**.

msql_listfields(*void*)

msql_listtables

See **msql_list_tables()**.

msql_listtables(*void*)

msql_list_dbs

Returns a result pointer containing the databases available from the current msql daemon. Use the **msql_dbname()** function to traverse this result pointer.

int **msql_list_dbs**(*void*)

msql_list_fields

Retrieves information about the given tablename. Arguments are the database name and the tablename. A result pointer is returned, which can be used with **msql_fieldflags()**, **msql_fieldlen()**, **msql_fieldname()**, and **msql_fieldtype()**. A query identifier is a positive integer. The function returns -1 if a error occurs. A string describing the error will be placed in **$phperrmsg**, and unless the function was called as **@msql_list_fields()**, then this error string will also be printed out. See also **msql_error()**.

int **msql_list_fields**(*string* database, *string* tablename)

msql_list_tables

Takes a database name and result pointer much like the **msql()** function. The **msql_table-name()** function should be used to extract the actual table names from the result pointer.

int **msql_list_tables**(*string* database)

msql_numfields

Identical to **msql_num_fields()**.

> *int* **msql_numfields**(*int* query_identifier)

msql_numrows

Identical to **msql_num_rows()**.

> *int* **msql_numrows**(*void*)

msql_num_fields

Returns the number of fields in a result set. See also **msql()**, **msql_query()**, **msql_fetch_field()**, and **msql_num_rows()**.

> *int* **msql_num_fields**(*int* query_identifier)

msql_num_rows

Returns the number of rows in a result set. See also **msql()**, **msql_query()**, and **msql_fetch_row()**.

> *int* **msql_num_rows**(*int* query_identifier)

msql_pconnect

Returns a positive mSQL persistent link identifier on success, or false on error. **msql_pconnect()** acts very much like **msql_connect()** with two major differences. First, when connecting, the function would first try to find a (persistent) link that's already open with the same host. If one is found, an identifier for it will be returned instead of opening a new connection. Second, the connection to the SQL server will not be closed when the execution of the script ends. Instead, the link will remain open for future use (**msql_close()** will not close links established by **msql_pconnect()**). This type of links is therefore called "persistent."

> *int* **msql_pconnect**([*string* hostname], [*string* :port], [*string* username], [*string* password])

msql_query

Sends a query to the currently active database on the server that's associated with the specified link identifier. If the link identifier isn't specified, the last opened link is assumed. If no link is open, the function tries to establish a link as if **msql_connect()** was called, and then uses it. Returns a positive mSQL query identifier on success, or false on error. See also **msql()**, **msql_select_db()**, and **msql_connect()**.

> *int* **msql_query**(*string* query, *int* link_identifier)

msql_regcase

See **sql_regcase()**.

   msql_regcase(*void*)

msql_result

Returns the contents of the cell at the row and offset in the specified mSQL result set. **msql_result()** returns the contents of one cell from a mSQL result set. The field argument can be the field's offset, the field's name, or the field's table dot field's name (fieldname.tablename). If the column name has been aliased ('select foo as bar from . . . '), use the alias instead of the column name. When working on large result sets, you should consider using one of the functions that fetch an entire row. As these functions return the contents of multiple cells in one function call, they are much quicker than **msql_result()**. Also, note that specifying a numeric offset for the field argument is much quicker than specifying a fieldname or tablename.fieldname argument. The following are some recommended high-performance alternatives: **msql_fetch_row()**, **msql_fetch_array()**, and **msql_fetch_object()**.

   int **msql_result**(*int* query_identifier, *int* i, *mixed* field)

msql_selectdb

See **msql_select_db()**.

   msql_selectdb(*void*)

msql_select_db

Returns true on success, false on error. **msql_select_db()** sets the current active database on the server that's associated with the specified link identifier. If no link identifier is specified, the last opened link is assumed. If no link is open, the function will try to establish a link as if **msql_connect()** was called, and then uses it. Every subsequent call to **msql_query()** will be made on the active database. See also **msql_connect()**, **msql_pconnect()**, and **msql_query()**.

   int **msql_select_db**(*string* database_name, *int* link_identifier)

msql_tablename

Takes a result pointer returned by the **msql_list_tables()** function, as well as an integer index, and returns the name of a table. The **msql_numrows()** function may be used to determine the number of tables in the result pointer.

   string **msql_tablename**(*int* query_identifier, *int* field)

   Example: msql_tablename()

```
<?php
msql_connect ("localhost");
$result = msql_list_tables ("wisconsin");
$i = 0;
while ($i < msql_numrows ($result)) {
    $tb_names[$i] = msql_tablename ($result, $i);
    echo $tb_names[$i] . "<BR>";
    $i++;
}
?>
```

mssql_close

Returns true on success, false on error. Closes the link to a MS SQL Server database that's associated with the specified link identifier. If the link identifier isn't specified, the last opened link is assumed.

Note: This isn't usually necessary because non-persistent open links are automatically closed at the end of the script's execution. **Mssql_close()** will not close persistent links generated by **mssql_pconnect()**. See also **mssql_connect()**, and **mssql_pconnect()**.

int **mssql_close**([*int* link_identifier])

mssql_connect

Returns a positive MS SQL link identifier on success, or false on error. Establishes a connection to a MS SQL server. The servername argument has to be a valid servername that is defined in the interfaces file. In case a second call is made to **mssql_connect()** with the same arguments, no new link will be established Instead, the link identifier of the already opened link will be returned. The link to the server will be closed as soon as the execution of the script ends, unless it's closed earlier by explicitly calling **mssql_close()**. See also **mssql_pconnect()**, and **mssql_close()**.

int **mssql_connect**([*string* servername], [*string* username], [*string* password])

mssql_data_seek

Returns true on success, false on failure. **Mssql_data_seek()** moves the internal row pointer of the MS SQL result associated with the specified result identifier to point to the specified row number. The next call to **mssql_fetch_row()** would return that row. See also **mssql_data_seek()**.

int **mssql_data_seek**(*int* result_identifier, *int* row_number)

mssql_fetch_array

Returns an array that corresponds to the fetched row, or false if no more rows exist. **Mssql_fetch_array()** is an extended version of **mssql_fetch_row()**. In addition to storing the data in the numeric indices of the result array, it also stores the data in associative indices, using the field names as keys.

Note: Using **mssql_fetch_array()** is NOT significantly slower than using **mssql_fetch_row()**, it actually provides a significant added value. For further details, also see **mssql_fetch_row()**.

int **mssql_fetch_array**(*int* result)

mssql_fetch_field

Returns an object containing field information and can be used in order to obtain information about fields in a certain query result. If the field offset isn't specified, the next field that wasn't yet retrieved by **mssql_fetch_field()** is retrieved.

object **mssql_fetch_field**(*int* result, [*int* field_offset])

The properties of the object are as follows:

- name—Column name. If the column is a result of a function, this property is set to computed#N, where #N is a serial number.
- column_source—The table from which the column was taken.
- max_length—Maximum length of the column.
- numeric—1 if the column is numeric.

See also **mssql_field_seek()**.

mssql_fetch_object

Returns an object with properties that correspond to the fetched row, or false if no more rows are left. **Mssql_fetch_object()** is similar to **mssql_fetch_array()**, with one difference—an object is returned, instead of an array. Indirectly, that means that you can only access the data by the field names, not by their offsets (numbers are illegal property names). Speed-wise, the function is identical to **mssql_fetch_array()**, and almost as quick as **mssql_fetch_row()**; the difference is insignificant. See also **mssql_fetch_array()** and **mssql_fetch_row()**.

int **mssql_fetch_object**(*int* result)

mssql_fetch_row

Returns an array that corresponds to the fetched row, or false if no more rows exist. **Mssql_fetch_row()** fetches one row of data from the result associated with the specified result identifier. The row is returned as an array. Each result column is stored in an array offset, starting at offset 0. Subsequent call to **mssql_fetch_rows()** would return the next row in the result set, or false if no more rows are available. See also **mssql_fetch_array()**, **mssql_fetch_object()**, **mssql_data_seek()**, **mssql_fetch_lengths()**, and **mssql_result()**.

array **mssql_fetch_row**(*int* result)

mssql_field_length

int **mssql_field_length**(*int* result, [*int* offset])

mssql_field_name

int **mssql_field_name**(*int* result, [*int* offset])

mssql_field_seek

Seeks to the specified field offset. If the next call to **mssql_fetch_field**() won't include a field offset, this field would be returned. See also **mssql_fetch_field**().

int **mssql_field_seek**(*int* result, *int* field_offset)

mssql_field_type

string **mssql_field_type**(int result, [int offset])

mssql_free_result

Only needs to be called if you are worried about using too much memory while your script is running. All result memory will automatically be freed when the script ends. You may call **mssql_free_result**() with the result identifier as an argument, and the associated result memory will be freed.

int **mssql_free_result**(*int* result)

mssql_get_last_message

string mssql_get_last_message(*void*)

mssql_min_error_severity

void **mssql_min_error_severity**(*int* severity)

mssql_min_message_severity

void **mssql_min_message_severity**(*int* severity)

mssql_num_fields

Returns the number of fields in a result set. See also **mssql_db_query**(), **mssql_query**(), **mssql_fetch_field**(), and **mssql_num_rows**().

int **mssql_num_fields**(*int* result)

mssql_num_rows

Returns the number of rows in a result set. See also **mssql_db_query()**, **mssql_query()**, and **mssql_fetch_row()**.

int **mssql_num_rows**(*string* result)

mssql_pconnect

Returns a positive MS SQL persistent link identifier on success, or false on error. Acts very much like **mssql_connect()** with two major differences. First, when connecting, the function would first try to find a (persistent) link that's already open with the same host, username, and password. If one is found, an identifier for it will be returned instead of opening a new connection. Second, the connection to the SQL server will not be closed when the execution of the script ends. Instead, the link will remain open for future use (**mssql_close()** will not close links established by **mssql_pconnect()**). This type of links is therefore called "persistent".

int **mssql_pconnect**([*string* servername], [*string* username], [*string* password])

mssql_query

Returns a positive MS SQL result identifier on success, or false on error. **Mssql_query()** sends a query to the currently active database on the server that's associated with the specified link identifier. If the link identifier isn't specified, the last opened link is assumed. If no link is open, the function tries to establish a link as if **mssql_connect()** was called, and then uses it. See also **mssql_db_query()**, **mssql_select_db()**, and **mssql_connect()**.

int **mssql_query**(*string* query, [*int* link_identifier])

mssql_result

Returns the contents of one cell from a MS SQL result set. The field argument can be the field's offset, the field's name, or the field's table dot field's name (tablename.fieldname). If the column name has been aliased ('select foo as bar from . . .'), it uses the alias instead of the column name. When working on large result sets, you should consider using one of the functions that fetch an entire row. As these functions return the contents of multiple cells in one function call, they are much quicker than **mssql_result()**.

Note: specifying a numeric offset for the field argument is much quicker than specifying a fieldname or tablename.fieldname argument. The following are recommended high-performance alternatives: **mssql_fetch_row()**, **mssql_fetch_array()**, **and mssql_fetch_object()**.

int **mssql_result**(*int* result, *int* i, *mixed* field)

mssql_select_db

Returns true on success, false on error. **Mssql_select_db()** sets the current active database on the server that's associated with the specified link identifier. If no link identifier is specified, the last opened link is assumed. If no link is open, the function will try to establish a link as if **mssql_connect()** was called, and then uses it. Every subsequent call to **mssql_query()** will be made on the active database. See also **mssql_connect()**, **mssql_pconnect()**, and **mssql_query()**.

int **mssql_select_db**(*string* database_name, [*int* link_identifier])

mt_getrandmax

Returns the maximum value that can be returned by a call to **mt_rand()**. See also **mt_rand()**, **mt_srand()**, **rand()**, **srand()**, and **getrandmax()**.

int **mt_getrandmax**(*void*)

mt_rand

Many random number generators of older libcs have dubious or unknown characteristics and are slow. By default, PHP uses the libc random number generator with the **rand()** function. **mt_rand()** function is a drop-in replacement for this. It uses a random number generator with known characteristics, the Mersenne Twister, which will produce random numbers that should be suitable for seeding some kinds of cryptography (see the home pages for details) and is four times faster than what the average libc provides. The Homepage of the Mersenne Twister can be found at *http://www.math.keio.ac.jp/~matumoto/emt.html*, and an optimized version of the MT source is available at *http://www.scp.syr.edu/~marc/hawk/twister.html*.

int **mt_rand**([*int* min], [*int* max])

If called without the optional **$min**, **$max** arguments **mt_rand()** returns a pseudo-random value between 0 and RAND_MAX . If you want a random number between 5 and 15 (inclusive), for example, use mt_rand *(5, 15)*. Remember to seed the random number generator before use with **mt_srand()**.

Note: In versions before 3.0.7, the meaning of **$max** was **$range**. To get the same results in these versions, the short example should be *mt_rand (5, 11)* to get a random number between 5 and 15. See also **mt_srand()**, **mt_getrandmax()**, **srand()**, **rand()** and **getrandmax()**.

mt_srand

Seeds the random number generator with **$seed**.

void **mt_srand**(*int* seed)

```
// seed with microseconds since last "whole" second
mt_srand ((double) microtime() * 1000000);
$randval = mt_rand();
```

See also **mt_rand()**, **mt_getrandmax()**, **srand()**, **rand()**, and **getrandmax()**.

mysql_affected_rows

Returns the number of rows affected by the last INSERT, UPDATE, or DELETE query on the server associated with the specified link identifier. If the link identifier isn't specified, the last opened link is assumed. If the last query was a DELETE query with no WHERE clause, all of the records will have been deleted from the table, but this function will return zero. This command is not effective for SELECT statements, only on statements that modify records. To retrieve the number of rows returned from a SELECT, use **mysql_num_rows()**.

int **mysql_affected_rows**([*int* link_identifier])

mysql_change_user

Changes the logged in user of the current active connection, or the connection given by the optional parameter link_identifier. If a database is specified, this will default the current database after the user has been changed. If the new user and password authorization fails, the current connected user stays active.

Note: This function was introduced in PHP 3.0.13 and requires MySQL 3.23.3 or higher.

int **mysql_change_user**(*string* user, *string* password, [*string* database], [*int* link_identifier])

mysql_close

Returns true on success, false on error. **mysql_close()** closes the connection to the MySQL server that's associated with the specified link identifier. If **$link_identifier** isn't specified, the last opened link is used. Using **mysql_close()** isn't usually necessary because non-persistent open links are automatically closed at the end of the script's execution. **Note: mysql_close()** will not close persistent links created by **mysql_pconnect()**.

int **mysql_close**([*int* link_identifier])

Example: MySQL close

```php
<?php
    $link = mysql_connect ("kraemer", "marliesle", "secret")
        or die ("Could not connect");
    print ("Connected successfully");
    mysql_close ($link);
?>
```

See also **mysql_connect()**, and **mysql_pconnect()**.

mysql_connect

Returns a positive MySQL link identifier on success, or an error message on failure. Establishes a connection to a MySQL server. The following defaults are assumed for missing optional parameters: $host:port = 'localhost:3306', $username = name of the user that owns the server process and $password = empty password. The hostname string can also include a port number. e.g. "hostname:port" or a path to a socket e.g. ":/path/to/socket" for the localhost.

Note: Support for ":port" was added in PHP 3.0B4. Support for ":/path/to/socket" was added in PHP 3.0.10. You can suppress the error message on failure by prepending '@' to the function name. If a second call is made to **mysql_connect()** with the same arguments, no new link will be established. Instead, the link identifier of the already opened link will be returned. The link to the server will be closed as soon as the execution of the script ends, unless it's closed earlier by explicitly calling **mysql_close()**.

int **mysql_connect**([*string* :/path/to/socket], [*string* username], [*string* password])

Example: MySQL connect

```php
<?php
    $link = mysql_connect ("kraemer", "marliesle", "secret")
        or die ("Could not connect");
    print ("Connected successfully");
    mysql_close ($link);
?>
```

See also **mysql_pconnect()**, and **mysql_close()**.

mysql_create_db

Attempts to create a new database on the server associated with the specified link identifier.

int **mysql_create_db**(*string* database name, [*int* link_identifier])

Example: MySQL create database

```php
<?php
    $link = mysql_pconnect ("kron", "jutta", "geheim")
        or die ("Could not connect");
    if (mysql_create_db ("my_db")) {
        print ("Database created successfully\n");
    } else {
        printf ("Error creating database: %s\n", mysql_error ());
    }
?>
```

For downwards compatibility, **mysql_createdb()** can also be used. See also **mysql_drop_db()**.

mysql_data_seek

Returns true on success, false on failure. **mysql_data_seek()** moves the internal row pointer of the MySQL result, associated with the specified result identifier, to point to the specified row number. The next call to **mysql_fetch_row()** would return that row. **$Row_number** starts at 0.

int **mysql_data_seek**(*int* result_identifier, *int* row_number)

Example: MySQL data seek

```php
<?php
    $link = mysql_pconnect ("kron", "jutta", "geheim")
        or die ("Could not connect");
    mysql_select_db ("samp_db")
        or die ("Could not select database");
    $query = "SELECT last_name, first_name FROM friends";
```

```
    $result = mysql_query ($query)
        or die ("Query failed");

    # fetch rows in reverse order
    for ($i = mysql_num_rows ($result) - 1; $i >=0; $i--) {
        if (!mysql_data_seek ($result, $i)) {
            printf ("Cannot seek to row %d\n", $i);
            continue;
        }
        if(!($row = mysql_fetch_object ($result)))
            continue;
        printf ("%s %s<BR>\n", $row->last_name, $row->first_name);
    }
    mysql_free_result ($result);
?>
```

mysql_db_name

Takes as its first parameter the result pointer from a call to **mysql_list_dbs()**. The **$row** parameter is an index into the result set. If an error occurs, false is returned. Use **mysql_errno()** and **mysql_error()** to determine the nature of the error.

int **mysql_db_name**(*int* result, *int* row, [*mixed* field])

Example: Mysql_db_name()

```
<?php
error_reporting(E_ALL);
mysql_connect('dbhost', 'username', 'password');
$db_list = mysql_list_dbs();
$i = 0;
$cnt = mysql_numrows($db_list);
while ($i < $cnt) {
    echo mysql_db_name($db_list, $i) . "\n";
    $i++;
}
?>
```

For backward compatibility, **mysql_dbname()** is also accepted. This is deprecated, however.

mysql_db_query

Returns a positive MySQL result identifier to the query result, or false on error. **mysql_db_query()** selects a database and executes a query on it. If the optional link identifier isn't specified, the function will try to find an open link to the MySQL server. If no such link is found, it will try to create one as if **mysql_connect()** was called with no arguments. See also **mysql_connect()**. For downwards compatibility, **mysql()** can also be used.

int **mysql_db_query**(*string* database, *string* query, [*int* link_identifier])

mysql_drop_db

Returns true on success, false on failure. **mysql_drop_db()** attempts to drop (remove) an entire database from the server associated with the specified link identifier. See also **mysql_create_db()**. For downward compatibility, **mysql_dropdb()** can also be used.

int **mysql_drop_db**(*string* database_name, [*int* link_identifier])

mysql_errno

Returns the error number from the last mySQL function, or 0 (zero) if no error occurred. Errors coming back from the mySQL database backend no longer issue warnings. Instead, use **mysql_errno()** to retrieve the error code.

Note: This function only returns the error code from the most recently executed mySQL function (not including **mysql_error()** and **mysql_errno()**). So if you want to use it, make sure you check the value before calling another mySQL function.

int **mysql_errno**([*int* link_identifier])

```php
<?php
mysql_connect("marliesle");
echo mysql_errno().": ".mysql_error()."<BR>";
mysql_select_db("nonexistentdb");
echo mysql_errno().": ".mysql_error()."<BR>";
$conn = mysql_query("SELECT * FROM nonexistenttable");
echo mysql_errno().": ".mysql_error()."<BR>";
?>
```

See also **mysql_error()**.

mysql_error

Returns the error text from the last mySQL function, or "" (the empty string) if no error occurred. Errors coming back from the mySQL database backend no longer issue warnings. Instead, use **mysql_error()** to retrieve the error text.

Note: This function only returns the error text from the most recently executed mySQL function (not including **mysql_error()** and **mysql_errno()**). So if you want to use it, make sure you check the value before calling another mySQL function.

string **mysql_error**([*int* link_identifier])

```php
<?php
mysql_connect("marliesle");
echo mysql_errno().": ".mysql_error()."<BR>";
mysql_select_db("nonexistentdb");
echo mysql_errno().": ".mysql_error()."<BR>";
$conn = mysql_query("SELECT * FROM nonexistenttable");
echo mysql_errno().": ".mysql_error()."<BR>";
?>
```

See also **mysql_errno()**.

mysql_fetch_array

Returns an array that corresponds to the fetched row, or false if no more rows exist. **mysql_fetch_array()** is an extended version of **mysql_fetch_row()**. In addition to storing the data in the numeric indices of the result array, it also stores the data in associative indices, using the field names as keys. If two or more columns of the result have the same field names, the last column will take precedence. To access the other column(s) of the same name, you must use the numeric index of the column or make an alias for the column.

array **mysql_fetch_array**(*int* result, [*int* result_type])

```
select t1.f1 as foo t2.f1 as bar from t1, t2
```

An important thing to note is that using **mysql_fetch_array()** is NOT significantly slower than using **mysql_fetch_row(),** it actually provides a significant added value. The optional second argument **$result_type** in **mysql_fetch_array()** is a constant and can take the following values: MYSQL_ASSOC, MYSQL_NUM, and MYSQL_BOTH. (This feature was added in PHP 3.0.7). For further details, see also **mysql_fetch_row()** and **mysql_fetch_assoc()**.

Example: Mysql_fetch_array()

```php
<?php
mysql_connect ($host, $user, $password);
$result = mysql_db_query ("database","select user_id, fullname from table");
while ($row = mysql_fetch_array ($result)) {
    echo "user_id: ".$row["user_id"]."<br>\n";
    echo "user_id: ".$row[0]."<br>\n";
    echo "fullname: ".$row["fullname"]."<br>\n";
    echo "fullname: ".$row[1]."<br>\n";
}
mysql_free_result ($result);
?>
```

mysql_fetch_assoc

Returns an associative array that corresponds to the fetched row, or false if no more rows exist. **mysql_fetch_assoc()** is equivalent to calling **mysql_fetch_array()** with MYSQL_ASSOC for the optional second parameter. It only returns an associative array. This is the way **mysql_fetch_array()** originally worked. If you need the numeric indices as well as the associative, use **mysql_fetch_array()**. If two or more columns of the result have the same field names, the last column will take precedence. To access the other column(s) of the same name, you must use **mysql_fetch_array()** and have it return the numeric indices as well. An important thing to note is that using **mysql_fetch_assoc()** is NOT significantly slower than using **mysql_fetch_row()**, it actually provides a significant added value. For further details, see also **mysql_fetch_row()** and **mysql_fetch_array()**.

array **mysql_fetch_assoc**(*int* result)

Example: Mysql_fetch_assoc()

```php
<?php
mysql_connect ($host, $user, $password);
$result = mysql_db_query ("database","select * from table");
while ($row = mysql_fetch_assoc ($result)) {
    echo $row["user_id"];
    echo $row["fullname"];
}
mysql_free_result ($result);
?>
```

mysql_fetch_field

Returns an object containing field information. Can be used in order to obtain information about fields in a certain query result. If the field offset isn't specified, the next field that wasn't yet retrieved by **mysql_fetch_field**() is retrieved.

object **mysql_fetch_field**(*int* result, [*int* field_offset])

The properties of the object are as follows:

- name—column name
- table—name of the table to which the column belongs
- max_length—maximum length of the column
- not_null—1 if the column cannot be null
- primary_key —1 if the column is a primary key
- unique_key—1 if the column is a unique key
- multiple_key—1 if the column is a non-unique key
- numeric—1 if the column is numeric
- blob—1 if the column is a BLOB
- type—the type of column
- unsigned—1 if the column is unsigned
- zerofill—1 if the column is zero-filled

Example: Mysql_fetch_field()

```php
<?php
mysql_connect ($host, $user, $password)
    or die ("Could not connect");
$result = mysql_db_query ("database", "select * from table")
    or die ("Query failed");
# get column metadata
$i = 0;
while ($i < mysql_num_fields ($result)) {
    echo "Information for column $i:<BR>\n";
    $meta = mysql_fetch_field ($result);
    if (!$meta) {
        echo "No information available<BR>\n";
    }
```

```
    echo "<PRE>
blob:          $meta->blob
max_length:    $meta->max_length
multiple_key:  $meta->multiple_key
name:          $meta->name
not_null:      $meta->not_null
numeric:       $meta->numeric
primary_key:   $meta->primary_key
table:         $meta->table
type:          $meta->type
unique_key:    $meta->unique_key
unsigned:      $meta->unsigned
zerofill:      $meta->zerofill
</PRE>";
    $i++;
}
mysql_free_result ($result);
?>
```

See also **mysql_field_seek()**.

mysql_fetch_lengths

Returns an array that corresponds to the lengths of each field in the last row fetched by **mysql_fetch_row()**, or false on error. **mysql_fetch_lengths()** stores the lengths of each result column in the last row returned by **mysql_fetch_row()**, **mysql_fetch_array()**, and **mysql_fetch_object()** in an array, starting at offset 0. See also **mysql_fetch_row()**.

array **mysql_fetch_lengths**(*int* result)

mysql_fetch_object

Returns an object with properties that correspond to the fetched row, or false if no more rows exist. **mysql_fetch_object()** is similar to **mysql_fetch_array()**, with one difference—an object is returned, instead of an array. Indirectly, that means that you can only access the data by the field names, and not by their offsets (numbers are illegal property names). The optional argument **$result_type** is a constant and can take the following values: MYSQL_ASSOC, MYSQL_NUM, and MYSQL_BOTH. Speed-wise, the function is identical to **mysql_fetch_array()**, and almost as quick as **mysql_fetch_row()**; the difference is insignificant).

object **mysql_fetch_object**(*int* result, [*int* result_type])

Example: mysql_fetch_object()

```
<?php
mysql_connect ($host, $user, $password);
$result = mysql_db_query ("database", "select * from table");
while ($row = mysql_fetch_object ($result)) {
    echo $row->user_id;
    echo $row->fullname;
}
mysql_free_result ($result);
?>
```

See also **mysql_fetch_array**() and **mysql_fetch_row**().

mysql_fetch_row

Returns an array that corresponds to the fetched row, or false if no more rows exist. Fetches one row of data from the result associated with the specified result identifier. The row is returned as an array. Each result column is stored in an array offset, starting at offset 0. Subsequent call to **mysql_fetch_row**() would return the next row in the result set, or false if no more rows exist. See also **mysql_fetch_array**(), **mysql_fetch_object**(), **mysql_data_seek**(), **mysql_fetch_lengths**(), and **mysql_result**().

array **mysql_fetch_row**(*int* result)

mysql_field_flags

Returns the field flags of the specified field. The flags are reported as a single word per flag, separated by a single space so that you can split the returned value using **explode**(). The following flags are reported, if your version of MySQL is current enough to support them: "not_null", "primary_key", "unique_key", "multiple_key", "blob", "unsigned", "zerofill", "binary", "enum", "auto_increment", and "timestamp". For downward compatibility, **mysql_fieldflags**() can also be used.

string **mysql_field_flags**(*int* result, *int* field_offset)

mysql_field_len

Returns the length of the specified field. For downward compatibility, **mysql_fieldlen**() can also be used.

int **mysql_field_len**(*int* result, *int* field_offset)

mysql_field_name

Returns the name of the specified field index. **$result** must be a valid result identifier, and **$field_index** is the numerical offset of the field.

Note: $field_index starts at 0. For example, the index of the third field would actually be 2, the index of the fourth field would be 3, and so on.

string **mysql_field_name**(*int* result, *int* field_index)

Example: mysql_field_name()

```
// The users table consists of three fields:
//   user_id
//   username
//   password.
$res = mysql_db_query("users", "select * from users", $link);
echo mysql_field_name($res, 0) . "\n";
echo mysql_field_name($res, 2);
```

The previous example would produce the following output:

```
user_id
password
```

For downwards compatibility, **mysql_fieldname()** can also be used.

mysql_field_seek

Seeks to the specified field offset. If the next call **to mysql_fetch_field()** doesn't include a field offset, the field offset specified in **mysql_field_seek()** will be returned. See also **mysql_fetch_field()**.

int **mysql_field_seek**(*int* result, *int* field_offset)

mysql_field_table

Returns the name of the table where the specified field is. For downward compatibility, **mysql_fieldtable()** can also be used.

string **mysql_field_table**(*int* result, *int* field_offset)

mysql_field_type

Similar to the **mysql_field_name()** function. The arguments are identical, but the field type is returned instead. The field type will be one of "int", "real", "string", "blob", and others as detailed in the MySQL documentation(URL).

string **mysql_field_type**(*int* result, *int* field_offset)

Example: mysql field types

```php
<?php
mysql_connect ("localhost:3306");
mysql_select_db ("wisconsin");
$result = mysql_query ("SELECT * FROM onek");
$fields = mysql_num_fields ($result);
$rows   = mysql_num_rows ($result);
$i = 0;
$table = mysql_field_table ($result, $i);
echo "Your '".$table."' table has ".$fields." fields and ".$rows." records <BR>";
echo "The table has the following fields <BR>";
while ($i < $fields) {
    $type  = mysql_field_type  ($result, $i);
    $name  = mysql_field_name  ($result, $i);
    $len   = mysql_field_len   ($result, $i);
    $flags = mysql_field_flags ($result, $i);
    echo $type." ".$name." ".$len." ".$flags."<BR>";
    $i++;
}
mysql_close ();
?>
```

For downward compatibility, **mysql_fieldtype()** can also be used.

mysql_free_result

Frees all memory associated with the result identifier **$result**. **mysql_free_result()** only needs to be called if you are concerned about how much memory is being used for queries that return large result sets. All associated result memory is automatically freed at the end of the script's execution. For downward compatibility, **mysql_freeresult()** can also be used.

    int **mysql_free_result**(*int* result)

mysql_insert_id

Returns the ID generated for an AUTO_INCREMENT column by the previous INSERT query using the given **$link_identifier**. If **$link_identifier** isn't specified, the last opened link is assumed. **mysql_insert_id()** returns 0 if the previous query does not generate an AUTO_INCREMENT value. If you need to save the value for later, be sure to call **mysql_insert_id()** immediately after the query that generates the value.

    Note: The value of the MySQL SQL function, LAST_INSERT_ID(), always contains the most recently generated AUTO_INCREMENT value, and it is not reset between queries. **mysql_insert_id()** converts the return type of the native MySQL C API function, **mysql_insert_id()**, to a type of long. If your AUTO_INCREMENT column has a column type of BIGINT, the value returned by **mysql_insert_id()** will be incorrect. Instead, use the internal MySQL SQL function LAST_INSERT_ID().

    int **mysql_insert_id**([*int* link_identifier])

mysql_list_dbs

Returns a result pointer containing the databases available from the current mysql daemon. Use the **mysql_tablename()** function to traverse this result pointer.

    Note: The previous code would work just as easily with **mysql_fetch_row()** or other similar functions. For downward compatibility, **mysql_listdbs()** can also be used.

    int **mysql_list_dbs**([*int* link_identifier])

Example: mysql_list_dbs()

```
$link = mysql_connect('localhost', 'myname', 'secret');
$db_list = mysql_list_dbs($link);
while ($row = mysql_fetch_object($db_list)) {
  echo $row->Database . "\n";
}
```

The previous example would produce the following output:

```
database1
database2
database3
...
```

mysql_list_fields

Retrieves information about the given table name. Arguments are the database name and the table name. A result pointer is returned, which can be used with **mysql_field_flags()**, **mysql_field_len()**, **mysql_field_name()**, and **mysql_field_type()**. A result identifier is a positive integer. The function returns -1 if an error occurs. A string describing the error will be placed in **$phperrmsg**. Unless the function was called as **@mysql()**, this error string will also be printed out. For downward compatibility, **mysql_listfields()** can also be used.

int **mysql_list_fields**(*string* database_name, *string* table_name, [*int* link_identifier])

Example: mysql_list_fields()

```
$link = mysql_connect('localhost', 'myname', 'secret');
$fields = mysql_list_fields("database1", "table1", $link);
$columns = mysql_num_fields($fields);
for ($i = 0; $i < $columns; $i++) {
  echo mysql_field_name($fields, $i) . "\n";;
}
```

The previous example would produce the following output:

```
field1
field2
field3
...
```

mysql_list_tables

Takes a database name and returns a result pointer, much like the **mysql_db_query()** function. The **mysql_tablename()** function should be used to extract the actual table names from the result pointer. For downward compatibility, **mysql_listtables()** can also be used.

int **mysql_list_tables**(*string* database, [*int* link_identifier])

mysql_num_fields

Returns the number of fields in a result set. See also **mysql_db_query()**, **mysql_query()**, **mysql_fetch_field()**, and **mysql_num_rows()**. For downward compatibility, **mysql_numfields()** can also be used.

int **mysql_num_fields**(*int* result)

mysql_num_rows

Returns the number of rows in a result set. This command is only valid for SELECT statements. To retrieve the number of rows returned from an INSERT, UPDATE, or DELETE, use **mysql_affected_rows()**. See also **mysql_db_query()**, **mysql_query()** and **mysql_fetch_row()**. For downward compatibility, **mysql_numrows()** can also be used.

int **mysql_num_rows**(*int* result)

mysql_pconnect

Returns a positive MySQL persistent link identifier on success, or false on error. Establishes a connection to a MySQL server. The following defaults are assumed for missing optional parameters: **$host:port** = 'localhost:3306', **$username** = name of the user that owns the server process, and **$password** = empty password. The hostname string can also include a port number. For example, "hostname:port" or a path to a socket, such as ":/path/to/socket" for the localhost.

Note: Support for ":port" was added in 3.0B4. Support for the ":/path/to/socket" was added in 3.0.10.

int **mysql_pconnect**([*string* :/path/to/socket], [*string* username], [*string* password])

mysql_pconnect() acts very much like **mysql_connect()** with two major differences. First, when connecting, the function would first try to find a (persistent) link that's already open with the same host, username, and password. If one is found, an identifier for it will be returned instead of opening a new connection. Second, the connection to the SQL server will not be closed when the execution of the script ends. Instead, the link will remain open for future use (**mysql_close()** will not close links established by **mysql_pconnect()**). This type of link is therefore called "persistent."

mysql_query

Sends a query to the currently active database on the server that's associated with the specified link identifier. If **$link_identifier** isn't specified, the last opened link is assumed. If no link is open, the function tries to establish a link as if **mysql_connect()** was called with no arguments, and then use it.

Note: The query string should not end with a semicolon. **mysql_query()** returns true (nonzero) or false to indicate whether or not the query succeeded. A return value of true means that the query was legal and could be executed by the server. It does not indicate anything about the number of rows affected or returned. It is perfectly possible for a query to succeed but affect no rows or return no rows.

int **mysql_query**(*string* query, [*int* link_identifier])

The following query is syntactically invalid, so **mysql_query()** fails and returns false:
Example: mysql_query()

```
<?php
$result = mysql_query ("SELECT * WHERE 1=1")
    or die ("Invalid query");
?>
```

The following query is semantically invalid if *my_col* is not a column in the table *my_tbl* , so **mysql_query()** fails and returns false:
Example: mysql_query()

```
<?php
$result = mysql_query ("SELECT my_col FROM my_tbl")
    or die ("Invalid query");
?>
```

mysql_query() will also fail and return false if you don't have permission to access the table(s) referenced by the query. Assuming the query succeeds, you can call **mysql_num_rows()** to find out how many rows were returned for a SELECT statement or **mysql_affected_rows()** to find out how many rows were affected by a DELETE, INSERT, REPLACE, or UPDATE statement. For SELECT statements, **mysql_query()** returns a new result identifier that you can pass to **mysql_result()**. When you are finished with the result set, you can free the resources associated with it by calling **mysql_free_result()**. Although, the memory will automatically be freed at the end of the script's execution. See also **mysql_affected_rows()**, **mysql_db_query()**, **mysql_free_result()**, **mysql_result()**, **mysql_select_db()**, and **mysql_connect()**.

mysql_result

Returns the contents of one cell from a MySQL result set. The field argument can be the field's offset, the field's name, or the field's table dot field's name (fieldname.tablename). If the column name has been aliased ('select foo as bar from . . . '), use the alias instead of the column name. When working on large result sets, you should consider using one of the functions that fetch an entire row. As these functions return the contents of multiple cells in one function call, they're much quicker than **mysql_result()**. Also, note that specifying a numeric offset for the field argument is much quicker than specifying a fieldname or tablename.fieldname argument. Calls to **mysql_result()** should not be mixed with calls to other functions that deal with the result set. Recommended high-performance alternatives are: **mysql_fetch_row()**, **mysql_fetch_array()**, and **mysql_fetch_object()**.

mixed **mysql_result**(*int* result, *int* row, [*mixed* field])

mysql_select_db

Returns true on success, false on error. Sets the current active database on the server that's associated with the specified link identifier. If no link identifier is specified, the last opened link is assumed. If no link is open, the function will try to establish a link as if **mysql_connect()** was called, and then use it. Every subsequent call to **mysql_query()** will be made on the active database. See also **mysql_connect()**, **mysql_pconnect()**, and **mysql_query()**. For downward compatibility, **mysql_selectdb()** can also be used.

int **mysql_select_db**(*string* database_name, [*int* link_identifier])

mysql_tablename

Takes a result pointer returned by the **mysql_list_tables()** function, as well as an integer index, and returns the name of a table. The **mysql_num_rows()** function may be used to determine the number of tables in the result pointer.

string **mysql_tablename**(*int* result, *int* i)

Example: Mysql_tablename()

```
<?php
mysql_connect ("localhost:3306");
```

```
$result = mysql_list_tables ("wisconsin");
$i = 0;
while ($i < mysql_num_rows ($result)) {
    $tb_names[$i] = mysql_tablename ($result, $i);
    echo $tb_names[$i] . "<BR>";
    $i++;
}
?>
```

natcasesort

Implements a sort algorithm that orders alphanumeric strings in the way a human being would. This is described as a "natural ordering." **natcasesort()** is a case insensitive version of **natsort()**. See **natsort()** for an example of the difference between this algorithm and the regular computer string sorting algorithms. For more information see Martin Pool's Natural Order String Comparison (*http://www.linuxcare.com.au/projects/natsort/*) page. See also **sort()**, **natsort()**, **strnatcmp()** and **strnatcasecmp()**.

void **natcasesort**(*array* array)

natsort

Implements a sort algorithm that orders alphanumeric strings in the way a human being would. This is described as a "natural ordering." An example of the difference between this algorithm and the regular computer string sorting algorithms (used in **sort()**) can be seen in the following example.

void **natsort**(*array* array)

Example: natsort()

```
$array1 = $array2 = array ("img12.png","img10.png","img2.png","img1.png");
sort($array1);
echo "Standard sorting\n";
print_r($array1);
natsort($array2);
echo "\nNatural order sorting\n";
print_r($array2);
```

The previous code will generate the following output:

```
Standard sorting
Array
(
    [0] => img1.png
    [1] => img10.png
    [2] => img12.png
    [3] => img2.png
)
Natural order sorting
Array
```

```
(
    [3] => img1.png
    [2] => img2.png
    [1] => img10.png
    [0] => img12.png
)
```

For more information see Martin Pool's Natural Order String Comparison *(http://www.linux-care.com.au/projects/natsort/)* page. See also **natcasesort()**, **strnatcmp()** and **strnat-casecmp()**.

next

Returns the array element in the next place that's pointed by the internal array pointer, or false if no more elements exist. **Next()** behaves like **current()**, with one difference. It advances the internal array pointer one place forward before returning the element, which means it returns the next array element and advances the internal array pointer by one. If advancing the internal array pointer results in going beyond the end of the element list, **next()** returns false. If the array contains empty elements or elements that have a key value of 0, then this function will return false for these elements as well. To properly traverse an array which may contain empty elements or elements with key values of 0, see the **each()** function. See also **current()**, **end()**, **prev()**, and **reset()**.

mixed **next**(*array* array)

nl2br

Returns string with '<BR>' inserted before all newlines. See also **htmlspecialchars()**, **htmlentities()** and **word_wrap()**.

string **nl2br**(*string* string)

number_format

Returns a formatted version of **$number**. This function accepts either one, two, or four parameters (not three). If only one parameter is given, **$number** will be formatted without decimals, but with a comma (",") between every group of thousands. If two parameters are given, **$number** will be formatted with **$decimals** decimals with a dot (".") in front, and a comma (",") between every group of thousands. If all four parameters are given, **$number** will be formatted with **$decimals** decimals, **$dec_point** instead of a dot (".") before the decimals, and **$thousands_sep** instead of a comma (",") between every group of thousands.

string **number_format**(*float* number, *int* decimals, *string* dec_point, *string* thousands_sep)

ob_end_clean

Discards the contents of the output buffer and turns off output buffering. See also **ob_start()** and **ob_end_flush()**.

void **ob_end_clean**(*void*)

ob_end_flush

Sends the contents of the output buffer (if any) and turns output buffering off. If you want to further process the buffer's contents, you have to call **ob_get_contents()** before **ob_end_flush()** because the buffer contents are discarded after **ob_get_contents()** is called. See also **ob_start()**, **ob_get_contents()**, and **ob_end_clean()**.

> *void* **ob_end_flush**(*void*)

ob_get_contents

Returns the contents of the output buffer or false, if output buffering isn't active. See also **ob_start()** and **ob_get_length()**.

> *string* **ob_get_contents**(*void*)

ob_get_length

Returns the length of the contents in the output buffer or false, if output buffering isn't active. See also **ob_start()** and **ob_get_contents()**.

> *string* **ob_get_length**(*void*)

ob_implicit_flush

Turns implicit flushing on or off (if no **$flag** is given, it defaults to on). Implicit flushing will result in a flush operation after every output call, so that explicit calls to **flush()** will no longer be needed. Turning implicit flushing on will disable output buffering, and the output buffers current output will be sent as if **ob_end_flush()** had been called. See also **flush()**, **ob_start()**, and **ob_end_flush()**.

> *void* **ob_implicit_flush**([*int* flag])

ob_start

Turns output buffering on. While output buffering is active, no output is sent from the script. Instead, the output is stored in an internal buffer. The contents of this internal buffer may be copied into a string variable using **ob_get_contents()**. To output what is stored in the internal buffer, use **ob_end_flush()**. Alternatively, **ob_end_clean()** will silently discard the buffer contents. See also **ob_get_contents()**, **ob_end_flush()**, **ob_end_clean()**, and **ob_implicit_flush()**.

> *void* **ob_start**(*void*)

OCIBindByName

Binds the PHP variable **$variable** to the Oracle placeholder **$ph_name**. Whether it will be used for input or output will be determined run-time, and the necessary storage space will be allocated. The **$length** parameter sets the maximum length for the bind. If you set **$length** to -1, OCIBindByName() will use the current length of **$variable** to set the maximum length. If you need to bind an abstract Datatype (LOB/ROWID/BFILE), you need to allocate it first using **OCINewDescriptor()** function. The **$length** is not used for abstract datatypes and should be set to -1. The **$type** variable tells oracle what kind of descriptor we want to use. Possible values are as follows: OCI_B_FILE (Binary-File), OCI_B_CFILE (Character-File), OCI_B_CLOB (Character-LOB), OCI_B_BLOB (Binary-LOB), and OCI_B_ROWID (ROWID).

int **OCIBindByName**(int stmt, string ph_name, & variable, int length, [int type])

Example: OCIDefineByName

```php
<?php
/* OCIBindByPos example thies@digicol.de (980221)
   inserts 3 records into emp, and uses the ROWID for updating the
   records just after the insert.
*/
$conn = OCILogon("scott","tiger");
$stmt = OCIParse($conn,"insert into emp (empno, ename) ".
                       "values (:empno,:ename) ".
                       "returning ROWID into :rid");
$data = array(1111 => "Larry", 2222 => "Bill", 3333 => "Jim");
$rowid = OCINewDescriptor($conn,OCI_D_ROWID);
OCIBindByName($stmt,":empno",&$empno,32);
OCIBindByName($stmt,":ename",&$ename,32);
OCIBindByName($stmt,":rid",&$rowid,-1,OCI_B_ROWID);
$update = OCIParse($conn,"update emp set sal = :sal where ROWID = :rid");
OCIBindByName($update,":rid",&$rowid,-1,OCI_B_ROWID);
OCIBindByName($update,":sal",&$sal,32);
$sal = 10000;
while (list($empno,$ename) = each($data)) {
    OCIExecute($stmt);
    OCIExecute($update);
}
$rowid->free();
OCIFreeStatement($update);
OCIFreeStatement($stmt);
$stmt = OCIParse($conn,"select * from emp where empno in (1111,2222,3333)");
OCIExecute($stmt);
while (OCIFetchInto($stmt,&$arr,OCI_ASSOC)) {
    var_dump($arr);
}
OCIFreeStatement($stmt);
/* delete our "junk" from the emp table.... */
$stmt = OCIParse($conn,"delete from emp where empno in (1111,2222,3333)");
OCIExecute($stmt);
OCIFreeStatement($stmt);
OCILogoff($conn);
?>
```

It is a bad idea to use magic quotes and **OciBindByName()** simultaneously because no quoting is needed on quoted variables. Any quotes magically applied will be written into your database because **OciBindByName()** is not able to distinguish magically added quotes from those added by intention.

OCIColumnIsNULL

Returns true if the returned column **$column** in the result from the statement **$stmt** is NULL. You can use either the column-number (1-Based) or the column-name for the **$col** parameter. See also **OCINumCols()**, **OCIColumnType()**, and **OCIColumnSize()**.

int **OCIColumnIsNULL**(int stmt, mixed column)

OCIColumnName

Returns the name of the column corresponding to the column number (1-based) that is passed in.

string **OCIColumnName**(*int* stmt, *int* col)

Example: OCIColumnName

```php
<?php
    print "<HTML><PRE>\n";
    $conn = OCILogon("scott", "tiger");
    $stmt = OCIParse($conn,"select * from emp");
    OCIExecute($stmt);
    print "<TABLE BORDER=\"1\">";
    print "<TR>";
    print "<TH>Name</TH>";
    print "<TH>Type</TH>";
    print "<TH>Length</TH>";
    print "</TR>";
    $ncols = OCINumCols($stmt);
    for ( $i = 1; $i <= $ncols; $i++ ) {
        $column_name  = OCIColumnName($stmt,$i);
        $column_type  = OCIColumnType($stmt,$i);
        $column_size  = OCIColumnSize($stmt,$i);
        print "<TR>";
        print "<TD>$column_name</TD>";
        print "<TD>$column_type</TD>";
        print "<TD>$column_size</TD>";
        print "</TR>";
    }
    OCIFreeStatement($stmt);
    OCILogoff($conn);
    print "</PRE>";
    print "</HTML>\n";
?>
```

OCIColumnSize

Returns the size of the column as given by Oracle. You can use either the column-number (1-based) or the column-name for the **$col** parameter. See also **OCINumCols()**, **OCIColumnName()**, and **OCIColumnSize()**.

int **OCIColumnSize**(*int* stmt, *mixed* column)

Example: OCIColumnSize

```php
<?php
    print "<HTML><PRE>\n";
    $conn = OCILogon("scott", "tiger");
    $stmt = OCIParse($conn,"select * from emp");
    OCIExecute($stmt);
    print "<TABLE BORDER=\"1\">";
    print "<TR>";
    print "<TH>Name</TH>";
    print "<TH>Type</TH>";
    print "<TH>Length</TH>";
    print "</TR>";
    $ncols = OCINumCols($stmt);
    for ( $i = 1; $i <= $ncols; $i++ ) {
        $column_name  = OCIColumnName($stmt,$i);
        $column_type  = OCIColumnType($stmt,$i);
        $column_size  = OCIColumnSize($stmt,$i);
        print "<TR>";
        print "<TD>$column_name</TD>";
        print "<TD>$column_type</TD>";
        print "<TD>$column_size</TD>";
        print "</TR>";
    }
    print "</TABLE>";
    OCIFreeStatement($stmt);
    OCILogoff($conn);
    print "</PRE>";
    print "</HTML>\n";
?>
```

OCIColumnType

Returns the data type of the column corresponding to the column number (1-based) that is passed in. See also **OCINumCols()**, **OCIColumnName()**, and **OCIColumnSize()**.

mixed **OCIColumnType**(*int* stmt, *int* col)

Example: OCIColumnType

```php
<?php
    print "<HTML><PRE>\n";
    $conn = OCILogon("scott", "tiger");
    $stmt = OCIParse($conn,"select * from emp");
    OCIExecute($stmt);
    print "<TABLE BORDER=\"1\">";
    print "<TR>";
    print "<TH>Name</TH>";
    print "<TH>Type</TH>";
    print "<TH>Length</TH>";
    print "</TR>";
    $ncols = OCINumCols($stmt);
    for ( $i = 1; $i <= $ncols; $i++ ) {
        $column_name  = OCIColumnName($stmt,$i);
        $column_type  = OCIColumnType($stmt,$i);
        $column_size  = OCIColumnSize($stmt,$i);
        print "<TR>";
        print "<TD>$column_name</TD>";
```

```
        print "<TD>$column_type</TD>";
        print "<TD>$column_size</TD>";
        print "</TR>";
    }
    OCIFreeStatement($stmt);
    OCILogoff($conn);
    print "</PRE>";
    print "</HTML>\n";
?>
```

OCICommit

Commits all outstanding statements for Oracle connection **$connection**.

    int **OCICommit**(*int* connection)

OCIDefineByName

Uses fetches SQL-Columns into user-defined PHP-Variables. Be careful that the Oracle user is ALL-UPPERCASE column-names, whereby in your select you can also write lower-case. **OCIDefineByName()** expects the **$Column-Name** to be in uppercase. If you define a variable that doesn't exists in your select statement, no error will be given. If you need to define an abstract Datatype (LOB/ROWID/BFILE), you need to allocate it first using **OCINewDescriptor()** function. See also the **OCIBindByName()** function.

    int **OCIDefineByName**(*int* stmt, *string* Column-Name, & variable, [*int* type])

Example: OCIDefineByName

```
<?php
/* OCIDefineByPos example thies@digicol.de (980219) */
$conn = OCILogon("scott","tiger");
$stmt = OCIParse($conn,"select empno, ename from emp");
/* the define MUST be done BEFORE ociexecute! */
OCIDefineByName($stmt,"EMPNO",&$empno);
OCIDefineByName($stmt,"ENAME",&$ename);
OCIExecute($stmt);
while (OCIFetch($stmt)) {
    echo "empno:".$empno."\n";
    echo "ename:".$ename."\n";
}
OCIFreeStatement($stmt);
OCILogoff($conn);
?>
```

OCIError

Returns the last error found. If the optional **$stmt | conn | global** is not provided, the last error encountered is returned. If no error is found, **OCIError()** returns false. **OCIError()** returns the error as an associative array. In this array, **$code** consists of the oracle error code and **$message**, the oracle errorstring.

    array **OCIError**([*int* stmt | conn | global])

OCIExecute

Executes a previously parsed statement (see **OCIParse()**). The optional **$mode** enables you to specify the execution mode (default is OCI_COMMIT_ON_SUCCESS). If you don't want statements to be committed automatically, specify OCI_DEFAULT as your mode.

int **OCIExecute**(*int* statement, [*int* mode])

OCIFetch

Fetches the next row (for SELECT statements) into the internal result-buffer.

int **OCIFetch**(*int* statement)

OCIFetchInto

Fetches the next row (for SELECT statements) into the **$result** array. **OCIFetchInto()** will overwrite the previous content of **$result**. By default, **$result** will contain a one-based array of all columns that are not NULL. The **$mode** parameter enables you to change the default behavior. You can specify more than one flag by simply adding them up, for example, OCI_ASSOC+OCI_RETURN_NULLS.

int **OCIFetchInto**(*int* stmt, *&* result, [*int* mode])

The known flags are as follows:

- OCI_ASSOC—Return an associative array.
- OCI_NUM—Return a numbered array starting with one. (DEFAULT)
- OCI_RETURN_NULLS—Return empty columns.
- OCI_RETURN_LOBS—Return the value of a LOB instead of the descriptor.

OCIFetchStatement

Fetches all the rows from a result into a user-defined array. **OCIFetchStatement()** returns the number of rows fetched.

int **OCIFetchStatement**(*int* stmt, *&* variable)

Example: OCIFetchStatement

```php
<?php
/* OCIFetchStatement example mbritton@verinet.com (990624) */
$conn = OCILogon("scott","tiger");
$stmt = OCIParse($conn,"select * from emp");
OCIExecute($stmt);
$nrows = OCIFetchStatement($stmt,$results);
if ( $nrows > 0 ) {
    print "<TABLE BORDER=\"1\">\n";
    print "<TR>\n";
    while ( list( $key, $val ) = each( $results ) ) {
```

```
        print "<TH>$key</TH>\n";
    }
    print "</TR>\n";
    for ( $i = 0; $i < $nrows; $i++ ) {
        reset($results);
        print "<TR>\n";
        while ( $column = each($results) ) {
            $data = $column['value'];
            print "<TD>$data[$i]</TD>\n";
        }
        print "</TR>\n";
    }
    print "</TABLE>\n";
} else {
    echo "No data found<BR>\n";
}
print "$nrows Records Selected<BR>\n";
OCIFreeStatement($stmt);
OCILogoff($conn);
?>
```

OCIFreeCursor

Returns true if successful, or false if unsuccessful.

int **OCIFreeCursor**(*int* stmt)

OCIFreeDesc

Returns true if successful, or false if unsuccessful.

int **OCIFreeDesc**(*object* lob)

OCIFreeStatement

Returns true if successful, or false if unsuccessful.

int **OCIFreeStatement**(*int* stmt)

OCIInternalDebug

Enables internal debug output. Set **$onoff** to 0 to turn debug output off, 1 to turn it on.

void **OCIInternalDebug**(*int* onoff)

OCILogOff

Closes an Oracle connection.

int **OCILogOff**(*int* connection)

OCILogon

Returns a connection identifier needed for most other OCI calls. The optional third parameter can contain either the name of the local Oracle instance or the name of the entry in tnsnames.ora to which you want to connect. If the optional third parameter is not specified, PHP uses the environment variables ORACLE_SID (Oracle instance) or TWO_TASK (tnsnames.ora) to determine to which database to connect. Connections are shared at the page level when using **OCILogon**(). This means that commits and rollbacks apply to all open transactions in the page, even if you have created multiple connections. The following example demonstrates how the connections are shared.

int **OCILogon**(*string* username, *string* password, [*string* db])

Example: OCILogon

```php
<?php
print "<HTML><PRE>";
$db = "";
$c1 = ocilogon("scott","tiger",$db);
$c2 = ocilogon("scott","tiger",$db);
function create_table($conn)
{ $stmt = ociparse($conn,"create table scott.hallo (test varchar2(64))");
  ociexecute($stmt);
  echo $conn." created table\n\n";
}
function drop_table($conn)
{ $stmt = ociparse($conn,"drop table scott.hallo");
  ociexecute($stmt);
  echo $conn." dropped table\n\n";
}
function insert_data($conn)
{ $stmt = ociparse($conn,"insert into scott.hallo
            values('$conn' || ' ' || to_char(sysdate,'DD-MON-YY HH24:MI:SS'))");
  ociexecute($stmt,OCI_DEFAULT);
  echo $conn." inserted hallo\n\n";
}
function delete_data($conn)
{ $stmt = ociparse($conn,"delete from scott.hallo");
  ociexecute($stmt,OCI_DEFAULT);
  echo $conn." deleted hallo\n\n";
}
function commit($conn)
{ ocicommit($conn);
  echo $conn." commited\n\n";
}
function rollback($conn)
{ ocirollback($conn);
  echo $conn." rollback\n\n";
}
function select_data($conn)
{ $stmt = ociparse($conn,"select * from scott.hallo");
  ociexecute($stmt,OCI_DEFAULT);
  echo $conn."----selecting\n\n";
  while (ocifetch($stmt))
```

```
        echo $conn." <".ociresult($stmt,"TEST").">\n\n";
    echo $conn."----done\n\n";
}
create_table($c1);
insert_data($c1);       // Insert a row using c1
insert_data($c2);       // Insert a row using c2
select_data($c1);       // Results of both inserts are returned
select_data($c2);
rollback($c1);          // Rollback using c1
select_data($c1);       // Both inserts have been rolled back
select_data($c2);
insert_data($c2);       // Insert a row using c2
commit($c2);            // commit using c2
select_data($c1);       // result of c2 insert is returned
delete_data($c1);       // delete all rows in table using c1
select_data($c1);       // no rows returned
select_data($c2);       // no rows returned
commit($c1);            // commit using c1
select_data($c1);       // no rows returned
select_data($c2);       // no rows returned
drop_table($c1);
print "</PRE></HTML>";
?>
```

See also **OCIPLogon()** and **OCINLogon()**.

OCINewCursor

Allocates a new statement handle on the specified connection.

int **OCINewCursor**(*int* conn)

Example: Using a REF CURSOR from a stored procedure

```
<?php
// suppose your stored procedure info.output returns a ref cursor in :data
$conn = OCILogon("scott","tiger");
$curs = OCINewCursor($conn);
$stmt = OCIParse($conn,"begin info.output(:data); end;");

ocibindbyname($stmt,"data",&$curs,-1,OCI_B_CURSOR);
ociexecute($stmt);
ociexecute($curs);
while (OCIFetchInto($curs,&$data)) {
    var_dump($data);
}
OCIFreeCursor($stmt);
OCIFreeStatement($curs);
OCILogoff($conn);
?>
```

Example: Using a REF CURSOR in a select statement

```
<?php
print "<HTML><BODY>";
$conn = OCILogon("scott","tiger");
```

```
$count_cursor = "CURSOR(select count(empno) num_emps from emp " .
                "where emp.deptno = dept.deptno) as EMPCNT from dept";
$stmt = OCIParse($conn,"select deptno,dname,$count_cursor");
ociexecute($stmt);
print "<TABLE BORDER=\"1\">";
print "<TR>";
print "<TH>DEPT NAME</TH>";
print "<TH>DEPT #</TH>";
print "<TH># EMPLOYEES</TH>";
print "</TR>";
while (OCIFetchInto($stmt,&$data,OCI_ASSOC)) {
    print "<TR>";
    $dname  = $data["DNAME"];
    $deptno = $data["DEPTNO"];
    print "<TD>$dname</TD>";
    print "<TD>$deptno</TD>";
    ociexecute($data[ "EMPCNT" ]);
    while (OCIFetchInto($data[ "EMPCNT" ],&$subdata,OCI_ASSOC)) {
        $num_emps = $subdata["NUM_EMPS"];
        print  "<TD>$num_emps</TD>";
    }
    print "</TR>";
}
print "</TABLE>";
print "</BODY></HTML>";
OCIFreeStatement($stmt);
OCILogoff($conn);
?>
```

OCINewDescriptor

Allocates storage to hold descriptors or LOB locators. Valid values for the valid **$type** are: OCI_D_FILE, OCI_D_LOB, and OCI_D_ROWID. For LOB descriptors, the methods load, save, and savefile are associated with the descriptor. The load method exists for BFILE only. See the second example usage hints.

string **OCINewDescriptor**(*int* connection, [*int* type])

Example: OCINewDescriptor

```
<?php
    /* This script is designed to be called from a HTML form.
     * It expects $user, $password, $table, $where, and $commitsize
     * to be passed in from the form.  The script then deletes
     * the selected rows using the ROWID and commits after each
     * set of $commitsize rows. (Use with care, there is no rollback)
     */
    $conn = OCILogon($user, $password);
    $stmt = OCIParse($conn,"select rowid from $table $where");
    $rowid = OCINewDescriptor($conn,OCI_D_ROWID);
    OCIDefineByName($stmt,"ROWID",&$rowid);
    OCIExecute($stmt);
    while ( OCIFetch($stmt) ) {
        $nrows = OCIRowCount($stmt);
        $delete = OCIParse($conn,"delete from $table where ROWID = :rid");
        OCIBindByName($delete,":rid",&$rowid,-1,OCI_B_ROWID);
```

```
        OCIExecute($delete);
        print "$nrows\n";
        if ( ($nrows % $commitsize) == 0 ) {
            OCICommit($conn);
        }
    }
    $nrows = OCIRowCount($stmt);
    print "$nrows deleted...\n";
    OCIFreeStatement($stmt);
    OCILogoff($conn);
?>
<?php
    /* This script demonstrates file upload to LOB columns
     * The formfield used for this example looks like this
     * <form action="upload.php3" method="post" enctype="multipart/form-data">
     * <input type="file" name="lob_upload">
     * ...
     */
  if(!isset($lob_upload) || $lob_upload == 'none'){
?>
<form action="upload.php3" method="post" enctype="multipart/form-data">
Upload file: <input type="file" name="lob_upload"><br>
<input type="submit" value="Upload"> - <input type="reset">
</form>
<?php
  } else {
      // $lob_upload contains the temporary filename of the uploaded file
      $conn = OCILogon($user, $password);
      $lob = OCINewDescriptor($conn, OCI_D_LOB);
      $stmt = OCIParse($conn,"insert into $table (id, the_blob)
                values(my_seq.NEXTVAL, EMPTY_BLOB()) returning the_blob into
:the_blob");
      OCIBindByName($stmt, ':the_blob', &$lob, -1, OCI_B_BLOB);
      OCIExecute($stmt);
      if($lob->savefile($lob_upload)){
          OCICommit($conn);
          echo "Blob successfully uploaded\n";
      }else{
          echo "Couldn't upload Blob\n";
      }
      OCIFreeDesc($lob);
      OCIFreeStatement($stmt);
      OCILogoff($conn);
  }
?>
```

OCINLogon

Creates a new connection to an Oracle 8 database and logs on. The optional third parameter can either contain the name of the local Oracle instance or the name of the entry in tnsnames.ora to which you want to connect. If the optional third parameter is not specified, PHP uses the environment variables ORACLE_SID (Oracle instance) or TWO_TASK (tnsnames.ora) in order to determine to which database to connect. **OCINLogon()** forces a new connection. This should be used if you need to isolate a set of transactions. By default, connections are shared at the page level if using **OCILogon()** or at the Web server process level if using **OCIPLogon()**. If you have multiple connections open using **OCINLogon()**, all commits and rollbacks apply to the specified connection only. This example demonstrates how the connections are separated. See also **OCILogon()** and **OCIPLogon()**.

int **OCINLogon**(*string* username, *string* password, [*string* db])

Example: OCINLogon

```php
<?php
print "<HTML><PRE>";
$db = "";
$c1 = ocilogon("scott","tiger",$db);
$c2 = ocinlogon("scott","tiger",$db);
function create_table($conn)
{ $stmt = ociparse($conn,"create table scott.hallo (test
varchar2(64))");
  ociexecute($stmt);
  echo $conn." created table\n\n";
}
function drop_table($conn)
{ $stmt = ociparse($conn,"drop table scott.hallo");
  ociexecute($stmt);
  echo $conn." dropped table\n\n";
}
function insert_data($conn)
{ $stmt = ociparse($conn,"insert into scott.hallo
            values('$conn' || ' ' || to_char(sysdate,'DD-MON-YY HH24:MI:SS'))");
  ociexecute($stmt,OCI_DEFAULT);
  echo $conn." inserted hallo\n\n";
}
function delete_data($conn)
{ $stmt = ociparse($conn,"delete from scott.hallo");
  ociexecute($stmt,OCI_DEFAULT);
  echo $conn." deleted hallo\n\n";
}
function commit($conn)
{ ocicommit($conn);
  echo $conn." commited\n\n";
}
function rollback($conn)
{ ocirollback($conn);
  echo $conn." rollback\n\n";
}
function select_data($conn)
{ $stmt = ociparse($conn,"select * from scott.hallo");
  ociexecute($stmt,OCI_DEFAULT);
  echo $conn."----selecting\n\n";
  while (ocifetch($stmt))
    echo $conn." <".ociresult($stmt,"TEST").">\n\n";
  echo $conn."----done\n\n";
}
create_table($c1);
insert_data($c1);
select_data($c1);
select_data($c2);
rollback($c1);
select_data($c1);
```

```
    select_data($c2);
    insert_data($c2);
    commit($c2);
    select_data($c1);
    delete_data($c1);
    select_data($c1);
    select_data($c2);
    commit($c1);
    select_data($c1);
    select_data($c2);
    drop_table($c1);
    print "</PRE></HTML>";
    ?>
```

OCINumCols

Returns the number of columns in a statement.

int **OCINumCols**(*int* stmt)

Example: OCINumCols

```
<?php
    print "<HTML><PRE>\n";
    $conn = OCILogon("scott", "tiger");
    $stmt = OCIParse($conn,"select * from emp");
    OCIExecute($stmt);
    while ( OCIFetch($stmt) ) {
        print "\n";
        $ncols = OCINumCols($stmt);
        for ( $i = 1; $i <= $ncols; $i++ ) {
            $column_name  = OCIColumnName($stmt,$i);
            $column_value = OCIResult($stmt,$i);
            print $column_name . ': ' . $column_value . "\n";
        }
        print "\n";
    }
    OCIFreeStatement($stmt);
    OCILogoff($conn);
    print "</PRE>";
    print "</HTML>\n";
?>
```

OCIParse

Parses the **$query** using **$conn**. It returns the statement identity if the query is valid, false if not. The **$query** can be any valid SQL statement.

int **OCIParse**(*int* conn, *string* query)

OCIPLogon

Creates a persistent connection to an Oracle 8 database and logs on. The optional third parameter can either contain the name of the local Oracle instance or the name of the entry in tnsnames.ora to which you want to connect. If the optional third parameter is not specified, PHP uses the environment variables ORACLE_SID (Oracle instance) or TWO_TASK (tnsnames.ora) to determine to which database to connect. See also **OCILogon()** and **OCINLogon()**.

int **OCIPLogon**(*string* username, *string* password, [*string* db])

OCIResult

Returns the data for column $column in the current row (see **OCIFetch()**). **OCIResult()** will return everything as strings, except for abstract types (ROWIDs, LOBs, and FILEs).

mixed **OCIResult**(*int* statement, *mixed* column)

OCIRollback

Rolls back all outstanding statements for Oracle connection **$connection**.

int **OCIRollback**(*int* connection)

OCIRowCount

Returns the number of rows affected for update-statements, for example. This funtion will not tell you the number of rows a select will return.

int **OCIRowCount**(*int* statement)

Example: OCIRowCount

```php
<?php
    print "<HTML><PRE>";
    $conn = OCILogon("scott","tiger");
    $stmt = OCIParse($conn,"create table emp2 as select * from emp");
    OCIExecute($stmt);
    print OCIRowCount($stmt) . " rows inserted.<BR>";
    OCIFreeStatement($stmt);
    $stmt = OCIParse($conn,"delete from emp2");
    OCIExecute($stmt);
    print OCIRowCount($stmt) . " rows deleted.<BR>";
    OCICommit($conn);
    OCIFreeStatement($stmt);
    $stmt = OCIParse($conn,"drop table emp2");
    OCIExecute($stmt);
    OCIFreeStatement($stmt);
    OCILogOff($conn);
    print "</PRE></HTML>";
?>
```

OCIServerVersion

string **OCIServerVersion**(*int* conn)

Example: OCIServerVersion

```php
<?php
   $conn = OCILogon("scott","tiger");
   print "Server Version: " . OCIServerVersion($conn);
   OCILogOff($conn);
?>
```

OCIStatementType

string **OCIStatementType**(*int* stmt)

OCIStatementType() returns one of the following values:

"SELECT"	"UPDATE"	"DELETE"
"INSERT"	"CREATE"	"DROP"
"ALTER"	"BEGIN"	"DECLARE"
"UNKNOWN"		

Example: Code examples

```php
<?php
   print "<HTML><PRE>";
   $conn = OCILogon("scott","tiger");
   $sql  = "delete from emp where deptno = 10";
   $stmt = OCIParse($conn,$sql);
   if ( OCIStatementType($stmt) == "DELETE" ) {
       die "You are not allowed to delete from this table<BR>";
   }
   OCILogoff($conn);
   print "</PRE></HTML>";
?>
```

octdec

Returns the decimal equivalent of the octal number represented by the octal_string argument. OctDec converts an octal string to a decimal number. The largest number that can be converted is 17777777777 or 2147483647 in decimal. See also **decoct()**.

int **octdec**(*string* octal_string)

odbc_autocommit

Without the **$OnOff** parameter, this function returns auto-commit status for **$connection_id.** True is returned if auto-commit is on, false if it is off or an error occurs. If **$OnOff** is true, auto-commit is enabled; if it is false auto-commit is disabled. Returns true on success, false on failure. By default, auto-commit is on for a connection. Disabling auto-commit is equivalent to starting a transaction. See also **odbc_commit()** and **odbc_rollback()**.

int **odbc_autocommit**(*int* connection_id, [*int* OnOff])

odbc_binmode

int **odbc_binmode**(*int* result_id, *int* mode)

(ODBC SQL types affected: BINARY, VARBINARY, and LONGVARBINARY)

- ODBC_BINMODE_PASSTHRU—Passthru BINARY data.
- ODBC_BINMODE_RETURN—Return as is.
- ODBC_BINMODE_CONVERT—Convert to char and return.

When binary SQL data is converted to character C data, each byte (8 bits) of source data is represented as two ASCII characters. These characters are the ASCII character representation of the number in its hexadecimal form. For example, a binary 00000001 is converted to *"01"* and a binary 11111111 is converted to *"FF"*.

LONGVARBINARY handling

binmode	longreadlen	result
ODBC_BINMODE_PASSTHRU	0	passthru
DBC_BINMODE_RETURN	0	passthru
ODBC_BINMODE_CONVERT	0	passthru
ODBC_BINMODE_PASSTHRU	0	passthru
ODBC_BINMODE_PASSTHRU	>0	passthru
ODBC_BINMODE_RETURN	>0	return as is
ODBC_BINMODE_CONVERT	>0	return as char

If **odbc_fetch_into()** is used, passthru means that an empty string is returned for these columns. If **$result_id** is *0*, the settings apply as default for new results.

Note: Default for longreadlen is *4096,* and binmode defaults to *ODBC_BINMODE_RETURN* . Handling of binary long columns is also affected by **odbc_longreadlen()**.

odbc_close

Closes down the connection to the database server associated with the given connection identifier. **Note:** This function will fail if any transactions are open on this connection. The connection will remain open in this case.

void **odbc_close**(*int* connection_id)

odbc_close_all

Closes down all connections to database server(s).
Note: This function will fail if any transactions are open on a connection. This connection will remain open in this case.

void **odbc_close_all**(*void*)

odbc_columnprivileges

Lists columns and associated privileges for the given table. Returns an ODBC result identifier or false on failure.

int **odbc_columnprivileges**(*int* connection_id, [*string* qualifier], [*string* owner], [*string* table_name], [*string* column_name])

The result set has the following columns:

- TABLE_QUALIFIER
- TABLE_OWNER
- TABLE_NAME
- GRANTOR
- GRANTEE
- PRIVILEGE
- IS_GRANTABLE

The result set is ordered by TABLE_QUALIFIER, TABLE_OWNER, and TABLE_NAME. The **$column_name** argument accepts search patterns ('%' to match zero or more characters and '_' to match a single character).

odbc_columns

Lists all columns in the requested range. Returns an ODBC result identifier or false on failure.

int **odbc_columns**(*int* connection_id, [*string* qualifier], [*string* owner], [*string* table_name], [*string* column_name])

The result set has the following columns:

TABLE_QUALIFIER	TABLE_OWNER	TABLE_NAME
COLUMN_NAME	DATA_TYPE	TYPE_NAME
PRECISION	LENGTH	SCALE
RADIX	NULLABLE	REMARKS

The result set is ordered by TABLE_QUALIFIER, TABLE_OWNER, and TABLE_NAME. The **$owner**, **$table_name,** and **$column_name** arguments accept search patterns ('%' to match zero or more characters and '_' to match a single character). See also **odbc_columnprivileges()** to retrieve associated privileges.

odbc_commit

Returns true on success, false on failure. All pending transactions on **$connection_id** are committed.

int **odbc_commit**(*int* connection_id)

odbc_connect

Returns an ODBC connection id or 0 (false) on error. The connection id returned by this function is needed by other ODBC functions. You can have multiple connections open at once. The optional fourth parameter sets the type of cursor to be used for this connection. This parameter is not normally needed, but can be useful for working around problems with some ODBC drivers. With some ODBC drivers, executing a complex stored procedure may fail with an error similar to: "Cannot open a cursor on a stored procedure that has anything other than a single select statement in it." Using SQL_CUR_USE_ODBC may avoid that error. Also, some drivers don't support the optional row_number parameter in **odbc_fetch_row()**. SQL_CUR_USE_ODBC might help in that case, too.

> *int* **odbc_connect**(*string* dsn, *string* user, *string* password, [*int* cursor_type])

The following constants are defined for cursortype:

- SQL_CUR_USE_IF_NEEDED
- SQL_CUR_USE_ODBC
- SQL_CUR_USE_DRIVER
- SQL_CUR_DEFAULT

For persistent connections, see **odbc_pconnect()**.

odbc_cursor

Returns a cursorname for the given result_id.

> *string* **odbc_cursor**(*int* result_id)

odbc_do

Executes a query on the given connection.

> *int* **odbc_do**(*int* conn_id, *string* query)

odbc_exec

Returns false on error. Returns an ODBC result identifier if the SQL command was executed successfully. **odbc_exec()** will send an SQL statement to the database server specified by **$connection_id.** This parameter must be a valid identifier returned by **odbc_connect()** or **odbc_pconnect()**. See also **odbc_prepare()** and **odbc_execute()** for multiple execution of SQL statements.

> *int* **odbc_exec**(*int* connection_id, *string* query_string)

odbc_execute

Executes a statement prepared with **odbc_prepare()**. Returns true on successful execution, false otherwise. The array **$arameters_array** only needs to be given if you really have parameters in your statement.

int **odbc_execute**(*int* result_id, [*array* parameters_array])

odbc_fetch_into

Returns the number of columns in the result; false on error. **$result_array** must be passed by reference, but it can be of any type since it will be converted to type array. The array will contain the column values starting at array index 0.

int **odbc_fetch_into**(*int* result_id, [*int* rownumber], *array* result_array)

odbc_fetch_row

If this function was successful (there was a row), true is returned. If there are no more rows, false is returned. Fetches a row of the data that was returned by **odbc_do()** / **odbc_exec()**. After **odbc_fetch_row()** is called, the fields of that row can be accessed with **odbc_result()**. If **$row_number** is not specified, **odbc_fetch_row()** will try to fetch the next row in the result set. Calls to **odbc_fetch_row()**, with and without **$row_number**, can be mixed. To step through the result more than once, you can call **odbc_fetch_row()** with **$row_number 1**, and then continue doing **odbc_fetch_row()** without **$row_number** to review the result. If a driver doesn't support fetching rows by number, the **$row_number** parameter is ignored.

int **odbc_fetch_row**(*int* result_id, [*int* row_number])

odbc_field_len

Returns the length of the field referenced by the number in the given ODBC result identifier. Field numbering starts at 1. See also **odbc_field_scale()** to get the scale of a floating point number.

int **odbc_field_len**(*int* result_id, *int* field_number)

odbc_field_name

Returns the name of the field occupying the given column number in the given ODBC result identifier. Field numbering starts at 1. False is returned on error.

string **odbc_field_name**(*int* result_id, *int* field_number)

odbc_field_num

Returns the number of the column slot that corresponds to the named field in the given ODBC result identifier. Field numbering starts at 1. False is returned on error.

int **odbc_field_num**(*int* result_id, *string* field_name)

odbc_field_precision

Returns the precision of the field referenced by number in the given ODBC result identifier. See also **odbc_field_scale()** to get the scale of a floating point number.

> *string* **odbc_field_precision**(*int* result_id, *int* field_number)

odbc_field_scale

Returns the scale of the field referenced by number in the given ODBC result identifier.

> *string* **odbc_field_scale**(*int* result_id, *int* field_number)

odbc_field_type

Returns the SQL type of the field referenced by number in the given ODBC result identifier. Field numbering starts at 1.

> *string* **odbc_field_type**(*int* result_id, *int* field_number)

odbc_foreignkeys

Retrieves information about foreign keys. Returns an ODBC result identifier or false on failure.

> *int* **odbc_foreignkeys**(*int* connection_id, *string* pk_qualifier, *string* pk_owner, *string* pk_table, *string* fk_qualifier, *string* fk_owner, *string* fk_table)

The result set has the following columns:

PKTABLE_QUALIFIER	PKTABLE_OWNER	PKTABLE_NAME
PKCOLUMN_NAME	FKTABLE_QUALIFIER	FKTABLE_OWNER
FKTABLE_NAME	FKCOLUMN_NAME	KEY_SEQ
UPDATE_RULE	DELETE_RULE	FK_NAME
PK_NAME		

If **$pk_table** contains a table name, **odbc_foreignkeys()** returns a result set containing the primary key of the specified table and all of the foreign keys that refer to it. If **$fk_table** contains a table name, **odbc_foreignkeys()** returns a result set containing all of the foreign keys in the specified table and the primary keys (in other tables) to which they refer. If both **$pk_table** and **$fk_table** contain table names, **odbc_foreignkeys()** returns the foreign keys in the table specified in **$fk_table** that refer to the primary key of the table specified in **$pk_table** . This should be one key at most.

odbc_free_result

Always returns true. Only needs to be called if you are worried about using too much memory while your script is running. All result memory will automatically be freed when the script is finished. But, if you are sure you are not going to need the result data anymore in a script, you may call **odbc_free_result()**, and the memory associated with **$result_id** will be freed.

Note: If auto-commit is disabled (see **odbc_autocommit()**) and you call **odbc_free_result()** before committing, all pending transactions are rolled back.

int **odbc_free_result**(*int* result_id)

odbc_gettypeinfo

Retrieves information about data types supported by the data source. Returns an ODBC result identifier or false on failure. The optional argument **$data_type** can be used to restrict the information to a single data type.

int **odbc_gettypeinfo**(*int* connection_id, [*int* data_type])

The result set has the following columns:

TYPE_NAME	DATA_TYPE	PRECISION
LITERAL_PREFIX	LITERAL_SUFFIX	CREATE_PARAMS
NULLABLE	CASE_SENSITIVE	SEARCHABLE
UNSIGNED_ATTRIBUTE	MONEY	AUTO_INCREMENT
LOCAL_TYPE_NAME	MINIMUM_SCALE	MAXIMUM_SCALE

The result set is ordered by DATA_TYPE and TYPE_NAME.

odbc_longreadlen

(ODBC SQL types affected: LONG, LONGVARBINARY) The number of bytes returned to PHP is controlled by the parameter length. If it is set to 0, long column data is passed through to the client.

Note: Handling of LONGVARBINARY columns is also affected by **odbc_binmode()**.

int **odbc_longreadlen**(*int* result_id, *int* length)

odbc_num_fields

Returns the number of fields (columns) in an ODBC result. This function will return -1 on error. The argument is a valid result identifier returned by **odbc_exec()**.

int **odbc_num_fields**(*int* result_id)

odbc_num_rows

Returns the number of rows in an ODBC result. This function will return -1 on error. For INSERT, UPDATE, and DELETE statements, **odbc_num_rows()** returns the number of rows affected. For a SELECT clause, this can be the number of rows available.

Note: Using **odbc_num_rows()** to determine the number of rows available after a SELECT will return -1 with many drivers.

int **odbc_num_rows**(*int* result_id)

odbc_pconnect

Returns an ODBC connection id or 0 (false) on error. This function is much like **odbc_connect()**, except that the connection is not really closed when the script has finished. Future requests for a connection with the same **$dsn, $user, $password** combination (via **odbc_connect()** and **odbc_pconnect()**) can reuse the persistent connection.

Note: Persistent connections have no effect if PHP is used as a CGI program. For information about the optional cursor_type parameter, see the **odbc_connect()** function. For more information on persistent connections, refer to the PHP FAQ.

int **odbc_pconnect**(*string* dsn, *string* user, *string* password, [*int* cursor_type])

odbc_prepare

Returns false on error. Returns an ODBC result identifier if the SQL command was prepared successfully. The result identifier can be used later to execute the statement with **odbc_execute()**.

int **odbc_prepare**(*int* connection_id, *string* query_string)

odbc_primarykeys

Returns the column names that comprise the primary key for a table. Returns an ODBC result identifier or false on failure.

int **odbc_primarykeys**(*int* connection_id, *string* qualifier, *string* owner, *string* table)

The result set has the following columns:

TABLE_QUALIFIER	TABLE_OWNER	TABLE_NAME
COLUMN_NAME	KEY_SEQ	PK_NAME

odbc_procedurecolumns

Returns the list of input and output parameters, as well as the columns that make up the result set for the specified procedures. Returns an ODBC result identifier or false on failure.

int **odbc_procedurecolumns**(*int* connection_id, [*string* qualifier], [*string* owner], [*string* proc], [*string* column])

The result set has the following columns:

PROCEDURE_QUALIFIER	PROCEDURE_OWNER	PROCEDURE_NAME
COLUMN_NAME	COLUMN_TYPE	DATA_TYPE
TYPE_NAME	PRECISION	LENGTH
SCALE	RADIX	NULLABLE
REMARKS		

The result set is ordered by PROCEDURE_QUALIFIER, PROCEDURE_OWNER, PROCE-

DURE_NAME, and COLUMN_TYPE. The **$owner**, **$proc,** and **$column** arguments accept search patterns ('%' to match zero or more characters and '_' to match a single character).

odbc_procedures
Lists all procedures in the requested range. Returns an ODBC result identifier or false on failure.

> *int* **odbc_procedures**(*int* connection_id, [*string* qualifier], [*string* owner], [*string* name])

The result set has the following columns:

PROCEDURE_QUALIFIER	PROCEDURE_OWNER	PROCEDURE_NAME
NUM_INPUT_PARAMS	NUM_OUTPUT_PARAMS	NUM_RESULT_SETS
REMARKS	PROCEDURE_TYPE	

The **$owner** and **$name** arguments accept search patterns ('%' to match zero or more characters and '_' to match a single character).

odbc_result
Returns the contents of the field. **$field** can either be an integer containing the column number of the field you want, or it can be a string containing the name of the field.

> *string* **odbc_result**(*int* result_id, *mixed* field)

Example:

```
$item_3 = odbc_result ($Query_ID, 3);
$item_val = odbc_result ($Query_ID, "val");
```

The first call to **odbc_result()** returns the value of the third field in the current record of the query result. The second function call to **odbc_result()** returns the value of the field whose field name is "val" in the current record of the query result. An error occurs if a column number parameter for a field is less than one or exceeds the number of columns (or fields) in the current record. Similarly, an error occurs if a field has a name that is not one of the fieldnames of the table(s) that is (are) being queried. Field indices start from 1. Regarding the way binary or long column data is returned, refer to **odbc_binmode ()** and **odbc_longreadlen().**

odbc_result_all
Returns the number of rows in the result, or false on error. **odbc_result_all()** will print all rows from a result identifier produced by **odbc_exec()**. The result is printed in HTML table format. With the optional string argument **$format**, additional overall table formatting can be done.

> *int* **odbc_result_all**(*int* result_id, [*string* format])

odbc_rollback

Rolls back all pending statements on **$connection_id**. Returns true on success, false on failure.

int **odbc_rollback**(*int* connection_id)

odbc_setoption

This function enables fiddling with the ODBC options for a particular connection or query result. It was written to help find workarounds to problems in quirky ODBC drivers. You should probably only use this function if you are an ODBC programmer and understand the effects of the various options. You will certainly need a good ODBC reference to explain all the different options and values that can be used. Different driver versions support different options.

int **odbc_setoption**(*int* id, *int* function, *int* option, *int* param)

Because the effects may vary depending on the ODBC driver, use of this function in scripts to be made publicly available is strongly discouraged. Also, some ODBC options are not available to this function because they must be set before the connection is established or the query is prepared. However, if on a particular job it can make PHP work so your boss doesn't tell you to use a commercial product, that's all that really matters. **$ID** is a connection id or result id on which to change the settings. For SQLSetConnectOption(), this is a connection id. For SQLSetStmtOption(), this is a result id. **$Function** is the ODBC function to use. The value should be 1 for SQLSetConnectOption() and 2 for SQLSetStmtOption(). Parameter **$option** is the option to set. Parameter **$param** is the value for the given **$option**.

Example: ODBC Setoption

```
// 1. Option 102 of SQLSetConnectOption() is SQL_AUTOCOMMIT.
//    Value 1 of SQL_AUTOCOMMIT is SQL_AUTOCOMMIT_ON.
//    This example has the same effect as
//    odbc_autocommit($conn, true);
odbc_setoption ($conn, 1, 102, 1);
// 2. Option 0 of SQLSetStmtOption() is SQL_QUERY_TIMEOUT.
//    This example sets the query to timeout after 30 seconds.
$result = odbc_prepare ($conn, $sql);
odbc_setoption ($result, 2, 0, 30);
odbc_execute ($result);
```

odbc_specialcolumns

When the type argument is SQL_BEST_ROWID, **odbc_specialcolumns()** returns the column or columns that uniquely identify each row in the table. When the type argument is SQL_ROWVER, **odbc_specialcolumns()** returns the optimal column or set of columns that, by retrieving values from the column or columns, enables any row in the specified table to be uniquely identified. This function returns an ODBC result identifier or false on failure.

int **odbc_specialcolumns**(*int* connection_id, *int* type, *string* qualifier, *string* owner, *string* table, *int* scope, *int* nullable)

The result set has the following columns:

SCOPE	COLUMN_NAME	DATA_TYPE
TYPE_NAME	PRECISION	LENGTH
SCALE	PSEUDO_COLUMN	

The result set is ordered by SCOPE.

odbc_statistics

Gets statistics about a table and its indexes. Returns an ODBC result identifier or false on failure.

> *int* **odbc_statistics**(*int* connection_id, *string* qualifier, *string* owner, *string* table_name, *int* unique, *int* accuracy)

The result set has the following columns:

TABLE_QUALIFIER	TABLE_OWNER	TABLE_NAME
NON_UNIQUE	INDEX_QUALIFIER	INDEX_NAME
TYPE	SEQ_IN_INDEX	COLUMN_NAME
COLLATION	CARDINALITY	PAGES
FILTER_CONDITION		

The result set is ordered by NON_UNIQUE, TYPE, INDEX_QUALIFIER, INDEX_NAME, and SEQ_IN_INDEX.

odbc_tableprivileges

Lists tables in the requested range and the privileges associated with each table. Returns an ODBC result identifier or false on failure.

> *int* **odbc_tableprivileges**(*int* connection_id, [*string* qualifier], [*string* owner], [*string* name])

The result set has the following columns:

TABLE_QUALIFIER	TABLE_OWNER	TABLE_NAME
GRANTOR	GRANTEE	PRIVILEGE
IS_GRANTABLE		

The result set is ordered by TABLE_QUALIFIER, TABLE_OWNER and TABLE_NAME. The **$owner** and **$name** arguments accept search patterns ('%' to match zero or more characters and '_' to match a single character).

odbc_tables

Lists all tables in the requested range. Returns an ODBC result identifier or false on failure.

> *int* **odbc_tables**(*int* connection_id, [*string* qualifier], [*string* owner], [*string* name], [*string* types])

The result set has the following columns:

| TABLE_QUALIFIER | TABLE_OWNER | TABLE_NAME |
| TABLE_TYPE | REMARKS | |

The result set is ordered by TABLE_TYPE, TABLE_QUALIFIER, TABLE_OWNER, and TABLE_NAME. The **$owner** and **$name** arguments accept search patterns ('%' to match zero or more characters and '_' to match a single character). To support enumeration of qualifiers, owners, and table types, the following special semantics for the **$qualifier, $owner, $name**, and **$table_type** are available:

If **$qualifier** is a single percent character (%) and **$owner** and **$name** are empty strings, then the result set contains a list of valid qualifiers for the data source. (All columns except the TABLE_QUALIFIER column contain NULLs.) If **$owner** is a single percent character (%) and **$qualifier** and **$name** are empty strings, then the result set contains a list of valid owners for the data source. (All columns except the TABLE_OWNER column contain NULLs.) If **$table_type** is a single percent character (%) and **$qualifier, $owner,** and **$name** are empty strings, then the result set contains a list of valid table types for the data source. (All columns except the TABLE_TYPE column contain NULLs.) If **$table_type** is not an empty string, it must contain a list of comma-separated values for the types of interest. Each value may be enclosed in single quotes (') or unquoted, for example, "'TABLE','VIEW'" or "TABLE, VIEW". If the data source does not support a specified table type, **odbc_tables()** does not return any results for that type. See also **odbc_tableprivileges()** to retrieve associated privileges.

opendir

Returns a directory handle to be used in subsequent **closedir()**, **readdir()**, and **rewinddir()** calls.

int **opendir**(*string* path)

openlog

Opens a connection to the system logger for a program. The string **$ident** is added to each message. Values for **$option** and **$facility** are given in the following table. The **$option** argument is used to indicate what logging options will be used when generating a log message. The **$facility** argument is used to specify what type of program is logging the message. This enables you to specify (in your machine's syslog configuration) how messages coming from different facilities will be handled. The use of **openlog()** is optional. It will automatically be called by **syslog()** if necessary, in which case $ident will default to false.

int **openlog**(*string* ident, *int* option, *int* facility)

Openlog() Options

Constant	Description
LOG_CONS	If an error occurs while sending data to the system logger, write directly to the system console.
LOG_NDELAY	Open the connection to the logger immediately.

LOG_ODELAY	(Default) Delay opening the connection until the first message is logged.
LOG_PERROR	Print log message also to standard error.
LOG_PID	Include PID with each message.

You can use one or more of these options. When using multiple options, you need to *OR* them, that is, open the connection immediately, write to the console, and include the PID in each message. You will use: *LOG_CONS | LOG_NDELAY | LOG_PID*

Openlog() Facilities

Constant	Description
LOG_AUTH	security/authorization messages (use LOG_AUTHPRIV instead in systems where that constant is defined)
LOG_AUTHPRIV	security/authorization messages (private)
LOG_CRON	clock daemon (cron and at)
LOG_DAEMON	other system daemons
LOG_KERN	kernel messages
LOG_LOCAL0 ... LOG_LOCAL7	reserved for local use
LOG_LPR	line printer subsystem
LOG_MAIL	mail subsystem
LOG_NEWS	USENET news subsystem
LOG_SYSLOG	messages generated internally by syslogd
LOG_USER	generic user-level messages
LOG_UUCP	UUCP subsystem

See also **define_syslog_variables()**, **syslog()** and **closelog()**.

Ora_Bind

Returns true if the bind succeeds, otherwise false. Details about the error can be retrieved using the **ora_error()** and **ora_errorcode()** functions. This function binds the named PHP variable with a SQL parameter. The SQL parameter must be in the form ":name". With the optional type parameter, you can define whether the SQL parameter is an in/out (0, default), in (1), or out (2) parameter. As of PHP 3.0.1, you can use the constants ORA_BIND_INOUT, ORA_BIND_IN, and ORA_BIND_OUT instead of the numbers. ora_bind must be called after **ora_parse()** and before **ora_exec()**. Input values can be given by assignment to the bound PHP variables, after calling **ora_exec()**. The bound PHP variables contain the output values if available.

int **Ora_Bind**(*int* cursor, *string* PHP variable name, *string* SQL parameter name, *int* length, [*int* type])

```php
<?php
ora_parse($curs, "declare tmp INTEGER; begin tmp := :in; :out := tmp; :x := 7.77;
```

```
     end;");
     ora_bind($curs, "result", ":x", $len, 2);
     ora_bind($curs, "input", ":in", 5, 1);
     ora_bind($curs, "output", ":out", 5, 2);
     $input = 765;
     ora_exec($curs);
     echo "Result: $result<BR>Out: $output<BR>In: $input";
     ?>
```

Ora_Close

Returns true if the close succeeds, otherwise false. Details about the error can be retrieved using the **ora_error()** and **ora_errorcode()** functions. This function closes a data cursor opened with **ora_open()**.

   int **Ora_Close**(*int* cursor)

Ora_ColumnName

Returns the name of the field/column **$column** on the cursor **$cursor**. The returned name is in all uppercase letters.

   string **Ora_ColumnName**(*int* cursor, *int* column)

Ora_ColumnSize

Returns the size of the Oracle column **$column** on the cursor **$cursor**.

   int **Ora_ColumnSize**(*int* cursor, *int* column)

Ora_ColumnType

Returns the Oracle data type name of the field/column **$column** on the cursor **$cursor**.

   string **Ora_ColumnType**(*int* cursor, *int* column)

   The returned type will be one of the following:

- "VARCHAR2"
- "VARCHAR"
- "CHAR"
- "NUMBER"
- "LONG"
- "LONG RAW"
- "ROWID"
- "DATE"
- "CURSOR"

Ora_Commit

Returns true on success, false on error. Details about the error can be retrieved using the **ora_error()** and **ora_errorcode()** functions. This function commits an Oracle transaction. A transaction is defined as all the changes on a given connection since the last commit/rollback, autocommit was turned off, or when the connection was established.

int **Ora_Commit**(*int* conn)

Ora_CommitOff

Returns true on success, false on error. Details about the error can be retrieved using the **ora_error()** and **ora_errorcode()** functions. This function turns off automatic commit after each **ora_exec()**.

int **Ora_CommitOff**(*int* conn)

Ora_CommitOn

This function turns on automatic commit after each **ora_exec()** on the given connection. Returns true on success, false on error. Details about the error can be retrieved using the **ora_error()** and **ora_errorcode()** functions.

int **Ora_CommitOn**(*int* conn)

Ora_Do

This function is a quick combination of **ora_parse()**, **ora_exec()**, and **ora_fetch()**. It will parse and execute a statement, then fetch the first result row. Returns true on success, false on error. Details about the error can be retrieved using the **ora_error()** and **ora_errorcode()** functions. See also **ora_parse()**, **ora_exec()**, and **ora_fetch()**.

int **Ora_Do**(*int* conn, *string* query)

Ora_Error

Returns an error message of the form XXX - NNNNN, where XXX is where the error comes from and NNNNN identifies the error message.

Note: Support for connection ids was added in 3.0.4.

string **Ora_Error**(*int* cursor_or_connection)

On UNIX versions of Oracle, you can find details about an error message like this:

$ oerr ora 00001 00001, 00000, "unique constraint (%s.%s) violated" // *Cause: An update or insert statement attempted to insert a duplicate key // For Trusted ORACLE configured in DBMS MAC mode, you may see // this message if a duplicate entry exists at a different level. // *Action: Either remove the unique restriction or do not insert the key

Ora_ErrorCode

Returns the numeric error code of the last executed statement on the specified cursor or connection. FIXME: should possible values be listed?

Note: Support for connection ids was added in 3.0.4.

int **Ora_ErrorCode**(*int* cursor_or_connection)

Ora_Exec

Returns true on success, false on error. Details about the error can be retrieved using the **ora_error()** and **ora_errorcode()** functions. See also **ora_parse()**, **ora_fetch()**, and **ora_do()**.

int **Ora_Exec**(*int* cursor)

Ora_Fetch

Returns true (a row was fetched) or false (no more rows, or an error occurred). If an error occurred, details can be retrieved using the **ora_error()** and **ora_errorcode()** functions. If no error occured, **ora_errorcode()** will return 0. Retrieves a row of data from the specified cursor. See also **ora_parse()**, **ora_exec()**, and **ora_do()**.

int **Ora_Fetch**(*int* cursor)

Ora_Fetch_Into

Fetches a row into an array.

Note: You need to fetch the array by reference. See also **ora_parse()**, **ora_exec()**, **ora_fetch()**, and **ora_do()**.

int **Ora_Fetch_Into**(*int* cursor, *array* result, [*int* flags])

Example: Oracle fetch into array

```php
<?php
array($results);
ora_fetch_into($cursor, &$results);
echo $results[0];
echo $results[1];
?>
```

Ora_GetColumn

Returns the column data. If an error occurs, false is returned and **ora_errorcode()** will return to a non-zero value. Note, however, that a test for false on the results from this function may be true in cases where an error did not occur (NULL result, empty string, the number 0, the string "0"). Fetches the data for a column or function result.

mixed **Ora_GetColumn**(*int* cursor, *mixed* column)

Ora_Logoff

Returns true on success, false on error. Details about the error can be retrieved using the **ora_error()** and **ora_errorcode()** functions. Logs out the user and disconnects from the server. See also **ora_logon()**.

   int **Ora_Logoff**(*int* connection)

Ora_Logon

Establishes a connection between PHP and an Oracle database with the given username and password.

   int **Ora_Logon**(*string* user, *string* password)

   Connections can be made using SQL*Net by supplying the TNS name to **$user** like this:

```
$conn = Ora_Logon ("user<EMPHASIS >@TNSNAME</EMPHASIS><\#34>, <\#34>pass<\#34>);
```

   If you have character data with non-ASCII characters, you should make sure that NLS_LANG is set in your environment. For server modules, you should set it in the server's environment before starting the server. Returns a connection index on success, or false on failure. Details about the error can be retrieved using the **ora_error()** and **ora_errorcode()** functions.

Ora_Numcols

Returns the number of columns in a result. Only returns meaningful values after a parse/exec/fetch sequence. See also **ora_parse()**, **ora_exec()**, **ora_fetch()**, and **ora_do()**.

   int **Ora_Numcols**(*int* cursor_ind)

Ora_Numrows

Returns the number of rows in a result.

   int **Ora_Numrows**(*int* cursor_ind)

Ora_Open

Opens an Oracle cursor associated with connection. Returns a cursor index or false on failure. Details about the error can be retrieved using the **ora_error()** and **ora_errorcode()** functions.

   int **Ora_Open**(*int* connection)

Ora_Parse

Parses an SQL statement or a PL/SQL block and associates it with the given cursor. Returns 0 on success or -1 on error. See also **ora_exec()**, **ora_fetch()**, and **ora_do()**.

   int **Ora_Parse**(*int* cursor_ind, *string* sql_statement, *int* defer)

Ora_pLogon

Establishes a persistent connection between PHP and an Oracle database with the given username and password. See also **ora_logon()**.

int **Ora_pLogon**(*string* user, *string* password)

Ora_Rollback

Undoes an Oracle transaction. (See **ora_commit()** for the definition of a transaction.) Returns true on success, false on error. Details about the error can be retrieved using the **ora_error()** and **ora_errorcode()** functions.

int **Ora_Rollback**(*int* connection)

OrbitEnum

This class represents the enumeration identified with the **$id parameter**. The **$id** can be either the name of the enumeration (for example, "MyEnum") or the full repository id (for example, "IDL:MyEnum:1.0").

new **OrbitEnum**(*string* id)

Example: Sample IDL file

```
enum MyEnum {
    a,b,c,d,e
};
```

Example: PHP code for accessing MyEnum

```
<?php
$enum = new OrbitEnum ("MyEnum");
echo $enum->a;      /* write 0 */
echo $enum->c;      /* write 2 */
echo $enum->e;      /* write 4 */
?>
```

OrbitObject

This class provides access to a CORBA object. The $ior parameter should be a string containing the *Interoperable Object Reference* (IOR) that identifies the remote object.

new **OrbitObject**(*string* ior)

Example: Sample IDL file

```
interface MyInterface {
    void SetInfo (string info);
    string GetInfo();
    attribute int value;
}
```

Example: PHP code for accessing MyInterface

```php
<?php
$obj = new OrbitObject ($ior);
$obj->SetInfo ("A 2GooD object");
echo $obj->GetInfo();
$obj->value = 42;
echo $obj->value;
?>
```

OrbitStruct

This class represents the structure identified with the **$id** parameter. The **$id** can be either the name of the struct (for example, "MyStruct") or the full repository id (for example, "IDL:MyStruct:1.0").

new **OrbitStruct**(*string* id)

Example: Sample IDL file

```
struct MyStruct {
    short shortvalue;
    string stringvalue;
};
interface SomeInterface {
  void SetValues (MyStruct values);
  MyStruct GetValues();
}
```

Example: PHP code for accessing MyStruct

```php
<?php
$obj = new OrbitObject ($ior);
$initial_values = new OrbitStruct ("IDL:MyStruct:1.0");
$initial_values->shortvalue = 42;
$initial_values->stringvalue = "HGTTG";
$obj->SetValues ($initial_values);
$values = $obj->GetValues();
echo $values->shortvalue;
echo $values->stringvalue;
?>
```

Ord

Returns the ASCII value of the first character of **$string**. This function complements **chr()**. See also **chr()**.

int **Ord**(*string* string)

Example: Ord()

```
if (ord ($str) == 10) {
    echo "The first character of \$str is a line feed.\n";
}
```

pack

Packs given arguments into binary string according to $format. Returns binary string containing data. The idea to this function was taken from Perl, and all formatting codes work the same. However, some formatting codes are missing, such as Perl's "u" format code. The format string consists of format codes followed by an optional repeater argument. The repeater argument can be either an integer value or * for repeating to the end of the input data. For a, A, h, H, the repeat count specifies how many characters of one data argument are taken. For @, it is the absolute position where to put the next data. For everything else, the repeat count specifies how many data arguments are consumed and packed into the resulting binary string.

string **pack**(*string* format, [*mixed* args])

The following are currently implemented:

- a—NUL-padded string
- A—SPACE-padded string
- h—Hex string, low nibble first
- H—Hex string, high nibble first
- c—signed char
- C—unsigned char
- s—signed short (always 16 bit, machine byte order)
- S—unsigned short (always 16 bit, machine byte order)
- n—unsigned short (always 16 bit, big endian byte order)
- v—unsigned short (always 16 bit, little endian byte order)
- i—signed integer (machine dependent size and byte order)
- I—unsigned integer (machine dependent size and byte order)
- l—signed long (always 32 bit, machine byte order)
- L—unsigned long (always 32 bit, machine byte order)
- N—unsigned long (always 32 bit, big endian byte order)
- V—unsigned long (always 32 bit, little endian byte order)
- f—float (machine dependent size and representation)
- d—double (machine dependent size and representation)
- x—NUL byte
- X—Back up one byte
- @—NUL-fill to absolute position

Example: Pack() format string

```
$binarydata = pack ("nvc*", 0x1234, 0x5678, 65, 66);
```

The resulting binary string will be 6 bytes long and contain the byte sequence 0x12, 0x34, 0x78, 0x56, 0x41, 0x42. **Note:** The distinction between signed and unsigned values only affects the function **unpack(),** where as function **pack()** gives the same result for signed and unsigned format codes. Also note that PHP internally stores integral values as signed values of a machine dependent size. If you give it an unsigned integral value too large to be stored that way, it is converted to a double, which often yields an undesired result.

parse_str

Parses **$str** as if it were the query string passed via an URL and sets variables in the current scope. If the second parameter $arr is present, variables are stored in this variable as array elements instead.

void **parse_str(** *string* str, [*array* arr])

Example: Using parse_str()

```
$str = "first=value&second[]=this+works&second[]=another";
parse_str($str);
echo $first;      /* prints "value" */
echo $second[0]; /* prints "this works" */
echo $second[1]; /* prints "another" */
```

parse_url

Returns an associative array returning any of the various components of the URL that are present. This includes the "scheme", "host", "port", "user", "pass", "path", "query", and "fragment".

array **parse_url(** *string* url)

passthru

Similar to the **Exec()** function in that it executes a **$command**. If the **$return_var** argument is present, the return status of the Unix command will be placed here. This function should be used in place of **Exec()** or **System()** when the output from the Unix command is binary data, which needs to be passed directly back to the browser. A common use for this is to execute something like the pbmplus utilities that can output an image stream directly. By setting the content-type to image/gif and then calling a pbmplus program to output a gif, you can create PHP scripts that output images directly.

Note: If you start a program using this function and want to leave it running in the background, you have to make sure that the output of that program is redirected to a file or some other output stream; otherwise, PHP will hang until the execution of the program ends. See also **exec()**, **system()**, **popen()**, **EscapeShellCmd()**, and the backtick operator.

void **passthru(** *string* command, [*int* return_var])

pdf_add_outline

Adds a bookmark with text **$text** that points to the current page. The bookmark is inserted as a child of **$parent** and is by default open, if **$open** is not 0. The return value is an identifier for the bookmark, which can be used as a parent for other bookmarks. Therefore you can build up hierarchies of bookmarks. Unfortunately, pdflib does not make a copy of the string, which forces PHP to allocate the memory. Currently, this piece of memory has not been freed by any PDF function, but it will be taken care of by the PHP memory manager.

int **pdf_add_outline**(int pdf document, string text, [int parent], [int open])

pdf_arc

Draws an arc with center at point (**$x-coor**, **$y-coor**) and radius **$radius**, starting at angle **$start** and ending at angle **$end**. See also **pdf_circle()** and **pdf_stroke()**.

void **pdf_arc**(int pdf document, double x-coor, double y-coor, double radius, double start, double end)

pdf_begin_page

Starts a new page with height **$height** and width **$width**. In order to create a valid document, you must call this function and **pdf_end_page()** at least once. See also **pdf_end_page()**.

void **pdf_begin_page**(int pdf document, double width, double height)

pdf_circle

Draws a circle with center at point (**$x-coor**, **$y-coor**) and radius **$radius**. See also **pdf_arc()** and **pdf_stroke()**.

void **pdf_circle**(int pdf document, double x-coor, double y-coor, double radius)

pdf_clip

Clips all drawing to the current path.

void **pdf_clip**(int pdf document)

pdf_close

Closes the pdf document. See also **pdf_open()** and **fclose()**.

void **pdf_close**(int pdf document)

pdf_closepath

Closes the current path. This means, it draws a line from current point to the point where the first line was started. Many functions like **pdf_moveto()**, **pdf_circle()**, and **pdf_rect()** start a new path.

void **pdf_closepath**(int pdf document)

pdf_closepath_fill_stroke

Closes, fills the interior of the current path with the current fill color, and draws current path. See also **pdf_closepath()**, **pdf_stroke()**, **pdf_fill()**, **pdf_setgray_fill()**, **pdf_setgray()**, **pdf_setrgbcolor_fill()**, and **pdf_setrgbcolor()**.

> void **pdf_closepath_fill_stroke**(int pdf document)

pdf_closepath_stroke

A combination of **pdf_closepath()** and **pdf_stroke()**. It also clears the path. See also **pdf_closepath()** and **pdf_stroke()**.

> void **pdf_closepath_stroke**(int pdf document)

pdf_close_image

Closes an image that has been opened with any of the **pdf_open_xxx()** functions. See also **pdf_open_jpeg()**, **pdf_open_gif()**, and **pdf_open_memory_image()**.

> void **pdf_close_image**(int image)

pdf_continue_text

Outputs the string in **$text** in the next line. The distance between the lines can be set with **pdf_set_leading()**. See also **pdf_show_xy()**, **pdf_set_leading()**, and **pdf_set_text_pos()**.

> void **pdf_continue_text**(int pdf document, string text)

pdf_curveto

Draws a Bezier curve from the current point to the point (**$x3**, **$y3**) using (**$x1**, **$y1**) and (**$x2**, **$y2**) as control points. See also **pdf_moveto()**, **pdf_lineto()**, and **pdf_stroke()**.

> void **pdf_curveto**(int pdf document, double x1, double y1, double x2, double y2, double x3, double y3)

pdf_endpath

Ends the current path but does not close it. See also **pdf_closepath()**.

> void **pdf_endpath**(int pdf document)

pdf_end_page

Ends a page. Once a page is ended, it cannot be modified anymore. See also **pdf_begin_page()**.

> void **pdf_end_page**(int pdf document)

pdf_execute_image

Displays an image that has been put in the PDF file with the **pdf_put_image()** function on the current page at the given coordinates. The image can be scaled while displaying it. A scale of 1.0 will show the image in the original size. **Note:** This function has become meaningless with version 2.01 of pdflib. It will just output a warning.

void **pdf_execute_image**(int pdf document, int image, double x-coor, double y-coor, double scale)

Example: Multiple show of an image

```php
<?php
$im = ImageCreate(100, 100);
$col1 = ImageColorAllocate($im, 80, 45, 190);
ImageFill($im, 10, 10, $col1);
$pim = pdf_open_memory_image($pdf, $im);
pdf_put_image($pdf, $pim);
pdf_execute_image($pdf, $pim, 100, 100, 1);
pdf_execute_image($pdf, $pim, 200, 200, 2);
pdf_close_image($pdf, $pim);
?>
```

pdf_fill

Fills the interior of the current path with the current fill color. See also **pdf_closepath()**, **pdf_stroke()**, **pdf_setgray_fill()**, **pdf_setgray()**, **pdf_setrgbcolor_fill()**, and **pdf_setrgbcolor()**.

void **pdf_fill**(int pdf document)

pdf_fill_stroke

Fills the interior of the current path with the current fill color and draws current path. See also **pdf_closepath()**, **pdf_stroke()**, **pdf_fill()**, **pdf_setgray_fill()**, **pdf_setgray()**, **pdf_setrgbcolor_fill()**, and **pdf_setrgbcolor()**.

void **pdf_fill_stroke**(int pdf document)

pdf_get_image_height

Returns the heights of a pdf image in pixel. See also **pdf_open_image_file()**, **pdf_open_memory_image()**, and **pdf_get_image_width()**.

string **pdf_get_image_height**(int pdf document, int image)

pdf_get_image_width

Returns the widths of a pdf image in pixel. See also **pdf_open_image_file()**, **pdf_open_memory_image()**, and **pdf_get_image_height()**.

string **pdf_get_image_width**(int pdf document, int image)

pdf_get_parameter

Gets several parameters of pdflib which are of the type string. The function parameter **$modifier** characterizes the parameter to get. If the modifier is not needed, it has to be 0 or not passed at all. See also **pdf_get_value()**, **pdf_set_value()**, and **pdf_set_parameter()**.

> string **pdf_get_parameter**(int pdf document, string name, [double modifier])

pdf_get_value

Gets several numerical parameters of pdflib. The function parameter **$modifier** characterizes the parameter to get. If the modifier is not needed, it has to be 0 or not passed at all. See also **pdf_set_value()**, **pdf_get_parameter()**, and **pdf_set_parameter()**.

> double **pdf_get_value**(int pdf document, string name, [double modifier])

pdf_lineto

Draws a line from the current point to the point with coordinates (**$x-coor**, **$y-coor**). See also **pdf_moveto()**, **pdf_curveto()**, **pdf_stroke()**.

> void **pdf_lineto**(int pdf document, double x-coor, double y-coor)

pdf_moveto

Sets the current point to the coordinates **$x-coor** and **$y-coor**.

> void **pdf_moveto**(int pdf document, double x-coor, double y-coor)

pdf_open

Opens a new pdf document. The corresponding file has to be opened with **fopen()** and the file descriptor passed as argument **$file**. If you do not pass any parameters, the document will be created in memory and outputted page by page either to stdout or to the Web browser.

Note: The return value is needed as the first parameter in all other functions writing to the pdf document. See also **fopen()**, and **pdf_close()**.

> int **pdf_open**(int file)

pdf_open_gif

Opens an image stored in the file with the name **$filename**. The format of the image has to be gif. The function returns a pdf image identifier.

Note: This function shouldn't be used anymore. Please use the function **pdf_open_image_file()** instead. See also **pdf_close_image()**, **pdf_open_jpeg()**, **pdf_open_memory_image()**, **pdf_execute_image()**, **pdf_place_image()**, and **pdf_put_image()**.

> int **pdf_open_gif**(int pdf document, string filename)

Example: Including a gif image

```php
<?php
$im = pdf_open_gif($pdf, "test.gif");
pdf_place_image($pdf, $im, 100, 100, 1);
pdf_close_image($pdf, $im);
?>
```

pdf_open_image_file

Reads an image of format **$format** from the file **$filename**. Possible formats are 'png', 'tiff', 'jpeg', and 'gif'. The function returns a pdf image identifier. See also **pdf_close_image()**, **pdf_open_jpeg()**, **pdf_open_gif()**, **pdf_open_tiff()**, **pdf_open_png()**, **pdf_execute_image()**, **pdf_place_image()**, and **pdf_put_image()**.

int **pdf_open_image_file**(int PDF-document, string format, string filename)

Example: Inserting an image

```php
<?php
$pim = pdf_open_image_file($pdf, "png", "picture.png");
pdf_place_image($pdf, $pim, 100, 100, 1);
pdf_close_image($pdf, $pim);
?>
```

pdf_open_jpeg

Opens an image stored in the file with the name **$filename**. The format of the image has to be jpeg. The function returns a pdf image identifier.

Note: This function shouldn't be used anymore. Please use the function **pdf_open_image_file()** instead. See also **pdf_close_image()**, **pdf_open_gif()**, **pdf_open_png()**, **pdf_open_memory_image()**, **pdf_execute_image()**, **pdf_place_image()**, and **pdf_put_image()**.

int **pdf_open_jpeg**(int pdf document, string filename)

pdf_open_memory_image

Takes an image created with the PHP's image functions and makes it available for the pdf document. The function returns a pdf image identifier. See also **pdf_close_image()**, **pdf_open_jpeg()**, **pdf_open_gif()**, **pdf_open_png()**, **pdf_execute_image()**, **pdf_place_image()**, and **pdf_put_image()**.

int **pdf_open_memory_image**(int pdf document, int image)

Example: Including a memory image

```php
<?php
$im = ImageCreate(100, 100);
$col = ImageColorAllocate($im, 80, 45, 190);
ImageFill($im, 10, 10, $col);
$pim = pdf_open_memory_image($pdf, $im);
```

```
ImageDestroy($im);
pdf_place_image($pdf, $pim, 100, 100, 1);
pdf_close_image($pdf, $pim);
?>
```

pdf_open_png

Opens an image stored in the file with the name **$filename**. The format of the image has to be png. The function returns a pdf image identifier.

Note: This function shouldn't be used anymore. Please use the function **pdf_open_image_file()** instead. See also **pdf_close_image()**, **pdf_open_jpeg()**, **pdf_open_gif()**, **pdf_open_memory_image()**, **pdf_execute_image()**, **pdf_place_image()**, and **pdf_put_image()**.

> int **pdf_open_png**(int pdf, string png_file)

> **Example: Including a PNG image**

```
<?php
$im = pdf_open_png ($pdf, "test.png");
pdf_place_image ($pdf, $im, 100, 100, 1);
pdf_close_image ($pdf, $im);
?>
```

pdf_open_tiff

Opens an image stored in the file with the name **$filename**. The format of the image has to be tiff. The function returns a pdf image identifier.

Note: This function shouldn't be used anymore. Please use the function **pdf_open_image_file()** instead. See also **pdf_close_image()**, **pdf_open_gif()**, **pdf_open_jpeg()**, **pdf_open_png()**, **pdf_open_memory_image()**, **pdf_execute_image()**, **pdf_place_image()**, and **pdf_put_image()**.

> int **pdf_open_tiff**(int PDF-document, string filename)

pdf_place_image

Places an image on the page at position (**$x-coor , $x-coor**). The image can be scaled at the same time. See also **pdf_put_image()**.

> void **pdf_place_image**(int pdf document, int image, double x-coor, double y-coor, double scale)

pdf_put_image

Places an image in the PDF file without showing it. The stored image can be displayed with the **pdf_execute_image()** function as many times as needed. This is useful when using the same image multiple times in order to keep the file size small. Using **pdf_put_image()** and **pdf_exe-**

cute_image() is highly recommended for larger images (several kb) if they show up more than once in the document.

Note: This function has become meaningless with version 2.01 of pdflib. It will just output a warning. See also **pdf_put_image()**, **pdf_place_image()**, and **pdf_execute_image()**.

> void **pdf_put_image**(int pdf document, int image)

pdf_rect

Draws a rectangle with its lower-left corner at point (**$x-coor, $y-coor**). This width is set to **$width**. This height is set to **$height**. See also **pdf_stroke()**.

> void **pdf_rect**(int pdf document, double x-coor, double y-coor, double width, double height)

pdf_restore

Restores the environment saved with **pdf_save()**. It works like the postscript command restore. See also **pdf_save()**.

> void **pdf_restore**(int pdf document)

> **Example: Save and Restore**

```php
<?php pdf_save($pdf);
// do all kinds of rotations, transformations, ...
pdf_restore($pdf) ?>
```

pdf_rotate

Sets the rotation in degrees to **$angle**.

> void **pdf_rotate**(int pdf document, double angle)

pdf_save

Saves the current environment. It works like the postscript command save. Very useful if you want to translate or rotate an object without affecting other objects. **pdf_save()** should always be followed by **pdf_restore()** to restore the environment before **pdf_save()**. See also **pdf_restore()**.

> void **pdf_save**(int pdf document)

pdf_scale

Sets the scaling factor in both directions. The following example scales x and y direction by 72. The following line will therefore be drawn one inch in both directions.

> void **pdf_scale**(int pdf document, double x-scale, double y-scale)

> **Example: Scaling**

```php
<?php pdf_scale($pdf, 72.0, 72.0);
pdf_lineto($pdf, 1, 1);
pdf_stroke($pdf);
?>
```

pdf_setdash

Sets the dash pattern **$white** white points and **$black** black points. If both are 0, a solid line is set.

void **pdf_setdash**(int pdf document, double white, double black)

pdf_setflat

Sets the flatness to a value between 0 and 100.

void **pdf_setflat**(int pdf document, double value)

pdf_setgray

Sets the current drawing and filling color to the given gray value. See also **pdf_setrgbcolor_stroke()** and **pdf_setrgbcolor_fill()**.

void **pdf_setgray**(int pdf document, double gray value)

pdf_setgray_fill

Sets the current gray value to fill a path. See also **pdf_setrgbcolor_fill()**.

void **pdf_setgray_fill**(int pdf document, double gray value)

pdf_setgray_stroke

Sets the current drawing color to the given gray value. See also **pdf_setrgbcolor_stroke()**.

void **pdf_setgray_stroke**(int pdf document, double gray value)

pdf_setlinecap

Sets the linecap parameter between a value of 0 and 2.

void **pdf_setlinecap**(int pdf document, int value)

pdf_setlinejoin

Sets the linejoin parameter between a value of 0 and 2.

void **pdf_setlinejoin**(int pdf document, long value)

pdf_setlinewidth

Sets the line width to **$width**.

> void **pdf_setlinewidth**(int pdf document, double width)

pdf_setmiterlimit

Sets the miter limit to a value greater than or equal to 1.

> void **pdf_setmiterlimit**(int pdf document, double value)

pdf_setrgbcolor

Sets the current drawing and filling color to the given rgb color value. See also **pdf_setrgbcolor_stroke()** and **pdf_setrgbcolor_fill()**.

> void **pdf_setrgbcolor**(int pdf document, double red value, double green value, double blue value)

pdf_setrgbcolor_fill

Sets the current rgb color value to fill a path. See also **pdf_setrgbcolor_fill()**.

> void **pdf_setrgbcolor_fill**(int pdf document, double red value, double green value, double blue value)

pdf_setrgbcolor_stroke

Sets the current drawing color to the given rgb color value. See also **pdf_setrgbcolor_stroke()**.

> void **pdf_setrgbcolor_stroke**(int pdf document, double red value, double green value, double blue value)

pdf_set_border_color

Sets the color of the surrounding box of links and annotations. The three color components have to have a value between 0.0 and 1.0. See also **pdf_set_border_style()** and **pdf_set_border_dash()**.

> void **pdf_set_border_color**(int pdf document, double red, double green, double blue)

pdf_set_border_dash

Sets the length of black and white areas of a dashed line of the surrounding box of links and annotations. See also **pdf_set_border_style()** and **pdf_set_border_color()**.

> void **pdf_set_border_dash**(int pdf document, double black, double white)

pdf_set_border_style

Sets the style and width of the surrounding box of links and annotations. The parameter **$style** can be solid or dashed. See also **pdf_set_border_color()** and **pdf_set_border_dash()**.

> void **pdf_set_border_style**(int pdf document, string style, double width)

pdf_set_char_spacing

Sets the spacing between characters. See also **pdf_set_word_spacing()** and **pdf_set_leading()**.

> void **pdf_set_char_spacing**(int pdf document, double space)

pdf_set_duration

Sets the duration between following pages in seconds. See **also pdf_set_transition()**.

> void **pdf_set_duration**(int pdf document, double duration)

pdf_set_font

Sets the current font face, font size, and encoding. If you use pdflib 0.6, you will need to provide the Adobe Font Metrics (afm-files) for the font in the font path (default is ./fonts). If you use php3 or a version of pdflib older than 2.20, the fourth parameter $encoding can take the following values: 0 = builtin, 1 = pdfdoc, 2 = macroman, 3 = macexpert, 4 = winansi. An encoding greater than 4 and less than 0 will default to winansi. winansi is often a good choice. If you use php4 and a version of pdflib >= 2.20, the encoding parameter has changed to a string. Use 'winansi', 'builtin', 'host', 'macroman', and so on instead. If the last parameter is set to 1, the font is embedded into the pdf document; otherwise, it is not. To embed a font is usually a good idea if the font is not widely spread, and you cannot ensure that the person watching your document has access to fonts in the document. A font is only embedded once, even if you call **pdf_set_font()** several times.

> void **pdf_set_font**(int pdf document, string font name, double size, string encoding, [int embed])

Note: This function has to be called after **pdf_begin_page()** in order to create a valid pdf document. Also note that if you reference a font in a .upr file, make sure the name in the afm file and the font name are the same. Otherwise, the font will be embedded several times (Thanks to Paul Haddon for finding this).

pdf_set_horiz_scaling

Sets the horizontal scaling to **$scale** percent.

> void **pdf_set_horiz_scaling**(int pdf document, double scale)

pdf_set_info

Sets an information field of a pdf document. Possible values for the fieldname are 'Subject', 'Title', 'Creator', 'Author', 'Keywords', and one user-defined name. It can be called before beginning a page.

Note: This function replaces **pdf_set_info_keywords()**, **pdf_set_info_title()**, **pdf_set_info_subject()**, **pdf_set_info_creator()**, and **pdf_set_info_sybject()**.

void **pdf_set_info**(int pdf document, string fieldname, string value)

Example: Setting document information

```php
<?php
$fd = fopen("test.pdf", "w");
$pdfdoc = pdf_open($fd);
pdf_set_info($pdfdoc, "Author", "Uwe Steinmann");
pdf_set_info($pdfdoc, "Creator", "Uwe Steinmann");
pdf_set_info($pdfdoc, "Title", "Testing Info Fields");
pdf_set_info($pdfdoc, "Subject", "Test");
pdf_set_info($pdfdoc, "Keywords", "Test, Fields");
pdf_set_info($pdfdoc, "CustomField", "What ever makes sense");
pdf_begin_page($pdfdoc, 595, 842);
pdf_end_page($pdfdoc);
pdf_close($pdfdoc);
?>
```

pdf_set_leading

Sets the distance between text lines. This will be used if text is output by **pdf_continue_text()**. See also **pdf_continue_text()**.

void **pdf_set_leading**(int pdf document, double distance)

pdf_set_parameter

Sets several parameters of pdflib which are of the type string. See also **pdf_get_value()**, **pdf_set_value()**, and **pdf_get_parameter()**.

void **pdf_set_parameter**(int pdf document, string name, string value)

pdf_set_text_matrix

Sets a matrix that describes a transformation applied on the current text font. The matrix has to pass as an array with six elements.

Note: This function is not available anymore since pdflib 2.3.

void **pdf_set_text_matrix**(int pdf document, array matrix)

pdf_set_text_pos

Sets the position of text for the next **pdf_show()** function call. See also **pdf_show()** and **pdf_show_xy()**.

>   void **pdf_set_text_pos**(int pdf document, double x-coor, double y-coor)

pdf_set_text_rendering

Determines how text is rendered. The possible values for **$mode** are 0=fill text, 1=stroke text, 2=fill and stroke text, 3=invisible, 4=fill text and add it to clipping path, 5=stroke text and add it to clipping path, 6=fill and stroke text and add it to clipping path, and 7=add it to clipping path.

>   void **pdf_set_text_rendering**(int pdf document, int mode)

pdf_set_text_rise

Sets the text rising to **$rise** points.

>   void **pdf_set_text_rise**(int pdf document, double rise)

pdf_set_transition

Sets the transition between following pages. See also **pdf_set_duration()**.

>   void **pdf_set_transition**(int pdf document, int transition)

>   The value of **$transition** can be as follows:

- 0 for none.
- 1 for two lines sweeping across the screen reveal the page.
- 2 for multiple lines sweeping across the screen reveal the page.
- 3 for a box reveals the page.
- 4 for a single line sweeping across the screen reveals the page.
- 5 for the old page dissolves to reveal the page.
- 6 for the dissolve effect moves from one screen edge to another.
- 7 for the old page is simply replaced by the new page (default).

pdf_set_value

Sets several numerical parameters of pdflib. See also **pdf_get_value()**, **pdf_get_parameter()**, and **pdf_set_parameter()**.

>   void **pdf_set_value**(int pdf document, string name, double value)

pdf_set_word_spacing

Sets the spacing between words. See also **pdf_set_char_spacing()** and **pdf_set_leading()**.

> void **pdf_set_word_spacing**(int pdf document, double space)

pdf_show

Outputs the string **$text** at the current text position using the current font. See also **pdf_show_xy()**, **pdf_show_boxed()**, **pdf_set_text_pos()**, and **pdf_set_font()**.

> void **pdf_show**(int pdf document, string text)

pdf_show_boxed

Outputs the string **$text** in a box with its lower left position at (**$x-coor, $y-coor**). The dimension of the box is **$height** by **$width**. The parameter **$mode** determines how the text is type set. If **$width** and **$height** are zero, the **$mode** can be left, right, or center. If **$width** or **$height** is unequal zero, it can also be justify and fulljustify. If the parameter **$feature** is set to "blind", the text is not shown. Returns the number of characters that could not be processed because they did not fit into the box. See also **pdf_show()** and **pdf_show_xy()**.

> int **pdf_show_boxed**(int pdf document, string text, double x-coor, double y-coor, double width, double height, string mode, [string feature])

pdf_show_xy

Outputs the string **$text** at position (**$x-coor, $y-coor**). See also **pdf_show()** and **pdf_show_boxed()**.

> void **pdf_show_xy**(int pdf document, string text, double x-coor, double y-coor)

pdf_skew

Skews the coordinate system by **$alpha** (x) and **$beta** (y) degrees. **$alpha** and **$beta** may not be 90 or 270 degrees.

> void **pdf_skew**(int pdf document, double alpha, double beta)

pdf_stringwidth

Returns the width of the string in **$text** by using the current font. It requires a font to be set before with **pdf_set_font()**. See also **pdf_set_font()**.

> double **pdf_stringwidth**(int pdf document, string text)

pdf_stroke

Draws a line along the current path. The current path is the sum of all line drawing. Without this function, the line would not be drawn. See also **pdf_closepath()** and **pdf_closepath_stroke()**.

> void **pdf_stroke**(int pdf document)

pdf_translate

Sets the origin of the coordinate system to the point (**$x-coor, $y-coor**), relative to the current origin. The following example draws a line from (0, 0) to (200, 200), relative to the initial coordinate system. You have to set the current point after **pdf_translate()** and before you start drawing more objects.

> void **pdf_translate**(int pdf document, double x-coor, double y-coor)

Example: Translation

```
<?php pdf_moveto($pdf, 0, 0);
pdf_lineto($pdf, 100, 100);
pdf_stroke($pdf);
pdf_translate($pdf, 100, 100);
pdf_moveto($pdf, 0, 0);
pdf_lineto($pdf, 100, 100);
pdf_stroke($pdf);
?>
```

pfpro_cleanup

Used to shutdown the Payflow Pro library cleanly. It should be called after you have processed any transactions and before the end of your script. However, you may omit this call, in which case this extension will automatically call **pfpro_cleanup()** after your script terminates. See also **pfpro_init()**.

> void **pfpro_cleanup**(void)

pfpro_init

Used to initialize the Payflow Pro library. You may omit this call, in which case this extension will automatically call **pfpro_init()** before the first transaction. See also **pfpro_cleanup()**.

> void **pfpro_init**(void)

pfpro_process

Returns an associative array containing the response. **pfpro_process()** processes a transaction with Payflow Pro. The first parameter is an associative array containing keys and values that will be encoded and passed to the processor. The second parameter is optional and specifies the host to which to connect. By default, this is "test.signio.com", so you will certainly want to change this to "connect.signio.com" in order to process live transactions. The third parameter specifies the port on which to connect. It defaults to 443, the standard SSL port. The fourth parameter specifies the timeout to be used, in seconds. This defaults to 30 seconds.

Note: This timeout appears to only begin once a link to the processor has been established, so your script could potentially continue for a very long time in the event of DNS or network problems. The fifth parameter, if required, specifies the hostname of your SSL proxy. The sixth parameter specifies the port to use. The seventh and eighth parameters specify the logon identity and password to use on the proxy. The function returns an associative array of the keys and values in the response.

Note: Be sure to read the Payflow Pro Developers Guide for full details of the required parameters.

array **pfpro_process**(array parameters, [string address], [int port], [int timeout], [string proxy address], [int proxy port], [string proxy logon], [string proxy password])

Example: Payflow Pro

```php
<?php
pfpro_init();
$transaction = array(USER    => 'mylogin',
          PWD      => 'mypassword',
          TRXTYPE  => 'S',
          TENDER   => 'C',
          AMT      => 1.50,
          ACCT     => '4111111111111111',
          EXPDATE  => '0904'
          );
$response = pfpro_process($transaction);
if (!$response) {
  die("Couldn't establish link to Verisign.\n");
}
echo "Verisign response code was ".$response[RESULT];
echo ", which means: ".$response[RESPMSG]."\n";
echo "\nThe transaction request: ";
print_r($transaction);
echo "\nThe response: ";
print_r($response);
pfpro_cleanup();
?>
```

pfpro_process_raw

Returns a string containing the response. **pfpro_process_raw()** processes a raw transaction string with Payflow Pro. You should really use **pfpro_process()** instead, as the encoding rules of these transactions are non-standard. The first parameter in this case is a string containing the raw transaction request. All other parameters are the same as with **pfpro_process()**. The return value is a string containing the raw response.

Note: Be sure to read the Payflow Pro Developers Guide for full details of the required parameters and encoding rules. You would be well advised to use **pfpro_process()** instead.

string **pfpro_process_raw**(string parameters, [string address], [int port], [int timeout], [string proxy address], [int proxy port], [string proxy logon], [string proxy password])

Example: Payflow Pro raw

```php
<?php
pfpro_init();
$response =
pfpro_process("USER=mylogin&PWD[5]=m&ndy&TRXTYPE=S&TENDER=C&AMT=1.50&ACCT=4111111111111
111&EXPDATE=0904");
if (!$response) {
   die("Couldn't establish link to Verisign.\n");
}
echo "Verisign raw response was ".$response;
pfpro_cleanup();
?>
```

pfpro_version

Returns the version string of the Payflow Pro library. At the time of writing, this was L211.

string **pfpro_version**(void)

pfsockopen

Behaves exactly as **fsockopen()** with the difference that the connection is not closed after the script finishes. It is the persistent version of **fsockopen()**.

int **pfsockopen**(string hostname, int port, [int errno], [string errstr], [int timeout])

pg_client_encoding

The function returns the client encoding as the string. The returned string should be either: SQL_ASCII, EUC_JP, EUC_CN, EUC_KR, EUC_TW, UNICODE, MULE_INTERNAL, LATINX (X=1 . . . 9), KOI8, WIN, ALT, SJIS, BIG5, or WIN1250.

Note: This function requires PHP-4.0.2 or higher and PostgreSQL-7.0 or higher. The function used to be called **pg_clientencoding()**. See also **pg_set_client_encoding()**.

string **pg_client_encoding**([int connection])

pg_close

Returns false if connection is not a valid connection index, true otherwise. Closes down the connection to a PostgreSQL database associated with the given connection index.

Note: This isn't usually necessary, as non-persistent open links are automatically closed at the end of the script's execution. **pg_close()** will not close persistent links generated by **pg_pconnect()**.

bool **pg_close**(int connection)

pg_cmdtuples

Returns the number of tuples (instances) affected by INSERT, UPDATE, and DELETE queries. If no tuple is affected, the function will return 0.

int **pg_cmdtuples**(int result_id)

Example: Pg_cmdtuples()

```
<?php
$result = pg_exec ($conn, "INSERT INTO publisher VALUES ('Author')");
$cmdtuples = pg_cmdtuples ($result);
echo $cmdtuples . " <- cmdtuples affected.";
?>
```

pg_connect

Returns a connection index on success, or false if the connection could not be made. Opens a connection to a PostgreSQL database. The arguments should be within a quoted string.

int **pg_connect**(string conn_string)

Example: Using pg_connect arguments

```
<?php
$dbconn = pg_Connect ("dbname=mary");
//connect to a database named "mary"
$dbconn2 = pg_Connect ("host=localhost port=5432 dbname=mary");
//connect to a database named "mary" on "localhost" at port "5432"
$dbconn3 = pg_Connect ("user=lamb password=baaaa dbname=mary ");
//connect to a database named "mary" with a username and password
?>
```

The arguments available include **$dbname $port**, **$host**, **$tty**, **$options**, **$user**, and **$password**. This function returns a connection index that is needed by other PostgreSQL functions. You can have multiple connections open at once. The previous syntax of: $conn = pg_connect ("host", "port", "options", "tty", "dbname") has been deprecated. See also **pg_pconnect()**.

pg_dbname

Returns the name of the database to which the given PostgreSQL connection index is connected, or false if connection is not a valid connection index.

string **pg_dbname**(int connection)

pg_end_copy

Syncs PostgreSQL front-end with the backend after doing a copy operation. It must be issued, or the backend may get "out of sync" with the front-end. Returns true if successful, false otherwise. For further details and an example, see also **pg_put_line()**.

bool **pg_end_copy**([resource connection])

pg_errormessage

Returns a string containing the error message, false on failure. Details about the error probably cannot be retrieved using the **pg_errormessage()** function. If an error occurred on the last database action for which a valid connection exists, this function will return a string containing the error message generated by the backend server.

string **pg_errormessage**(int connection)

pg_exec

Returns a result index if query could be executed, false on failure or if connection is not a valid connection index. Details about the error can be retrieved using the **pg_ErrorMessage()** function if connection is valid. Sends an SQL statement to the PostgreSQL database specified by the connection index. The connection must be a valid index that was returned by **pg_Connect()**. The return value of this function is an index to be used to access the results from other PostgreSQL functions.

Note: PHP/FI returns 1 if the query was not expected to return data (inserts or updates, for example) and greater than 1 even on selects that did not return anything. No such assumption can be made in PHP.

int **pg_exec**(int connection, string query)

pg_fetch_array

Returns an array that corresponds to the fetched row, or false if no more rows exist. **Pg_fetch_array()** is an extended version of **pg_fetch_row()**. In addition to storing the data in the numeric indices of the result array, it also stores the data in associative indices, using the field names as keys. The third optional argument **$result_type** in **pg_fetch_array()** is a constant and can take the following values: PGSQL_ASSOC, PGSQL_NUM, and PGSQL_BOTH.

Note: $Result_type was added in PHP 4.0. Also note that using **pg_fetch_array()** is NOT significantly slower than using **pg_fetch_row()**, it actually provides a significant added value. For further details, see also **pg_fetch_row()**.

array **pg_fetch_array**(int result, int row, [int result_type])

Example: PostgreSQL fetch array

```
<?php
$conn = pg_pconnect ("dbname=publisher");
if (!$conn) {
    echo "An error occured.\n";
    exit;
}
$result = pg_Exec ($conn, "SELECT * FROM authors");
if (!$result) {
    echo "An error occured.\n";
    exit;
}
$arr = pg_fetch_array ($result, 0);
echo $arr[0] . " <- array\n";
```

```php
$arr = pg_fetch_array ($result, 1);
echo $arr["author"] . " <- array\n";
?>
```

pg_fetch_object

Returns an object with properties that correspond to the fetched row, or false if no more rows are available. **Pg_fetch_object()** is similar to **pg_fetch_array()**, with one difference—an object is returned, instead of an array. Indirectly, that means that you can only access the data by the field names, and not by their offsets (numbers are illegal property names). The third optional argument $result_type in pg_fetch_object() is a constant and can take the following values: PGSQL_ASSOC, PGSQL_NUM, and PGSQL_BOTH.

Note: $Result_type was added in PHP 4.0. Speed-wise, the function is identical to **pg_fetch_array()**, and almost as quick as **pg_fetch_row()**; the difference is insignificant. See also **pg_fetch_array()** and **pg_fetch_row()**.

object **pg_fetch_object**(int result, int row, [int result_type])

Example: Postgres fetch object

```php
<?php
$database = "verlag";
$db_conn = pg_connect ("host=localhost port=5432 dbname=$database");
if (!$db_conn): ?>
    <H1>Failed connecting to Postgres database <? echo $database ?></H1> <?
    exit;
endif;
$qu = pg_exec ($db_conn, "SELECT * FROM verlag ORDER BY autor");
$row = 0; // postgres needs a row counter other dbs might not
while ($data = pg_fetch_object ($qu, $row)):
    echo $data->autor." (";
    echo $data->jahr ."): ";
    echo $data->titel."<BR>";
    $row++;
endwhile; ?>
<PRE><?php
$fields[] = Array ("autor", "Author");
$fields[] = Array ("jahr",  "  Year");
$fields[] = Array ("titel", " Title");
$row= 0; // postgres needs a row counter other dbs might not
while ($data = pg_fetch_object ($qu, $row)):
    echo "----------\n";
    reset ($fields);
    while (list (,$item) = each ($fields)):
        echo $item[1].": ".$data->$item[0]."\n";
    endwhile;
    $row++;
endwhile;
echo "----------\n"; ?>
</PRE> <?php
pg_freeResult ($qu);
pg_close ($db_conn);
?>
```

pg_fetch_row

Returns an array that corresponds to the fetched row, or false if no more rows are available. **Pg_fetch_row()** fetches one row of data from the result associated with the specified result identifier. The row is returned as an array. Each result column is stored in an array offset, starting at offset 0. See also **pg_fetch_array()**, **pg_fetch_object()**, and **pg_result()**.

array **pg_fetch_row**(int result, int row)

Example: Postgres fetch row

```php
<?php
$conn = pg_pconnect ("dbname=publisher");
if (!$conn) {
    echo "An error occured.\n";
    exit;
}
$result = pg_Exec ($conn, "SELECT * FROM authors");
if (!$result) {
    echo "An error occured.\n";
    exit;
}
$num = pg_numrows($result);
for ($i=0; $i<$num; $i++) {
  $r = pg_fetch_row($result, $i);
  for ($j=0; $j<count($r); $j++) {
    echo "$r[$j] ";
  }
  echo "<BR>";
}
?>
```

pg_fieldisnull

Test if a field is NULL or not. Returns 0 if the field in the given row is not NULL. Returns 1 if the field in the given row is NULL. Field can be specified as a number or fieldname. Row numbering starts at 0.

int **pg_fieldisnull**(int result_id, int row, mixed field).

pg_fieldname

Returns the name of the field occupying the given column number in the given PostgreSQL result identifier. Field numbering starts from 0.

string **pg_fieldname**(int result_id, int field_number)

pg_fieldnum

Returns the number of the column slot that corresponds to the named field in the given PosgreSQL result identifier. Field numbering starts at 0. This function will return -1 on error.

int **pg_fieldnum**(int result_id, string field_name)

pg_fieldprtlen

Returns the actual printed length (number of characters) of a specific value in a PostgreSQL result. Row numbering starts at 0. This function will return -1 on an error.

int **pg_fieldprtlen**(int result_id, int row_number, string field_name)

pg_fieldsize

Returns the internal storage size (in bytes) of the field number in the given PostgreSQL result. Field numbering starts at 0. A field size of -1 indicates a variable length field. This function will return false on error.

int **pg_fieldsize**(int result_id, int field_number)

pg_fieldtype

Returns a string containing the type name of the given field in the given PostgreSQL result identifier. Field numbering starts at 0.

string **pg_fieldtype**(int result_id, int field_number)

pg_freeresult

Only needs to be called if you are worried about using too much memory while your script is running. All result memory will automatically be freed when the script is finished. But, if you are sure you are not going to need the result data anymore in a script, you may call **pg_freeresult()** with the result identifier as an argument. The associated result memory then will be freed.

int **pg_freeresult**(int result_id)

pg_getlastoid

Used to retrieve the oid assigned to an inserted tuple if the result identifier is used from the last command sent via **pg_exec()** and was an SQL INSERT. This function will return a positive integer if a valid oid was available. It will return -1 if an error occurred or the last command sent via **pg_exec()** was not an INSERT.

int **pg_getlastoid**(int result_id)

pg_host

Returns the host name to which the given PostgreSQL connection identifier is connected.

string **pg_host**(int connection_id)

pg_loclose

Closes an Inversion Large Object. **$Fd** is a file descriptor for the large object from **pg_loopen()**.

void **pg_loclose**(int fd)

pg_locreate

Creates an Inversion Large Object and returns the oid of the large object. **$conn** specifies a valid database connection. PostgreSQL access modes INV_READ, INV_WRITE, and INV_ARCHIVE are not supported. The object always is created with both read and write access. INV_ARCHIVE has been removed from PostgreSQL itself (version 6.3 and above).

    int **pg_locreate**(int conn)

pg_loexport

The **$oid** argument specifies the object id of the large object to export, and the **$filename** argument specifies the pathname of the file. Returns false if an error occurred, true otherwise. Remember that handling large objects in PostgreSQL must happen inside a transaction.

    bool **pg_loexport**(int oid, int file, [int connection_id])

pg_loimport

The **$filename** argument specifies the pathname of the file to be imported as a large object. Returns false if an error occurred, object id of the just created large object otherwise. Remember that handling large objects in PostgreSQL must happen inside a transaction.

    int **pg_loimport**(int file, [int connection_id])

pg_loopen

Opens an Inversion Large Object and returns file descriptor of the large object. The file descriptor encapsulates information about the connection. Do not close the connection before closing the large object file descriptor. $objoid specifies a valid large object oid, and $mode can be either "r", "w", or "rw".

    int **pg_loopen**(int conn, int objoid, string mode)

pg_loread

Reads at most **$len** bytes from a large object and returns it as a string. **$fd** specifies a valid large object file descriptor, and $len specifies the maximum allowable size of the large object segment.

    string **pg_loread**(int fd, int len)

pg_loreadall

Reads a large object and passes it straight through to the browser after sending all pending headers. Mainly intended for sending binary data like images or sound.

    void **pg_loreadall**(int fd)

pg_lounlink

Deletes a large object with the **$lobjid** identifier for that large object.

    void **pg_lounlink**(int conn, int lobjid)

pg_lowrite

Writes, at most, to a large object from a variable **$buf** and returns the number of bytes actually written, or false in the case of an error. **$fd** is a file descriptor for the large object from **pg_loopen**().

    int **pg_lowrite**(int fd, string buf)

pg_numfields

Returns the number of fields (columns) in a PostgreSQL result. The argument is a valid result identifier returned by **pg_exec**(). This function will return -1 on error.

    int **pg_numfields**(int result_id)

pg_numrows

Returns the number of rows in a PostgreSQL result. The argument is a valid result identifier returned by **pg_exec**(). This function will return -1 on error.

    int **pg_numrows**(int result_id)

pg_options

Returns a string containing the options specified on the given PostgreSQL connection identifier.

    string **pg_options**(int connection_id)

pg_pconnect

Returns a connection index on success, or false if the connection could not be made. Opens a connection to a PostgreSQL database. The arguments should be within a quoted string. The arguments available include **$dbname**, **$port**, **$host**, **$tty**, **$options**, **$user**, and **$password**. This function returns a connection index that is needed by other PostgreSQL functions. You can have multiple connections open at once. The previous syntax of: **$conn** = pg_pconnect ("host", "port", "options", "tty", "dbname") has been deprecated. See also **pg_connect**().

    int **pg_pconnect**(string conn_string)

pg_port

Returns the port number to which the given PostgreSQL connection identifier is connected.

    int **pg_port**(int connection_id)

pg_put_line

Sends a NULL-terminated string to the PostgreSQL backend server. This is useful, for example, for very high-speed inserting of data into a table, initiated by starting a PostgreSQL copy operation. That final NULL-character is added automatically. Returns true if successful, false otherwise. **Note:** The application must explicitly send the two characters "\." on a final line to indicate to the backend that it has finished sending its data. See also **pg_end_copy()**.

bool **pg_put_line**([resource connection_id], string data)

Example: High-speed insertion of data into a table

```php
<?php
    $conn = pg_pconnect ("dbname=foo");
    pg_exec($conn, "create table bar (a int4, b char(16), d float8)");
    pg_exec($conn, "copy bar from stdin");
    pg_put_line($conn, "3\thello world\t4.5\n");
    pg_put_line($conn, "4\tgoodbye world\t7.11\n");
    pg_put_line($conn, "\\.\n");
    pg_end_copy($conn);
?>
```

pg_result

Returns values from a result identifier produced by **pg_Exec()**. The **$row_number** and **$fieldname** specify what cell in the table of results to return. Row numbering starts from 0. Instead of naming the field, you may use the field index as an unquoted number. Field indices start from 0. PostgreSQL has many built-in types, and only the basic ones are directly supported here. All forms of integer, boolean, and oid types are returned as integer values. All forms of float and real types are returned as double values. All other types, including arrays, are returned as strings formatted in the same default PostgreSQL manner that you would see in the psql program.

mixed **pg_result**(int result_id, int row_number, mixed fieldname)

pg_set_client_encoding

This function sets the client encoding. Returns 0 if successful or -1 if an error occurs. **$encoding** is the client encoding and can be one of the following: SQL_ASCII, EUC_JP, EUC_CN, EUC_KR, EUC_TW, UNICODE, MULE_INTERNAL, LATINX (X=1 . . . 9), KOI8, WIN, ALT, SJIS, BIG5, or WIN1250.

Note: This function requires PHP-4.0.2 or higher and PostgreSQL-7.0 or higher. The function used to be called **pg_setclientencoding()**. See also **pg_client_encoding()**.

int **pg_set_client_encoding**([int connection], string encoding)

pg_trace

Enables tracing of the PostgreSQL front-end/backend communication to a debugging file. To fully understand the results, one needs to be familiar with the internals of PostgreSQL communication protocol. For those who are not, it can still be useful for tracing errors in queries sent to the server. You could do, for example, grep '^To backend' trace.log and see what query actually was sent to the PostgreSQL server. $Filename and $mode are the same as in **fopen()** (**$mode** defaults to 'w'). **$connection** specifies the connection to trace and defaults to the last one opened. Returns true if $filename could be opened for logging, false otherwise. See also **fopen()** and **pg_untrace()**.

bool **pg_trace**(string filename, [string mode], [int connection]

pg_tty

Returns the tty name that server side debugging output is sent to on the given PostgreSQL connection identifier.

string **pg_tty**(int connection_id)

pg_untrace

Stops tracing started by **pg_trace()**. **$connection** specifies the connection that was traced, and it defaults to the last one opened. Returns always true. See also **pg_trace()**.

bool **pg_untrace**([int connection])

phpcredits

Prints out the credits listing the PHP developers, modules, and so on. It generates the appropriate HTML codes to insert the information in a page. A parameter indicating what will be printed (a pre-defined constant flag, see the following table) needs to be passed. See also **phpinfo()**, **phpversion()**, and **php_logo_guid()**.

void **phpcredits**(int flag)

For example, to print the general credits, you will use the following somewhere in your code:

```
...
phpcredits(CREDITS_GENERAL);
...
```

And if you want to print the core developers and the documentation group in a page of its own, you will use this:

```
<?php
  phpcredits(CREDITS_GROUP + CREDITS_DOCS + CREDITS_FULLPAGE);
?>
```

And if you feel like embedding all the credits in your page, then code like the one following will do it:

```
<html>
  <head>
    <title>My credits page</title>
  </head>
```

```
<body>
<?php
  // some code of your own
  phpcredits(CREDITS_ALL + CREDITS_FULLPAGE);
  // some more code
?>
</body>
</html>
```

Pre-defined phpcredits() flags

Name	Description
CREDITS_ALL	All the credits, equivalent to using: CREDITS_DOCS + CREDITS_GENERAL + CREDITS_GROUP + CREDITS_MODULES + CREDITS_FULLPAGE. It generates a complete stand-alone HTML page with the appropriate tags.
CREDITS_DOCS	The credits for the documentation team.
CREDITS_FULLPAGE	Usually used in combination with the other flags. Indicates that the complete stand-alone HTML page needs to be printed, including the information indicated by the other flags.
CREDITS_GENERAL	General credits: Language design and concept, PHP 4.0 authors, and SAPI module.
CREDITS_GROUP	A list of the core developers.
CREDITS_MODULES	A list of the extension modules for PHP and their authors.
CREDITS_SAPI	This flag is defined but, as of PHP 4.0.1pl2, it is not used.

phpinfo

Outputs a large amount of information about the current state of PHP. This includes information about PHP compilation options and extensions, the PHP version, server information and environment (if compiled as a module), the PHP environment, OS version information, paths, master and local values of configuration options, HTTP headers, and the PHP License.

     int **phpinfo**([int what])

The output may be customized by passing one or more of the following values together in the optional parameter **$what**. Returns a string containing the version of the currently running PHP parser. See also **phpinfo()**, **phpcredits()**, and **php_logo_guid()**.

INFO_GENERAL	INFO_CREDITS	INFO_CONFIGURATION
INFO_MODULES	INFO_ENVIRONMENT	INFO_VARIABLES
INFO_LICENSE	INFO_ALL	CREDITS_GROUP
CREDITS_GENERAL	CREDITS_SAPI	CREDITS_MODULES
CREDITS_DOCS	CREDITS_FULLPAGE	CREDITS_ALL

phpversion

Returns a string containing the version of the currently running PHP parser. See also **phpinfo()**, **phpcredits()**, and **php_logo_guid()**.

string **phpversion**(void)

Example: phpversion() example

```
// prints e.g. 'Current PHP version: 3.0rel-dev'
echo "Current PHP version: ".phpversion();
```

php_logo_guid

This functionality was added in PHP 4 Beta 4. See also **phpinfo()**, **phpversion()**, and **phpcredits()**.

string **php_logo_guid**(void)

php_sapi_name

Returns a lowercase string that describes the type of interface between Web server and PHP (Server API, SAPI). In CGI PHP, this string is "cgi", in mod_php for Apache, this string is "apache", and so on.

string **php_sapi_name**(void)

Example: Php_sapi_name()

```
$inter_type = php_sapi_name();
if ($inter_type == "cgi")
    print "You are using CGI PHP\n";
else
    print "You are not using CGI PHP\n";
```

php_uname

Returns a string with a description on which the operating system PHP is built.

string **php_uname**(void)

Example: php_uname()

```
if (substr(php_uname(), 0, 7) == "Windows") {
    die("Sorry, this script doesn't run on Windows.\n");
}
```

pi

Returns an approximation of pi.

double **pi**(void)

popen

Opens a pipe to a process executed by forking the command given by command. Returns a file pointer identical to that returned by **fopen()**, except that it is unidirectional (may only be used for reading or writing) and must be closed with **pclose()**. This pointer may be used with **fgets()**, **fgetss()**, and **fputs()**. If an error occurs, returns false. See also **pclose()**.

int **popen**(string command, string mode)

```
$fp = popen ("/bin/ls", "r");
```

pos

This is an alias for **current()**. See also **end()**, **next()**, **prev()**, and **reset()**.

mixed **pos**(array array)

posix_ctermid

string **posix_ctermid**(void)

posix_getcwd

string **posix_getcwd**(void)

posix_getegid

Returns the numeric effective group ID of the current process. See also **posix_getgrgid()** for information on how to convert this into a useable group name.

int **posix_getegid**(void)

posix_geteuid

Returns the numeric effective user ID of the current process. See also **posix_getpwuid()** for information on how to convert this into a useable username.

int **posix_geteuid**(void)

posix_getgid

Returns the numeric real group ID of the current process. See also **posix_getgrgid()** for information on how to convert this into a useable group name.

int **posix_getgid**(void)

posix_getgrgid

array **posix_getgrgid**(int gid)

posix_getgrnam

array **posix_getgrnam**(string name)

posix_getgroups

Returns an array of integers containing the numeric group ids of the group set of the current process. See also **posix_getgrgid()** for information on how to convert this into useable group names.

array **posix_getgroups**(void)

posix_getlogin

Returns the login name of the user owning the current process. See **posix_getpwnam()** for information how to get more information about this user.

string **posix_getlogin**(void)

posix_getpgid

Returns the process group identifier of the process **$pid**. This is not a POSIX function but is common on BSD and System V systems. If your system does not support this function at system level, this PHP function will always return false.

int **posix_getpgid**(int pid)

posix_getpgrp

Returns the process group identifier of the current process. See POSIX.1 and the getpgrp manual page on your POSIX system for more information on process groups.

int **posix_getpgrp**(void).

posix_getpid

Returns the process identifier of the current process.

int **posix_getpid**(void)

posix_getppid

Returns the process identifier of the parent process of the current process.

int **posix_getppid**(void).

posix_getpwnam

Returns an associative array containing information about a user referenced by an alphanumeric username, passed in the **$username** parameter.

array **posix_getpwnam**(string username)

The array elements returned are shown in the following table:

Element	Description
name	The name element contains the username of the user. This is a short, usually less than 16-character "handle" of the user, not her real, full name. This should be the same as the **$username** parameter used when calling the function, and hence redundant.
passwd	The passwd element contains the user's password in an encrypted format. Often on a system employing "shadow" passwords, for example, an asterisk is returned instead.
uid	User ID of the user in numeric form.
gid	The group ID of the user. Use the function **posix_getgrgid**() to resolve the group name and a list of its members.
gecos	GECOS is an obsolete term that refers to the finger information field on a Honeywell batch processing system. The field lives on, however, and its contents have been formalized by POSIX. The field contains a comma separated list containing the user's full name, office phone, office number, and home phone number. On most systems, only the user's full name is available.
dir	This element contains the absolute path to the home directory of the user.
shell	The shell element contains the absolute path to the executable of the user's default shell.

posix_getpwuid

Returns an associative array containing information about a user referenced by a numeric user ID, passed in the **$uid** parameter.

array **posix_getpwuid**(int uid)

The array elements returned are shown in the following table:

Element	Description
name	The name element contains the username of the user. This is a short, usually less than 16-character "handle" of the user, not her real, full name.
passwd	The passwd element contains the user's password in an encrypted format. Often on a system employing "shadow" passwords, for example, an asterisk is returned instead.
uid	User ID should be the same as the **$uid** parameter used when calling the function, and hence, redundant.
gid	The group ID of the user. Use the function **posix_getgrgid**() to resolve the group name and a list of its members.

gecos	GECOS is an obsolete term that refers to the finger information field on a Honeywell batch processing system. The field lives on, however, and its contents have been formalized by POSIX. The field contains a comma separated list containing the user's full name, office phone, office number, and home phone number. On most systems, only the user's full name is available.
dir	This element contains the absolute path to the home directory of the user.
shell	The shell element contains the absolute path to the executable of the user's default shell.

posix_getrlimit

array **posix_getrlimit**(void)

posix_getsid

Returns the sid of the process **$pid**. If **$pid** is 0, the sid of the current process is returned. This is not a POSIX function, but is common on System V systems. If your system does not support this function at system level, this PHP function will always return false.

int **posix_getsid**(int pid)

posix_getuid

Returns the numeric real user ID of the current process. See also **posix_getpwuid**() for information on how to convert this into a useable username.

int **posix_getuid**(void)

posix_isatty

bool **posix_isatty**(int fd)

posix_kill

Sends the signal **$sig** to the process with the process identifier **$pid**. Returns false, if unable to send the signal, true otherwise. See also the kill manual page of your POSIX system, which contains additional information about negative process identifiers, the special pid 0, the special pid -1, and the signal number 0.

bool **posix_kill**(int pid, int sig)

posix_mkfifo

bool **posix_mkfifo**(*string* pathname, *int* mode)

posix_setgid

Sets the real group ID of the current process. This is a privileged function and you need appropriate privileges (usually root) on your system to be able to perform this function. The appropriate order of function calls is **posix_setgid()** first and **posix_setuid()** last. Returns true on success, false otherwise.

bool **posix_setgid**(*int* gid)

posix_setpgid

Lets the process **$pid** join the process group **$pgid**. See POSIX.1 and the setsid manual page on your POSIX system for more information on process groups and job control. Returns true on success, false otherwise.

int **posix_setpgid**(*int* pid, *int* pgid)

posix_setsid

Makes the current process a session leader. See POSIX.1 and the setsid manual page on your POSIX system for more information on process groups and job control. Returns the session id.

int **posix_setsid**(*void*)

posix_setuid

Sets the real user ID of the current process. This is a privileged function and you need appropriate privileges (usually root) on your system to be able to perform this function. Returns true on success, false otherwise. See also **posix_setgid()**.

bool **posix_setuid**(*int* uid)

posix_times

Returns a hash of strings with information about the current process CPU usage.

array **posix_times**(*void*)

The indices of the hash are ticks—the number of clock ticks that have elapsed since reboot.

- utime—User time used by the current process.
- stime—System time used by the current process.
- cutime—User time used by current process and children.
- cstime—System time used by current process and children.

posix_ttyname

string **posix_ttyname**(*int* fd)

posix_uname

Returns a hash of strings with information about the system.

array **posix_uname**(*void*)

The indices of the hash are as follows:

- sysname—operating system name (for example, Linux)
- nodename—system name (for example, valiant)
- release—operating system release (for example, 2.2.10)
- version—operating system version (for example, #4 Tue Jul 20 17:01:36 MEST 1999)
- machine—system architecture (for example, i586)
- domainname—DNS domainname (for example,. php.net)

domainname is a GNU extension and not part of POSIX.1, so this field is only available on GNU systems or when using the GNU libc. Posix requires that you must not make any assumptions about the format of the values. For example, you cannot rely on three digit version numbers or anything else returned by this function.

pow

Returns base raised to the power of exp. See also **exp()**.

float **pow**(*float* base, *float* exp)

preg_grep

Returns the array consisting of the elements of the $input array that match the given **$pattern**.

array **preg_grep**(*string* pattern, *array* input)

Example: preg_grep()

```
// return all array elements
// containing floating point numbers
$fl_array = preg_grep ("/^(\d+)?\.\d+$/", $array);
```

preg_match

Searches **$subject** for a match to the regular expression given in **$pattern**. If **$matches** is provided, then it is filled with the results of the search. **$matches[0]** will contain the text that match the full pattern, **$matches[1]** will have the text that matched the first captured parenthesized subpattern, and so on. Returns true if a match for **$pattern** was found in the subject string, or false if no match was found or an error occurred. See also **preg_match_all()**, **preg_replace()**, and **preg_split()**.

int **preg_match**(*string* pattern, *string* subject, [*array* matches])

Example: Find the string of text "php"

```
// the "i" after the pattern delimiter indicates a case-insensitive search
if (preg_match ("/php/i", "PHP is the web scripting language of choice.")) {
    print "A match was found.";
} else {
    print "A match was not found.";
}
```

Example: Find the word "web"

```
// the \b in the pattern indicates a word boundary, so only the distinct
// word "web" is matched, and not a word partial like "webbing" or "cobweb"
if (preg_match ("/\bweb\b/i", "PHP is the web scripting language of choice.")) {
    print "A match was found.";
} else {
    print "A match was not found.";
}
if (preg_match ("/\bweb\b/i", "PHP is the website scripting language of choice.")) {
    print "A match was found.";
} else {
    print "A match was not found.";
}
```

Example: Getting the domain name out of a URL

```
// get host name from URL
preg_match("/^(http:\/\/)?([^\/]+)/i",
"http://www.php.net/index.html", $matches);
$host = $matches[2];
// get last two segments of host name
preg_match("/[^\.\/]+\.[^\.\/]+$/",$host,$matches);
echo "domain name is: ".$matches[0]."\n";
        This example will produce:
domain name is: php.net
```

preg_match_all

Searches **$subject** for all matches to the regular expression given in **$pattern** and puts them in **$matches** in the order specified by **$order**. After the first match is found, the subsequent searches continue from the end of the last match.

int **preg_match_all**(*string* pattern, *string* subject, *array* matches, [*int* order])

$order can be one of two things:

1. **PREG_PATTERN_ORDER**   Orders results so that $matches[0] is an array of full pattern matches, $matches[1] is an array of strings matched by the first parenthesized subpattern, and so on.

```
preg_match_all ("|<[^>]+>(.*)</[^>]+>|U",
    "<b>example: </b><div align=left>this is a test</div>",
    $out, PREG_PATTERN_ORDER);
```

```
print $out[0][0].", ".$out[0][1]."\n";
print $out[1][0].", ".$out[1][1]."\n"
```

This example will produce the following:

```
<b>example: </b>, <div align=left>this is a test</div>
example: , this is a test
```

So, $out[0] contains array of strings that matched full pattern, and $out[1] contains array of strings enclosed by tags.

2. **PREG_SET_ORDER**   Orders result so that $matches[0] is an array of the first set of matches, $matches[1] is an array of the second set of matches, and so on.

```
preg_match_all ("|<[^>]+>(.*)</[^>]+>|U",
    "<b>example: </b><div align=left>this is a test</div>",
    $out, PREG_SET_ORDER);
print $out[0][0].", ".$out[0][1]."\n";
print $out[1][0].", ".$out[1][1]."\n"
```

This example will produce the following:

```
<b>example: </b>, example:
<div align=left>this is a test</div>, this is a test
```

In this case, $matches[0] is the first set of matches, and $matches[0][0] has text matched by full pattern, $matches[0][1] has text matched by first subpattern, and so on. Similarly, $matches[1] is the second set of matches, and so on. If **$order** is not specified, it is assumed to be PREG_PATTERN_ORDER. Returns the number of full pattern matches, or false if no match is found or an error occurred. See also **preg_match(), preg_replace(),** and **preg_split()**.

Example: Getting all phone numbers out of some text.

```
preg_match_all ("/\(? (\d{3})? \)?  (?(1)  [\-\s] ) \d{3}-\d{4}/x",
               "Call 555-1212 or 1-800-555-1212", $phones);
```

Example: Find matching HTML tags (greedy)

```
// the \\2 is an example of backreferencing. This tells pcre that
// it must match the 2nd set of parenthesis in the regular expression
// itself, which would be the ([\w]+) in this case.
$html = "<b>bold text</b><a href=howdy.html>click me</a>
preg_match_all ("/(<([\w]+)[^>]*>)(.*)(<\/\\2>)/", $html, $matches);
for ($i=0; $i< count($matches[0]); $i++) {
echo "matched: ".$matches[0][$i]."\n";
echo "part 1: ".$matches[1][$i]."\n";
echo "part 2: ".$matches[3][$i]."\n";
echo "part 3: ".$matches[4][$i]."\n\n";
}
```

This example will produce the following:

```
matched: <b>bold text</b>
part 1: <b>
part 2: bold text
part 3: </b>
matched: <a href=howdy.html>click me</a>
part 1: <a href=howdy.html>
part 2: click me
part 3: </a>
```

preg_quote

Takes **$str** and puts a backslash in front of every character that is part of the regular expression syntax. This is useful if you have a run-time string that you need to match in some text, and the string may contain special regex characters. If the optional **$delimiter** is specified, it will also be escaped. This is useful for escaping the delimiter that is required by the PCRE functions. The / is the most commonly used delimiter.

string **preg_quote**(*string* str, [*string* delimiter])

The special regular expression characters are as follows:

```
. \\ + * ? [ ^ ] $ ( ) { } = ! < > | :
```

Example 1:

```
$keywords = "$40 for a g3/400";
$keywords = preg_quote ($keywords, "/");
echo $keywords; // returns \$40 for a g3\/400
```

Example 2: Italicizing a word within some text

```
// In this example, preg_quote($word) is used to keep the
// asterisks from having special meaning to the regular
// expression.

$textbody = "This book is *very* difficult to find.";
$word = "*very*";
$textbody = preg_replace ("/".preg_quote($word)."/",
                          "<i>".$word."</i>",
                          $textbody);
```

preg_replace

Searches **$subject** for matches to **$pattern** and replaces them with **$replacement**. If **$limit** is specified, then only **$limit** matches will be replaced; if **$limit** is omitted or is -1, then all matches are replaced. **$Replacement** may contain references of the form \\ n . Every such reference will be replaced by the text captured by the n'th parenthesized pattern. n can be from 0 to 99, and \\0 refers to the text matched by the whole pattern. Opening parentheses are counted from left to right (starting from 1) in order to obtain the number of the capturing subpattern.

mixed **preg_replace**(*mixed* pattern, *mixed* replacement, *mixed* subject, [*int* limit])

If no matches are found in **$subject**, then it will be returned unchanged. Every parameter to **preg_replace()** can be an array. If **$subject** is an array, then the search and replace is performed on every entry of **$subject**, and the return value is an array as well. If **$pattern** and **$replacement** are arrays, then **preg_replace()** takes a value from each array and uses them to do search and replace on **$subject**. If **$replacement** has fewer values than **$pattern**, then empty string is used for the rest of replacement values. If **$pattern** is an array and **$replacement** is a string, then this replacement string is used for every value of **$pattern**. However, the converse would not make sense. /e modifier makes **preg_replace()** treat the **$replacement** parameter as PHP code after the appropriate references substitution is done. **Tip:** Make sure that **$replacement** constitutes a valid PHP code string, otherwise PHP will complain about a parse error at the line containing **preg_replace()**. Parameter **$limit** was added after PHP 4.0.1pl2. See also **preg_match()**, **preg_match_all()**, and **preg_split()**.

Example: Replacing several values

```
$patterns = array ("/(19|20)(\d{2})-(\d{1,2})-(\d{1,2})/",
                   "/^\s*{(\w+)}\s*=/");
$replace = array ("\\3/\\4/\\1\\2", "$\\1 =");
print preg_replace ($patterns, $replace, "{startDate} = 1999-5-27");
        This example will produce:
$startDate = 5/27/1999
```

Example: Using /e modifier

```
preg_replace ("/(<\/?)(\w+)([^>]*>)/e",
              "'\\1'.strtoupper('\\2').'\\3'",
              $html_body);
```

This would capitalize all HTML tags in the input text.

Example: Convert HTML to text

```
// $document should contain an HTML document.
// This will remove HTML tags, javascript sections
// and white space. It will also convert some
// common HTML entities to their text equivalent.
$search = array ("'<script[^>]*?>.*?</script>'si",  // Strip out javascript
                 "'<[\/\!]*?[^<>]*?>'si",  // Strip out html tags
                 "'([\r\n])[\s]+'",  // Strip out white space
                 "'&(quot|#34);'i",  // Replace html entities
                 "'&(amp|#38);'i",
                 "'&(lt|#60);'i",
                 "'&(gt|#62);'i",
                 "'&(nbsp|#160);'i",
                 "'&(iexcl|#161);'i",
                 "'&(cent|#162);'i",
                 "'&(pound|#163);'i",
                 "'&(copy|#169);'i",
                 "'&#(\d+);'e");  // evaluate as php
$replace = array ("",
                  "",
                  "\\1",
                  "\"",
                  "&",
                  "<",
```

```
            ">",
            " ",
            chr(161),
            chr(162),
            chr(163),
            chr(169),
            "chr(\\1)");
$text = preg_replace ($search, $replace, $document);
```

preg_split

Parameter **$flags** was added in PHP 4 Beta 3. Returns an array containing substrings of **$subject** split along boundaries matched by **$pattern**. If **$limit** is specified, then only substrings up to **$limit** are returned. If **$flags** is PREG_SPLIT_NO_EMPTY, then only non-empty pieces will be returned by **preg_split()**.

array preg_split **preg_split**(*string* pattern, *string* subject, [*int* limit], [*int* flags])

Example: preg_split()
Get the parts of a search string.

```
// split the phrase by any number of commas or space characters,
// which include " ", \r, \t, \n and \f
$keywords = preg_split ("/[\s,]+/", "hypertext language, programming<\#34>);
```

Splitting a string into component characters.

```
$str = 'string';
$chars = preg_split('//', $str, 0, PREG_SPLIT_NO_EMPTY);
print_r($chars);
```

See also **preg_match()**, **preg_match_all()**, and **preg_replace()**.

prev

Returns the array element in the previous place that's pointed by the internal array pointer, or false if no more elements are available. If the array contains empty elements, then this function will return false for these elements as well. In order to properly traverse an array which may contain empty elements, see the **each()** function. **Prev()** behaves just like **next()**, except it rewinds the internal array pointer one place instead of advancing it. See also **current()**, **end()**, **next()**, and **reset()**.

mixed **prev**(*array* array)

print

Outputs **$arg**. See also **echo()**, **printf()**, and **flush()**.

print(*string* arg)

printf

Produces output according to $format, which is described in the documentation for **sprintf()**. See also **print()**, **sprintf()**, **sscanf()**, **fscanf(),** and **flush()**.

int **printf**(*string* format, [*mixed* args])

print_r

Displays information about the values of variables in a way that's readable by humans. If given a string, integer or double, the value itself will be printed. If given an array, values will be presented in a format that shows keys and elements. Similar notation is used for objects. Compare **print_r()** to **var_dump()**.

void **print_r**(*mixed* expression)

```
<?php
$a = array (1, 2, array ("a", "b", "c"));
print_r ($a);
?>
```

This function will continue forever if given an array or object that contains a direct or indirect reference to itself or one that contains an array or object on a deeper level that does so. This is especially true for *print_r($GLOBALS)* because *$GLOBALS* is itself a global variable and contains a reference to itself as such.

pspell_add_to_personal

Adds a word to the personal wordlist. If you used **pspell_new_config()** with **pspell_config_personal()** to open the dictionary, you can save the wordlist later with **pspell_save_wordlist()**. **Note:** This function will not work unless you have pspell .11.2 and aspell .32.5 or later.

int **pspell_add_to_personal**(*int* dictionary_link, *string* word)

Example: Pspell_add_to_personal()

```
$pspell_config = pspell_config_create ("en");
pspell_config_personal ($pspell_config, "/var/dictionaries/custom.pws");
$pspell_link = pspell_new_config ($pspell_config);
pspell_add_to_personal ($pspell_link, "Vlad");
pspell_save_wordlist ($pspell_link);
```

pspell_add_to_session

Adds a word to the wordlist associated with the current session. It is very similar to **pspell_add_to_personal()**.

int **pspell_add_to_session**(*int* dictionary_link, *string* word)

pspell_check

Checks the spelling of a word and returns true if the spelling is correct, false if not.

boolean **pspell_check**(*int* dictionary_link, *string* word)

Example: Pspell_check()

```
$pspell_link = pspell_new ("en");
if (pspell_check ($pspell_link, "testt")) {
    echo "This is a valid spelling";
} else {
    echo "Sorry, wrong spelling";
}
```

pspell_clear_session

Clears the current session. The current wordlist becomes blank, and if you try to save it with **pspell_save_wordlist**(), for example, nothing happens.

int **pspell_clear_session**(*int* dictionary_link)

Example: Pspell_add_to_personal()

```
$pspell_config = pspell_config_create ("en");
pspell_config_personal ($pspell_config, "/var/dictionaries/custom.pws");
$pspell_link = pspell_new_config ($pspell_config);
pspell_add_to_personal ($pspell_link, "Vlad");
pspell_clear_session ($pspell_link);
pspell_save_wordlist ($pspell_link);        //"Vlad" will not be saved
```

pspell_config_create

Has a very similar syntax to **pspell_new**(). In fact, using **pspell_config_create**() immediately followed by **pspell_new_config**() will produce the exact same result. However, after creating a new config, you can also use **pspell_config_*()** functions before calling **pspell_new_config**() to take advantage of some advanced functionality. The language parameter is the language code that consists of the two letter ISO 639 language code and an optional two letter ISO 3166 country code after a dash or underscore. The spelling parameter is the requested spelling for languages with more than one spelling such as English. Known values are 'american', 'british', and 'canadian'. The jargon parameter contains extra information in order to distinguish two different word lists that have the same language and spelling parameters. The encoding parameter is the encoding that words are expected to be in. Valid values are 'utf-8', 'iso8859-*', 'koi8-r', 'viscii', 'cp1252', 'machine unsigned 16', and 'machine unsigned 32'. This parameter is largely untested, so be careful when using.

int **pspell_config_create**(*string* language, [*string* spelling], [*string* jargon], [*string* encoding])

The mode parameter is the mode in which spellchecker will work. Several modes are available:

- PSPELL_FAST—Fast mode (least number of suggestions)
- PSPELL_NORMAL—Normal mode (more suggestions)
- PSPELL_BAD_SPELLERS—Slow mode (a lot of suggestions)

For more information and examples, check out inline manual pspell Web site: *http://pspell.sourceforge.net/*.

Example: Pspell_config_create()

```
$pspell_config = pspell_config_create ("en");
pspell_config_personal ($pspell_config, "/var/dictionaries/custom.pws");
pspell_config_repl ($pspell_config, "/var/dictionaries/custom.repl");
$pspell_link = pspell_new_personal (pspell_config);
```

pspell_config_ignore

Used on a config before calling **pspell_new_config()**. This function enables short words to be skipped by the spellchecker. Words less then n characters will be skipped.

int **pspell_config_ignore**(*int* dictionary_link, *int* n)

Example: Pspell_config_ignore()

```
$pspell_config = pspell_config_create ("en");
pspell_config_ignore($pspell_config, 5);
$pspell_link = pspell_new_config($pspell_config);
pspell_check($pspell_link, "abcd");//will not result in an error
```

pspell_config_mode

Should be used on a config before calling **pspell_new_config()**. This function determines how many suggestions will be returned by **pspell_suggest()**.

int **pspell_config_mode**(*int* dictionary_link, *int* mode)

The mode parameter is the mode in which spellchecker will work. Several modes are available:

- PSPELL_FAST—Fast mode (least number of suggestions)
- PSPELL_NORMAL—Normal mode (more suggestions)
- PSPELL_BAD_SPELLERS—Slow mode (a lot of suggestions)

Example: Pspell_config_mode()

```
$pspell_config = pspell_config_create ("en");
pspell_config_mode($pspell_config, PSPELL_FAST);
$pspell_link = pspell_new_config($pspell_config);
pspell_check($pspell_link, "thecat");
```

pspell_config_personal

Should be used on a config before calling **pspell_new_config()**. The personal wordlist will be loaded and used in addition to the standard one after you call **pspell_new_config()**. If the file does not exist, it will be created. The file is also the file to where **pspell_save_wordlist()** will save personal wordlist. The file should be writeable by whoever php runs as (that is, nobody).

Note: This function will not work unless you have pspell .11.2 and aspell .32.5 or later.

int **pspell_config_personal**(*int* dictionary_link, *string* file)

Example: Pspell_config_personal()

```
$pspell_config = pspell_config_create ("en");
pspell_config_personal ($pspell_config, "/var/dictionaries/custom.pws");
$pspell_link = pspell_new_config ($pspell_config);
pspell_check ($pspell_link, "thecat");
```

pspell_config_repl

Should be used on a config before calling **pspell_new_config()**. The replacement pairs improve the quality of the spellchecker. When a word is misspelled and a proper suggestion was not found in the list, **pspell_store_replacement()** can be used to store a replacement pair and then **pspell_save_wordlist()** to save the wordlist along with the replacement pairs. The file should be writeable by whoever php runs as (that is, nobody).

Note: This function will not work unless you have pspell .11.2 and aspell .32.5 or later.

int **pspell_config_repl**(*int* dictionary_link, *string* file)

Example: Pspell_config_repl()

```
$pspell_config = pspell_config_create ("en");
pspell_config_personal ($pspell_config, "/var/dictionaries/custom.pws");
pspell_config_repl ($pspell_config, "/var/dictionaries/custom.repl");
$pspell_link = pspell_new_config ($pspell_config);
pspell_check ($pspell_link, "thecat");
```

pspell_config_runtogether

Should be used on a config before calling **pspell_new_config()**. This function determines whether run-together words will be treated as legal compounds. That is, "thecat" will be a legal compound, although a space should be present between the two words. Changing this setting only affects the results returned by **pspell_check()**; **pspell_suggest()** will still return suggestions.

int **pspell_config_runtogether**(*int* dictionary_link, *boolean* flag)

Example: Pspell_config_runtogether()

```
$pspell_config = pspell_config_create ("en");
pspell_config_runtogether ($pspell_config, true);
$pspell_link = pspell_new_config ($pspell_config);
pspell_check ($pspell_link, "thecat");
```

pspell_config_save_repl

Should be used on a config before calling **pspell_new_config()**. It determines whether **pspell_save_wordlist()** will save the replacement pairs along with the wordlist. Usually using this function is unnecessary because if **pspell_config_repl()** is used, the replacement pairs will be saved by **pspell_save_wordlist()** anyway. If it is not, the replacement pairs will not be saved. **Note:** This function will not work unless you have pspell .11.2 and aspell .32.5 or later.

int **pspell_config_save_repl**(*int* dictionary_link, *boolean* flag)

pspell_new

Opens up a new dictionary and returns the dictionary link identifier for use in other pspell functions. The language parameter is the language code that consists of the two letter ISO 639 language code and an optional two letter ISO 3166 country code after a dash or underscore. The spelling parameter is the requested spelling for languages with more than one spelling such as English. Known values are 'american', 'british', and 'canadian'. The jargon parameter contains extra information to distinguish two different word lists that have the same language and spelling parameters. The encoding parameter is the encoding that words are expected to be in. Valid values are 'utf-8', 'iso8859-*', 'koi8-r', 'viscii', 'cp1252', 'machine unsigned 16', and 'machine unsigned 32'. This parameter is largely untested, so be careful when using.

int **pspell_new**(*string* language, [*string* spelling], [*string* jargon], [*string* encoding], [*int* mode])

The mode parameter is the mode in which spellchecker will work. Several modes are available:

■ PSPELL_FAST—Fast mode (least number of suggestions).

■ PSPELL_NORMAL—Normal mode (more suggestions).

■ PSPELL_BAD_SPELLERS—Slow mode (a lot of suggestions).

■ PSPELL_RUN_TOGETHER—Consider run-together words as legal compounds. That is, "thecat" will be a legal compound, although a space should be present between the two words. Changing this setting only affects the results returned by **pspell_check()**; **pspell_suggest()** will still return suggestions.

Mode is a bit mask constructed from different constants previously listed. However, PSPELL_FAST, PSPELL_NORMAL, and PSPELL_BAD_SPELLERS are mutually exclusive, so you should select only one of them. For more information and examples, check out inline manual pspell Web site: *http://pspell.sourceforge.net/*.

Example: Pspell_new()

```
$pspell_link = pspell_new ("en", "", "", "",
                    (PSPELL_FAST|PSPELL_RUN_TOGETHER));
```

pspell_new_config

Opens up a new dictionary with settings specified in a config, created with **pspell_config_create()** and modified with **pspell_config_*()** functions. This method provides you with the most flexibility and has all the functionality provided by **pspell_new()** and **pspell_new_personal()**. The config parameter is the one returned by **pspell_config_create()** when the config was created.

int **pspell_new_config**(*int* config)

Example: Pspell_new_config()

```
$pspell_config = pspell_config_create ("en");
pspell_config_personal ($pspell_config, "/var/dictionaries/custom.pws");
pspell_config_repl ($pspell_config, "/var/dictionaries/custom.repl");
$pspell_link = pspell_new_personal (pspell_config);
```

pspell_new_personal

Opens up a new dictionary with a personal wordlist and returns the dictionary link identifier for use in other pspell functions. The wordlist can be modified and saved with **pspell_save_wordlist()**, if desired. However, the replacement pairs are not saved. In order to save replacement pairs, you should create a config using **pspell_config_create()**, set the personal wordlist file with **pspell_config_personal()**, set the file for replacement pairs with **pspell_config_repl()**, and open a new dictionary with **pspell_new_config()**.

int **pspell_new_personal**(*string* personal, *string* language, [*string* spelling], [*string* jargon], [*string* encoding], [*int* mode])

The personal parameter specifies the file where words added to the personal list will be stored. It should be an absolute filename beginning with '/'; otherwise, it will be relative to $HOME, which is "/root" for most systems and is probably not what you want. The language parameter is the language code that consists of the two letter ISO 639 language code and an optional two letter ISO 3166 country code after a dash or underscore. The spelling parameter is the requested spelling for languages with more than one spelling such as English. Known values are 'american', 'british', and 'canadian'. The jargon parameter contains extra information to distinguish two different word lists that have the same language and spelling parameters. The encoding parameter is the encoding that words are expected to be in. Valid values are 'utf-8', 'iso8859-*', 'koi8-r', 'viscii', 'cp1252', 'machine unsigned 16', and 'machine unsigned 32'. This parameter is largely untested, so be careful when using.

The mode parameter is the mode in which spellchecker will work. Several modes are available:

■ PSPELL_FAST—Fast mode (least number of suggestions).

■ PSPELL_NORMAL—Normal mode (more suggestions).

■ PSPELL_BAD_SPELLERS—Slow mode (a lot of suggestions).

■ PSPELL_RUN_TOGETHER—Consider run-together words as legal compounds. That is, "thecat" will be a legal compound, although a space should be present between the two words. Changing this setting only affects the results returned by **pspell_check()**; **pspell_suggest()** will still return suggestions.

Mode is a bit mask constructed from different constants previously listed. However,

PSPELL_FAST, PSPELL_NORMAL, and PSPELL_BAD_SPELLERS are mutually exclusive, so you should select only one of them. For more information and examples, check out inline manual pspell Web site: *http://pspell.sourceforge.net/*.

Example: Pspell_new_personal()

```
$pspell_link = pspell_new_personal ("/var/dictionaries/custom.pws",
    "en", "", "", "", PSPELL_FAST|PSPELL_RUN_TOGETHER));
```

pspell_save_wordlist

Saves the personal wordlist from the current session. The dictionary has to be opened with **pspell_new_personal()**, and the location of files has to be saved specifically with **pspell_config_personal()** and (optionally) **pspell_config_repl()**.

Note: This function will not work unless you have pspell .11.2 and aspell .32.5 or later.

int **pspell_save_wordlist**(int dictionary_link)

Example: Pspell_add_to_personal()

```
$pspell_config = pspell_config_create ("en");
pspell_config_personal ($pspell_config, "/tmp/dicts/newdict");
$pspell_link = pspell_new_config ($pspell_config);
pspell_add_to_personal ($pspell_link, "Vlad");
pspell_save_wordlist ($pspell_link);
```

pspell_store_replacement

Stores a replacement pair for a word, so that replacement can be returned by **pspell_suggest()** later. In order to be able to take advantage of this function, you have to use **pspell_new_personal()** to open the dictionary. In order to permanently save the replacement pair, you have to use **pspell_config_personal()** and **pspell_config_repl()** to set the path where to save your custom wordlists. Then use **pspell_save_wordlist()** for the changes to be written to the disk.

Note: This function will not work unless you have pspell .11.2 and aspell .32.5 or later.

int **pspell_store_replacement**(int dictionary_link, string misspelled, string correct)

Example: Pspell_store_replacement()

```
$pspell_config = pspell_config_create ("en");
pspell_config_personal ($pspell_config, "/var/dictionaries/custom.pws");
pspell_config_repl ($pspell_config, "/var/dictionaries/custom.repl");
$pspell_link = pspell_new_config ($pspell_config);
pspell_store_replacement ($pspell_link, $misspelled, $correct);
pspell_save_wordlist ($pspell_link);
```

pspell_suggest

Returns an array of possible spellings for the given word.

array **pspell_suggest**(int dictionary_link, string word)

Example: Pspell_suggest()

```
$pspell_link = pspell_new ("en");
if (!pspell_check ($pspell_link, "testt")) {
    $suggestions = pspell_suggest ($pspell_link, "testt");
    for ($i=0; $i < count ($suggestions); $i++) {
        echo "Possible spelling: " . $suggestions[$i] . "<br>";
    }
}
```

putenv

Adds **$setting** to the server environment.

void **putenv**(string setting)

Example: Setting an Environment Variable

```
putenv ("UNIQID=$uniqid");
```

quoted_printable_decode

Returns an 8-bit binary string corresponding to the decoded quoted printable string. This function is similar to imap_qprint(), except this one does not require the IMAP module to work.

string quoted_printable_decode(string str)

quotemeta

Returns a version of str with a backslash character (\ ) before every character that is among the following: . \\ + * ? [^] ($). See also **addslashes()**, **htmlentities()**, **htmlspecialchars()**, **nl2br()**, and **stripslashes()**.

string **quotemeta**(string str)

rad2deg

Converts **$number** from radian to degrees. See also **deg2rad()**.

double **rad2deg**(double number)

rand

If called without the optional **$min**, **$max** arguments **rand()** returns a pseudo-random value between 0 and RAND_MAX . If you want a random number between 5 and 15 (inclusive), for example, use rand (5, 15). Remember to seed the random number generator before use with **srand()**. **Note:** In versions before 3.0.7, the meaning of **$max** was **$range**. To get the same results in these versions, the short example should be rand (5, 11) to get a random number between 5 and 15. See also **srand()**, **getrandmax()**, **mt_rand()**, **mt_srand()**, and **mt_getrandmax()**.

    int **rand**([double int min], [double int max])

range

Returns an array of integers from **$low** to **$high**, inclusive. See **shuffle()** for an example of its use.

    array **range**(int low, int high)

rawurldecode

Returns a string in which the sequences with percent (%) signs followed by two hex digits have been replaced with literal characters. For example, the string foo%20bar%40baz decodes into foo bar@baz. See also **rawurlencode()**, **urldecode()**, and **urlencode()**.

    string **rawurldecode**(string str)

rawurlencode

Returns a string in which all non-alphanumeric characters, except -_. have been replaced with a percent (%) sign followed by two hex digits. This is the encoding described in RFC1738 for protecting literal characters from being interpreted as special URL delimiters, and for protecting URL's from being mangled by transmission media with character conversions (like some email systems). The following is an example for if you want to include a password in an ftp url:

    string **rawurlencode**(string str)

    Example 1: Rawurlencode()

```
echo '<A HREF="ftp://user:', rawurlencode ('foo @+%/'),
    '@ftp.my.com/x.txt">';
```

Or, if you pass information in a path info component of the url:
Example 2: Rawurlencode()

```
echo '<A HREF="http://x.com/department_list_script/',
    rawurlencode ('sales and marketing/Miami'), '">';
```

See also **rawurldecode()**, **urldecode()**, **urlencode()**.

readdir

Returns the filename of the next file from the directory. The filenames are not returned in any particular order.

    string **readdir**(int dir_handle)

Example: List all files in the current directory

```
// Note that !== did not exist until 4.0.0-RC2
<?php
$handle=opendir('.');
echo "Directory handle: $handle\n";
echo "Files:\n";
while (($file = readdir($handle))!==false) {
    echo "$file\n";
}
closedir($handle);
?>
```

Note: readdir() will return the . and .. entries. If you don't want these, simply strip them out.
Example: List all files in the current directory and strip out . and ..

```
<?php
$handle=opendir('.');
while (false!==($file = readdir($handle))) {
    if ($file != "." && $file != "..") {
        echo "$file\n";
    }
}
closedir($handle);
?>
```

readfile

Reads a file and writes it to standard output. Returns the number of bytes read from the file. If an error occurs, false is returned. Unless the function was called as @readfile, an error message is printed. If **$filename** begins with "http://" (not case sensitive), an HTTP 1.0 connection is opened to the specified server and the text of the response is written to standard output. Does not handle HTTP redirects, so you must include trailing slashes on directories. If **$filename** begins with "ftp://" (not case sensitive), an ftp connection to the specified server is opened and the requested file is written to standard output. If the server does not support passive mode ftp, this will fail. If **$filename** begins with neither of these strings, the file will be opened from the filesystem and its contents written to standard output. You can use the optional second parameter and set it to "1" if you want to search for the file in the **include_path()**, too. See also **fpassthru()**, **file()**, **fopen()**, **include()**, **require()**, and **virtual()**.

int **readfile**(string filename, [int use_include_path])

readgzfile

Reads a file, decompresses it, and writes it to standard output. **Readgzfile()** can be used to read a file that is not in gzip format. In this case, **readgzfile()** will directly read from the file without decompression. Returns the number of (uncompressed) bytes read from the file. If an error occurs, false is returned, and unless the function was called as @readgzfile, an error message is printed. The file **$filename** will be opened from the filesystem and its contents written to standard output. You can use the optional second parameter and set it to "1" if you want to search for the file in the **include_path()**, too. See also **gzpassthru()**, **gzfile()**, and **gzopen()**.

> int **readgzfile**(string filename, [int use_include_path])

readline

Returns a single string from the user. You may specify a string with which to prompt the user. The line returned has the ending newline removed. You must add this line to the history yourself using **readline_add_history()**.

> string **readline**([string prompt])

> **Example: Readline()**

```
//get 3 commands from user
for ($i=0; $i < 3; $i++) {
        $line = readline ("Command: ");
        readline_add_history ($line);
}
//dump history
print_r (readline_list_history());

//dump variables
print_r (readline_info());
```

readline_add_history

Adds a line to the command line history.

> void **readline_add_history**(string line)

readline_clear_history

Clears the entire command line history.

> boolean readline_clear_history(void)

readline_completion_function

Registers a completion function. You must supply the name of an existing function that accepts a partial command line and returns an array of possible matches. This is the same kind of functionality you would get if you hit your tab key while using Bash.

> *boolean* readline_completion_function(*string* line)

readline_info

If called with no parameters, this function returns an array of values for all the setting readline uses. The elements will be indexed by the following values: done, end, erase_empty_line, library_version, line_buffer, mark, pending_input, point, prompt, readline_name, and terminal_name.

If called with one parameter, the value of that setting is returned. If called with two parameters, the setting will be changed to the given value.

mixed **readline_info**([*string* varname], [*string* newvalue])

readline_list_history

Returns an array of the entire command line history. The elements are indexed by integers starting at zero.

array readline_list_history(*void*)

readline_read_history

This function reads a command history from a file.

boolean **readline_read_history**(*string* filename)

readline_write_history

This function writes the command history to a file.

boolean **readline_write_history**(*string* filename)

readlink

Performs like the readlink C function and returns the contents of the symbolic link path or 0 in case of error. See also **symlink()**, **readlink()**, and **linkinfo()**. This function does not work on Windows' systems.

string **readlink**(*string* path)

read_exif_data

Reads the EXIF headers from a JPEG image file. It returns an associative array where the indexes are the Exif header names and the values are the values associated with those Exif headers. Exif headers tend to be present in JPEG images generated by digital cameras. Unfortunately, each digital camera maker has a different idea of how to actually tag their images, so you can't always rely on a specific Exif header being present.

This function is only available in PHP 4 compiled using --enable-exif. This function does not require the GD image library.

array **read_exif_data**(*string* filename)

Example: read_exif_data

```php
<?php
 $exif = read_exif_data ('p0001807.jpg');
 while(list($k,$v)=each($exif)) {
   echo "$k: $v<br>\n";
 }
?>
```

Output is as follows:

```
FileName: p0001807.jpg
FileDateTime: 929353056
FileSize: 378599
CameraMake: Eastman Kodak Company
CameraModel: KODAK DC265 ZOOM DIGITAL CAMERA (V01.00)
DateTime: 1999:06:14 01:37:36
Height: 1024
Width: 1536
IsColor: 1
FlashUsed: 0
FocalLength:  8.0mm
RawFocalLength: 8
ExposureTime:  0.004 s (1/250)
RawExposureTime: 0.0040000001899898
ApertureFNumber: f/ 9.5
RawApertureFNumber: 9.5100002288818
FocusDistance: 16.66m
RawFocusDistance: 16.659999847412
Orientation: 1
ExifVersion: 0200
```

realpath

Expands all symbolic links and resolves references to '/./', '/../', and extra '/' characters in the input **$path** and returns the canonicalized absolute pathname. The resulting path will have no symbolic link, '/./' or '/../' components.

string **realpath**(*string* path)

Example: realpath()

```
$real_path = realpath ("../../index.php");
```

recode

This function is an alias for **recode_string()**. It has been added in PHP 4.

string **recode**(*string* request, *string* string)

recode_file

Recodes the file referenced by file handle **$input** into the file referenced by file handle **$output** according to the recode request. Returns false if unable to comply, true otherwise. This function does not currently process file handles referencing remote files (URLs). Both file handles must refer to local files.

bool **recode_file**(*int* input, *int* output)

recode_string

Recodes the string **$string** according to the recode request **$request** . Returns false if unable to comply, true otherwise.

A simple recode request may be "lat1..iso646-de". See also the GNU Recode documentation of your installation for detailed instructions about recode requests.

string **recode_string**(*string* request, *string* string)

register_shutdown_function

Registers the function named by **$func** to be executed when script processing is complete.

int register_shutdown_function(*string* func)

Common Pitfalls: Because no output is allowed to the browser in this function, you will be unable to debug it using statements such as print or echo.

rename

Attempts to rename **$oldname** to **$newname**. Returns true on success and false on failure.

int **rename**(*string* oldname, *string* newname)

reset

Rewinds the internal pointer of **$array** to the first element. **Reset()** returns the value of the first array element. See also **current()**, **each()**, **next()**, and **prev()**.

mixed **reset**(*array* array)

restore_error_handler

Used after changing the error handler function using **set_error_handler()** to revert to the previous error handler (which could be the built-in or a user defined function). See also **error_reporting()**, **set_error_handler()**, **trigger_error()**, and **user_error()**

void restore_error_handler(*void*)

rewind

Sets the file position indicator for fp to the beginning of the file stream. If an error occurs, returns 0. The file pointer must be valid and must point to a file successfully opened by **fopen()**. See also **fseek()** and **ftell()**.

int **rewind**(*int* fp)

rewinddir

Resets the directory stream indicated by **$dir_handle** to the beginning of the directory.

void **rewinddir**(*int* dir_handle)

rmdir

Attempts to remove the directory named by pathname. The directory must be empty, and the relevant permissions must permit this. If an error occurs, returns 0. See also **mkdir()**.

int **rmdir**(*string* dirname)

round

Returns the rounded value of **$val** to specified precision. See also **ceil()** and **floor()**.

double **round**(*double* val, [*int* precision])

```
$foo = round (3.4);    // $foo == 3.0
$foo = round (3.5);    // $foo == 4.0
$foo = round (3.6);    // $foo == 4.0
$foo = round (1.95583, 2);   // $foo == 1.96
```

rsort

This function sorts an array in reverse order (highest to lowest).

void **rsort**(*array* array, [*int* sort_flags])

Example: Rsort()

```
$fruits = array ("lemon", "orange", "banana", "apple");
rsort ($fruits);
reset ($fruits);
while (list ($key, $val) = each ($fruits)) {
    echo "$key -> $val\n";
}
```

This example would display the following:

```
fruits[0] = orange
fruits[1] = lemon
fruits[2] = banana
fruits[3] = apple
```

The fruits have been sorted in reverse alphabetical order. You may modify the behavior of the sort using the optional parameter **$sort_flags**, for details see **sort()**. See also **arsort()**, **asort()**, **ksort()**, **sort()**, and **usort()**.

rtrim

Returns the argument string without trailing whitespace, including newlines. This is an alias for **chop()**. See also **trim()**, **ltrim()**, and **rtrim()**.

rtrim(*void*)

Example: rtrim( )

```
$trimmed = rtrim ($line);
```

satellite_caught_exception

This function returns true if an exception has been caught.

bool satellite_caught_exception( )

Example: Sample IDL file

```
/* ++?????++ Out of Cheese Error. Redo From Start. */
exception OutOfCheeseError {
    int parameter;
}
interface AnotherInterface {
    void AskWhy() raises (OutOfCheeseError);
}
```

Example: PHP code for handling CORBA exceptions

```
<?php
$obj = new OrbitObject ($ior);
$obj->AskWhy();
if (satellite_caught_exception()) {
    if ("IDL:OutOfCheeseError:1.0" == satellite_exception_id()) {
        $exception = satellite_exception_value();
        echo $exception->parameter;
    }
}
?>
```

satellite_exception_id

Returns a repository id string, for example, "IDL:MyException:1.0". For example usage, see **satellite_caught_exception().**

string satellite_exception_id( )

satellite_exception_value

Returns an exception struct. For example usage, see **satellite_caught_exception().**

OrbitStruct satellite_exception_value( )

sem_acquire

Returns true on success, false on error. **Sem_acquire()** blocks (if necessary) until the semaphore can be acquired. A process attempting to acquire a semaphore that it has already acquired will block forever, if acquiring the semaphore would cause its max_acquire value to be exceeded.

After processing a request, any semaphores acquired by the process, but not explicitly released, will be released automatically, and a warning will be generated. See also **sem_get()** and **sem_release()**.

int **sem_acquire**(*int* sem_identifier)

sem_get

Returns a positive semaphore identifier on success, or false on error. **Sem_get()** returns an id that can be used to access the System V semaphore with the given key. The semaphore is created, if necessary, using the permission bits specified in perm (defaults to 0666). The number of processes that can acquire the semaphore simultaneously is set to max_acquire (defaults to 1). Actually, this value is set only if the process finds it is the only process currently attached to the semaphore.

A second call to **sem_get()** for the same key will return a different semaphore identifier, but both identifiers access the same underlying semaphore. See also **sem_acquire()** and **sem_release()**. This function does not work on Windows' systems.

int **sem_get**(*int* key, [*int* max_acquire], [*int* perm])

sem_release

Returns true on success, false on error. **Sem_release()** releases the semaphore if it is currently acquired by the calling process, otherwise a warning is generated.

After releasing the semaphore, **sem_acquire()** may be called to re-acquire it. See also **sem_get()** and **sem_acquire()**. This function does not work on Windows' systems.

int **sem_release**(*int* sem_identifier)

serialize

Returns a string containing a byte-stream representation of **$value** that can be stored anywhere. This is useful for storing or passing PHP values around without losing their type and structure.

To make the serialized string into a PHP value again, use **unserialize()**. **Serialize()** handles the types integer, double, string, array (multidimensional), and object (object properties will be serialized, but methods are lost).

string **serialize**(*mixed* value)

Example: Serialize()

```
// $session_data contains a multi-dimensional array with session
// information for the current user.  We use serialize() to store
// it in a database at the end of the request.
$conn = odbc_connect ("webdb", "php", "chicken");
$stmt = odbc_prepare ($conn,
      "UPDATE sessions SET data = ? WHERE id = ?");
$sqldata = array (serialize($session_data), $PHP_AUTH_USER);
if (!odbc_execute ($stmt, &$sqldata)) {
    $stmt = odbc_prepare($conn,
      "INSERT INTO sessions (id, data) VALUES(?, ?)");
```

```
        if (!odbc_execute($stmt, &$sqldata)) {
        /* Something went wrong.  Bitch, whine and moan. */
        }
}
```

session_cache_limiter

Returns the name of the current cache limiter. If **$cache_limiter** is specified, the name of the current cache limiter is changed to the new value. The cache limiter controls the cache control HTTP headers sent to the client. These headers determine the rules by which the page content may be cached. Setting the cache limiter to *nocache*, for example, would disallow any client-side caching. A value of *public*, however, would permit caching. It can also be set to *private*, which is slightly more restrictive than *public*.

The cache limiter is reset to the default value stored in *session.cache_limiter* at request startup time. Thus, you need to call **session_cache_limiter()** for every request (and before **session_start()** is called). This function was added in PHP 4.0.3.

string **session_cache_limiter**([*string* cache_limiter])

Example: session_cache_limiter()

```
<?php
# set the cache limiter to 'private'
session_cache_limiter('private');
$cache_limiter = session_cache_limiter();
echo "The cache limiter is now set to $cache_limiter<p>";
?>
```

session_decode

Decodes the session data in **$data**, setting variables stored in the session. This function was added in PHP 4.0.

bool **session_decode**(*string* data)

session_destroy

Destroys all of the data associated with the current session. This function returns true on success and false on failure to destroy the session data.

bool **session_destroy**(*void*)

session_encode

Returns a string with the contents of the current session encoded within. This function was added in PHP 4.0.

string **session_encode**(*void*)

session_get_cookie_params

Returns an array with the current session cookie information, the array contains the following items:

- "lifetime"—The lifetime of the cookie.
- "path"—The path where information is stored.
- "domain"—The domain of the cookie.

array session_get_cookie_params(*void*)

session_id

Returns the session id for the current session. If **$id** is specified, it will replace the current session id. The constant SID can also be used to retrieve the current name and session id as a string suitable for adding to URLs.

string **session_id**([*string* id])

session_is_registered

Returns true if a variable with the name **$name** is registered in the current session. This function was added in PHP 4.0.

bool session_is_registered(*string* name)

session_module_name

Returns the name of the current session module. If **$module** is specified, that module will be used instead. This function was added in PHP 4.0.

string **session_module_name**([*string* module])

session_name

Returns the name of the current session. If **$name** is specified, the name of the current session is changed to its value.

The session name references the session id in cookies and URLs. It should contain only alphanumeric characters; it should be short and descriptive (that is, for users with enabled cookie warnings). The session name is reset to the default value stored in *session.name* at request startup time. Thus, you need to call **session_name()** for every request (and before **session_start()** or **session_register()** are called). This function was added in PHP 4.0.

string **session_name**([*string* name])

Example: session_name()

```php
<?php
# set the session name to WebsiteID
$previous_name = session_name ("WebsiteID");
echo "The previous session name was $previous_name<p>";
?>
```

session_register

Variable number of arguments, any of which can be either a string holding the variable name or an array consisting of such variable names or other arrays. For each encountered variable name, **session_register()** registers the global variable named by it with the current session.

This function returns true when the variable is successfully registered with the session. This function was added in PHP 4.0.

bool **session_register**(*mixed* name, [*mixed* . . .])

session_save_path

Returns the path of the current directory used to save session data. If $path is specified, the path to which data is saved will be changed.

Note: In some operating systems, you may want to specify a path on a filesystem that handles many small files efficiently. For example, on Linux, reiserfs may provide better performance than ext2fs. This function was added in PHP 4.0.

string **session_save_path**([*string* path])

session_set_cookie_params

Sets cookie parameters defined in the php.ini file. The effect of this function only lasts for the duration of the script.

void **session_set_cookie_params**(*int* lifetime, [*string* path], [*string* domain])

session_set_save_handler

Sets the user-level session storage functions, which are used for storing and retrieving data associated with a session. This is most useful when a storage method, other than those supplied by PHP sessions, is preferred, for example, storing the session data in a local database.

void **session_set_save_handler**(*string* open, *string* close, *string* read, *string* write, *string* destroy, *string* gc)

Note: You must set the configuration option **$session.save_handler** to **$user** in your php.ini file for **session_set_save_handler()** to take effect.

The following example provides file-based session storage similar to the PHP sessions default save handler **$files**. This example could easily be extended to cover database storage using your favorite PHP supported database engine.

Example: session_set_save_handler()

```php
<?php
function open ($save_path, $session_name) {
  global $sess_save_path, $sess_session_name;
  $sess_save_path = $save_path;
  $sess_session_name = $session_name;
  return(true);
}
function close() {
  return(true);
}
function read ($id) {
  global $sess_save_path, $sess_session_name;
  $sess_file = "$sess_save_path/sess_$id";
  if ($fp = @fopen($sess_file, "r")) {
    $sess_data = fread($fp, filesize($sess_file));
    return($sess_data);
  } else {
    return("");
  }
}
function write ($id, $sess_data) {
  global $sess_save_path, $sess_session_name;
  $sess_file = "$sess_save_path/sess_$id";
  if ($fp = @fopen($sess_file, "w")) {
    return(fwrite($fp, $sess_data));
  } else {
    return(false);
  }
}
function destroy ($id) {
  global $sess_save_path, $sess_session_name;
  $sess_file = "$sess_save_path/sess_$id";
  return(@unlink($sess_file));
}
/*********************************************
 * WARNING - You will need to implement some *
 * sort of garbage collection routine here.  *
 *********************************************/
function gc ($maxlifetime) {
  return true;
}
session_set_save_handler ("open", "close", "read", "write", "destroy", "gc");
session_start();
// proceed to use sessions normally
?>
```

session_start

Creates a session or resumes the current one based on the session id being passed via a GET variable or a cookie. This function always returns true. This function was added in PHP 4.0.

bool **session_start**(*void*)

session_unregister

Unregisters (forgets) the global variable named $name from the current session. This function returns true when the variable is successfully unregistered from the session. This function was added in PHP 4.0.

bool **session_unregister**(*string* name)

session_unset

Frees all session variables currently registered.

void **session_unset**(*void*)

setcookie

Defines a cookie to be sent along with the rest of the header information. Cookies must be sent before any other headers are sent. This is a restriction of cookies, not PHP. This requires you to place calls to this function before any <html> or <head> tags.

int **setcookie**(*string* name, [*string* value], [*int* expire], [*string* path], [*string* domain], [*int* secure])

All the arguments, except the *name* argument, are optional. If only the name argument is present, the cookie by that name will be deleted from the remote client. You may also replace any argument with an empty string ("") in order to skip that argument. The *expire* and *secure* arguments are integers and cannot be skipped with an empty string. Use a zero (0) instead. The *expire* argument is a regular Unix time integer, as returned by the **time()** or **mktime()** functions. The *secure* indicates that the cookie should only be transmitted over a secure HTTPS connection.

Here are some common pitfalls:

■ Cookies will not become visible until the next loading of a page for which the cookie should be visible.

■ Cookies must be deleted with the same parameters with which they were set.

In PHP 3, multiple calls to **setcookie()** in the same script will be performed in reverse order. If you are trying to delete one cookie before inserting another, you should put the insert before the delete. In PHP 4, multiple calls to **setcookie()** are performed in the order called.

The following are some examples of how to send cookies:

Example 1: setcookie() send

```
setcookie ("TestCookie", "Test Value");
setcookie ("TestCookie", $value,time()+3600);   /* expire in 1 hour */
setcookie ("TestCookie", $value,time()+3600, "/~rasmus/", <\#34>.utoronto.ca<\#34>,
1);
```

Examples follow on how to delete cookies sent in the previous example:

Example 2: setcookie() delete

```
setcookie ("TestCookie");
// set the expiration date to one hour ago
setcookie ("TestCookie", "", time() - 3600);
```

```
setcookie ("TestCookie", "", time() - 3600, <\#34>/≅rasmus/<\#34>,
<\#34>.utoronto.ca<\#34>, 1);
```

When deleting a cookie, you should assure that the expiration date is in the past, in order to trigger the removal mechanism in your browser.

Note: The value portion of the cookie will automatically be urlencoded when you send the cookie. When it is received, it is automatically decoded and assigned to a variable by the same name as the cookie name. To see the contents of our test cookie in a script, simply use one of the following examples:

```
echo $TestCookie;
echo $HTTP_COOKIE_VARS["TestCookie"];
```

You may also set array cookies by using array notation in the cookie name. This has the effect of setting as many cookies as you have array elements. However, when the cookie is received by your script, the values are all placed in an array with the cookie's name:

```
setcookie ("cookie[three]", "cookiethree");
setcookie ("cookie[two]", "cookietwo");
setcookie ("cookie[one]", "cookieone");
if (isset ($cookie)) {
    while (list ($name, $value) = each ($cookie)) {
        echo "$name == $value<br>\n";
    }
}
```

For more information on cookies, see Netscape's cookie specification at *http://www.netscape.com/newsref/std/cookie_spec.html*.

Microsoft Internet Explorer 4 with Service Pack 1 applied does not correctly deal with cookies that have their path parameter set. Netscape Communicator 4.05 and Microsoft Internet Explorer 3.x appear to handle cookies incorrectly when the path and time are not set.

setlocale

$Category is a string specifying the category of the functions affected by the locale setting:

- LC_ALL for all of the below.
- LC_COLLATE for string comparison—not currently implemented in PHP.
- LC_CTYPE for character classification and conversion, for example **strtoupper()**.
- LC_MONETARY for localeconv()—not currently implemented in PHP.
- LC_NUMERIC for decimal separator.
- LC_TIME for date and time formatting with **strftime()**.

string **setlocale**(*string* category, *string* locale)

If **$locale** is the empty string *""*, the locale names will be set from the values of environment variables with the same names as the previous categories, or from "LANG". If locale is zero or *"0"*, the locale setting is not affected, only the current setting is returned.

Setlocale returns the new current locale, or false if the locale functionality is not implemented in the platform. The specified locale does not exist; otherwise, the category name is invalid. An invalid category name also causes a warning message.

settype

Sets the type of variable **$var** to **$type**.

int **settype**(*string* var, *string* type)

Possible values of **$type** are as follows:

- "integer"
- "double"
- "string"
- "array"
- "object"

Returns true if successful; otherwise returns false. See also **gettype()**.

set_error_handler

Sets a user function (**$error_handler**) to handle errors in a script. Returns the previously defined error handler (if any), or false on error. This function can be used for defining your own way of handling errors during runtime, for example, in applications in which you need to do cleanup of data/files when a critical error happens, or when you need to trigger an error under certain conditions (using **trigger_error()**).

The user function needs to accept two parameters: the error code and a string describing the error. The following example shows the handling of internal exceptions by triggering errors and handling them with a user defined function.

string **set_error_handler**(*string* error_handler)

Example: Error handling with **set_error_handler()** and **trigger_error()**

```php
<?php
// redefine the user error constants - PHP 4 only
define (FATAL,E_USER_ERROR);
define (ERROR,E_USER_WARNING);
define (WARNING,E_USER_NOTICE);
// set the error reporting level for this script
error_reporting  (FATAL + ERROR + WARNING);
// error handler function
function myErrorHandler ($errno, $errstr) {
    switch ($errno) {
    case FATAL:
    echo "<b>FATAL</b> [$errno] $errstr<br>\n";
    echo "  Fatal error in line ".__LINE__." of file ".__FILE__;
    echo ", PHP ".PHP_VERSION." (".PHP_OS.")<br>\n";
    echo "Aborting...<br>\n";
    exit -1;
    break;
```

```
            case ERROR:
            echo "<b>ERROR</b> [$errno] $errstr<br>\n";
            break;
            case WARNING:
            echo "<b>WARNING</b> [$errno] $errstr<br>\n";
            break;
            default:
            echo "Unkown error type: [$errno] $errstr<br>\n";
            break;
            }
}
// function to test the error handling
function scale_by_log ($vect, $scale) {
            if ( !is_numeric($scale) || $scale <= 0 )
            trigger_error("log(x) for x <= 0 is undefined, you used: scale = $scale",
                FATAL);
            if (!is_array($vect)) {
            trigger_error("Incorrect input vector, array of values expected", ERROR);
            return null;
            }
            for ($i=0; $i<count($vect); $i++) {
            if (!is_numeric($vect[$i]))
            trigger_error("Value at position $i is not a number, using 0 (zero)",
                WARNING);
            $temp[$i] = log($scale) * $vect[$i];
            }
            return $temp;
}
// set to the user defined error handler
$old_error_handler = set_error_handler("myErrorHandler");
// trigger some errors, first define a mixed array with a non-numeric item
echo "vector a\n";
$a = array(2,3,"foo",5.5,43.3,21.11);
print_r($a);
// now generate second array, generating a warning
echo "----\nvector b - a warning (b = log(PI) * a)\n";
$b = scale_by_log($a, M_PI);
print_r($b);
// this is trouble, we pass a string instead of an array
echo "----\nvector c - an error\n";
$c = scale_by_log("not array",2.3);
var_dump($c);
// this is a critical error, log of zero or negative number is undefined
echo "----\nvector d - fatal error\n";
$d = scale_by_log($a, -2.5);
?>
```

And when you run this sample script, the output will be as follows:

```
vector a
Array
(
    [0] => 2
    [1] => 3
    [2] => foo
    [3] => 5.5
    [4] => 43.3
    [5] => 21.11
)
----
```

```
vector b - a warning (b = log(PI) * a)
<b>WARNING</b> [1024] Value at position 2 is not a number, using 0 (zero)<br>
Array
(
    [0] => 2.2894597716988
    [1] => 3.4341896575482
    [2] => 0
    [3] => 6.2960143721717
    [4] => 49.566804057279
    [5] => 24.165247890281
)
----
vector c - an error
<b>ERROR</b> [512] Incorrect input vector, array of values expected<br>
NULL
----
vector d - fatal error
<b>FATAL</b> [256] log(x) for x <= 0 is undefined, you used: scale = -2.5<br>
  Fatal error in line 16 of file trigger_error.php, PHP 4.0.1p12 (Linux)<br>
Aborting...<br>
```

See also **error_reporting()**, **restore_error_handler()**, **trigger_error()**, and **user_error()**.

set_file_buffer

Outputs using **fwrite()** is normally buffered at 8K. This means that if two processes want to write to the same output stream (a file), each is paused after 8K of data to enable the other to write. **set_file_buffer()** sets the buffering for write operations on the given file pointer **$fp** to **$buffer** bytes. If **$buffer** is 0, then write operations are unbuffered. This ensures that all writes with **fwrite()** are completed before other processes are allowed to write to that output stream. See also **fopen()** and **fwrite()**.

int **set_file_buffer**(int fp, int buffer)

The function returns 0 on success, or EOF if the request cannot be honored.

The following example demonstrates how to use **set_file_buffer()** to create an unbuffered stream.

Example: set_file_buffer()

```
$fp=fopen($file, "w");
if($fp){
  set_file_buffer($fp, 0);
  fputs($fp, $output);
  fclose($fp);
}
```

set_magic_quotes_runtime

Sets the current active configuration setting of **magic_quotes_runtime()** (0 for off, 1 for on). See also **get_magic_quotes_gpc()** and **get_magic_quotes_runtime()**.

long **set_magic_quotes_runtime**(int new_setting)

set_time_limit

Sets the number of seconds a script is allowed to run. If this is reached, the script returns a fatal error. The default limit is 30 seconds or, if it exists, the max_execution_time value defined in the configuration **file().** If seconds is set to zero, no time limit is imposed.

When called, **set_time_limit()** restarts the timeout counter from zero. In other words, if the timeout is the default 30 seconds, and 25 seconds into script execution a call such as set_time_limit(20) is made, the script will run for a total of 45 seconds before timing out.

Note: set_time_limit() has no effect when PHP is running in safe mode. No workaround exists other than turning off safe mode or changing the time limit in the **configuration file().**

void **set_time_limit(** *int* seconds)

shm_attach

Returns an id that that can be used to access the System V shared memory with the given key. The first call creates the shared memory segment with mem_size (default: sysvshm.init_mem in the **configuration file(),** otherwise 10000 bytes) and the optional perm-bits (default: 0666).

A second call to **shm_attach()** for the same **$key** will return a different shared memory identifier, but both identifiers access the same underlying shared memory. **$Memsize** and **$perm** will be ignored. This function does not work on Windows' systems.

int **shm_attach(** *int* key, [*int* memsize], [*int* perm])

shm_close

Used to close a shared memory block. **shm_close()** takes the shmid, which is the shared memory block identifier created by **shm_open().**

int **shm_close(** *int* shmid)

Example: Closing shared memory block

```
<?php
shm_close($shm_id);
?>
```

This example will close shared memory block identified by *$shm_id* .

shm_delete

Used to delete a shared memory block. **shm_delete()** takes the shmid, which is the shared memory block identifier created by **shm_open().** On success, 1 is returned; on failure, 0 is returned.

int **shm_delete(** *int* shmid)

Example: Deleting shared memory block

```php
<?php
shm_delete($shm_id);
?>
```

This example will delete shared memory block identified by *$shm_id*.

shm_detach

Disconnects from the shared memory given by the **$shm_identifier** created by **shm_attach()**. Remember, that shared memory still exists in the Unix system and the data is still present.

int **shm_detach**(*int* shm_identifier)

shm_get_var

Returns the variable with a given **$variable_key**. The variable is still present in the shared memory. This function does not work on Windows' systems.

mixed **shm_get_var**(*int* id, *int* variable_key)

shm_open

Creates or opens a shared memory block. **shm_open()** takes four parameters. The first is the key, which is the system's id for the shared memory block. This parameter can be passed as a decimal or hex. The second parameter are the flags that you can use: "a" for access (sets IPC_EXCL)—use this flag when you need to open an existing shared memory segment. "c" for create (sets IPC_CREATE)—Use this flag when you need to create a new shared memory segment.

The third parameter is the mode, which are the permissions that you wish to assign to your memory segment. Those are the same as permission for a file. Permissions need to be passed in octal form ex. 0644. The last parameter is the size of the shared memory block you wish to create in bytes.

int **shm_open**(*int* key, *string* flags, *int* mode, *int* size)

Note: The third and fourth should be entered as 0 if you are opening an existing memory segment. On success, **shm_open()** will return an id that you can use to access the shared memory segment you have created.

Example: Create a new shared memory block

```php
<?php
$shm_id = shm_open(0x0fff, "c", 0644, 100);
?>
```

This example opened a shared memory block with a system id of 0x0fff.

shm_put_var

Inserts or updates a **$variable** with a given **$variable_key**. All variable-types (**double**, **int**, **string**, **array**) are supported. This function does not work on Windows' systems.

int **shm_put_var**(*int* shm_identifier, *int* variable_key, *mixed* variable)

shm_read

Reads a string from shared memory block. **shm_read()** takes three parameters: shmid, which is the shared memory block identifier created by **shm_open()**; offset from which to start reading; and count on the number of bytes to read.

string **shm_read**(*int* shmid, *int* start, *int* count)

Example: Reading shared memory block

```
<?php
$shm_data = shm_read($shm_id, 0, 50);
?>
```

This example will read 50 bytes from shared memory block and place the data inside *$shm_data*.

shm_remove

Removes shared memory from Unix systems. All data will be destroyed. This function does not work on Windows' systems.

int **shm_remove**(*int* shm_identifier)

shm_remove_var

Removes a variable with a given **$variable_key** and frees the occupied memory. This function does not work on Windows' systems.

int **shm_remove_var**(*int* id, *int* variable_key)

shm_size

Used to get the size, in bytes of the shared memory block. **shm_size()** takes the shmid, which is the shared memory block identifier created by **shm_open()**. The function will return and int, which represents the number of bytes the shared memory block occupies.

int **shm_size**(*int* shmid)

Example: Getting the size of the shared memory block

```php
<?php
$shm_size = shm_size($shm_id);
?>
```

This example will put the size of shared memory block identified by *$shm_id* into *$shm_size*.

shm_write

Writes a string into shared memory block. **shm_write()** takes three parameters: shmid, which is the shared memory block identifier created by **shm_open()**; data, a string that you want to write into shared memory block; and offset, which specifies where to start writing data inside the shared memory segment.

int **shm_write**(*int* shmid, *string* data, *int* offset)

Example: Writing to shared memory block

```php
<?php
$shm_bytes_written = shm_write($shm_id, $my_string, 0);
?>
```

This example will write data inside *$my_string* into shared memory block; *$shm_bytes_written* will contain the number of bytes written.

show_source

Prints out a syntax highlighted version of the code contained in **$filename** using the colors defined in the built-in syntax highlighter for PHP. **Note:** This function is an alias for the function **highlight_file()**. See also **highlight_string()** and **highlight_file()**.

void **show_source**(*string* filename)

shuffle

Shuffles (randomizes the order of the elements in) an array. See also **arsort()**, **asort()**, **ksort()**, **rsort()**, **sort()** and **usort()**.

void **shuffle**(*array* array)

Example: Shuffle()

```php
$numbers = range (1,20);
srand (time());
shuffle ($numbers);
while (list (, $number) = each ($numbers)) {
    echo "$number ";
}
```

similar_text

Calculates the similarity between two strings as described in Oliver [1993]. **Note:** This implementation does not use a stack as in Oliver's pseudo code. Instead, it uses recursive calls that may or may not speed up the whole process. Note also that the complexity of this algorithm is O(N**3), where N is the length of the longest string.

By passing a reference as third argument, **similar_text()** will calculate the similarity in percent for you. It returns the number of matching chars in both strings.

int **similar_text**(*string* first, *string* second, [*double* percent])

sin

Returns the sine of arg in radians. See also **cos()** and **tan()**.

float **sin**(*float* arg)

sizeof

Returns the number of elements in the array. See also **count()**.

int **sizeof**(*array* array)

sleep

Delays program execution for the given number of **$seconds**. See also **usleep()**.

void **sleep**(*int* seconds)

snmpget

Returns SNMP object value on success and false on error. This function is used to read the value of an SNMP object specified by the **$object_id**. SNMP agent is specified by the **$hostname** and the read community is specified by the **$community** parameter.

string **snmpget**(*string* hostname, *string* community, *string* object_id, [*int* timeout], [*int* retries])

```
$syscontact = snmpget("127.0.0.1", "public", <\#34>system.SysContact.0<\#34>);
```

snmpset

Sets the specified SNMP object value, returning true on success and false on error. The **snmpset()** function is used to set the value of an SNMP object specified by the **$object_id**. SNMP agent is specified by the **$hostname** and the read community is specified by the **$community** parameter.

bool **snmpset**(*string* hostname, *string* community, *string* object_id, *string* type, *mixed* value, [*int* timeout], [*int* retries])

snmpwalk

Returns an array of SNMP object values starting from the **object_id()** as root and false on error.

array **snmpwalk**(*string* hostname, *string* community, *string* object_id, [*int* timeout], [*int* retries])

snmpwalk() function is used to read all the values from an SNMP agent specified by the **$hostname**. **$Community** specifies the read community for that agent. A null **$object_id** is taken as the root of the SNMP objects tree, and all objects under that tree are returned as an array. If **$object_id** is specified, all the SNMP objects below that **$object_id** are returned.

```
$a = snmpwalk("127.0.0.1", "public", "");
```

The previous function call would return all the SNMP objects from the SNMP agent running on localhost. One can step through the values with a loop.

```
for ($i=0; $i<count($a); $i++) {
    echo $a[$i];
}
```

snmpwalkoid

Returns an associative array with object ids and their respective object value starting from the **$object_id** as root and false on error.

array **snmpwalkoid**(*string* hostname, *string* community, *string* object_id, [*int* timeout], [*int* retries])

snmpwalkoid() function is used to read all object ids and their respective values from an SNMP agent specified by the hostname. Community specifies the read **$community** for that agent. A null **$object_id** is taken as the root of the SNMP objects tree, and all objects under that tree are returned as an array. If **$object_id** is specified, all the SNMP objects below that **$object_id** are returned.

The existence of **snmpwalkoid()** and **snmpwalk()** has historical reasons. Both functions are provided for backward compatibility.

```
$a = snmpwalkoid("127.0.0.1", "public", "");
```

The previous function call would return all the SNMP objects from the SNMP agent running on localhost. One can step through the values with a loop.

```
for (reset($a); $i = key($a); next($a)) {
    echo "$i: $a[$i]<br>\n";
}
```

snmp_get_quick_print

Returns the current value stored in the UCD Library for quick_print. quick_print is off by default.

boolean snmp_get_quick_print(*void*)

```
$quickprint = snmp_get_quick_print();
```

The previous function call would return false if quick_print is on, and true if quick_print is on.

snmp_get_quick_print() is only available when using the UCD SNMP library. This function is not available when using the Windows SNMP library. See **snmp_set_quick_print()** for a full description of what quick_print does.

snmp_set_quick_print

Sets the value of quick_print within the UCD SNMP library. When this is set (1), the SNMP library will return "quick printed" values. This means that just the value will be printed. When quick_print is not enabled (default), the UCD SNMP library prints extra information including the type of the value (that is, IpAddress or OID). Additionally, if quick_print is not enabled, the library prints additional hex values for all strings of three characters or less.

void **snmp_set_quick_print**(*boolean* quick_print)

Setting quick_print is often used when using the information returned, rather then displaying it.

```
snmp_set_quick_print(0);
$a = snmpget("127.0.0.1", "public", ".1.3.6.1.2.1.2.2.1.9.1");
echo "$a<BR>\n";
snmp_set_quick_print(1);
$a = snmpget("127.0.0.1", "public", ".1.3.6.1.2.1.2.2.1.9.1");
echo "$a<BR>\n";
```

The first value printed might be 'Timeticks: (0) 0:00:00.00', whereas with quick_print enabled, just '0:00:00.00' would be printed.

By default, the UCD SNMP library returns verbose values. quick_print is used to return only the value.

Currently, strings are still returned with extra quotes. This will be corrected in a later release. **snmp_set_quick_print()** is only available when using the UCD SNMP library. This function is not available when using the Windows SNMP library.

socket

Creates a communication endpoint (a socket), and returns a descriptor to the socket.

int **socket**(*int* domain, *int* type, *int* protocol)

The **$domain** parameter sets the domain. Currently, AF_INET and AF_UNIX are understood. The **$type** parameter selects the socket type. This is one of SOCK_STREAM, SOCK_DGRAM, SOCK_SEQPACKET, SOCK_RAW, SOCK_RDM, or SOCK_PACKET. **$protocol** sets the protocol. Returns a valid socket descriptor on success, or a negative error code on failure. This code may be passed to **strerror()** to get a textual explanation of the error.

For more information on the usage of **socket()**, as well as on the meanings of the various parameters, see the Unix man page socket. See also **accept_connect()**, **bind()**, **connect()**, **listen()**, **strerror()**, and **socket_get_status()**.

socket_get_status

Returns information about an existing socket resource. Currently returns four entries in the result array:

- **$timed_out** (bool)—The socket timed out waiting for data.
- **$blocked** (bool)—The socket was blocked.

- **$eof** (bool)—Indicates EOF event.
- **$unread_bytes** (int)—Number of bytes left in the socket buffer.

See also **accept_connect()**, **bind()**, **connect()**, **listen()**, and **strerror()**.

array **socket_get_status**(*resource* socket_get_status)

socket_set_blocking

If **$mode** is false, the given socket descriptor will be switched to non-blocking mode, and if true, it will be switched to blocking mode. This affects calls like **fgets()** that read from the socket. In non-blocking mode, an **fgets()** call will always return right away. However, in blocking mode, it will wait for data to become available on the socket. This function was previously called as **set_socket_blocking()**, but this usage is deprecated.

int **socket_set_blocking**(*int* socket descriptor, *int* mode)

socket_set_timeout

Sets the timeout value on **$socket descriptor**, expressed in the sum of **$seconds** and **$microseconds**.

bool **socket_set_timeout**(*int* socket descriptor, *int* seconds, *int* microseconds)

Example: socket_set_timeout()

```php
<?php
$fp = fsockopen("www.php.net", 80);
if(!$fp) {
    echo "Unable to open\n";
} else {
    fputs($fp,"GET / HTTP/1.0\n\n");
    $start = time();
    socket_set_timeout($fp, 2);
    $res = fread($fp, 2000);
    var_dump(socket_get_status($fp));
    fclose($fp);
    print $res;
}
?>
```

This function was previously called as **set_socket_timeout()**, but this usage is deprecated. See also **fsockopen()** and **fopen()**.

sort

This function sorts an array. Elements will be arranged from lowest to highest when this function has completed.

void **sort**(*array* array, [*int* sort_flags])

Example: Sort()

```php
<?php
$fruits = array ("lemon", "orange", "banana", "apple");
sort ($fruits);
reset ($fruits);
while (list ($key, $val) = each ($fruits)) {
    echo "fruits[".$key."] = ".$val;
}
?>
```

This example would display the following:

```
fruits[0] = apple
fruits[1] = banana
fruits[2] = lemon
fruits[3] = orange
```

The fruits have been sorted in alphabetical order.

The optional second parameter **$sort_flags** may be used to modify the sorting behavior using these values.

Sorting type flags:

■ SORT_REGULAR—Compare items normally.

■ SORT_NUMERIC—Compare items numerically.

■ SORT_STRING—Compare items as strings.

See also **arsort()**, **asort()**, **ksort()**, **natsort()**, **natcasesort()**, **rsort()**, **usort()** and **uksort()**.

soundex

Calculates the soundex key of **$str**. Soundex keys have the property that words pronounced similarly produce the same soundex key, and can thus be used to simplify searches in databases where you know the pronunciation but not the spelling. This soundex function returns a string that is four characters long, starting with a letter.

string **soundex**(*string* str)

This particular soundex function is one described by Donald Knuth in "The Art Of Computer Programming, vol. 3: Sorting And Searching", Addison-Wesley (1973), pp. 391-392.

Example: Soundex

```
soundex ("Euler") == soundex ("Ellery") == 'E460';
soundex ("Gauss") == soundex ("Ghosh") == 'G200';
soundex ("Hilbert") == soundex ("Heilbronn") == 'H416';
soundex ("Knuth") == soundex ("Kant") == 'K530';
soundex ("Lloyd") == soundex ("Ladd") == 'L300';
soundex ("Lukasiewicz") == soundex ("Lissajous") == 'L222';
```

split

Returns an array of strings, each of which is a substring of $string formed by splitting it on boundaries formed by the regular expression $pattern. If $limit is set, the returned array will contain a maximum of $limit elements with the last element containing the whole rest of $string. If an error occurs, split() returns false.

array **split**(*string* pattern, *string* string, [*int* limit])

The following is an example of splitting off the first four fields from a line from /etc/passwd:
Example: Split()

```
$passwd_list = split (":", $passwd_line, 5);
```

The following is an example of parsing a date which may be delimited with slashes, dots, or hyphens:
Example: Split()

```
$date = "04/30/1973";   // Delimiters may be slash, dot, or hyphen
list ($month, $day, $year) = split ('[/.-]', $date);
echo "Month: $month; Day: $day; Year: $year<br>\n";
```

Note: $pattern is case-sensitive. If you don't require the power of regular expressions, it is faster to use **explode(),** which doesn't incur the overhead of the regular expression engine.

For users looking for a way to emulate Perl's $chars = split(", $str) behavior, please see the examples for **preg_split()**.

Note: $pattern is a regular expression. If you want to split on any of the characters which are considered special by regular expressions, you'll need to escape them first. If you think **split()** (or any other regex function, for that matter) is doing something weird, please read the file regex.7, included in the regex/ subdirectory of the PHP distribution. It's in manpage format, so you'll want to do something along the lines of man /usr/local/src/regex/regex.7 in order to read it. See also **spliti()**, **explode()**, and **implode()**.

spliti

This function is identical to **split()**, except that this ignores case distinction when matching alphabetic characters. See also **split()**, **explode()**, and **implode()**.

array **spliti**(*string* pattern, *string* string, [*int* limit])

sprintf

Returns a string produced according to the formatting string **$format**. See also **printf()**, **sscanf()**, **fscanf()**, and **number_format()**.

string **sprintf**(*string* format, [*mixed* args])

The format string is composed of zero or more directives: ordinary characters (excluding %) that are copied directly to the result and conversion specifications, each of which results in fetching its own parameter. This applies to both **sprintf()** and **printf()**.

Each conversion specification consists of a percent sign (%), followed by one or more of these elements, in order:

- An optional padding specifier that says what character will be used for padding the results to the right string size. This may be a space character or a *0* (zero character). The default is to pad with spaces. An alternate padding character can be specified by prefixing it with a single quote ('). See the following examples.

- An optional alignment specifier that says if the result should be left-justified or right-justified. The default is right-justified; a - character here will make it left-justified.

- An optional number, a width specifier that says how many characters (minimum) this conversion should result in.

- An optional precision specifier that says how many decimal digits should be displayed for floating-point numbers. This option has no effect for other types than double. (Another function useful for formatting numbers is **number_format()**.)

A type specifier says what type the argument data should be treated as. Here are the possible types:

- *%*—A literal percent character. No argument is required.
- *b*—The argument is treated as an integer and presented as a binary number.
- *c*—The argument is treated as an integer and presented as the character with that ASCII value.
- *d*—The argument is treated as an integer and presented as a decimal number.
- *f*—The argument is treated as a double and presented as a floating-point number.
- *o*—The argument is treated as an integer and presented as an octal number.
- *s*—The argument is treated as and presented as a string.
- *x*—The argument is treated as an integer and presented as a hexadecimal number (with lowercase letters).
- *X*—The argument is treated as an integer and presented as a hexadecimal number (with uppercase letters).

Example: Sprintf() : zero-padded integers

```
$isodate = sprintf ("%04d-%02d-%02d", $year, $month, $day);
```

Example: Sprintf() : formatting currency

```
$money1 = 68.75;
$money2 = 54.35;
$money = $money1 + $money2;
// echo $money will output "123.1";
$formatted = sprintf ("%01.2f", $money);
// echo $formatted will output "123.10"
```

sql_regcase

Returns a valid regular expression which will match **$string**, ignoring case. This expression is **$string** with each character converted to a bracket expression. This bracket expression contains that character's uppercase and lowercase form if applicable, otherwise it contains the original character twice.

string **sql_regcase**(*string* string)

Example: Sql_regcase()

```
echo sql_regcase ("Foo bar");
```

prints [Ff][Oo][Oo][ ][Bb][Aa][Rr] .
This can be used to achieve case insensitive pattern matching in products that support only case sensitive regular expressions.

sqrt

Returns the square root of **$arg**.

float **sqrt**(*float* arg)

srand

Seeds the random number generator with **$seed**. See also **rand()**, **getrandmax()**, **mt_rand()**, **mt_srand()**, and **mt_getrandmax()**.

void **srand**(*int* seed)

```
// seed with microseconds since last "whole" second
srand ((double) microtime() * 1000000);
$randval = rand();
```

sscanf

This function is the input analog of **printf()**. **Sscanf()** reads from the string **$str** and interprets it according to the specified **$format**. If only two parameters were passed to this function, the values parsed will be returned as an array. See also **fscanf()**, **printf()**, and **sprintf()**.

mixed **sscanf**(*string* str, *string* format, [*string* var1])

Example: Sscanf()

```
// getting the serial number
$serial = sscanf("SN/2350001","SN/%d");
// and the date of manufacturing
$mandate = "January 01 2000";
list($month, $day, $year) = sscanf($mandate,"%s %d %d");
```

```
echo "Item $serial was manufactured on: $year-<\#34>.substr($month,0,3).<\#34>-
$day\n<\#34>;
```

If optional parameters are passed, the function will return the number of assigned values. The optional parameters must be passed by reference.

Example: Sscanf() - using optional parameters

```
// get author info and generate DocBook entry
$auth = "24\tLewis Carroll";
$n = sscanf($auth,"%d\t%s %s", &$id, &$first, &$last);
echo "<author id='$id'>
    <firstname>$first</firstname>
    <surname>$last</surname>
</author>\n";
```

stat

Gathers the statistics of the file named by filename. See **clearstatcache()** for more details.

array **stat**(*string* filename)

Returns an array with the statistics of the file with the following elements:

device	inode	inode protection mode
number of links	user id of owner	group id owner
device type if inode device *	size in bytes	time of last access
time of last modification	time of last change	blocksize for filesystem I/O *
number of blocks allocated		

*—Only valid on systems supporting the st_blksize type—other systems, such as Windows, return -1. The results of this function are cached.

strcasecmp

Returns < 0 if *str1* is less than *str2*; > 0 if *str1* is greater than *str2*, and 0 if they are equal. See also **ereg()**, **strcmp()**, **substr()**, **stristr()**, and **strstr()**.

int **strcasecmp**(*string* str1, *string* str2)

Example 1: strcasecmp()

```
$var1 = "Hello";
$var2 = "hello";
if (!strcasecmp ($var1, $var2)) {
    echo '$var1 is equal to $var2 in a case-insensitive string comparison';
}
```

strchr

This function is an alias for **strstr()** and is identical in every way.

string **strchr**(*string* haystack, *string* needle)

strcmp

Returns < 0 if *str1* is less than *str2*; > 0 if *str1* is greater than *str2*, and 0 if they are equal.
Note: This comparison is case sensitive. See also **ereg()**, **strcasecmp()**, **substr()**, **stristr()**, **strncmp()**, and **strstr()**.

int **strcmp**(*string* str1, *string* str2)

strcspn

Returns the length of the initial segment of **$str1**, which does not contain any of the characters in **$str2**. See also **strspn()**.

int **strcspn**(*string* str1, *string* str2)

strerror

Takes as its **$errno** parameter the return value of one of the socket functions, and returns the corresponding explanatory text. This makes it somewhat more pleasant to figure out why something didn't work. For instance, instead of having to track down a system include file to find out what '-111' means, you just pass it to **strerror()**, which tells you what happened. See also **accept_connect()**, **bind()**, **connect()**, **listen()**, **socket()**, and **socket_get_status()**.

string **strerror**(*int* errno)

Example: strerror()

```
<?php
if (($socket = socket (AF_INET, SOCK_STREAM, 0)) < 0) {
    echo "socket() failed: reason: " . strerror ($socket) . "\n";
}
if (($ret = bind ($socket, '127.0.0.1', 80)) < 0) {
    echo "bind() failed: reason: " . strerror ($ret) . "\n";
}
?>
```

The expected output from the previous example (assuming the script is not run with root privileges): bind() failed: reason: Permission denied.

strftime

Returns a string formatted according to the given format string using the given **$timestamp** or the current local time if no timestamp is given. Month and weekday names and other language dependent strings respect the current locale set with **setlocale()**. See also **setlocale()** and **mktime()** and the Open Group specification of **strftime()**. (*http://www.opengroup.org/onlinepubs/7908799/xsh/strftime.html*).

string **strftime**(string format, [int timestamp])

The following conversion specifiers are recognized in the format string:

- %a—abbreviated weekday name according to the current locale
- %A—full weekday name according to the current locale
- %b—abbreviated month name according to the current locale
- %B—full month name according to the current locale
- %c—preferred date and time representation for the current locale
- %C—century number (the year divided by 100 and truncated to an integer, range 00 to 99)
- %d—day of the month as a decimal number (range 00 to 31)
- %D—same as %m/%d/%y
- %e—day of the month as a decimal number, a single digit is preceded by a space (range ' 1' to '31')
- %h—same as %b
- %H—hour as a decimal number using a 24-hour clock (range 00 to 23)
- %I—hour as a decimal number using a 12-hour clock (range 01 to 12)
- %j—day of the year as a decimal number (range 001 to 366)
- %m—month as a decimal number (range 01 to 12)
- %M—minute as a decimal number
- %n—newline character
- %p—either 'am' or 'pm' according to the given time value, or the corresponding strings for the current locale
- %r—time in a.m. and p.m. notation
- %R—time in 24 hour notation
- %S—second as a decimal number
- %t—tab character
- %T—current time, equal to %H:%M:%S
- %u—weekday as a decimal number [1,7], with 1 representing Monday
- %U—week number of the current year as a decimal number, starting with the first Sunday as the first day of the first week
- %V—The ISO 8601:1988 week number of the current year as a decimal number, range 01 to 53, where week one is the first week that has at least four days in the current year, and with Monday as the first day of the week.
- %W—week number of the current year as a decimal number, starting with the first Monday as the first day of the first week
- %w—day of the week as a decimal, Sunday being 0
- %x—preferred date representation for the current locale without the time
- %X—preferred time representation for the current locale without the date

- %y—year as a decimal number without a century (range 00 to 99)

- %Y—year as a decimal number including the century

- %Z—time zone or name or abbreviation

- %%—a literal '%' character

Example: Strftime()

```
setlocale ("LC_TIME", "C");
print (strftime ("%A in Finnish is "));
setlocale ("LC_TIME", "fi_FI");
print (strftime ("%A, in French "));
setlocale ("LC_TIME", "fr_CA");
print (strftime ("%A and in German "));
setlocale ("LC_TIME", "de_DE");
print (strftime ("%A.\n"));
```

This example works if you have the respective locales installed in your system.

stripcslashes

Returns a string with backslashes stripped off. Recognizes C-like \n , \r . . . , octal and hexadecimal representation.

Note: Added in PHP4b3-dev. See also **addcslashes()**.

string **stripcslashes**(string str)

stripslashes

Returns a string with backslashes stripped off. (\' becomes' and so on.) Double backslashes are made into a single backslash. See also **addslashes()**.

string **stripslashes**(string str)

strip_tags

This function tries to strip all HTML and PHP tags from the given string. It errors on the side of caution in case of incomplete or bogus tags. It uses the same tag stripping state machine as the **fgetss()** function. You can use the optional second parameter to specify tags which should not be stripped.

Note: $Allowable_tags was added in PHP 3.0.13, PHP4B3.

string **strip_tags**(string str, [string allowable_tags])

stristr

Returns all of **$haystack** from the first occurrence of **$needle** to the end. **$needle** and **$haystack** are examined in a case-insensitive manner. See also **strchr()**, **strrchr()**, **substr()**, and **ereg()**.

string **stristr**(string haystack, string needle)

If **$needle** is not found, returns false. If **$needle** is not a string, it is converted to an integer and applied as the ordinal value of a character.

strlen

Returns the length of **$string**.

int **strlen**(string str)

strnatcasecmp

Implements a comparison algorithm that orders alphanumeric strings in the way a human being would. The behavior of this function is similar to **strnatcmp()**, except that the comparison is not case sensitive. For more information see Martin Pool's Natural Order String Comparison (*http://www.linuxcare.com.au/projects/natsort/*) page. See also **ereg()**, **strcasecmp()**, **substr()**, **stristr()**, **strcmp()**, **strncmp()**, **strnatcmp()**, and **strstr()**.

int **strnatcasecmp**(*string* str1, *string* str2)

Similar to other string comparison functions, this one returns < 0 if str1 is less than str2; > 0 if str1 is greater than str2, and 0 if they are equal.

strnatcmp

Implements a comparison algorithm that orders alphanumeric strings in the way a human being would; this is described as a "natural ordering." See also **ereg()**, **strcasecmp()**, **substr()**, **stristr()**, **strcmp()**, **strncmp()**, **strnatcmp()**, and **strstr()**.

int **strnatcmp**(*string* str1, *string* str2)

The following is an example of the difference between this algorithm and the regular computer string sorting algorithms (used in **strcmp()**):

```
$arr1 = $arr2 = array ("img12.png","img10.png","img2.png","img1.png");
echo "Standard string comparison\n";
usort($arr1,"strcmp");
print_r($arr1);
echo "\nNatural order string comparison\n";
usort($arr2,"strnatcmp");
print_r($arr2);
```

The previous code will generate the following output:

```
Standard string comparison
Array
(
    [0] => img1.png
    [1] => img10.png
    [2] => img12.png
    [3] => img2.png
)
Natural order string comparison
Array
```

```
(
    [0] => img1.png
    [1] => img2.png
    [2] => img10.png
    [3] => img12.png
)
```

For more information see Martin Pool's Natural Order String Comparison (*http://www.linuxcare.com.au/projects/natsort/*) page.

Similar to other string comparison functions, this one returns < 0 if str1 is less than str2; > 0 if str1 is greater than str2, and 0 if they are equal.

strncmp

This function is similar to **strcmp()**, with the difference that you can specify the (upper limit of the) number of characters (**$len**) from each string to be used in the comparison. If any of the strings are shorter than **$len**, then the length of that string will be used for the comparison.

int **strncmp**(*string* str1, *string* str2, *int* len)

Returns < 0 if *str1* is less than *str2*; > 0 if *str1* is greater than *str2*, and 0 if they are equal. This comparison is case sensitive.

strpos

Returns the numeric position of the first occurrence of **$needle** in the **$haystack** string. Unlike the **strrpos()**, this function can take a full string as the **$needle** parameter, and the entire string will be used.

int **strpos**(*string* haystack, *string* needle, [*int* offset])

If **$needle** is not found, returns false. **Note:** It is easy to mistake the return values for "character found at position 0" and "character not found." Here's how to detect the difference:

```
// in PHP 4.0b3 and newer:
$pos = strpos ($mystring, "b");
if ($pos === false) { // note: three equal signs
    // not found...
}
// in versions older than 4.0b3:
$pos = strpos ($mystring, "b");
if (is_string ($pos) && !$pos) {
    // not found...
}
```

If **$needle** is not a string, it is converted to an integer and applied as the ordinal value of a character.

The optional **$offset** parameter enables you to specify which character in **$haystack** to start searching. The position returned is still relative to the beginning of **$haystack**. See also **strrpos()**, **strrchr()**, **substr()**, **stristr()**, and **strstr()**.

strrchr

This function returns the portion of **$haystack** which starts at the last occurrence of **$needle** and goes until the end of **$haystack**. See also **substr()**, **stristr()**, and **strstr()**.

string **strrchr**(*string* haystack, *string* needle)

Returns false if **$needle** is not found. If **$needle** contains more than one character, the first is used. If **$needle** is not a string, it is converted to an integer and applied as the ordinal value of a character.

Example: Strrchr()

```
// get last directory in $PATH
$dir = substr (strrchr ($PATH, ":"), 1);
// get everything after last newline
$text = "Line 1\nLine 2\nLine 3";
$last = substr (strrchr ($text, 10), 1 );
```

strrev

Returns **$string**, reversed.

string **strrev**(*string* string)

strrpos

Returns the numeric position of the last occurrence of **$needle** in the **$haystack** string.

Note: The needle in this case can only be a single character. If a string is passed as the needle, then only the first character of that string will be used.

int **strrpos**(*string* haystack, *char* needle)

If **$needle** is not found, returns false. If **$needle** is not a string, it is converted to an integer and applied as the ordinal value of a character. See also **strpos()**, **strrchr()**, **substr()**, **stristr()**, and **strstr()**.

strspn

Returns the length of the initial segment of **$str1**, which consists entirely of characters in **$str2**. See also **strcspn()**.

int **strspn**(*string* str1, *string* str2)

```
strspn ("42 is the answer, what is the question ...", <\#34>1234567890<\#34>);
```

will return 2 as the result.

strstr

Returns all of **$haystack** from the first occurrence of **$needle** to the end.

string **strstr**(*string* haystack, *string* needle)

If **$needle** is not found, returns false. If **$needle** is not a string, it is converted to an integer and applied as the ordinal value of a character. This function is case-sensitive. For case-insensitive searches, use **stristr()**. See also **stristr()**, **strrchr()**, **substr()**, and **ereg()**.

Example: Strstr()

```
$email = 'sterling@designmultimedia.com';
$domain = strstr ($email, '@');
print $domain; // prints @designmultimedia.com
```

strtok

Used to tokenize a string. That is, if you have a string like "This is an example string," you could tokenize this string into its individual words by using the space character as the token.

string **strtok**(*string* arg1, *string* arg2)

Example: Strtok()

```
$string = "This is an example string";
$tok = strtok ($string," ");
while ($tok) {
    echo "Word=$tok<br>";
    $tok = strtok (" ");
}
```

Note: Only the first call to strtok uses the string argument. Every subsequent call to strtok only needs the token to use, as it keeps track of where it is in the current string. To start over or to tokenize a new string, you simply call strtok with the string argument again to initialize it. Note that you may put multiple tokens in the token parameter. The string will be tokenized when any one of the characters in the argument are found.

Also be careful that your tokens may be equal to "0". This evaluates to false in conditional expressions. See also **split()** and **explode()**.

strtolower

Returns **$string** with all alphabetic characters converted to lowercase.

Note: 'alphabetic' is determined by the current locale. This means that in the default "C" locale, for example, characters such as umlaut-A (_) will not be converted. See also **strtoupper()** and **ucfirst()**.

string **strtolower**(*string* str)

Example: Strtolower()

```
$str = "Mary Had A Little Lamb and She LOVED It So";
$str = strtolower($str);
print $str; # Prints mary had a little lamb and she loved it so
```

strtotime

The function expects to be given a string containing an english date format and will try to parse that format into a UNIX timestamp.

int **strtotime**(*string* time, [*int* now])

Example: Strtotime()

```
echo strtotime ("now") . "\n";
echo strtotime ("10 September 2000") . "\n";
echo strtotime ("+1 day") . "\n";
echo strtotime ("+1 week") . "\n";
echo strtotime ("+1 week 2 days 4 hours 2 seconds") . "\n";
```

strtoupper

Returns **$string** with all alphabetic characters converted to uppercase.

Note: 'alphabetic' is determined by the current locale. For instance, the default "C" locale characters such as umlaut-a (ä) will not be converted. See also **strtolower()** and **ucfirst()**.

string **strtoupper**(*string* string)

Example: Strtoupper()

```
$str = "Mary Had A Little Lamb and She LOVED It So";
$str = strtoupper ($str);
print $str; # Prints MARY HAD A LITTLE LAMB AND SHE LOVED IT SO
```

strtr

Operates on **$str**, translating all occurrences of each character in **$from** to the corresponding character in **$to** and returning the result. If **$from** and **$to** are different lengths, the extra characters in the longer of the two are ignored.

string **strtr**(*string* str, *string* from, *string* to)

Example: Strtr()

```
$addr = strtr($addr, "äåö", "aao");
```

strtr() can be called with only two arguments. If called with two arguments, it behaves in a new way: *from* then has to be an array that contains string -> string pairs that will be replaced in the source string. **strtr()** will always look for the longest possible match first and will NOT try to replace stuff on which it has already worked.

Examples:

```
$trans = array ("hello" => "hi", "hi" => "hello");
echo strtr("hi all, I said hello", $trans) . "\n";
```

This will show: "hello all, I said hi",

Note: This feature (two arguments) was added in PHP 4.0. See also **ereg_replace()**.

strval

Returns the string value of **$var**. **$var** may be any scalar type. You cannot use **strval()** on arrays or objects. See also **doubleval()**, **intval()**, **settype()**, and Type Juggling.

> *string* **strval**(*mixed* var)

str_pad

Pads the **$input** string on the left, the right, or both sides to the specified padding length. If the optional argument **$pad_string** is not supplied, the **$input** is padded with spaces; otherwise, it is padded with characters from **$pad_string** up to the limit.

> *string* **str_pad**(*string* input, *int* pad_length, [*string* pad_string], [*int* pad_type])

Optional argument **$pad_type** can be STR_PAD_RIGHT, STR_PAD_LEFT, or STR_PAD_BOTH. If **$pad_type** is not specified, it is assumed to be STR_PAD_RIGHT.

If the value of **$pad_length** is negative or less than the length of the input string, no padding takes place.

Example: str_pad()

```
$input = "Alien";
print str_pad($input, 10);                       // produces "Alien     "
print str_pad($input, 10, "-=", STR_PAD_LEFT);   // produces "-=-=-Alien"
print str_pad($input, 10, "_", STR_PAD_BOTH);    // produces <\#34>__Alien___<\#34>
```

str_repeat

Returns **$input_str** repeated **$multiplier** times. **$multiplier** has to be greater than 0.

> *string* **str_repeat**(*string* input, *int* multiplier)

Example: Str_repeat()

```
echo str_repeat ("-=", 10);
```

This will output "-=-=-=-=-=-=-=-=-=-=". This function was added in PHP 4.0.

str_replace

This function replaces all occurrences of **$needle** in **$haystack** with the given **$str**. If you don't need fancy replacing rules, you should always use this function instead of ereg_replace(). This function is binary safe.

Note: Str_replace() was added in PHP 3.0.6, but was buggy up until PHP 3.0.8. See also **ereg_replace()** and **strtr()**.

> *string* **str_replace**(*string* needle, *string* str, *string* haystack)

Example: Str_replace()

```
$bodytag = str_replace ("%body%", "black", "<body text=%body%><\#34>);
```

substr

Returns the portion of **$string** specified by the **$start** and **$length** parameters.

string **substr**(*string* string, *int* start, [*int* length])

If **$start** is positive, the returned string will start at the **$start** 'th position in **$string**, counting from zero. For instance, in the string *'abcdef'*, the character at position *0* is ' *a* ', the character at position *2* is ' *c* ', and so forth.

Examples:

```
$rest = substr ("abcdef", 1);     // returns "bcdef"
$rest = substr ("abcdef", 1, 3); // returns "bcd"
```

If **$start** is negative, the returned string will start at the **$start** 'th character from the end of **$string** .

Examples:

```
$rest = substr ("abcdef", -1);     // returns "f"
$rest = substr ("abcdef", -2);     // returns "ef"
$rest = substr ("abcdef", -3, 1); // returns "d"
```

If **$length** is given and is positive, the string returned will end **$length** characters from **$start**. If this would result in a string with negative length (because the start is past the end of the string), then the returned string will contain the single character at **$start**.

If **$length** is given and is negative, the string returned will end **$length** characters from the end of **$string**. If this would result in a string with negative length, then the returned string will contain the single character at **$start**. See also **strrchr()** and **ereg()**.

Examples:

```
$rest = substr ("abcdef", 1, -1); // returns "bcde"
```

substr_count

Returns the number of times the **$needle** substring occurs in the **$haystack** string.

int **substr_count**(*string* haystrack, *string* needle)

Example: substr_count()

```
print substr_count("This is a test", "is"); // prints out 2
```

substr_replace

Replaces the part of $string delimited by the $start and (optionally) $length parameters with the string given in $replacement. The result is returned.

string **substr_replace**(*string* string, *string* replacement, *int* start, [*int* length])

If **$start** is positive, the replacing will begin at the **$start** 'th offset into **$string**. If **$start** is negative, the replacing will begin at the **$start** 'th character from the end of **$string**. If **$length** is given and is positive, it represents the length of the portion of **$string** which is to be replaced. If it is negative, it represents the number of characters from the end of **$string** at which to stop replacing. If it is not given, then it will default to strlen(**$string**); that is, end the replacing at the end of **$string**. See also **str_replace()** and **substr()**. **Substr_replace()** was added in PHP 4.0.

Example: Substr_replace()

```php
<?php
$var = 'ABCDEFGH:/MNRPQR/';
echo "Original: $var<hr>\n";
/* These two examples replace all of $var with 'bob'. */
echo substr_replace ($var, 'bob', 0) . "<br>\n";
echo substr_replace ($var, 'bob', 0, strlen ($var)) . "<br>\n";
/* Insert 'bob' right at the beginning of $var. */
echo substr_replace ($var, 'bob', 0, 0) . "<br>\n";
/* These next two replace 'MNRPQR' in $var with 'bob'. */
echo substr_replace ($var, 'bob', 10, -1) . "<br>\n";
echo substr_replace ($var, 'bob', -7, -1) . "<br>\n";
/* Delete 'MNRPQR' from $var. */
echo substr_replace ($var, '', 10, -1) . "<br>\n";
?>
```

swf_actiongeturl

Gets the URL specified by the parameter **$url** with the target **$target**.

void **swf_actiongeturl**(string url, string target)

swf_actiongotoframe

Goes to the frame specified by **$framenumber**, plays it, and then stops.

void **swf_actiongotoframe**(int framenumber)

swf_actiongotolabel

Displays the frame with the label given by the $label parameter and then stops.

void **swf_actiongotolabel**(string label)

swf_actionnextframe

Goes forward one frame.

void swf_actionnextframe(*void*)

swf_actionplay

Starts playing the flash movie from the current frame.

void **swf_actionplay**(*void*)

swf_actionprevframe

void swf_actionprevframe(*void*)

swf_actionsettarget

Sets the context for all actions. You can use this to control other flash movies that are currently playing.

void **swf_actionsettarget**(*string* target)

swf_actionstop

Stops playing the flash movie at the current frame.

void **swf_actionstop**(*void*)

swf_actiontogglequality

Toggles the flash movie between high and low quality.

void swf_actiontogglequality(*void*)

swf_actionwaitforframe

Checks to see if the frame specified by the **$framenumber** parameter has been loaded; if not, it will skip the number of actions specified by the **$skipcount** parameter. This can be useful for "Loading . . . " type animations.

void **swf_actionwaitforframe**(*int* framenumber, *int* skipcount)

swf_addbuttonrecord

Enables you to define the specifics of using a button. The first parameter, **$states**, defines what states the button can have. These can be any or all of the following constants: BSHitTest, BSDown, BSOver, or BSUp. The second parameter, the **$shapeid,** is the look of the button. This is usually the object id of the shape of the button. The **$depth** parameter is the placement of the button in the current frame.

void **swf_addbuttonrecord**(*int* states, *int* shapeid, *int* depth)

Example: Swf_addbuttonrecord()

```
swf_startButton ($objid, TYPE_MENUBUTTON);
    swf_addButtonRecord (BSDown|BSOver, $buttonImageId, 340);
    swf_onCondition (MenuEnter);
        swf_actionGetUrl ("http://www.designmultimedia.com", "_level1");
    swf_onCondition (MenuExit);
        swf_actionGetUrl ("", "_level1");
swf_endButton ();
```

swf_addcolor

Sets the global add color to the **$rgba** color specified. This color is then used (implicitly) by the **swf_placeobject()**, **swf_modifyobject(),** and the **swf_addbuttonrecord()** functions. The color of the object will be added by the **$rgba** values when the object is written on the screen. The **$rgba** values can be either positive or negative.

void **swf_addcolor**(*float* r, *float* g, *float* b, *float* a)

swf_closefile

Closes a file that was opened by the **swf_openfile()** function. If the **$return_file** parameter is set, then the contents of the SWF file are returned from the function.

void **swf_closefile**([*int* return_file])

Example: Creating a simple flash file based on user input, outputting it, and saving it in a database.

```php
<?php
// The $text variable is submitted by the
// user
// Global variables for database
// access (used in the swf_savedata() function)
$DBHOST = "localhost";
$DBUSER = "sterling";
$DBPASS = "secret";
swf_openfile ("php://stdout", 256, 256, 30, 1, 1, 1);
    swf_definefont (10, "Ligon-Bold");
        swf_fontsize (12);
        swf_fontslant (10);
    swf_definetext (11, $text, 1);
    swf_pushmatrix ();
        swf_translate (-50, 80, 0);
        swf_placeobject (11, 60);
    swf_popmatrix ();
    swf_showframe ();
    swf_startdoaction ();
        swf_actionstop ();
    swf_enddoaction ();
$data = swf_closefile (1);
$data ?
  swf_savedata ($data) :
  die ("Error could not save SWF file");
// void swf_savedata (string data)
// Save the generated file a database
// for later retrieval
function swf_savedata ($data)
{
    global $DBHOST,
           $DBUSER,
           $DBPASS;
    $dbh = @mysql_connect ($DBHOST, $DBUSER, $DBPASS);
    if (!$dbh) {
        die (sprintf ("Error [%d]: %s",
                      mysql_errno (), mysql_error ()));
    }
```

```
        $stmt = "INSERT INTO swf_files (file) VALUES ('$data')";
        $sth = @mysql_query ($stmt, $dbh);
        if (!$sth) {
            die (sprintf ("Error [%d]: %s",
                          mysql_errno (), mysql_error ()));
        }
        @mysql_free_result ($sth);
        @mysql_close ($dbh);
    }
    ?>
```

swf_definebitmap

Defines a bitmap given a GIF, JPEG, RGB, or FI image. The image will be converted into a Flash JPEG or Flash color map format.

void **swf_definebitmap**(*int* objid, *string* image_name)

swf_definefont

Defines a font given by the **$fontname** parameter and gives it the id specified by the **$fontid** parameter. It then sets the font given by **$fontname** to the current font.

void **swf_definefont**(*int* fontid, *string* fontname)

swf_defineline

Defines a line starting from the x coordinate given by **$x1** and the y coordinate given by **$y1** parameter, up to the x coordinate given by the **$x2** parameter and the y coordinate given by the **$y2** parameter. It will have a width defined by the **$width** parameter.

void **swf_defineline**(*int* objid, *float* x1, *float* y1, *float* x2, *float* y2, *float* width)

swf_definepoly

Defines a polygon given an array of x, y coordinates (the coordinates are defined in the parameter **$coords**). The parameter **$npoints** is the number of overall points that are contained in the array given by **$coords**. The **$width** is the width of the polygon's border; if set to 0.0, the polygon is filled.

void **swf_definepoly**(*int* objid, *array* coords, *int* npoints, *float* width)

swf_definerect

Defines a rectangle with an upper-left hand coordinate given by the x, **$x1**, the y, **$y1**, and a lower-right hand coordinate given by the x coordinate, **$x2** , and the y coordinate, $y2. Width of the rectangles border is given by the **$width** parameter; if the width is 0.0, then the rectangle is filled.

void **swf_definerect**(*int* objid, *float* x1, *float* y1, *float* x2, *float* y2, *float* width)

swf_definetext

Defines a text string (the **$str** parameter) using the current font and font size. The **$docenter** is where the word is centered. If **$docenter** is 1, then the word is centered in x.

void **swf_definetext**(*int* objid, *string* str, *int* docenter)

swf_endbutton

Ends the definition of the current button.

void **swf_endbutton**(*void*)

swf_enddoaction

Ends the current action started by the **swf_startdoaction()** function.

void **swf_enddoaction**(*void*)

swf_endshape

Completes the definition of the current shape.

void **swf_endshape**(*void*)

swf_endsymbol

Ends the definition of a symbol that was started by the **swf_startsymbol()** function.

void **swf_endsymbol**(*void*)

swf_fontsize

Changes the font size to the value given by the **$size** parameter.

void **swf_fontsize**(*float* size)

swf_fontslant

Sets the current font slant to the angle indicated by the $slant parameter. Positive values create a forward slant; negative values create a negative slant.

void **swf_fontslant**(*float* slant)

swf_fonttracking

Sets the font tracking to the value specified by the $tracking parameter. This function is used to increase the spacing between letters and text. Positive values increase the space and negative values decrease the space between letters.

void **swf_fonttracking**(*float* tracking)

swf_getbitmapinfo

Returns an array of information about a bitmap given by the **$bitmapid** parameter. The returned array has the following elements:

- "size"—The size in bytes of the bitmap.
- "width"—The width in pixels of the bitmap.
- "height"—The height in pixels of the bitmap.

array **swf_getbitmapinfo**(*int* bitmapid)

swf_getfontinfo

Returns an associative array with the following parameters:

- Aheight—The height in pixels of a capital A.
- xheight—The height in pixels of a lowercase x.

array **swf_getfontinfo**(*void*)

swf_getframe

Gets the number of the current frame.

int **swf_getframe**(*void*)

swf_labelframe

Labels the current frame with the name given by the **$name** parameter.

void **swf_labelframe**(string name)

swf_lookat

Defines a viewing transformation by giving the viewing position (the parameters **$view_x**, **$view_y**, and **$view_z**) and the coordinates of a reference point in the scene. The reference point is defined by the **$reference_x**, **$reference_y**, and **$reference_z** parameters. The **$twist** controls the rotation along with viewer's z-axis.

void **swf_lookat**(double view_x, double view_y, double view_z, double reference_x, double reference_y, double reference_z, double twist)

swf_modifyobject

Updates the position and/or color of the object at the specified depth, **$depth**. The parameter **$how** determines what is updated. **$how** can either be the constant MOD_MATRIX or MOD_COLOR or it can be a combination of both (MOD_MATRIX | MOD_COLOR).

void **swf_modifyobject**(int depth, int how)

MOD_COLOR uses the current mulcolor (specified by the function **swf_mulcolor()**) and add-color (specified by the function **swf_addcolor()**) to color the object. MOD_MATRIX uses the current matrix to position the object.

swf_mulcolor

Sets the global multiply color to the **$rgba** color specified. This color is then used (implicitly) by the **swf_placeobject()**, **swf_modifyobject()**, and the **swf_addbuttonrecord()** functions. The color of the object will be multiplied by the **$rgba** values when the object is written to the screen.

Note: The **$rgba** values can be either positive or negative.

void **swf_mulcolor**(float r, float g, float b, float a)

swf_nextid

Returns the next available object id.

int **swf_nextid**(void)

swf_oncondition

Describes a transition that will trigger an action list.

void **swf_oncondition**(int transition)

Several types of possible transitions are available. The following are for buttons defined as TYPE_MENUBUTTON:

- IdletoOverUp
- OverUptoIdle
- OverUptoOverDown
- OverDowntoOverUp
- IdletoOverDown
- OutDowntoIdle
- MenuEnter (IdletoOverUp | IdletoOverDown)
- MenuExit (OverUptoIdle | OverDowntoIdle)

  For TYPE_PUSHBUTTON, the following options are available:

- IdletoOverUp
- OverUptoIdle
- OverUptoOverDown
- OverDowntoOverUp
- OverDowntoOutDown
- OutDowntoOverDown

- OutDowntoIdle
- ButtonEnter (IdletoOverUp | OutDowntoOverDown)
- ButtonExit (OverUptoIdle | OverDowntoOutDown)

swf_openfile

Opens a new file named **$filename** with a width of **$width,** a height of **$height,** a frame rate of **$framerate,** a background with a red color of **$r,** a green color of **$g,** and a blue color of **$b.** The **swf_openfile()** must be the first function you call; otherwise, your script will cause a segfault. If you want to send your output to the screen, make the filename: "php://stdout" (support for this is in 4.0.1 and up).

void **swf_openfile**(string filename, float width, float height, float framerate, float r, float g, float b)

swf_ortho

Defines a orthographic mapping of user coordinates onto the current viewport.

void **swf_ortho**(double xmin, double xmax, double ymin, double ymax, double zmin, double zmax)

swf_ortho2

Defines a two dimensional orthographic mapping of user coordinates onto the current viewport. This defaults to one-to-one mapping of the area of the Flash movie. If a perspective transformation is desired, the **swf_perspective()** function can be used.

void **swf_ortho2**(double xmin, double xmax, double ymin, double ymax)

swf_perspective

Defines a perspective projection transformation. The **$fovy** parameter is field-of-view angle in the y direction. The **$aspect** parameter should be set to the aspect ratio of the viewport onto which is being drawn. The **$near** parameter is the near clipping plane and the **$far** parameter is the far clipping plane.

void **swf_perspective**(double fovy, double aspect, double near, double far)

Note: Various distortion artifacts may appear when performing a perspective projection. This is because Flash players only have a two dimensional matrix; some are not too pretty.

swf_placeobject

Places the object specified by **$objid** in the current frame at a depth of **$depth**. The **$objid** parameter and the **$depth** must be between 1 and 65,535. This uses the current mulcolor (specified by **swf_mulcolor()**) and the current addcolor (specified by **swf_addcolor()**) to color the object, and it uses the current matrix to position the object. **Note:** Full RGBA colors are supported.

void **swf_placeobject**(int objid, int depth)

swf_polarview

Defines the viewer's position in polar coordinates. The **$dist** parameter gives the distance between the viewpoint to the world space origin. The **$azimuth** parameter defines the azimuthal angle in the x,y coordinate plane, measured in distance from the y-axis. The **$incidence** parameter defines the angle of incidence in the y,z plane, measured in distance from the z-axis. The incidence angle is defined as the angle of the viewport relative to the z-axis. Finally, the **$twist** specifies the amount that the viewpoint is to be rotated about the line of sight using the right hand rule.

    void **swf_polarview**(double dist, double azimuth, double incidence, double twist)

swf_popmatrix

Pushes the current transformation matrix back onto the stack.

    void **swf_popmatrix**(void)

swf_posround

Enables or disables the rounding of the translation when objects are placed or moved. Situations occur when text becomes more readable because rounding has been enabled. The **$round** is whether to enable rounding or not. If set to the value of 1, then rounding is enabled; if set to 0, then rounding is disabled.

    void **swf_posround**(int round)

swf_pushmatrix

Pushes the current transformation matrix back onto the stack.

    void **swf_pushmatrix**(void)

swf_removeobject

Removes the object at the depth specified by **$depth**.

    void **swf_removeobject**(int depth)

swf_rotate

Rotates the current transformation by the angle given by the **$angle** parameter around the axis given by the **$axis** parameter. Valid values for the axis are 'x' (the x-axis), 'y' (the y-axis) or 'z' (the z-axis).

    void **swf_rotate**(double angle, string axis)

swf_scale

Scales the x coordinate of the curve by the value of the **$x** parameter, the y coordinate of the curve by the value of the **$y** parameter, and the z coordinate of the curve by the value of the **$z** parameter.

void **swf_scale**(*double* x, *double* y, *double* z)

swf_setfont

Sets the current font to the value given by the **$fontid** parameter.

void **swf_setfont**(*int* fontid)

swf_setframe

Changes the active frame to the frame specified by **$framenumber**.

void **swf_setframe**(*int* framenumber)

swf_shapearc

Draws a circular arc from angle A given by the **$ang1** parameter to angle B given by the **$ang2** parameter. The center of the circle has an x coordinate given by the **$x** parameter and a y coordinate given by the **$y**, the radius of the circle is given by the **$r** parameter.

void **swf_shapearc**(*float* x, *float* y, *float* r, *float* ang1, *float* ang2)

swf_shapecurveto

Draws a quadratic Bezier curve from the x coordinate given by **$x1** and the y coordinate given by **$y1** to the x coordinate given by **$x2** and the y coordinate given by **$y2**. The current position is then set to the x,y coordinates given by the **$x2** and **$y2** parameters.

void **swf_shapecurveto**(*float* x1, *float* y1, *float* x2, *float* y2)

swf_shapecurveto3

Draws a cubic Bezier curve using the x,y coordinate pairs **$x1**, **$y1** and **$x2**, **$y2** as off curve control points and the x,y coordinate **$x3**, **$y3** as an endpoint. The current position is then set to the x,y coordinate pair given by **$x3**, **$y3**.

void **swf_shapecurveto3**(*float* x1, *float* y1, *float* x2, *float* y2, *float* x3, *float* y3)

swf_shapefillbitmapclip

Sets the fill to bitmap clipped, empty spaces will be filled by the bitmap given by the **$bitmapid** parameter.

void swf_shapefillbitmapclip(*int* bitmapid)

swf_shapefillbitmaptile

Sets the fill to bitmap tile. Empty spaces will be filled by the bitmap given by the **$bitmapid** parameter (tiled).

void swf_shapefillbitmaptile(*int* bitmapid)

swf_shapefilloff

Turns off filling for the current shape.

void **swf_shapefilloff**(*void*)

swf_shapefillsolid

Sets the current fill style to solid, and then sets the fill color to the values of the **$rgba** parameters.

void **swf_shapefillsolid**(*float* r, *float* g, *float* b, *float* a)

swf_shapelinesolid

Sets the current line style to the color of the **$rgba** parameters and width to the **$width** parameter. If 0.0 is given as a width, then no lines are drawn.

void **swf_shapelinesolid**(*float* r, *float* g, *float* b, *float* a, *float* width)

swf_shapelineto

Draws a line to the x,y coordinates given by the **x** parameter and the **y** parameter. The current position is then set to the x,y parameters.

void **swf_shapelineto**(*float* x, *float* y)

swf_shapemoveto

Moves the current position to the x coordinate given by the **$x** parameter and the y position given by the **$y** parameter.

void **swf_shapemoveto**(float x, float y)

swf_showframe

Outputs the current frame.

void **swf_showframe**(void)

swf_startbutton

Starts off the definition of a button. The **$type** parameter can either be TYPE_MENUBUTTON or TYPE_PUSHBUTTON. The TYPE_MENUBUTTON constant enables the focus to travel from the button when the mouse is down. TYPE_PUSHBUTTON does not allow the focus to travel when the mouse is down.

> void **swf_startbutton**(int objid, int type)

swf_startdoaction

Starts the description of an action list for the current frame. This must be called before actions are defined for the current frame.

> *void* **swf_startdoaction**(*void*)

swf_startshape

Starts a complex shape with an object id given by the **$objid** parameter.

> *void* **swf_startshape**(*int* objid)

swf_startsymbol

Defines an object id as a symbol. Symbols are tiny flash movies that can be played simultaneously. The **$objid** parameter is the object id you want to define as a symbol.

> *void* **swf_startsymbol**(*int* objid)

swf_textwidth

Provides the width of the string, **$str**, in pixels, using the current font and font size.

> *float* **swf_textwidth**(*string* str)

swf_translate

Translates the current transformation by the **$x**, **$y**, and **$z** values given.

> *void* **swf_translate**(*double* x, *double* y, *double* z)

swf_viewport

Selects an area for future drawing for **$xmin** to **$xmax** and **$ymin** to **$ymax**. If this function is not called, the area defaults to the size of the screen.

> *void* **swf_viewport**(*double* xmin, *double* xmax, *double* ymin, *double* ymax)

sybase_affected_rows

Returns the number of affected rows by the last query. Returns the number of rows affected by the last INSERT, UPDATE, or DELETE query on the server associated with the specified link identifier. If the link identifier isn't specified, the last opened link is assumed.

This command is not effective for SELECT statements, only on statements which modify records. To retrieve the number of rows returned from a SELECT, use **sybase_num_rows()**.

Note: This function is only available using the CT library interface to Sybase, not the DB library.

int **sybase_affected_rows**([*int* link_identifier])

sybase_close

Returns true on success, false on error. Closes the link to a Sybase database that's associated with the specified link identifier. If the link identifier isn't specified, the last opened link is assumed.

Note: This isn't usually necessary because non-persistent open links are automatically closed at the end of the script's execution. **sybase_close()** will not close persistent links generated by sybase_pconnect(). See also **sybase_connect()** and **sybase_pconnect()**.

int **sybase_close**(*int* link_identifier)

sybase_connect

Returns a positive Sybase link identifier on success, or false on error. Establishes a connection to a Sybase server. The servername argument has to be a valid servername that is defined in the interfaces file.

int **sybase_connect**(*string* servername, *string* username, *string* password, [*string* charset])

In case a second call is made to **sybase_connect()** with the same arguments, no new link will be established. Instead, the link identifier of the already opened link will be returned.

The link to the server will be closed as soon as the execution of the script ends, unless it's closed earlier by explicitly calling **sybase_close()**. See also **sybase_pconnect()** and **sybase_close()**.

sybase_data_seek

Returns true on success, false on failure. Moves the internal row pointer of the Sybase result associated with the specified result identifier to pointer to the specified row number. The next call to **sybase_fetch_row()** would return that row. See also **sybase_data_seek()**.

int **sybase_data_seek**(*int* result_identifier, *int* row_number)

sybase_fetch_array

Returns an array that corresponds to the fetched row, or false if no more rows are available. This function is an extended version of **sybase_fetch_row()**. In addition to storing the data in the numeric indices of the result array, it also stores the data in associative indices using the field names as keys.

int **sybase_fetch_array**(*int* result)

Note: Using **sybase_fetch_array()** is NOT significantly slower than using **sybase_fetch_row()**, it actually provides a significant added value. For further details, also see **sybase_fetch_row()**.

sybase_fetch_field

Returns an object containing field information. This function can be used in order to obtain information about fields in a certain query result. If the field offset isn't specified, the next field that wasn't yet retrieved by **sybase_fetch_field()** is retrieved. See also **sybase_field_seek()**.

object **sybase_fetch_field**(*int* result, *int* field_offset)

The properties of the object are as follows:

- name—Column name. If the column is a result of a function, this property is set to computed#N, where #N is a serial number.
- column_source—The table from which the column was taken.
- max_length—Maximum length of the column.
- numeric—1 if the column is numeric.

sybase_fetch_object

Returns an object with properties that correspond to the fetched row, or false if no more rows are available. This function is similar to **sybase_fetch_array()**, with one difference—an object is returned, instead of an array. Indirectly, that means that you can only access the data by the field names, not by their offsets (numbers are illegal property names).

int sybase_fetch_object(*int* result)

Speed-wise, the function is identical to **sybase_fetch_array()**, and almost as quick as **sybase_fetch_row()**; the difference is insignificant. See also **sybase_fetch_array()** and **sybase_fetch_row()**.

sybase_fetch_row

Returns an array that corresponds to the fetched row, or false if no more rows are available. Fetches one row of data from the result associated with the specified result identifier. The row is returned as an array. Each result column is stored in an array offset, starting at offset 0.

array **sybase_fetch_row**(*int* result)

Subsequent call to **sybase_fetch_rows()** would return the next row in the result set, or false if no more rows are available. See also **sybase_fetch_array()**, **sybase_fetch_object()**, **sybase_data_seek()**, **sybase_fetch_lengths()**, and **sybase_result()**.

sybase_field_seek

Seeks to the specified field offset. If the next call to **sybase_fetch_field()** won't include a field offset, this field would be returned. See also **sybase_fetch_field()**.

int **sybase_field_seek**(*int* result, *int* field_offset)

sybase_free_result

This function only needs to be called if you are worried about using too much memory while your script is running. All result memory will automatically be freed when the script ends. You may call **sybase_free_result()** with the result identifier as an argument and the associated result memory will be freed.

int **sybase_free_result**(*int* result)

sybase_num_fields

Returns the number of fields in a result set. See also **sybase_db_query()**, **sybase_query()**, **sybase_fetch_field()**, and **sybase_num_rows()**.

int **sybase_num_fields**(*int* result)

sybase_num_rows

Returns the number of rows in a result set. See also **sybase_db_query()**, **sybase_query()**, and **sybase_fetch_row()**.

int **sybase_num_rows**(*string* result)

sybase_pconnect

Returns a positive Sybase persistent link identifier on success, or false on error. Acts very much like **sybase_connect()** with two major differences.

int **sybase_pconnect**(*string* servername, *string* username, *string* password, [*string* charset])

First, when connecting, the function would try to find a (persistent) link that's already open with the same host, username, and password. If one is found, an identifier for it will be returned instead of opening a new connection.

Secondly, the connection to the SQL server will not be closed when the execution of the script ends. Instead, the link will remain open for future use (**sybase_close()** will not close links established by **sybase_pconnect()**). This type of links is therefore called "persistent."

sybase_query

Returns a positive Sybase result identifier on success, or false on error. Sends a query to the currently active database on the server that's associated with the specified link identifier. If the link identifier isn't specified, the last opened link is assumed. If no link is open, the function tries to establish a link as if **sybase_connect()** was called, and then uses it. See also **sybase_db_query()**, **sybase_select_db()**, and **sybase_connect()**.

int **sybase_query**(*string* query, *int* link_identifier)

sybase_result

Returns the contents of the cell at the row and offset in the specified Sybase result set. Returns the contents of one cell from a Sybase result set. The field argument can be the field's offset, the field's name, or the field's table dot field's name (tablename.fieldname). If the column name has been aliased ('select foo as bar from . . . '), use the alias instead of the column name.

int **sybase_result**(*int* result, *int* row, *mixed* field)

When working on large result sets, you should consider using one of the functions that fetch an entire row. As these functions return the contents of multiple cells in one function call, they're much quicker than sybase_result().

Note: Specifying a numeric offset for the field argument is much quicker than specifying a fieldname or tablename.fieldname argument. Recommended high-performance alternatives are as follows: **sybase_fetch_row()**, **sybase_fetch_array()**, and **sybase_fetch_object()**.

sybase_select_db

Returns true on success, false on error. Sets the current active database on the server that's associated with the specified link identifier. If no link identifier is specified, the last opened link is assumed. If no link is open, the function will try to establish a link as if **sybase_connect()** was called, and use it.

Every subsequent call to **sybase_query()** will be made on the active database. See also **sybase_connect()**, **sybase_pconnect()**, and **sybase_query()**.

int **sybase_select_db**(*string* database_name, *int* link_identifier)

symlink

Creates a symbolic link from the existing **$target** with the specified name **$link**. See also **link()** to create hard links, and **readlink()** along with **linkinfo()**. **Note:** This function does not work on Windows' systems.

int **symlink**(*string* target, *string* link)

syslog

Generates a log message that will be distributed by the system logger. $priority is a combination of the facility and the level, values for which are given in the next section. The remaining argument is the message to send, except that the two characters %m will be replaced by the error message string (strerror) corresponding to the present value of errno.

int **syslog**(*int* priority, *string* message)

Syslog() Priorities (in descending order)

Constant	Description
LOG_EMERG	system is unusable
LOG_ALERT	action must be taken immediately
LOG_CRIT	critical conditions
LOG_ERR	error conditions
LOG_WARNING	warning conditions
LOG_NOTICE	normal, but significant, condition
LOG_INFO	informational message
LOG_DEBUG	debug-level message

Example: Using **syslog()**

```php
<?php
define_syslog_variables();
// open syslog, include the process ID and also send
// the log to standard error, and use a user defined
// logging mechanism
openlog("myScripLog", LOG_PID | LOG_PERROR, LOG_LOCAL0);
// some code
if (authorized_client()) {
    // do something
} else {
    // unauthorized client!
    // log the attempt
    $access = date("Y/m/d H:i:s");
    syslog(LOG_WARNING,"Unauthorized client: $access $REMOTE_ADDR ($HTTP_USER_AGENT)");
}
closelog();
?>
```

For information on setting up a user defined log handler, see the syslog.conf 5 Unix manual page. More information on the syslog facilities and option can be found in the man pages for syslog 3 on Unix machines. On Windows NT, the syslog service is emulated using the Event Log. See also **define_syslog_variables()**, **openlog()**, and **closelog()**.

system

Similar to the C version of the function in that it executes the given $command and outputs the result. If a variable is provided as the second argument, then the return status code of the executed command will be written to this variable.

string **system**(*string* command, [*int* return_var])

Note: If you are going to allow data coming from user input to be passed to this function, then you should be using the **EscapeShellCmd()** function to make sure that users cannot trick the system into executing arbitrary commands. Also note that if you start a program using this function and want to leave it running in the background, you have to make sure that the output of that program is redirected to a file or some other output stream; otherwise, PHP will hang until the execution of the program ends.

The **System()** call also tries to automatically flush the Web server's output buffer after each line of output if PHP is running as a server module. Returns the last line of the command output on success, and false on failure.

If you need to execute a command and have all the data from the command passed directly back without any interference, use the **PassThru()** function. See also **exec()**, **PassThru()**, **popen()**, **EscapeShellCmd()**, and the **backtick operator()**.

tan

Returns the tangent of arg in radians. See also **sin()** and **cos()**.

float **tan**(*float* arg)

tempnam

Creates a unique temporary filename in the specified directory. If the directory does not exist, **tempnam()** may generate a filename in the system's temporary directory. See also **tmpfile()**.

string **tempnam**(*string* dir, *string* prefix)

The behavior of the **tempnam()** function is system dependent. On Windows, the TMP environment variable will override the **$dir** parameter. On Linux, the TMPDIR environment variable has precedence, although SVR4 will always use your **$dir** parameter, if the directory it points to exists. Consult your system documentation on the tempnam(3) function if in doubt.

Returns the new temporary filename, or the null string on failure.

Example: Tempnam()

```
$tmpfname = tempnam ("/tmp", "FOO");
```

textdomain

Sets the domain to search within when calls are made to gettext(), usually the named after an application. The previous default domain is returned. Call it with no parameters, in order to get the current setting without changing it.

int **textdomain**([*string* library])

time

Returns the current time measured in the number of seconds since the Unix Epoch (January 1 1970 00:00:00 GMT). See also **date()**.

int **time**(*void*)

tmpfile

Creates a temporary file with an unique name in write mode, returning a file handle similar to the one returned by **fopen()**. The file is automatically removed when closed (using **fclose()**), or when the script ends. For details, consult your system documentation on the *tmpfile(3)* function, as well as the stdio.h header file. See also **tempnam()**.

> *int* **tmpfile**(*void*)

touch

Attempts to set the modification time of the file named by filename to the value given by time. If the option time is not given,the present time is used.

> *int* **touch**(*string* filename, [*int* time])

If the file does not exist, it is created. Returns true on success and false otherwise.
Example: Touch()

```
if (touch ($FileName)) {
    print "$FileName modification time has been
          changed to todays date and time";
} else {
    print "Sorry Could Not change modification time of $FileName";
}
```

trigger_error

Used to trigger a user error condition. It can be used in conjunction with the built-in error handler, or with a user defined function that has been set as the new error handler (**set_error_handler()**). This function is useful when you need to generate a particular response to an exception at runtime.

> *void* **trigger_error**(*string* error_msg, [*int* error_type])

Example:

```
if (assert ($divisor == 0))
    trigger_error ("Cannot divide by zero", E_USER_ERROR);
```

Note: See **set_error_handler()** for a more extensive example. See also **error_reporting()**, **set_error_handler()**, **restore_error_handler()**, and **user_error()**.

trim

Strips whitespace from the start and the end of a string and returns the stripped string. The whitespace characters it currently strips are: "\n", "\r", "\t", "\v", "\0", and a plain space. See also **chop()**, **rtrim()**, and **ltrim()**.

> *string* **trim**(*string* str)

uasort

This function sorts an array such that array indices maintain their correlation with the array elements with which they are associated. This is used mainly when sorting associative arrays where the actual element order is significant. The comparison function is user-defined.

void **uasort**(*array* array, *function* cmp_function)

Note: Please see **usort()** and **uksort()** for examples of user-defined comparison functions. See also **usort()**, **uksort()**, **sort()**, **asort()**, **arsort()**, **ksort()**, and **rsort()**.

ucfirst

Capitalizes the first character of **$str**, if that character is alphabetic.

string **ucfirst**(*string* str)

Note: 'alphabetic' is determined by the current locale. For instance, in the default "C," locale characters such as umlaut-a (_) will not be converted.

Example: Ucfirst()

```
$text = 'mary had a little lamb and she loved it so.';
$text = ucfirst ($text); // $text is now Mary had a little lamb
                         // and she loved it so.
```

See also **strtoupper()** and **strtolower()**.

ucwords

Capitalizes the first character of each word in **$str**, if that character is alphabetic.

string **ucwords**(*string* str)

Example: ucwords()

```
$text = "mary had a little lamb and she loved it so.";
$text = ucwords($text); // $text is now: Mary Had A Little
                        // Lamb And She Loved It So.
```

See also **strtoupper()**, **strtolower()**, and **ucfirst()**.

uksort

Sorts the keys of an array using a user-supplied comparison function. If the array you wish to sort needs to be sorted by some non-trivial criteria, you should use this function. See also **usort()**, **uasort()**, **sort()**, **asort()**, **arsort()**, **ksort()**, **natsort()**, and **rsort()**.

void **uksort**(*array* array, *function* cmp_function)

Example: Uksort()

```
function cmp ($a, $b) {
    if ($a == $b) return 0;
```

```
    return ($a > $b) ? -1 : 1;
}
$a = array (4 => "four", 3 => "three", 20 => "twenty", 10 => "ten");
uksort ($a, "cmp");
while (list ($key, $value) = each ($a)) {
    echo "$key: $value\n";
}
```

This example would display the following:

```
20: twenty
10: ten
4: four
3: three
```

umask

Sets PHP's umask to mask & 0777 and returns the old umask. When PHP is being used as a server module, the umask is restored when each request is finished. **Umask()** without arguments simply returns the current umask.

Note: This function may not work on Windows systems.

int **umask**(*int* mask)

uniqid

Returns a prefixed unique identifier based on the current time in microseconds. The prefix can be useful, for instance, if you generate identifiers simultaneously on several hosts that might happen to generate the identifier at the same microsecond. **$Prefix** can be up to 114 characters long.

int **uniqid**(*string* prefix, [*boolean* lcg])

If the optional **$lcg** parameter is true, **uniqid()** will add additional "combined LCG" entropy at the end of the return value, which should make the results more unique.

With an empty **$prefix** , the returned string will be 13 characters long. If **$lcg** is true, it will be 23 characters.

Note: The **$lcg** parameter is only available in PHP 4 and PHP 3.0.13 and later.

If you need a unique identifier or token and you intend to give out that token to the user via the network (that is, session cookies), it is recommended that you use something along the lines of the following:

```
$token = md5 (uniqid ("")); // no random portion
$better_token = md5 (uniqid (rand())); // better, difficult to guess
```

This will create a 32-character identifier (a 128-bit hex number) that is extremely difficult to predict.

unixtojd

Returns the Julian Day for a UNIX **$timestamp** (seconds since 1.1.1970), or for the current day if no **$timestamp** is given. See also **jdtounix()**.
Note: This function is only available in PHP versions after PHP4RC1.

int **unixtojd**([*int* timestamp])

unlink

Deletes **$filename**. Similar to the Unix C unlink() function. Returns 0 or false on an error. See also **rmdir()** for removing directories.
Note: This function may not work on Windows systems.

int **unlink**(*string* filename)

unpack

From binary string into array according to **$format**. Returns array containing unpacked elements of binary string. **Unpack()** works slightly different from Perl as the unpacked data is stored in an associative array. To accomplish this you have to name the different format codes and separate them by a slash /.

array **unpack**(*string* format, *string* data)

Example: Unpack() format string

```
$array = unpack ("c2chars/nint", $binarydata);
```

The resulting array will contain the entries "chars1", "chars2", and "int". For an explanation of the format codes, see **pack()**.
Note: PHP internally stores integral values as signed. If you unpack a large unsigned long and it is of the same size as PHP internally stored values, the result will be a negative number even though unsigned unpacking was specified.

unserialize

Takes a single serialized variable (see **serialize()**) and converts it back into a PHP value. The converted value is returned, and can be an integer, double, string, array, or object. If an object was serialized, its methods are not preserved in the returned value.

mixed **unserialize**(*string* str)

Example: Unserialize()

```
// Here, we use unserialize() to load session data from a database
// into $session_data.    This example complements the one described
// with <FUNCTION >serialize</FUNCTION>.
$conn = odbc_connect ("webdb", "php", "chicken");
$stmt = odbc_prepare ($conn, "SELECT data FROM sessions WHERE id = ?");
$sqldata = array ($PHP_AUTH_USER);
```

```
if (!odbc_execute ($stmt, &$sqldata) || !odbc_fetch_into ($stmt, &$tmp)) {
    // if the execute or fetch fails, initialize to empty array
    $session_data = array();
} else {
    // we should now have the serialized data in $tmp[0].
    $session_data = unserialize ($tmp[0]);
    if (!is_array ($session_data)) {
    // something went wrong, initialize to empty array
    $session_data = array();
    }
}
```

unset

Destroys the specified variables and returns true. See also **isset()** and **empty()**.

int **unset**(*mixed* var, [*mixed* var], [*mixed* . . .])

Example: Unset()

```
// destroy a single variable
unset ($foo);
// destroy a single element of an array
unset ($bar['quux']);
// destroy more than one variable
unset ($foo1, $foo2, $foo3);
```

The behavior of **unset()** inside of a function can vary depending on what type of variable you are attempting to destroy.

If a globalized variable is **unset()** inside of a function, only the local variable is destroyed. The variable in the calling environment will retain the same value as before **unset()** was called.

```
function destroy_foo() {
    global $foo;
    unset($foo);
}
$foo = 'bar';
destroy_foo();
echo $foo;
```

The previous example would output the following:

```
bar
```

If a variable that is PASSED BY REFERENCE is **unset()** inside of a function, only the local variable is destroyed. The variable in the calling environment will retain the same value as before **unset()** was called.

```
function foo(&$bar) {
    unset($bar);
    $bar = "blah";
}
$bar = 'something';
echo "$bar\n";
```

```
foo($bar);
echo "$bar\n";
```

The previous example would output the following:

```
something
something
```

If a static variable is **unset()** inside of a function, **unset()** unsets the reference to the static variable, rather than the static variable itself.

```
function foo() {
    static $a;
    $a++;
        echo "$a\n";
    unset($a);
}
foo();
foo();
foo();
```

The previous example would output the following:

```
1
2
3
```

If you would like to **unset()** a global variable inside of a function, you can use the **$$GLOBALS** array to do so:

```
function foo() {
    unset($GLOBALS['bar']);
}
$bar = "something";
foo();
```

urldecode

Decodes any % ## encoding in the given string. The decoded string is returned.

string **urldecode**(*string* str)

Example: Urldecode()

```
$a = split ('&', $querystring);
$i = 0;
while ($i < count ($a)) {
    $b = split ('=', $a [$i]);
    echo 'Value for parameter ', htmlspecialchars (urldecode ($b [0])),
        ' is ', htmlspecialchars (urldecode ($b [1])), "<BR>";
    $i++;
}
```

See also **urlencode()**, **rawurlencode()**, and **rawurldecode()**.

urlencode

Returns a string in which all non-alphanumeric characters except -_. have been replaced with a percent (%) sign followed by two hex digits and spaces encoded as plus (+) signs. It is encoded the same way that the posted data from a WWW form is encoded, that is, the same way as in application/x-www-form-urlencoded media type. This differs from the RFC1738 encoding (see **rawurlencode()**) in that for historical reasons, spaces are encoded as plus (+) signs.

string **urlencode**(*string* str)

This function is a convenient way to pass variables to the next page when encoding a string to be used in a query part of an URL :

Example 1: Urlencode()

```
echo '<A HREF="mycgi?foo=', urlencode ($userinput), '">';
```

Note: Be careful about variables that may match HTML entities. Things like &amp, &copy, and &pound are parsed by the browser, and the actual entity is used instead of the desired variable name. This is an obvious hassle that the W3C has been telling people about for years. The reference is here: *http://www.w3.org/TR/html4/appendix/notes.html#h-B.2.2*. PHP supports changing the argument separator to the W3C-suggested semi-colon through the arg_separator .ini directive. Unfortunately, most user agents do not send form data in this semi-colon separated format. A more portable way around this is to use &amp, instead of &, as the separator. You don't need to change PHP's arg_separator for this. Leave it as &, but simply encode your URLs using htmlentities((urlencode($data)).

Example 2: Urlencode/htmlentities() example

```
echo '<A HREF="mycgi?foo=', htmlentities (urlencode ($userinput) ), '<\#34>>';
```

See also **urldecode()**, **htmlentities()**, **rawurldecode()**, and **rawurlencode()**.

user_error

This is an alias for the function **trigger_error()**. See also **error_reporting()**, **set_error_handler()**, **restore_error_handler()**, and **trigger_error()**.

void **user_error**(*string* error_msg, [*int* error_type])

usleep

Delays program execution for the given number of $micro_seconds. See also **sleep()**. This function does not work on Windows systems.

void **usleep**(*int* micro_seconds)

usort

This function will sort an array by its values using a user-supplied comparison function. If the array you wish to sort needs to be sorted by some non-trivial criteria, you should use this function.

void **usort**(*array* array, *string* cmp_function)

The comparison function must return an integer less than, equal to, or greater than zero if the first argument is considered to be respectively less than, equal to, or greater than the second. If two members compare as equal, their order in the sorted array is undefined.

Example: Usort()

```
function cmp ($a, $b) {
    if ($a == $b) return 0;
    return ($a > $b) ? -1 : 1;
}
$a = array (3, 2, 5, 6, 1);
usort ($a, "cmp");
while (list ($key, $value) = each ($a)) {
    echo "$key: $value\n";
}
```

This example would display the following:

```
0: 6
1: 5
2: 3
3: 2
4: 1
```

Note: Obviously in this trivial case the **rsort()** function would be more appropriate.

Example: Usort() example using multi-dimensional array

```
function cmp ($a, $b) {
    return strcmp($a["fruit"],$b["fruit"]);
}
$fruits[0]["fruit"] = "lemons";
$fruits[1]["fruit"] = "apples";
$fruits[2]["fruit"] = "grapes";
usort($fruits, "cmp");
while (list ($key, $value) = each ($fruits)) {
    echo "\$fruits[$key]: " . $value["fruit"] . "\n";
}
```

When sorting a multi-dimensional array, $a and $b contain references to the first index of the array.

This example would display the following:

```
$fruits[0]: apples
$fruits[1]: grapes
$fruits[2]: lemons
```

The underlying quicksort function in some C libraries (such as on Solaris systems) may cause PHP to crash if the comparison function does not return consistent values. See also **uasort()**, **uksort()**, **sort()**, **asort()**, **arsort()**, **ksort()**, **natsort()**, and **rsort()**.

utf8_decode

This function decodes **$data**, assumed to be UTF-8 encoded, to ISO-8859-1. See **utf8_encode()** for an explanation of UTF-8 encoding.

   string **utf8_decode**(*string* data)

utf8_encode

This function encodes the string **$data** to *UTF-8*, and returns the encoded version. *UTF-8* is a standard mechanism used by Unicode for encoding wide character values into a byte stream. *UTF-8* is transparent to plain ASCII characters, is self-synchronized (meaning it is possible for a program to figure out where in the bytestream characters start), and can be used with normal string comparison functions for sorting and such.

   string **utf8_encode**(string data)

   PHP encodes *UTF-8* characters in up to four bytes, like this:

UTF-8 encoding

bytes	bits	representation
1	7	0bbbbbbb
2	11	110bbbbb 10bbbbbb
3	16	1110bbbb 10bbbbbb 10bbbbbb
4	21	11110bbb 10bbbbbb 10bbbbbb 10bbbbbb

Each b represents a bit that can be used to store character data.

var_dump

This function returns structured information about an expression that includes its type and value. Arrays are explored recursively with values indented to show structure.

   void **var_dump**(mixed expression)

   Compare **var_dump()** to **print_r()**.

```
<pre>
<?php
    $a = array (1, 2, array ("a", "b", "c"));
    var_dump ($a);
?>
</pre>
```

virtual

This is an Apache-specific function which is equivalent to <!—#include virtual . . . —> in mod_include. It performs an Apache sub-request. It is useful for including CGI scripts, .shtml files, or anything else that you would parse through Apache.

Note: For a CGI script, the script must generate valid CGI headers. At the minimum, that means it must generate a Content-type header. For PHP files, you need to use **include()** or **require()**; **virtual()** cannot be used to include a document which is itself a PHP file.

   int **virtual**(string filename)

vm_addalias

Adds an alias to a virtual user. **$username** is the email login name and **$alias** is an alias for this vuser.

   int **vm_addalias**(string vdomain, string basepwd, string username, string alias)

vm_adduser

Adds a new virtual user with a password. **$newusername** is the email login name and **$newuserpassword** is the password for this user.

   int **vm_adduser**(string vdomain, string basepwd, string newusername, string newuserpassword)

vm_delalias

Removes an alias.

   int **vm_delalias**(string vdomain, string basepwd, string alias)

vm_deluser

Removes a virtual user.

   int **vm_deluser**(string vdomain, string username)

vm_passwd

Changes a virtual users password. **$username** is the email login name, **$password** the old password for the vuser, and **$newpassword** the new password.

   int **vm_passwd**(*string* vdomain, *string* username, *string* password, *string* newpassword)

wddx_add_vars

Used to serialize passed variables and adds the result to the packet specified by the **$packet_id**. The variables to be serialized are specified in exactly the same way as **wddx_serialize_vars()**.

   wddx_add_vars(int packet_id, mixed name_var, [mixed . . .])

wddx_deserialize

Takes a **$packet** string and deserializes it. It returns the result which can be string, number, or array.

Note: Structures are deserialized into associative arrays.

mixed **wddx_deserialize**(string packet)

wddx_packet_end

Ends the WDDX packet specified by the **$packet_id** and returns the string with the packet.

string **wddx_packet_end**(int packet_id)

wddx_packet_start

Starts a new WDDX packet for incremental addition of variables. It takes an optional **$comment** string and returns a packet ID for use in later functions. It automatically creates a structure definition inside the packet to contain the variables.

int **wddx_packet_start**([string comment])

wddx_serialize_value

Used to create a WDDX packet from a single given value. It takes the value contained in **$var** and an optional **$comment** string that appears in the packet header, and returns the WDDX packet.

string **wddx_serialize_value**(mixed var, [string comment])

wddx_serialize_vars

Used to create a WDDX packet with a structure that contains the serialized representation of the passed variables. This function takes a variable number of arguments, each of which can be either a string naming a variable or an array containing strings naming the variables or another array, and so on.

string **wddx_serialize_vars**(mixed var_name, [mixed . . .])

Example: wddx_serialize_vars

```
<?php
$a = 1;
$b = 5.5;
$c = array("blue", "orange", "violet");
$d = "colors";
$clvars = array("c", "d");
print wddx_serialize_vars("a", "b", $clvars);
?>
```

The previous example will produce the following:

```
<wddxPacket version='1.0'><header/><data><struct><var name='a'><number>1</number></var>
<var name='b'><number>5.5</number></var><var name='c'><array length='3'>
<string>blue</string><string>orange</string><string>violet</string></array></var>
<var name='d'><string>colors</string></var></struct></data></wddxPacket>
```

wordwrap

Wraps the string **$str** at the column number specified by the (optional) **$width** parameter. The line is broken using the (optional) **$break** parameter. See also **nl2br()**.

string **wordwrap**(string str, [int width], [string break], [int cut])

wordwrap() will automatically wrap at column 75 and break using '\n' (newline), if **$width** or **$break** are not given.

If the **$cut** is set to 1, the string is always wrapped at the specified width. So if you have a word that is larger than the given width, it is broken apart. (See Example 2).

Example 1: wordwrap()

```
$text = "The quick brown fox jumped over the lazy dog.";
$newtext = wordwrap( $text, 20 );
echo "$newtext\n";
```

This example would display the following:

```
The quick brown fox
jumped over the lazy dog.
```

Example 2: wordwrap()

```
$text = "A very long woooooooooooord.";
$newtext = wordwrap( $text, 8, "\n", 1);
echo "$newtext\n";
```

This example would display the following:

```
A very
long
woooooooo
ooooord.
```

xmldoc

Parses the XML document in **$str** and returns an object of class "Dom document", having the properties "doc" (resource), "version" (string), and "type" (long).

object **xmldoc**(string str)

xmldocfile

Parses the XML document in the file named $filename and returns an object of class "Dom document", having the properties "doc" (resource) and "version" (string).

object **xmldocfile**(string filename)

xmltree

Parses the XML document in $str and returns a tree PHP objects as the parsed document.

object **xmltree**(string str)

xml_error_string

Returns a string with a textual description of the error code $code, or false if no description was found.

string **xml_error_string**(int code)

$code is an error code from **xml_get_error_code()**.

xml_get_current_byte_index

Returns false if **$parser** does not refer to a valid parser; otherwise, it returns which byte index the parser is currently at in its data buffer (starting at 0).

int xml_get_current_byte_index(int parser)

$parser is a reference to the XML parser from where to get byte index.

xml_get_current_column_number

Returns false if **$parser** does not refer to a valid parser, otherwise it returns which column on the current line (as given by **xml_get_current_line_number()**) where the parser is currently.

int xml_get_current_column_number(int parser)

$parser is a reference to the XML parser from where to get column number.

xml_get_current_line_number

Returns false if **$parser** does not refer to a valid parser, otherwise it returns which line the parser is currently at in its data buffer.

int xml_get_current_line_number(int parser)

$parser is reference to the XML parser from where to get line number.

xml_get_error_code

Returns false if **$parser** does not refer to a valid parser, otherwise it returns one of the error codes listed in the error codes section().

int **xml_get_error_code**(int parser)

$parser is a reference to the XML parser from where to get error code.

xml_parse

When the XML document is parsed, the handlers for the configured events are called as many times as necessary, after which this function returns true or false.

True is returned if the parse was successful, false if it was not successful or if **$parser** does not refer to a valid parser. For unsuccessful parses, error information can be retrieved with **xml_get_error_code()**, **xml_error_string()**, **xml_get_current_line_number()**, **xml_get_current_column_number()**, and **xml_get_current_byte_index()**.

int **xml_parse**(int parser, string data, [int isFinal])

$parser is a reference to the XML parser to use.

$data is a chunk of data to parse. A document may be parsed piece-wise by calling **xml_parse()** several times with new data, as long as the **$isFinal** parameter is set and true when the last data is parsed.

$isFinal (optional) If set and true, **$data** is the last piece of data sent in this parse.

xml_parser_create

This function creates an XML parser and returns a handle for use by other XML functions. Returns false on failure.

int **xml_parser_create**([string encoding])

$encoding (optional) is the character encoding the parser should use. The following character encodings are supported:

- *ISO-8859-1* (default)
- *US-ASCII*
- *UTF-8*

xml_parser_free

Returns false if **$parser** does not refer to a valid parser, otherwise it frees the parser and returns true.

string **xml_parser_free**(int parser)

$parser A reference to the XML parser to free.

xml_parser_get_option

Returns false if **$parser** does not refer to a valid parser or if the option could not be set. Otherwise, the option's value is returned. See **xml_parser_set_option**() for the list of options.

> mixed **xml_parser_get_option**(int parser, int option)

> **$parser** is a reference to the XML parser from where to get an option.
> **$option** is the option to fetch. See **xml_parser_set_option**() for a list of options.

xml_parser_set_option

Returns false if **$parser** does not refer to a valid parser or if the option could not be set. Otherwise, the option is set and true is returned.

> int **xml_parser_set_option**(int parser, int option, mixed value)

> **$parser** is a reference to the XML parser in which to set an option.
> **$option** is the option to set. See the following table.
> **$value** is the option's new value.
> The following options are available:

XML parser options

Option constant	Data type	Description
XML_OPTION_CASE_FOLDING	Integer	Controls whether **case-folding**() is enabled for this XML parser. Enabled by default.
XML_OPTION_TARGET_ENCODING	String	Sets which target **encoding**() to use in this XML parser.

By default, it is set to the same as the source encoding used by **xml_parser_create**(). Supported target encodings are *ISO-8859-1* , *US-ASCII* and *UTF-8*.

xml_parse_into_struct

Parses an XML file into two parallel array structures, one (**$index**) containing pointers to the location of the appropriate values in the **$values** array. These last two parameters must be passed by reference.

> int **xml_parse_into_struct**(int parser, string data, array values, array index)

The following is an example that illustrates the internal structure of the arrays being generated by the function. We use a simple *note* tag embedded inside a *para* tag, and then we parse this and print out the structures generated:

```
$simple = "<para><note>simple note</note></para>";
$p = xml_parser_create();
xml_parse_into_struct($p,$simple,&$vals,&$index);
```

```
xml_parser_free($p);
echo "Index array\n";
print_r($index);
echo "\nVals array\n";
print_r($vals);
```

When that code is run, the output will beas follows:

```
Index array
Array
(
    [PARA] => Array
        (
            [0] => 0
            [1] => 2
        )
=> Array
        (
            [0] => 1
        )
)
Vals array
Array
(
    [0] => Array
        (
            [tag] => PARA
            [type] => open
            [level] => 1
        )
    [1] => Array
        (
            [tag] => NOTE
            [type] => complete
            [level] => 2
            [value] => simple note
        )
    [2] => Array
        (
            [tag] => PARA
            [type] => close
            [level] => 1
        )
)
```

Event-driven parsing (based on the expat library) can get complicated when you have an XML document that is complex. This function does not produce a DOM style object, but it generates structures amenable of being transversed in a tree fashion. Thus, objects representing the data in the XML file can easily be created. Consider the following XML file representing a small database of amino acids information:

Example: moldb.xml - small database of molecular information

```
<?xml version="1.0"?>
<moldb>
<molecule>
    <name>Alanine</name>
    <symbol>ala</symbol>
```

```
        <code>A</code>
        <type>hydrophobic</type>
</molecule>
<molecule>
        <name>Lysine</name>
        <symbol>lys</symbol>
        <code>K</code>
        <type>charged</type>
</molecule>
</moldb>
```

The following is an example of some code to parse the document and generate the appropriate objects:

Example: parsemoldb.php - parses moldb.xml into and array of molecular objects

```php
<?php
class AminoAcid {
var $name;   // aa name
var $symbol; // three letter symbol
var $code;   // one letter code
var $type;   // hydrophobic, charged or neutral
function AminoAcid ($aa) {
    foreach ($aa as $k=>$v)
            $this->$k = $aa[$k];
}
}
function readDatabase($filename) {
// read the xml database of aminoacids
$data = implode("",file($filename));
$parser = xml_parser_create();
xml_parser_set_option($parser,XML_OPTION_CASE_FOLDING,0);
xml_parser_set_option($parser,XML_OPTION_SKIP_WHITE,1);
xml_parse_into_struct($parser,$data,&$values,&$tags);
xml_parser_free($parser);
// loop through the structures
foreach ($tags as $key=>$val) {
    if ($key == "molecule") {
            $molranges = $val;
            // each contiguous pair of array entries are the
            // lower and upper range for each molecule definition
            for ($i=0; $i < count($molranges); $i+=2) {
                    $offset = $molranges[$i] + 1;
                    $len = $molranges[$i + 1] - $offset;
                    $tdb[] = parseMol(array_slice($values, $offset, $len));
            }
    } else {
            continue;
    }
}
return $tdb;
}
function parseMol($mvalues) {
for ($i=0; $i < count($mvalues); $i++)
    $mol[$mvalues[$i]["tag"]] = $mvalues[$i]["value"];
return new AminoAcid($mol);
}
$db = readDatabase("moldb.xml");
```

```
echo "** Database of AminoAcid objects:\n";
print_r($db);
?>
```

After executing parsemoldb.php, the variable *$db* contains an array of *AminoAcid* objects, and the output of the script confirms the following:

```
** Database of AminoAcid objects:
Array
(
    [0] => aminoacid Object
        (
            [name] => Alanine
            [symbol] => ala
            [code] => A
            [type] => hydrophobic
        )
    [1] => aminoacid Object
        (
            [name] => Lysine
            [symbol] => lys
            [code] => K
            [type] => charged
        )
)
```

xml_set_character_data_handler

Sets the character data handler function for the XML parser **$parser**. **$handler** is a string containing the name of a function that must exist when **xml_parse()** is called for **$parser**.

int xml_set_character_data_handler(int parser, string)

The function named by **$handler** must accept two parameters: **$parser,** the first parameter, is a reference to the XML parser calling the handler. The second parameter, **$data**, contains the character data as a string.

If a handler function is set to an empty string, or false, the handler in question is disabled. True is returned if the handler is set up, false if **$parser** is not a parser.

Currently, no support is available for object/method handlers. See **xml_set_object()** for using the XML parser within an object.

xml_set_default_handler

Sets the default handler function for the XML parser **$parser**. **$handler** is a string containing the name of a function that must exist when **xml_parse()** is called for **$parser**.

int **xml_set_default_handler**(int parser, string)

The function named by **$handler** must accept two parameters: **$parser,** the first parameter, is a reference to the XML parser calling the handler. The second parameter, **$data** , contains the character data. This may be the XML declaration, document type declaration, entities or other data for which no other handler exists.

If a handler function is set to an empty string, or false, the handler in question is disabled. True is returned if the handler is set up, false if **$parser** is not a parser.

Currently no support is available for object/method handlers. See **xml_set_object()** for using the XML parser within an object.

xml_set_element_handler

Sets the element handler functions for the XML parser **$parser**. **$startElementHandler** and **$endElementHandler** are strings containing the names of functions that must exist when **xml_parse()** is called for **$parser**.

int **xml_set_element_handler**(int parser, string startElementHandler, string endElementHandler)

The function named by **$startElementHandler** must accept three parameters: **$parser,** the first parameter, is a reference to the XML parser calling the handler. **$name,** the second parameter, contains the name of the element for which this handler is called. If **case-folding** is in effect for this parser, the element name will be in uppercase letters. **$attribs,** the third parameter, contains an associative array with the element's attributes (if any). The keys of this array are the attribute names; the values are the attribute values. Attribute names are **case-folded** on the same criteria as element names. Attribute values are not case-folded.

The original order of the attributes can be retrieved by walking through **$attribs** the normal way, using **each()**. The first key in the array was the first attribute, and so on.

The function named by **$endElementHandler** must accept two parameters: **$parser,** the first parameter, is a reference to the XML parser calling the handler. **$name,** the second parameter, contains the name of the element for which this handler is called. If **case-folding** is in effect for this parser, the element name will be in uppercase letters.

If a handler function is set to an empty string, or false, the handler in question is disabled. True is returned if the handlers are set up, false if **$parser** is not a parser.

Currently no support is available for object/method handlers. See **xml_set_object()** for using the XML parser within an object.

xml_set_external_entity_ref_handler

Sets the notation declaration handler function for the XML parser **$parser**. **$handler** is a string containing the name of a function that must exist when **xml_parse()** is called for **$parser**.

int xml_set_external_entity_ref_handler(int parser, string handler)

The function named by **$handler** must accept five parameters, and should return an integer value. If the value returned from the handler is false (which it will be if no value is returned), the XML parser will stop parsing and **xml_get_error_code()** will return XML_ERROR_EXTERNAL_ENTITY_HANDLING.

$parser,** the first parameter, is a reference to the XML parser calling the handler. **$openEntityNames, the second parameter, is a space-separated list of the names of the entities that are open for the parse of this entity (including the name of the referenced entity). **$base** is the base for resolving the system identifier (**$systemid**) of the external entity. Currently, this parameter will always be set to an empty string. **$systemId,** the fourth parameter, is the system identifier as specified in the entity declaration. **$publicId,** the fifth parameter, is the public identifier as specified in the entity declaration, or an empty string if none was specified. The whitespace in the public identifier will have been normalized as required by the XML spec.

If a handler function is set to an empty string, or false, the handler in question is disabled. True is returned if the handler is set up, false if **$parser** is not a parser.

Currently no support is available for object/method handlers. See **xml_set_object**() for using the XML parser within an object.

xml_set_notation_decl_handler

Sets the notation declaration handler function for the XML parser **$parser**. **$handler** is a string containing the name of a function that must exist when **xml_parse**() is called for **$parser**.

> int **xml_set_notation_decl_handler**(int parser, string handler)

A notation declaration is part of the document's DTD and has the following format:

```
<!NOTATION
    <PARAMETER >name</PARAMETER> {<PARAMETER >systemId</PARAMETER> |
    <PARAMETER >publicId</PARAMETER>}>
```

See section 4.7 of the XML 1.0 spec *(http://www.w3.org/TR/1998/REC-xml-19980210#*Notations) for the definition of notation declarations.

The function named by **$handler** must accept five parameters: **$parser,** the first parameter, is a reference to the XML parser calling the handler. **$notationName** is the notation's **$name**, as per the notation format described above. **$base** is the base for resolving the system identifier (**$systemId**) of the notation declaration. Currently, this parameter will always be set to an empty string. **$systemId** is the system identifier of the external notation declaration. **$publicId** is the public identifier of the external notation declaration.

If a handler function is set to an empty string, or false, the handler in question is disabled. True is returned if the handler is set up, false if **$parser** is not a parser.

Currently no support is available for object/method handlers. See **xml_set_object**() for using the XML parser within an object.

xml_set_object

This function enables you to use **$parser** inside **$object**. All callback functions could be set with **xml_set_element_handler**() and so on, and can be assumed to be methods of $object.

> void **xml_set_object**(int parser, object object)

```php
<?php
class xml  {
var $parser;
function xml() {
    $this->parser = xml_parser_create();
    xml_set_object($this->parser,&$this);
    xml_set_element_handler($this->parser,"tag_open","tag_close");
    xml_set_character_data_handler($this->parser,"cdata");
}
```

```
function parse($data) {
    xml_parse($this->parser,$data);
}
function tag_open($parser,$tag,$attributes) {
    var_dump($parser,$tag,$attributes);
}
function cdata($parser,$cdata) {
    var_dump($parser,$cdata);
}
function tag_close($parser,$tag) {
    var_dump($parser,$tag);
}
} // end of class xml
$xml_parser = new xml();
$xml_parser->parse("<A ID=\"hallo\">PHP</A>");
?>
```

xml_set_processing_instruction_handler

Sets the *processing instruction* (PI) handler function for the XML parser **$parser**. **$handler** is a string containing the name of a function that must exist when **xml_parse()** is called for **$parser**.

> int xml_set_processing_instruction_handler(int parser, string handler)

A processing instruction has the following format:

```
<?
        <REPLACEABLE >target</REPLACEABLE>
        <REPLACEABLE >data</REPLACEABLE>?>
```

You can put PHP code into such a tag, but be aware of one limitation: in an XML PI, the PI end tag (?>) can not be quoted, so this character sequence should not appear in the PHP code you embed with PIs in XML documents. If it does, the rest of the PHP code, as well as the "real" PI end tag, will be treated as character data.

The function named by **$handler** must accept three parameters: **$parser,** the first parameter, is a reference to the XML parser calling the handler. **$target,** the second parameter, contains the PI target. **$data**, contains the PI data.

If a handler function is set to an empty string, or false, the handler in question is disabled. True is returned if the handler is set up, false if **$parser** is not a parser.

Currently no support is available for object/method handlers. See **xml_set_object()** for using the XML parser within an object.

xml_set_unparsed_entity_decl_handler

Sets the unparsed entity declaration handler function for the XML parser **$parser**. **$handler** is a string containing the name of a function that must exist when **xml_parse()** is called for **$parser**.

> int xml_set_unparsed_entity_decl_handler(int parser, string handler)

This handler will be called if the XML parser encounters an external entity declaration with an NDATA declaration, like the following:

```
<!ENTITY <PARAMETER >name</PARAMETER> {<PARAMETER >publicId</PARAMETER> | <PARAMETER
>systemId</PARAMETER>}
          NDATA <PARAMETER >notationName</PARAMETER>>
```

See section 4.2.2 of *the XML 1.0* spec *(http://www.w3.org/TR/1998/REC-xml-19980210#sec-external-ent)* for the definition of notation declared external entities.

The function named by **$handler** must accept six parameters: **$parser**, the first parameter, is a reference to the XML parser calling the handler. **$entityName** is the name of the entity that is about to be defined. **$base** is the base for resolving the system identifier (**$systemId**) of the external entity. Currently, this parameter will always be set to an empty string. **$systemId** is the system identifier for the external entity. **$publicId** is the public identifier for the external entity. **$notationName** is the name of the notation of this entity (see **xml_set_notation_decl_handler()**).

If a handler function is set to an empty string, or false, the handler in question is disabled. True is returned if the handler is set up, false if **$parser** is not a parser.

Currently no support is available for object/method handlers. See **xml_set_object()** for using the XML parser within an object.

yaz_addinfo

Returns additional error message for target (last request). An empty string is returned if last operation was a success or if no additional information was provided by the target.

    int **yaz_addinfo**(int id)

yaz_close

Closes a connection to a target. The application can no longer refer to the target with the given ID.

    int **yaz_close**(int id)

yaz_connect

Prepares for a connection to a Z39.50 target. The zurl argument takes the form host[&port][/database]. If port is omitted, 210 is used. If database is omitted, default is used. This function is non-blocking and doesn't attempt to establish a socket—it merely prepares a connection to be performed later when **yaz_wait()** is called.

    int **yaz_connect**(string zurl)

yaz_errno

Returns error for target (last request). A positive value is returned if the target returned a diagnostic code; a value of zero is returned if no errors occurred (success). Negative value is returned for other errors that targets didn't indicate the error in question.

Yaz_errno() should be called after network activity for each target (after **yaz_wait()** returns) to determine the success or failure of the last operation (for example, search).

> int **yaz_errno**(int id)

yaz_error

Returns error message for target (last request). An empty string is returned if last operation was a success. **Yaz_error()** returns an english message corresponding to the last error number as returned by **yaz_errno()**.

> int **yaz_error**(int id)

yaz_hits

Returns number of hits for last search.

> int **yaz_hits**(int id)

yaz_range

This function is used in conjunction with **yaz_search()** to specify the maximum number of records to retrieve (number) and the first record position (start). If this function is not invoked (only **yaz_search()**), start is set to 1 and number is set to 10. Returns true on success, false on error.

> int **yaz_range**(int id, int start, int number)

yaz_record

Returns record at position or empty string if no record exists at given position. This function inspects a record in the current result set at the position specified. If no database record exists at the given position, an empty string is returned. The argument type specifies the form of the returned record. If type is "string," the record is returned in a string representation suitable for printing (for XML and SUTRS). If type is "array," the record is returned as an array representation (for structured records).

> int **yaz_record**(int id, int pos, string type)

yaz_search

Prepares for a search on the target with given id. The type represents the query type—only "rpn" is supported now, in which case the third argument specifies a Type-1 query (RPN). Like yaz_connect(), this function is non-blocking and only prepares for a search to be executed later, when yaz_wait() is called.

> int **yaz_search**(int id, string type, string query)

The RPN query

The RPN query is a textual representation of the Type-1 query, as defined by the Z39.50 standard. However in the text representation, as used by YAZ, a prefix notation is used, that is, the operator precedes the operands. The query string is a sequence of tokens where white space is ignored unless surrounded by double quotes. Tokens beginning with an at-character (@) are considered operators; otherwise, they are treated as search terms.

RPN Operators

Syntax	Description
@*and query1 query2*	Intersection of query1 and query2.
@*or query1 query2*	Union of query1 and query2.
@*not query1 query2*	Query1 and not query2.
@*set name*	Result set reference.
@*attrset set query*	Specifies attribute-set for query.

This construction is only allowed once—in the beginning of the whole query *@attr set type*=value query applies attribute to query. The type and value are integers specifying the attribute-type and attribute-value, respectively. The set, if given, specifies the attribute-set. The following illustrates valid query constructions: computer Matches documents where "computer" occur. No attributes are specified.

"donald knuth"   Matches documents where "donald knuth" occur.

@attr 1=4 art   Attribute type is 1 (Bib-1 use), attribute value is 4 Title), so this should match documents where "art" occur in the title.

@attrset gils @and @attr 1=4 art @attr 1=1003 "donald knuth"   The query as a whole uses the GILS attributeset. The query matches documents where "art" occur in the title and in which "donald knuth" occur in the author.

yaz_syntax

The syntax may be specified in a raw dot-notation (like 1.2.840.10003.5.10) or as one of the known record syntaxes (sutrs, usmarc, grs1, xml, and so on). This function is used in conjunction with yaz_search() to specify the preferred record syntax for retrieval.

int **yaz_syntax**(int id, string syntax)

yaz_wait

This function carries out networked (blocked) activity for outstanding requests, which have been prepared by the functions yaz_connect() and yaz_search(). yaz_wait() returns when all targets have either completed all requests or otherwise completed (in case of errors).

int **yaz_wait**(int id, string syntax)

yp_first

Returns the first key-value pair from the named map in the named domain, otherwise false. See also **yp_get_default_domain**().

array **yp_first**(string domain, string map)

Example for the NIS first:

```php
<?php
    $entry = yp_first($domain, "passwd.byname");
    $key = key($entry);
    echo "First entry in this map has key " . $key
        . " and value " . $entry[$key];
?>
```

yp_get_default_domain

Returns the default domain of the node or false. Can be used as the domain parameter for successive NIS calls. A NIS domain can be described as a group of NIS maps. Every host that needs to look up information binds itself to a certain domain. Refer to the documents mentioned at the beginning for more detailed information.

int yp_get_default_domain(*void*)

Example: Example for the default domain

```php
<?php
$domain = yp_get_default_domain();
echo "Default NIS domain is: " . $domain;
?>
```

yp_master

Returns the machine name of the master NIS server for a map. See also **yp_get_default_domain**().

string **yp_master**(*string* domain, *string* map)

Example: Example for the NIS master

```php
<?php
$number = yp_master ($domain, $mapname);
echo "Master for this map is: " . $master;
?>
```

yp_match

Returns the value associated with the passed key out of the specified map or false. This key must be exact. See also **yp_get_default_domain**().

string **yp_match**(*string* domain, *string* map, *string* key)

Example: Example for NIS match

```php
<?php
$entry = yp_match ($domain, "passwd.byname", "joe");
echo "Matched entry is: " . $entry;
?>
```

In this case, this could be: joe:##joe:11111:100:Joe User:/home/j/joe:/usr/local/bin/bash

yp_next

Returns the next key-value pair in the named map after the specified key or false. See also **yp_get_default_domain**().

array **yp_next**(string domain, string map, string key)

Example: Example for NIS next

```php
<?php
$entry = yp_next ($domain, "passwd.byname", "joe");
if (!$entry) {
    echo yp_errno(). ": " . yp_err_string();
}
$key = key ($entry);
echo "The next entry after joe has key " . $key
     . " and value " . $entry[$key];
?>
```

yp_order

Returns the order number for a map or false. See also **yp_get_default_domain**().

int **yp_order**(string domain, string map)

Example: Example for the NIS order

```php
<?php
    $number = yp_order($domain,$mapname);
    echo "Order number for this map is: " . $order;
?>
```

zend_logo_guid

This functionality was added in PHP 4 Beta 4.

string **zend_logo_guid**(void)

PHP Predefined Variables and Constants

Variables

For a list of all predefined variables and other useful information, please see and use **phpinfo()**. This list is neither exhaustive nor intended to be. It is simply a guideline as to what sorts of predefined variables you can expect to have access to in your script.

Apache Variables

These variables are created by the Apache Web server. If you are running another Web server, no guarantee exists that it will provide the same variables; it may omit some, or provide others not listed here. That said, a large number of these variables are accounted for in the CGI 1.1 specification, so you should be able to expect those. Note that few, if any, of these will be available, (or indeed have any meaning), if running PHP on the command line.

GATEWAY_INTERFACE The revision of the CGI specification that the server is using, such as CGI/1.1.

SERVER_NAME The name of the server host under which the current script is executing. If the script is running on a virtual host, this will be the value defined for that virtual host.

SERVER_SOFTWARE Server identification string, given in the headers when responding to requests.

SERVER_PROTOCOL Name and revision of the information protocol by which the page was requested, such as HTTP/1.0.

REQUEST_METHOD The request method used to access the page, such as GET, HEAD, POST, and PUT.

QUERY_STRING The query string, if any, by which the page is accessed.

DOCUMENT_ROOT The document root directory under which the current script is executing, as defined in the server's configuration file.

HTTP_ACCEPT   Contents of the **Accept**: header from the current request, if there is one.

HTTP_ACCEPT_CHARSET   Contents of the **Accept-Charset**: header from the current request, if there is one. Example: iso-8859-1,*,utf-8.

HTTP_ENCODING   Contents of the **Accept-Encoding**: header from the current request, if there is one. Example: gzip.

HTTP_ACCEPT_LANGUAGE   Contents of the **Accept-Language**: header from the current request, if there is one. Example: en.

HTTP_CONNECTION   Contents of the **Connection**: header from the current request, if there is one. Example: Keep-Alive.

HTTP_HOST   Contents of the **Host**: header from the current request, if there is one.

HTTP_REFERER   The address of the page (if any) which refers the browser to the current page. This is set by the user's browser; not all browsers will set this.

HTTP_USER_AGENT   Contents of the **User_Agent**: header from the current request, if there is one. This is a string denoting the browser software being used to view the current page; for example, *Mozilla/4.5 [en] (X11; U; Linux 2.2.9 i586)*. Among other things, you can use this value with **get_browser()** to tailor your page's functionality to the capabilities of the user's browser.

REMOTE_ADDR   The IP address from which the user is viewing the current page.

REMOTE_PORT   The port being used on the user's machine to communicate with the Web server.

SCRIPT_FILENAME   The absolute pathname of the currently executing script.

SERVER_ADMIN   The value given to the SERVER_ADMIN (for Apache) directive in the Web server configuration file. If the script is running on a virtual host, this will be the value defined for that virtual host.

SERVER_PORT   The port on the server machine being used by the Web server for communication. For default setups, this will be 80; using SSL, for instance, will change this to whatever your defined secure HTTP port is.

SERVER_SIGNATURE String containing the server version and virtual host name which are added to server-generated pages, if enabled.

PATH_TRANSLATED Filesystem- (not document root-) based path to the current script, after the server has done any virtual-to-real mapping.

SCRIPT_NAME Contains the current script's path. This is useful for pages that need to point to themselves.

REQUEST_URI The URI that was given in order to access this page; for instance, /index.html.

Environment Variables

These variables are imported into PHP's global namespace from the environment under which the PHP parser is running. Many are provided by the shell under which PHP is running and different systems are likely running different kinds of shells, so a definitive list is impossible. Please see your shell's documentation for a list of defined environment variables. Other environment variables include the CGI variables, placed there regardless of whether PHP is running as a server module or CGI processor.

PHP Variables

These variables are created by PHP itself. The **$HTTP_*_VARS** variables are available only if the **track_vars** configuration is turned on. As for PHP 4.0.3, **track_vars** is always turned on, regardless of the configuration file setting.

If the **register_globals** directive is set, then these variables will also be made available in the global scope of the script; for example, separate from the **$HTTP_*_VARS** arrays. This feature should be used with care, and turned off if possible; while the **$HTTP_*_VARS** variables are safe, the bare global equivalents can be overwritten by user input, with possibly malicious intent. If you cannot turn off **register_globals**, you must take whatever steps are necessary to ensure that the data you are using is safe.

argv   Array of arguments passed to the script. When the script is run on the command line, this gives C-style access to the command line parameters. When called via the GET method, this will contain the query string.

argc   Contains the number of command line parameters passed to the script, (if run on the command line).

PHP_SELF   The filename of the currently executing script, relative to the document root. If PHP is running as a command-line processor, this variable is not available.

HTTP_COOKIE_VARS   An associative array of variables passed to the current script via HTTP cookies.

HTTP_GET_VARS   An associative array of variables passed to the current script via the HTTP GET method.

HTTP_POST_VARS   An associative array of variables passed to the current script via the HTTP POST method.

HTTP_POST_FILES   An associative array of variables containing information about files uploaded via the HTTP POST method. **$HTTP_POST_FILES** is available only in PHP 4.0.0 and later.

HTTP_ENV_VARS   An associative array of variables passed to the current script via the parent environment.

HTTP_SERVER_VARS   An associative array of variables passed to the current script from the HTTP server. These variables are analogous to the Apache variables described previously.

Constants

__FILE__   The name of the script file presently being parsed. If used within a file that has been included or required, then the name of the included file is given, and not the name of the parent file.

__LINE__   The number of the line within the current script file that is being parsed. If used within a file that has been included or required, then the position within the included file is given.

PHP_VERSION   The string representation of the version of the PHP parser presently in use; for example, 3.0.8-dev.

PHP_OS   The name of the operating system on which the PHP parser is executing; for example, Linux.

TRUE   A true value.

FALSE   A false value.

E_ERROR   Denotes an error other than a parsing error from which recovery is not possible.

E_WARNING   Denotes a condition where PHP knows something is wrong, but will continue anyway; these can be caught by the script itself. An example would be an invalid regexp in **ereg()**.

E_PARSE   The parser choked on invalid syntax in the script file. Recovery is not possible.

E_NOTICE   Something happened which may or may not be an error. Execution continues. Examples include using an unquoted string as a hash index, or accessing a variable which has not been set.

E_ALL   All of the E_* constants rolled into one. If used with **error_reporting()**, it will cause any and all problems noticed by PHP to be reported.

APPENDIX C

PHP Build Options

Database

--with-adabas[=DIR] Include Adabas D support. DIR is the Adabas base install directory, and defaults to /usr/local.

--enable-dba=shared Build DBA as a shared module.

--enable-dbase Enable the bundled dbase library. No external libraries are required.

--with-db2[=DIR] Include Berkeley DB2 support.

--with-db3[=DIR] Include Berkeley DB3 support.

--with-dbm[=DIR] Include DBM support.

--with-dbmaker[=DIR] Include DBMaker support. DIR is the DBMaker base install directory, and defaults to where the latest version of DBMaker is installed, such as /home/dbmaker/3.6.

--with-empress[=DIR] Include Empress support. DIR is the Empress base install directory, and defaults to $EMPRESSPATH.

--enable-filepro Enable the bundled read-only filePro support. No external libraries are required.

--with-gdbm[=DIR] Include GDBM support.

--with-hyperwave Include Hyperwave support.

--with-ibm-db2[=DIR] Include IBM DB2 support. DIR is the DB2 base install directory, and defaults to /home/db2inst1/sqllib.

--with-informix[=DIR] Include Informix support. DIR is the Informix base install directory, and defaults to nothing.

--with-ingres[=DIR] Include Ingres II support. DIR is the Ingres base directory; the default is /II/ingres.

--with-interbase[=DIR] Include InterBase support. DIR is the InterBase base install directory, which defaults to /usr/interbase.

--with-ldap[=DIR] Include LDAP support. DIR is the LDAP base install directory. This provides LDAP (Lightweight Directory Access Protocol support). The parameter is the LDAP base install directory, and defaults to /usr/local/ldap.

--with-msql[=DIR] Enables mSQL support. The parameter to this option is the mSQL install directory, and defaults to /usr/local/Hughes. This is the default directory, of the mSQL 2.0 distribution. **configure** automatically detects which mSQL version you are running and PHP supports both 1.0 and 2.0, but if you compile PHP with mSQL 1.0, you can only access mSQL 1.0 databases, and vice versa. *See also* mSQL Configuration Directives in Appendix D.

--with-mysql[=DIR] Include MySQL support. DIR is the MySQL base directory. If unspecified, the bundled MySQL library will be used. This option is turned on by default. *See also* MySQL Configuration Directives in Appendix D.

--with-ndbm[=DIR] Include NDBM support.

--with-oci8[=DIR] Include Oracle-oci8 support. Default DIR is ORACLE_HOME.

--with-oracle[=DIR] Include Oracle-oci7 support. Default DIR is ORACLE_HOME. Includes Oracle support. Has been tested and should be working at least with Oracle versions 7.0 through 7.3. The parameter is the ORACLE_HOME directory. You do not have to specify this parameter if your Oracle environment has been set up.

--with-pgsql[=DIR] Include PostgreSQL support. DIR is the PostgreSQL base install directory, which defaults to /usr/local/pgsql. Set DIR to **shared** to build as a dl, or **shared,DIR** to build as a dl and still specify DIR.

--with-solid[=DIR] Include Solid support. DIR is the Solid base install directory, which defaults to /usr/local/solid.

--with-sybase-ct[=DIR] Include Sybase-CT support. DIR is the Sybase home directory, which defaults to /home/sybase.

--with-sybase[=DIR] Include Sybase-DB support. DIR is the Sybase home directory, which defaults to /home/sybase.

--with-openlink[=DIR] Include OpenLink ODBC support. DIR is the OpenLink base install directory, which defaults to /usr/local/openlink.

--with-iodbc[=DIR] Include iODBC support. DIR is the iODBC base install directory, which defaults to /usr/local. This feature was first developed for iODBC Driver Manager, a freely redistributable ODBC driver manager which runs under many flavors of UNIX.

--with-custom-odbc[=DIR]   Includes support for an arbitrary custom ODBC library. The parameter is the base directory and defaults to /usr/local. This option implies that you have defined CUSTOM_ODBC_LIBS when you run the configure script. You also must have a valid odbc.h header somewhere in your include path. If you don't have one, create it and include your specific header from there. Your header may also require some extra definitions, particularly when it is multiplatform. Define them in CFLAGS. For example, you can use Sybase SQL Anywhere on QNX as follows:

```
CFLAGS=-DODBC_QNX LDFLAGS=-lunix CUSTOM_ODBC_LIBS="-ldblib -lodbc"
./configure --with-custom-odbc=/usr/lib/sqlany50
```

--with-unixODBC[=DIR]   Include unixODBC support. DIR is the unixODBC base install directory, which defaults to /usr/local.

--with-velocis[=DIR]   Include Velocis support. DIR is the Velocis base install directory, which defaults to /usr/local/velocis.

E-commerce

--with-ccvs[=DIR]   Compile CCVS support into PHP4. Please specify your CCVS base install directory as DIR.

--with-cybercash[=DIR]   Include CyberCash support. DIR is the CyberCash MCK install directory.

--with-pfpro[=DIR]   Include Verisign Payflow Pro support.

Graphics

--enable-freetype-4bit-antialias-hack   Include support for FreeType2 (experimental).

--with-gd[=DIR]   Include GD support (DIR is GD's install dir). Set DIR to **shared** to build as a dl, or **shared,DIR** to build as a dl and still specify DIR.

--without-gd   Disable GD support.

--with-jpeg-dir[=DIR]   jpeg dir for pdflib 3.x

--with-png-dir[=DIR]   png dir for pdflib 3.x

--with-t1lib[=DIR]   Include T1lib support.

--with-tiff-dir[=DIR]   tiff dir for pdflib 3.x

--with-ttf[=DIR]   Include FreeType support.

--with-xpm-dir[=DIR]   xpm dir for gd-1.8+

Miscellaneous

--disable-libtool-lock   avoid locking, which might break parallel builds.

--disable-pear   Do not install PEAR.

--disable-pic   Disable PIC for shared objects.

--disable-posix   Disable POSIX-like functions.

--disable-rpath   Disable passing additional runtime library search paths.

--disable-session   Disable session support.

--enable-bcmath   Compile with bc style precision math functions. Read README-BCMATH for instructions on how to get this module installed. These functions allow you to operate with numbers outside of the ranges allowed by regular integers and floats.

--enable-c9x-inline   Enable C9x-inline semantics.

--enable-calendar   Enable support for calendar conversion.

--enable-debug   Compile with debugging symbols.

--enable-discard-path   If this is enabled, the PHP CGI binary can safely be placed outside of the Web tree and people will not be able to circumvent .htaccess security.

--enable-dmalloc   Enable dmalloc.

--enable-exif   Enable exif support.

--enable-experimental-zts   This will most likely break your build.

--enable-fast-install[=PKGS]   Optimize for fast installation. Default is yes.

--enable-force-cgi-redirect   Enable the security check for internal server redirects. You should use this if you are running the CGI version with Apache.

--enable-inline-optimization   If you have much memory and are using gcc, you might try this.

--enable-libgcc   Enable explicitly linking against libgcc.

--enable-maintainer-mode   Enable makes rules and dependencies not useful (and sometimes confusing) to the casual installer.

--enable-memory-limit   Compile with memory limit support.

--enable-safe-mode   Enable safe mode by default.

--enable-satellite   Enable CORBA support via Satellite (Requires ORBit).

--enable-shared[=PKGS]   Build shared libraries. Default is yes.

--enable-sigchild   Enable PHP's own SIGCHLD handler.

--enable-static[=PKGS]   Build static libraries. Default is yes.

--enable-sysvsem   Enable the System V semaphore support.

--enable-sysvshm   Enable the System V shared memory support.

--enable-trans-sid   Enable transparent session id propagation.

--with-cdb[=DIR]   Include CDB support.

--with-config-file-path=PATH   Sets the path in which to look for php.ini. Defaults to /usr/local/lib.

--with-cpdflib[=DIR]   Include cpdflib support (requires cpdflib >= 2). DIR is the cpdfllib install directory, and defaults to /usr.

--with-esoob[=DIR]   Include Easysoft OOB support. DIR is the OOB base install directory, and defaults to /usr/local/easysoft/oob/client.

--with-exec-dir[=DIR]   Only allow executables in DIR when in safe mode. Defaults to /usr/local/php/bin.

--with-fdftk[=DIR]   Include fdftk support. DIR is the fdftk install directory, and defaults to /usr/local.

--with-gnu-ld   Assume the C compiler uses GNU ld. Default is no.

--with-icap[=DIR]   Include ICAP support.

--with-imap[=DIR]   Include IMAP support. DIR is the IMAP include and c-client.a directory.

--with-java[=DIR]   Include Java support. DIR is the base install directory for the JDK. This extension can only be built as a shared dl.

--with-kerberos[=DIR]   Include Kerberos support in IMAP.

--with-mcal[=DIR]   Include MCAL support.

--with-mcrypt[=DIR]   Include mcrypt support. DIR is the mcrypt install directory.

--with-mhash[=DIR]   Include mhash support. DIR is the mhash install directory.

--with-mm[=DIR]   Include mm support for session storage.

--with-mod_charset   Enable transfer tables for mod_charset (Rus Apache).

--with-pdflib[=DIR]   Include pdflib 3.x support. DIR is the pdflib install directory, which defaults to /usr/local.

--with-readline[=DIR]   Include readline support. DIR is the readline install directory.

--with-regex=TYPE   Regex library type: system, apache, php.

--with-servlet[=DIR]   Include servlet support. DIR is the base install directory for the JSDK. This SAPI requires that the Java extension be built as a shared dl.

--with-swf[=DIR]   Include swf support.

--with-tsrm-pth[=pth-config]   Use GNU Pth.

--with-tsrm-pthreads   Use POSIX threads (default).

--with-zlib-dir[=DIR]   zlib dir for pdflib 3.x or include zlib support.

--with-zlib[=DIR]   Include zlib support (requires zlib >= 1.0.9). DIR is the zlib install directory, and defaults to /usr.

--without-pcre-regex   Do not include Perl Compatible Regular Expressions support. Use --with-pcre-regex=DIR to specify DIR where PCRE's include and library files are located, if not using bundled library.

Networking

--with-curl[=DIR]   Include CURL support.

--enable-ftp   Enable FTP support.

--disable-url-fopen-wrapper   Disable the URL-aware fopen wrapper that enables accessing files via http or ftp. This switch is only available for PHP versions up to 4.0.3, newer versions provide an INI parameter called **allow_url_fopen** instead of forcing you to decide upon this feature at compile time.

--with-mod-dav=DIR   Include DAV support through Apache's mod_dav. DIR is mod_dav's installation directory, (applies to Apache module version only).

--with-openssl[=DIR]   Include OpenSSL support in SNMP.

--with-snmp[=DIR]   Include SNMP support. DIR is the SNMP base install directory, defaults to searching through a number of common locations for the snmp install. Set DIR to **shared** to build as a dl, or **shared,DIR** to build as a dl and still specify DIR.

--enable-ucd-snmp-hack   Enable UCD SNMP hack.

--enable-sockets   Enable sockets support.

--with-yaz[=DIR]   Include YAZ support (ANSI/NISO Z39.50). DIR is the YAZ bin install directory.

--enable-yp   Include YP support.

PHP Behavior

--enable-magic-quotes   Enable magic quotes by default.

--disable-short-tags   Disable the short-form < start tag by default.

Server

--with-aolserver-src=DIR   Specify path to the source distribution of AOLserver.

--with-aolserver=DIR   Specify path to the installed AOLserver.

--with-apache[=DIR] Build Apache module. DIR is the top-level Apache build directory, and defaults to /usr/local/etc/httpd.

--with-apxs[=FILE]   Build shared Apache module. FILE is the optional pathname to the Apache apxs tool; defaults to apxs.

--enable-versioning   Export only required symbols. *See* INSTALL for more information.

--with-fhttpd[=DIR]   Build fhttpd module. DIR is the fhttpd sources directory; defaults to /usr/local/src/fhttpd.

--with-nsapi=DIR   Specify path to the installed Netscape.

--with-pi3web=DIR Build PHP as a module for use with Pi3Web.

--with-roxen=DIR Build PHP as a Pike module. DIR is the base Roxen directory, normally /usr/local/roxen/server.

--enable-roxen-zts Build the Roxen module using Zend Thread Safety.

--with-zeus=DIR Build PHP as an ISAPI module for use with Zeus.

Text and language

--with-aspell[=DIR] Include ASPELL support.

--with-gettext[=DIR] Include GNU gettext support. DIR is the gettext install directory; defaults to /usr/local.

--with-pspell[=DIR] Include PSPELL support.

--with-recode[=DIR] Include recode support. DIR is the recode install directory.

XML

--with-dom[=DIR] Include DOM support (requires libxml >= 2.0). DIR is the libxml install directory; defaults to /usr.

--enable-sablot-errors-descriptive Enable Descriptive errors.

--with-sablot[=DIR] Include Sablotron support.

--enable-wddx Enable WDDX support.

--disable-xml Disable XML support using bundled expat lib.

APPENDIX D

General Configuration Directives

allow_url_fopen: boolean This option enables the URL-aware fopen wrappers that enable accessing URL object-like files. Default wrappers are provided for the access of remote files using the ftp or http protocol, some extensions like zlib may register additional wrappers. This option was introduced immediately after the release of version 4.0.3. For versions up to and including 4.0.3, you can only disable this feature at compile time by using the configuration switch **--disable-url-fopen-wrapper**.

asp_tags: boolean Enables the use of ASP-like <% %> tags in addition to the usual <?php ?> tags. This includes the variable-value printing shorthand of <%= $value %>. Support for ASP-style tags was added in 3.0.4.

auto_append_file: string Specifies the name of a file that is automatically parsed after the main file. The file is included as if it was called with the **include()** function, so include_path is used. The special value none disables auto-appending. If the script is terminated with **exit()**, auto-append will not occur.

auto_prepend_file: string Specifies the name of a file that is automatically parsed before the main file. The file is included as if it was called with the **include()** function, so include_path is used. The special value none disables auto-prepending.

cgi_ext: string

display_errors: boolean This determines whether errors should be printed to the screen as part of the HTML output or not.

doc_root: string PHP's root directory on the server. Only used if non-empty. If PHP is configured with safe mode, no files outside this directory are served.

engine: boolean This directive is really only useful in the Apache module version of PHP. It is used by sites that would like to turn PHP parsing on and off on a per-directory or per-virtual server basis.

By putting engine off in the appropriate places in the httpd.conf file, PHP can be enabled or disabled.

error_log: string   Name of file where script errors should be logged. If the special value syslog is used, the errors are sent to the system logger instead. On UNIX, this means syslog(3) and on Windows NT it means the event log. The system logger is not supported on Windows 95.

error_reporting: integer   Set the error reporting level. See the **error_reporting()** function for details.

open_basedir: string   Limit the files that can be opened by PHP to the specified directory-tree. When a script tries to open a file with, for example, fopen or gzopen, the location of the file is checked. When the file is outside the specified directory-tree, PHP will refuse to open it. All symbolic links are resolved, so it's not possible to avoid this restriction with a symlink. The special value "." indicates that the directory in which the script is stored will be used as base-directory. Under Windows, separate the directories with a semicolon. On all other systems, separate the directories with a colon. As an Apache module, open_basedir paths from parent directories are now automatically inherited. Support for multiple directories was added in 3.0.7. The default is to enable all files to be opened.

gpc_order: string   Set the order of GET/POST/COOKIE variable parsing. The default setting of this directive is GPC. Setting this to GP, for example, will cause PHP to completely ignore cookies and to overwrite any GET method variables with POST-method variables of the same name.

ignore_user_abort: string   On by default. If changed to Off scripts will be terminated as soon as they try to output something after a client has aborted their connection. *See also* **ignore_user_abort()**.

include_path: string   Specifies a list of directories where the **require()**, **include()** and **fopen_with_path()** functions look for files. The format is like the system's **PATH** environment variable: a list of directories separated with a colon in UNIX or semicolon in Windows. The default value for this directive is "." (only the current directory).

isapi_ext: string

log_errors: boolean   Tells whether script error messages should be logged to the server's error log. This option is thus server-specific.

magic_quotes_gpc: boolean   Sets the magic_quotes state for GPC (Get/Post/Cookie) operations. When magic_quotes are on, all ' (single-quote), " (double quote), \ (backslash) and NULs are escaped with a backslash automatically. If **magic_quotes_sybase** is also on, a single-quote is escaped with a single-quote instead of a backslash.

magic_quotes_runtime: boolean   If **magic_quotes_runtime** is enabled, most functions that return data from any sort of external source including databases and text files will have quotes escaped with a backslash. If **magic_quotes_sybase** is also on, a single-quote is escaped with a single-quote instead of a backslash.

magic_quotes_sybase: boolean   If **magic_quotes_sybase** is on, a single-quote is escaped with a single-quote instead of a backslash if magic_quotes_gpc or **magic_quotes_runtime** is enabled.

max_execution_time: integer   This sets the maximum time in seconds a script is allowed to take before it is terminated by the parser. This helps prevent poorly written scripts from tying up the server. The default setting is 30.

memory_limit integer   This sets the maximum amount of memory in bytes that a script is allowed to allocate. This helps prevent poorly written scripts for eating up all available memory on a server.

nsapi_ext: string

register_globals boolean   Tells whether or not to register the EGPCS (Environment, GET, POST, Cookie, Server) variables as global variables. You may want to turn this off if you don't want to clutter your scripts' global scope with user data. This makes the most sense when coupled with **track_vars-** in which case you can access all of the EGPCS variables through the **$HTTP_ENV_VARS**, **$HTTP_GET_VARS**, **$HTTP_POST_VARS**, **$HTTP_COOKIE_VARS**, and **$HTTP_SERVER_VARS** arrays in the global scope.

short_open_tag: boolean   Tells whether the short form <? ?> of PHP's open tag should be enabled. If you want to use PHP in combination with XML, you have to disable this option. If disabled, you must use the long form of the open tag (<?php ?>).

sql.safe_mode: boolean

track_errors: boolean   If enabled, the last error message will always be present in the global variable **$php_errormsg**.

track_vars: boolean   If enabled, then Environment, GET, POST, Cookie, and Server variables can be found in the global associative arrays **$HTTP_ENV_VARS, $HTTP_GET_VARS, $HTTP_POST_VARS, $HTTP_COOKIE_VARS**, and

$HTTP_SERVER_VARS. Note that as of PHP 4.0.3, **track_vars** is always turned on.

upload_tmp_dir: string   The temporary directory used for storing files when doing file upload. Must be writable by whatever user PHP is running as.

user_dir: string   The base name of the directory used on a user's home directory for PHP files, for example public_html.

warn_plus_overloading: boolean   If enabled, this option makes PHP output a warning when the plus ("+") operator is used on strings. This is to make it easier to find scripts that need to be rewritten to using the string concatenator instead (".").

Mail Configuration Directives

SMTP: string   DNS name or IP address of the SMTP server PHP under Windows should use for mail sent with the **mail()** function.

sendmail_from: string   The From: mail address that should be used in mail sent from PHP under Windows.

sendmail_path: string   Where the **sendmail** program can be found, usually /usr/sbin/sendmail or /usr/lib/sendmail. **configure** does an honest attempt of locating this one for you and set a default, but if it fails, you can set it here. Systems not using sendmail should set this directive to the sendmail wrapper/replacement their mail system offers, if any. For example, Qmail users can normally set it to /var/qmail/bin/sendmail.

Safe Mode Configuration Directives

safe_mode: boolean   Whether to enable PHP's safe mode.

safe_mode_exec_dir: string   If PHP is used in safe mode, **system()** and the other functions executing system programs refuse to start programs that are not in this directory.

Debugger Configuration Directives

debugger.host: string   DNS name or IP address of host used by the debugger.

debugger.port: string   Port number used by the debugger.

debugger.enabled: boolean   Whether the debugger is enabled.

Extension Loading Directives

enable_dl: boolean   This directive is really only useful in the Apache module version of PHP. You can turn dynamic loading of PHP extensions with **dl()** on and off per virtual server or per directory. The main reason for turning dynamic loading off is security. With dynamic loading, it's possible to ignore all the safe_mode and open_basedir restrictions. The default is to allow dynamic loading, except when using safe-mode. In safe-mode, it's always impossible to use **dl()**.

extension_dir: string   In what directory PHP should look for dynamically loadable extensions.

extension: string   Which dynamically loadable extensions to load when PHP starts up.

MySQL Configuration Directives

mysql.allow_persistent: boolean   Whether to allow persistent MySQL connections.

mysql.default_host: string   The default server host to use when connecting to the database server if no other host is specified.

mysql.default_user: string   The default user name to use when connecting to the database server if no other name is specified.

mysql.default_password: string   The default password to use when connecting to the database server if no other password is specified.

mysql.max_persistent: integer   The maximum number of persistent MySQL connections per process.

mysql.max_links: integer   The maximum number of MySQL connections per process, including persistent connections.

mSQL Configuration Directives

msql.allow_persistent: boolean   Whether to allow persistent mSQL connections.

msql.max_persistent: integer   The maximum number of persistent mSQL connections per process.

msql.max_links: integer   The maximum number of mSQL connections per process, including persistent connections.

Postgres Configuration Directives

pgsql.allow_persistent: boolean   Whether to allow persistent Postgres connections.

pgsql.max_persistent: integer   The maximum number of persistent Postgres connections per process.

pgsql.max_links: integer   The maximum number of Postgres connections per process, including persistent connections.

Sybase Configuration Directives

sybase.allow_persistent: boolean   Whether to allow persistent Sybase connections.

sybase.max_persistent: integer   The maximum number of persistent Sybase connections per process.

sybase.max_links: integer   The maximum number of Sybase connections per process, including persistent connections.

Sybase-CT Configuration Directives

sybct.allow_persistent: boolean   Whether to allow persistent Sybase-CT connections. The default is on.

sybct.max_persistent: integer   The maximum number of persistent Sybase-CT connections per process. The default is -1, meaning unlimited.

sybct.max_links: integer   The maximum number of Sybase-CT connections per process, including persistent connections. The default is -1, meaning unlimited.

sybct.min_server_severity: integer   Server messages with severity greater than or equal to sybct.min_server_severity will be reported as warnings. This value can also be set from a script by calling **sybase_min_server_severity()**. The default is 10, which reports errors of information severity or greater.

sybct.min_client_severity: integer   Client library messages with severity greater than or equal to sybct.min_client_severity will be reported as warnings. This value can also be set from a script by calling **sybase_min_client_severity()**. The default is 10 which effectively disables reporting.

sybct.login_timeout: integer   The maximum time in seconds to wait for a connection attempt to succeed before returning failure. Note that if max_execution_time has been exceeded when a connection attempt times out, your script will be terminated before it can take action on failure. The default is one minute.

sybct.timeout: integer   The maximum time in seconds to wait for a select_db or query operation to succeed before returning failure. Note that if max_execution_time has been exceeded when an operation times out, your script will be terminated before it can take action on failure. The default is no limit.

sybct.hostname: string   The name of the host you claim to be connecting from, for display by sp_who. The default is none.

Informix Configuration Directives

ifx.allow_persistent: boolean   Whether to allow persistent Informix connections.

ifx.max_persistent: integer   The maximum number of persistent Informix connections per process.

ifx.max_links: integer   The maximum number of Informix connections per process, including persistent connections.

ifx.default_host: string   The default host to connect to when no host is specified in **ifx_connect()** or **ifx_pconnect()**.

ifx.default_user: string   The default user id to use when none is specified in **ifx_connect()** or **ifx_pconnect()**.

ifx.default_password: string   The default password to use when none is specified in **ifx_connect()** or **ifx_pconnect()**.

ifx.blobinfile: boolean   Set to true if you want to return blob columns in a file, false if you want them in memory. You can override the setting at runtime with **ifx_blobinfile_mode()**.

ifx.textasvarchar: boolean   Set to true if you want to return TEXT columns as normal strings in select statements, false if you want to use blob id parameters. You can override the setting at runtime with **ifx_textasvarchar()**.

ifx.byteasvarchar: boolean   Set to true if you want to return BYTE columns as normal strings in select queries, false if you want to use blob id parameters. You can override the setting at runtime with **ifx_textasvarchar()**.

ifx.charasvarchar: boolean   Set to true if you want to trim trailing spaces from CHAR columns when fetching them.

ifx.nullformat: boolean   Set to true if you want to return NULL columns as the literal string "NULL", false if you want them returned as the empty string "". You can override this setting at runtime with **ifx_nullformat()**.

BC Math Configuration Directives

bcmath.scale: integer   Number of decimal digits for all bcmath functions.

Browser Capability Configuration Directives

browscap: string   Name of browser capabilities file. *See also* **get_browser()**.

Unified ODBC Configuration Directives

uodbc.default_db: string   ODBC data source to use if none is specified in **odbc_connect()** or **odbc_pconnect()**.

uodbc.default_user: string   User name to use if none is specified in **odbc_connect()** or **odbc_pconnect()**.

uodbc.default_pw: string   Password to use if none is specified in **odbc_connect()** or **odbc_pconnect()**.

uodbc.allow_persistent: boolean   Whether to allow persistent ODBC connections.

uodbc.max_persistent: integer   The maximum number of persistent ODBC connections per process.

uodbc.max_links: integer   The maximum number of ODBC connections per process, including persistent connections.

APPENDIX E

Internet Resources

The primary resource for PHP is the official PHP Web site at http://www.php.net. There you can find information about mailing lists, other sites of interest as well as a full online reference for the PHP language. The following table provides a short list of some of the other interesting PHP Web sites available.

URL	Description
`http://www.php4devguide.com/`	The companion Web site to this book. This site contains links and updates related to this text.
`http://www.mysql.com/`	The official MySQL database Web site.
`http://www.phpbuilder.com/`	A nice site consisting of articles, code samples and more related to PHP development.
`http://www.thewebmasters.net/`	Home of FastTemplate and other PHP class libraries used in this book.
`http://phplib.netuse.de/`	The home of PHPLib, the class library used in this book for some database, sessions, and authentication examples.

APPENDIX F

Bibliography

Bibliography

Fournier, Roger. 1998. *A Methodology for Client/Server and Web Application Development*. New Jersey: Prentice Hall PTR.

McConnell, Steve. 1993. *Code Complete*. Washington: Microsoft Press.

McConnell, Steve. 1996. *Rapid Development*. Washington: Microsoft Press.

INDEX

Symbols

\, escape sequences, 24

`, execution operator, 33

{}, template variables, 236

$, variable designation, 27

&, assigning variables, 28

., dot operator, 25

?, ternary operator, 33

@

    error control operator, 33

    suppressing internal MySQL warnings, 95

A

access counts, Web pages, 76

access sockets, servers, 78

add_next_index_double() function, 210

advanced error handling, 192

alternate PHP syntax, 40

amortization schedules, 206

ampersand (&), assigning variables by
    reference, 28

Apache servers

    authentication, 140–141

    building PHP, 8, 12–13

    configuring, 11–12

    error log script, 186

    installing PHP, 7

    Java support, 214

APIs (Application Programming Interfaces)

    Cloanto Currency Server, 218–220

    Java, 215

application state, 114

applications

    debugging, 177

    development, 226–227

    testing, 179

apxs script, 214

architecture issues and projects, 177

arithmetic operators, 30

array() function, 26

ArrayAverage() function, 181

arrays, 26

array_init() function, 210

assert() function, 180

assert() function script, 190

assert_options() function, 191

assign() method, 236–237

assigning variables by reference or
    value, 28

assignment operators, 31

associative arrays, 26, 77

Auth class, 149, 153

authentication, 145

    Apache Web server, 140–141

    checking for valid users via Htpasswd
        class, 143–144

    header information, 147–148

    PHPLIB, 149–151

    scripts, 144

R